JUST MARRIED

How to Celebrate Your Wedding in Style

gestalten

Content

Preface
004

Talia & Zac
006

Leigh & Brad
020

Visra & Chris
030

Jose & Joel
036

**So, You're
Getting Married...**
044

Laura & Mike
048

Shona & Luke
058

Rin & Joe
062

Natasha & Len
070

Toni & Colin
076

Claire & Gary
082

Kristen & Michael
086

**The All-Important
Location**
098

Anna & Paul
102

Stacy & Josh
108

Sarah & Justin
118

Zoe & Phil
130

Suzy & Dmitry
134

Kelly & Curtis
140

The Guestlist
150

Anna & Brandon
154

Gwyneth & Monko
160

Sarah & Dawn
166

Lynette & Gris
172

Fiona & Jonny
184

The Journey
190

Emily & Louis
194

Kirstyn & Adam
200

Trishia & Justin
210

**The Decadence is in
the Decoration**
216

Julie & Bo
220

Caroline & Johnny
232

Garovs & Ryan
236

Kim & Robbie
244

Index
250

Imprint
256

Preface

by Fiona Leahy

The celebration of marriage is one of the most evocative occasions most of us will experience, either as a participant or as a guest.

There is an alchemy involved that is completely unique, a celebration of the romantic, the sentimental, the spiritual, and the creative, where the restrictions of everyday life can be cast aside. I feel incredibly fortunate to have forged a career that gives me the chance to experience first-hand the personal mix of imagination and artistry that is unique to each wedding.

My first ever event was actually a wedding. It just happened to be an extraordinary wedding between two wonderful creatives: Dita Von Teese and Marilyn Manson. Set in the splendor of an Irish castle, it was an occasion like no other; a complete rejection of the uptight and traditional. Fusing Gothic and Victorian aesthetics, it was a vivacious celebration that reflected the couple's very defined sense of personal style. It transformed my entire perspective of weddings and opened my eyes to the immense design potential they possess.

I knew from that moment on that this bewitching occasion had changed my life. I had found an outlet that fused art, creativity, and happiness in an entirely tangible way. It completely shifted my vision of what is possible and shaped what I have embraced in all the weddings I have undertaken since then—the desire to capture the essence of a couple and translate it into a joyful occasion.

Since that first, serendipitous celebration, I have worked on a huge array of weddings all over the world; from intimate weddings with simply the betrothed present to huge weddings in the Middle East for over a thousand guests.

It struck me during this time just how much weddings have evolved and changed. Weddings have moved entirely beyond the traditional and perfunctory in favor of becoming more of a visual and spiritual form of self-expression.

The Internet and the meteoric rise of wedding blogs, Pinterest, and specialist online publications have led to a heightened visibility of creative possibilities. With inspiration and aspiration so accessible, couples are far more informed and trend aware than ever before.

This empowering shift has stimulated couples to get more involved with the whole planning process. My favorite weddings to work on have been where the couple has thrown their own ideas into the mix. A wedding will always turn out better when the creative process has been a collaborative effort, because it is such a personal celebration.

Getting married, for some couples, has become an opportunity and an outlet for creative expression. I would say that weddings, such as these featured, are interactive forms of art; transforming a love and connection between two people into an experience and memory that will last beyond the day.

I hope this book inspires couples to embrace a much broader creative scope. Playful design and personal meaning can be brought into each step of the planning process from the invitations to the location. Even the smallest details are an opportunity to be creative. An important part of what I do is putting the fun into functional; elevating what could be mundane event essentials and transforming them into engaging and beautiful design elements.

Every wedding no matter how small or how simple should have an element of beauty, and by this I don't mean elaborate and I don't necessarily mean luxurious. Beauty does not need to be expensive. An abundance of one inexpensive element can be more breathtaking than a frugal amount of an expensive one, and I hope that the weddings we have chosen to show in this book illustrate that point.

One wedding in particular is a striking example of this: Emily and Louis who handmade nearly every item for their rainbow-hued wedding. From cooking the canapés to making all of the decorations, this dedicated couple took DIY to another level. Emily even screen printed all of their table linen and Louis brewed the beer.

Being able to share ideas and pool inspiration online has fuelled an explosion of incredible variety in weddings. As you can see from the ones featured in this book, when it comes to getting married the possibilities are endless and even the oldest of traditions are open to interpretation. Who says bouquets have to be made of flowers or that your dress has to be white?

Just take a look at Ryan and Garov's incredible wedding in the Philippines, where instead of floral displays lining their aisle they had billowing white fluffy clouds. Suzy and Dimitri opted for a bejeweled contortionist over the traditional bridesmaids and groomsmen in their extravagant Gothic celebration.

Your wedding is a day of huge importance that you will remember for the rest of your life, so make it an enjoyable one filled with laughter and love. Convey your personality by including things that you like, not what you think you should like. Just as you've found the person that's right for you, the way you celebrate that amazing connection has to be right for you too.

You might not have a style as defined as Dita & Manson but you will have a personal aesthetic. The first step to making your wedding a spectacular success is figuring out what it is. To do that it's all about being authentic and in touch with who you are, so start by asking yourselves: what distinguishes you from everyone else? What makes you tick? Aside from the obvious, each other, think about what you really love in this world. I'd say look inwards at your interests and passions and from that draw upon what you would like to emphasize. For another couple featured in this book, Kim and Robbie, that was *Napoleon Dynamite*. Their table numbers were quotes from the film and their reception venue was decorated in the colors of the school featured in the cult classic. Their shared love of the movie never fails to bring them together so they wanted to reflect this when celebrating their love for each other at their wedding—true authenticity.

It's these personal stories that I like to play on when creating an event for a client because, for me, that's where the best ideas come from. By adding depth and meaning, they transform a standard element of any wedding into a unique and special feature that will be forever remembered.

We had a couple recently where the bride was a passionate horse rider so, inspired by her show jumping prizes, we created these bespoke rosettes and used them as place cards. Guests were so enamored with them that most took them home and some even pinned them on their outfit, so they doubled as name badges and inadvertently helped everyone get to know each other.

Discovering the fabulous weddings and rediscovering the past projects featured in the following pages has been an incredible journey of inspiration that has made me want to get married ten different times in ten completely different ways!

The weddings featured in this book are in my mind living breathing experiential works of art; each one entirely unique and each one just as inspiring.

From a Russian palace to a backyard in Australia, this book is a celebration of celebrations! I hope that it shows that whilst the quintessential white wedding is wonderful, it isn't for everyone. This book proves that with some imagination and a few inspired touches you can make your special day match your own personal vision of perfection.

If art is the expression of Spirit then look through the manifestations on these pages and prepare to be inspired.

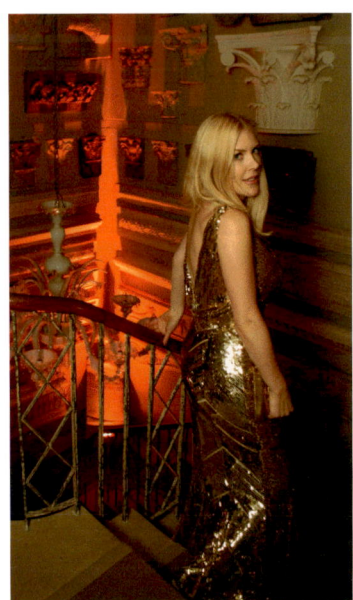

Fiona Leahy began her career as a fashion stylist. She then went on to work alongside Jade Jagger art directing at Garrard, the British Crown Jewelers. This involvement in fashion and fine jewelry has greatly influenced Fiona's current work: creating weddings and events that are distinguished by their visual decadence.

The wedding of Dita Von Teese and Marilyn Manson was Fiona's first. Now, 8 years on, Fiona and her team work on weddings all over the world in addition to creating events for global fashion houses such as Louis Vuitton, Dior, and Christian Louboutin.

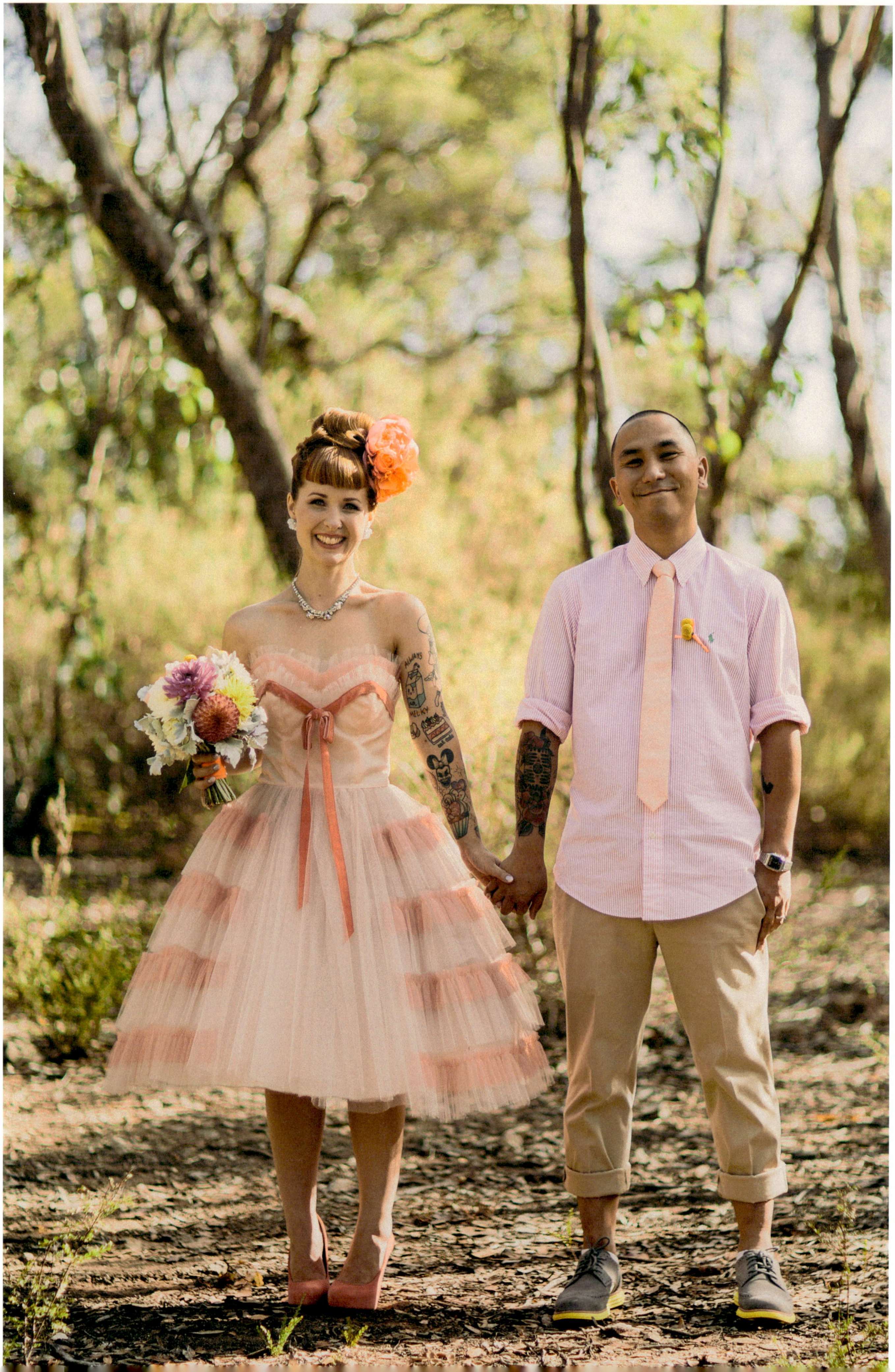

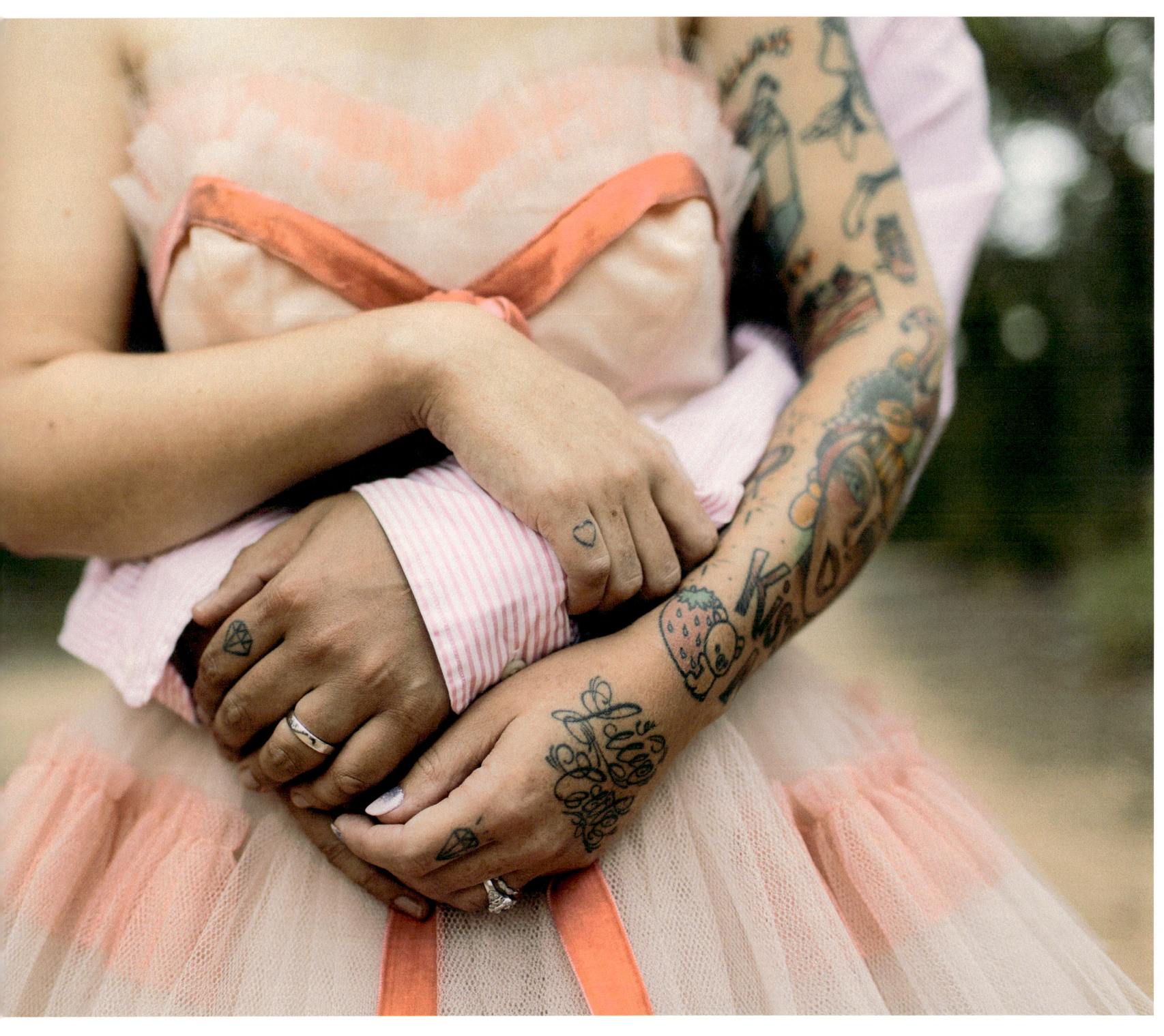

Talia & Zac

Talia and Zac are not white-wedding types. When they tied the knot, Talia wore pink, Zac rolled up his trousers, and they invited everyone to a houseparty in the Australian outback. The credits for creating the eclectic style read like a magazine photo shoot: chandeliers and invitations by Talia, signs by her brother, wedding favor bowls by her mum, coffee by her dad, Malaysian treats by Zac's parents. Tables with checked cloths and clusters of flowers were pure picnic magic, and the cake buffet kept energy levels up for the party.

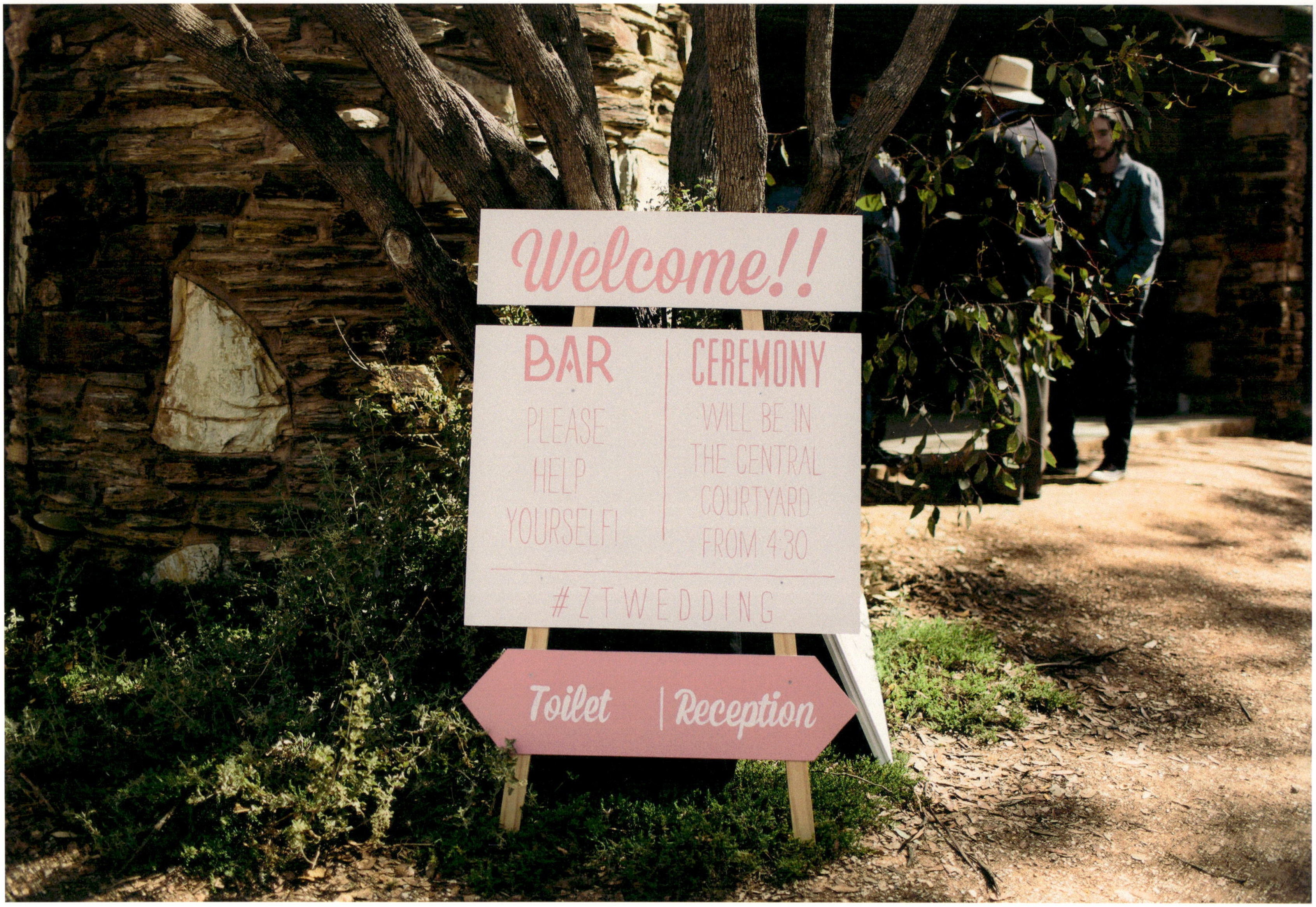

Welcome!!

BAR | CEREMONY

PLEASE HELP YOURSELF! | WILL BE IN THE CENTRAL COURTYARD FROM 4:30

#ZTWEDDING

Toilet | Reception

Welcome to Our Wedding...

You probably want your guests to spend their time celebrating and having fun, not searching for the bar or the powder room, right? Handpainted welcome signs, like the one Talia's brother made for her and Zac, are brilliant little helpers on the day. They let you tell it exactly like it is and leave everyone free to worry about more important things—like whether they should have that third glass of champagne before they sign the guestbook, or after...

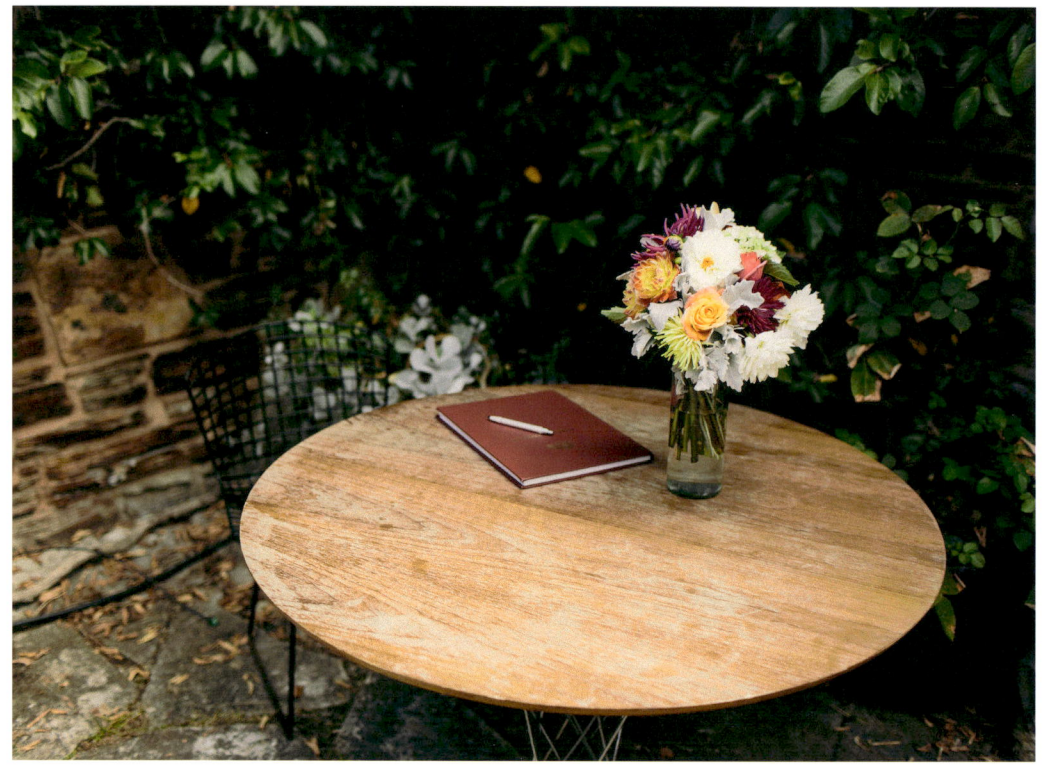

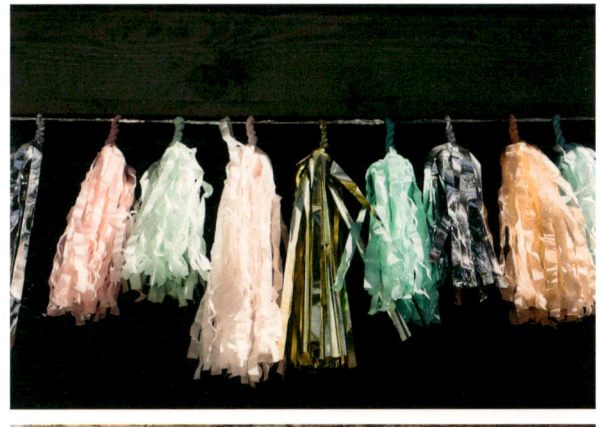

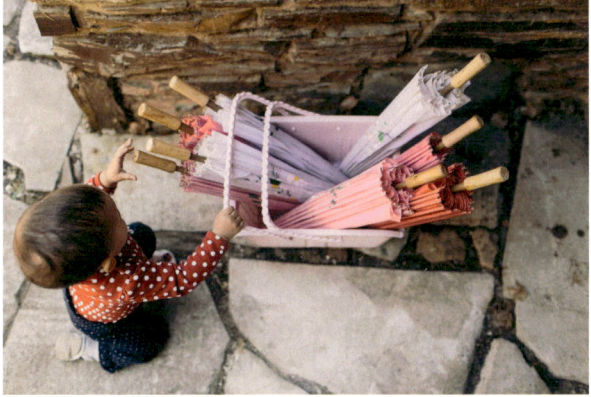

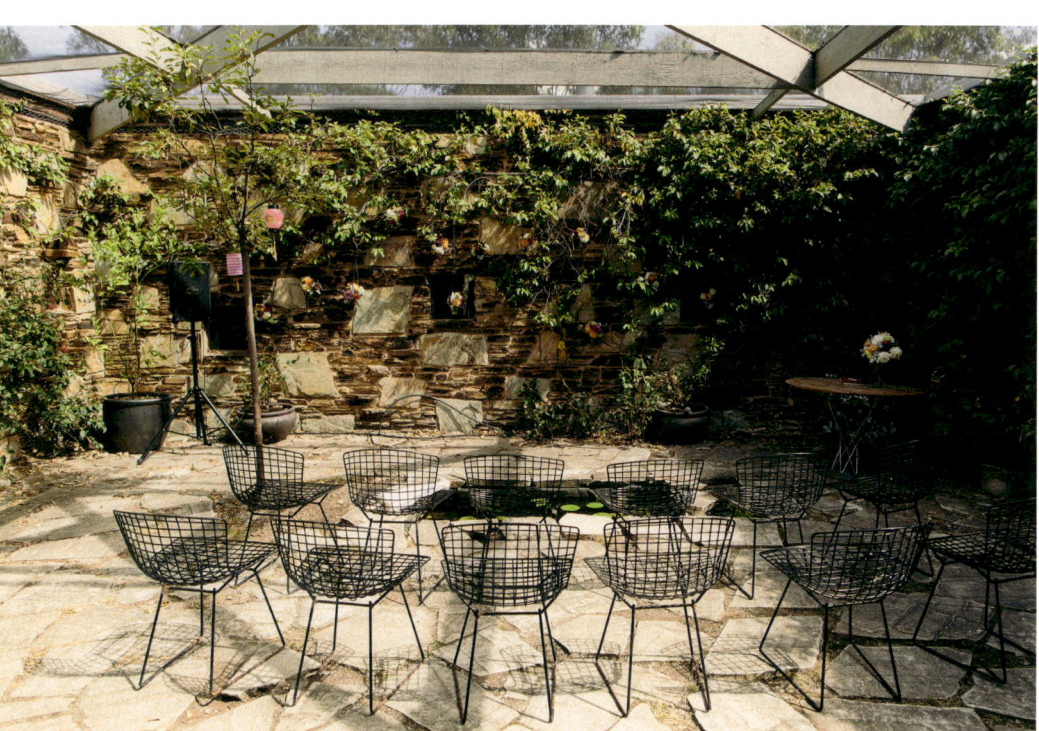

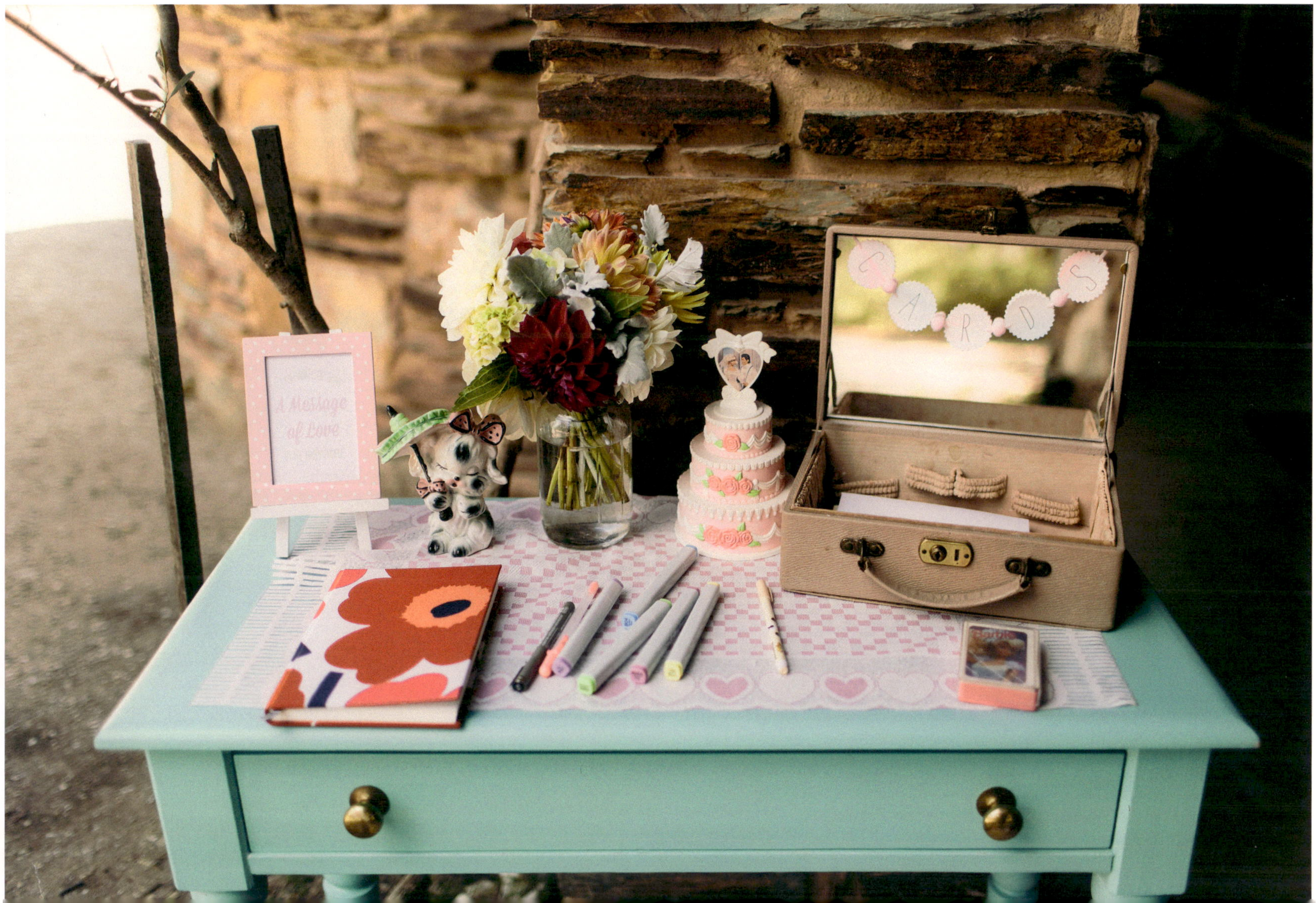

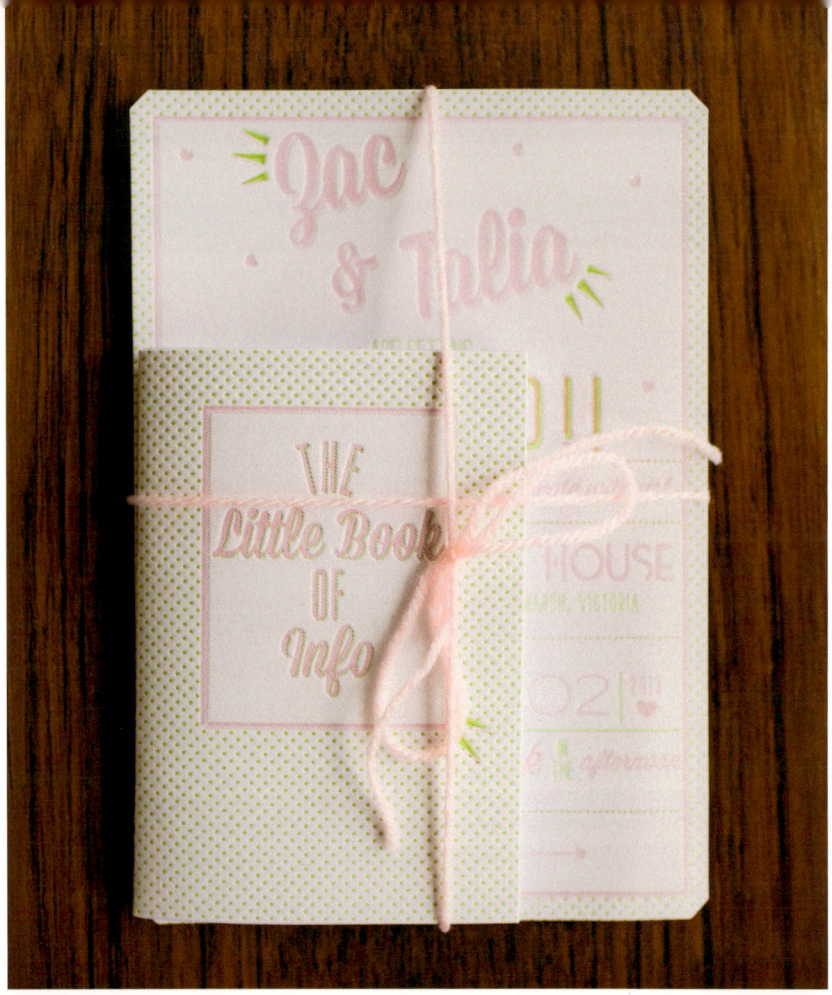

Little Book of Info

Weddings! There's so much you have to tell everyone. With all the details about how to get to the venue, what to wear, where to stay, presents (yes or no), and plans for the day after, you could write a book. So why don't you? It might not win you a Pulitzer, but it will be an inspired addition to your invites. It also has the added benefit of being hard to lose—even the most absent-minded of your guests will be able to keep hold of a little beauty like this.

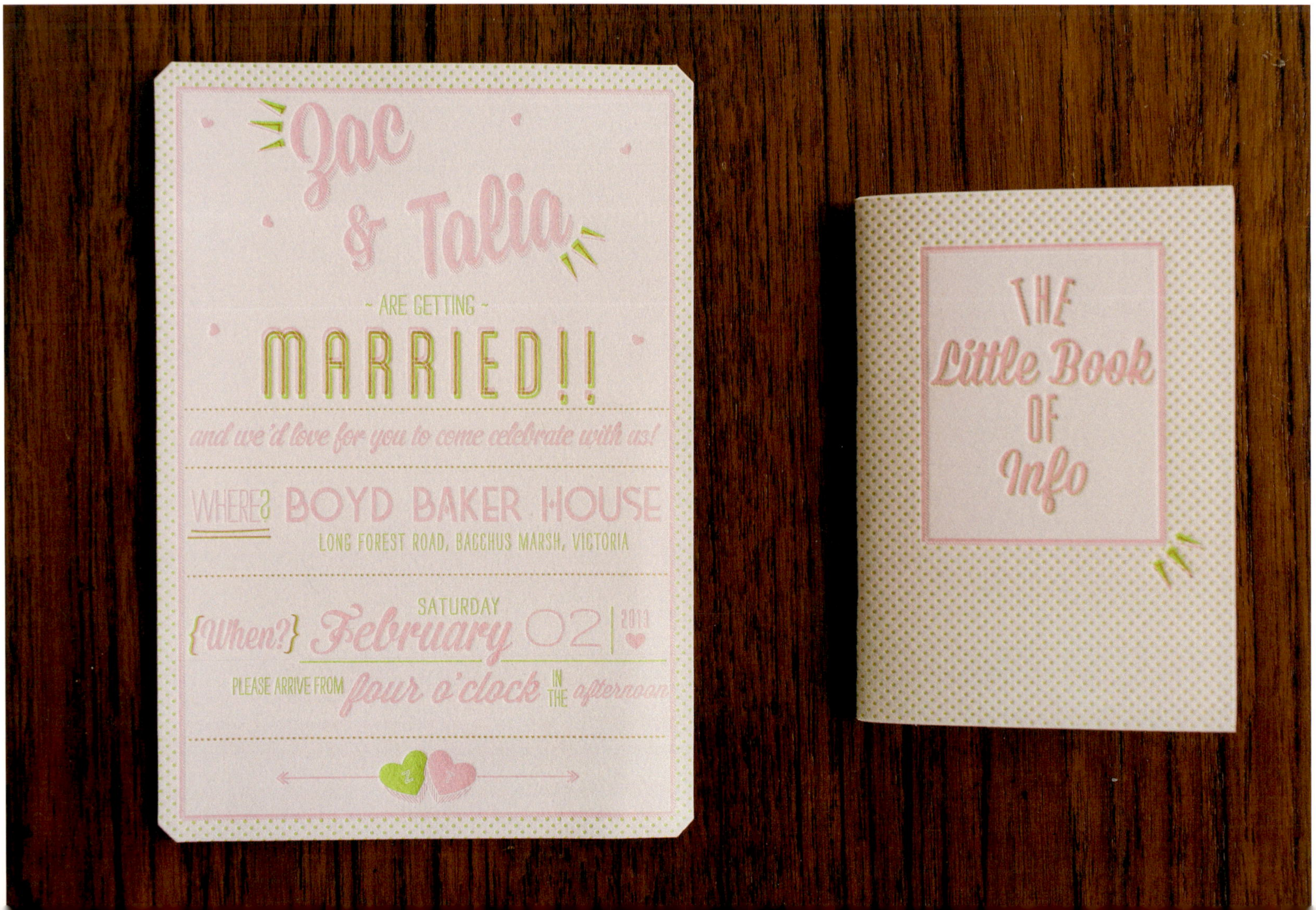

Zac & Talia

~ ARE GETTING ~

MARRIED!!

and we'd love for you to come celebrate with us!

WHERE? BOYD BAKER HOUSE
LONG FOREST ROAD, BACCHUS MARSH, VICTORIA

{When?} SATURDAY February 02 2013
PLEASE ARRIVE FROM four o'clock in the afternoon

THE Little Book OF Info

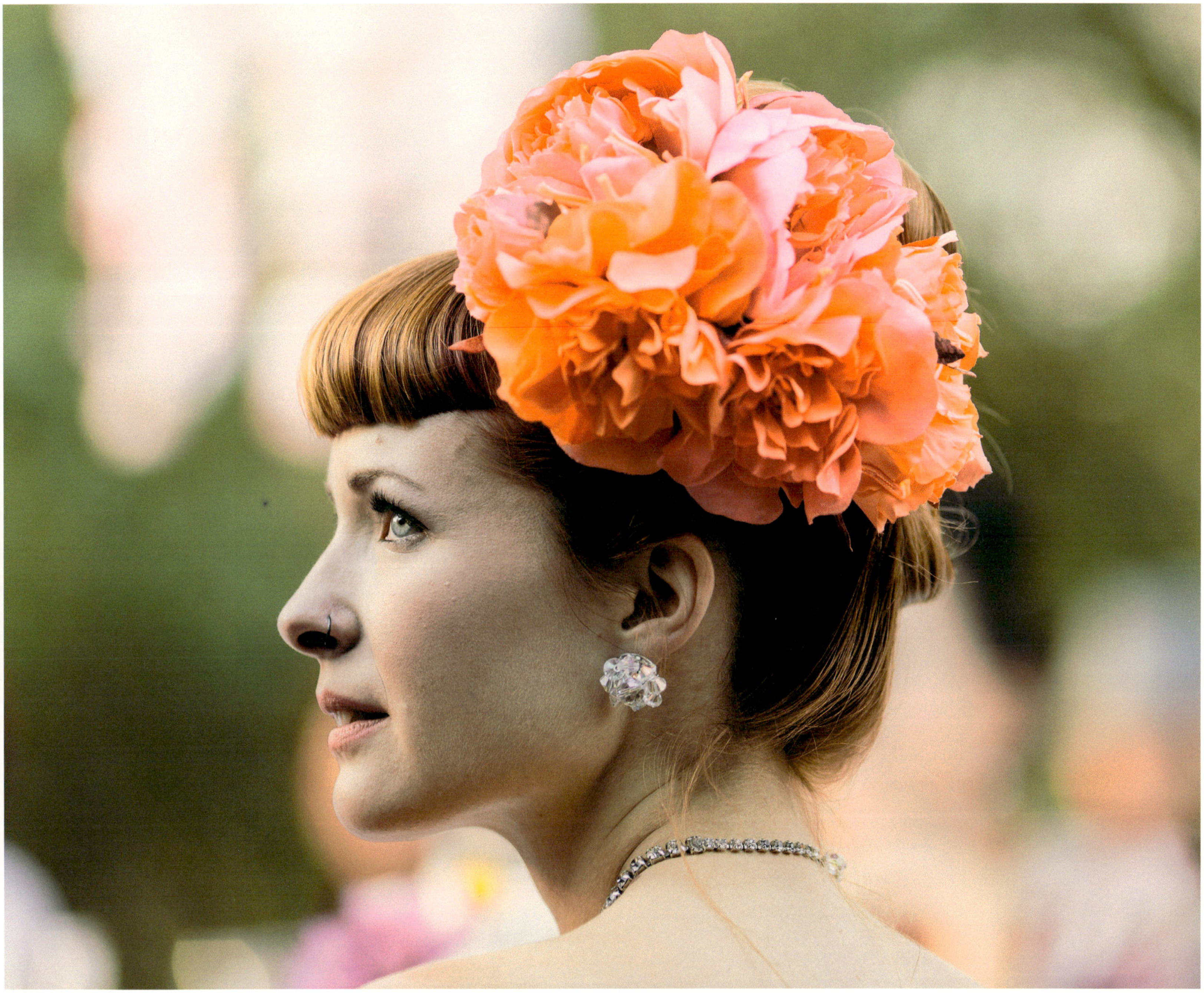

The dress doesn't have to do all the work, and a veil is not the only way to go. Talia's bold headpiece of orange and pink flowers was a fabulous addition to her fifties-style outfit.

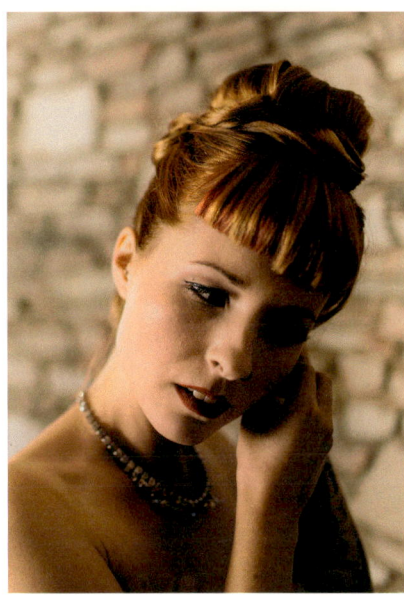

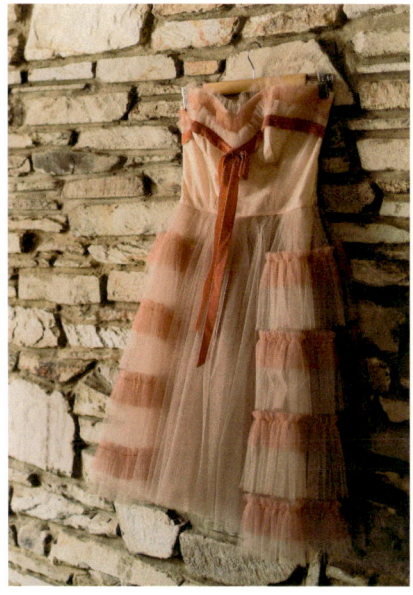

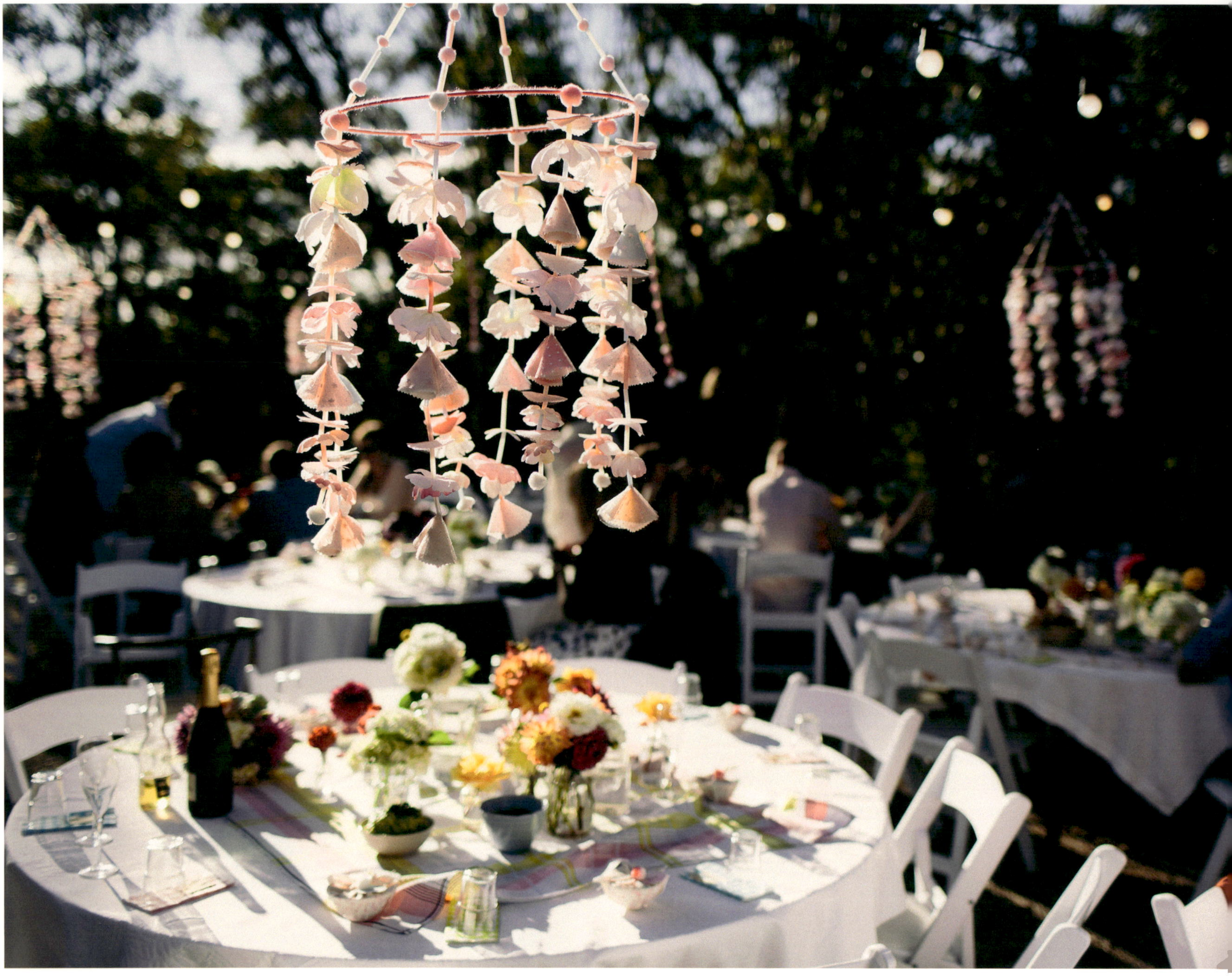

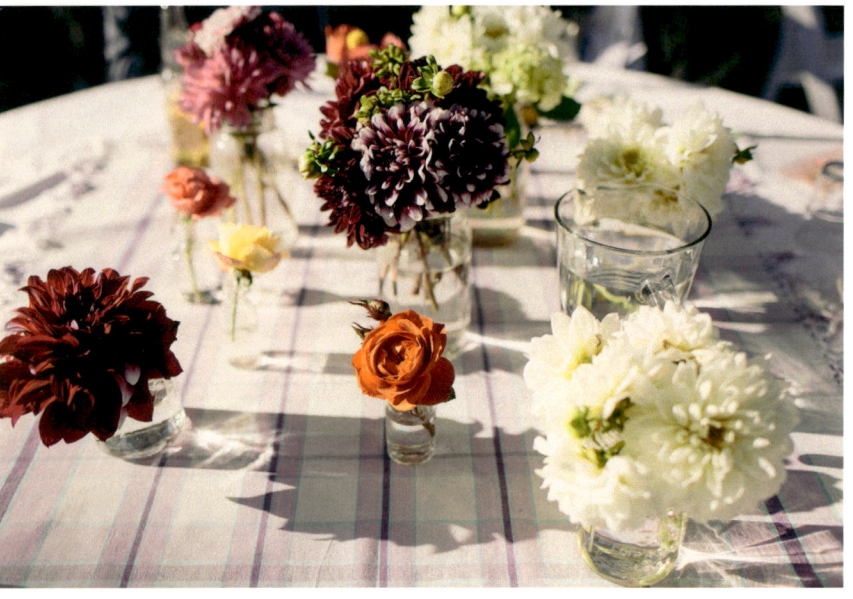

Blooming Marvelous

1. Mismatched jars and cute posies bring picnic chic to a celebration in the sun.

2. Talia spent ages cutting out the fabric for these chandeliers—and it was worth every snip.

3. Guests took home pottery bowls (mother of the bride) wrapped in hand-stamped fabric.

4. These tables are a far cry from formal dining, but who said a wedding had to be formal?

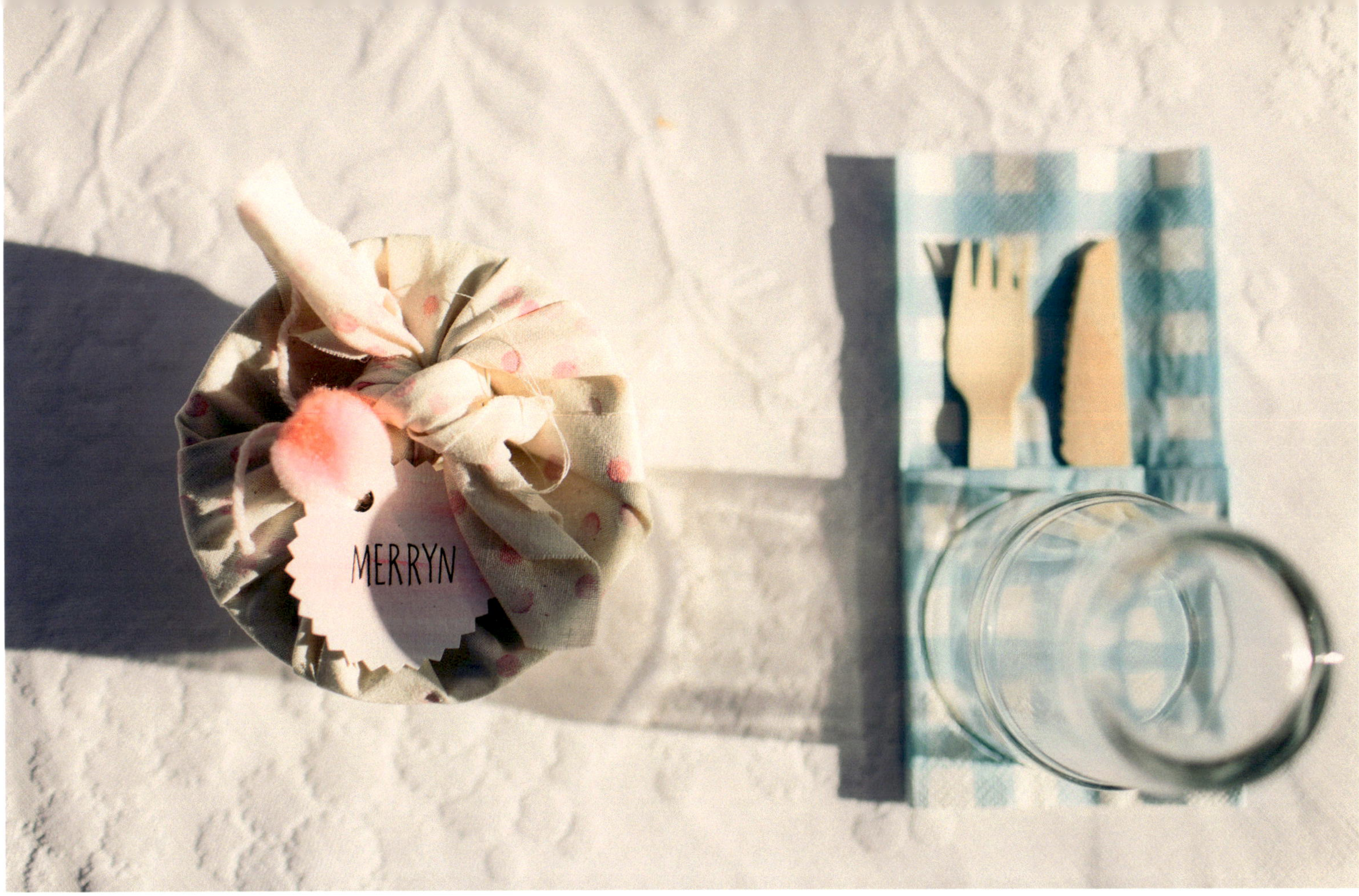

MERRYN

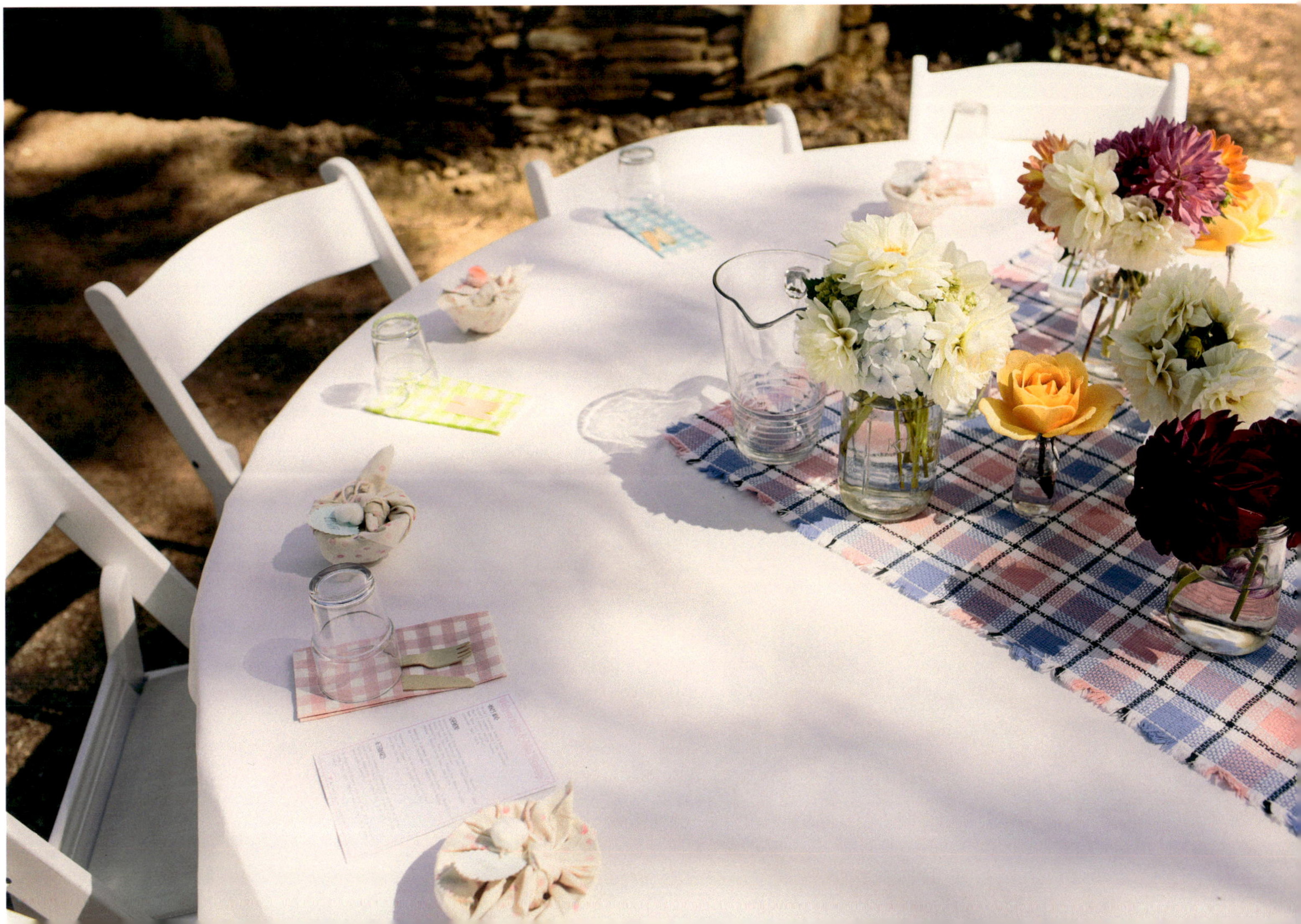

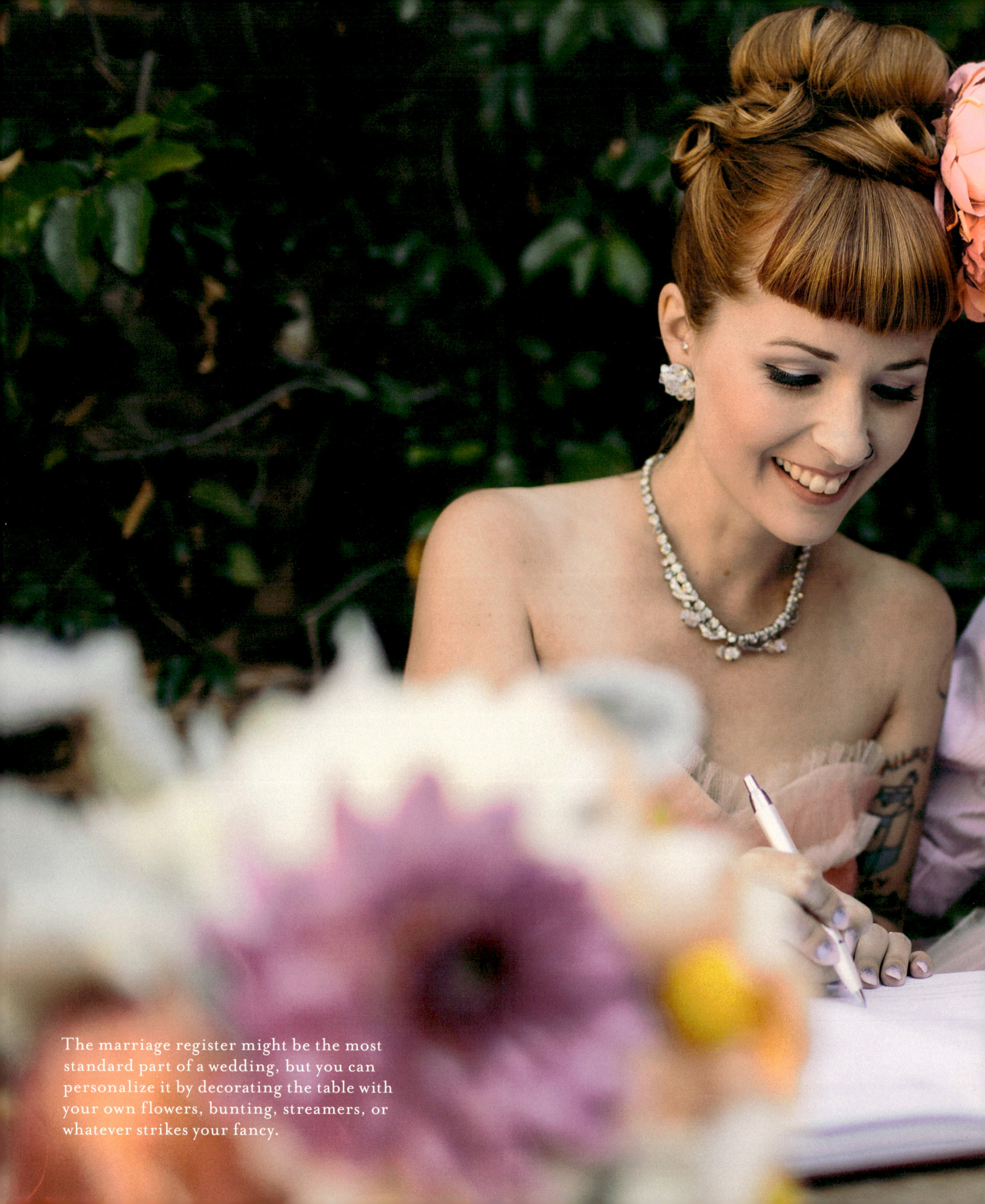

The marriage register might be the most standard part of a wedding, but you can personalize it by decorating the table with your own flowers, bunting, streamers, or whatever strikes your fancy.

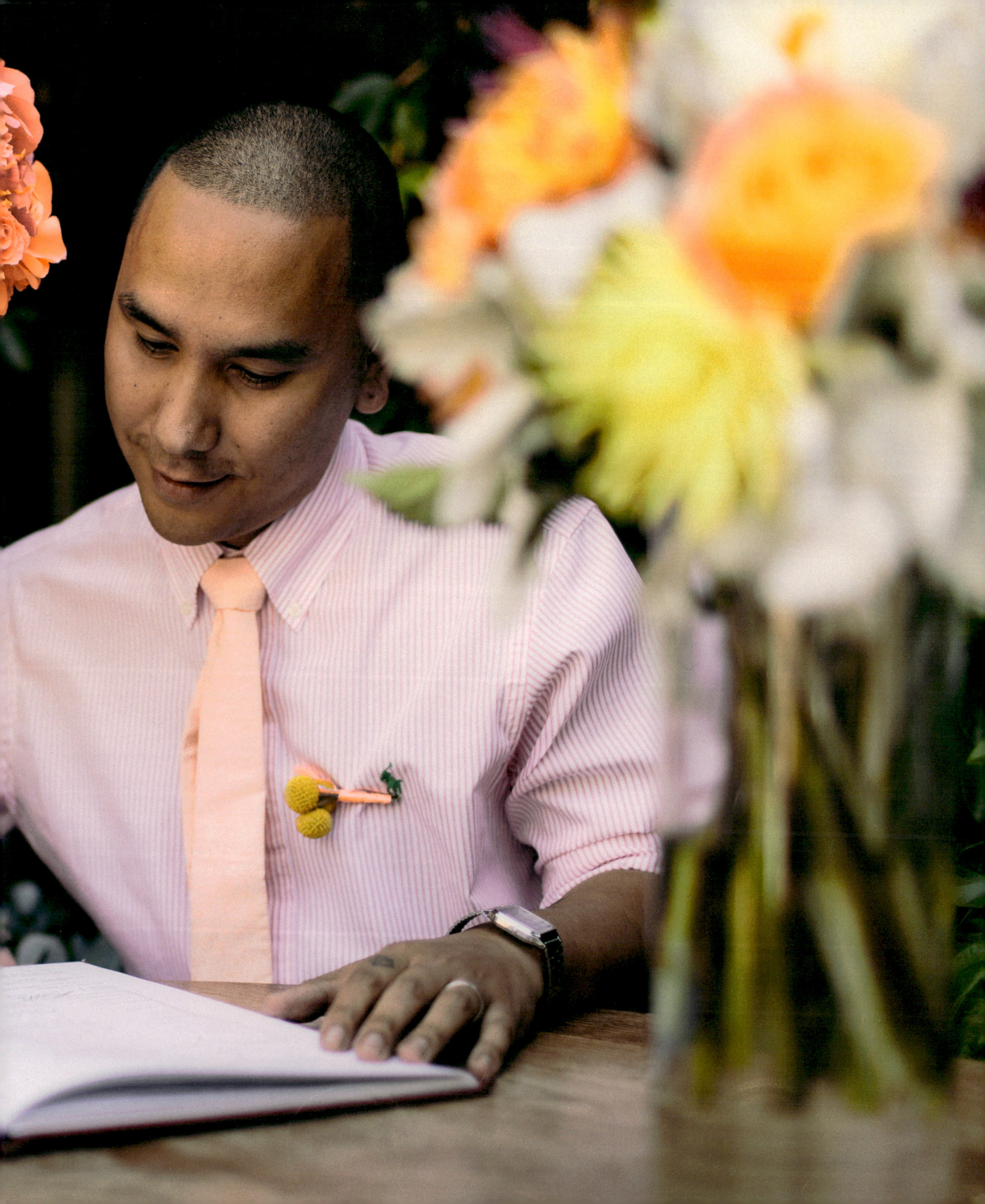

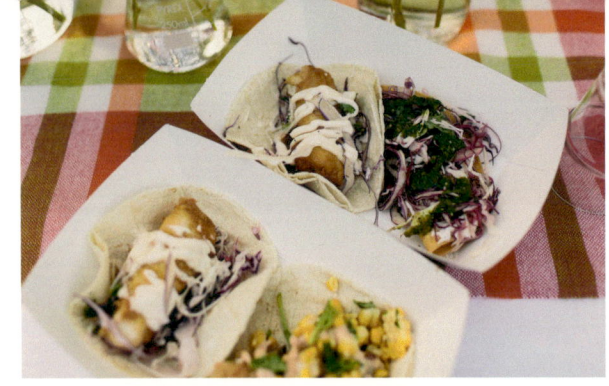

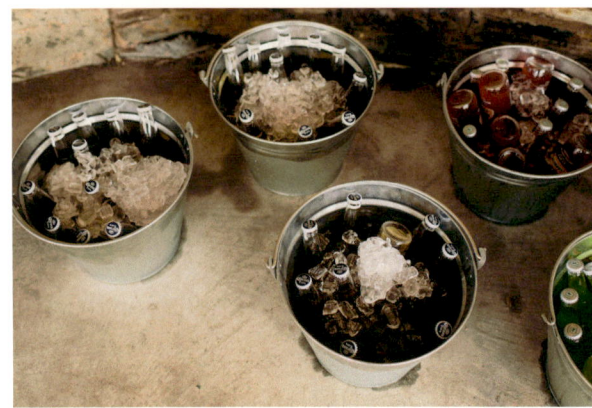

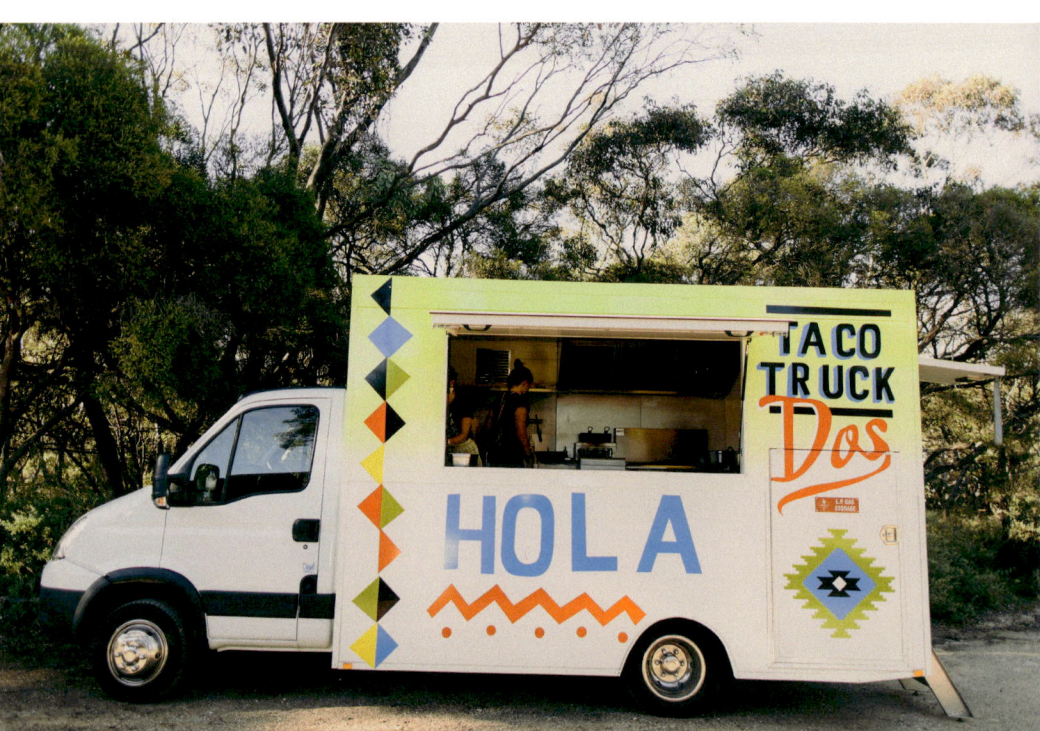

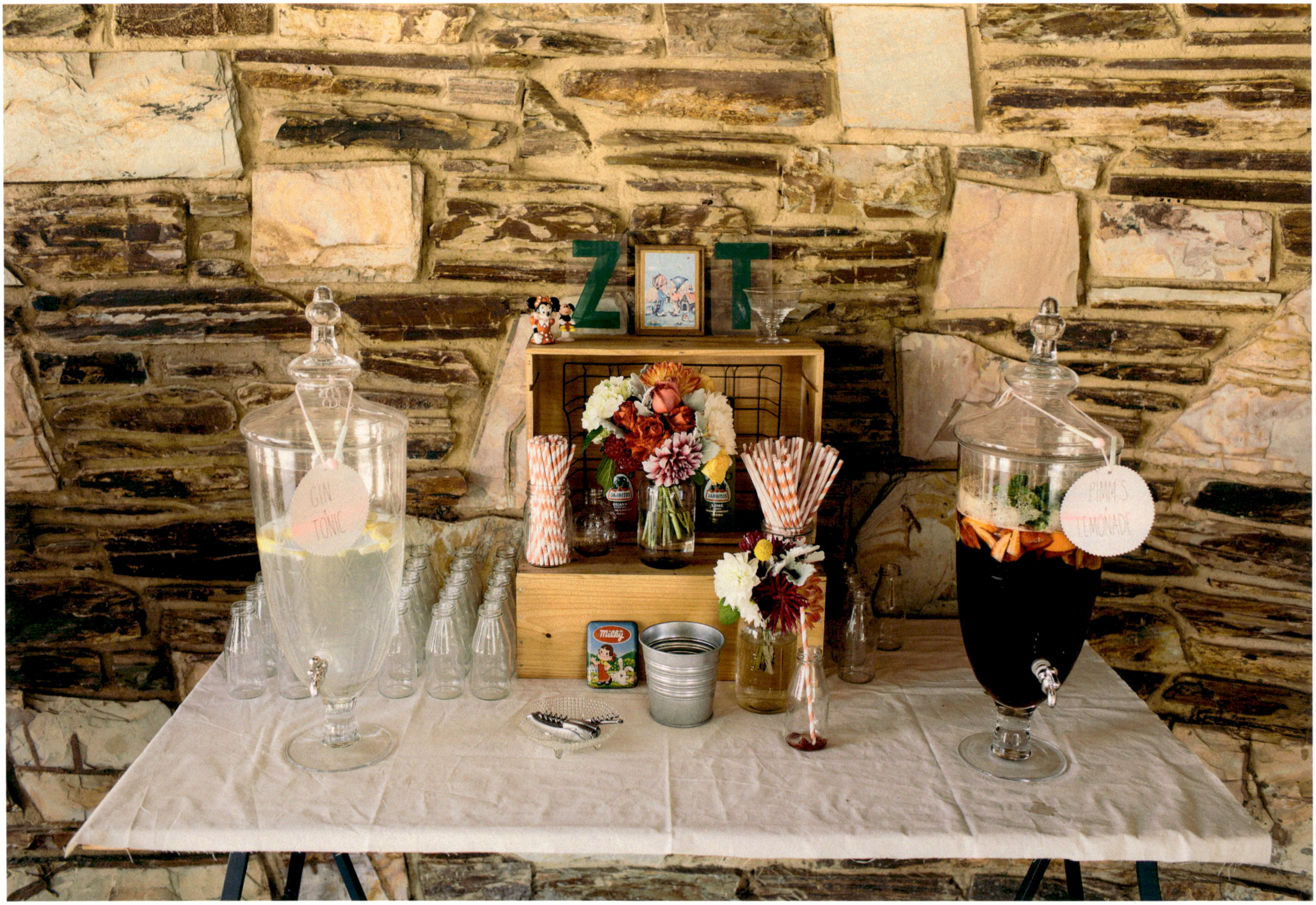

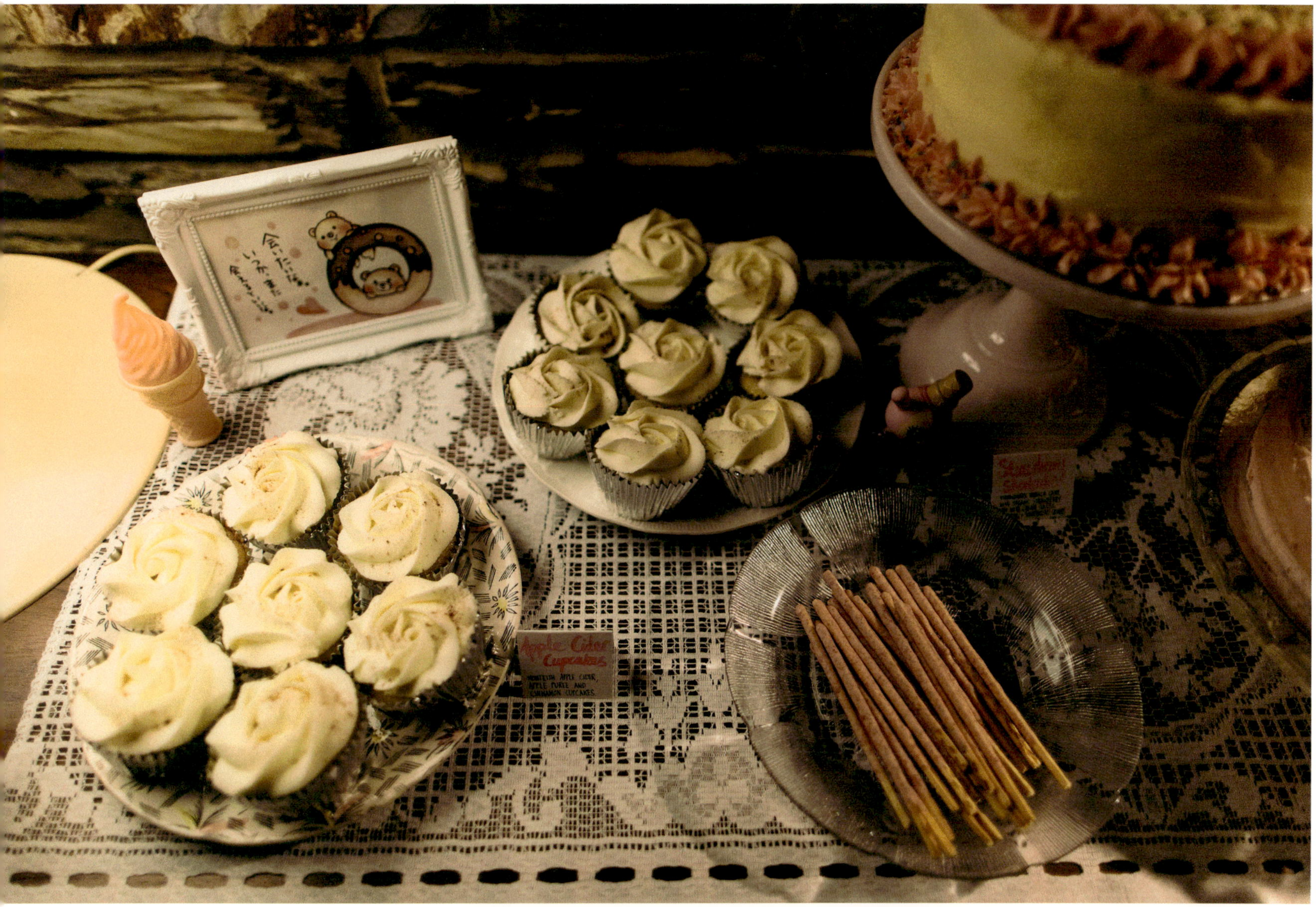

Tacos and Treats

When it comes to refreshments, any good houseparty host knows that the best thing is to let everyone get on with it themselves. Zac and Talia's guests were free to pour drinks from elegant glass dispensers and to grab their own tacos from the truck for dinner.

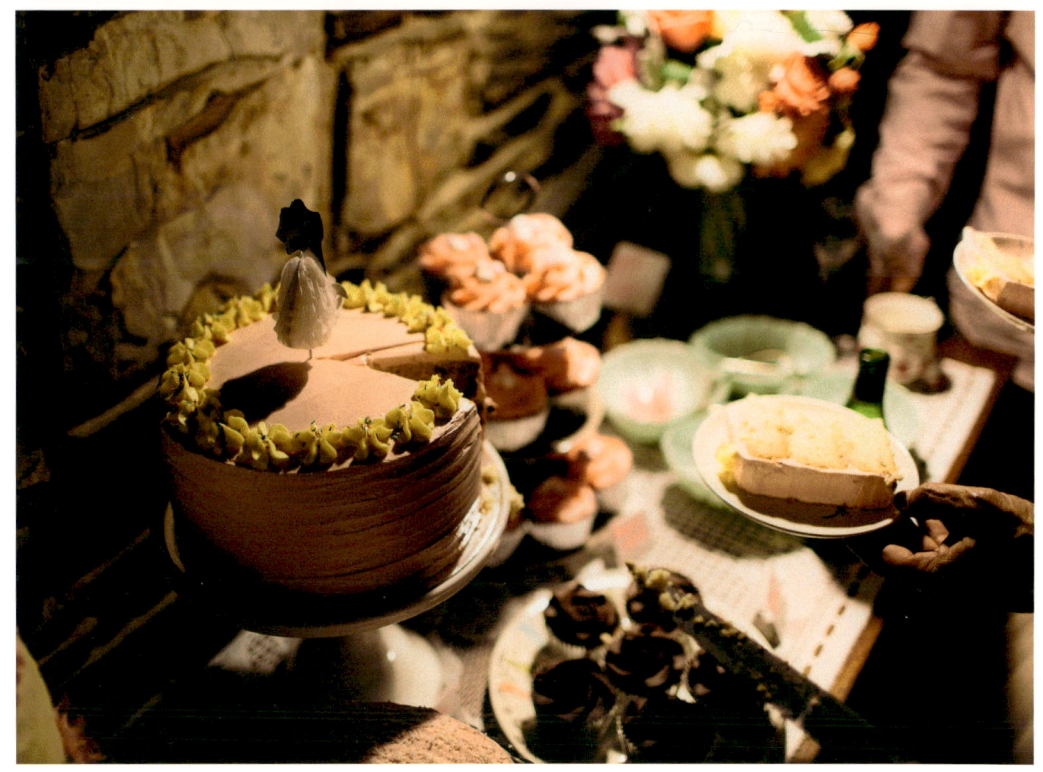

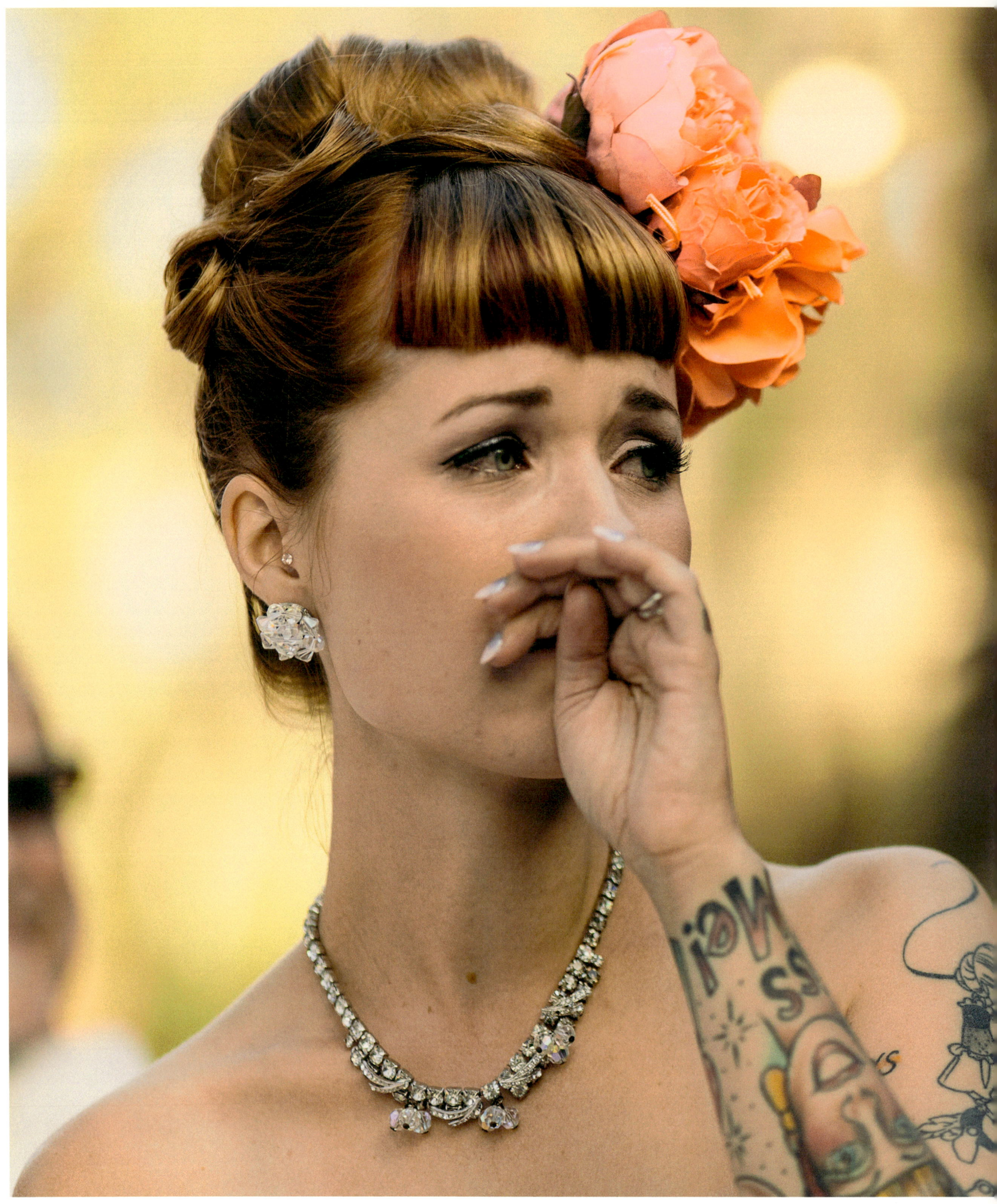

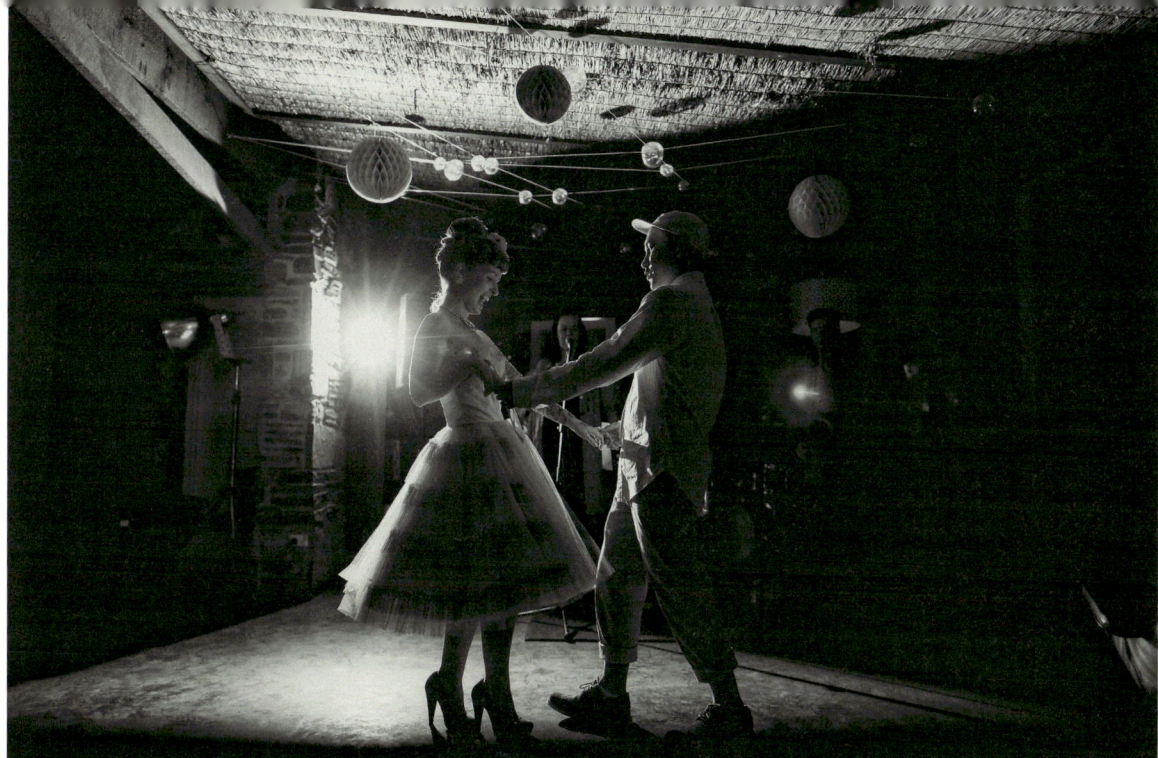

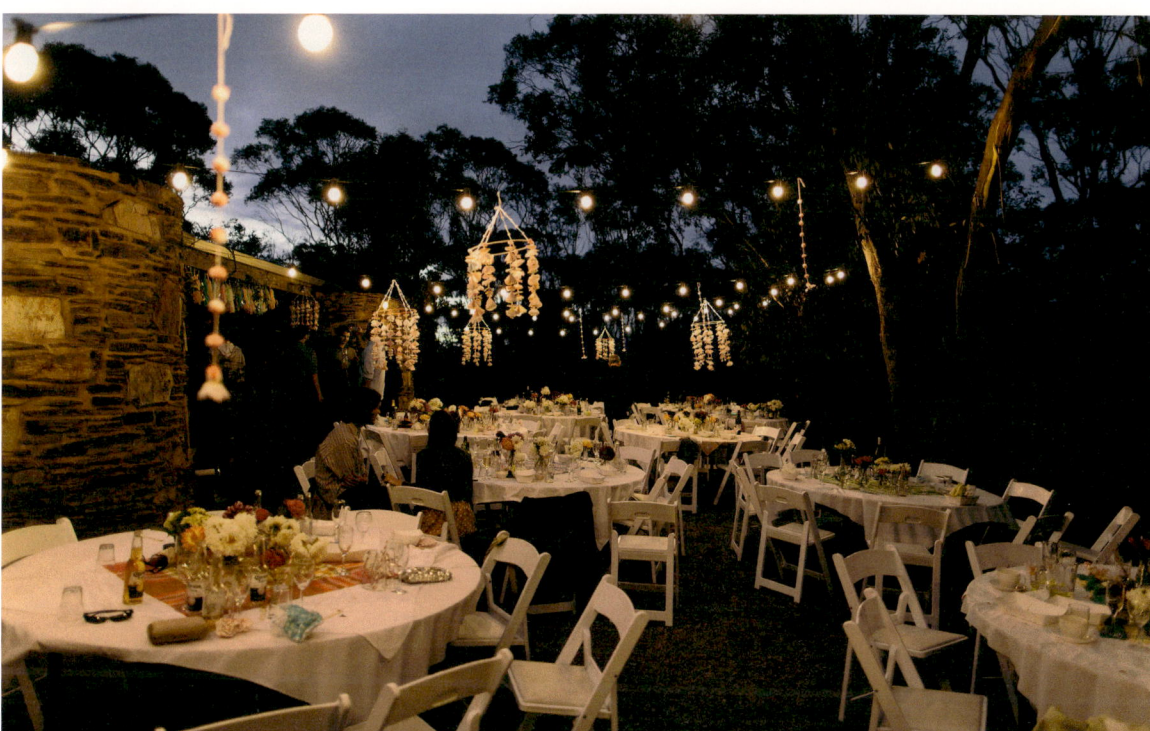

Weddings are the best kind of emotional roll-ercoasters. Talia went from happy tears during the speeches to hoots of laughter as she and Zac danced their first dance. With a live band playing and homemade decorations overhead, the couple created an intimate, relaxed atmosphere for the evening celebrations.

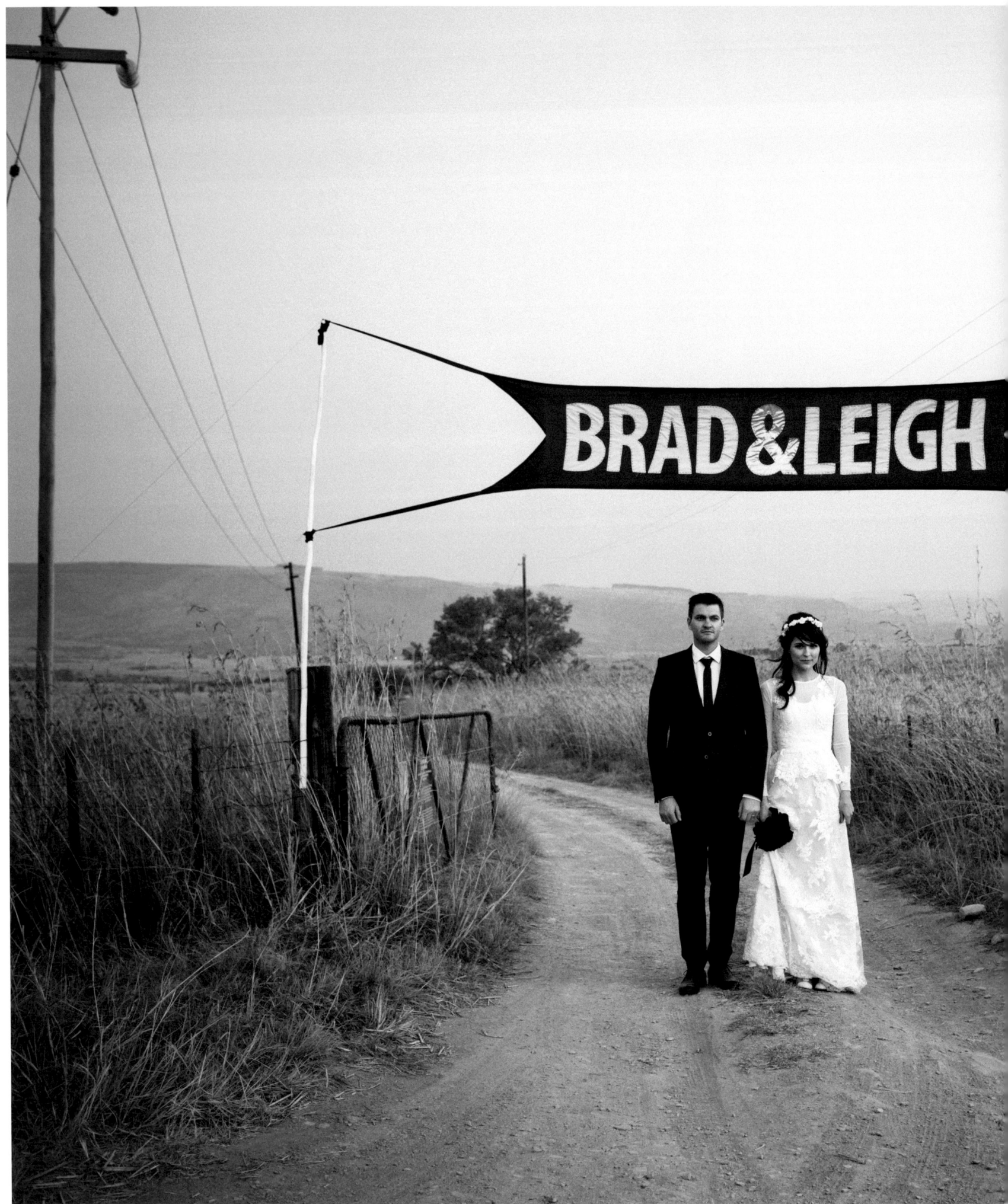

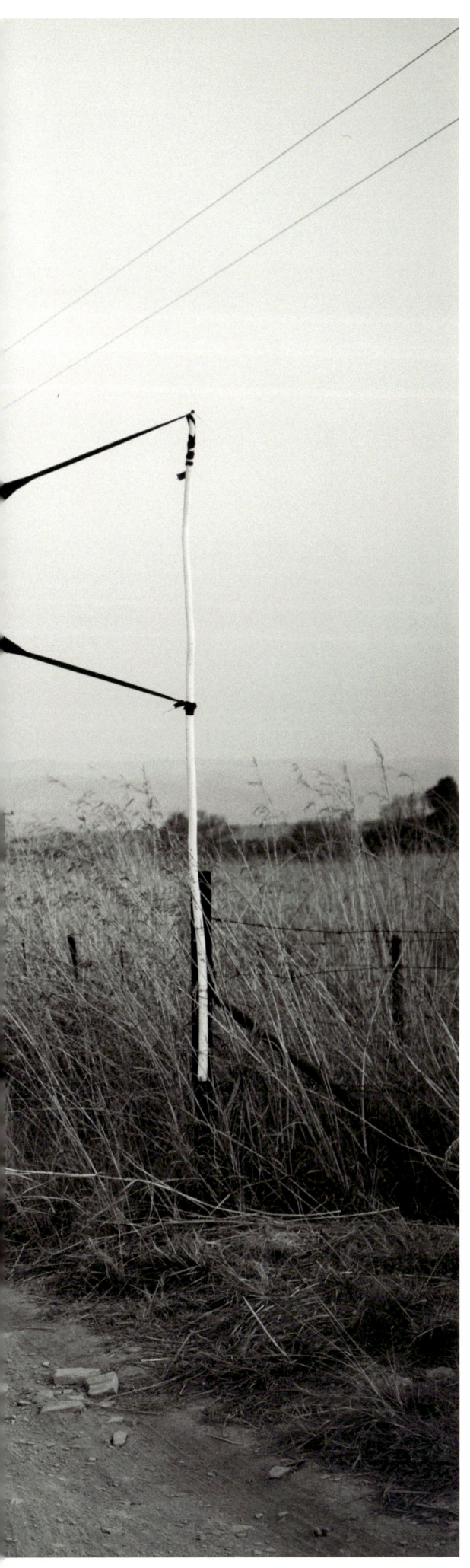

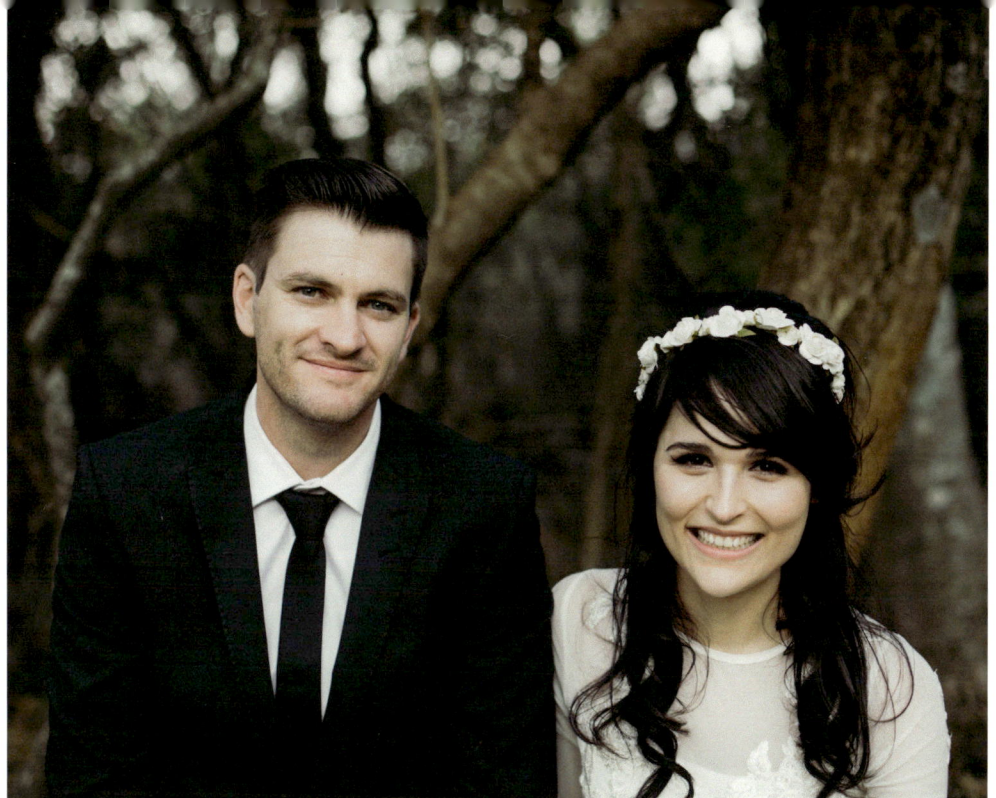

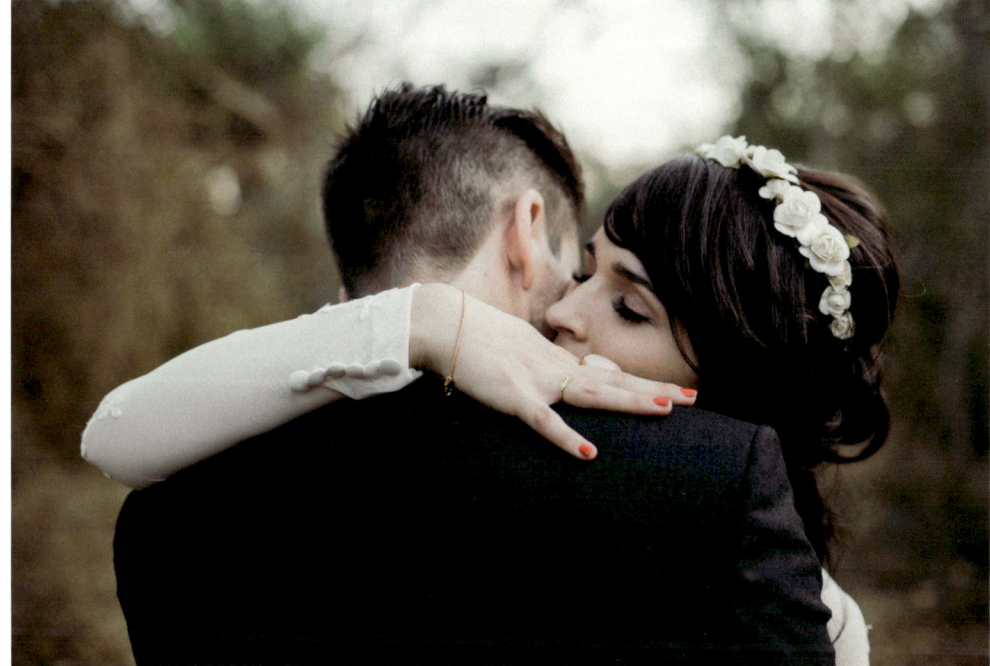

Leigh & Brad

Gathered in the shade, a small group of people look on as a young couple make their vows. The scene is so intimate and relaxed that it is almost as if the bride and groom just woke up that morning and said: let's do it today. That kind of spontaneous feel is exactly what Leigh and Brad wanted. Friends helped out with the preparations, and the groom's father performed the ceremony.

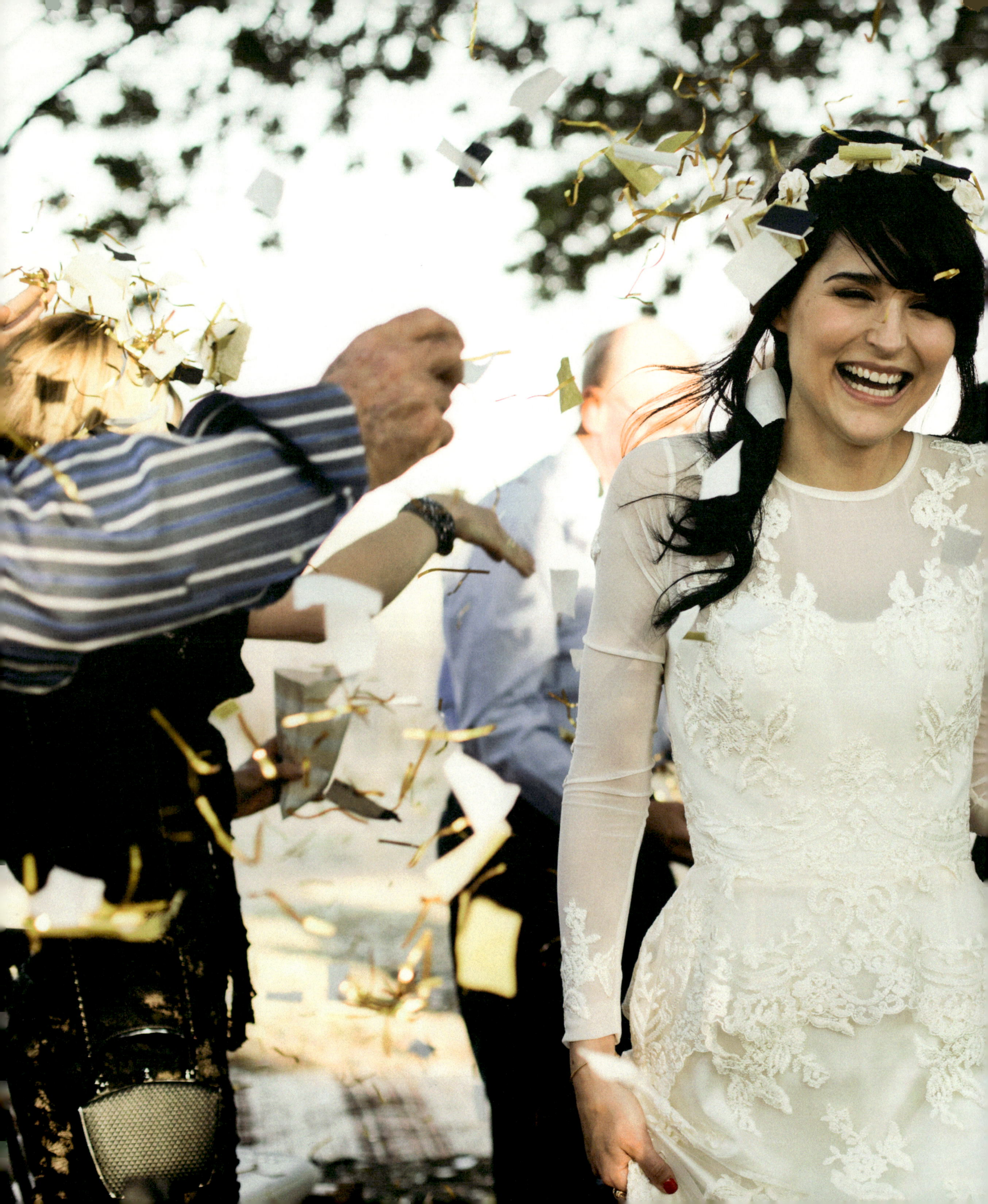

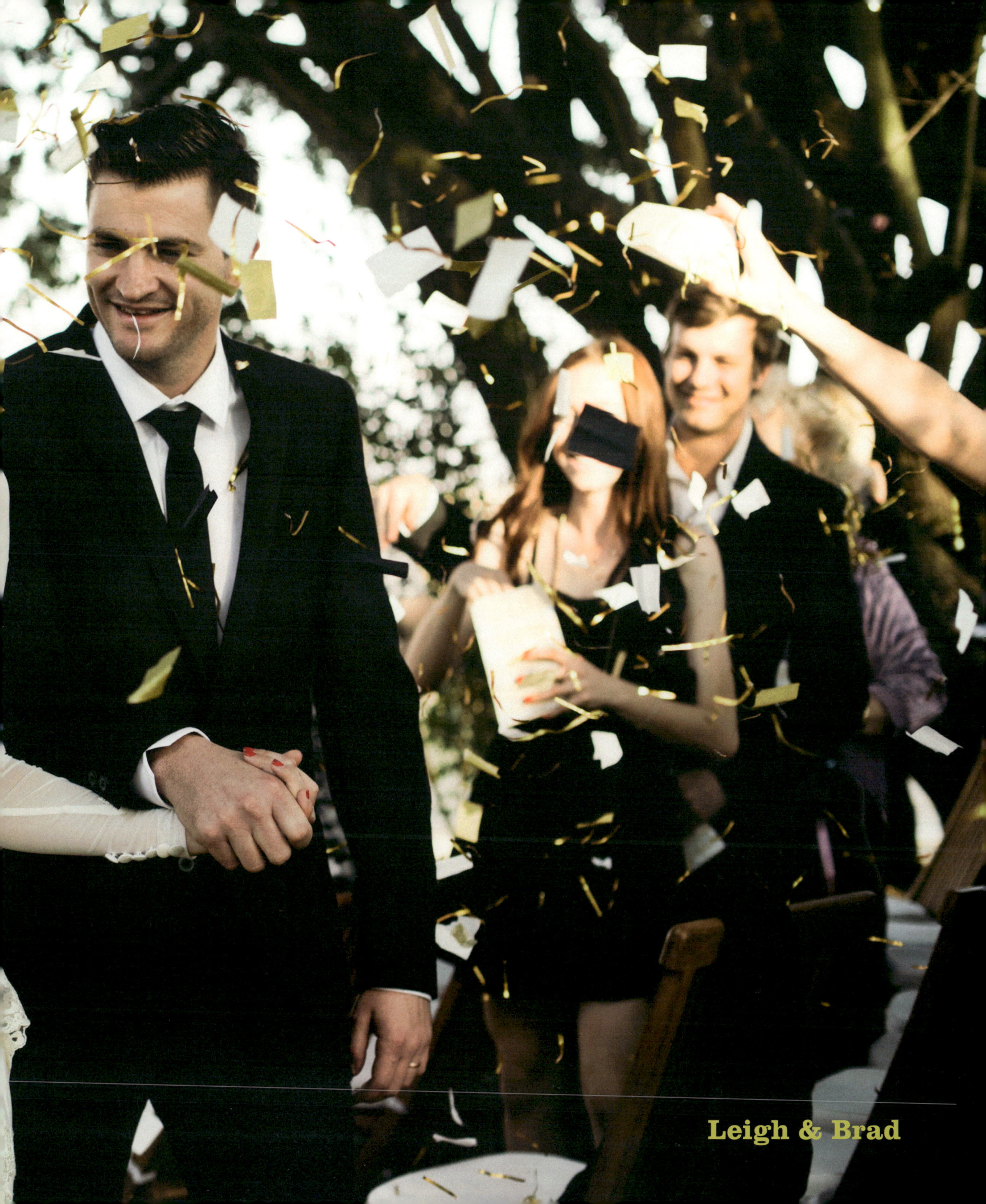

Leigh & Brad

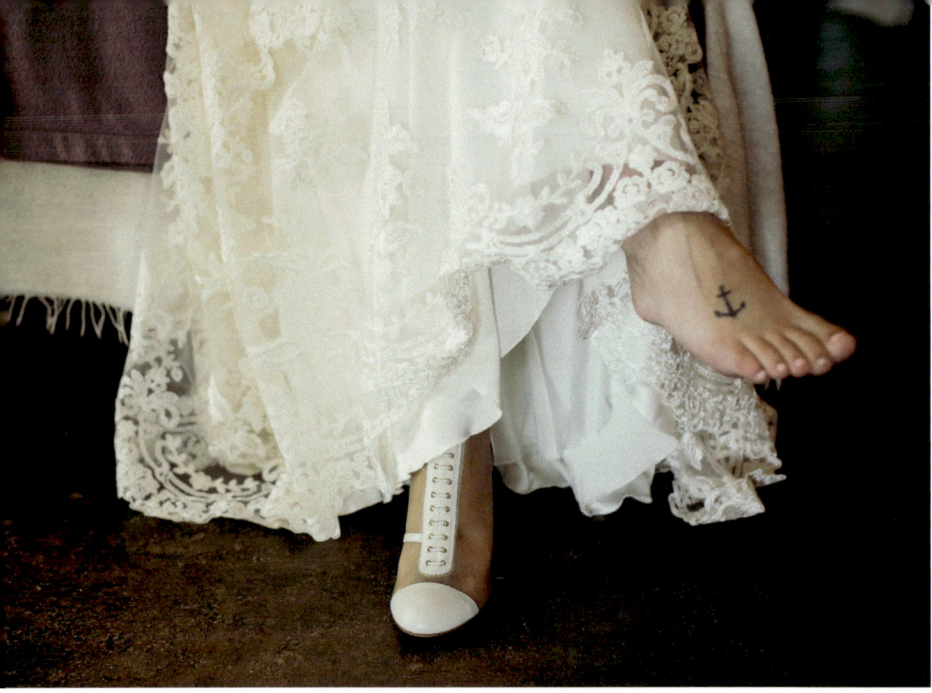

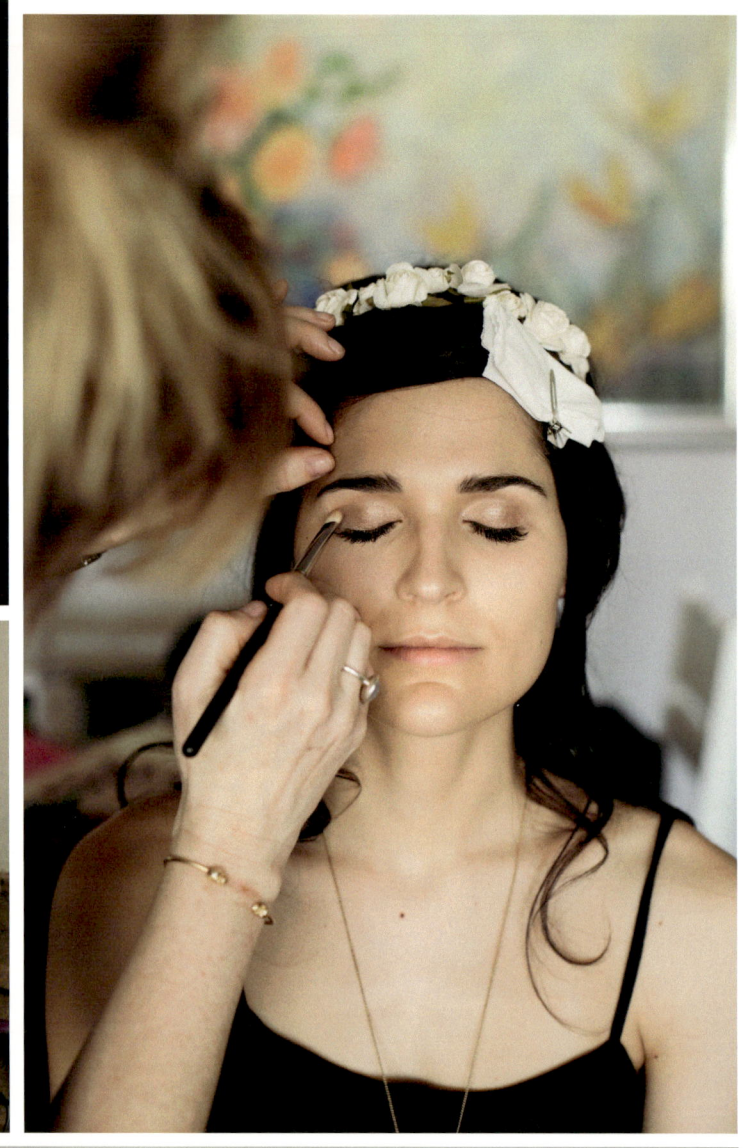

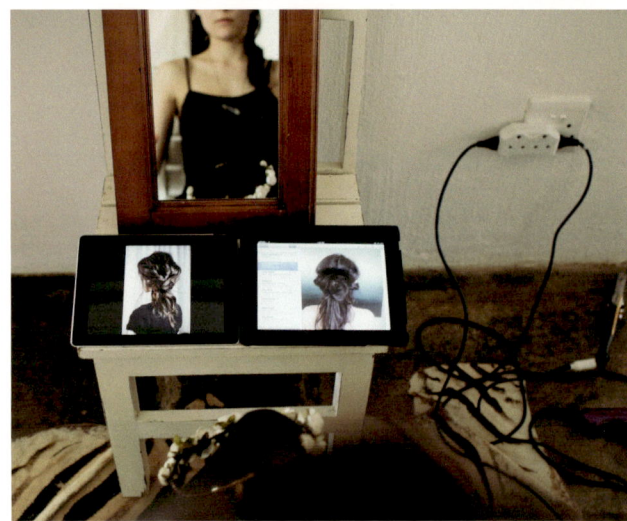

Lace, tattoos, and tablet computers: three very different worlds, one happy bride.

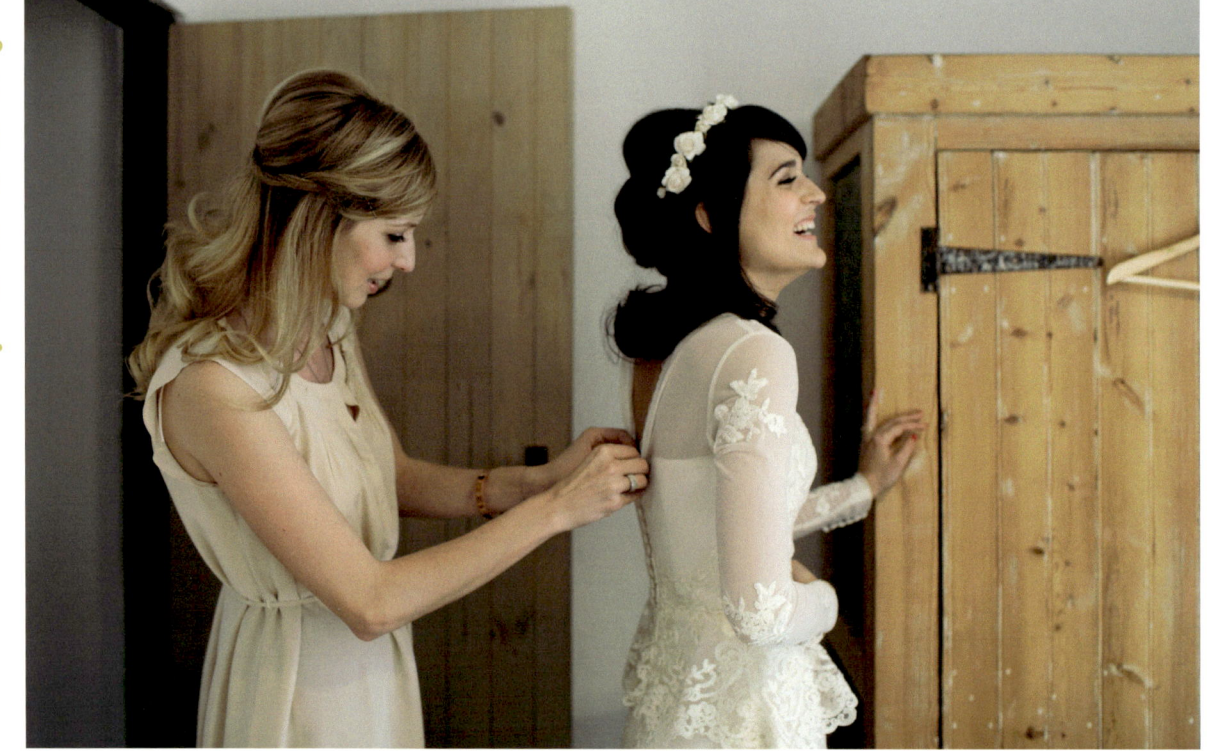

Strike a Pose

Official photos are gorgeous, no question. But a photo-booth sticks around all night and is on hand to capture you and your guests when you're feeling at your most creative, most silly, or most in the mood for voguing it up like you were born to be in a music video.

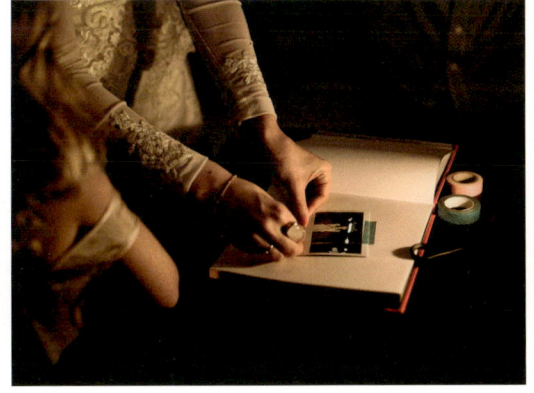

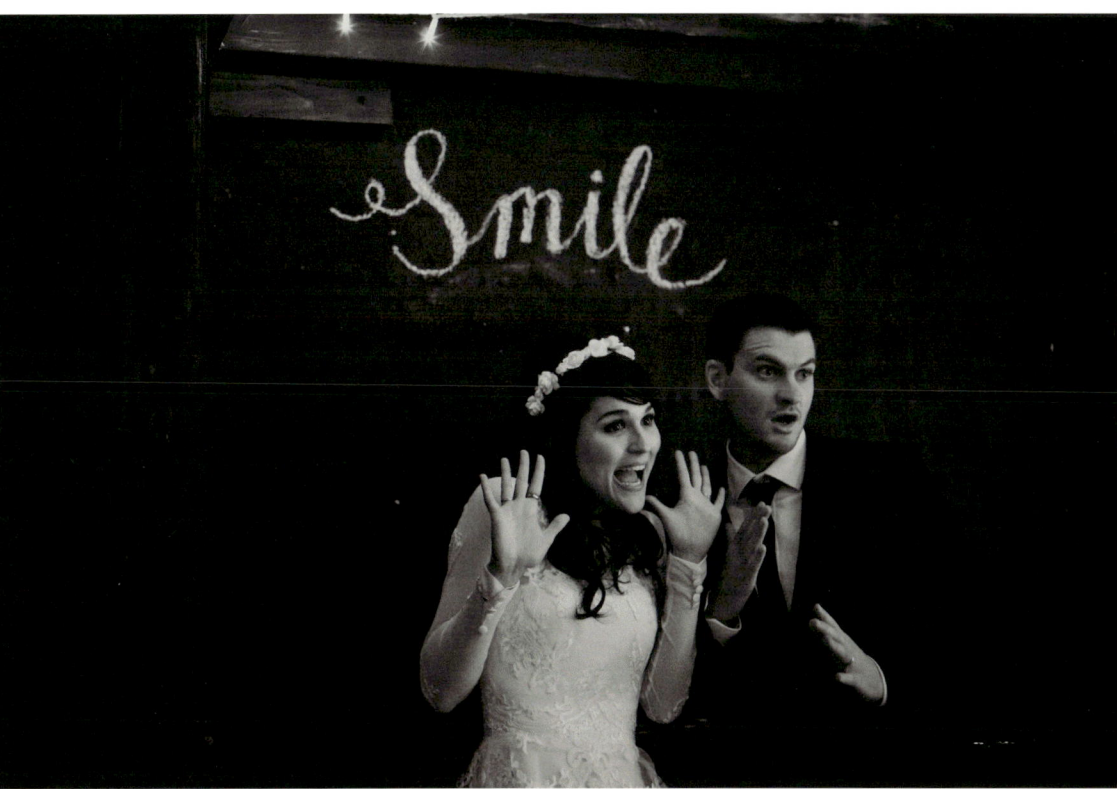

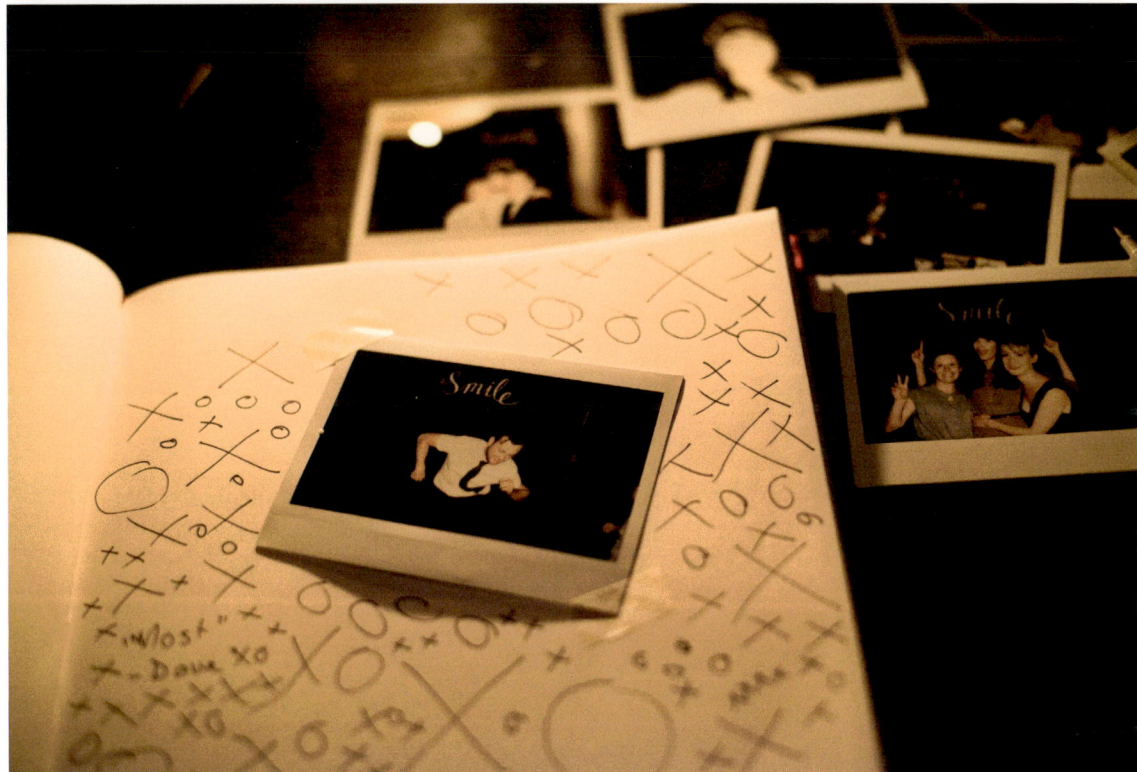

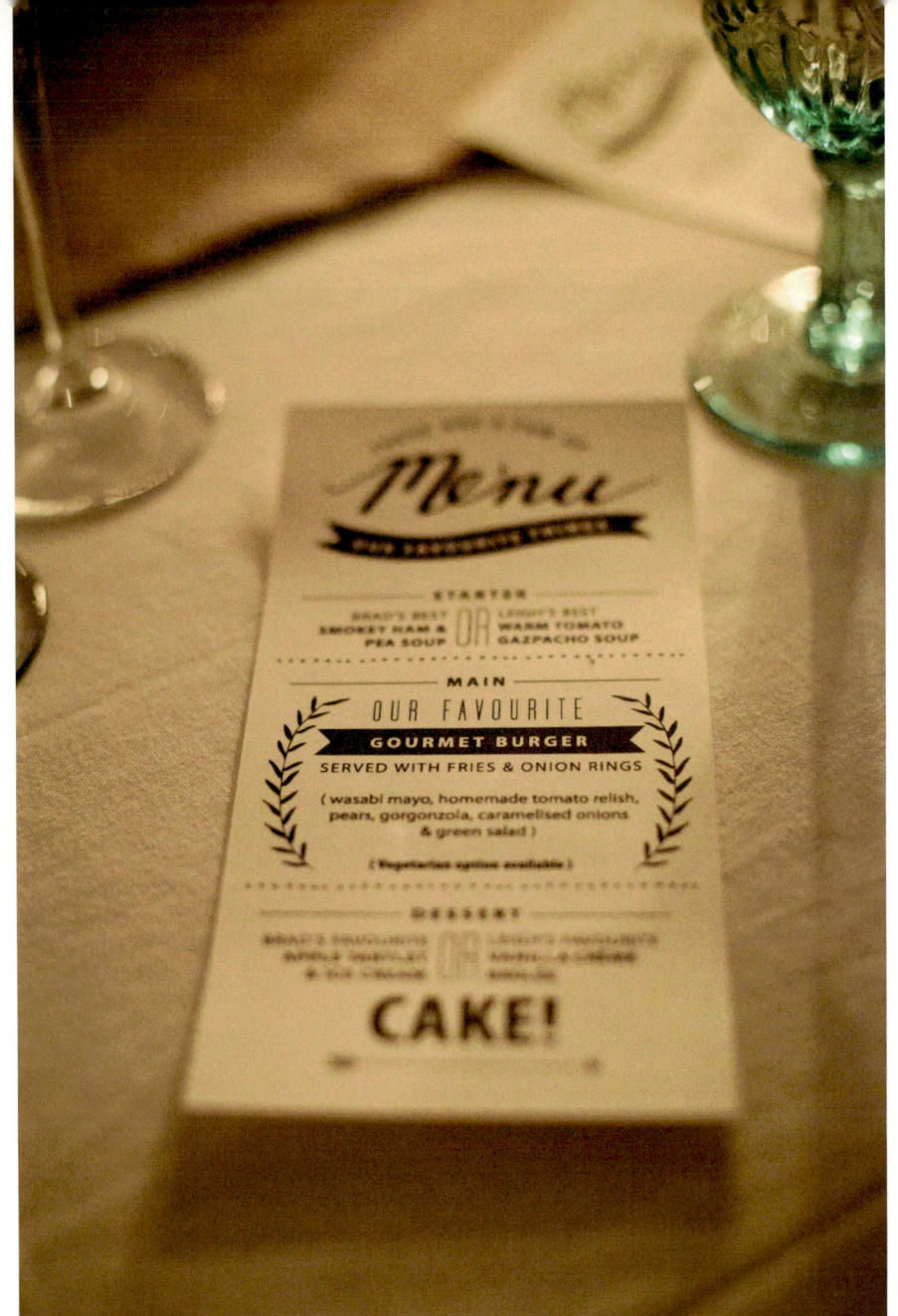

Sharing the Limelight

Vintage blacks, whites, and golds merge with bright bohemian flair. Pink drinks sparkle happily in the sun. Fairy lights twinkle in the rafters, and candles flicker from inside glass jars. For this one day, the vast beauty of the South African bush has let the lime-light shine elsewhere.

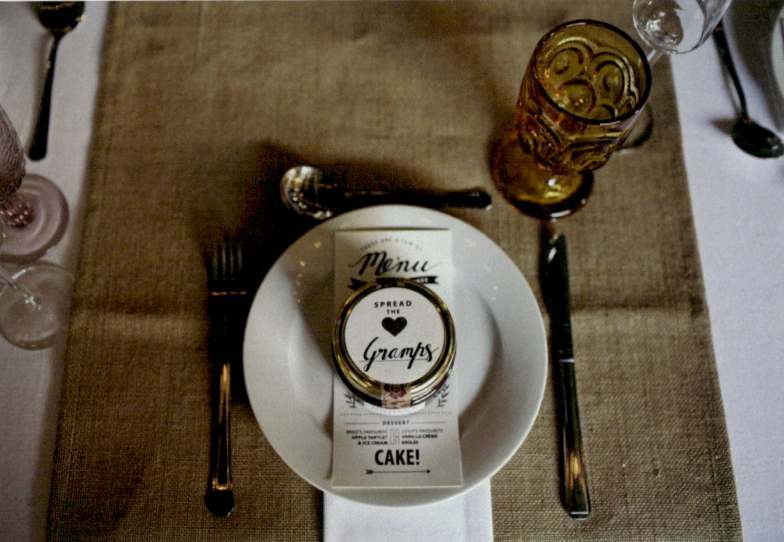

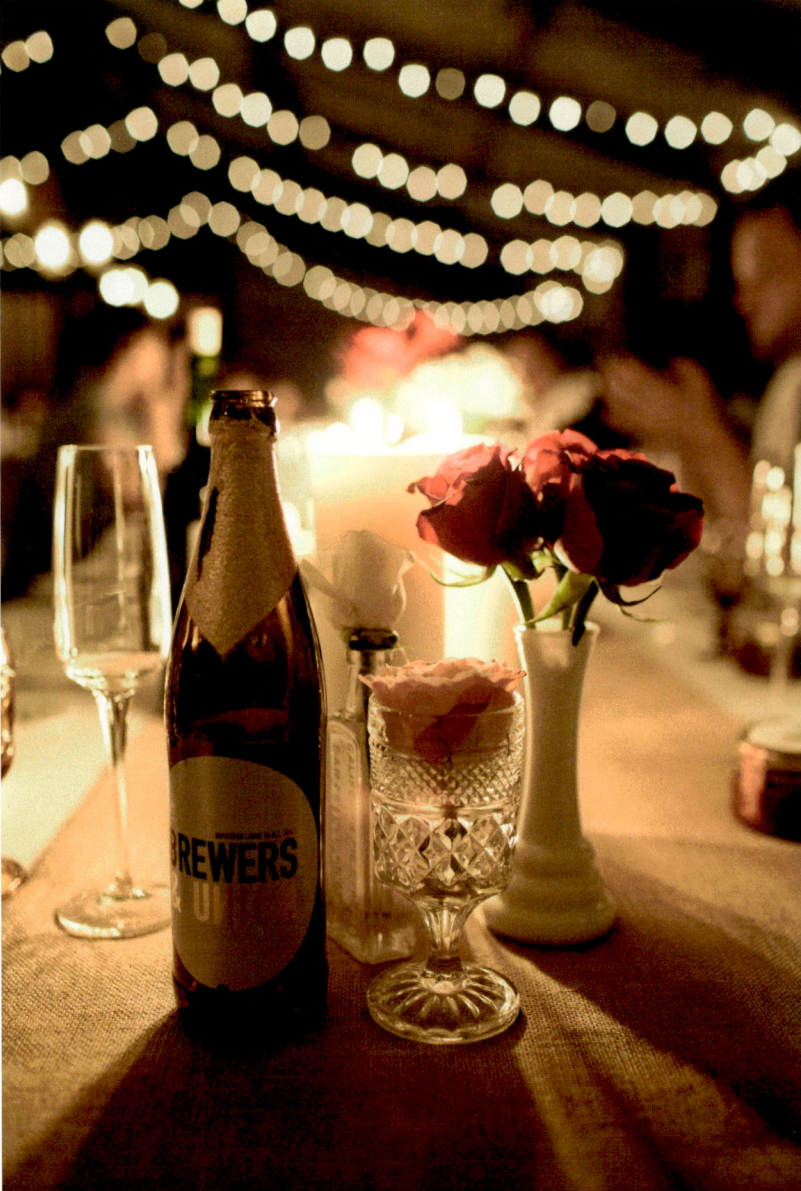

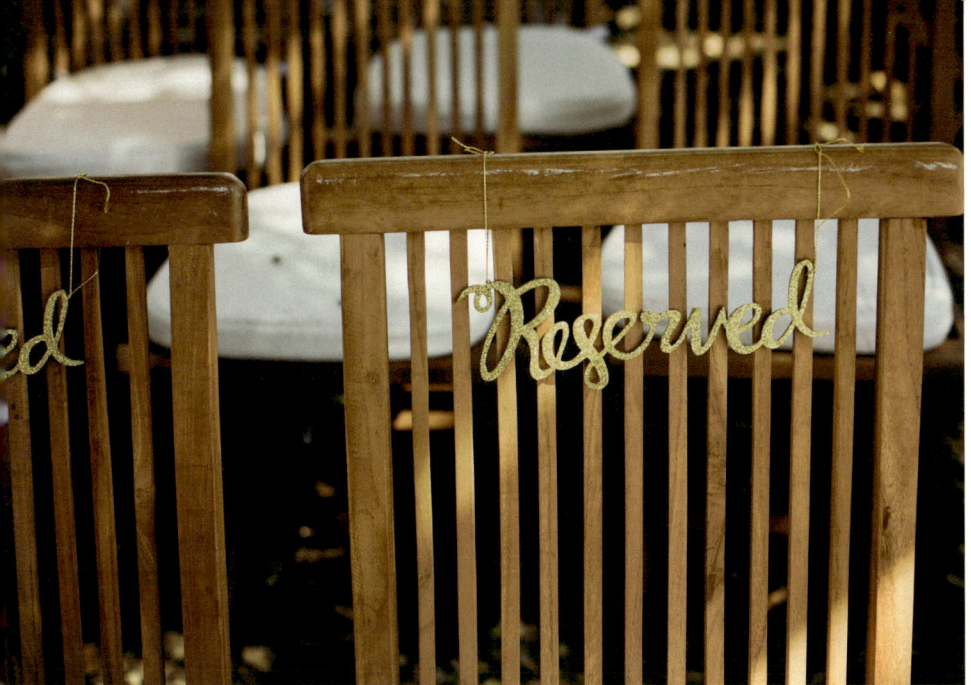

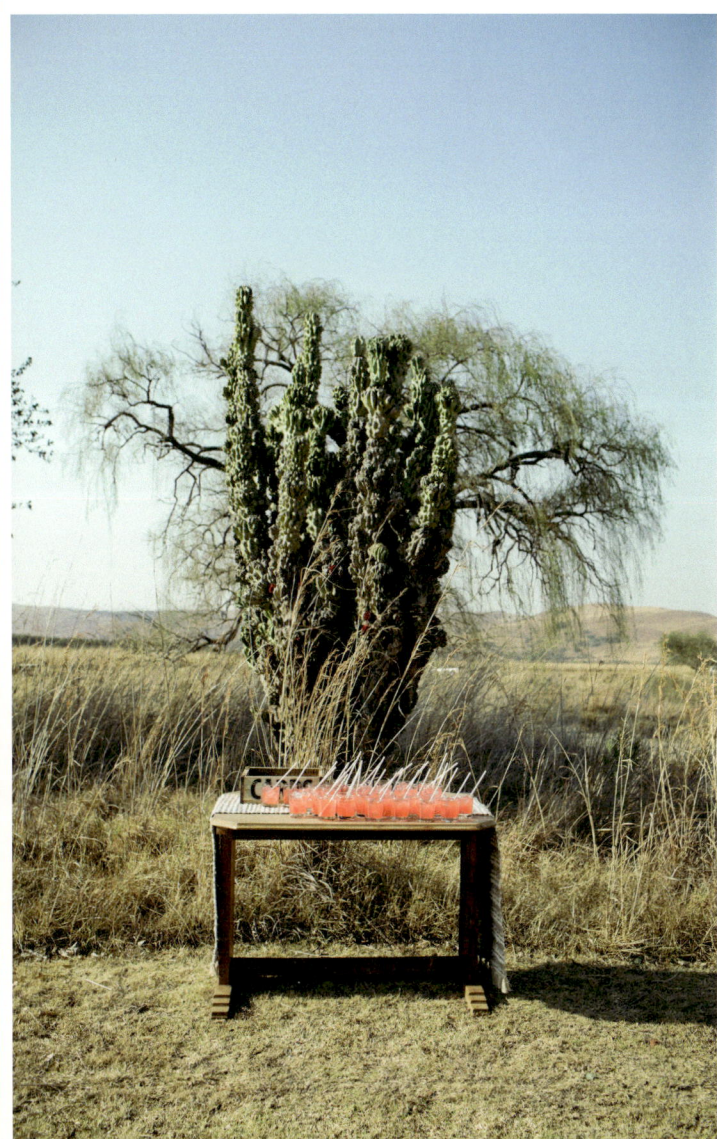

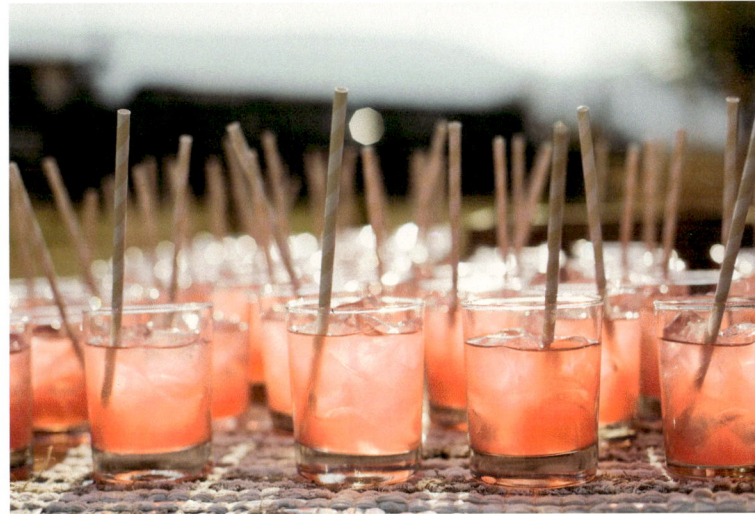

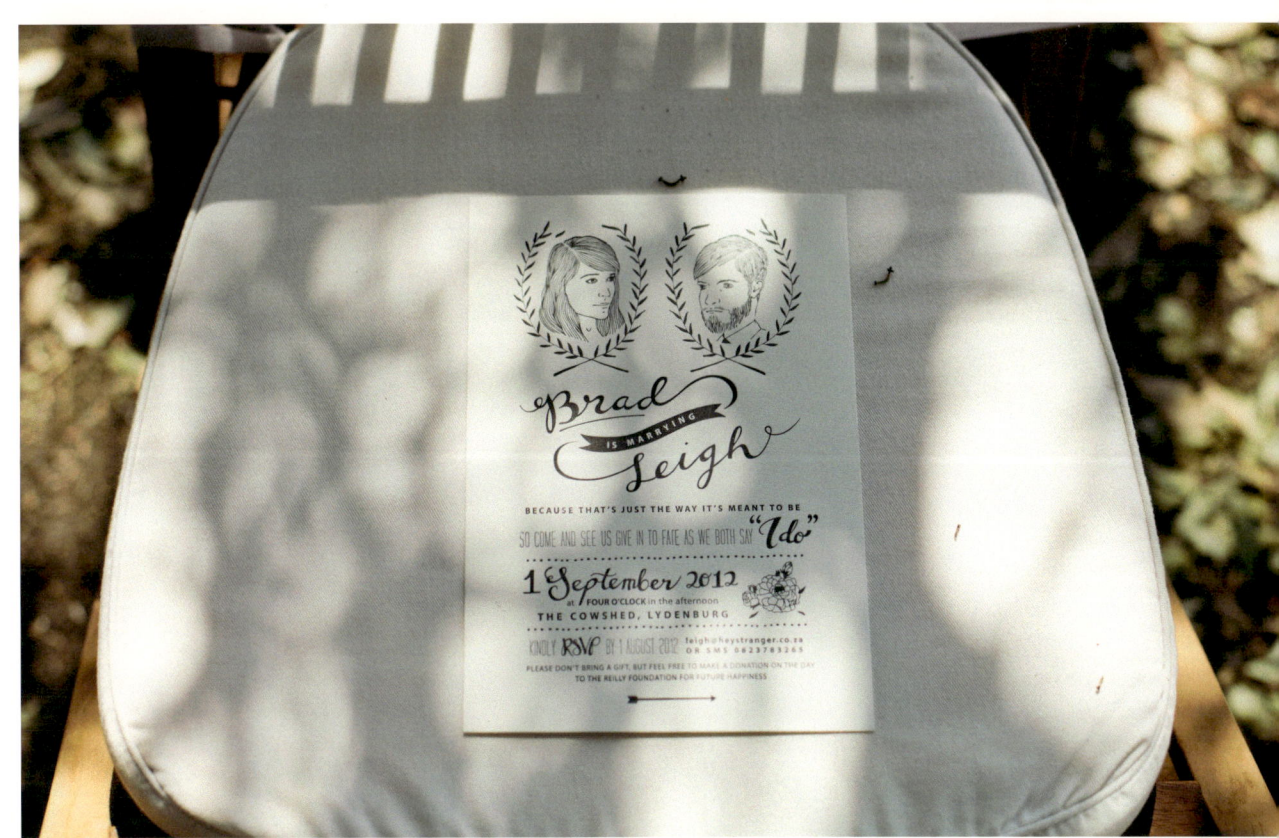

Brad

IS MARRYING

Leigh

BECAUSE THAT'S JUST THE WAY IT'S MEANT TO BE

SO COME AND SEE US GIVE IN TO FATE AS WE BOTH SAY "I do"

1 *September* 2012

AT FOUR O'CLOCK in the afternoon
THE COWSHED, LYDENBURG

KINDLY RSVP BY 1 AUGUST 2012
OR SMS 0823785265

PLEASE DON'T BRING A GIFT, BUT FEEL FREE TO MAKE A DONATION ON THE DAY
TO THE REILLY FOUNDATION FOR FUTURE HAPPINESS

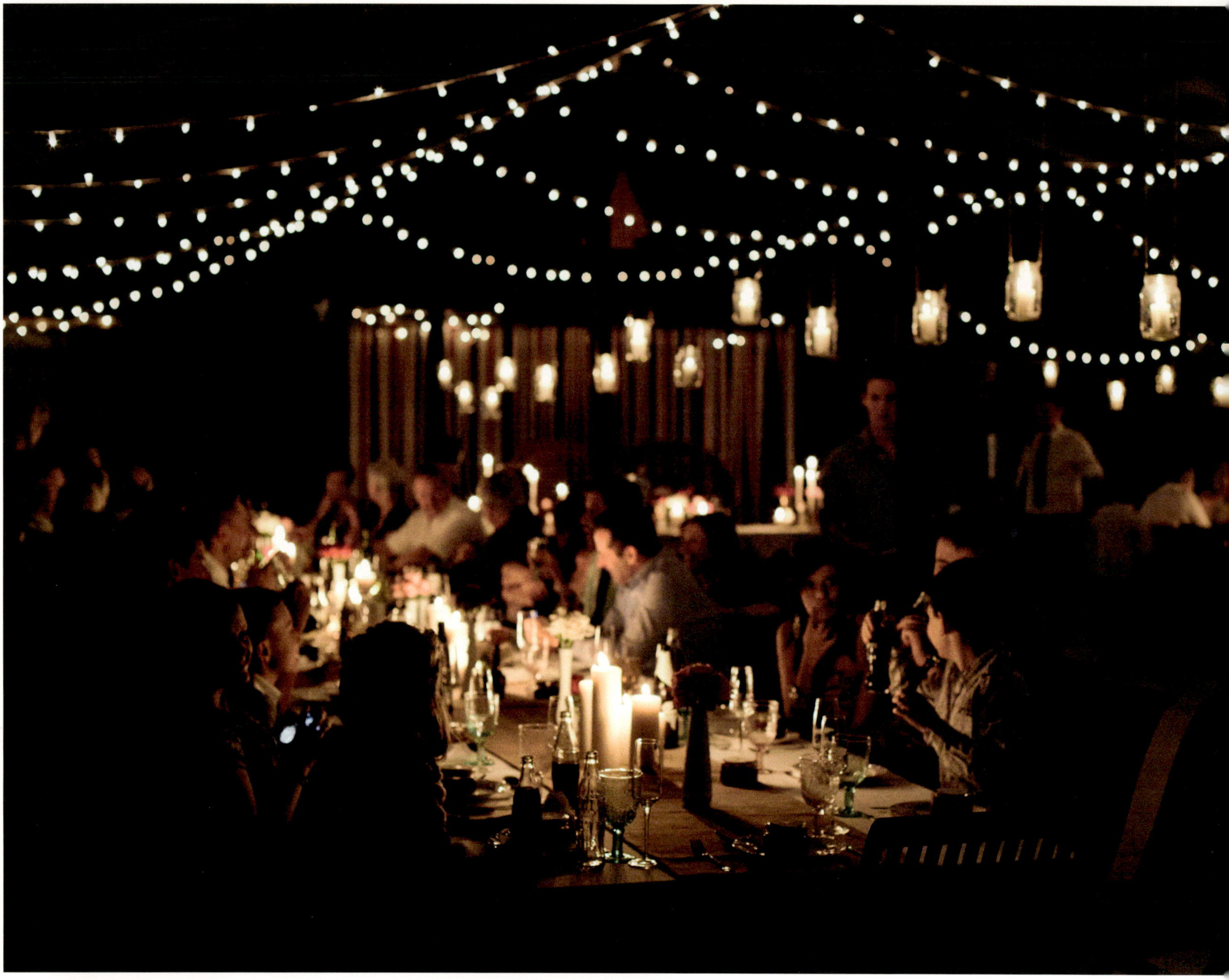

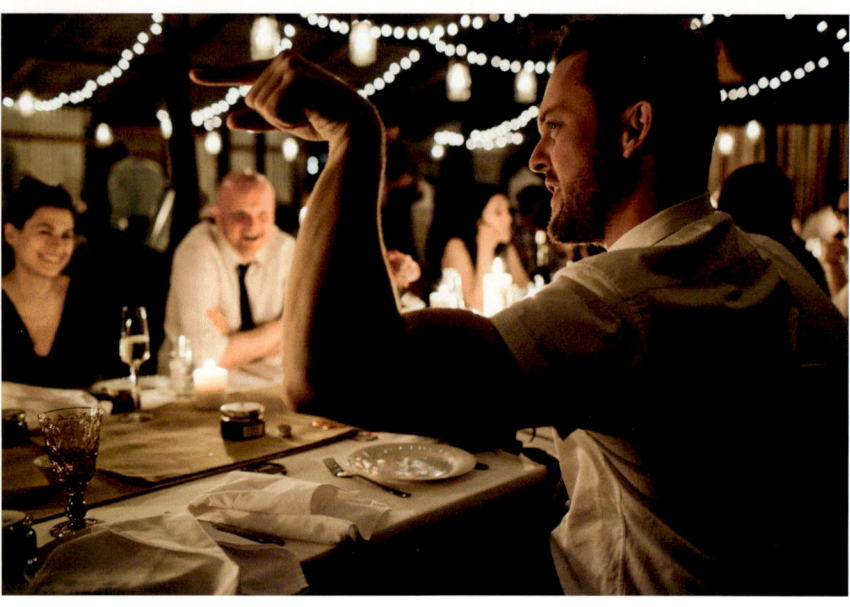

It's great to have your friends help out at your wedding. Even better if they can sing and play the guitar...

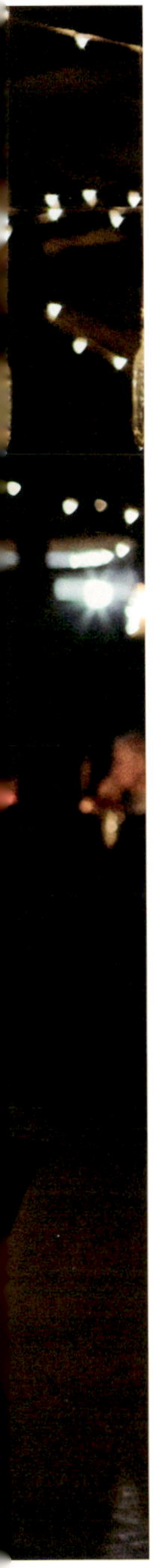

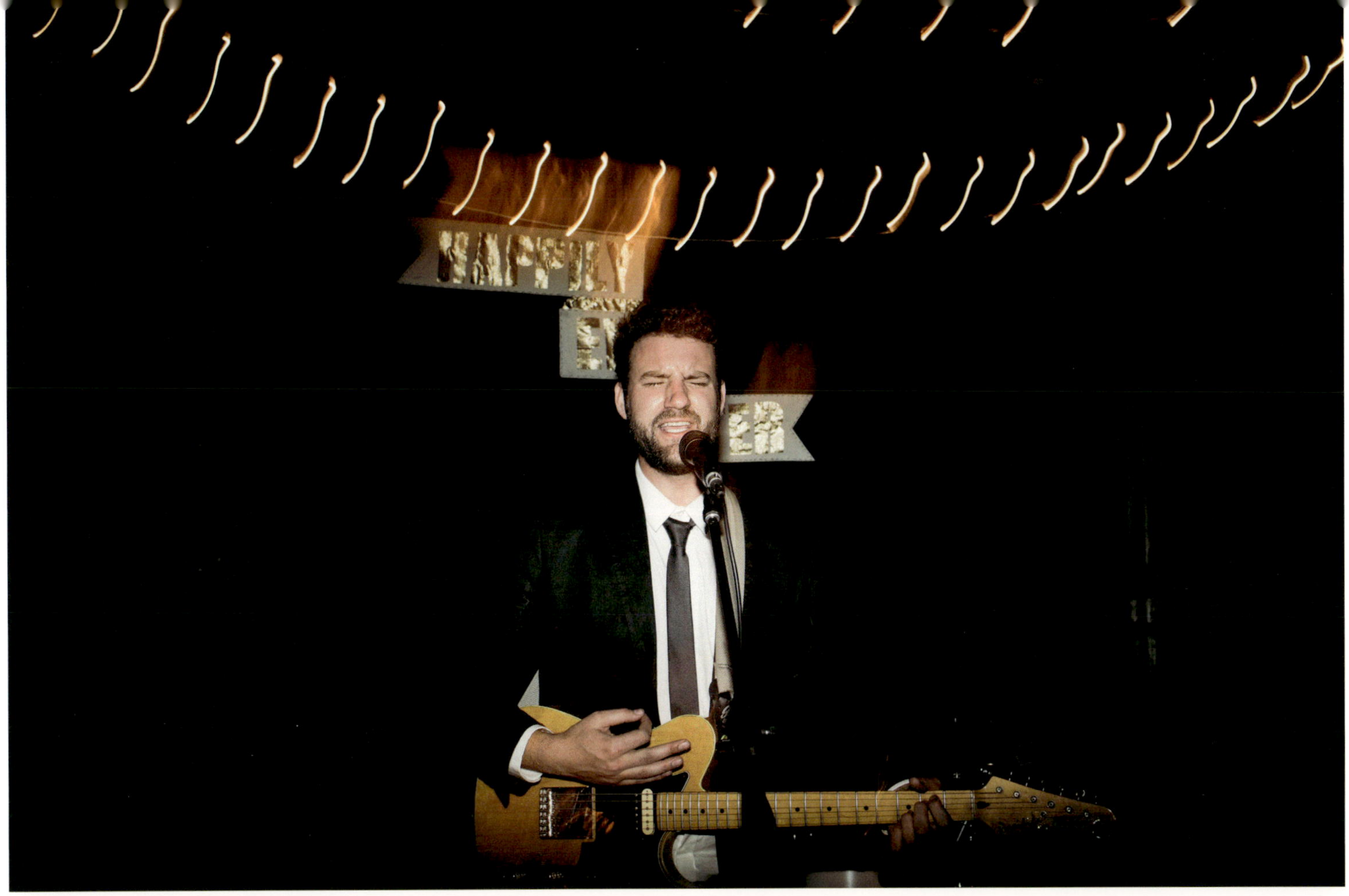
HAPPILY

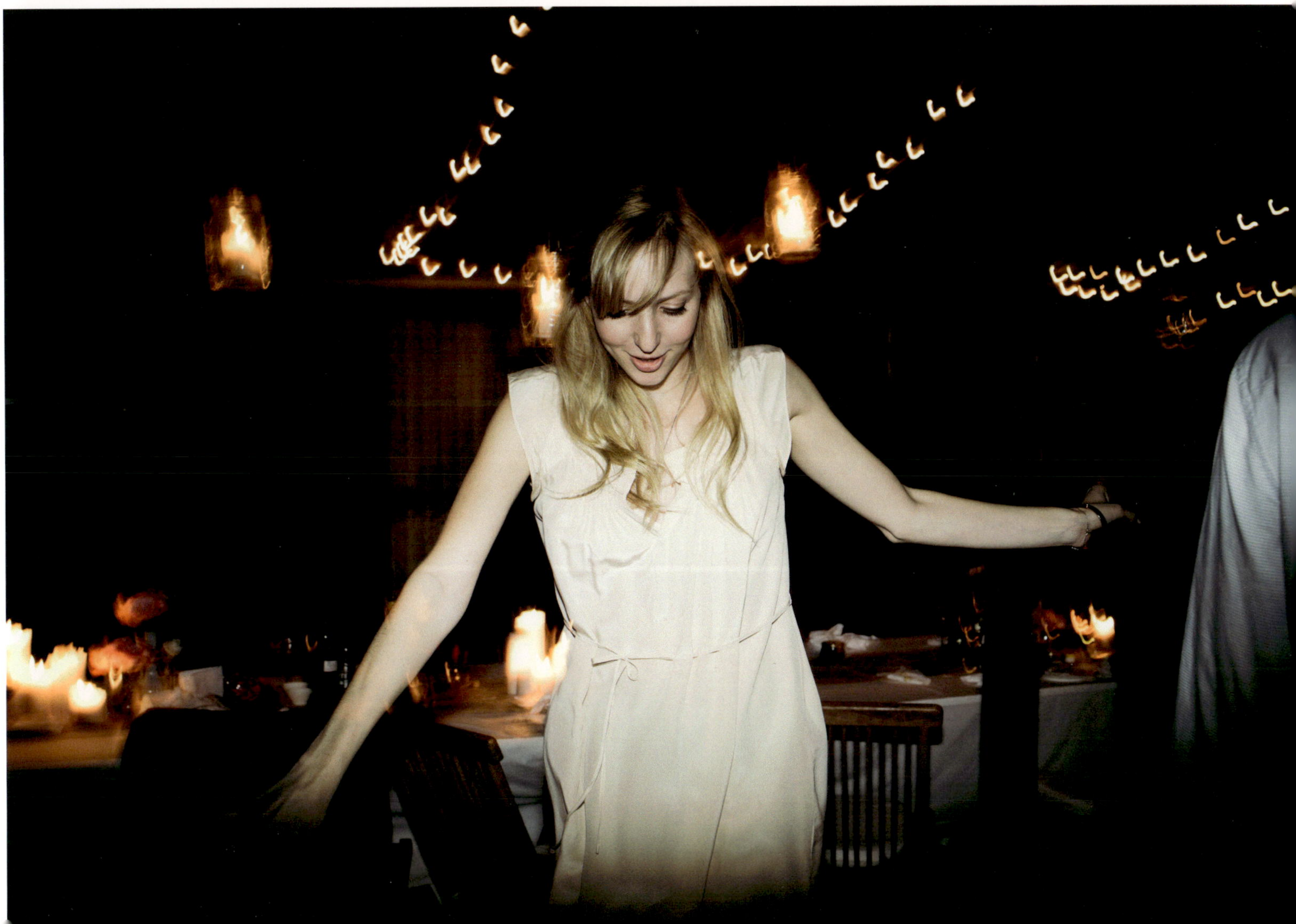

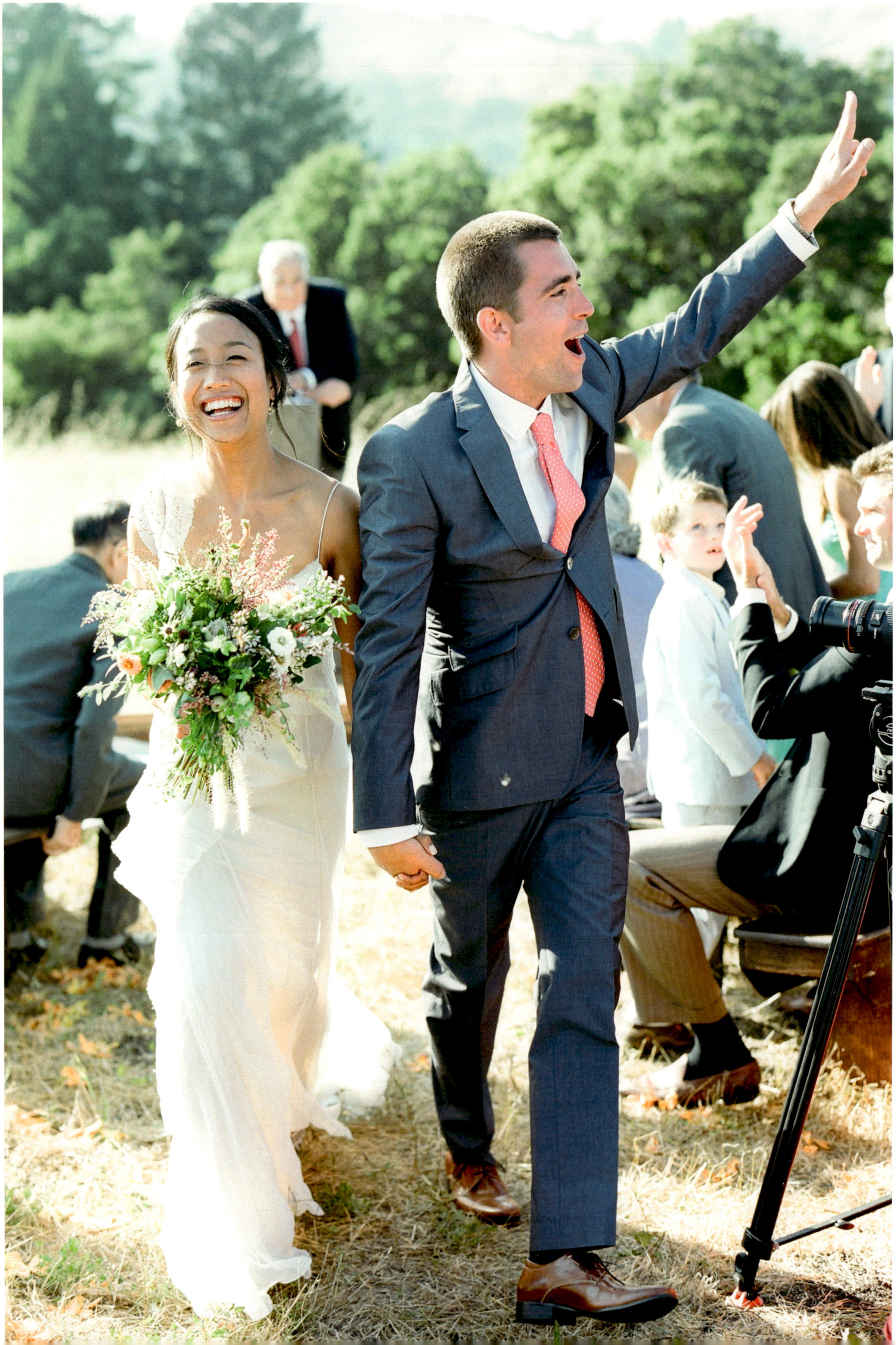

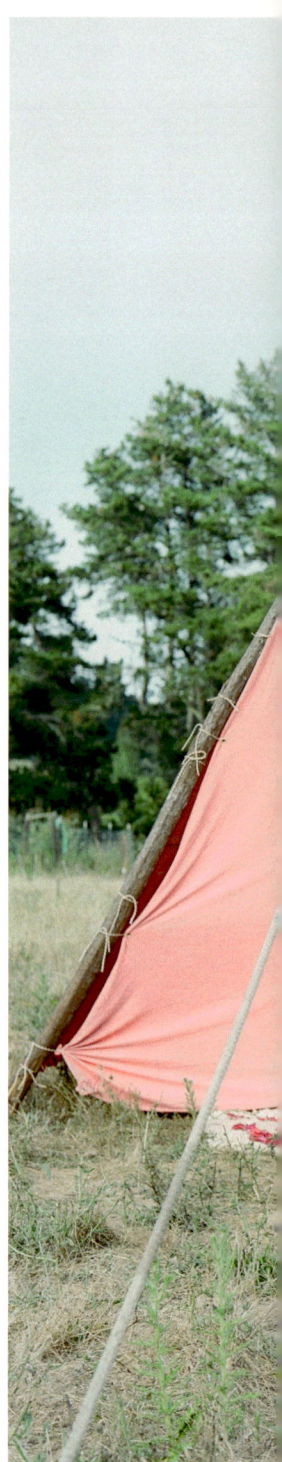

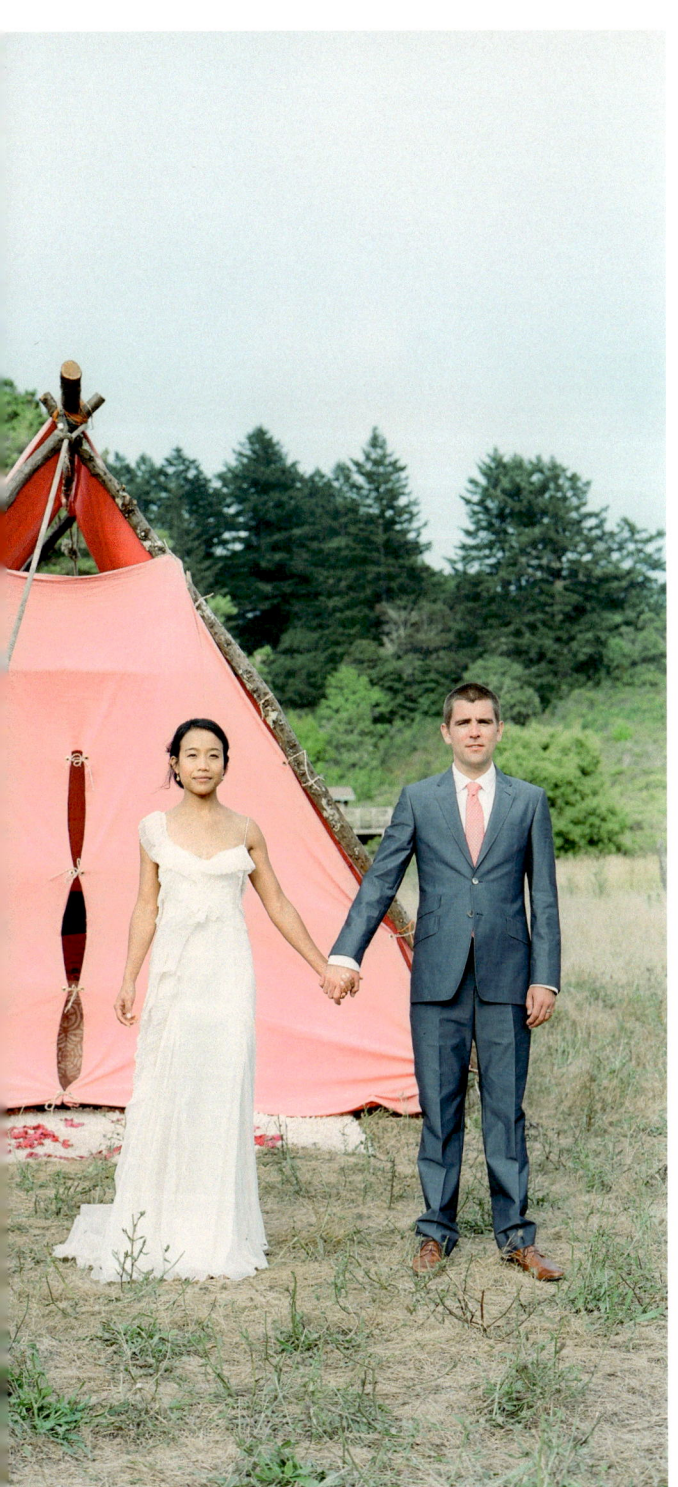

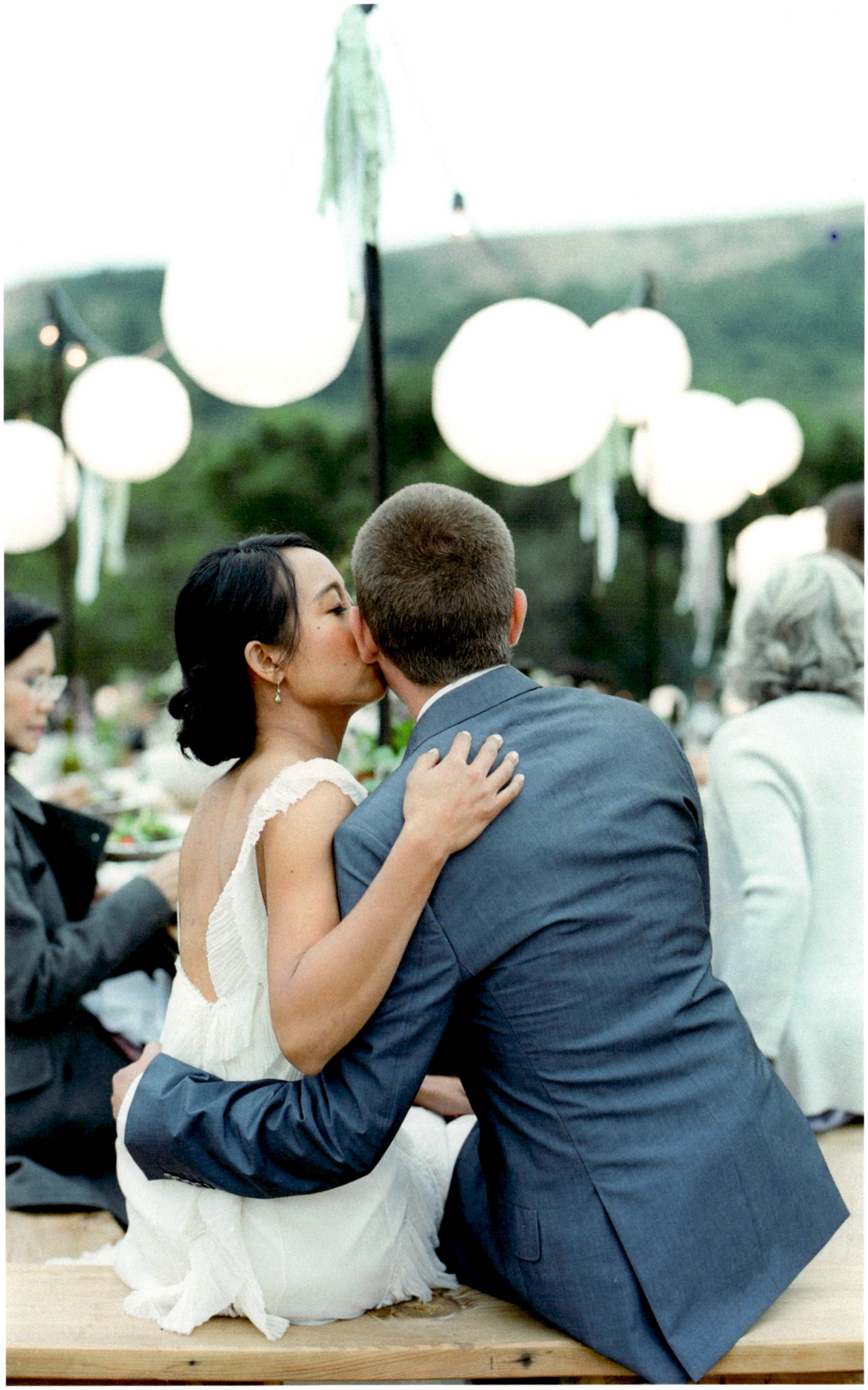

Visra & Chris

This California wedding had all the makings of an exclusive music festival. Headliners Visra and Chris put on an amazing show for their guests. There were vintage mirrors at outdoor sinks, a tent city nestled in the trees, and mismatched chairs waiting patiently for cocktail hour to come around. Everyone crowded onto wide wooden benches for the ceremony, which was framed by majestic trees and rolling sand-colored hills. Unusual for a festival, the support act came on later, when dinner was served at the vast triangular table that Visra, Chris, and the artist Drew Bennett had worked on for six months.

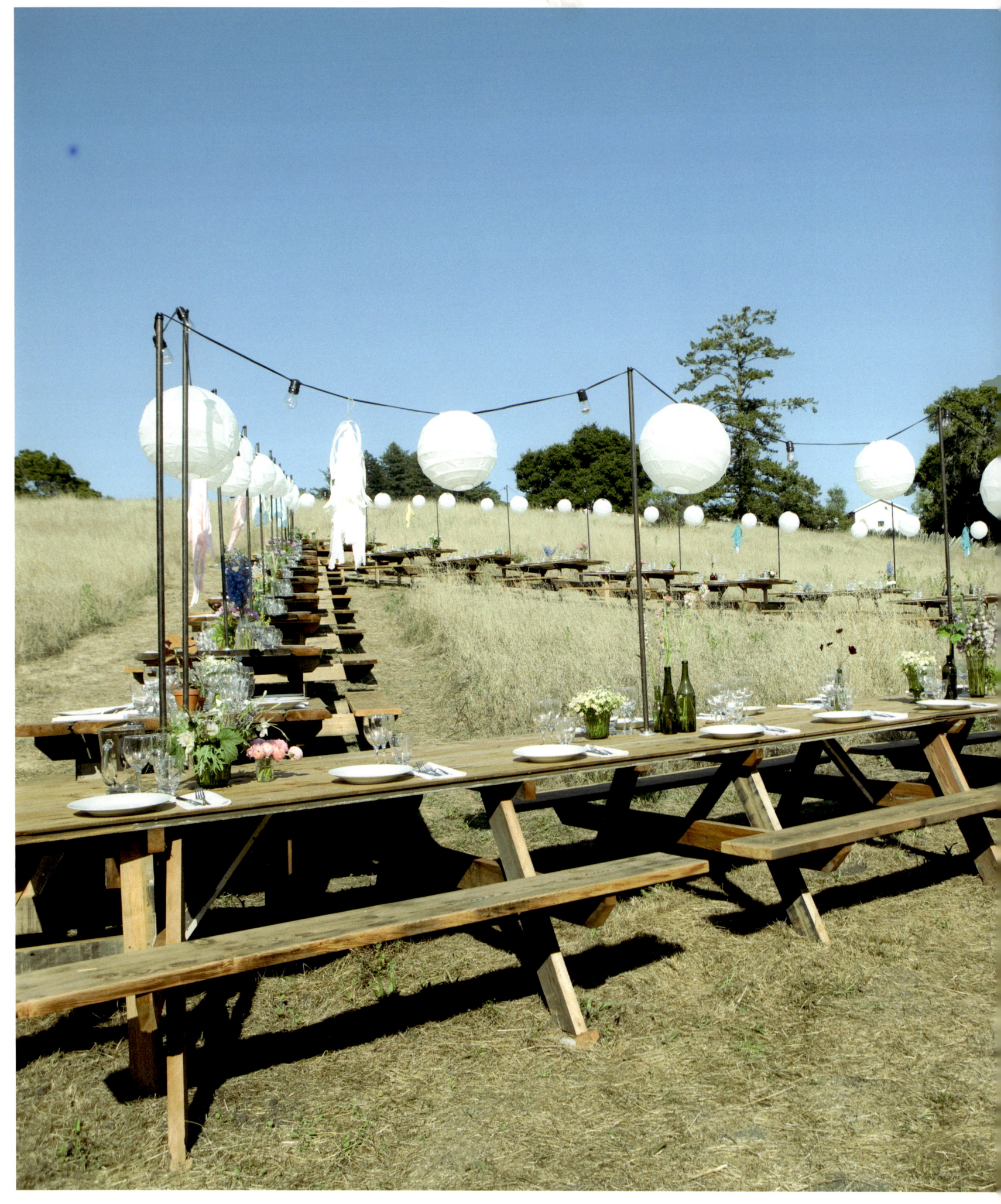

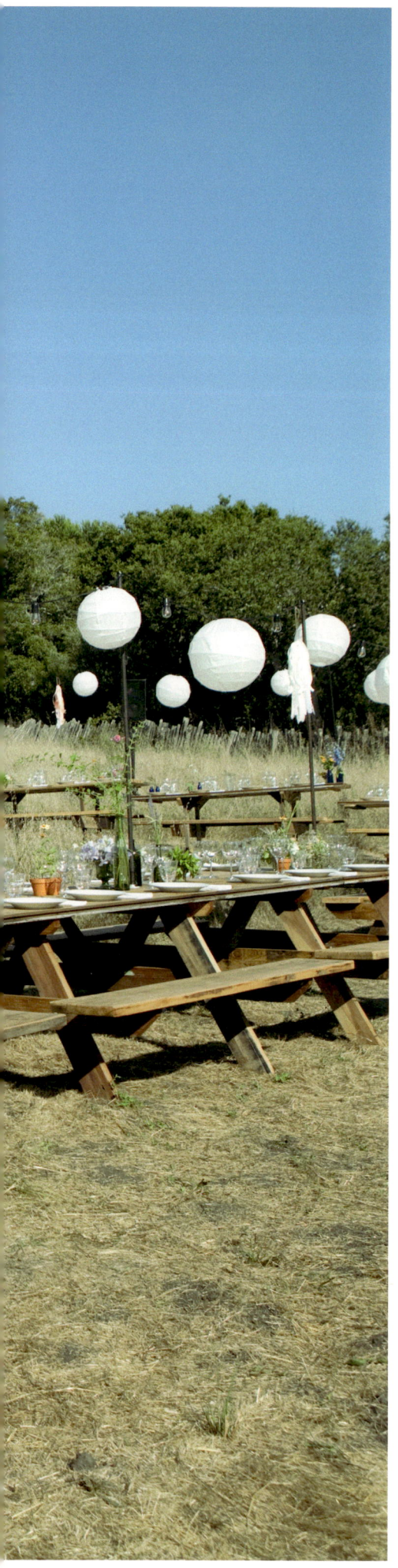

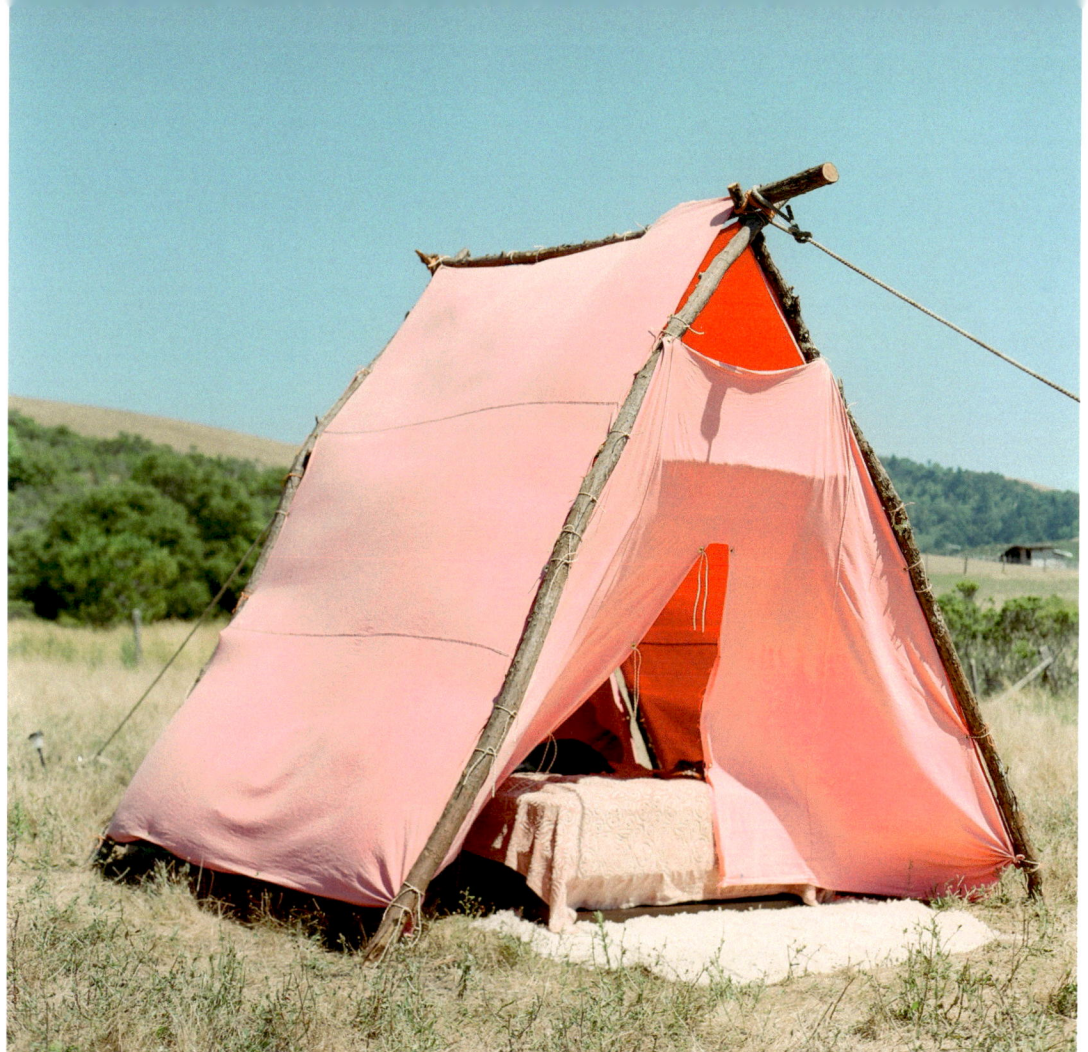

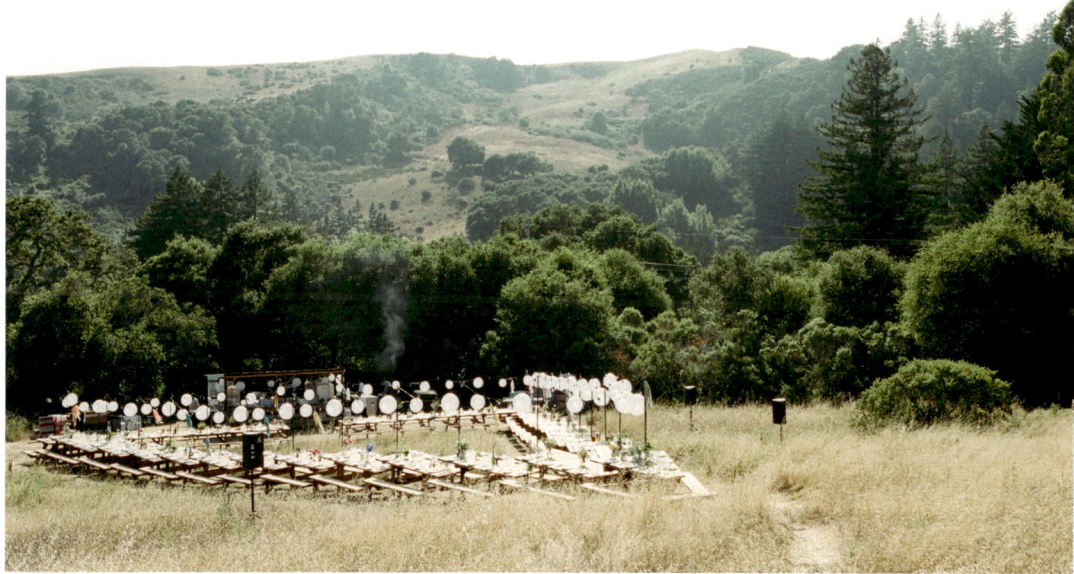

The amazing table meant that everyone could sit to-gether and celebrate as paper lanterns and simple white bulbs dripped pools of light onto the jars of flowers and plates of oysters below.

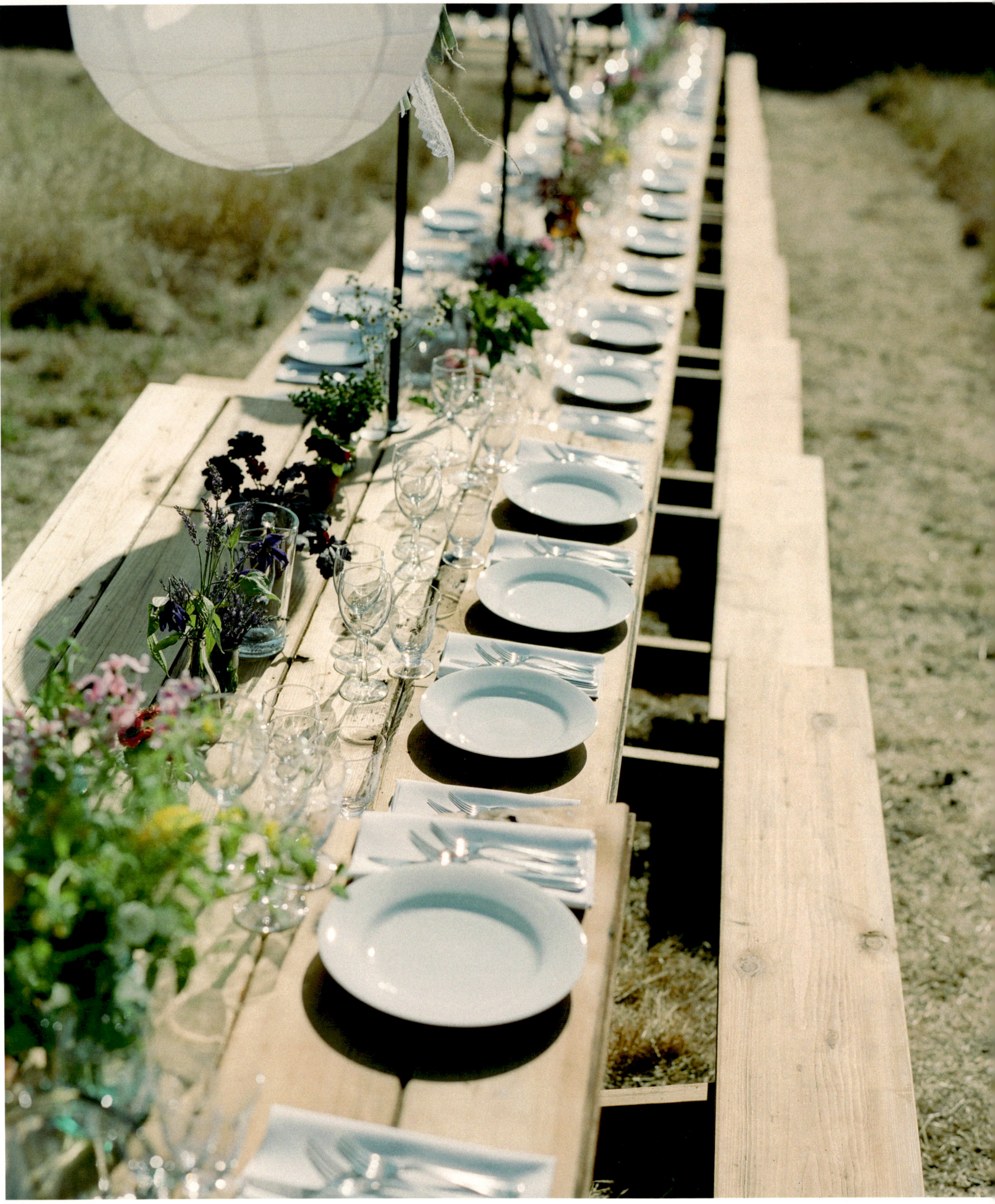

1. Brown glass bottles add a rustic feel to the table décor.

2. Roses don't have to be on stems and in vases to look good.

3. Flowers in pots could come live in your garden afterwards.

4. Pink looks amazing against the sandy wood of this picnic table.

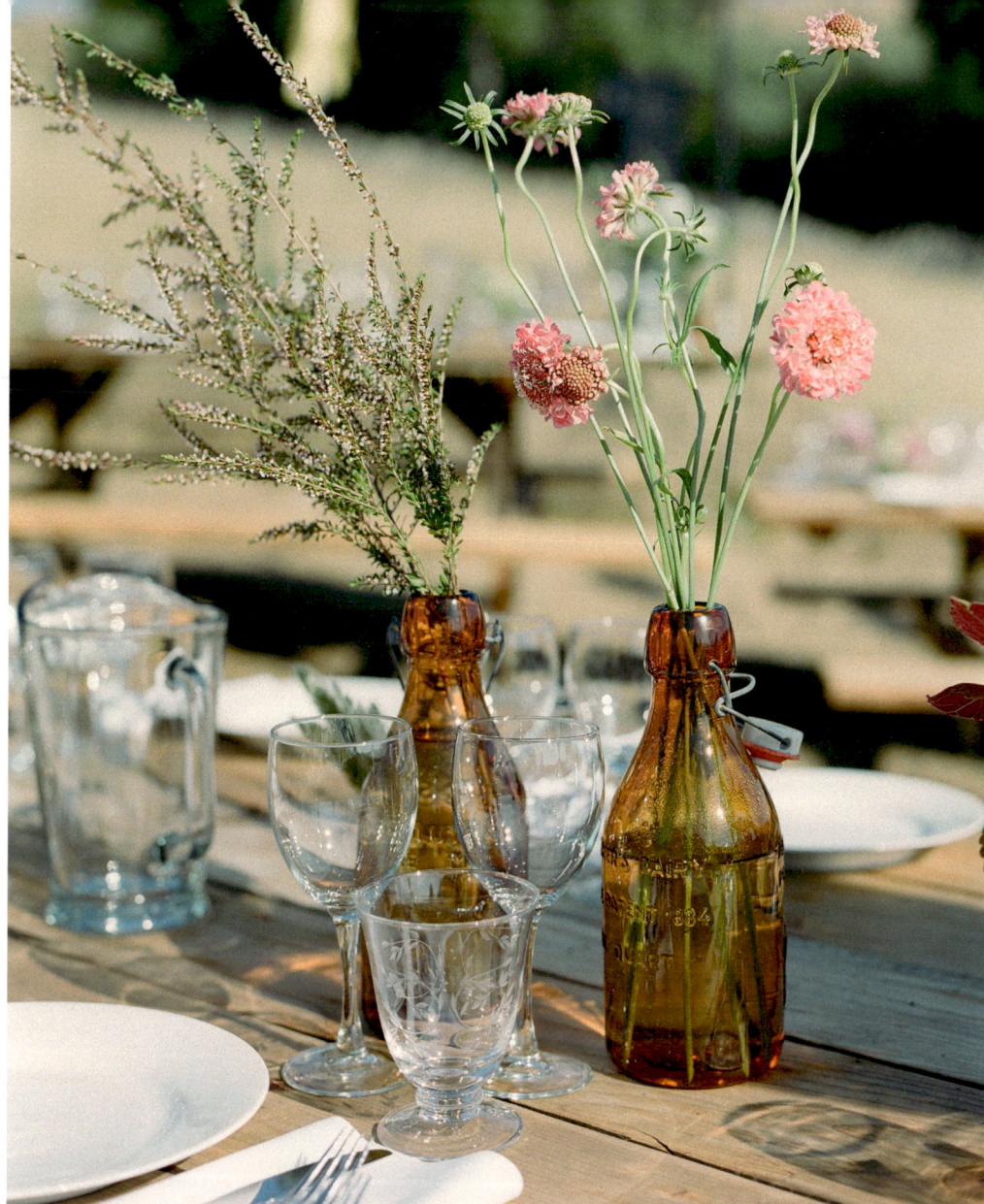

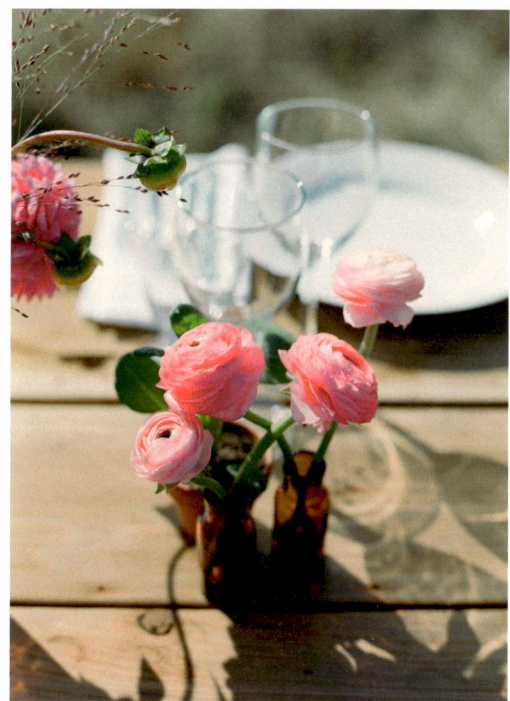

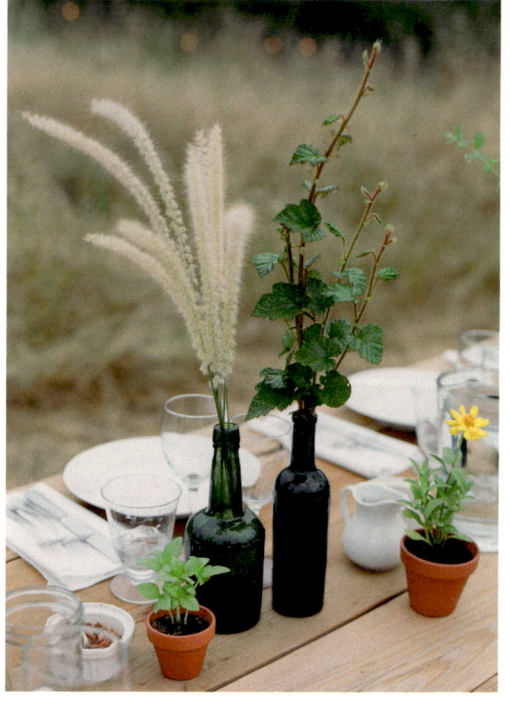

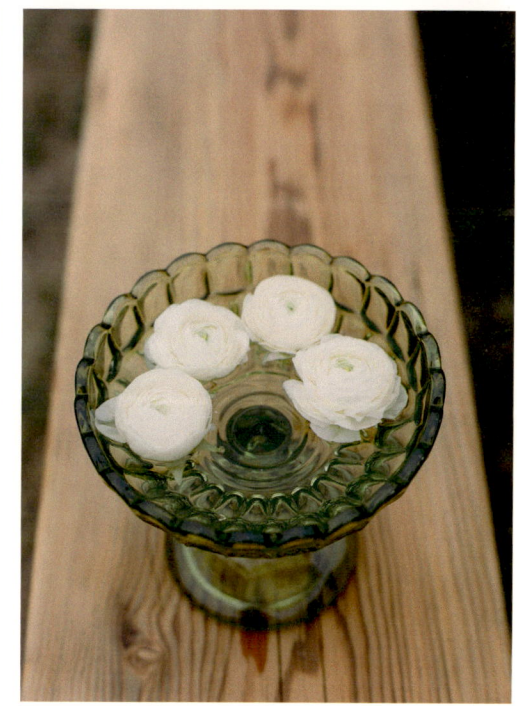

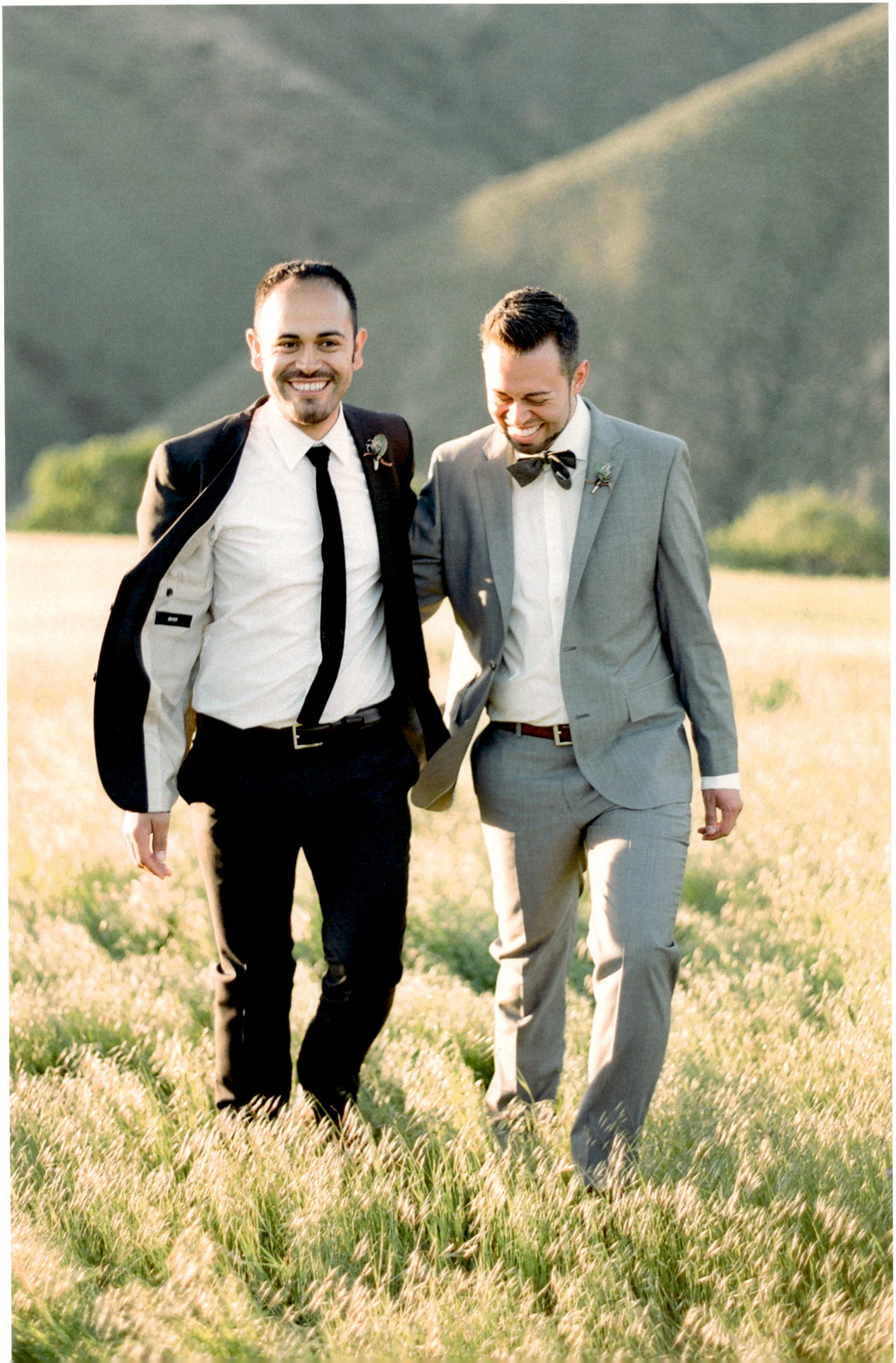

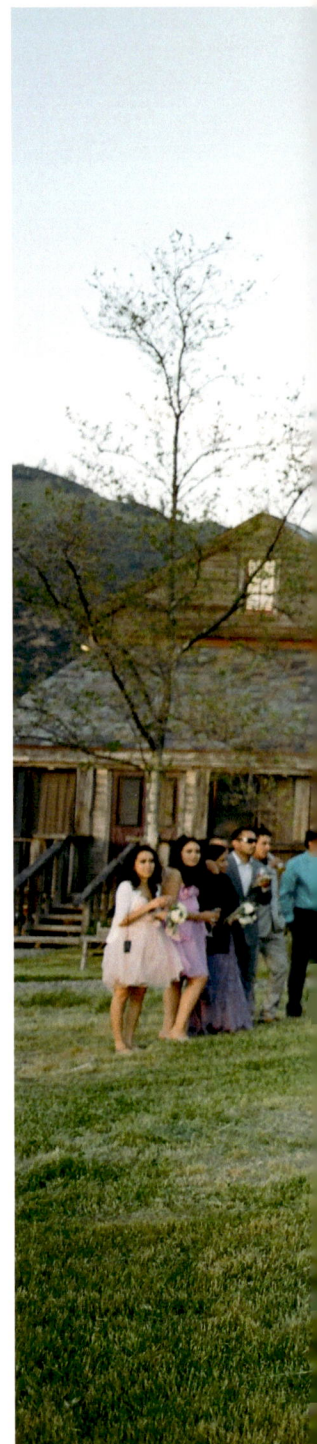

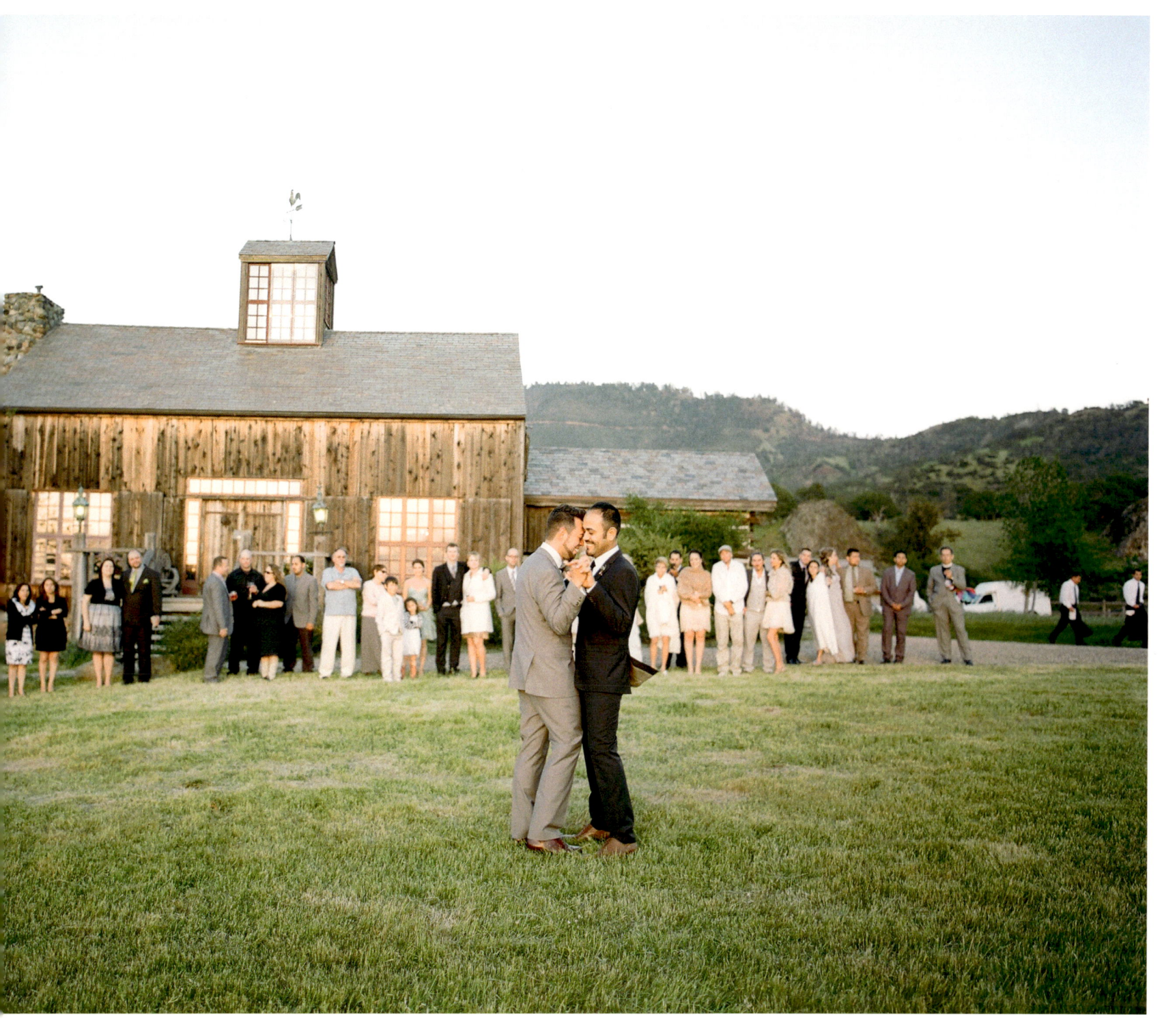

Jose & Joel

Rather than have a single theme for their wedding, Jose and Joel chose a few elements to shape their day and make it all about them. The tiny classic camera that Joel gave Jose before they married expressed their shared love of photography and cinematography. An elegant J+J monogram was carried through, from the invitations sent out in advance to the muslin bags of Mexican sweets that the guests took home. The couple's Mexican heritage was also featured at the dessert bar, which was laden with all kinds of traditional specialties, and at the reception, where heart-shaped cacti adorned the centerpieces.

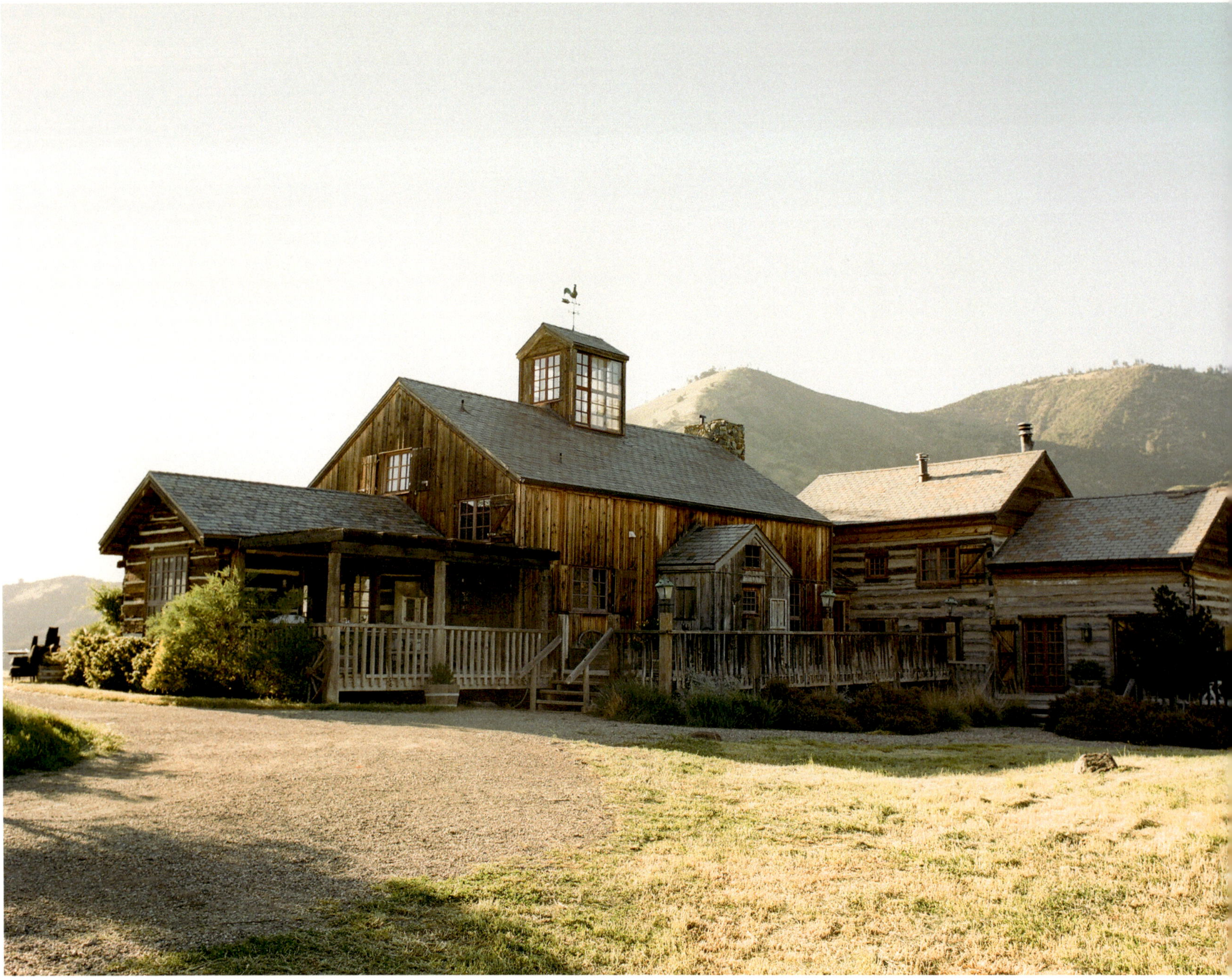

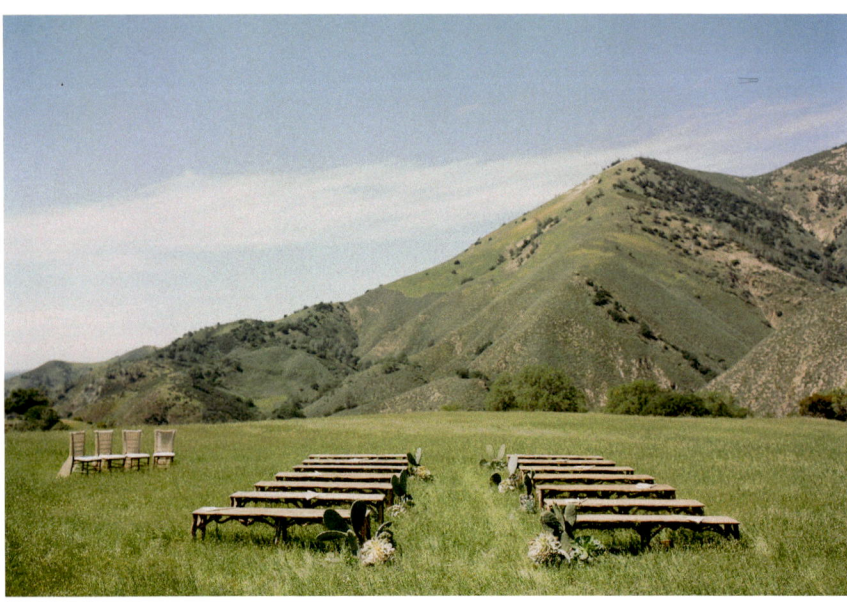

Marrying on a mountaintop is about as close to Cloud 9 as you can get.

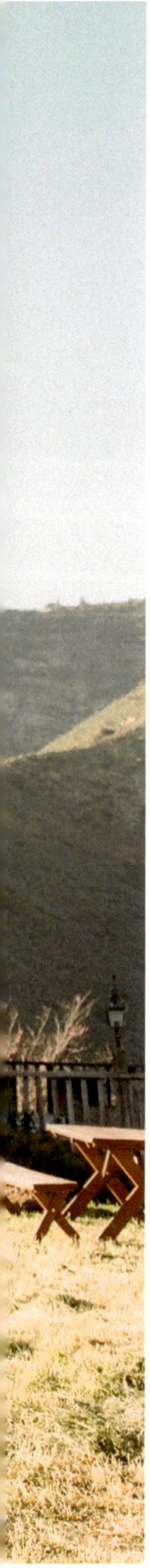

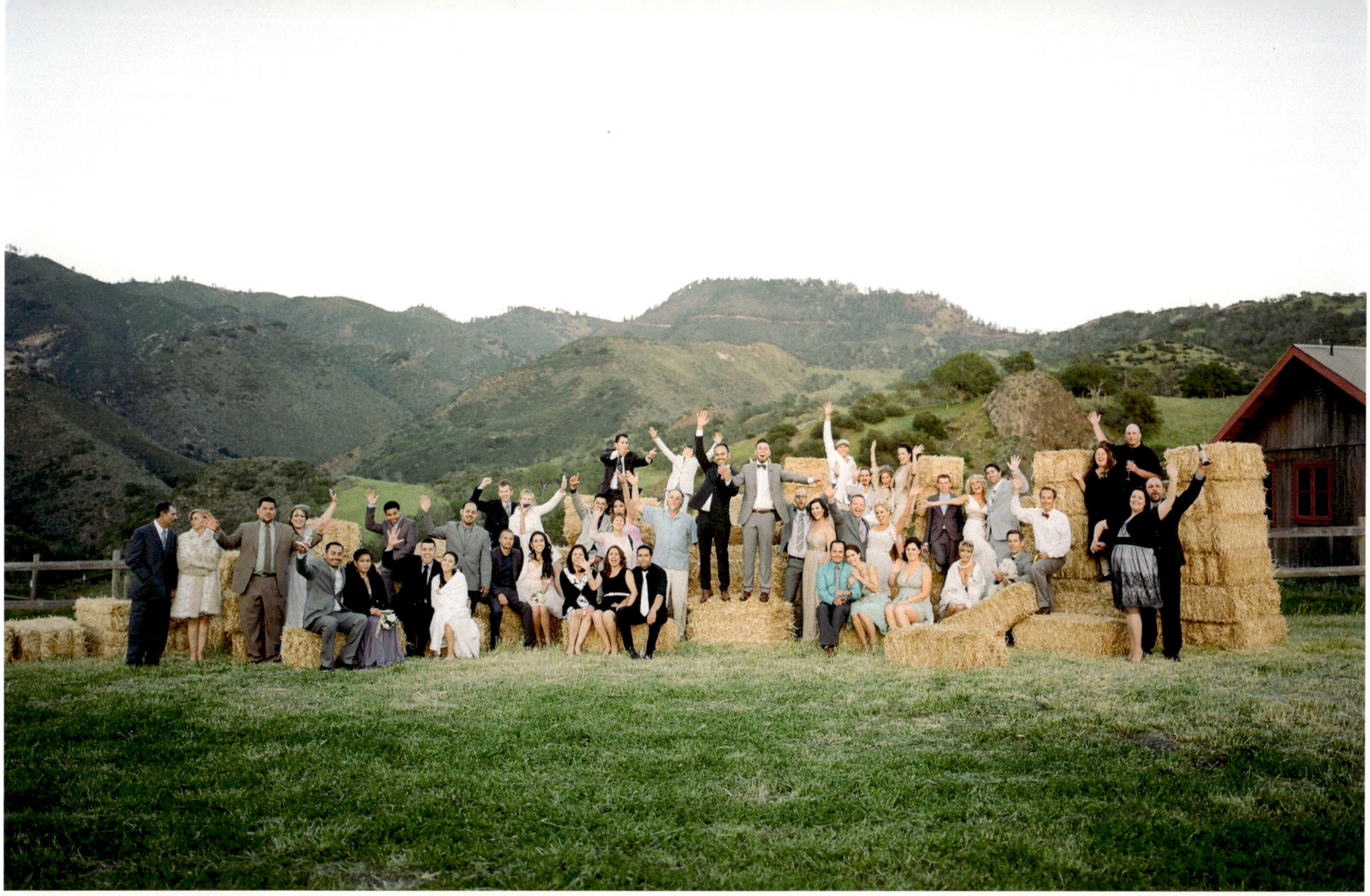

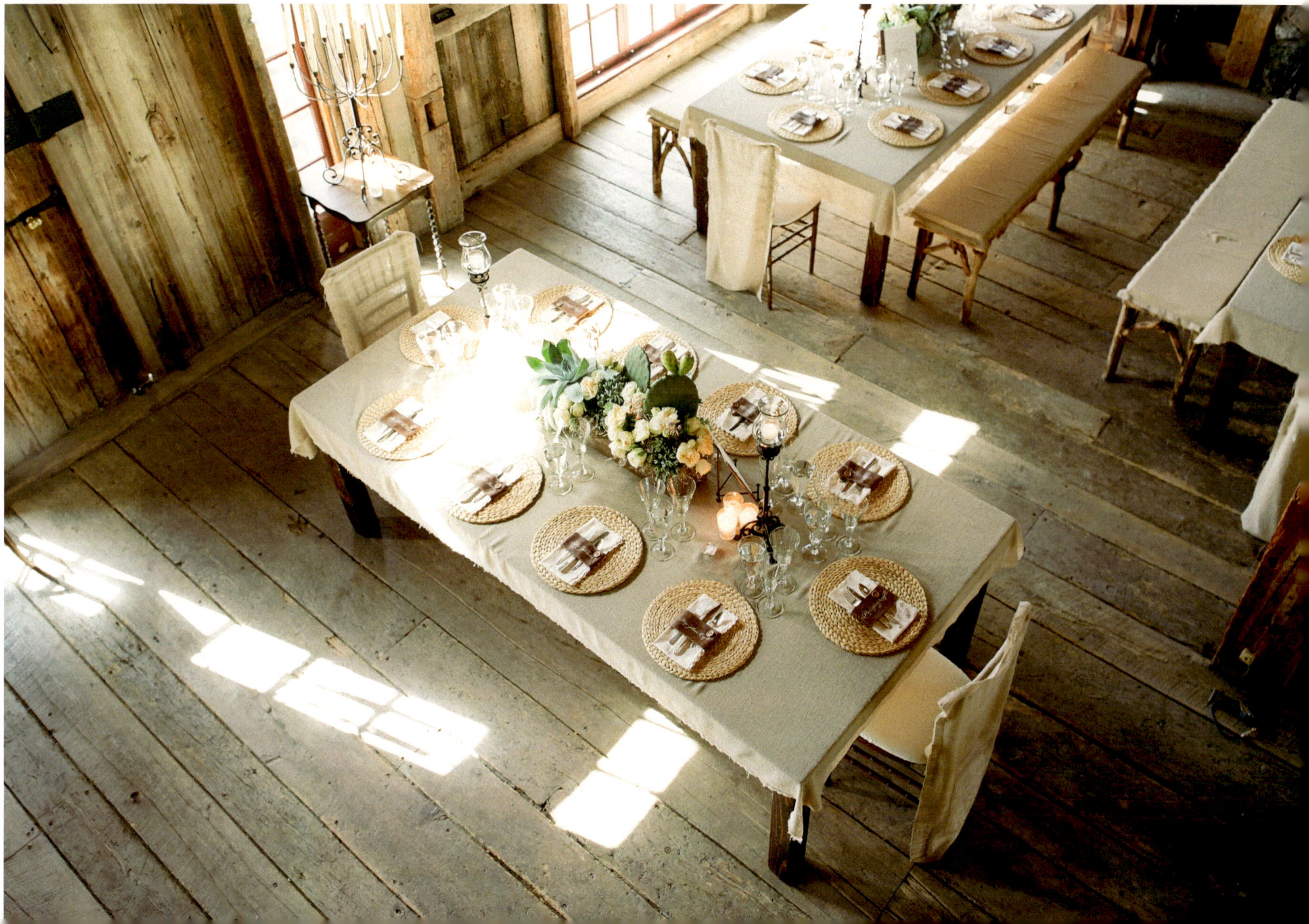

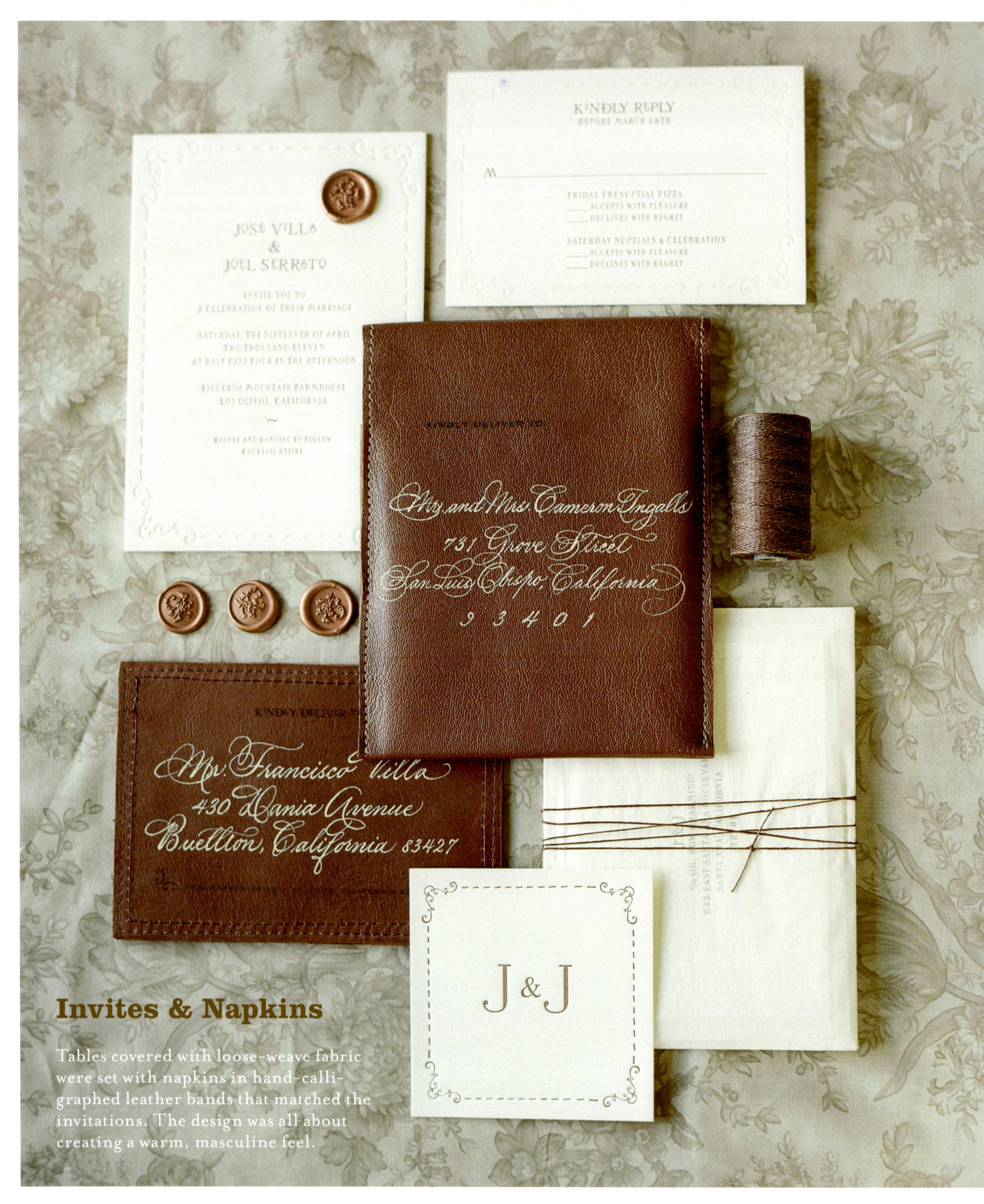

JOSE VILLA
&
JOEL SERRATO

INVITE YOU TO
A CELEBRATION OF THEIR MARRIAGE

SATURDAY, THE SIXTEENTH OF APRIL
TWO THOUSAND ELEVEN
AT HALF PAST FOUR IN THE AFTERNOON

FIGUEROA MOUNTAIN FARMHOUSE
LOS OLIVOS, CALIFORNIA

DINNER AND DANCING TO FOLLOW
COCKTAIL ATTIRE

KINDLY REPLY
BEFORE MARCH 18TH

M _____

FRIDAY PRENUPTIAL PIZZA
_____ ACCEPTS WITH PLEASURE
_____ DECLINES WITH REGRET

SATURDAY NUPTIALS & CELEBRATION
_____ ACCEPTS WITH PLEASURE
_____ DECLINES WITH REGRET

KINDLY DELIVER TO

Mr. Francisco Villa
430 Dania Avenue
Buellton, California 83427

KINDLY DELIVER TO

Mr. and Mrs. Cameron Ingalls
731 Grove Street
San Luis Obispo, California
9 3 4 0 1

J & J

Invites & Napkins

Tables covered with loose-weave fabric
were set with napkins in hand-calli-
graphed leather bands that matched the
invitations. The design was all about
creating a warm, masculine feel.

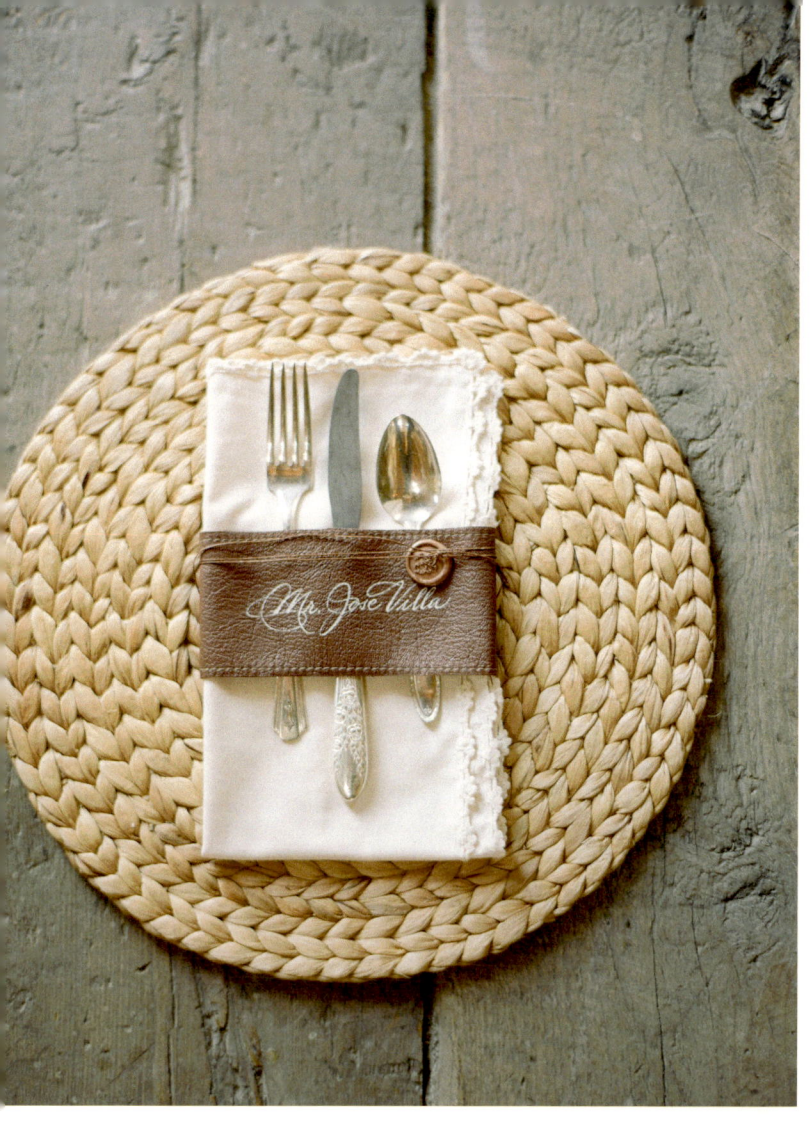

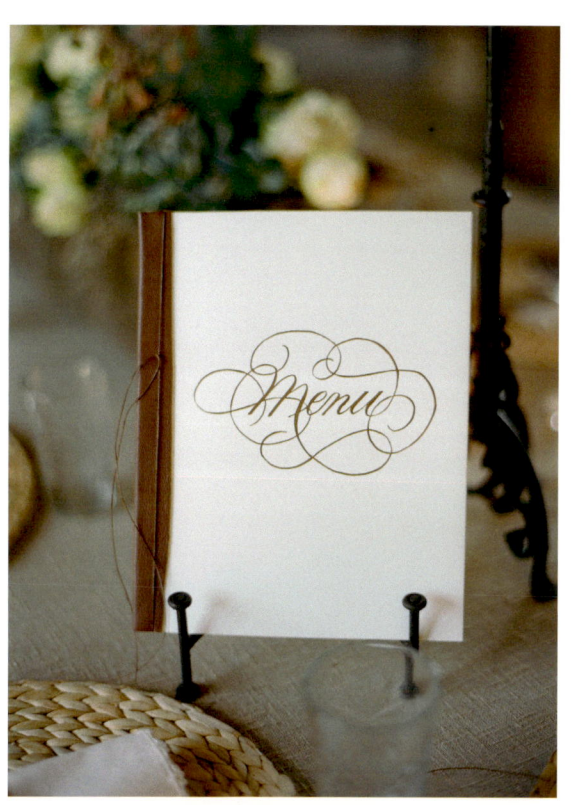

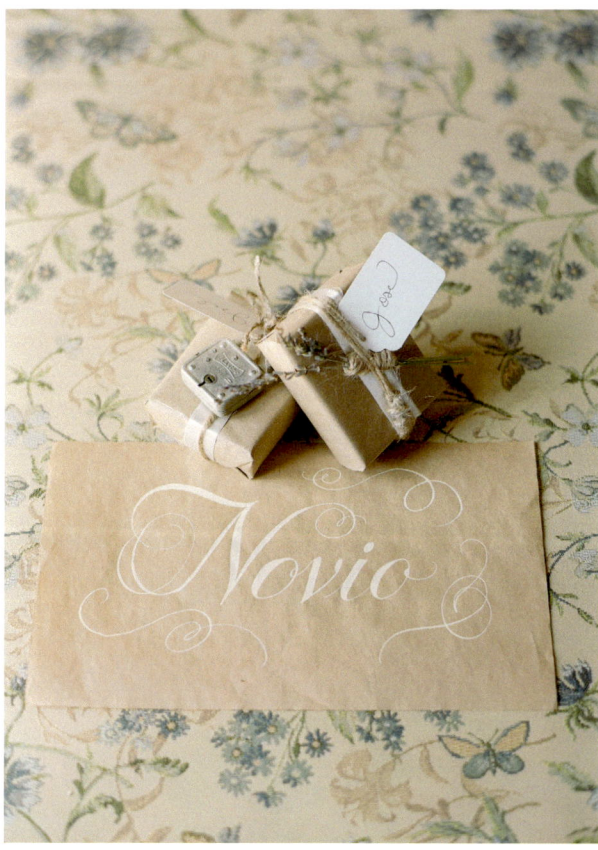

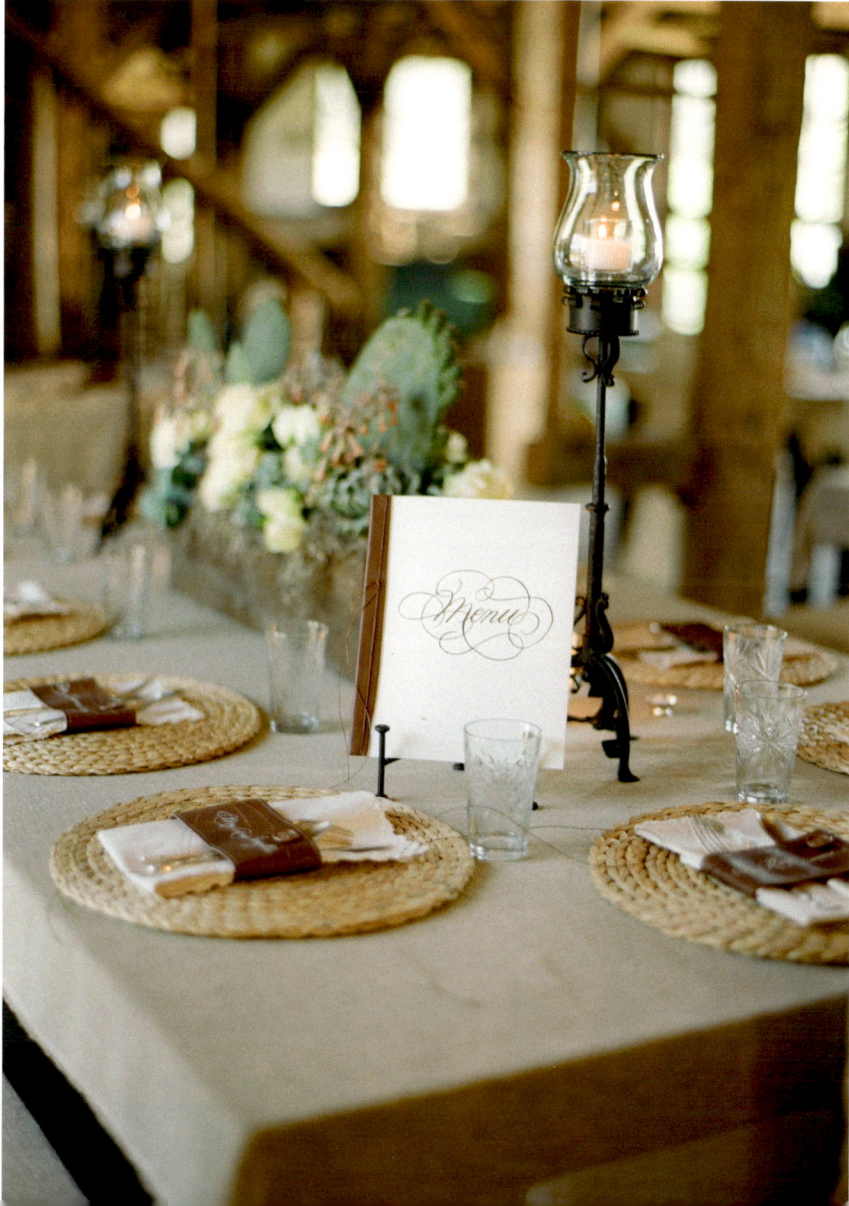

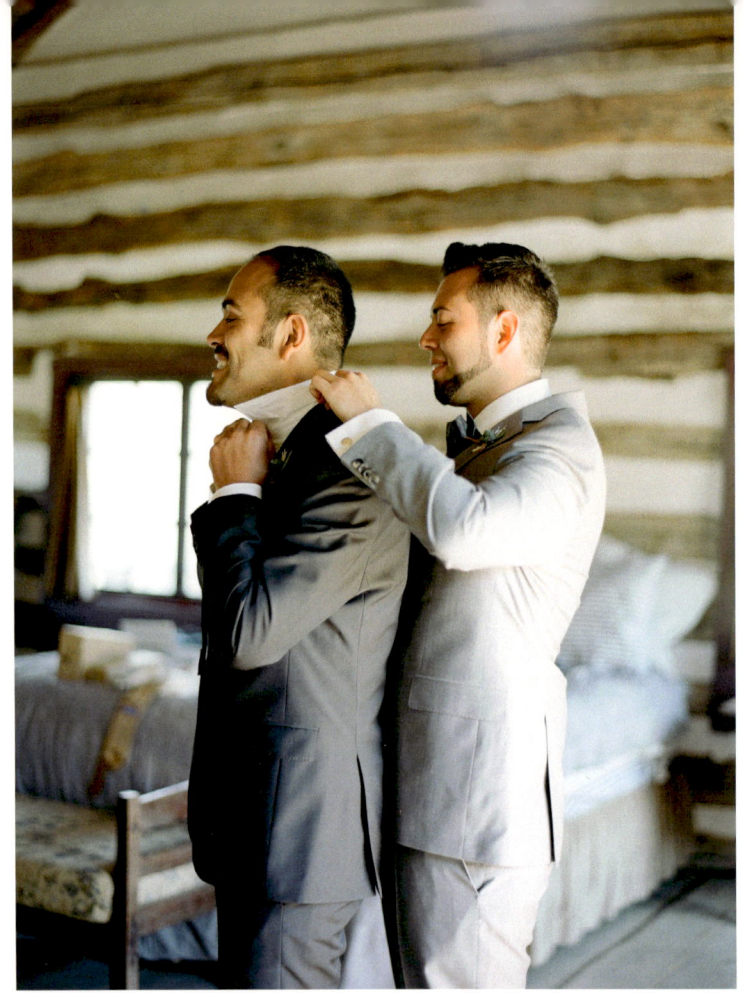
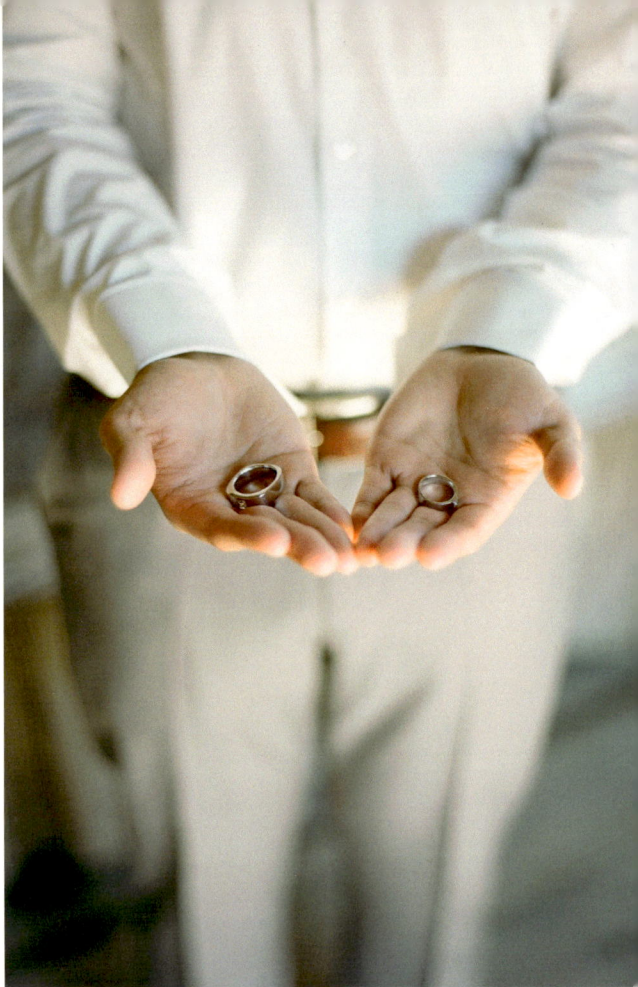

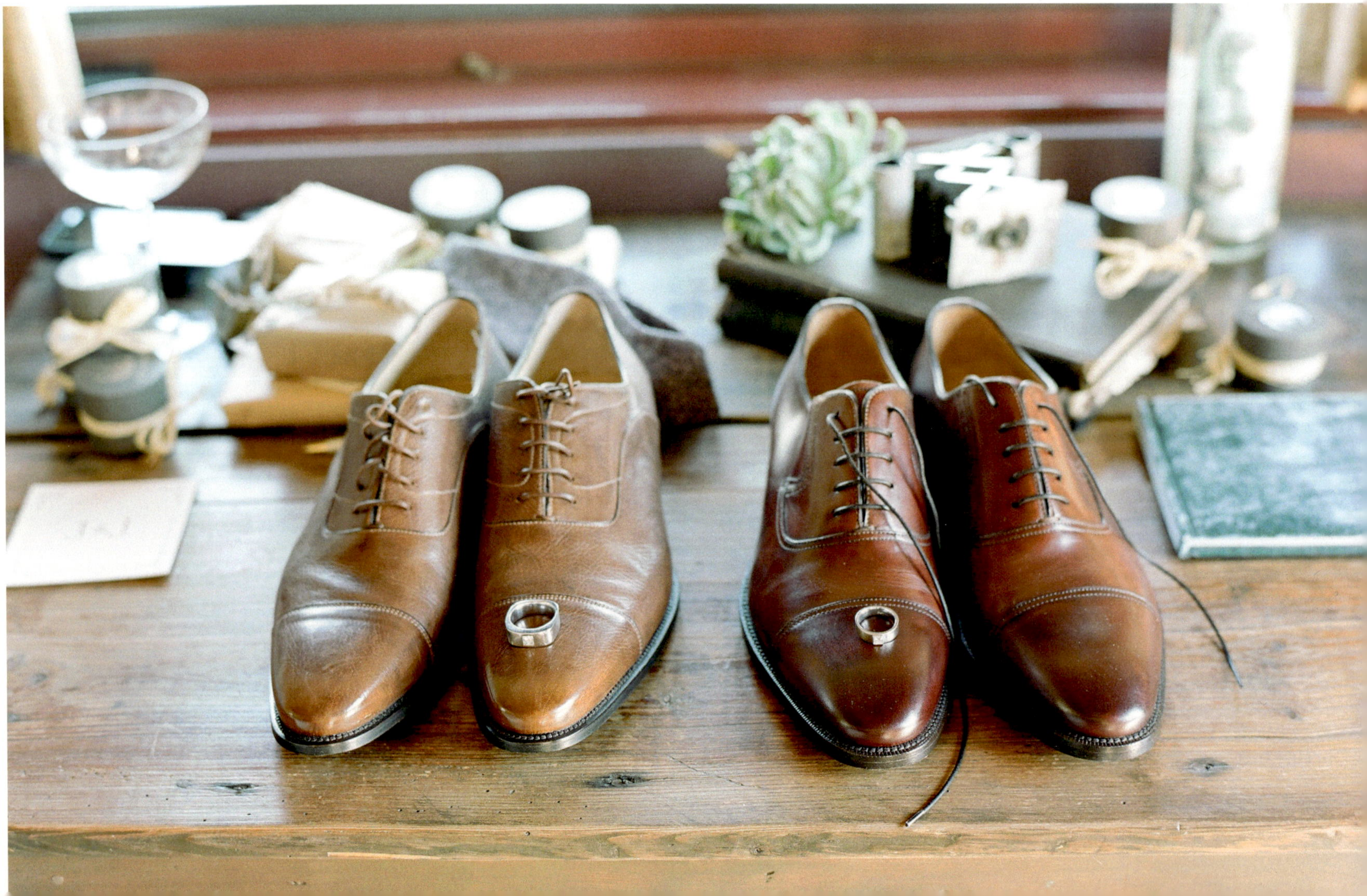

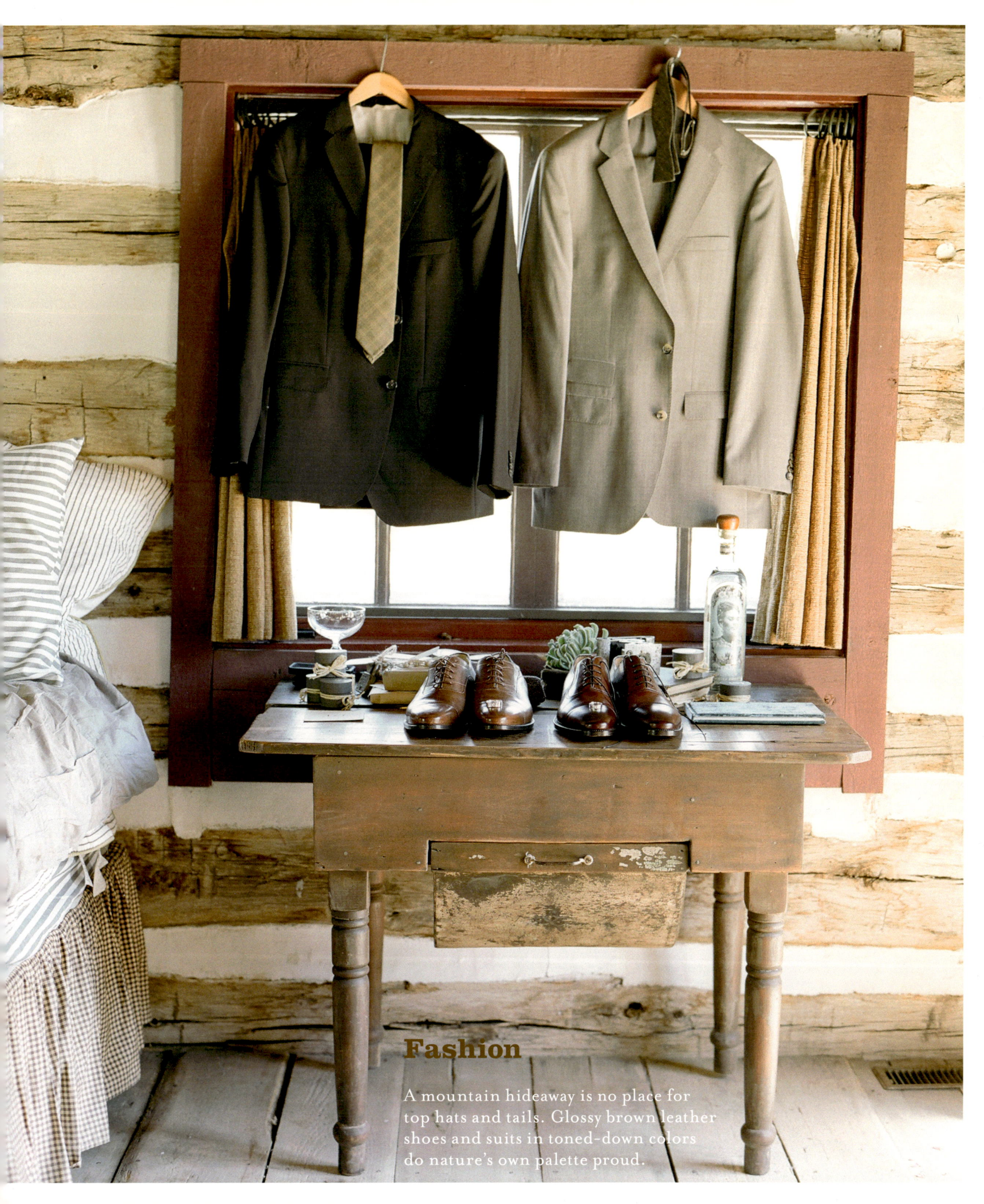

Fashion

A mountain hideaway is no place for top hats and tails. Glossy brown leather shoes and suits in toned-down colors do nature's own palette proud.

So, You're Getting Married...

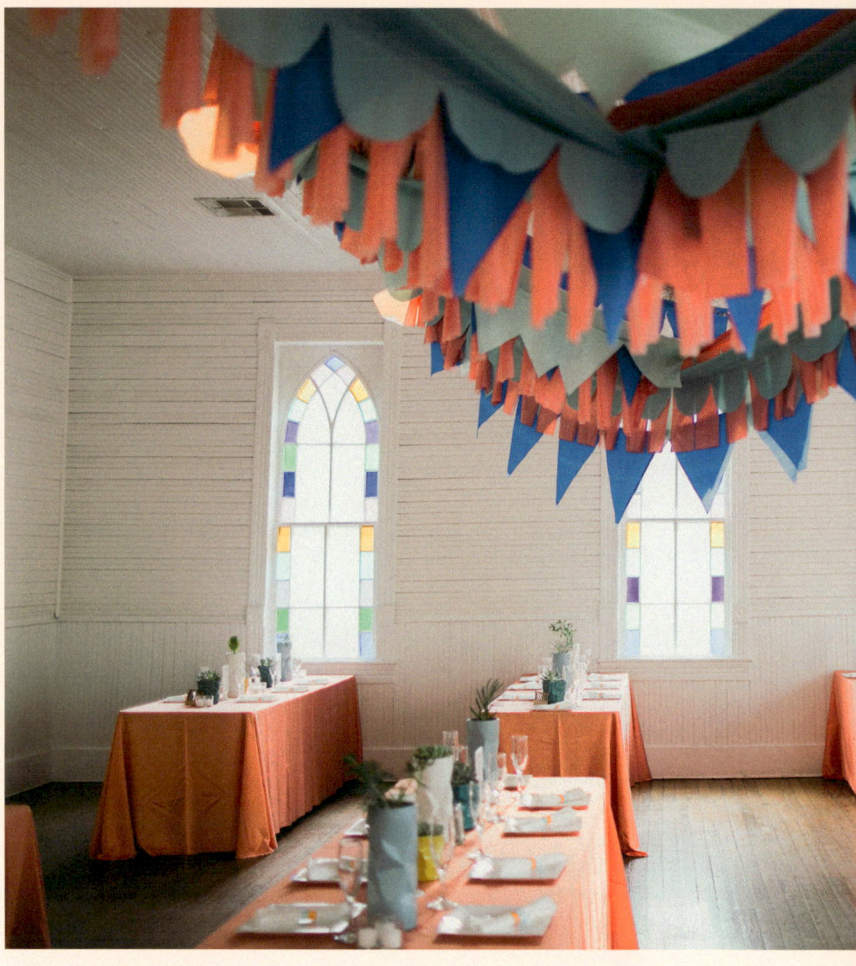

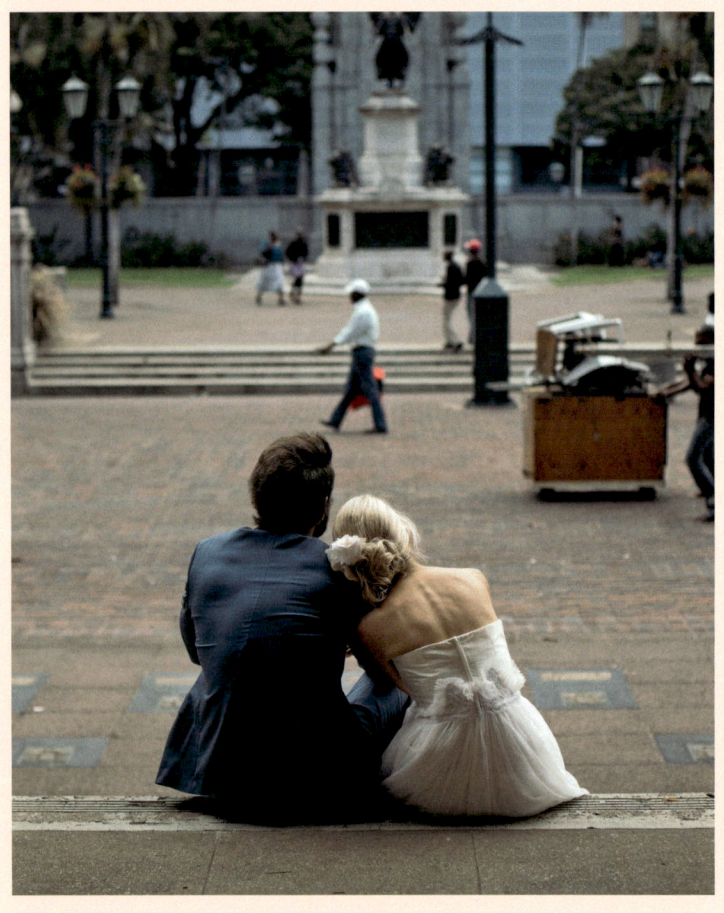

Deciding on how you want your wedding to look and feel can be a challenge. There are so many different styles out there that it can seem overwhelming to try and pick just one.

A theme is not always necessary: it is just as appropriate to convey a feeling or a mood.

Before you get carried away with centerpieces and party favors, strip it back and think about what really inspires you. What makes you smile? What captures your true essence?

Think about what defines you both as individuals and try to incorporate this into the day in a way that symbolizes you coming together as a couple.

When clients come to me for their initial consultation, the first thing I ask them to do is to start keeping images or tear sheets of whatever inspires them.

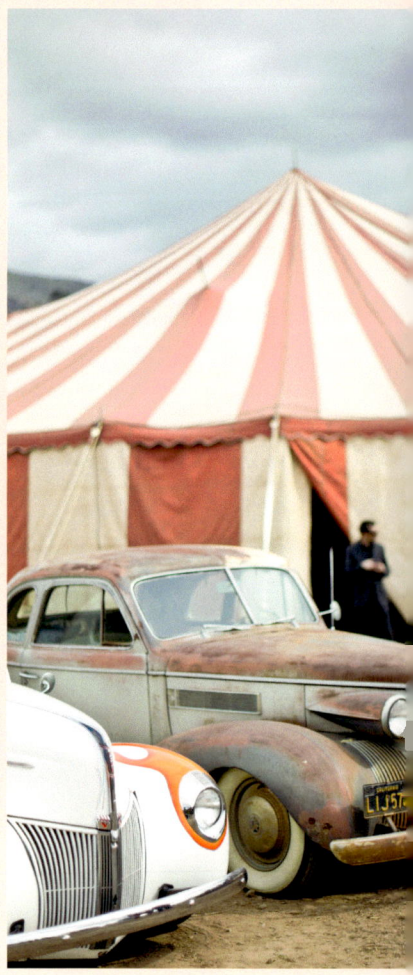

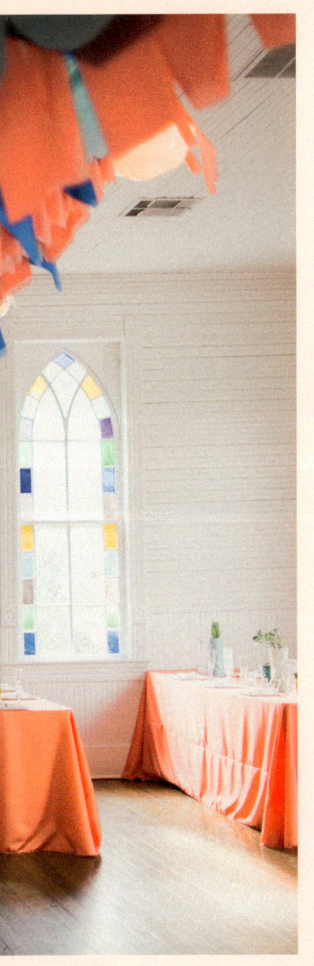

It can be absolutely anything: a color, a pattern, a flower, a piece of art. It doesn't have to be at all related to weddings. There are no rules and there are no right or wrong answers.

This process of cataloging inspiration can help to find your design aesthetic. As you begin to collate your images (the particularly enthusiastic keep scrapbooks), these become your own personal style guide that you can refer back to at each step of creating your wedding.

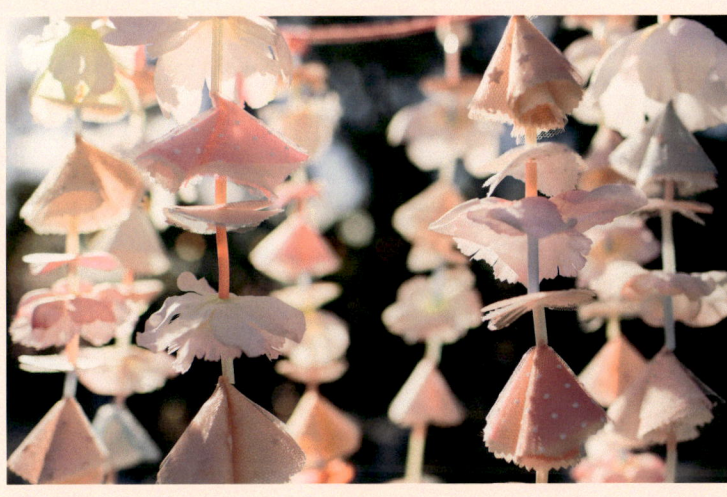

It might be that a very distinctive style emerges, like Talia and Zac's Japanese *kawaii* wedding, or that you decide upon a clear theme like Stacey and Josh did with their vintage circus wedding. It could be that what develops is a subtle thread that delicately ties all your wedding elements together like a favorite flower or a color you love. The simplest idea can elevate a wedding from the ordinary to the sublime.

Once you have your style clearly defined, you can then apply it to your wedding design.

First things first:

1. Start creating a mood board of all your favorite colors, flowers, and ideas.

2. Decide whether you're going all out for a big occasion or whether you want a small and intimate affair.

3. Is your wedding home or away?

4. Decide on the time of year as this will influence atmosphere and style.

5. Once you know when, get it on everyone's calendar with save the date cards.

Inviting your guests not just for a day or an evening, but for a little two-day escape from everyday life provides a couple of advantages. Everyone can arrive, mingle, and get to know each other before the main event. You might want to look for a countryside mansion that allows your guests to stay over so no one has to walk more than a few meters once the party is over.

Start incorporating your theme from the very beginning: whether it's your invitations or save the dates.

Interesting invitations to me are vital. They are the first interaction with guests and set the tone, the feeling, and the aesthetic of what's to come.

Whether invitations are a bespoke comic book for a geek chic event or embroidered onto vintage lace handkerchiefs for a 1950s-inspired wedding, they give guests a preview of what they can expect on the day.

A well designed, simple, hand-illustrated note can be just as beautiful as an elaborate invitation. However, don't be afraid to be playful. In the past we have made kaleidoscopes that reveal a different detail with each twist and viewfinders loaded with pictures of the bride and groom. Consider your theme, but ultimately choose what feels right for you.

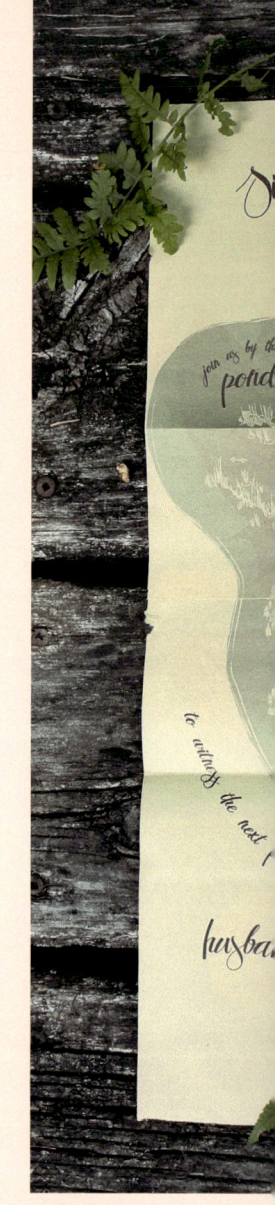

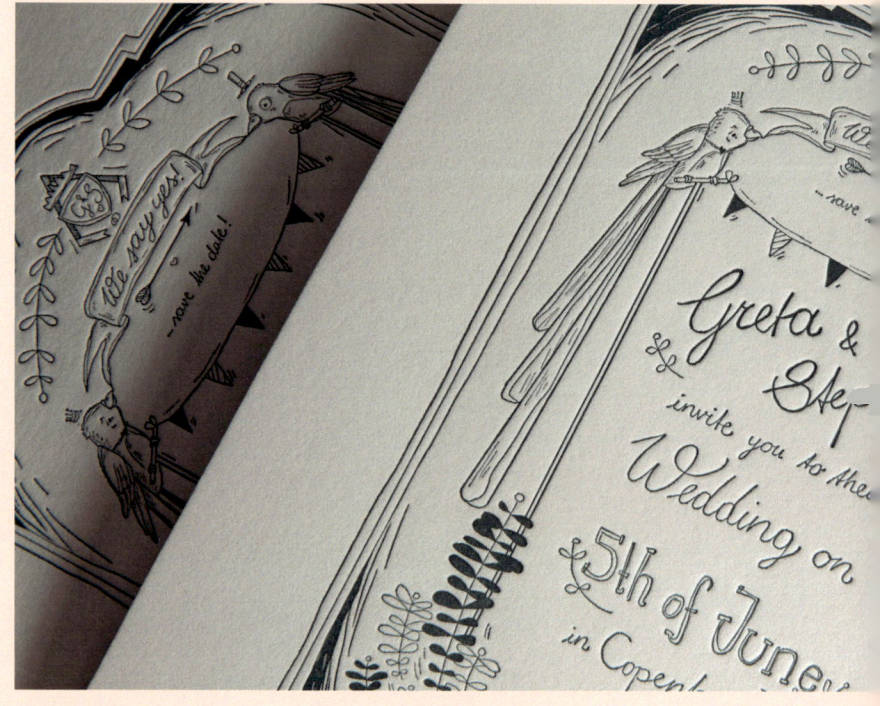

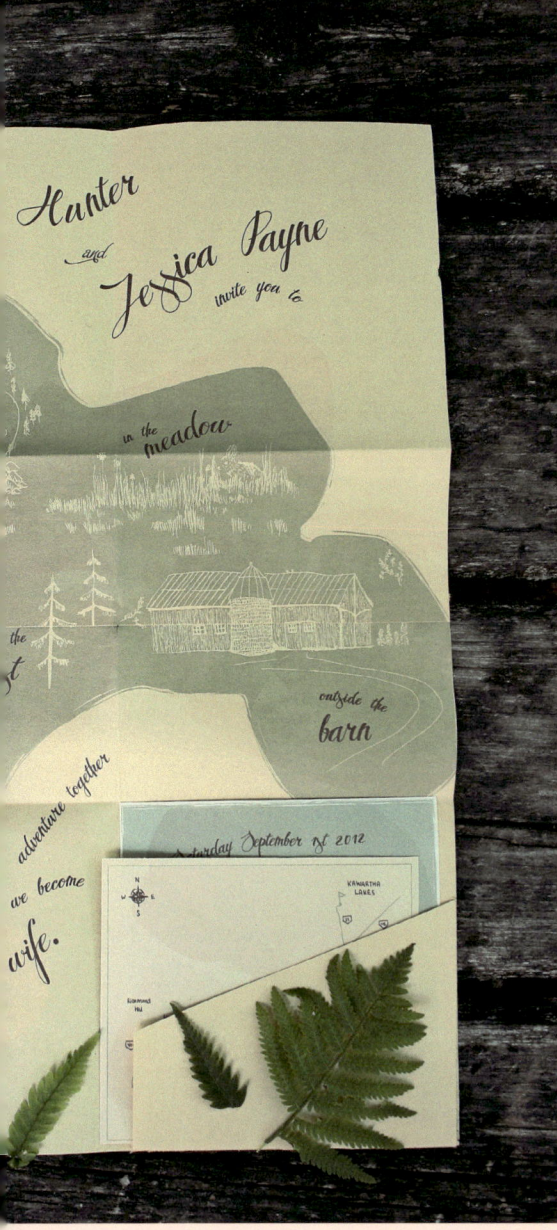

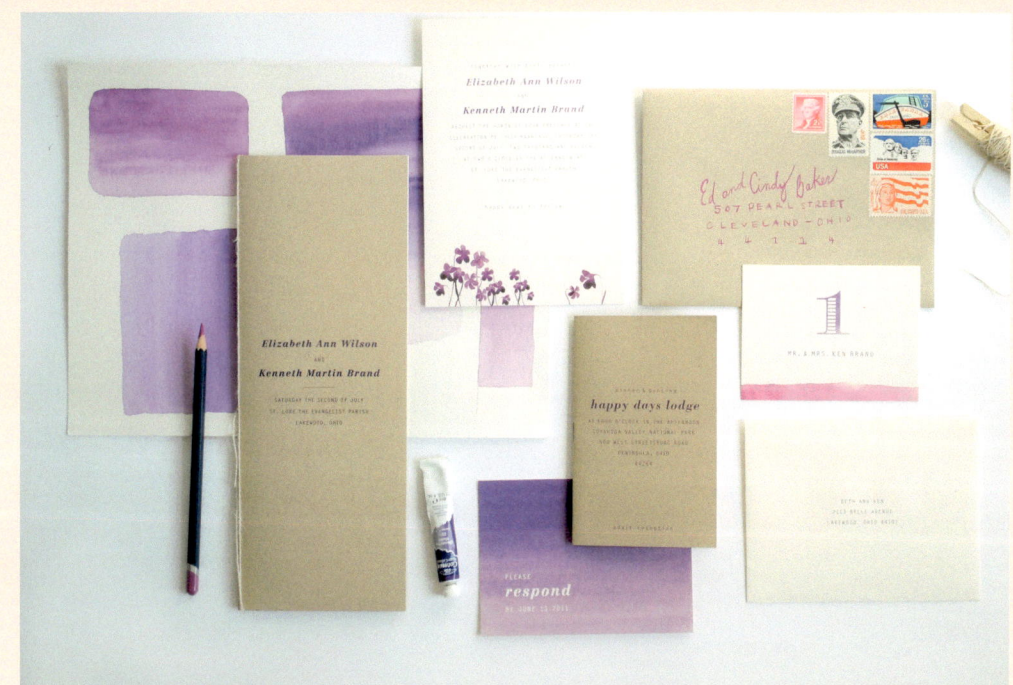

After the invitations, work in stages, moving onto the venue, décor, entertainment and so on. Every part of the wedding should have a dialogue. A good theme, no matter how subtle, will help the day flow. When planning your wedding, it might help to look at each part as a piece of a puzzle. When all the pieces are assembled they will make your wedding's atmosphere. Separately each piece may be spectacular, but if they are disjointed when put together, then your atmosphere will be, too.

On the other hand, if each piece complements the other and fit together beautifully, then you will have an incredible atmosphere and an incredible wedding.

From a practical point of view, invitations should include all the information guests will need for the day, including the schedule, location, and dress code. Remember, if your wedding is going to be on a mountain top, to let your guests know to leave their stilettos at home.

For me, "the decadence is in the detail" and it starts with the invitations.

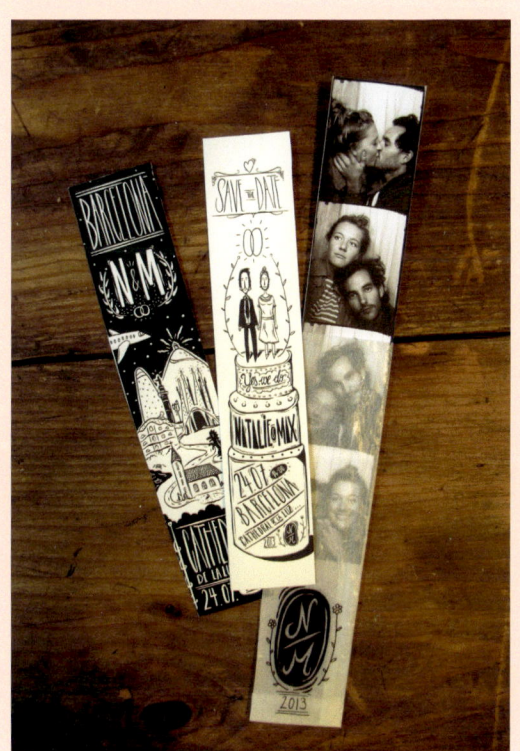

The weddings included in this book are fabulous examples of well-executed themes. They express personality and individuality but keep the heart and meaning of the day intact.

Remember: there is no wrong or right way to get married, but there is an enjoyable way to get married. If it looks right, if it feels right, then it is right and this book will hopefully show you how others have shunned the traditional with delightful results.

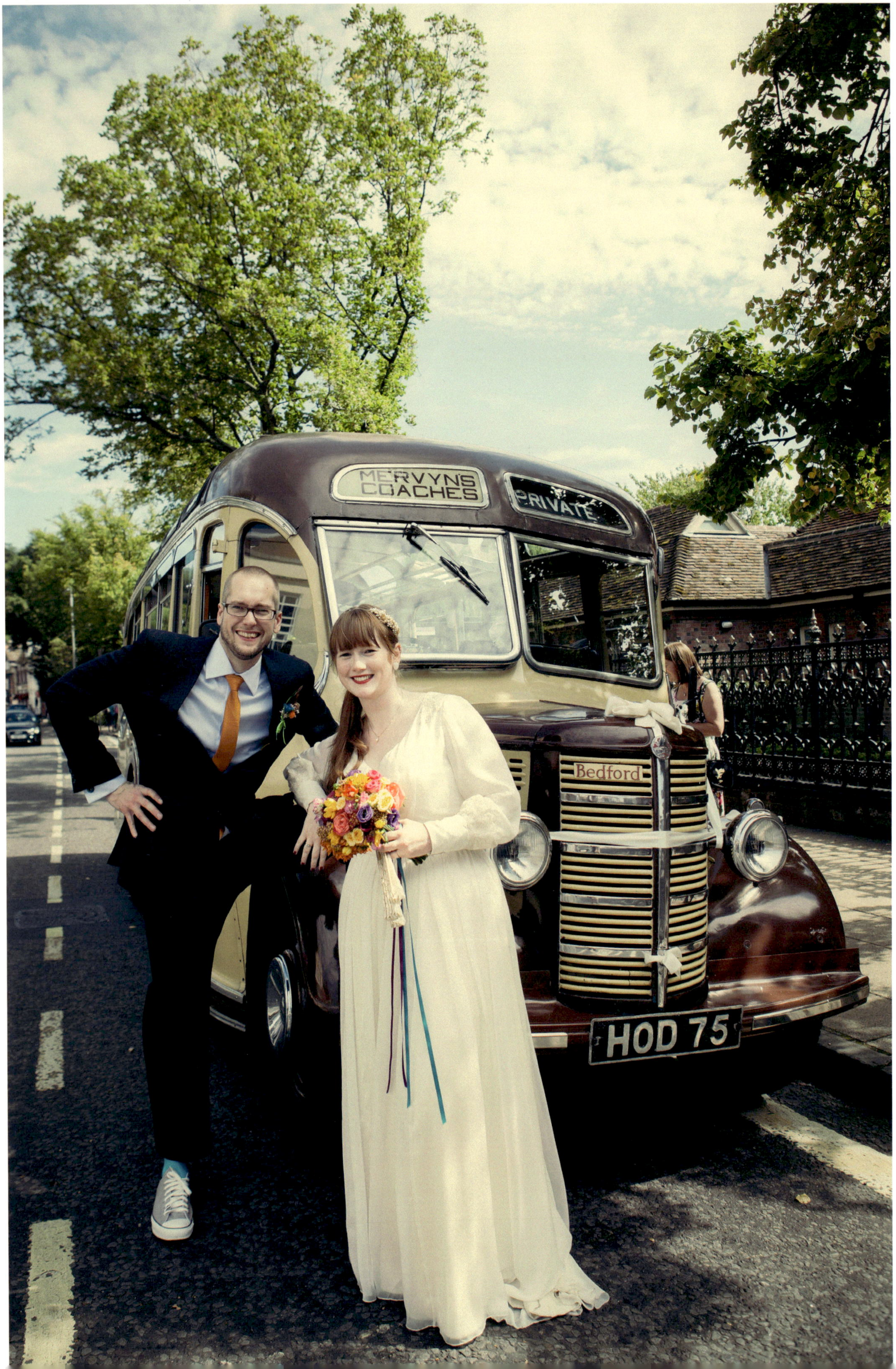

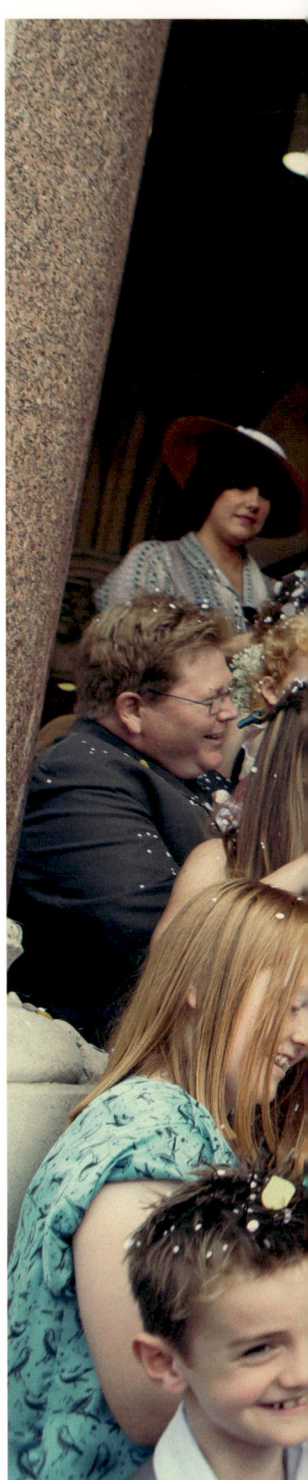

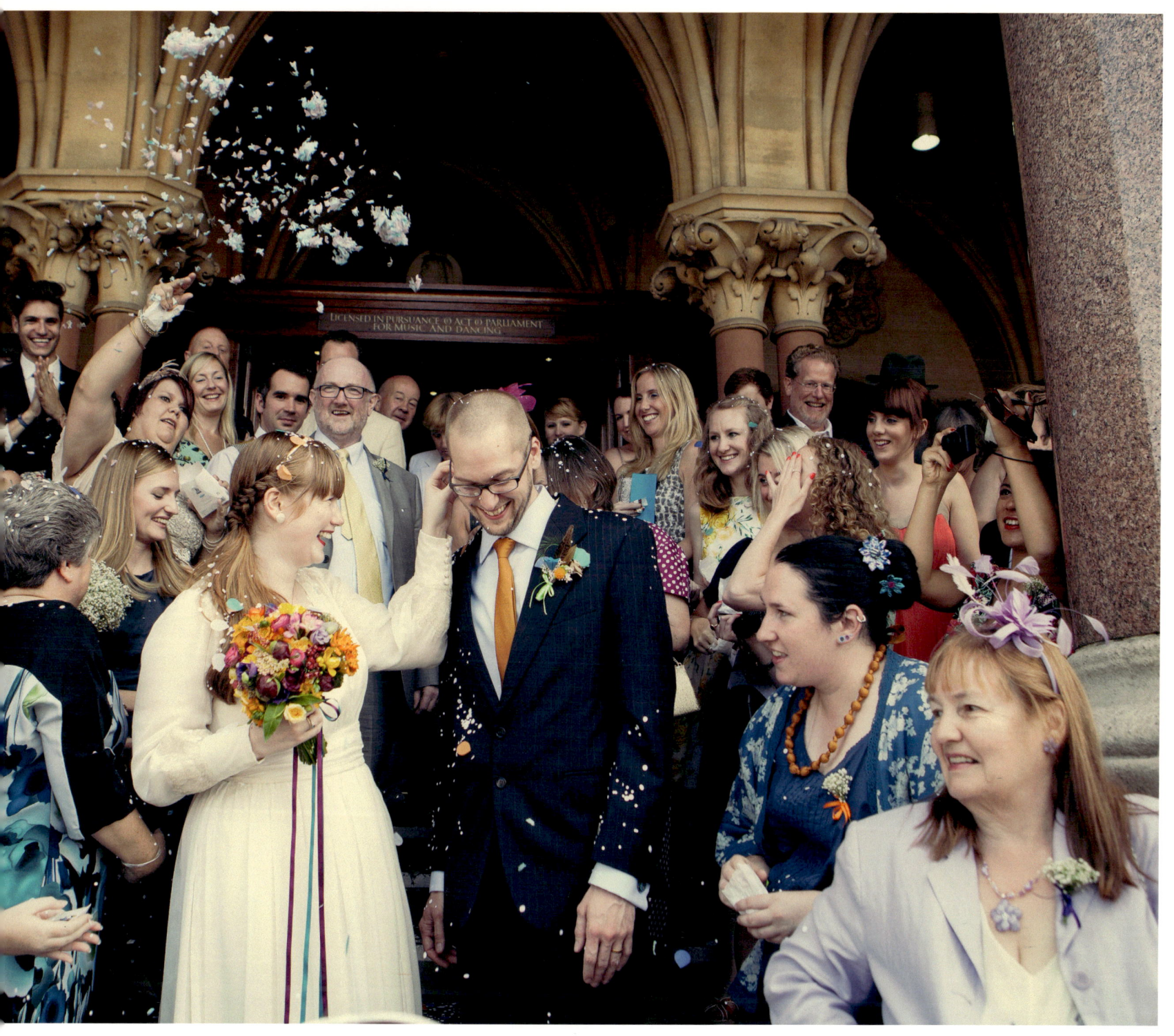

Laura & Mike

Laura and Mike's wedding is unlikely to make you think of DIY. The games on the lawn, the streamers hanging from trees, the table of cakes shiny with icing and wrapped in bright bows—it all adds up to a dreamy summer's day, not a hammers-and-nails project. But meanings were made to be broken, and Laura, Mike, and their family and friends did this all themselves. One of the few things that came ready-made was the vintage bus the couple traveled in. Even the most talented of wedding planners have to draw the line somewhere.

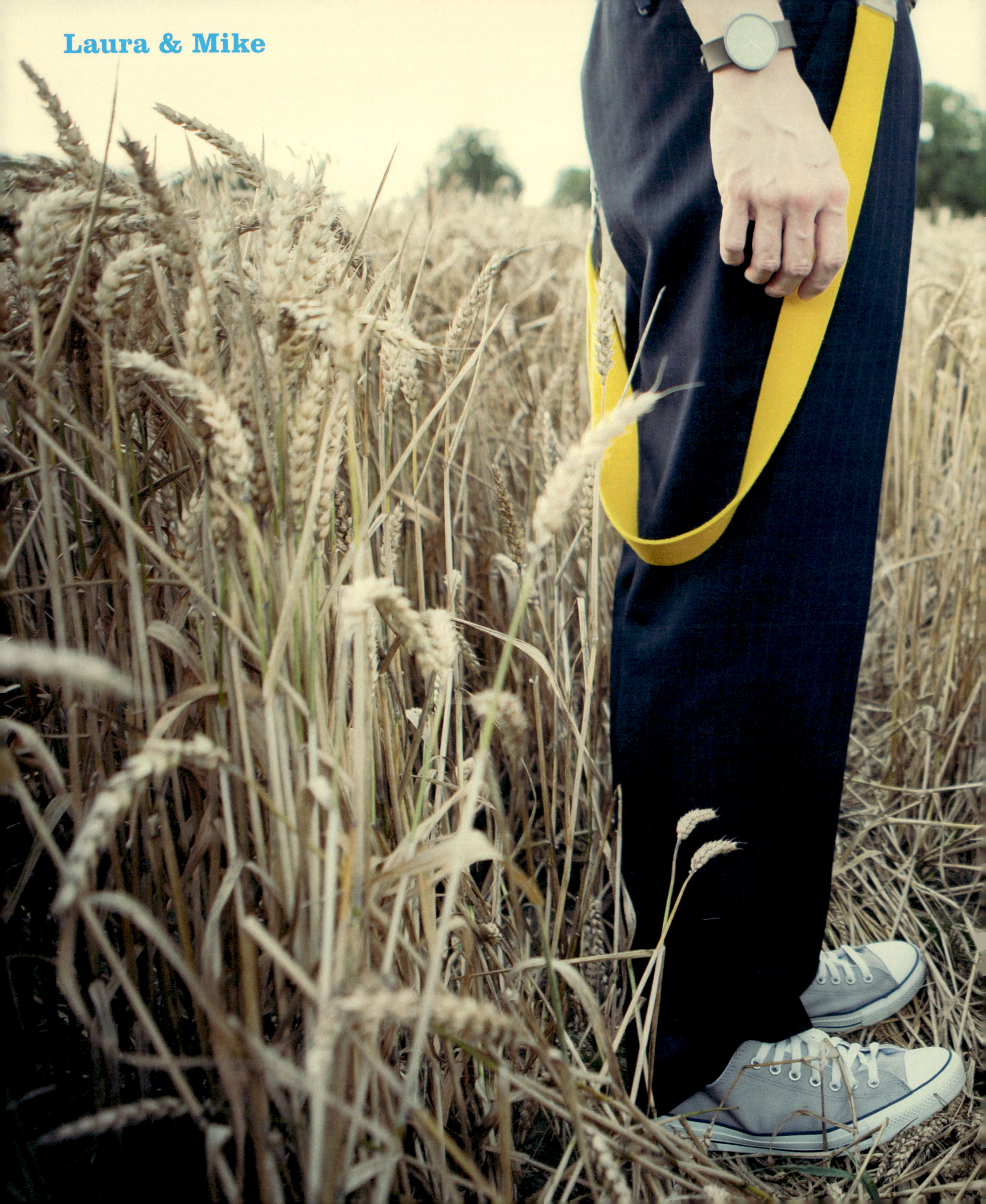

Laura & Mike

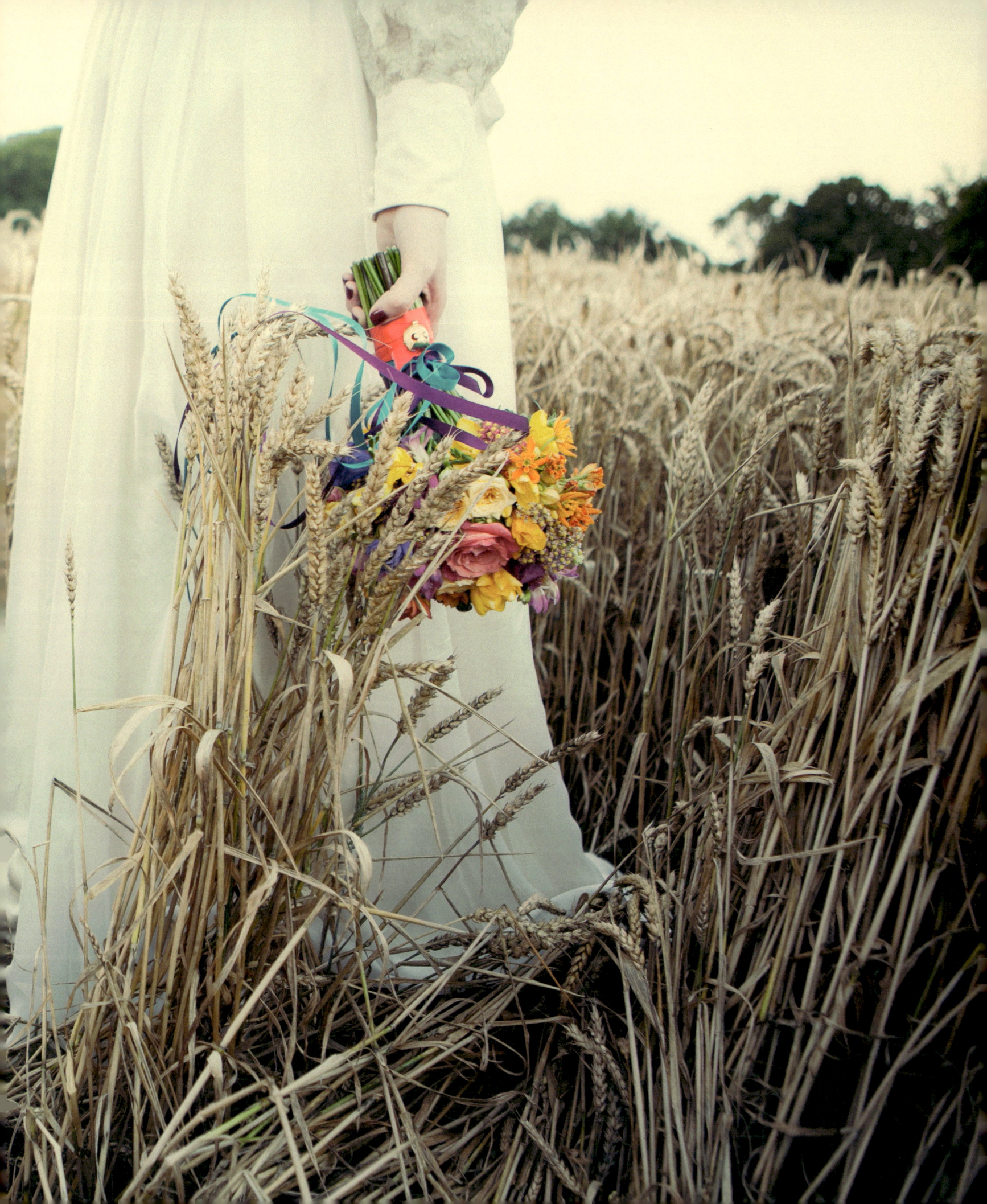

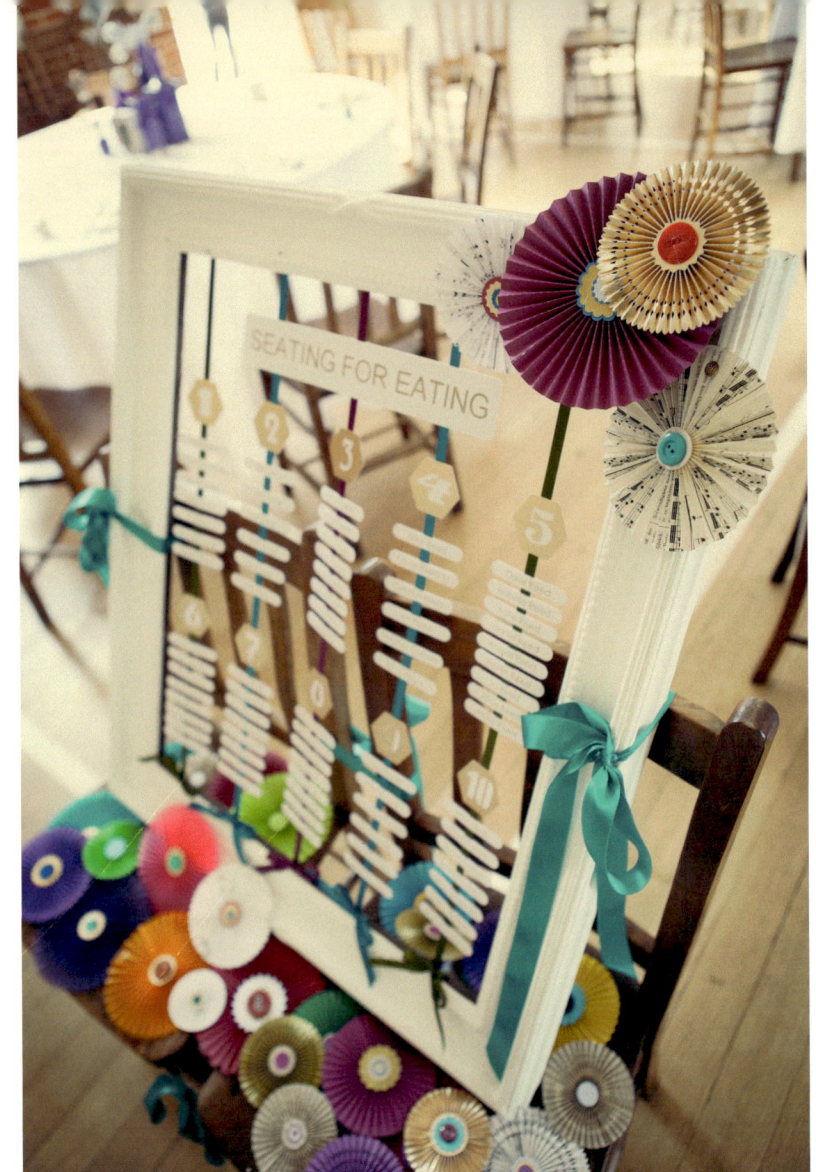

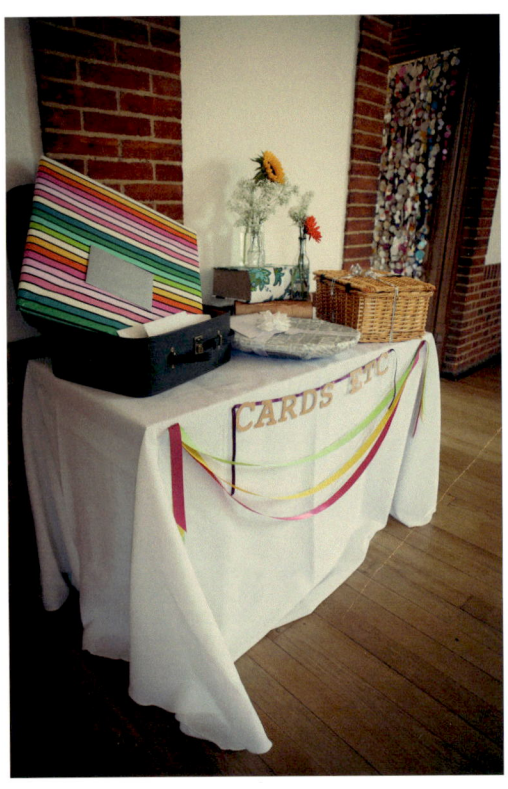

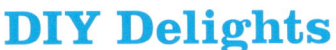

DIY Delights

From the bride's dress and the groom's photographs, to the invitations, flowers, paper decorations, and the iPod mix that got everyone dancing after dark, this celebration was homemade to perfection.

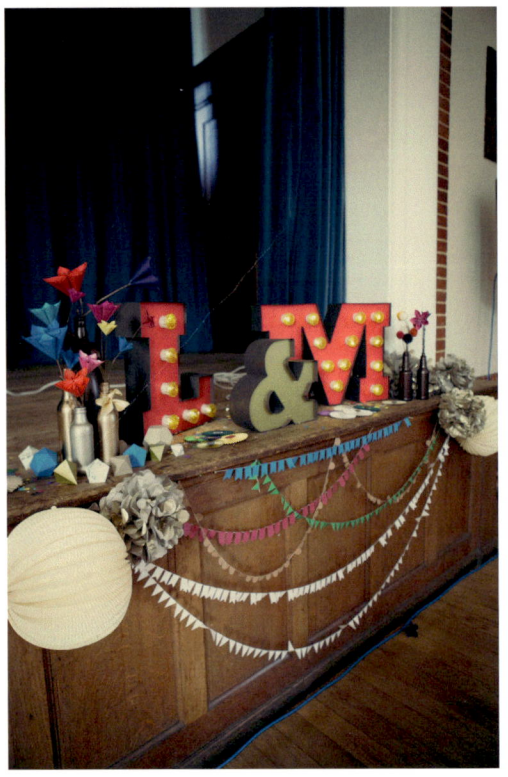

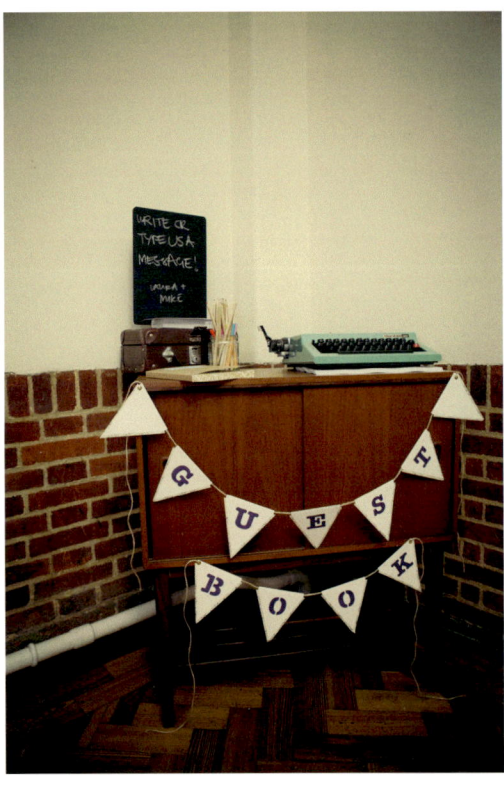

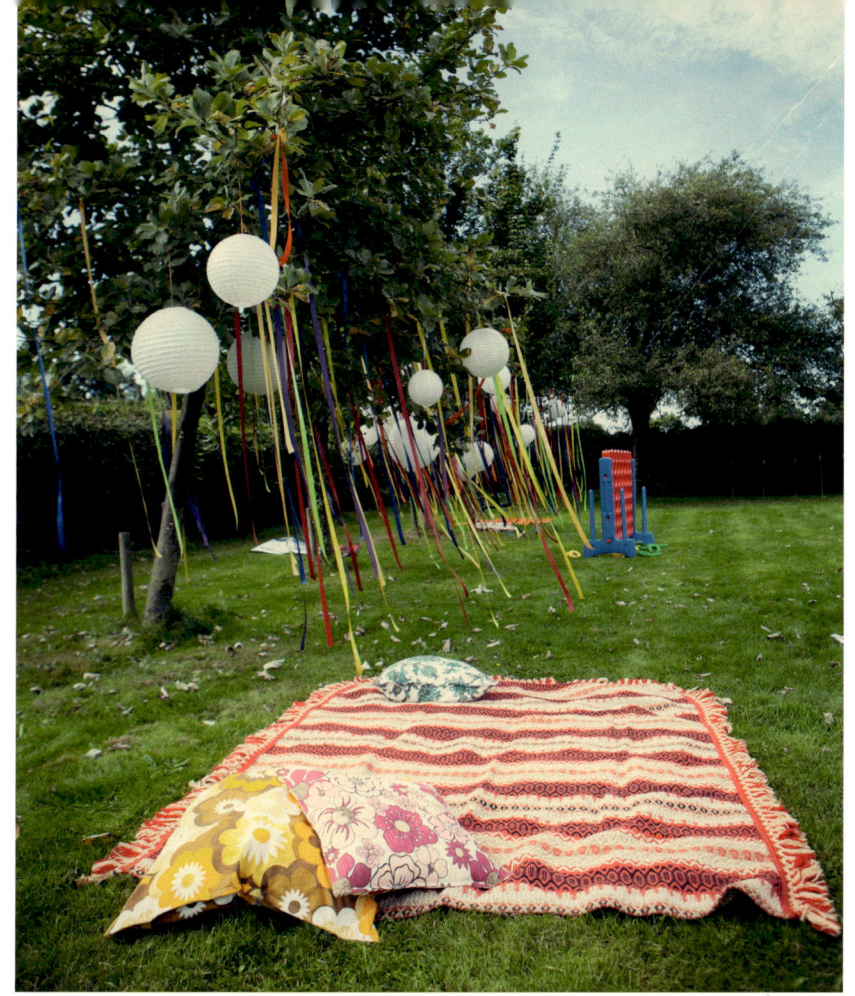
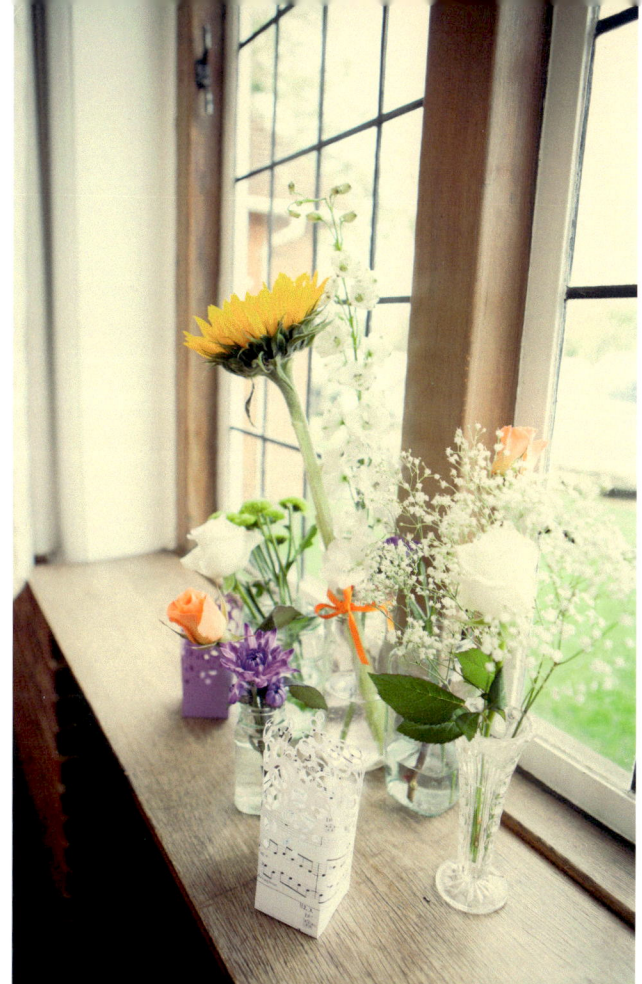

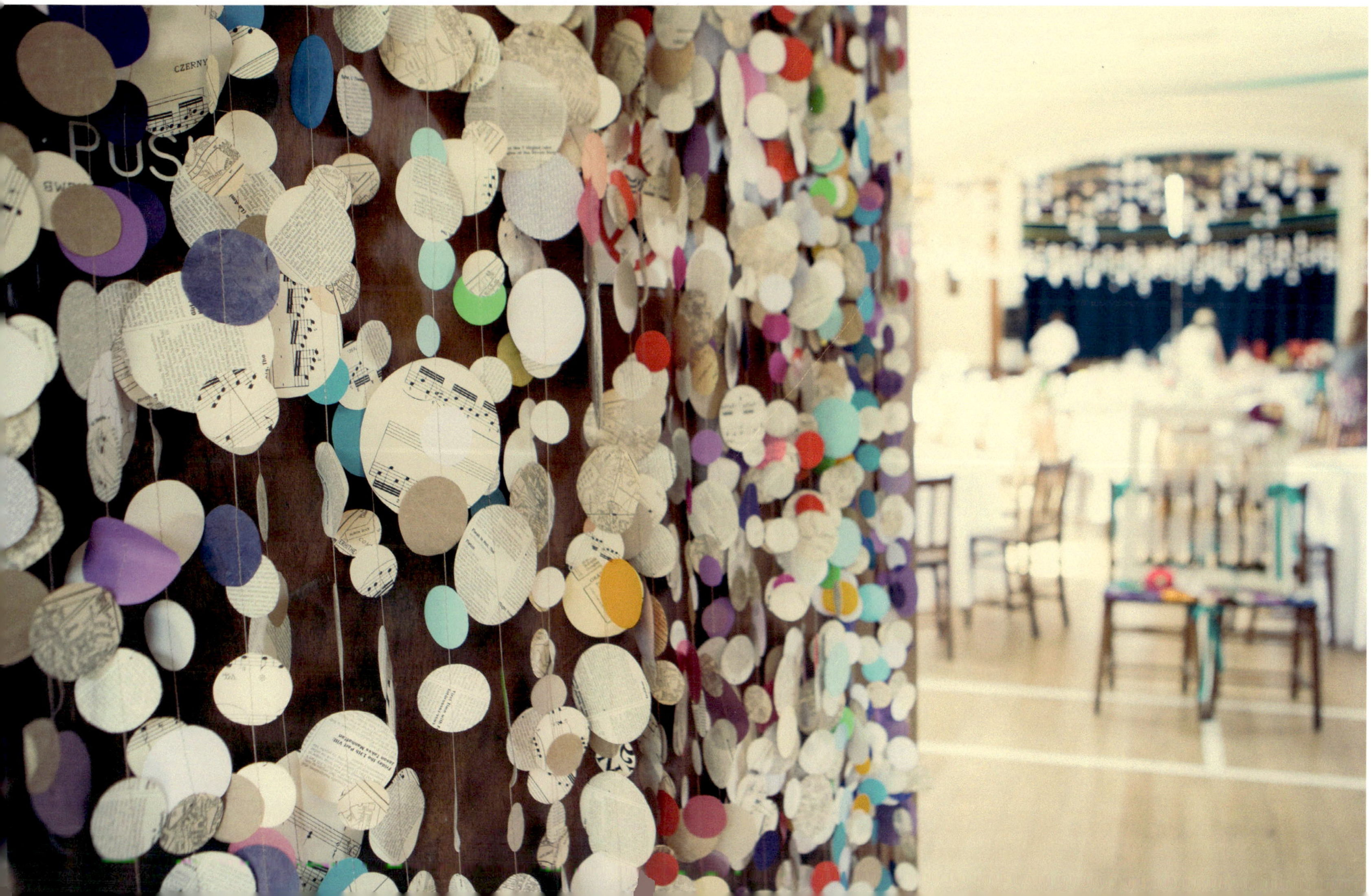

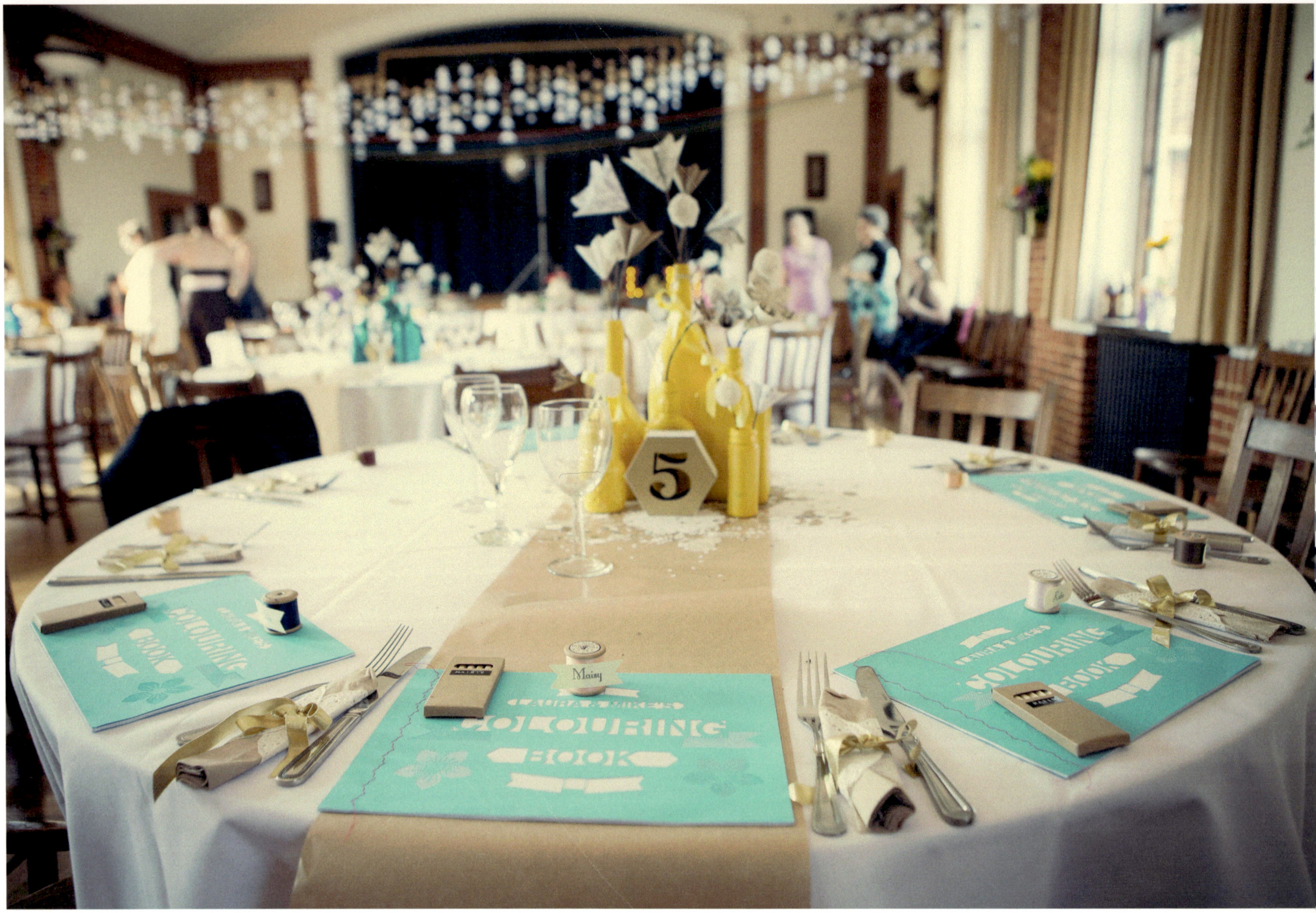

Dinner is Served

Tables set with colored bottles, paper flowers, and spools of thread for place cards matched the country feel of the village hall that hosted the reception. Personalized coloring books kept the kids entertained over dinner and were a cute souvenir of the day.

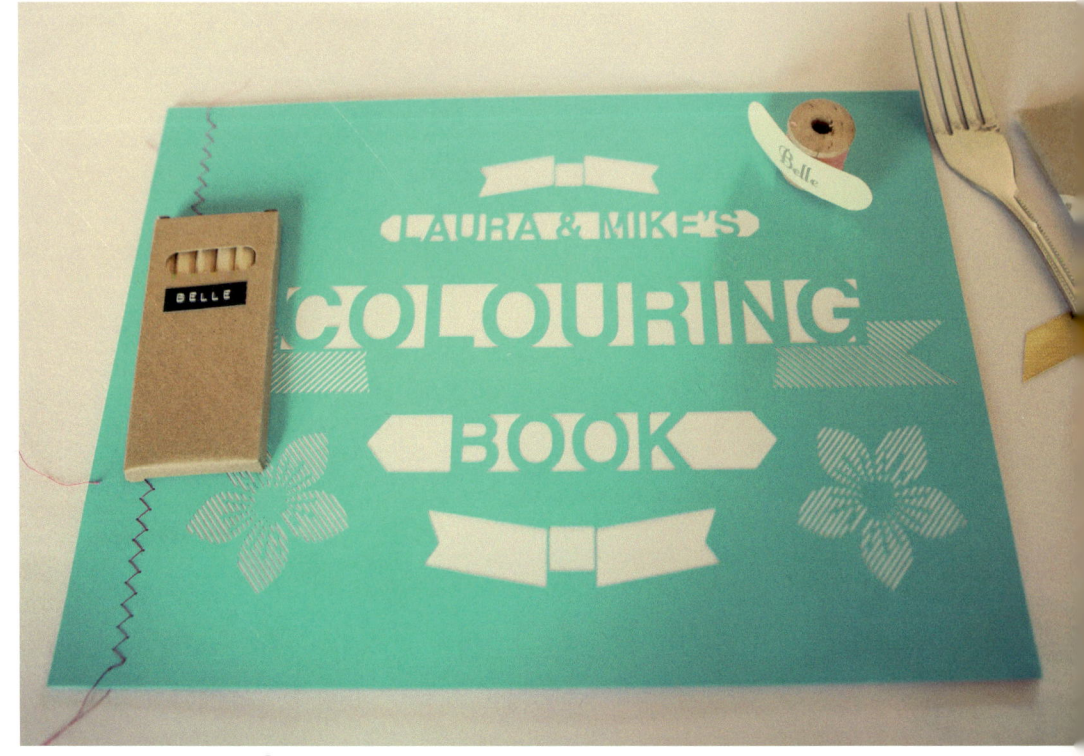

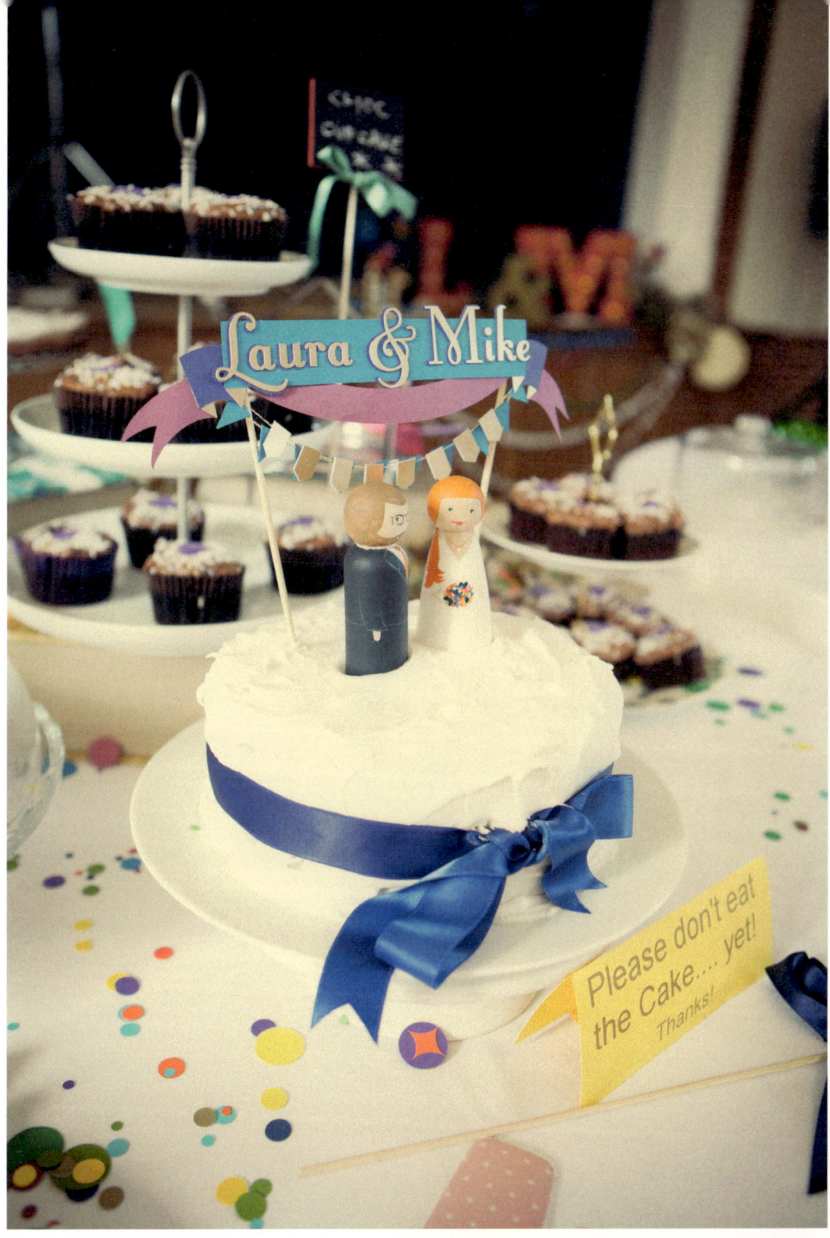

1. Do those cake toppers remind you of anyone?

2. A sprinkling of colorful confetti brings out the best in any tablecloth.

3. A whole candy store, just for us!

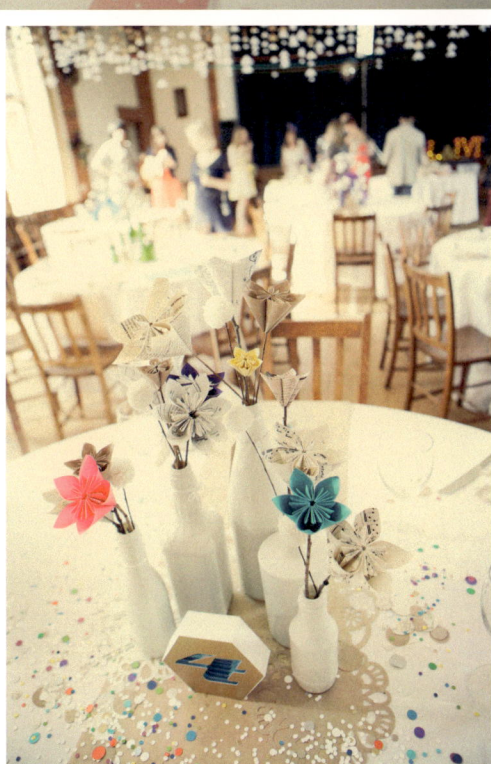

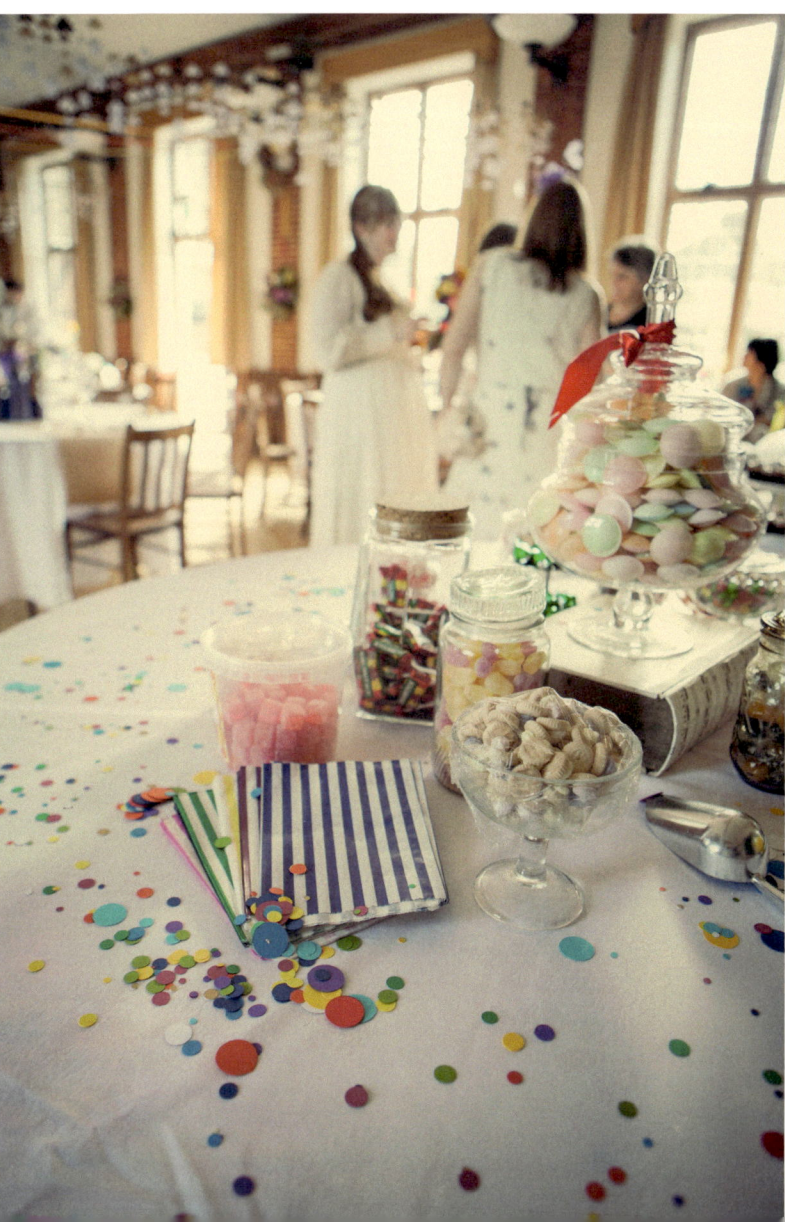

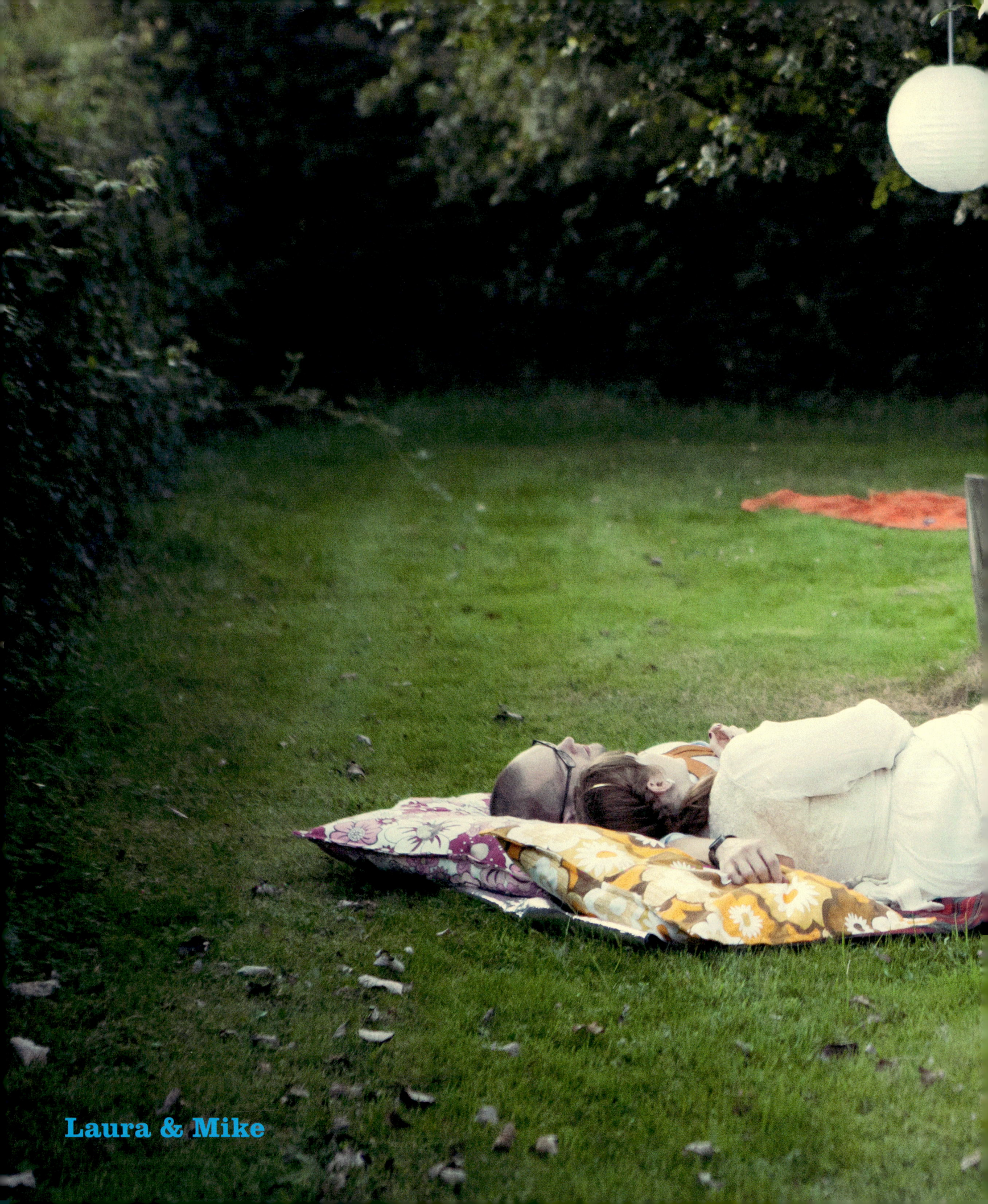

Laura & Mike

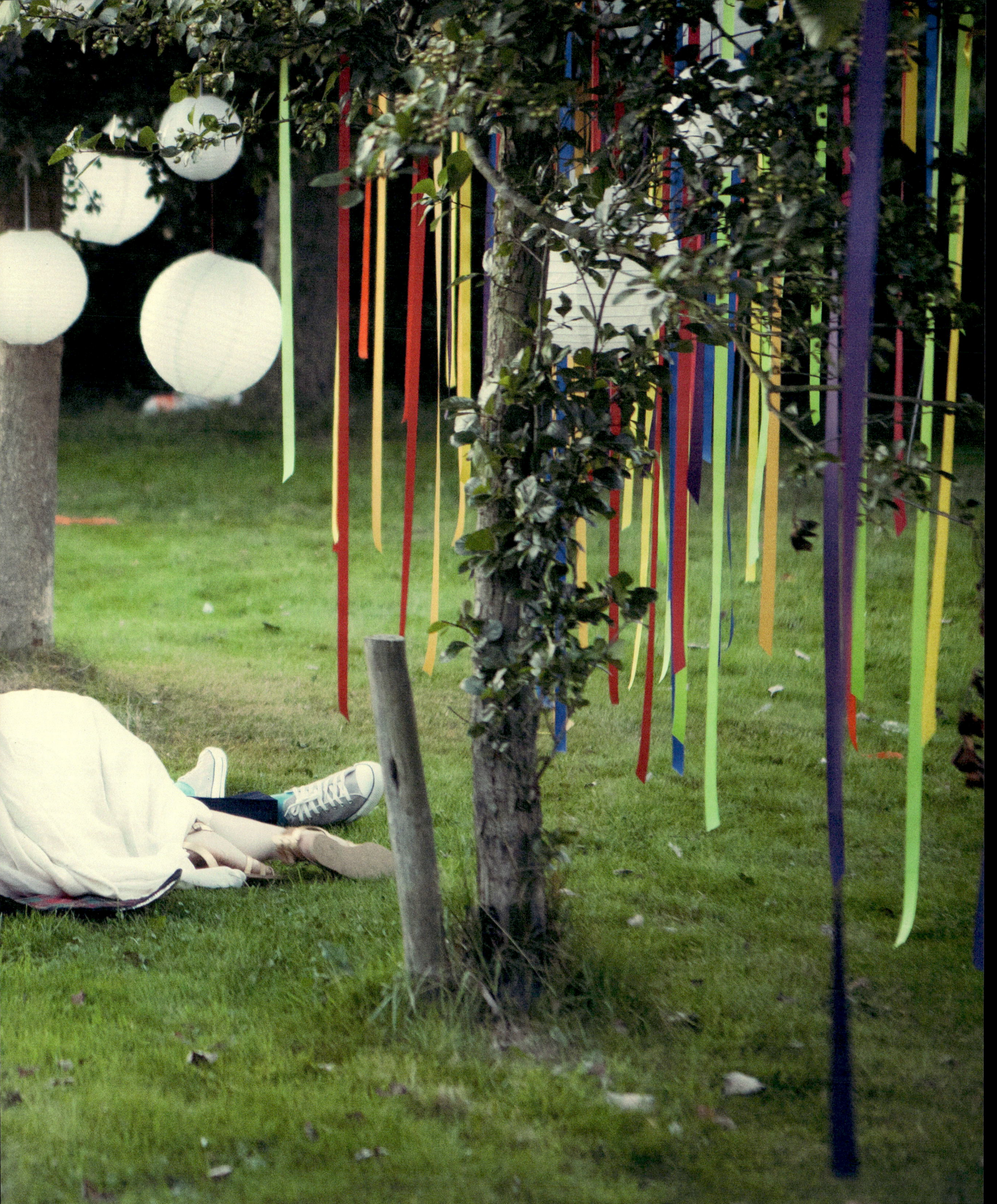

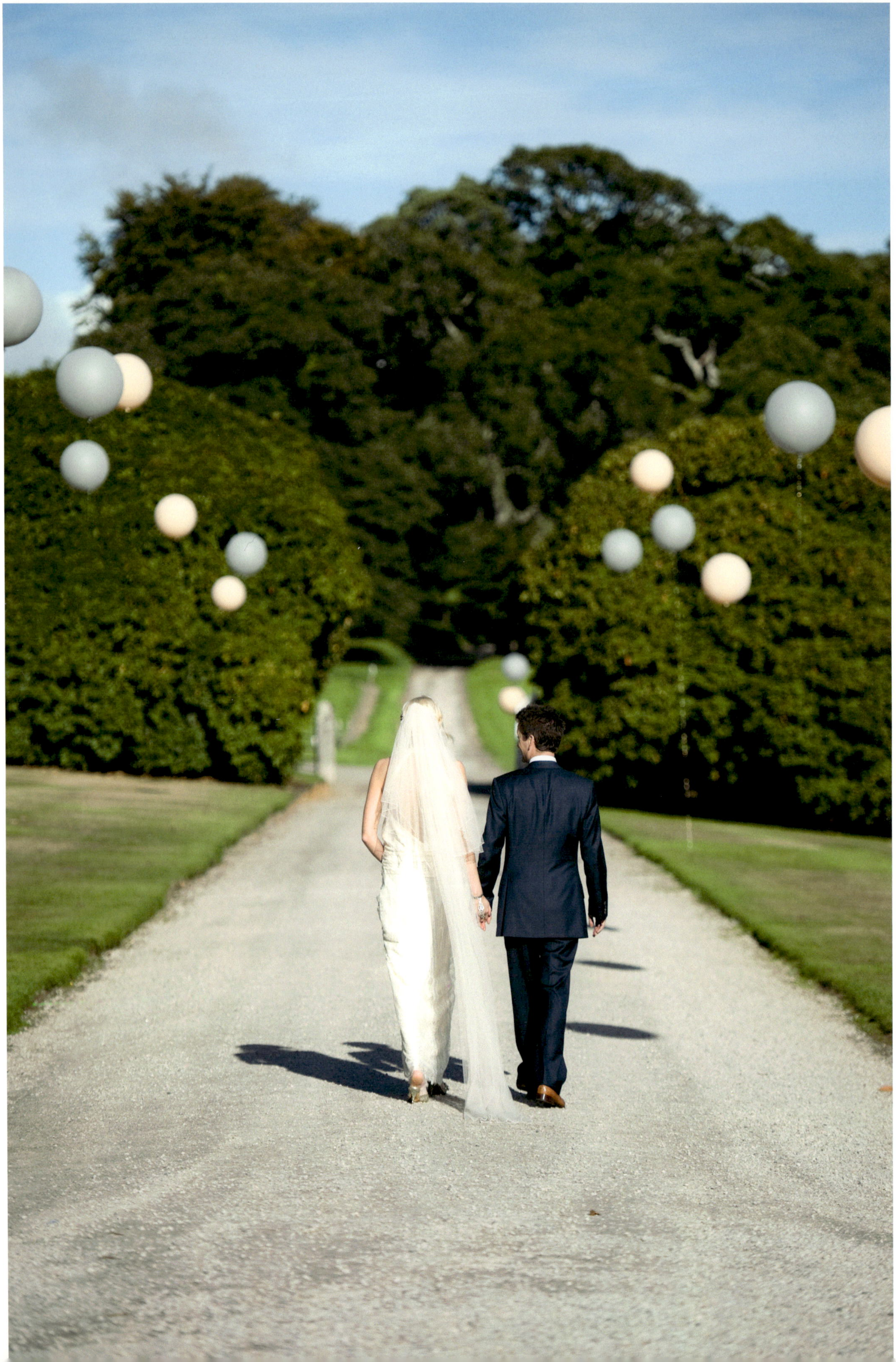

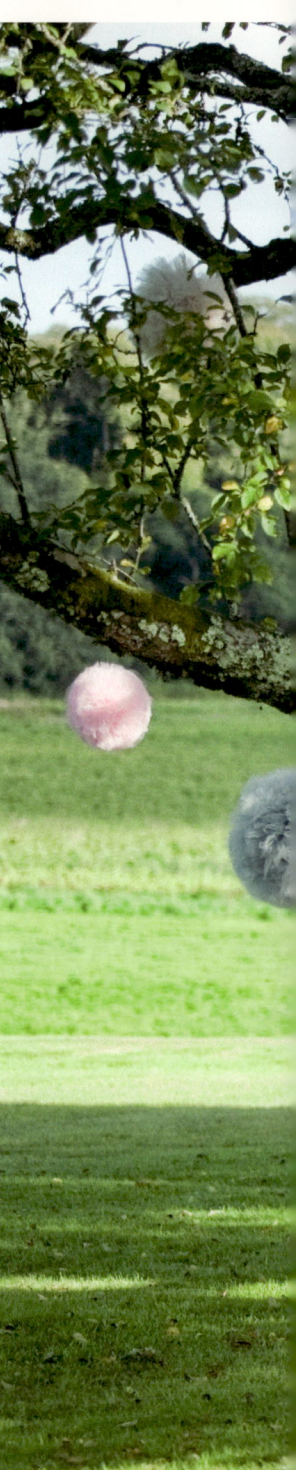

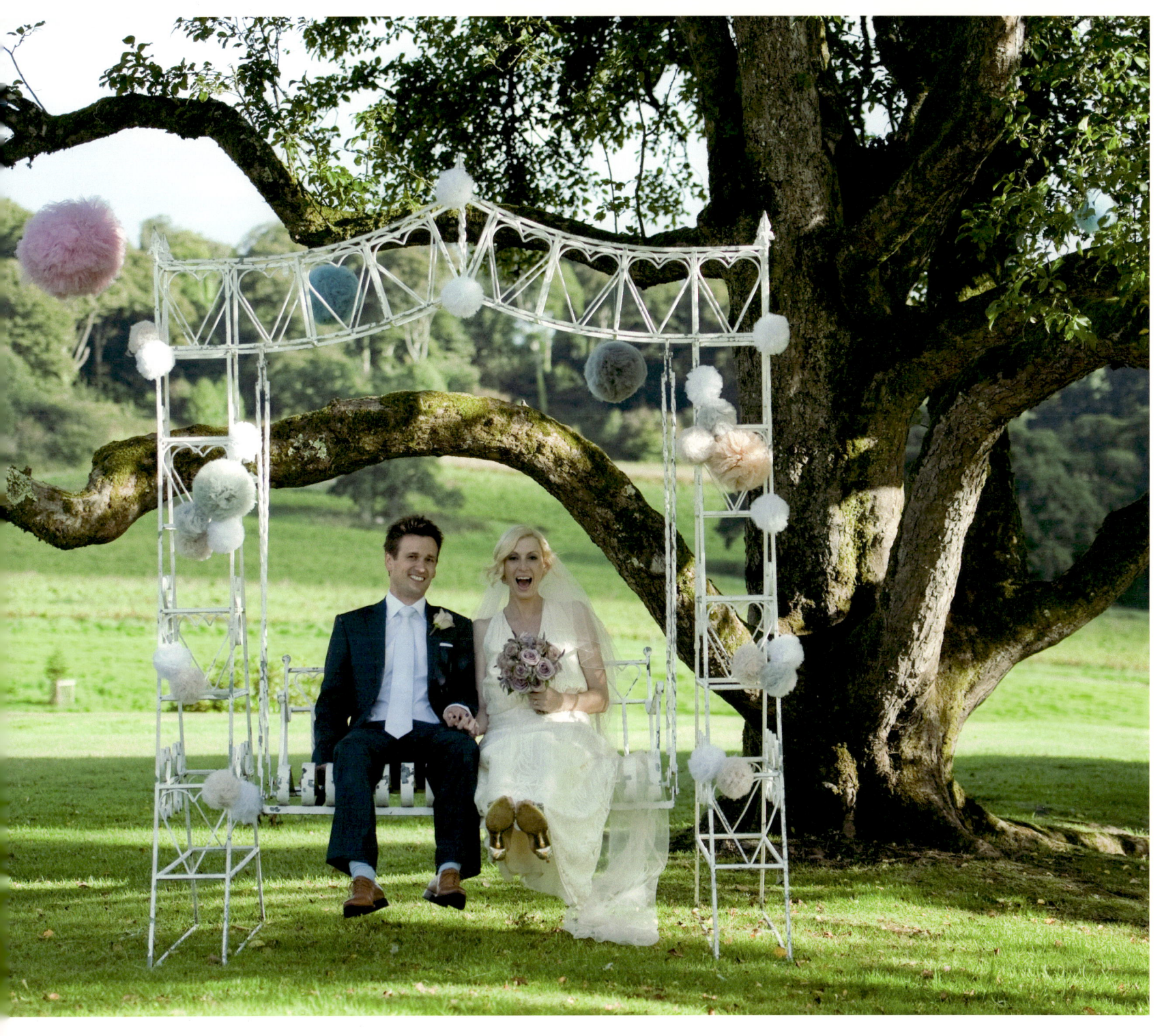

Shona & Luke

Shona and Luke's wedding fused the Roaring Twenties with eighteenth-century France. Shona's dress was inspired by the dropped-hem styles of the flappers, while her kitten heels gave the outfit a modern twist. Designer Fiona Leahy worked duck-egg blues, lemon yellows, and ornate candelabras into the decorations, which picked up the palette and look of Sofia Coppola's film, *Marie Antoinette*. Outside, guests relaxed on hay bales covered in gray linen, drank mojitos made with fresh mint, and enjoyed Falmouth Bay oysters.

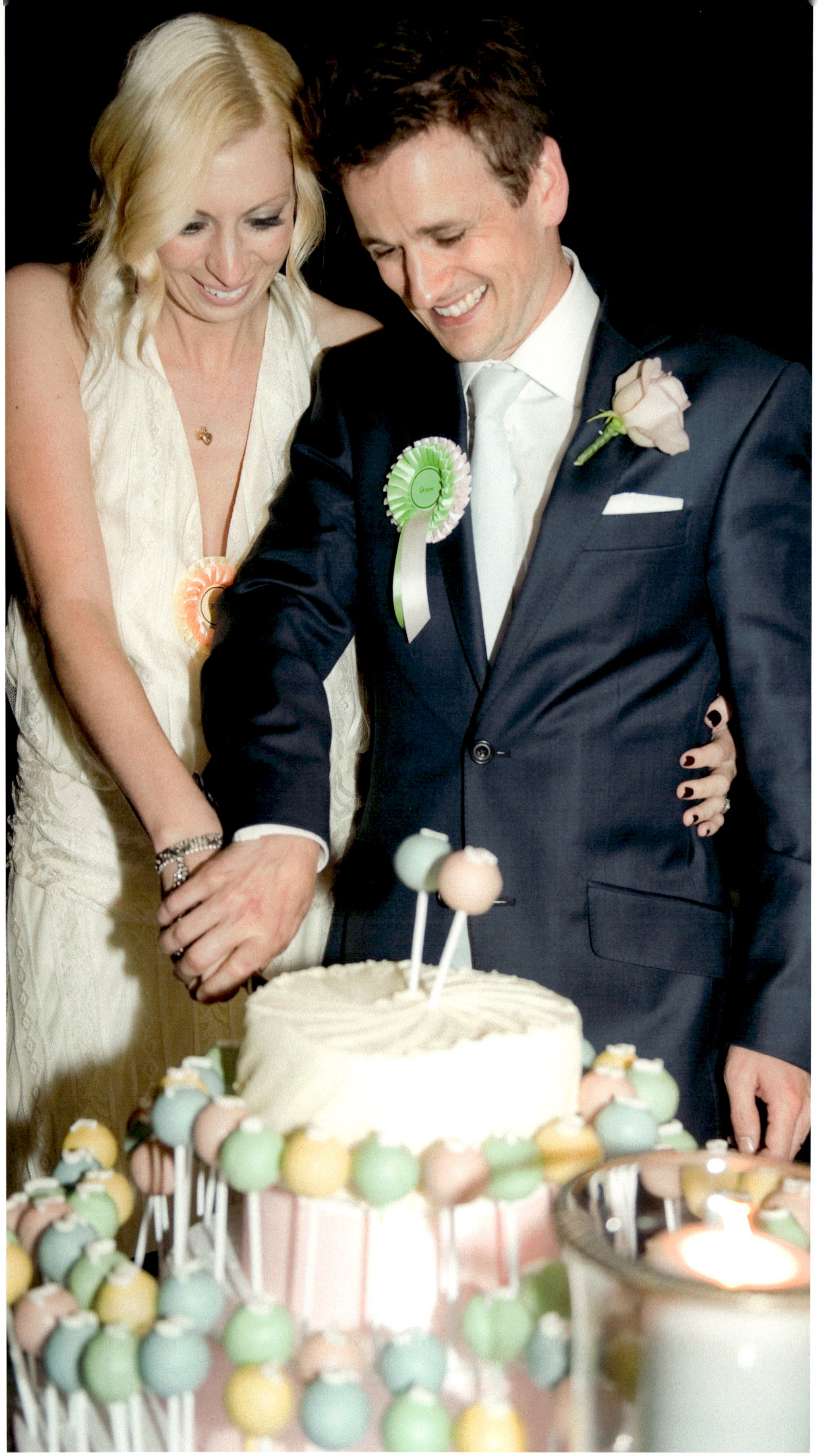

Oh, lollipops!

Cake pops are the latest thing in baked goods, so this sweet ensemble (one Victoria Sponge, two tiers of pastel pops) was right on trend.

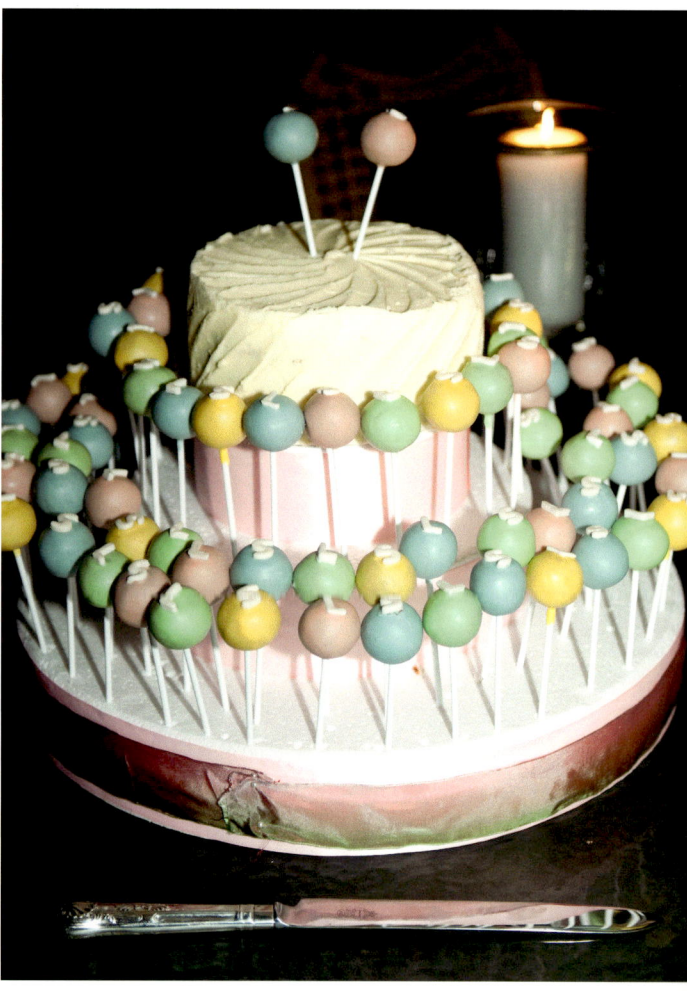

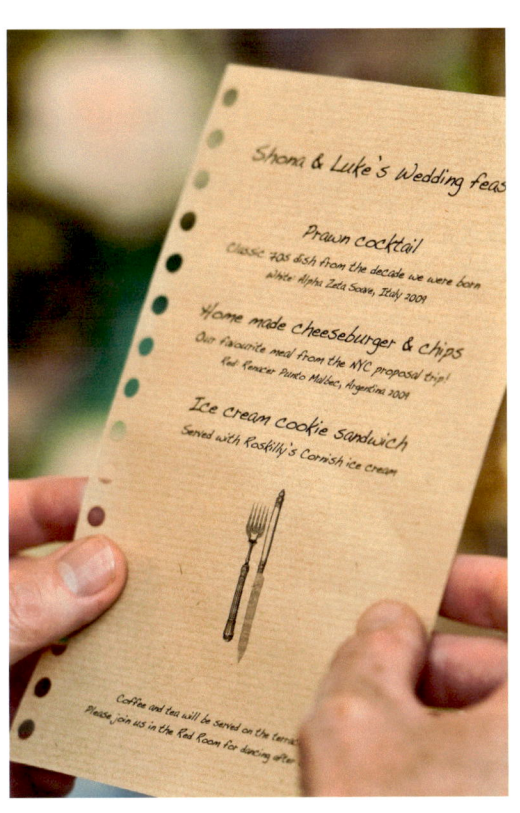

Shona & Luke's Wedding feast

Prawn cocktail
Classic 70s dish from the decade we were born
White Alpha Zeta Soave, Italy 2009

Home made cheeseburger & chips
Our favourite meal from the NYC proposal trip!
Red Reneve Punto Malbec, Argentina 2009

Ice cream cookie sandwich
Served with Roskilly's Cornish ice cream

Coffee and tea will be served on the terrace.
Please join us in the Red Room for dancing after.

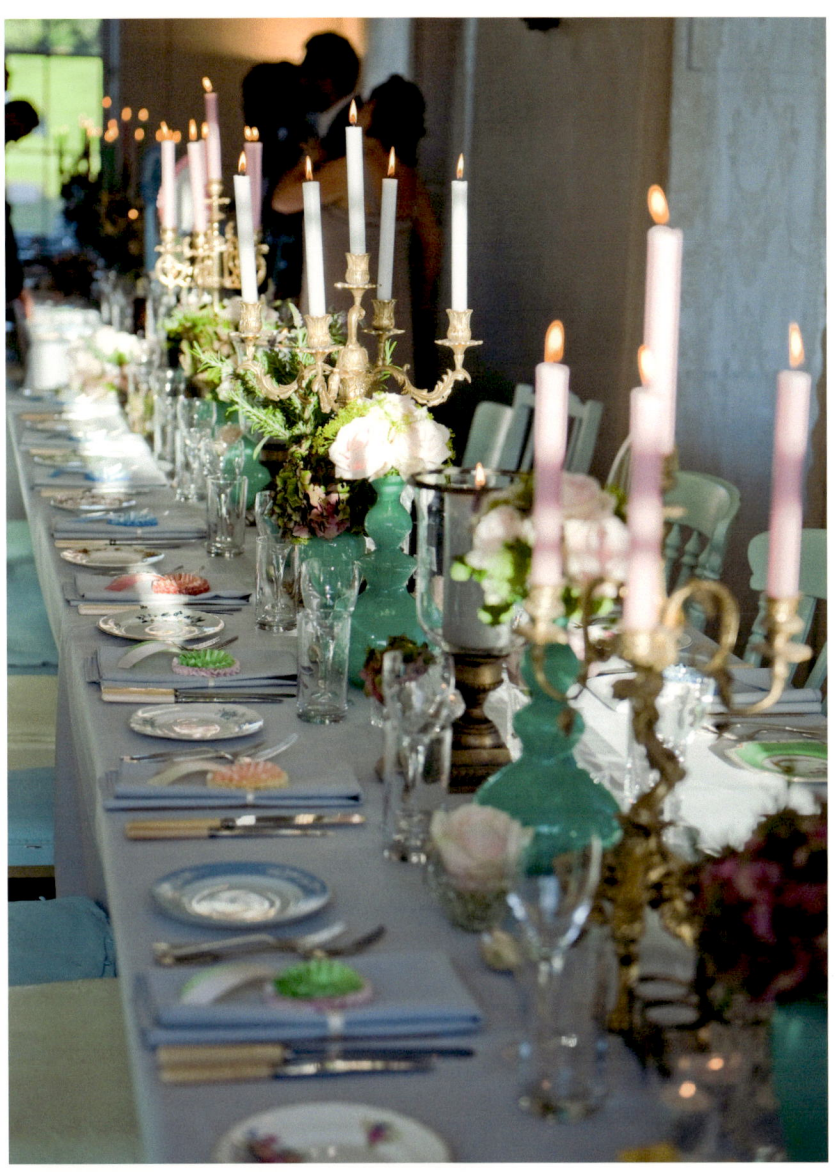

The rosette place cards were such a hit that guests pinned them on and wore them all night.

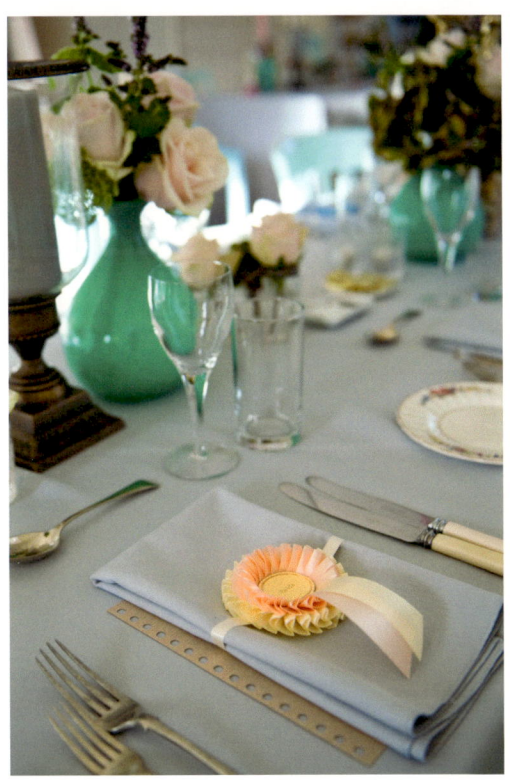

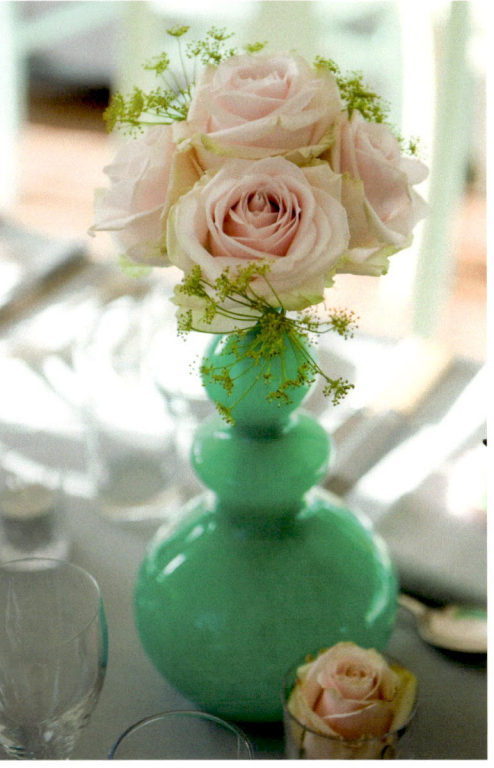

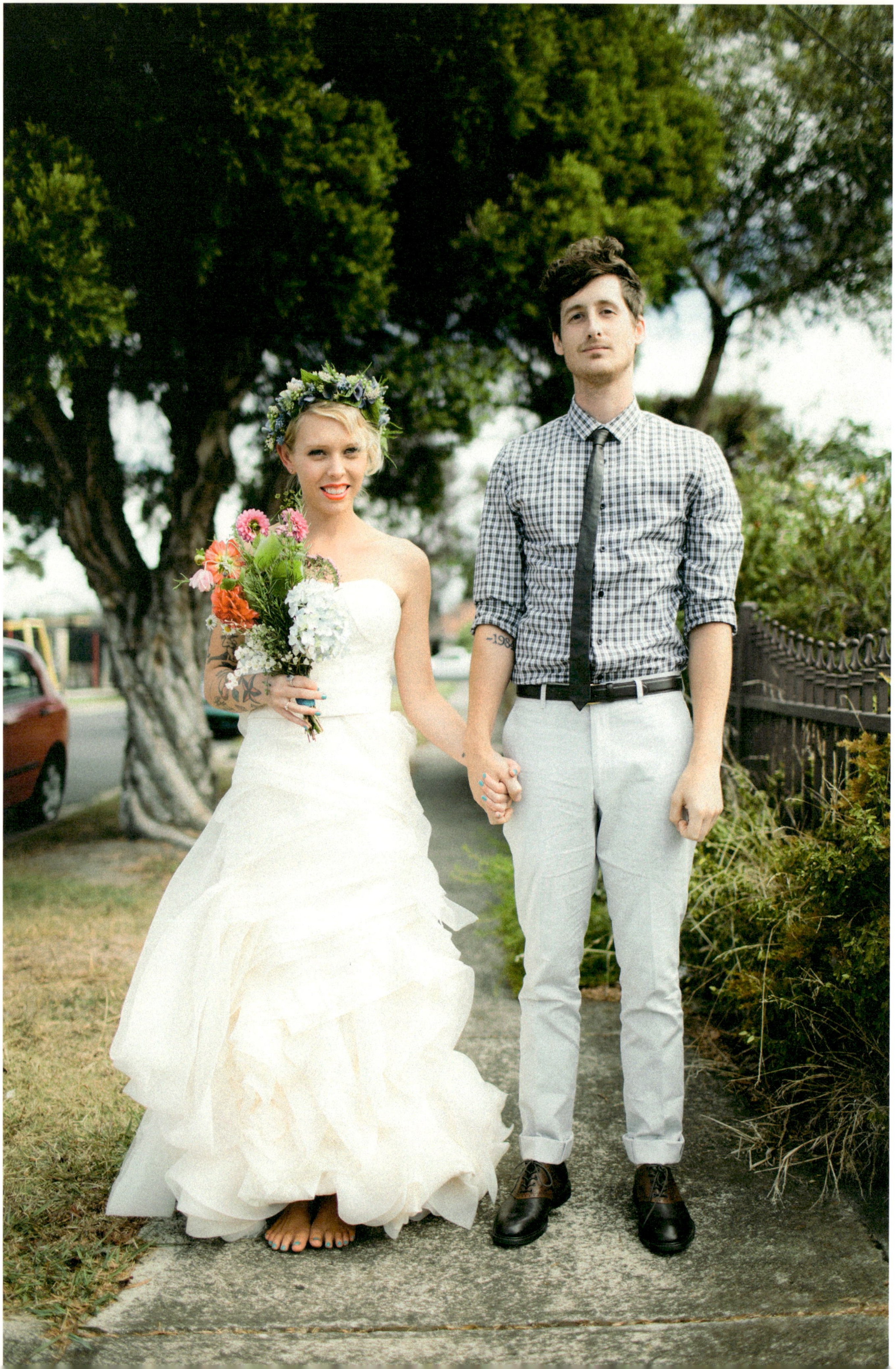

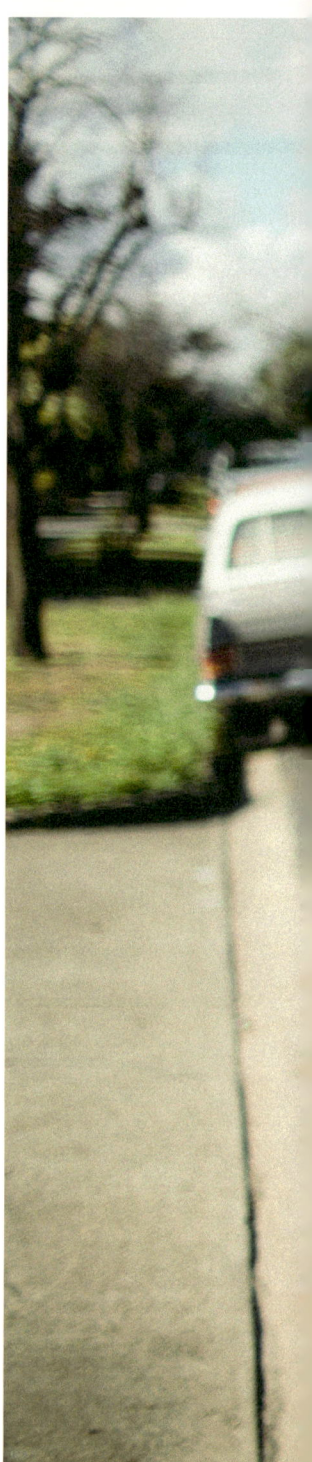

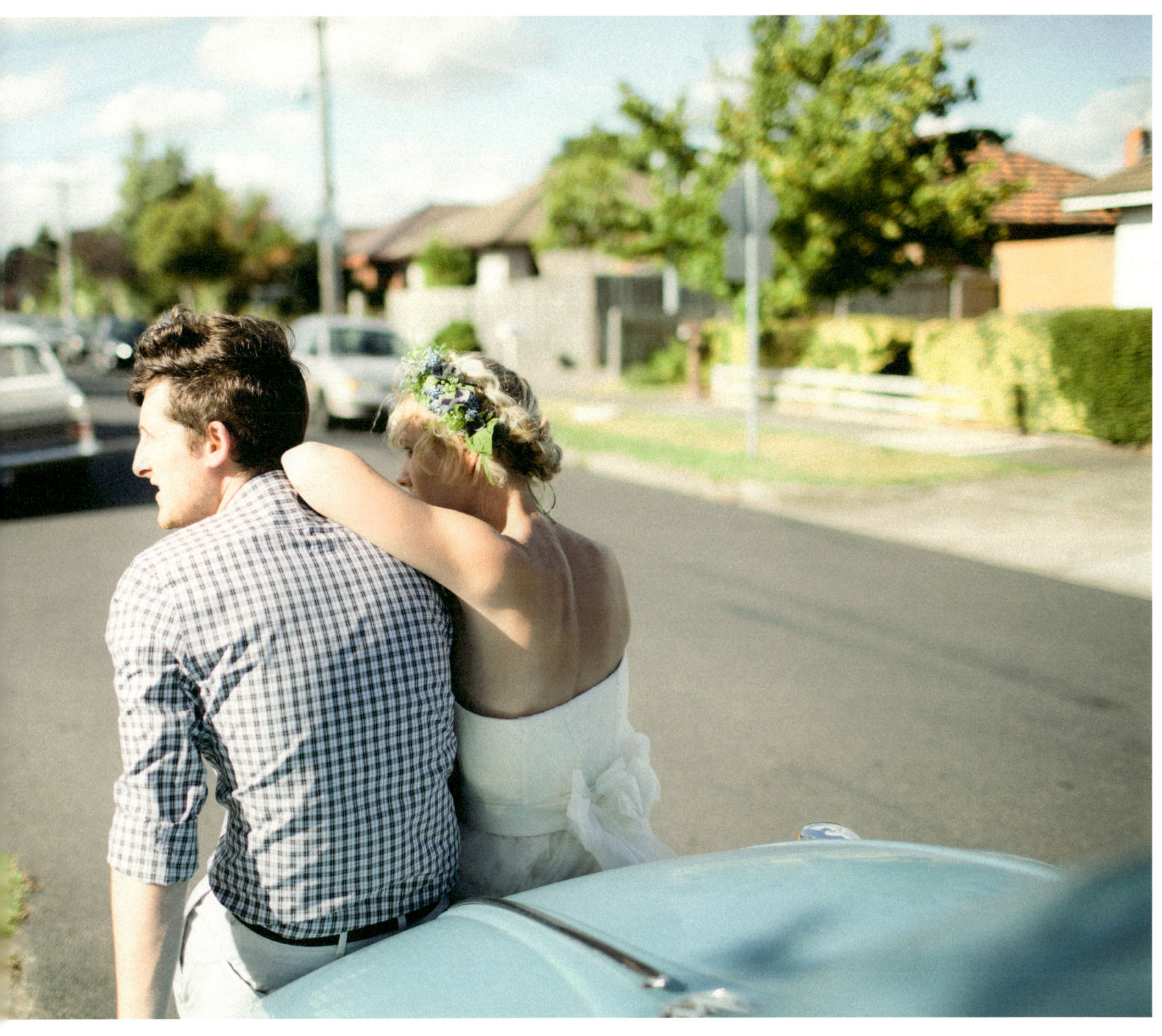

Rin & Joe

This looks like the kind of neighborhood where boy meets girl. They become friends, ride bikes, and have adventures. One day they grow up, friendship turns to love and suddenly a wedding is in the air. As Rin and Joe rest against the car outside their home, you could imagine this was their story. Rin dressed her bare feet up in blue nail polish and wore a flower crown in her summer-blonde hair, Joe wore a plaid shirt and skinny tie, and together they organized a backyard wedding where guests lounged on the lawn, kids cooled down with sno-cones, and the newlyweds went head to head on the badminton court.

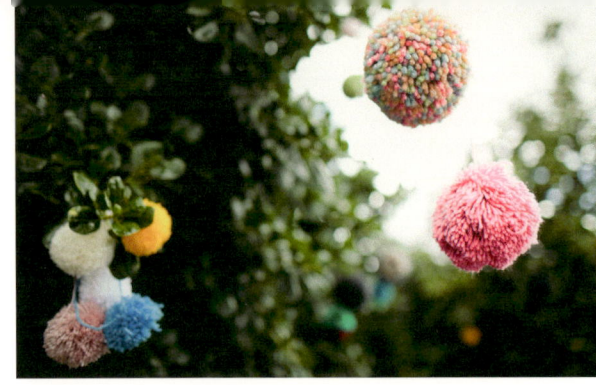

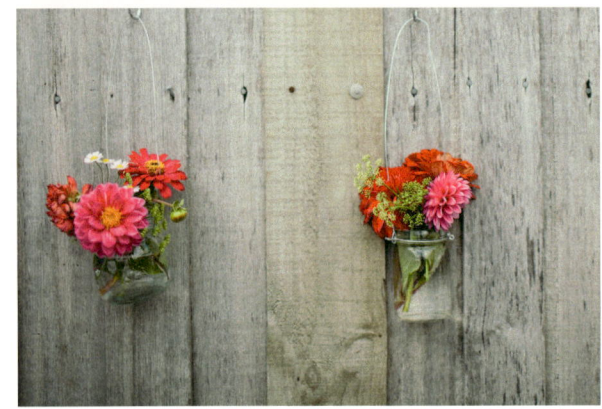

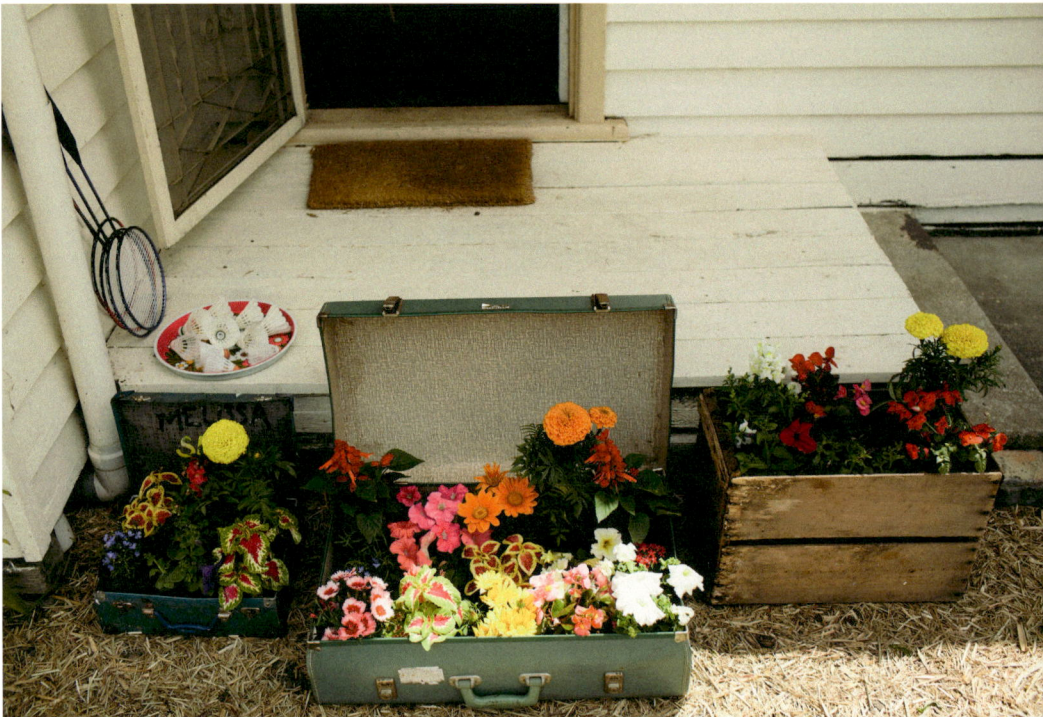

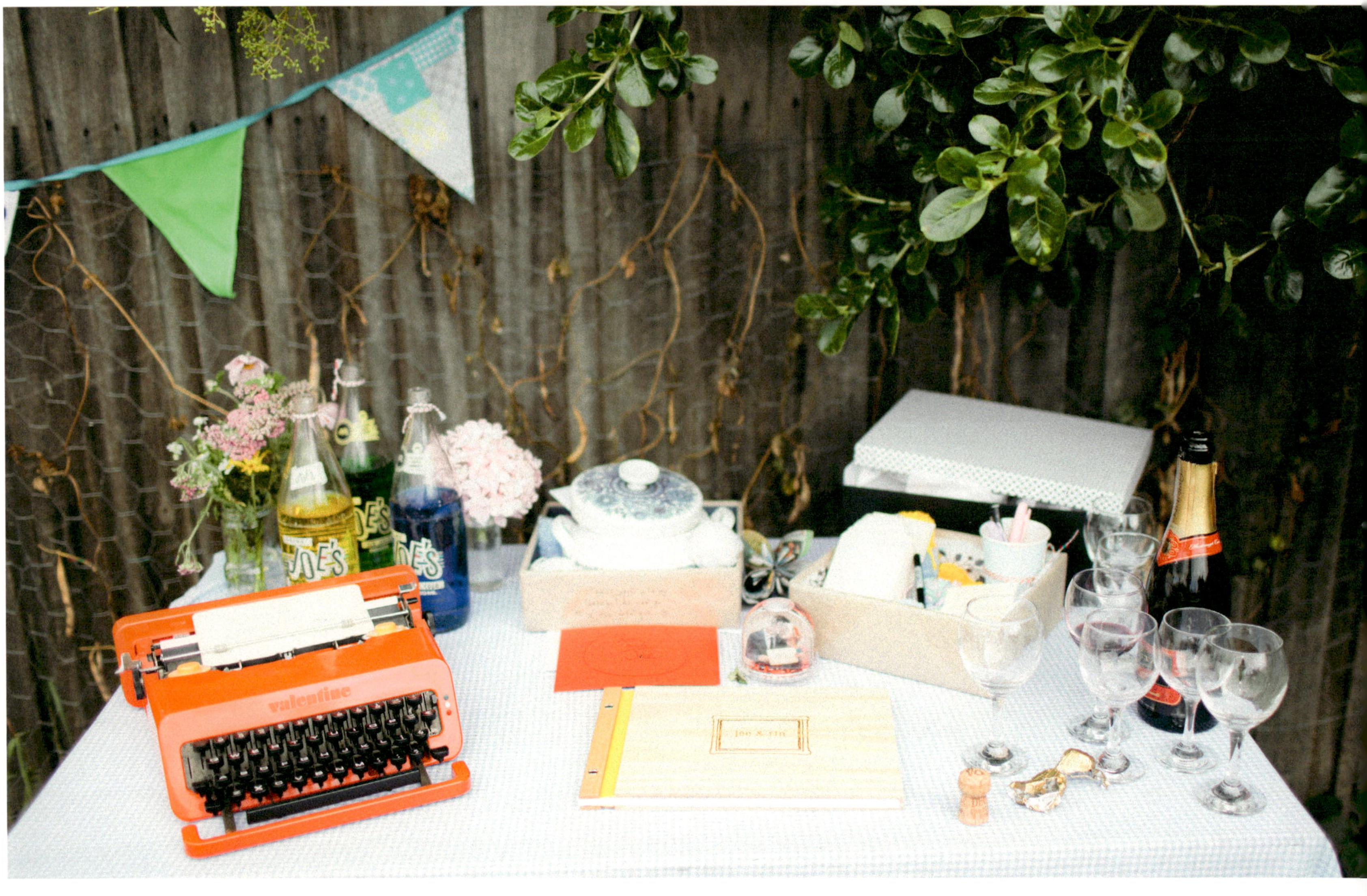

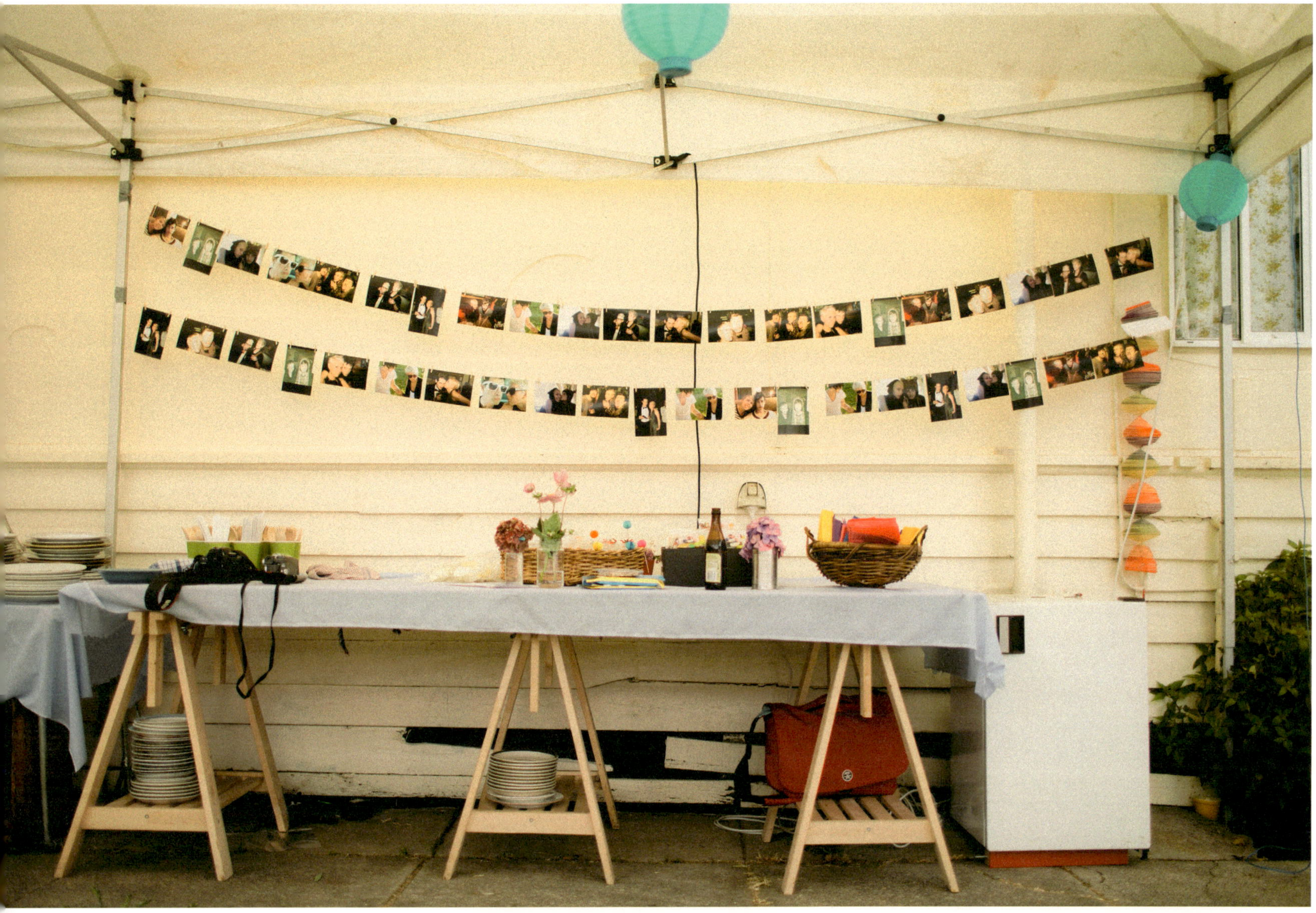

Picture Perfect

1. Photographs on strings tell Rin and Joe's story.

2. Clothes pegs clutch special wedding pics that were the backdrop to the ceremony.

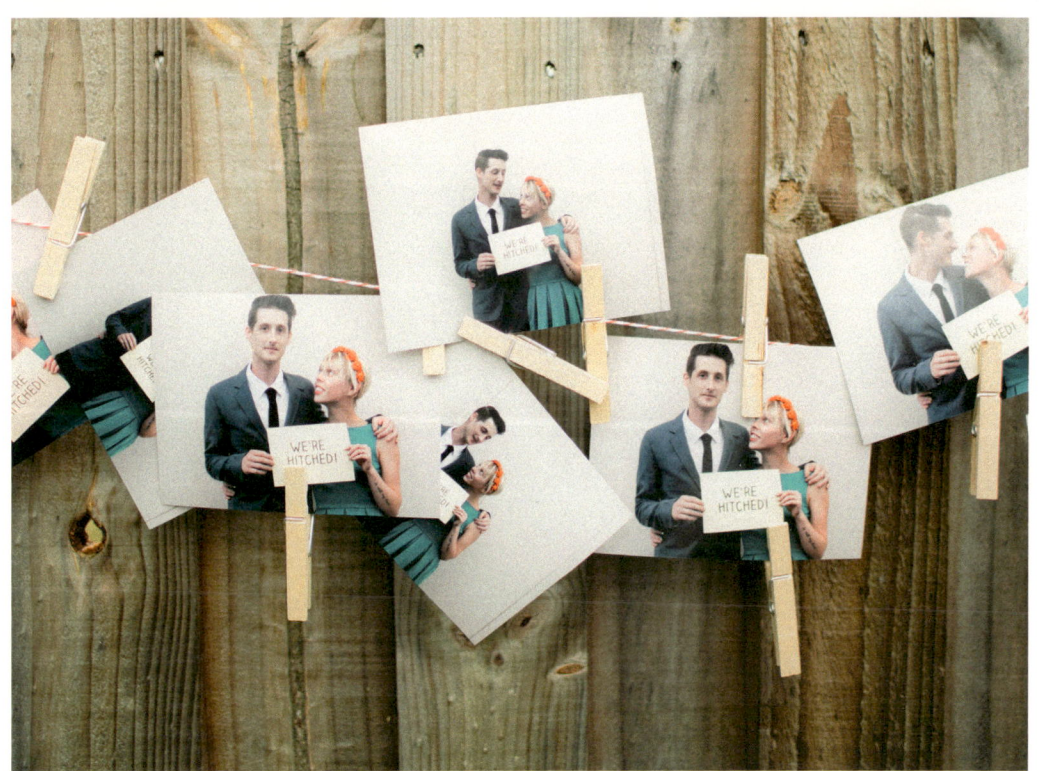

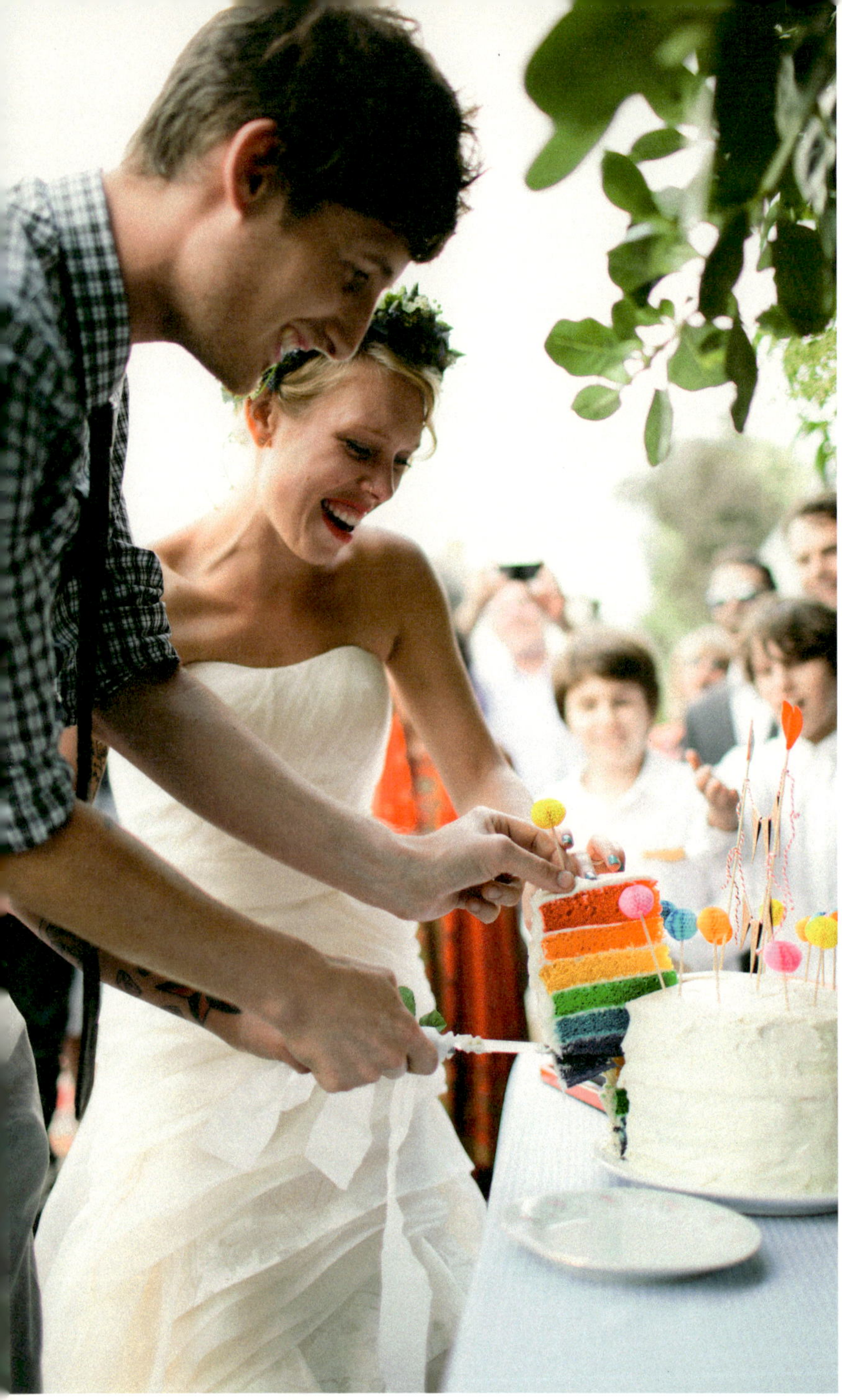

The Food

Homemade pizzas—yum—
followed by a buffet of Rin and
Joe's favorite childhood cakes.
Slice of typewriter, anyone?
The star of the show was a six-
layer rainbow cake decorated
with paper pompoms.

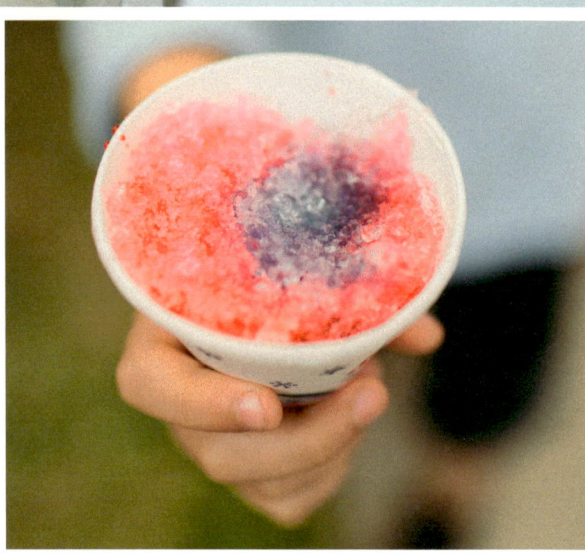

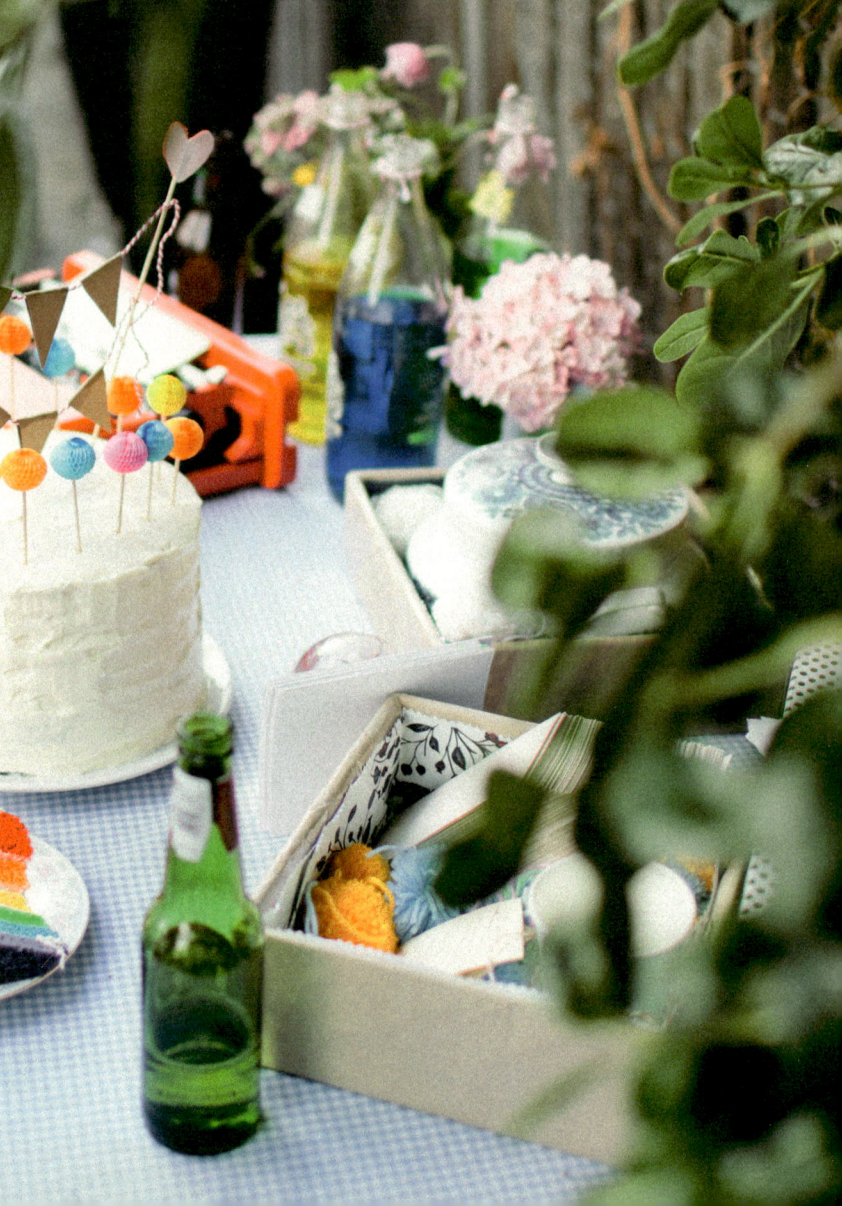

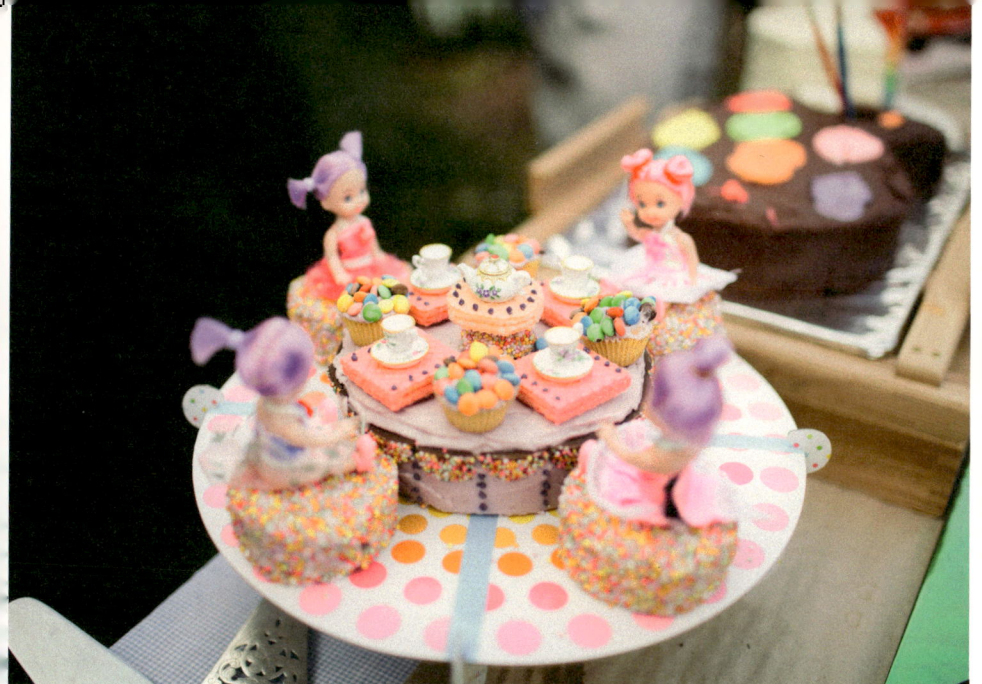

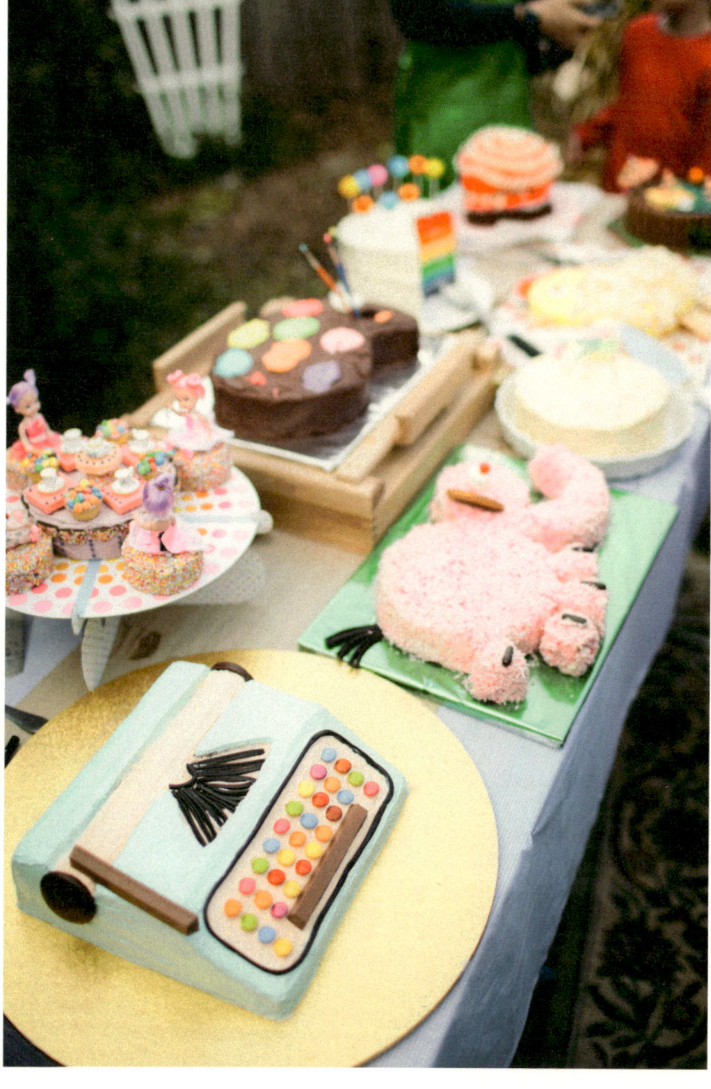

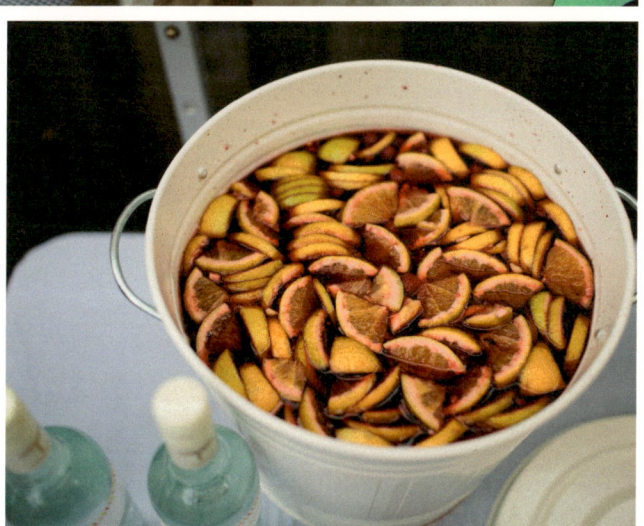

Pink elephants, Pimm's, and pizzas: peachy!

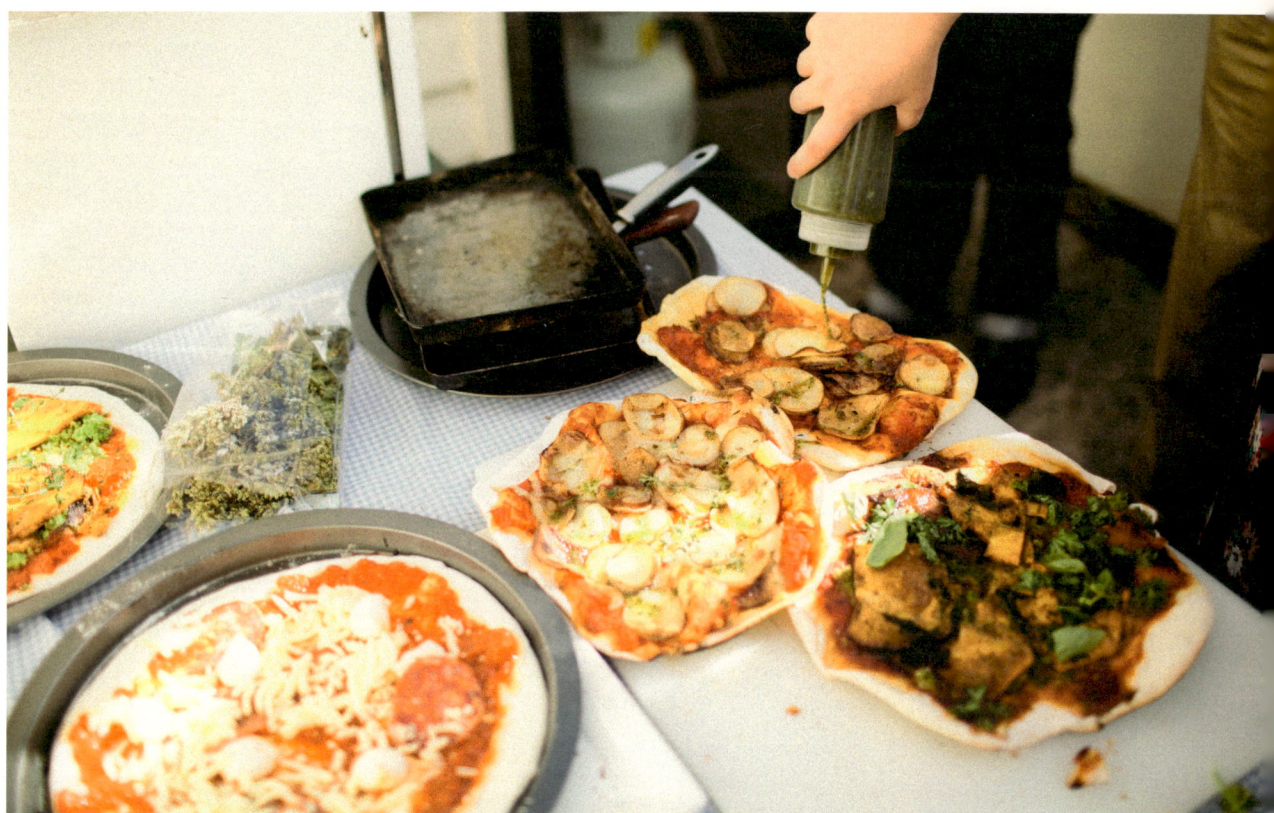

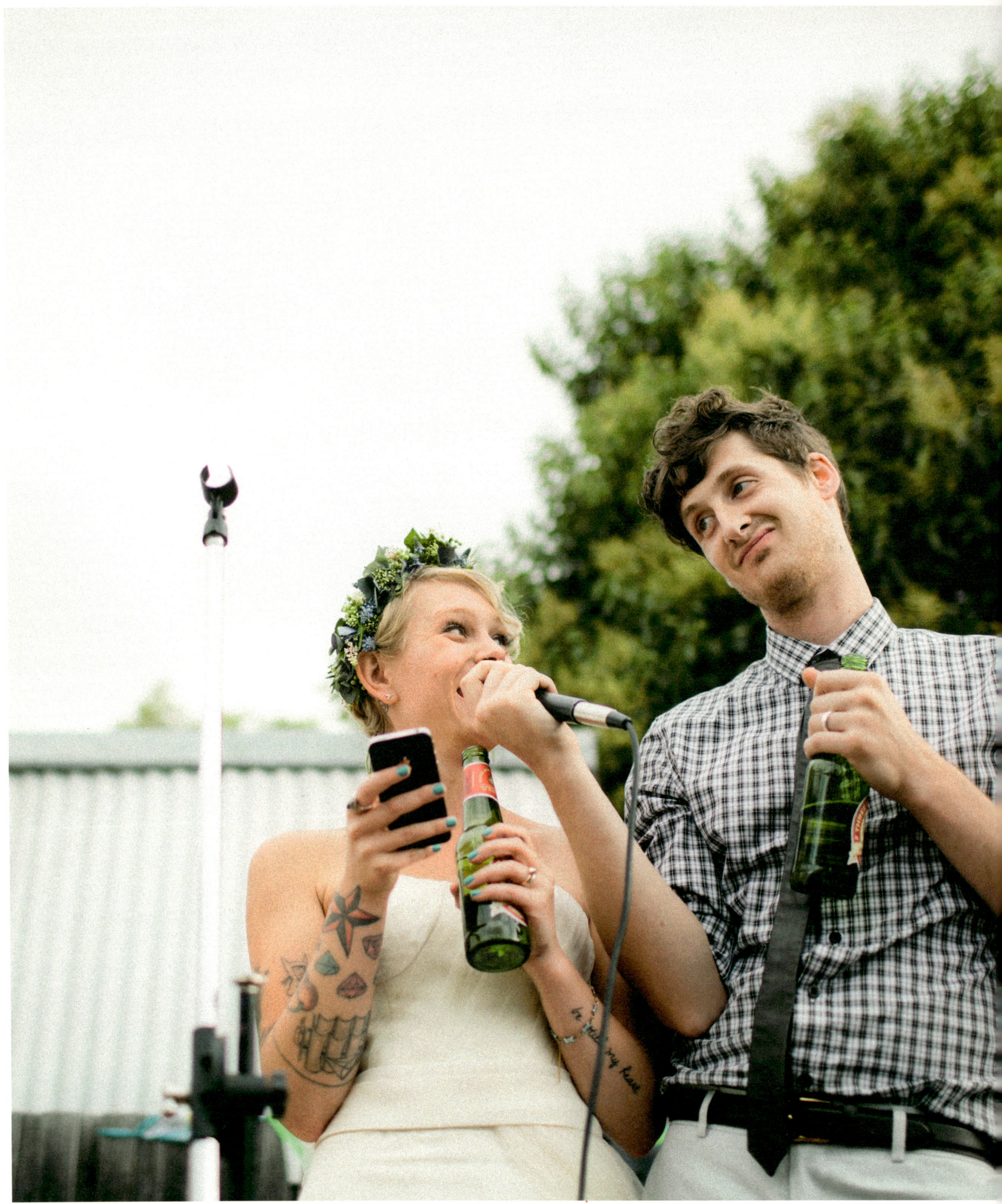

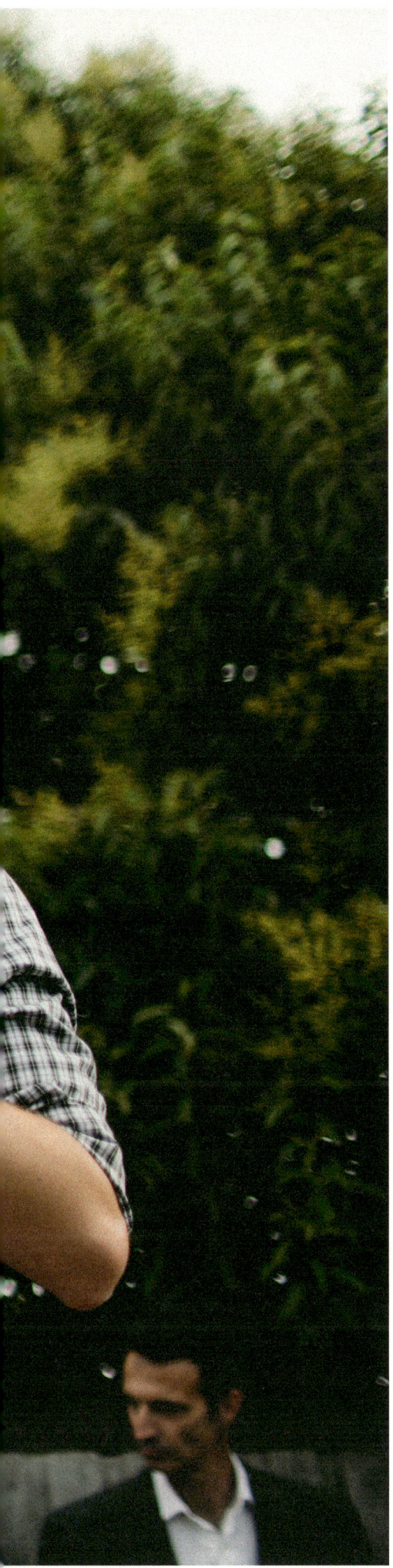

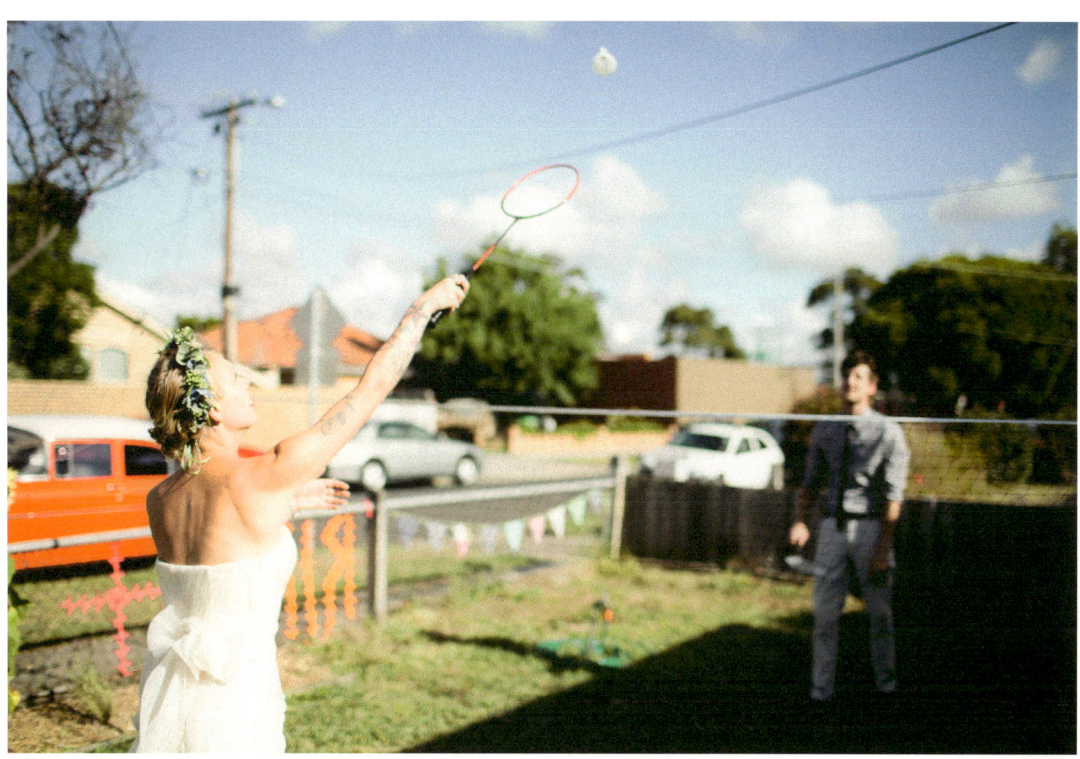

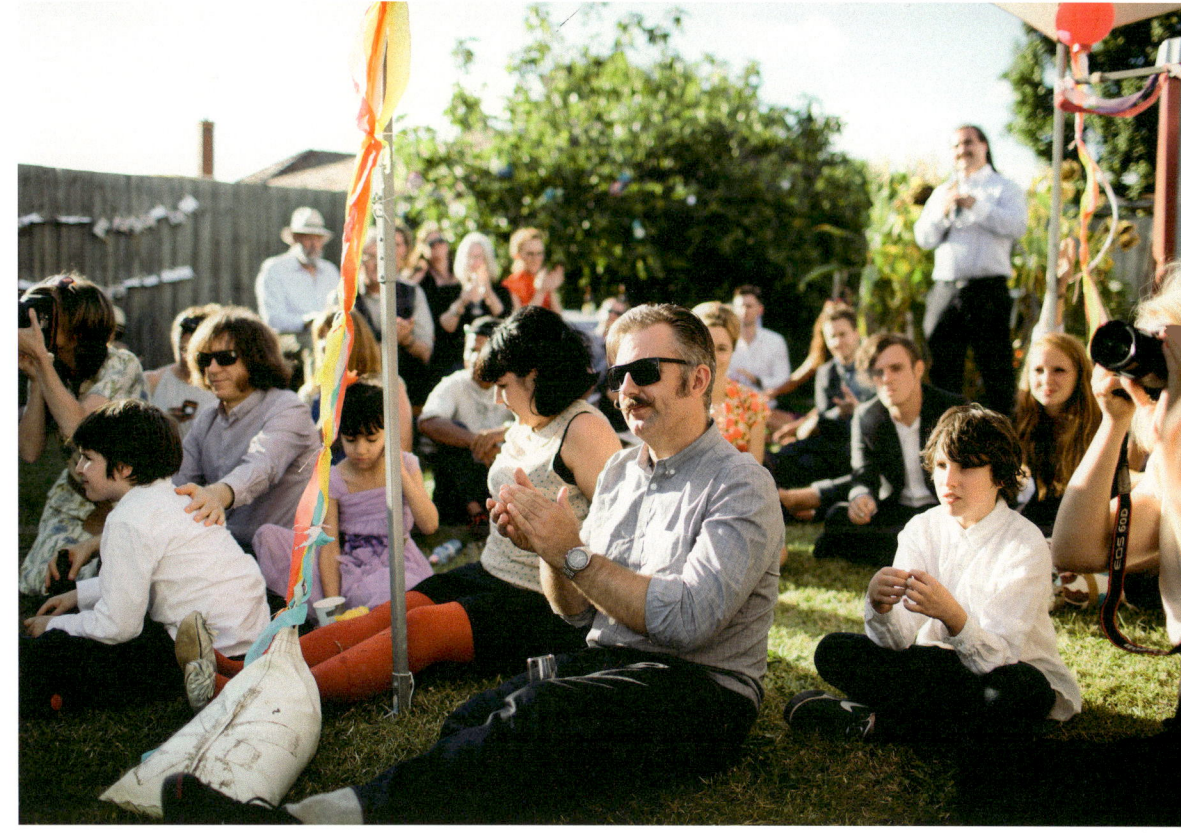

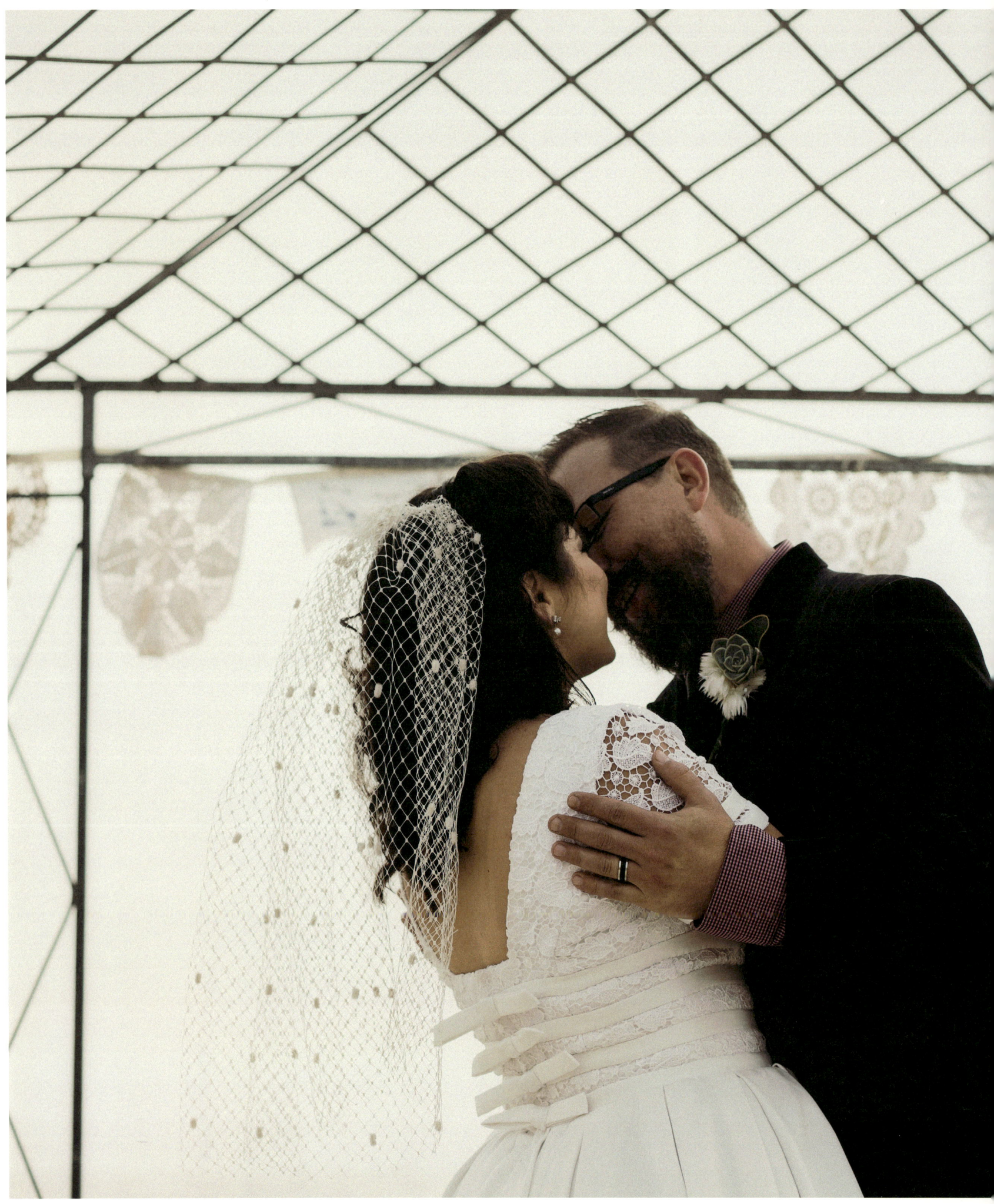

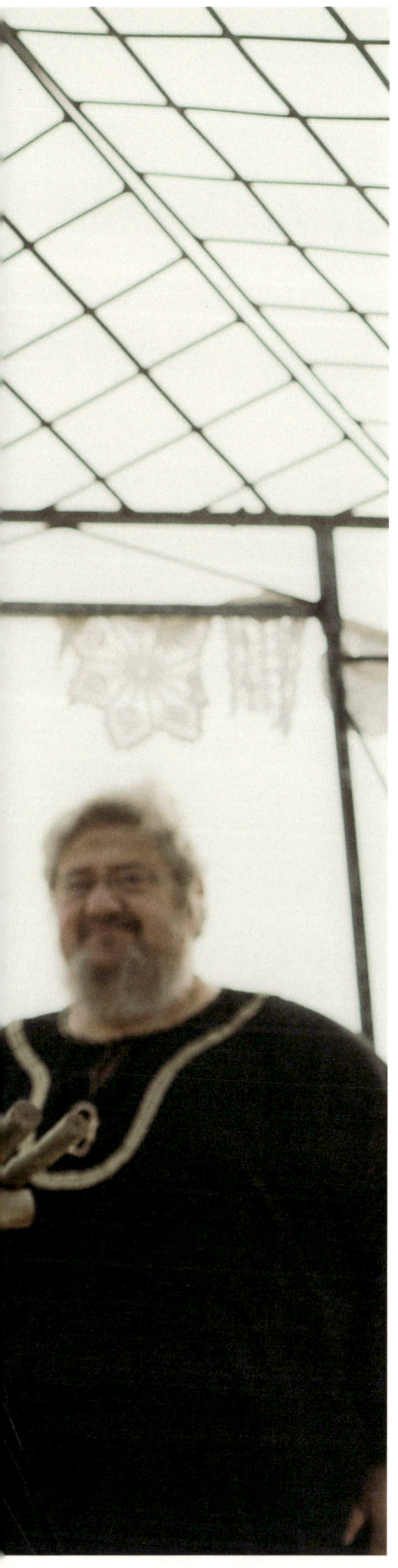

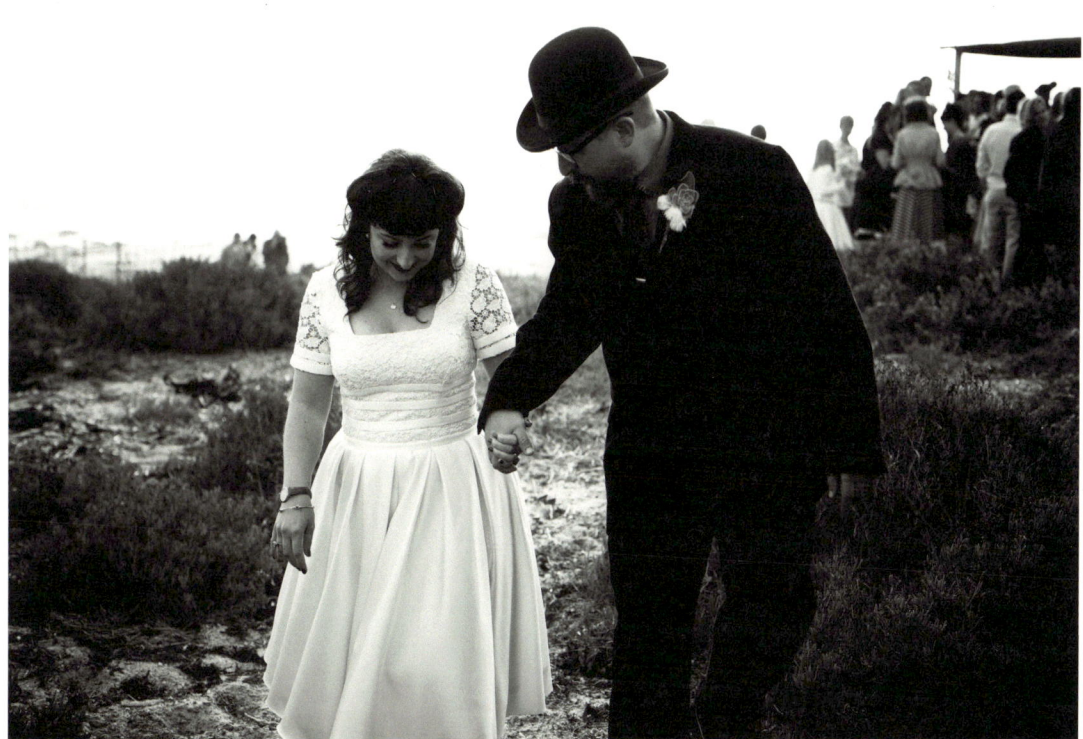

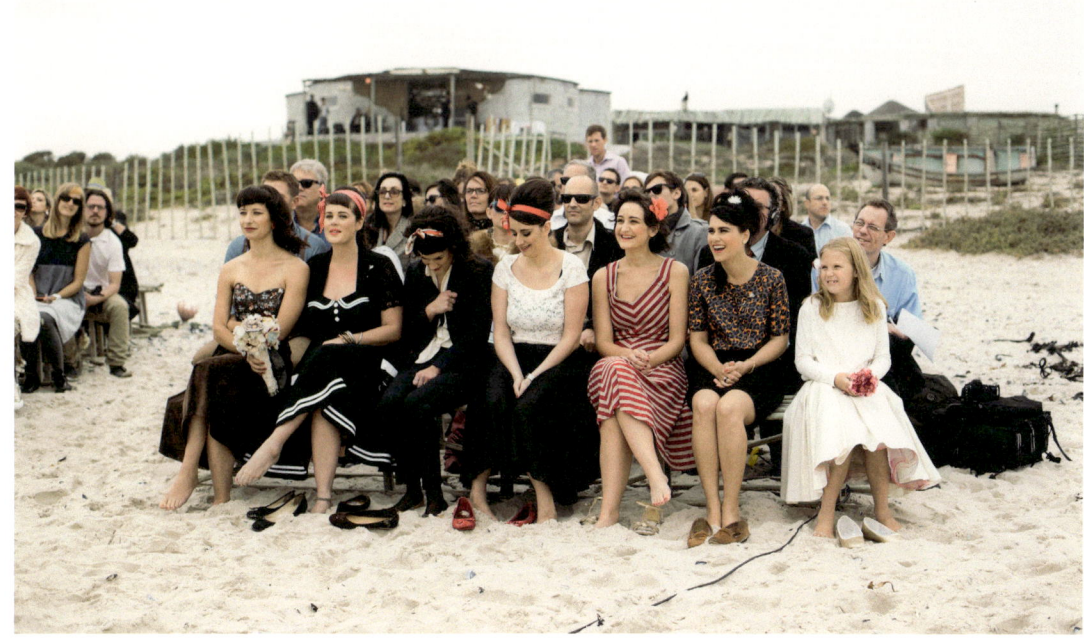

Natasha & Len

Len and Natasha brought two very different cultures together on their wedding day. The ceremony on the west coast of South Africa, the reception in the dunes, and the dinner cooked over the hot coals of a braai were all expressions of their Afrikaans heritage. Meanwhile, Natasha's 1950s dress, her rock-n-roll bridesmaids, and Len's wingtip shoes showed off their love of all things rockabilly.

71

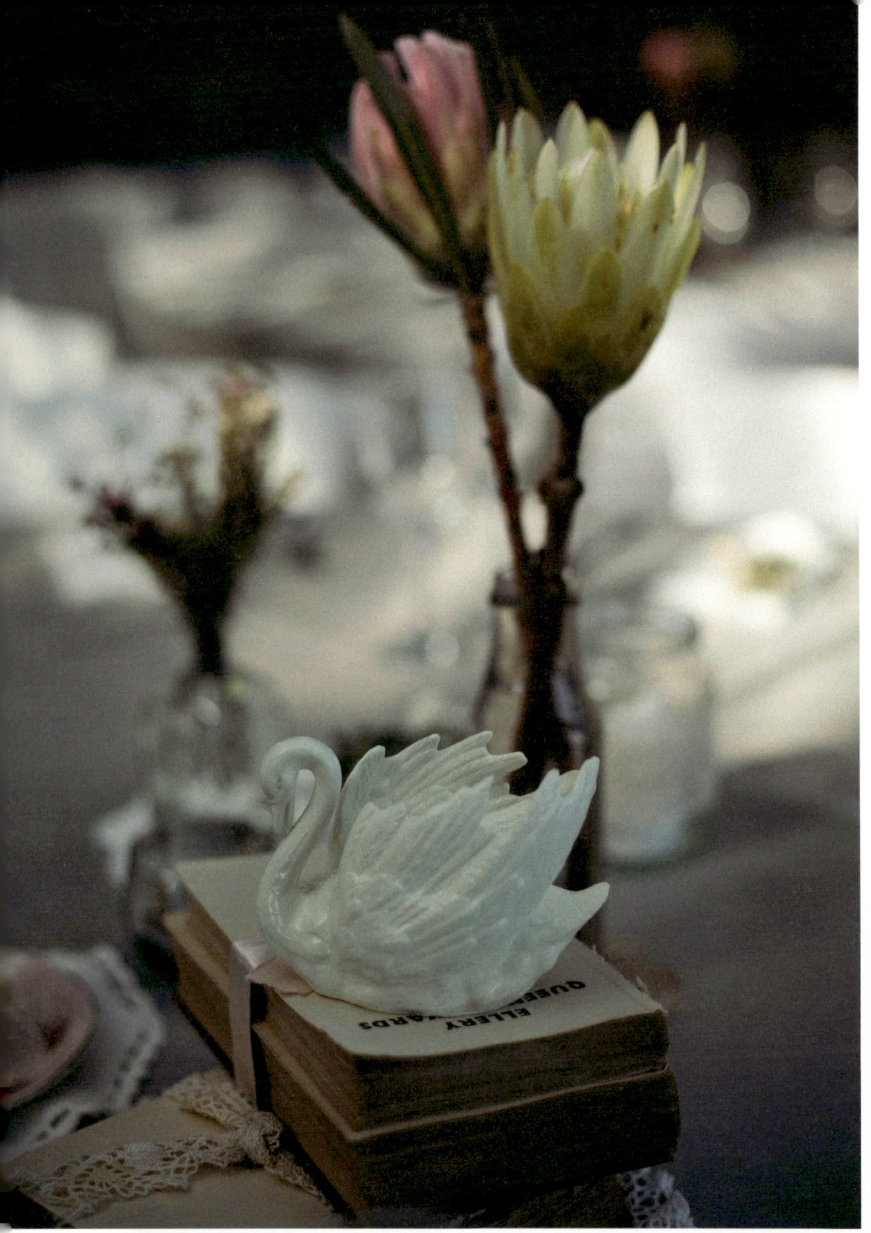

Flowers and Music

Wild Fynbos flowers native to the area lent their color to the celebrations, and a live band had everyone rocking the night away.

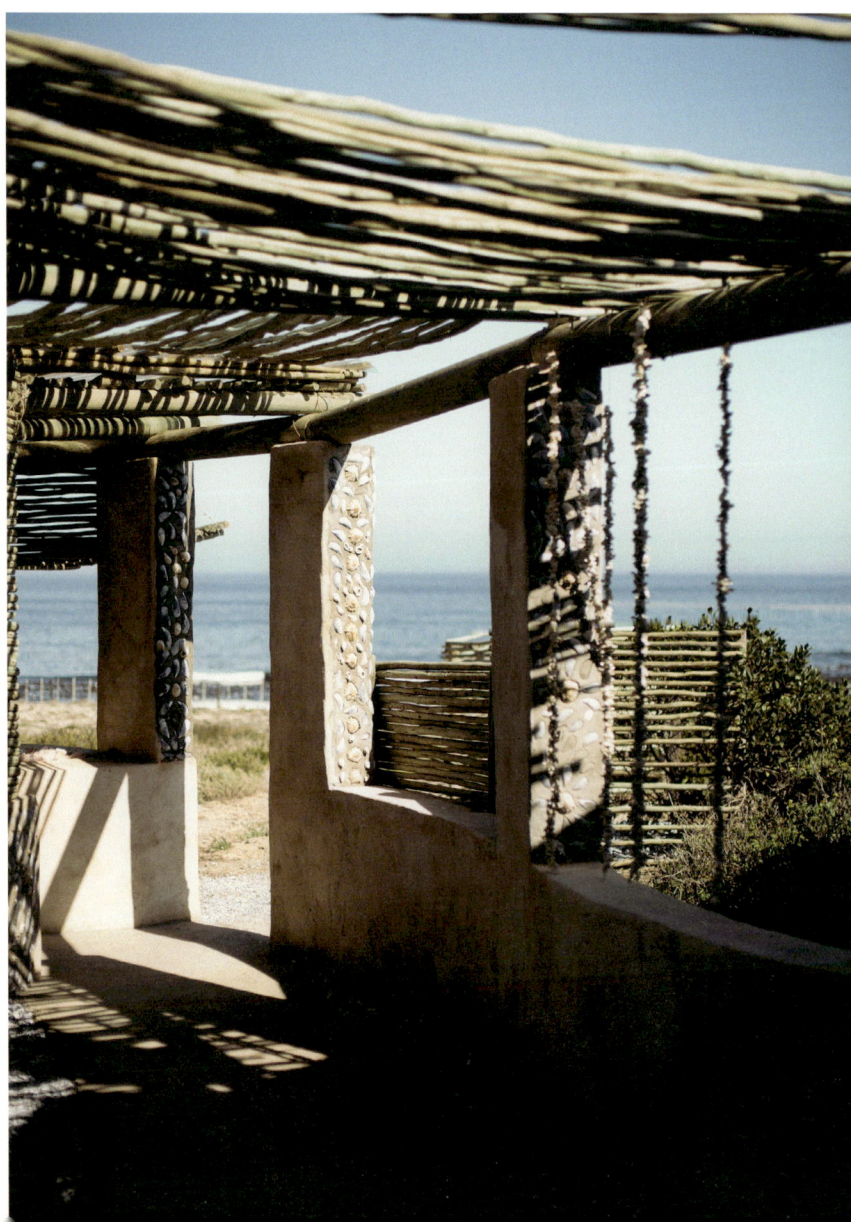

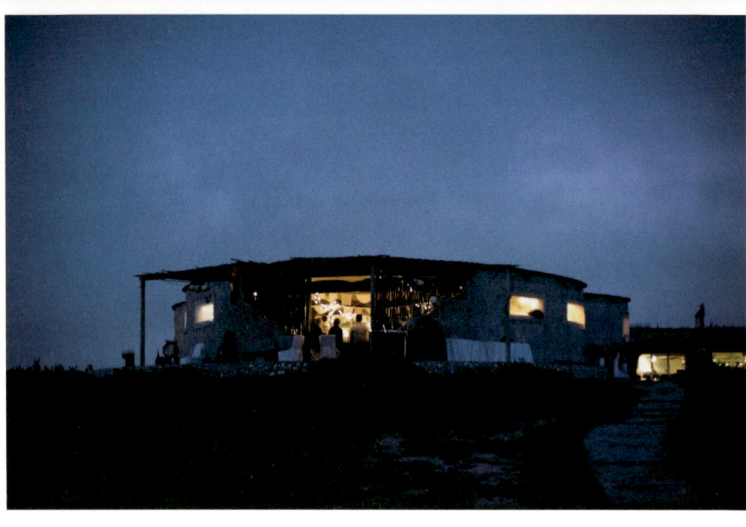

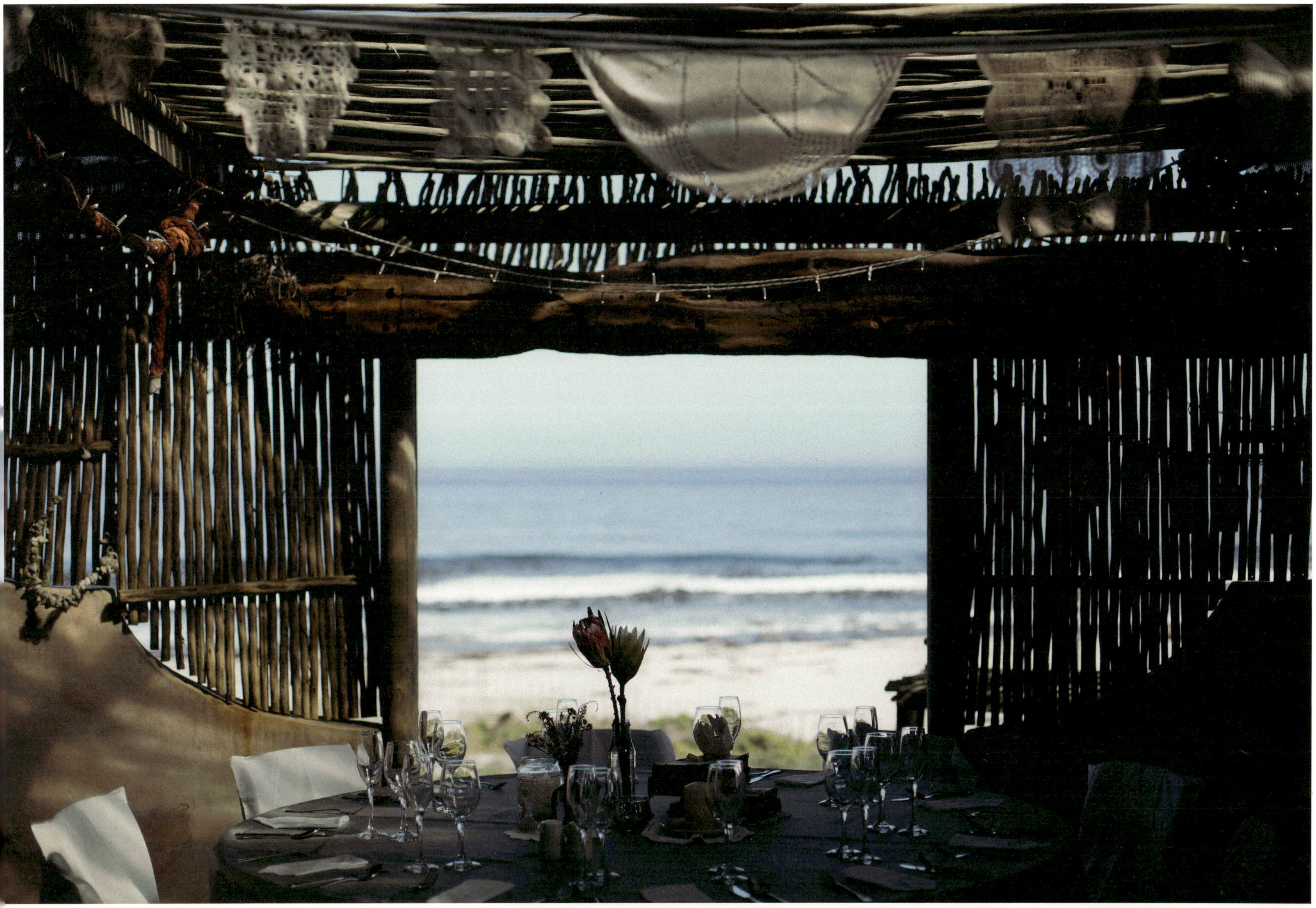

1. With the South African coastline as their backdrop, Len and Natasha kept their tables sleek and simple.

2. Decorations were a mixture of hand-stamped place cards, miniature figurines painted ivory, and crocheted doilies strung overhead like bunting.

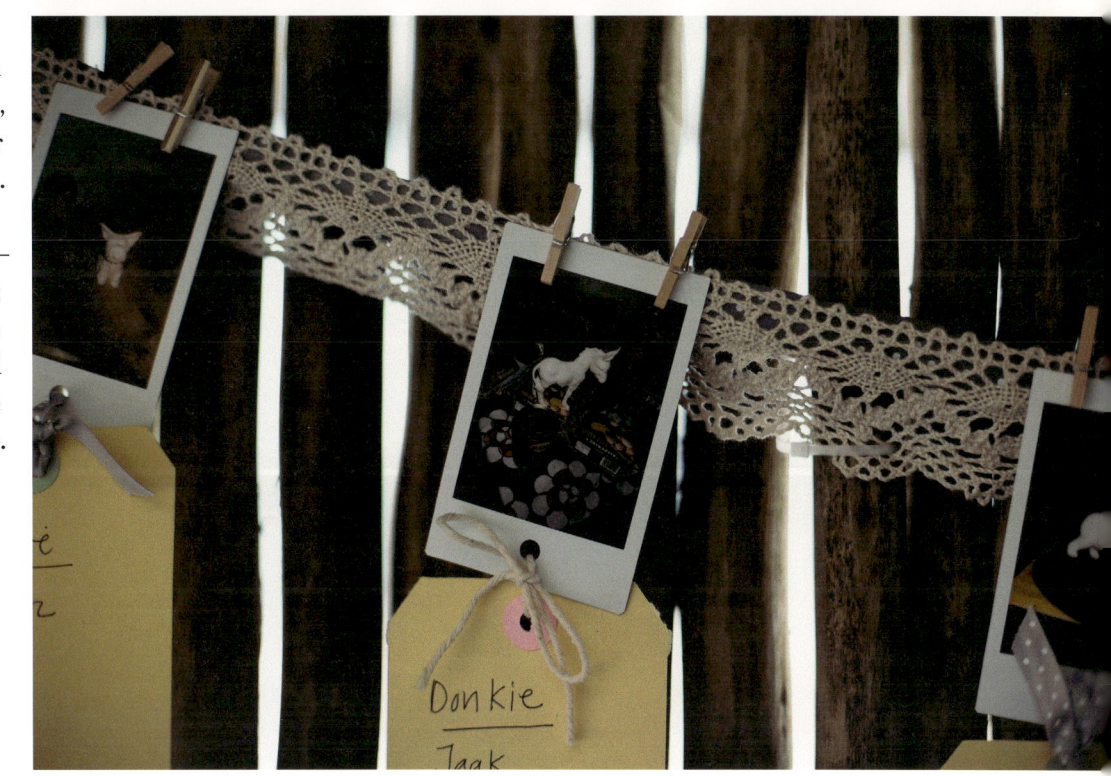

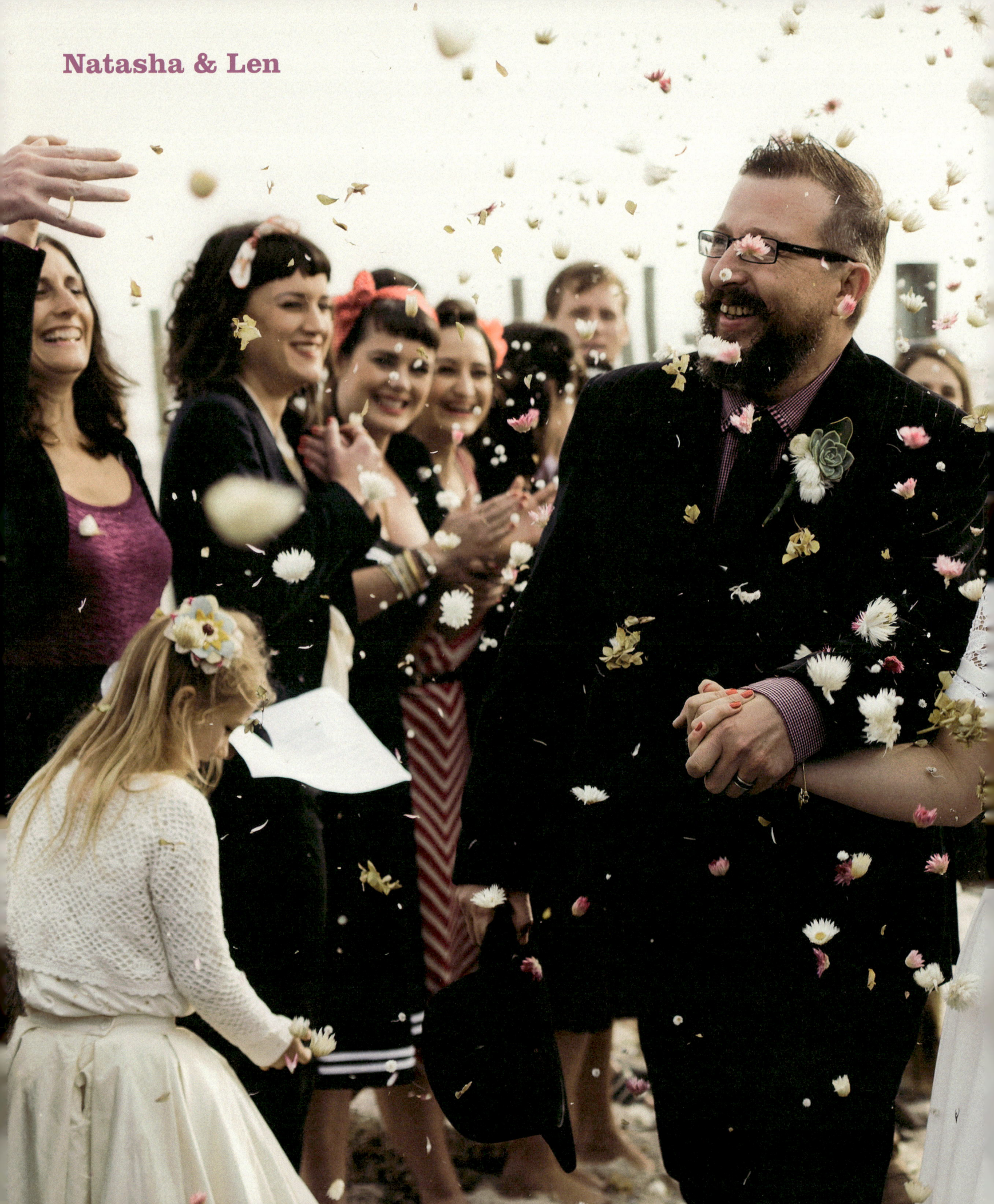

Natasha & Len

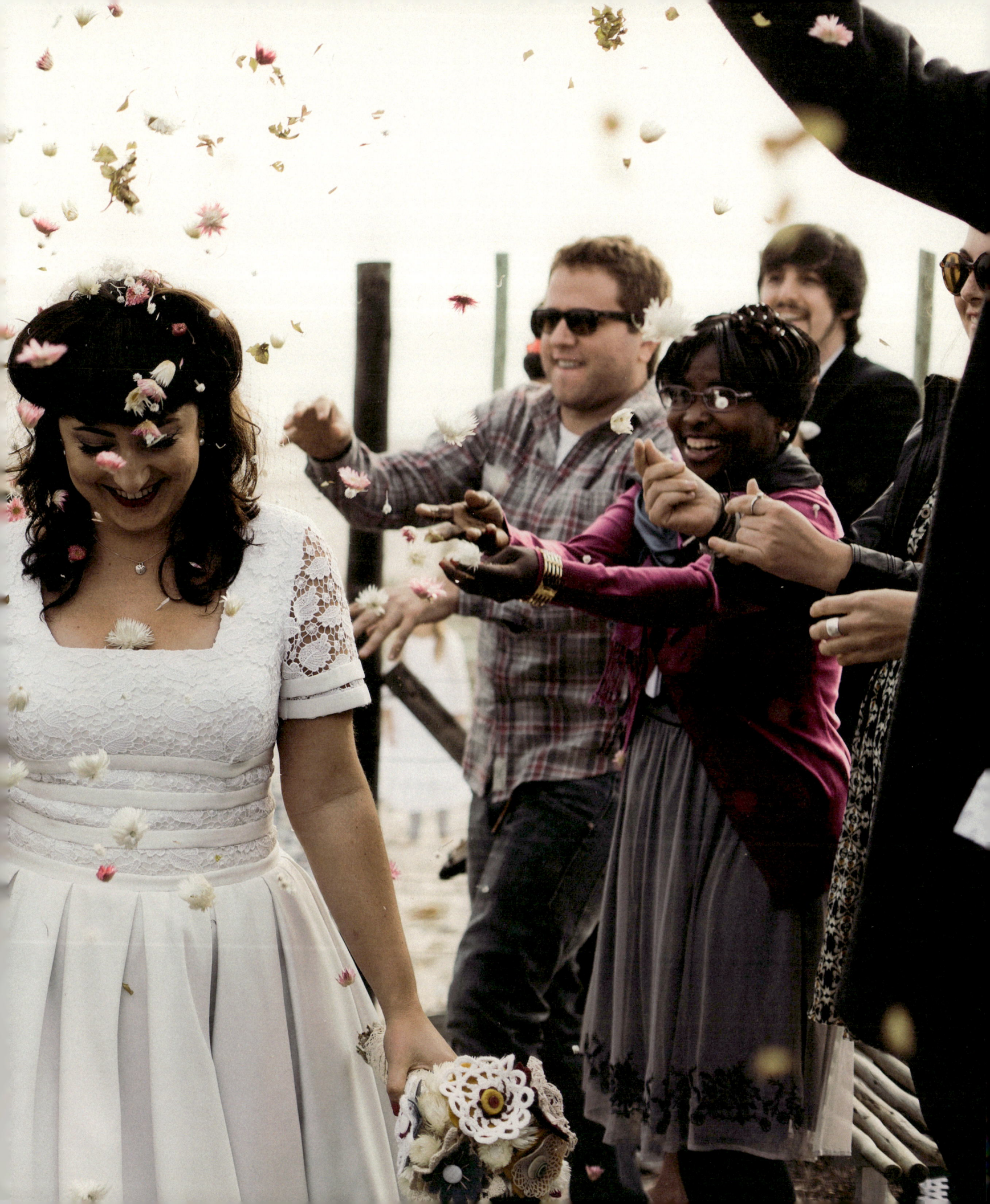

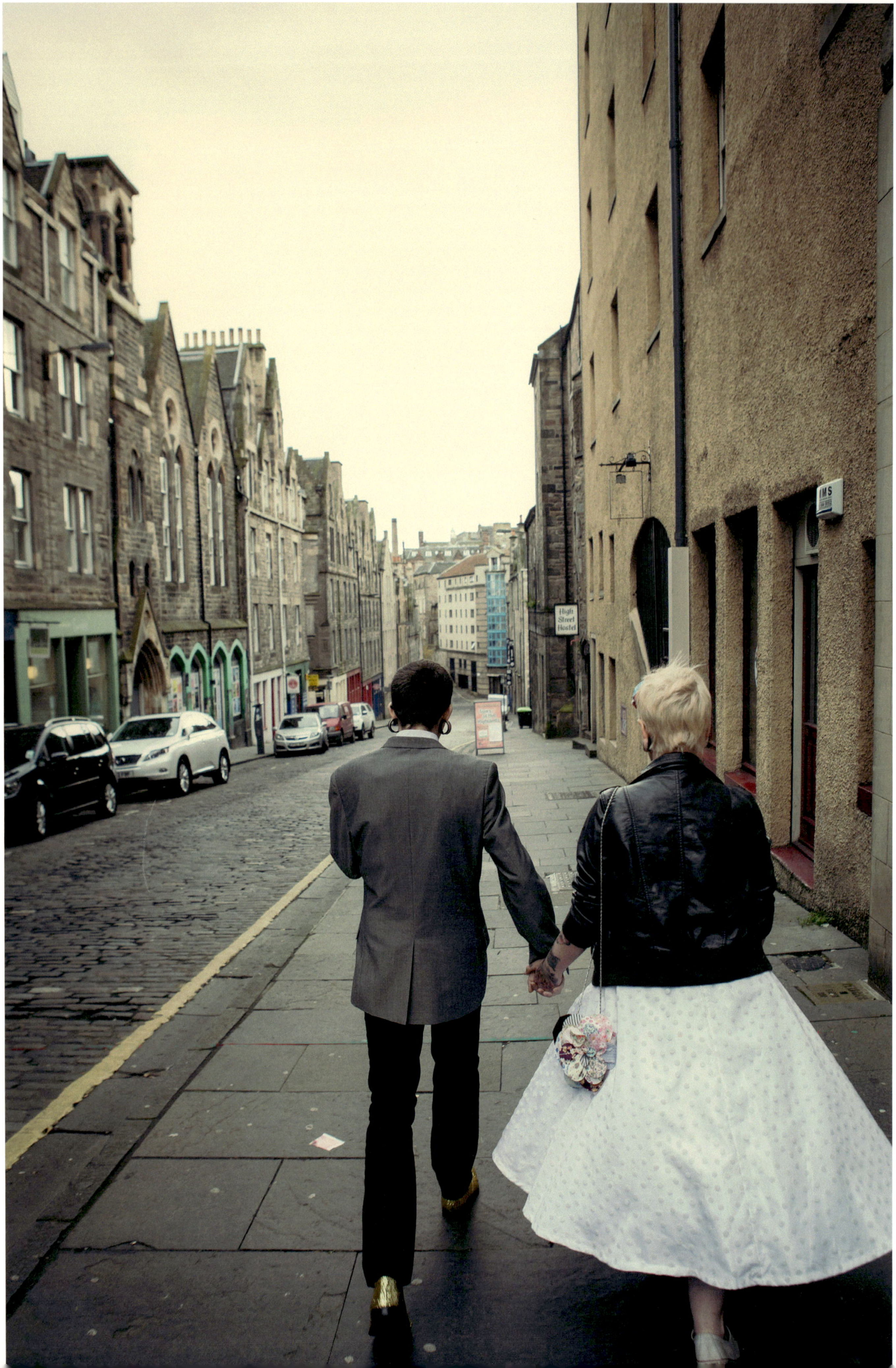

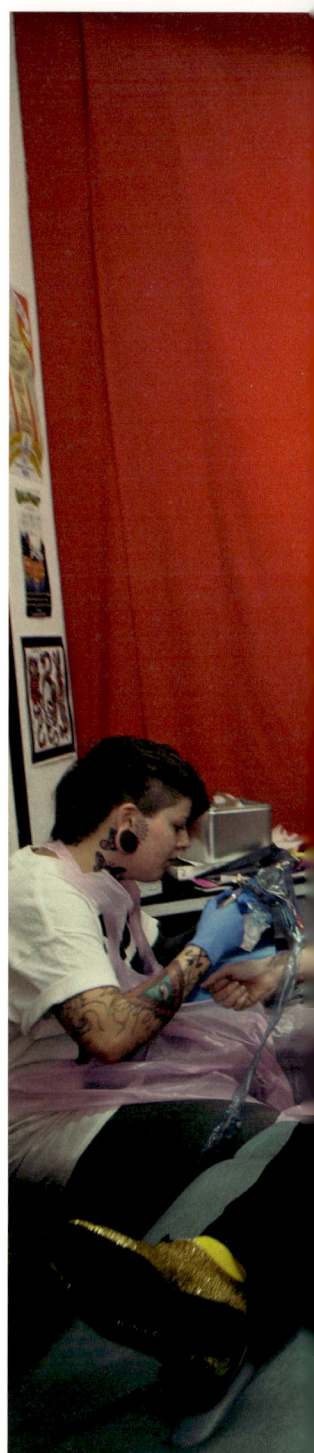

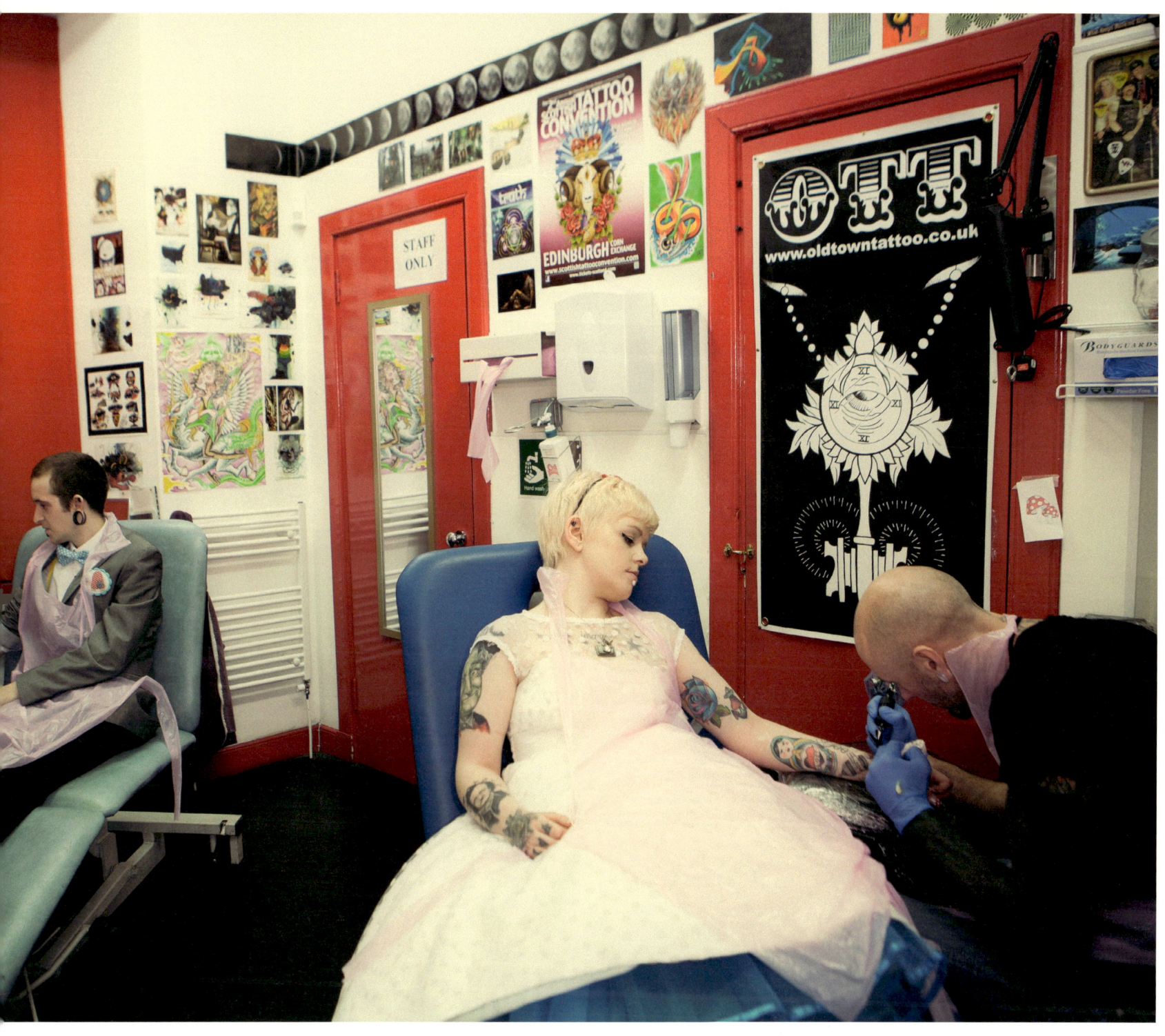

Toni & Colin

People often say cities can act as characters in films. On a cold November day in Edinburgh, Toni and Colin proved they could also do a good turn as wedding guests. The slate gray tenements and atmospheric closes played the perfect supporting role to the electric blue of Toni's petticoat, the gold sparkle of Colin's shoes, and the orange-red light of the neon signs in the café where they had their first look. Bursts of color continued at the reception, which was a patchwork of playful ornaments. But unlike the usual throwaway wedding favors, the cute characters and cartoon lettering followed Toni and Colin home after the party.

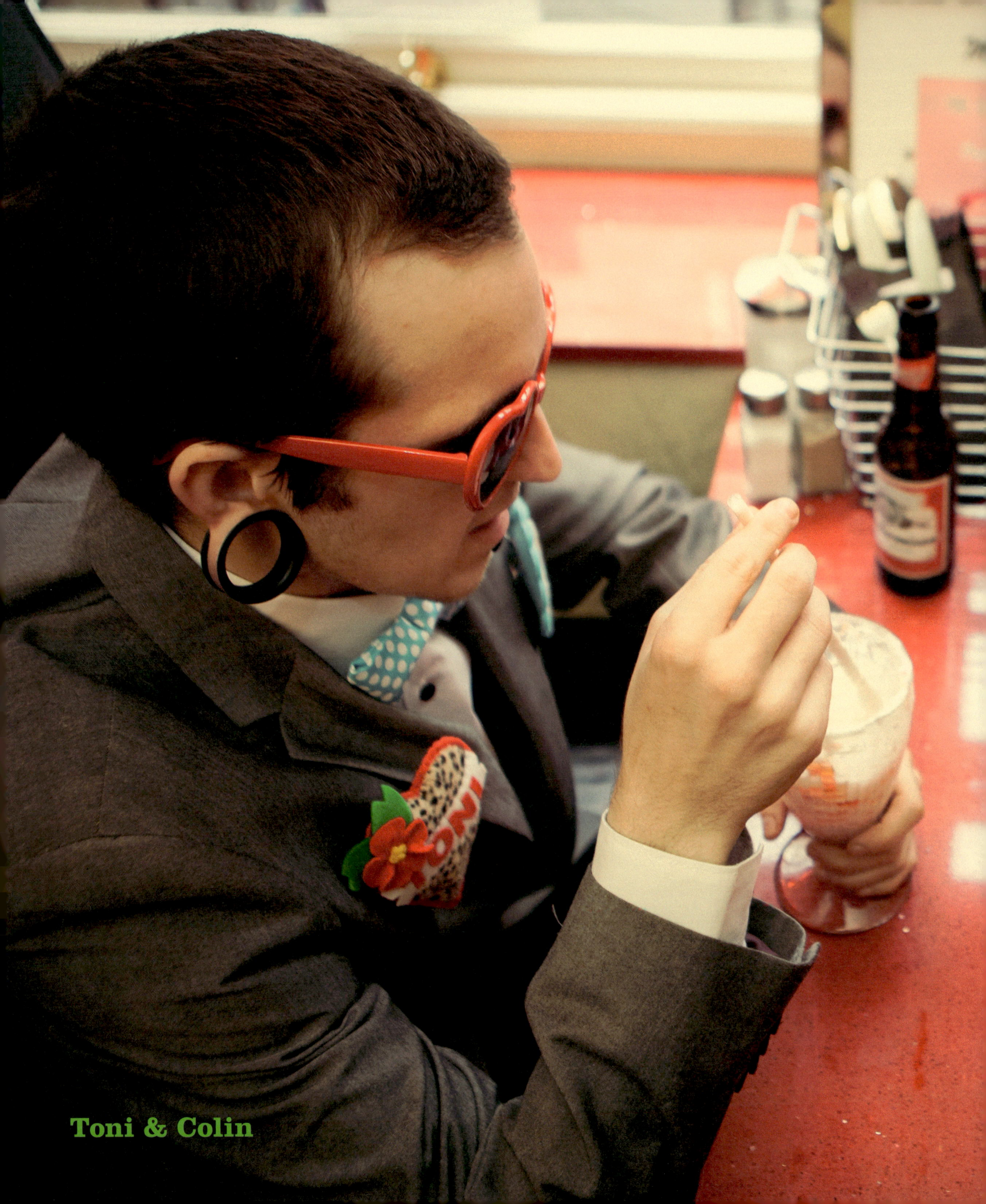

Toni & Colin

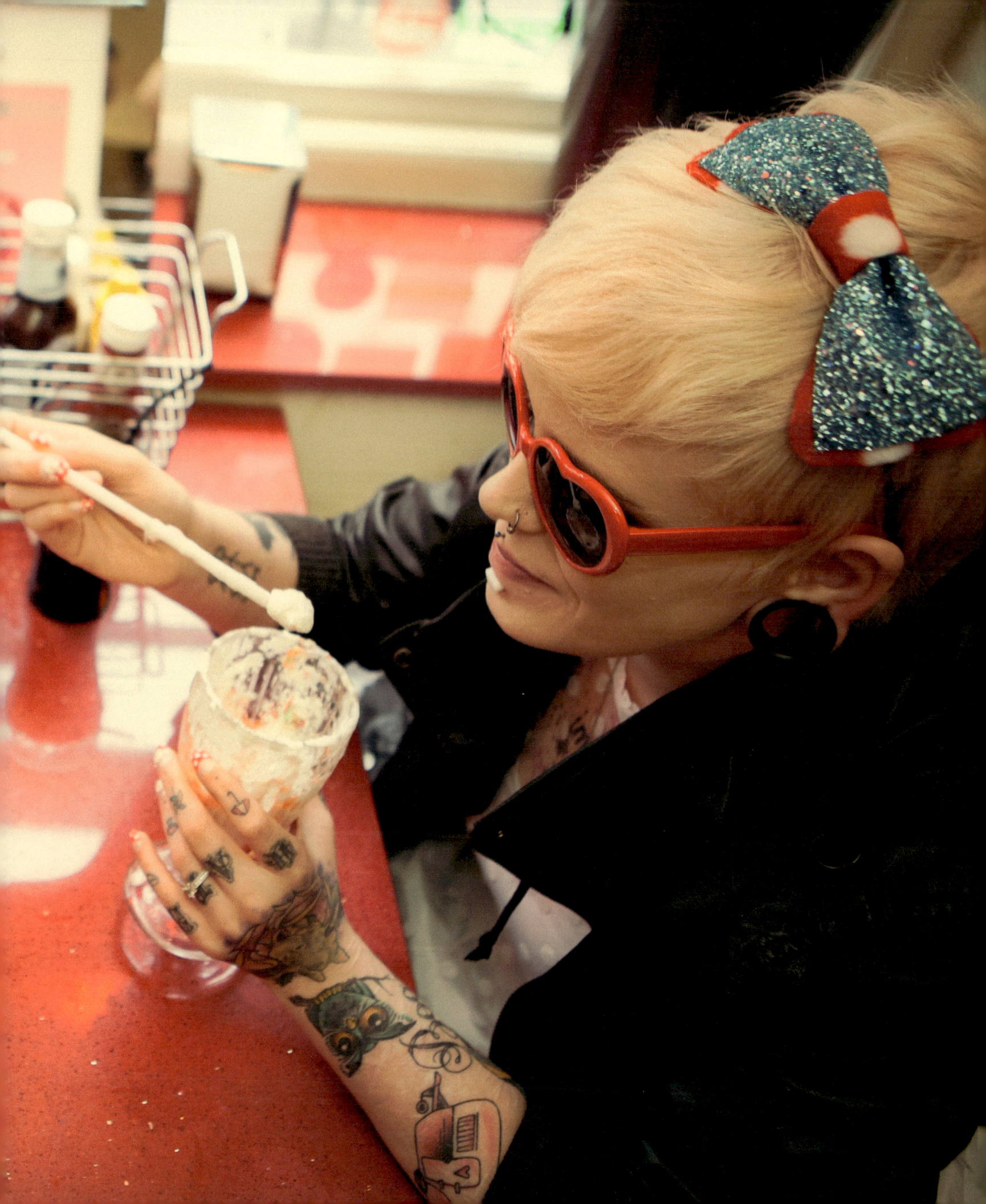

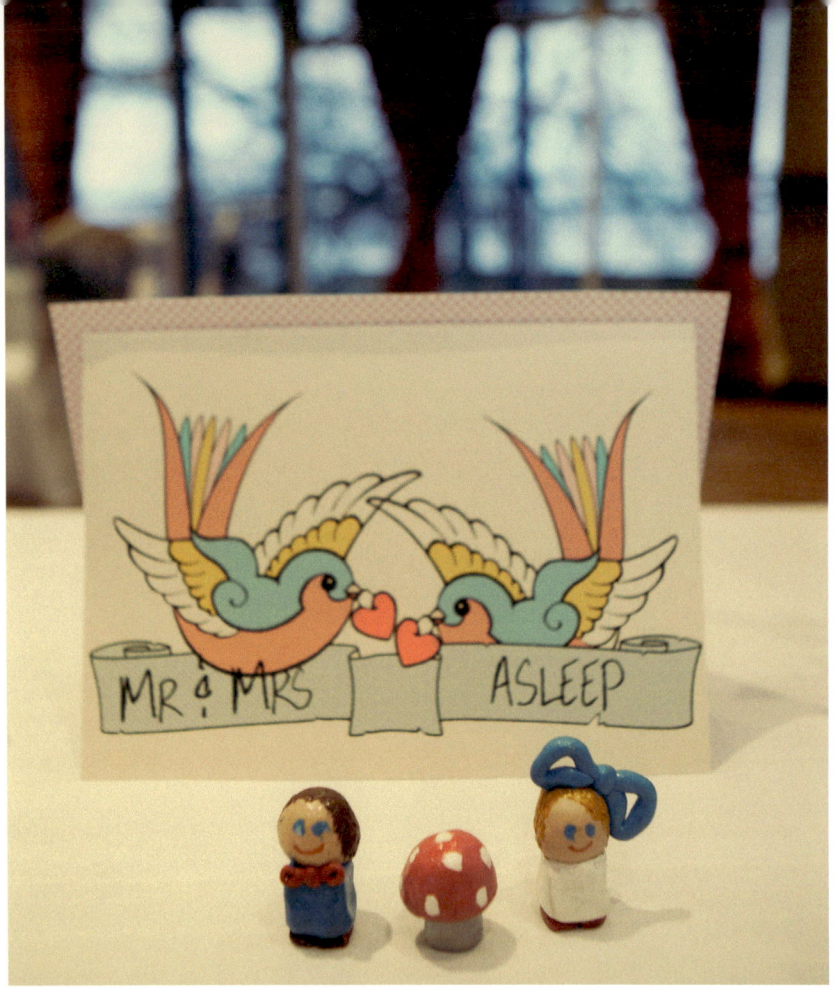

The Decoration

Everyone knows opposites attract, so why not go for the craziest mix of decorations you can think of? Toni and Colin pulled out all the stops for their reception — and everything fit together so well that now we're wondering how we never thought of pairing a flock of owls with a vintage typewriter!

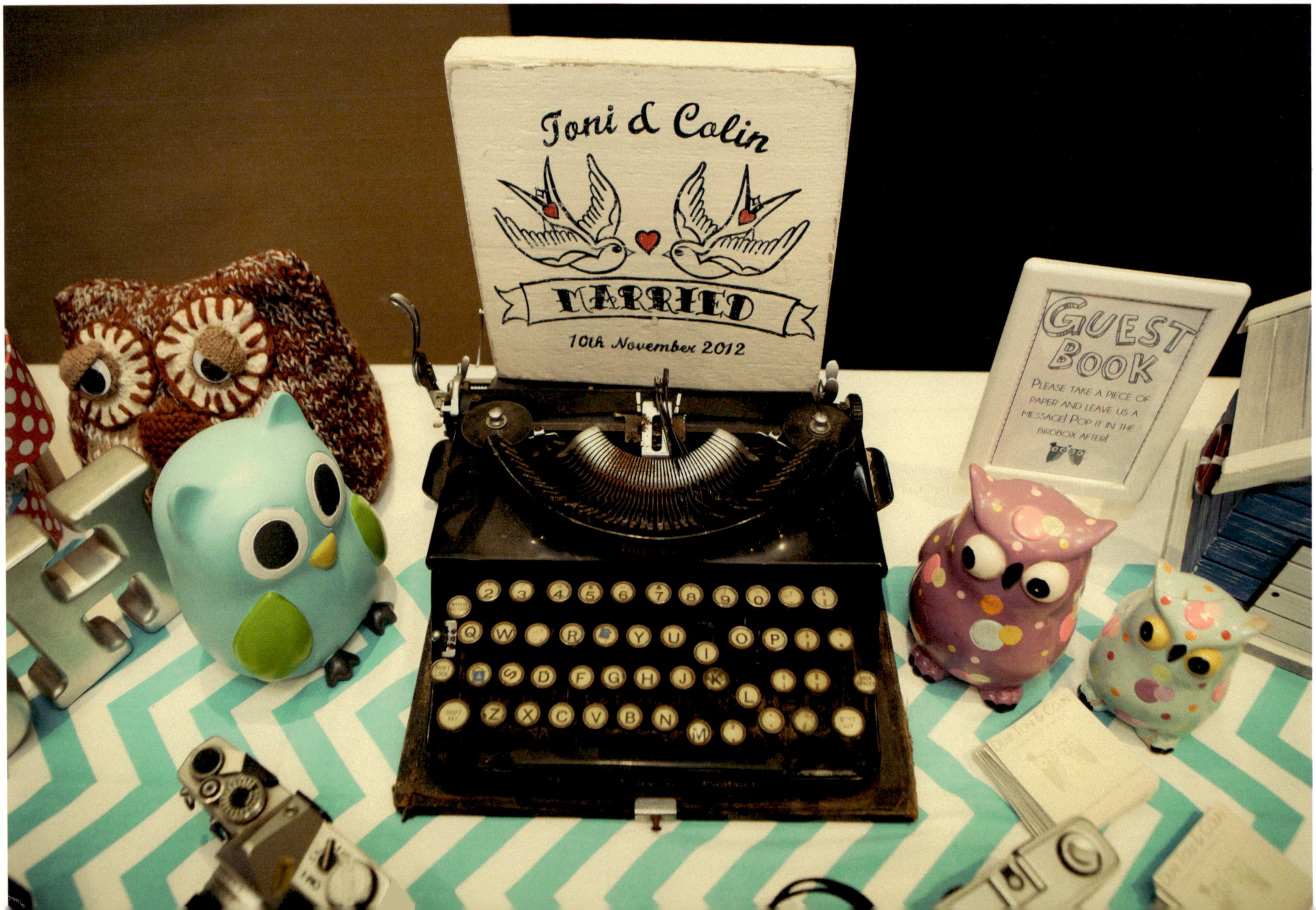

1. Zig-zag table runners cut bold lines across a white background.

2. Polka-dot stages are a sweet common denominator for mismatched centerpieces.

3. Polaroid cameras are a really fun addition to the party—a kind of portable photobooth!

4. A wedding is the start of a great adventure, just like the drink was for Alice!

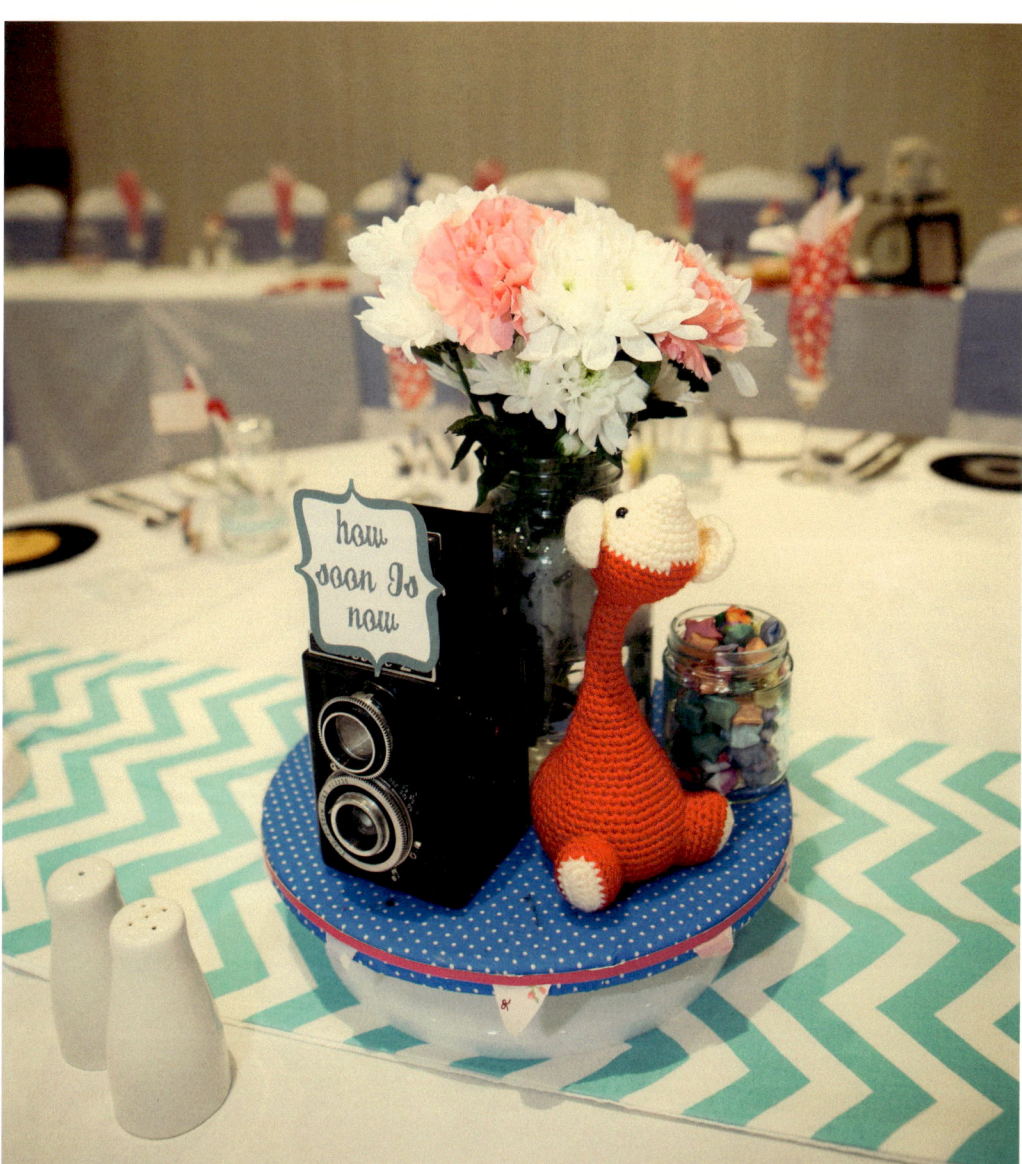

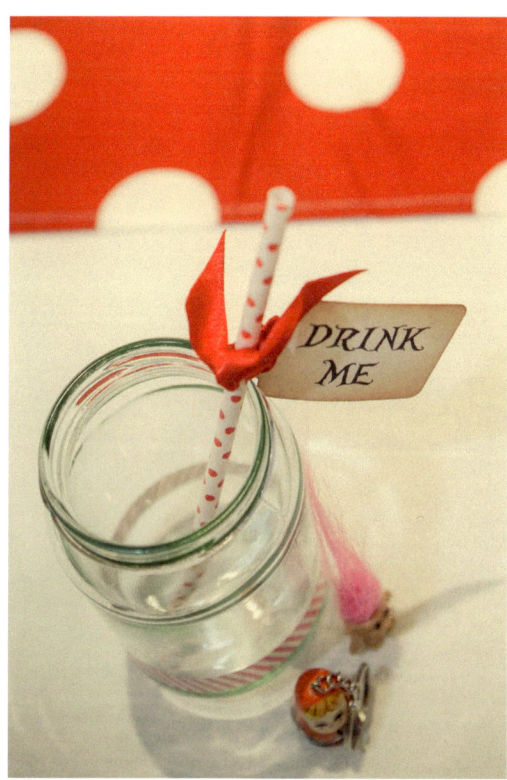

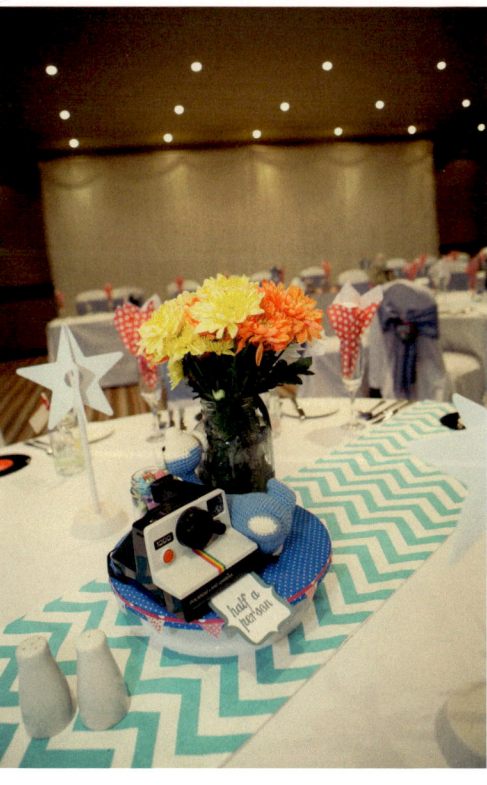

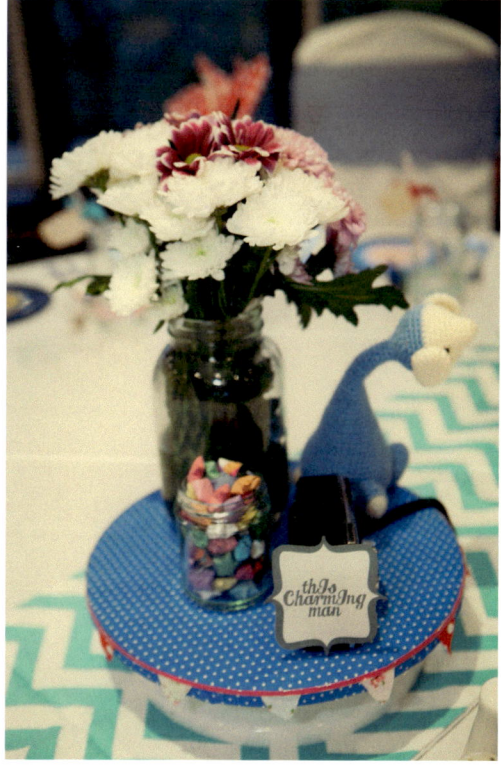

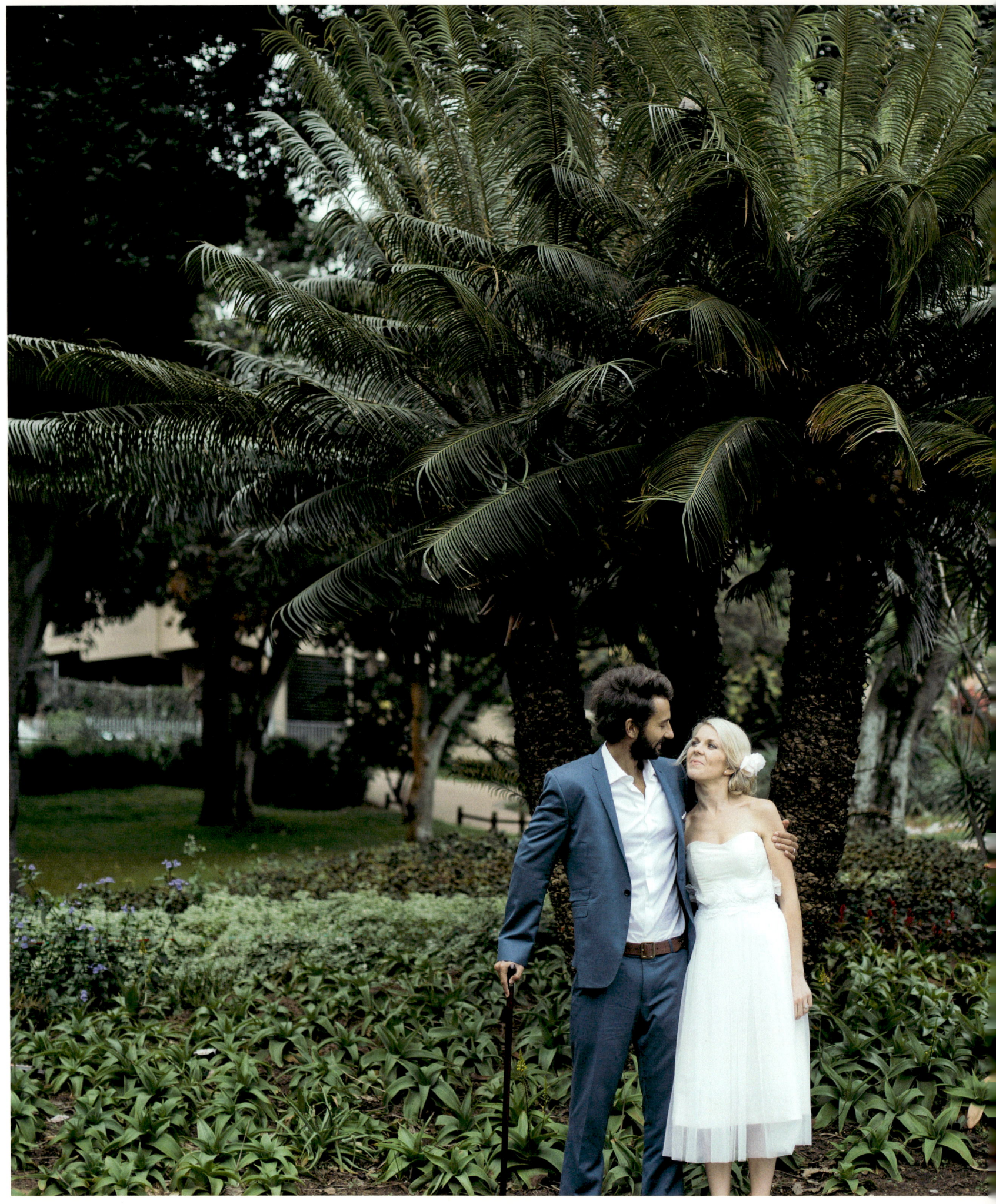

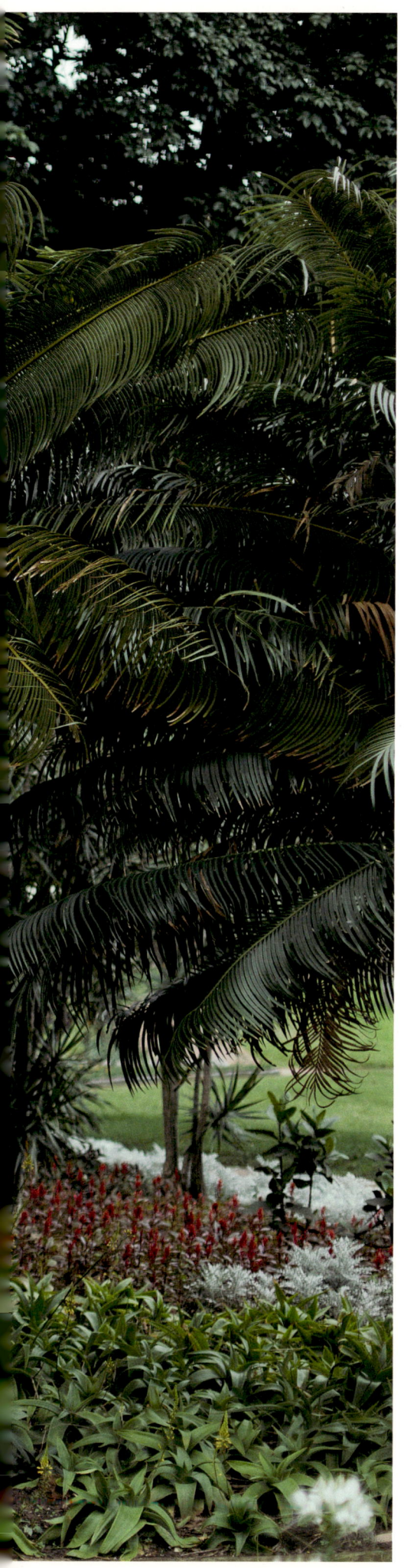

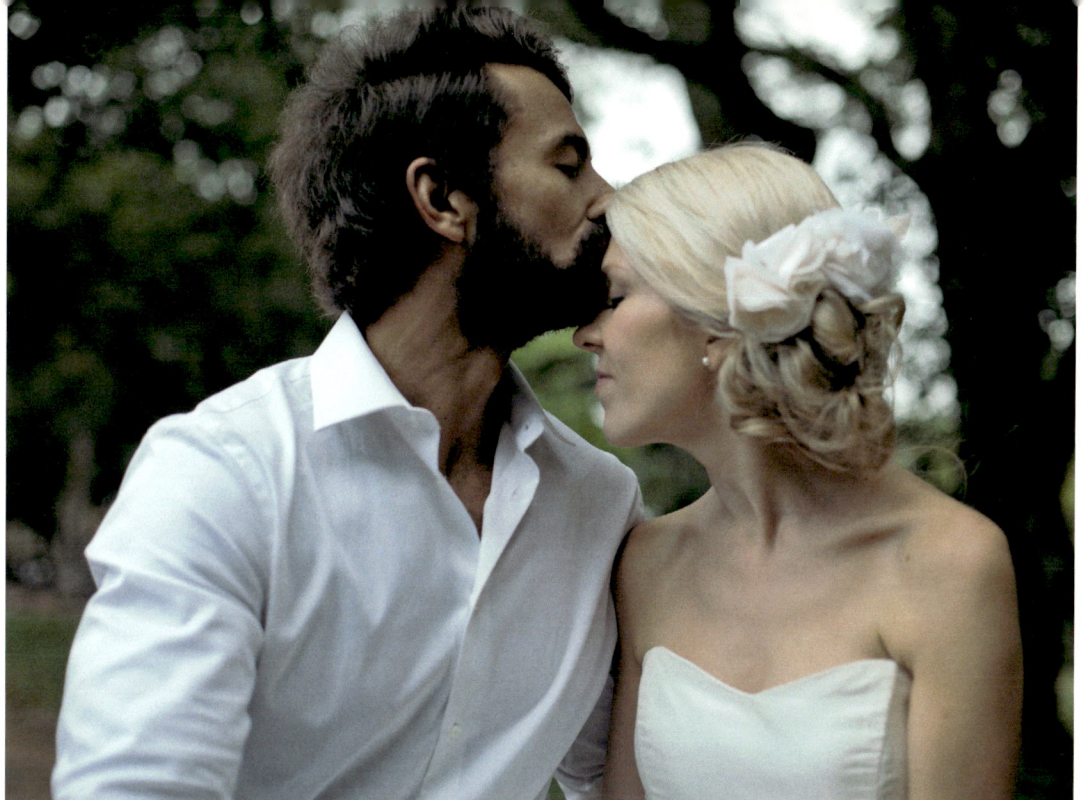

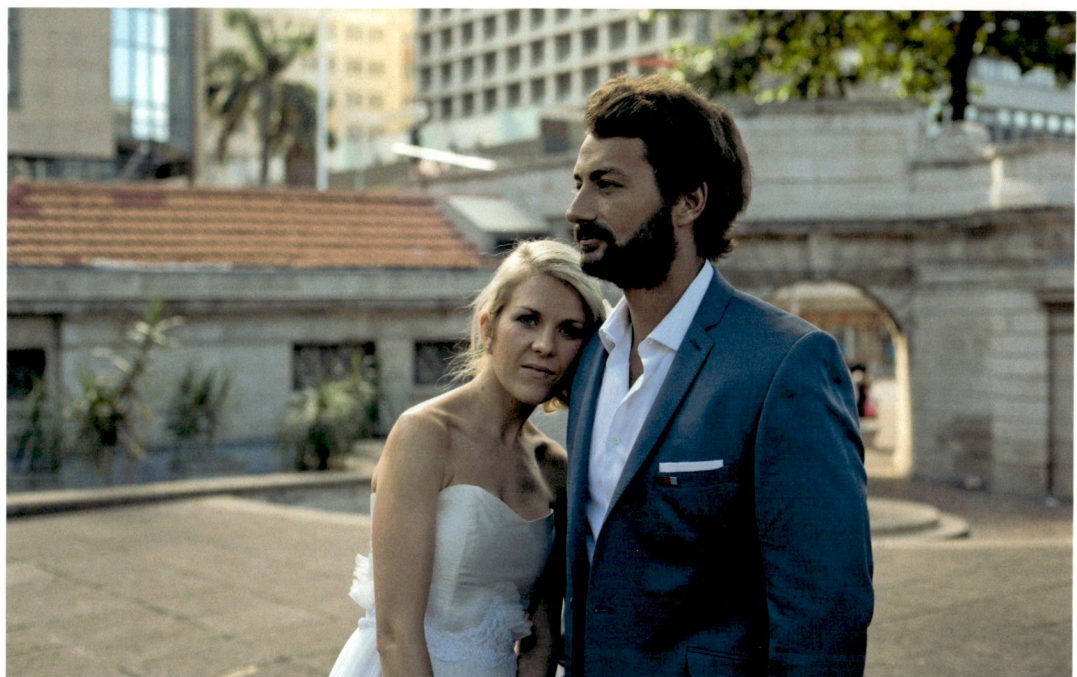

Claire & Gary

Posing in front of stone walls, high-rise buildings, and urban squares, there is clearly nowhere that Gary and Claire would rather be. They both have Durban in their blood, so they wanted it, and all its dog-eared charm, to be with them on their wedding day. Palm trees appeared in nearly every shot, and later the bottle-green fronds joined in with the reception color scheme to produce a trio of bold, subtle, and earthy tones.

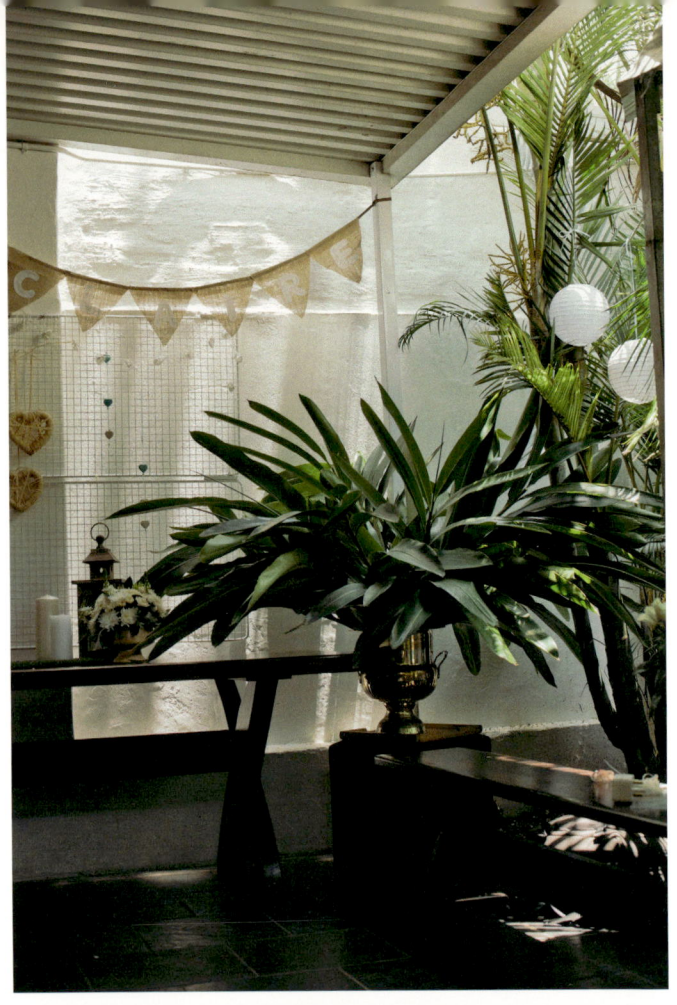

The Decoration

The families handled the decorations and kept them secret until the day. With personalized bunting, fat bunches of flowers, and warm lighting casting shadows on the wall, they created the low-key intimate setting that Gary and Claire were dreaming of.

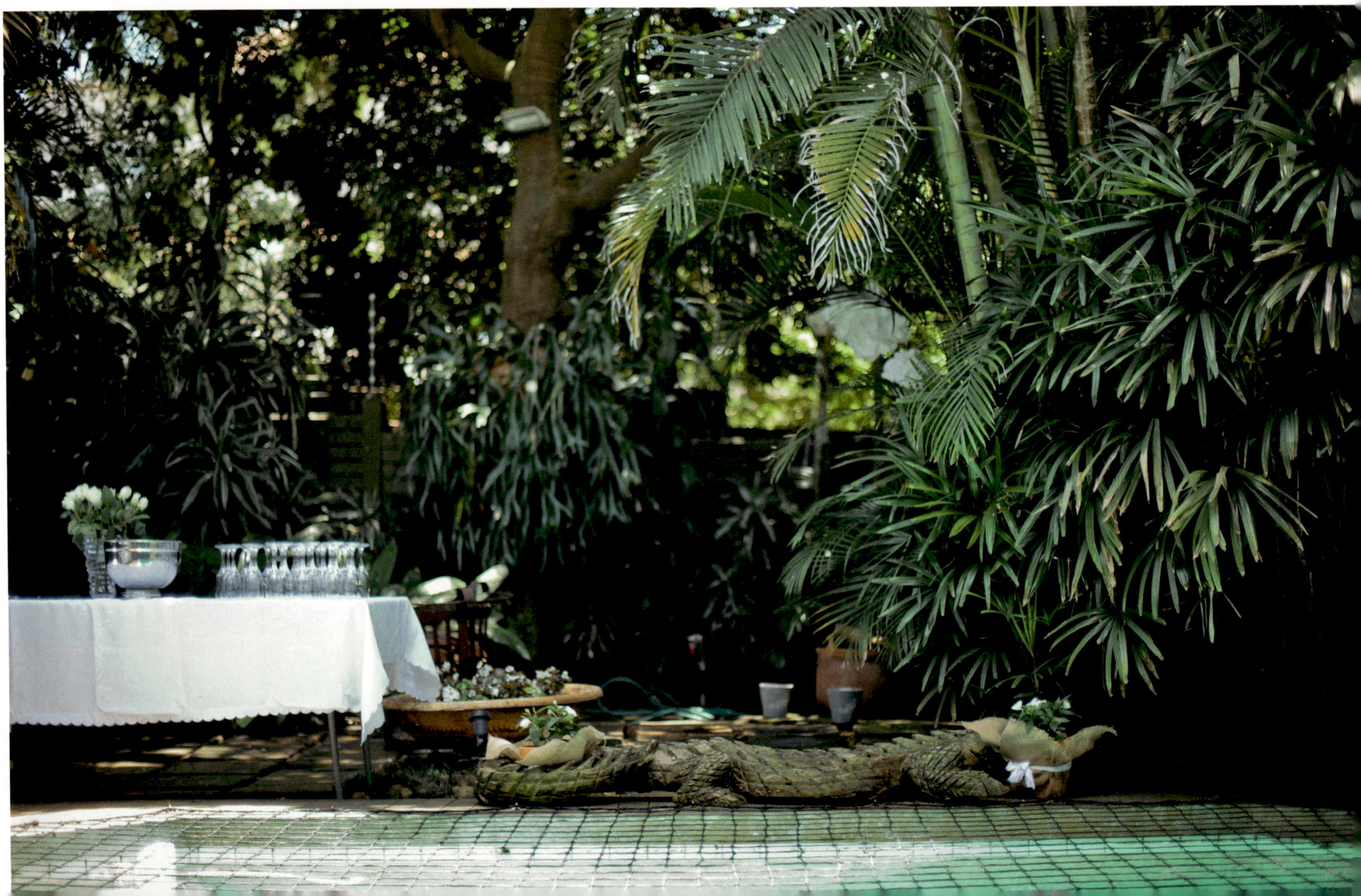

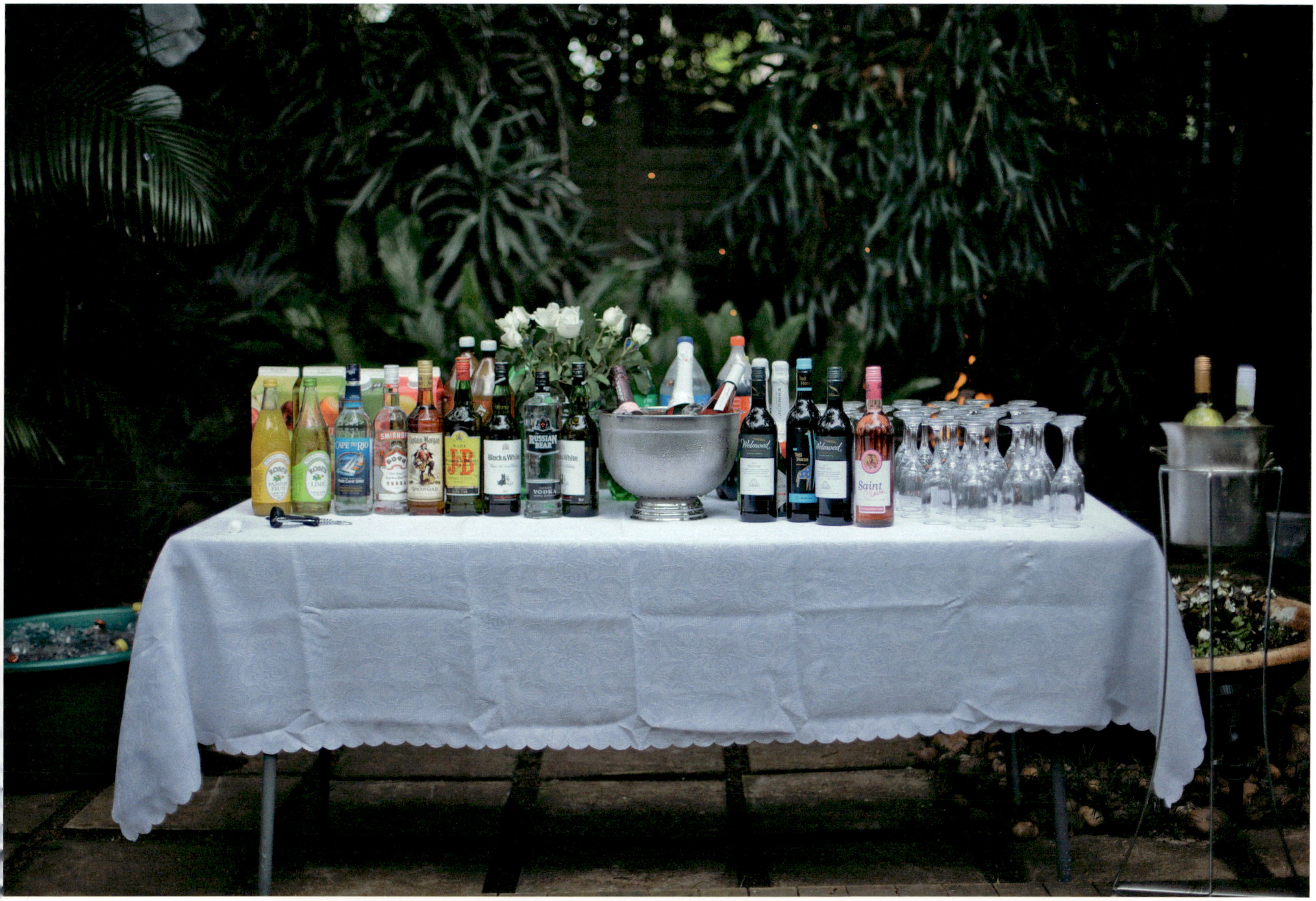

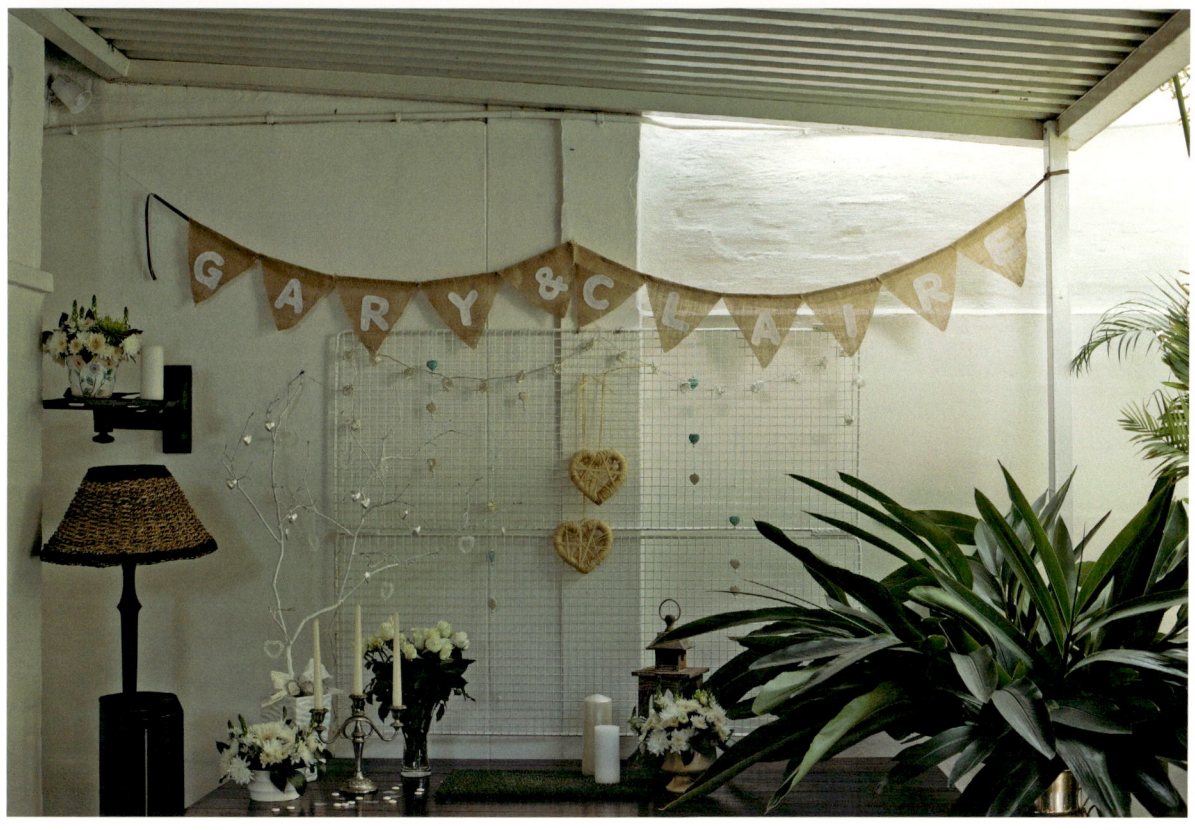

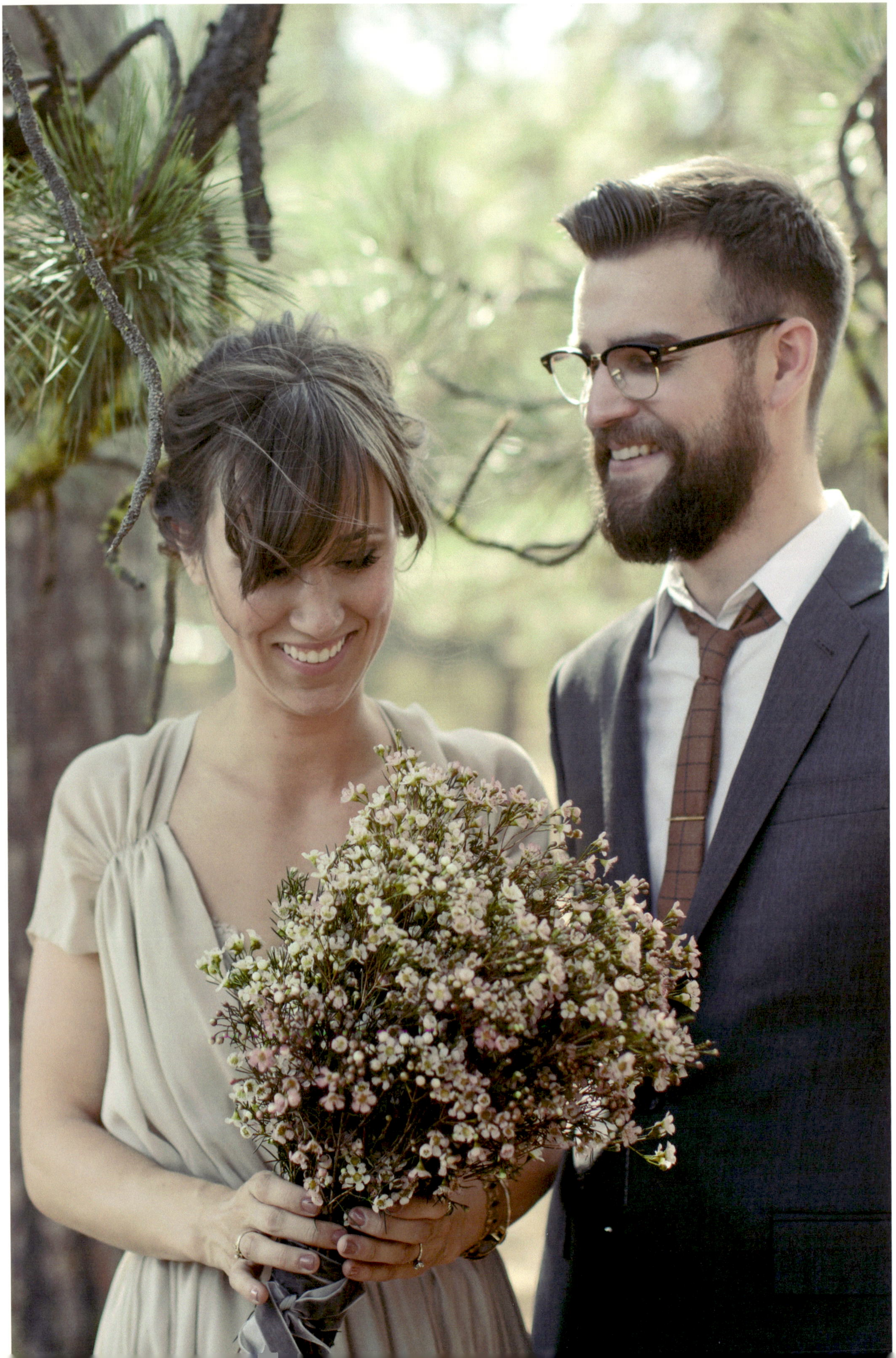

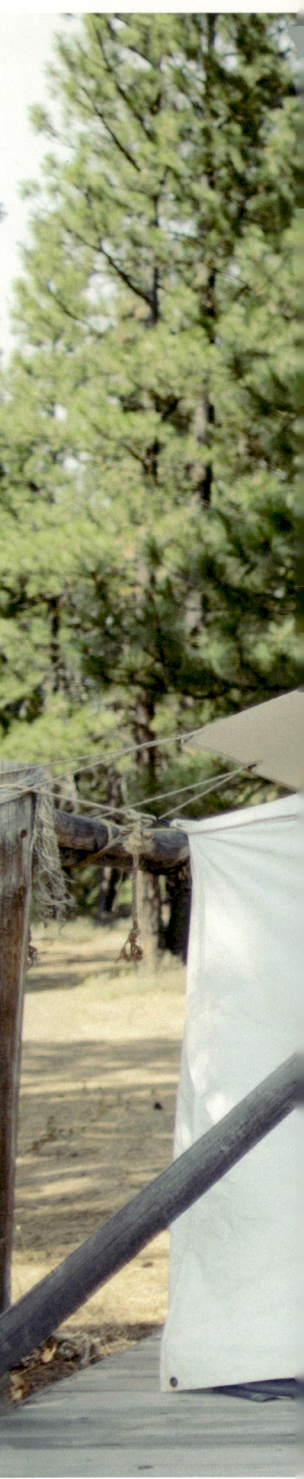

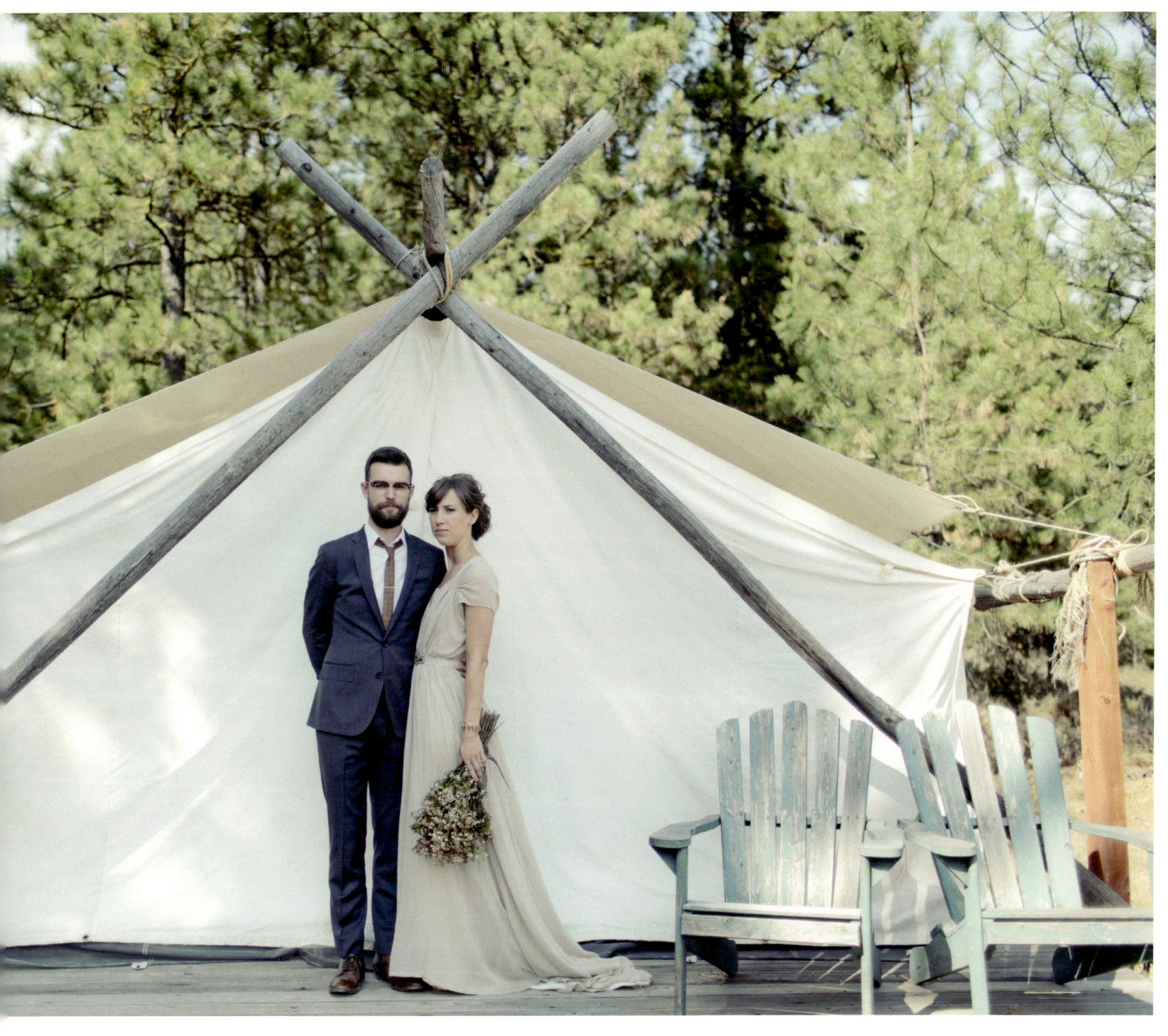

Kristen & Michael

Kristen and Michael wanted a simple wedding with the people they loved, good food, and good music. The bride and bridesmaids wore dresses in subdued tones and paired them with boots for a pretty prairie-girl look. The boys arrived in jeans with turnups and suspenders, and the groom wore a sleek suit and skinny tie. The ceremony was held at a beautiful homestead in Washington state, where the clapboard cabins and rustic beauty matched the vintage feel of the wedding.

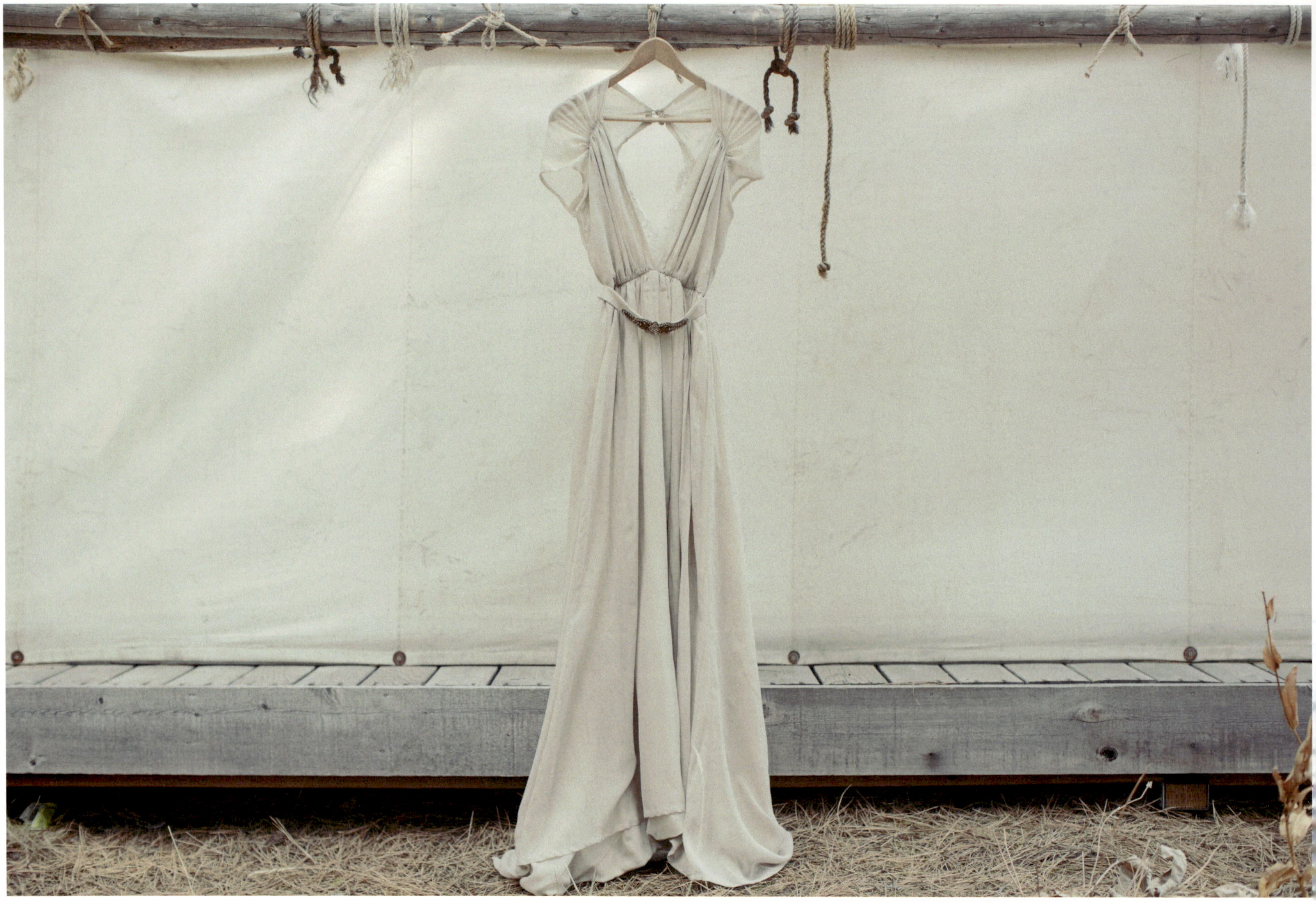

Brown shoes and
antique jewelry
make a vintage
dress sing.

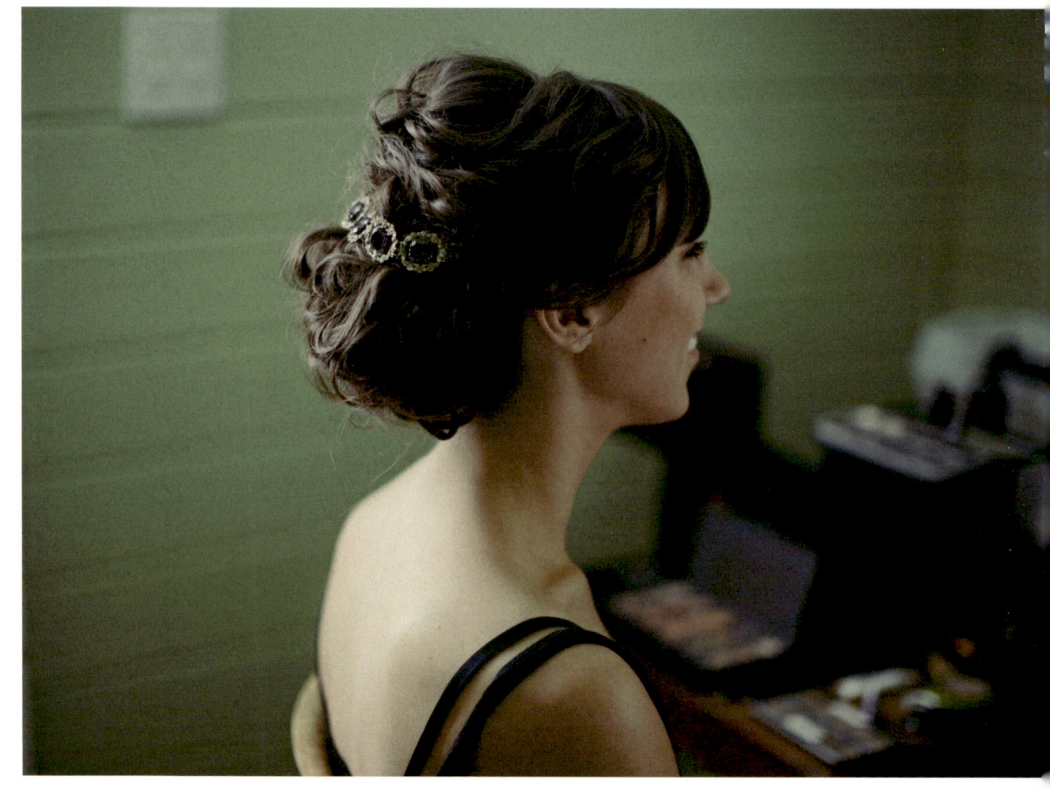

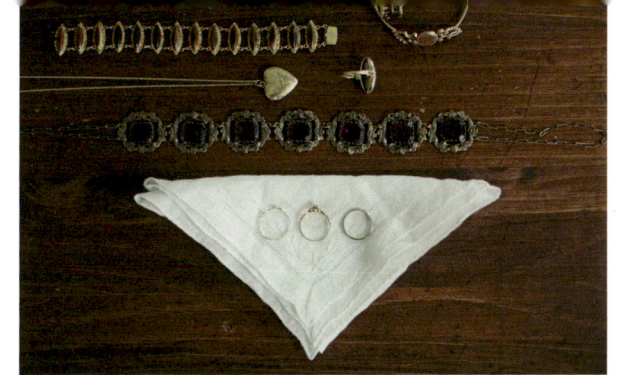

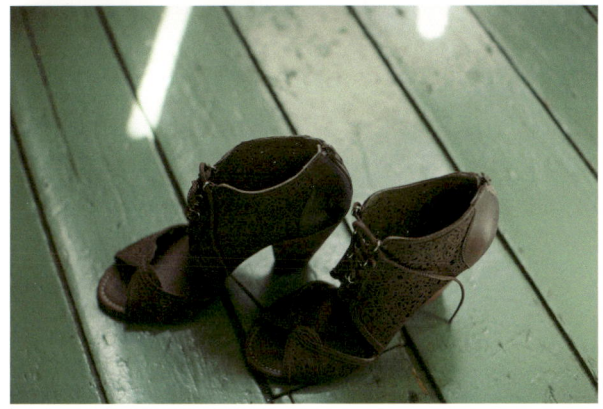

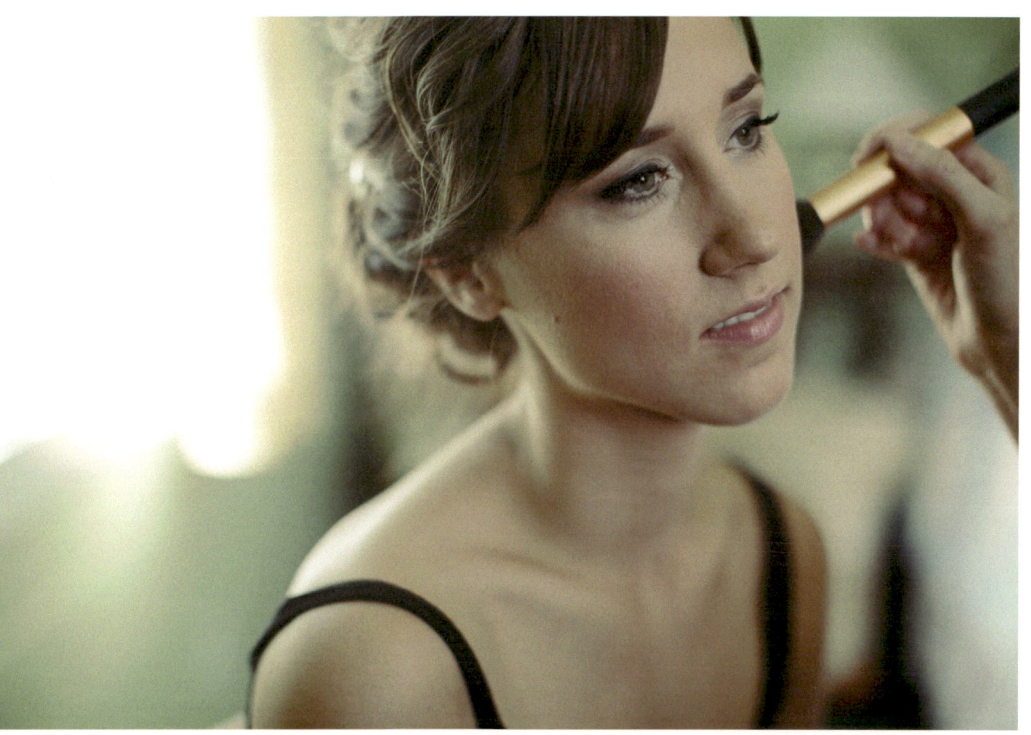

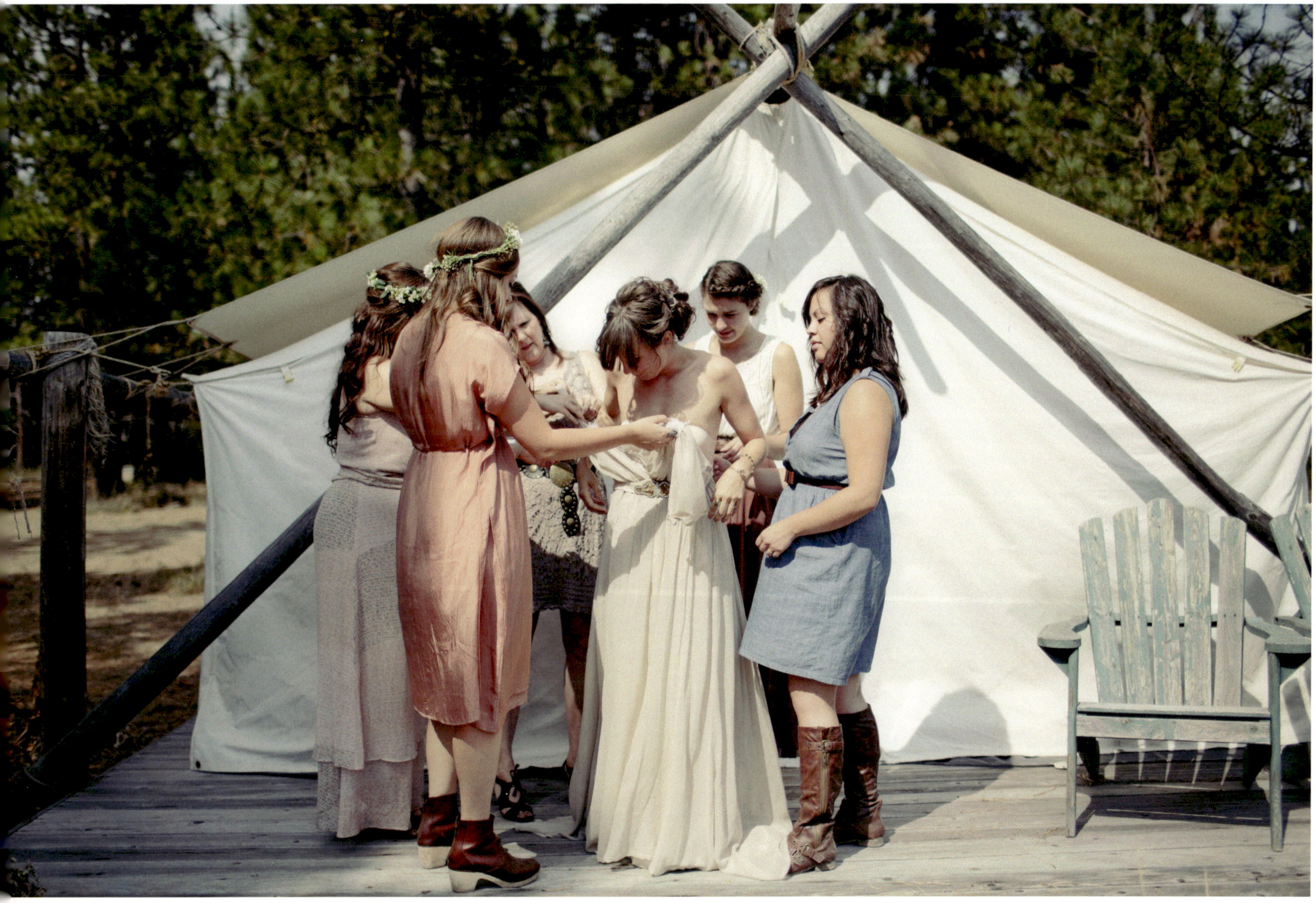

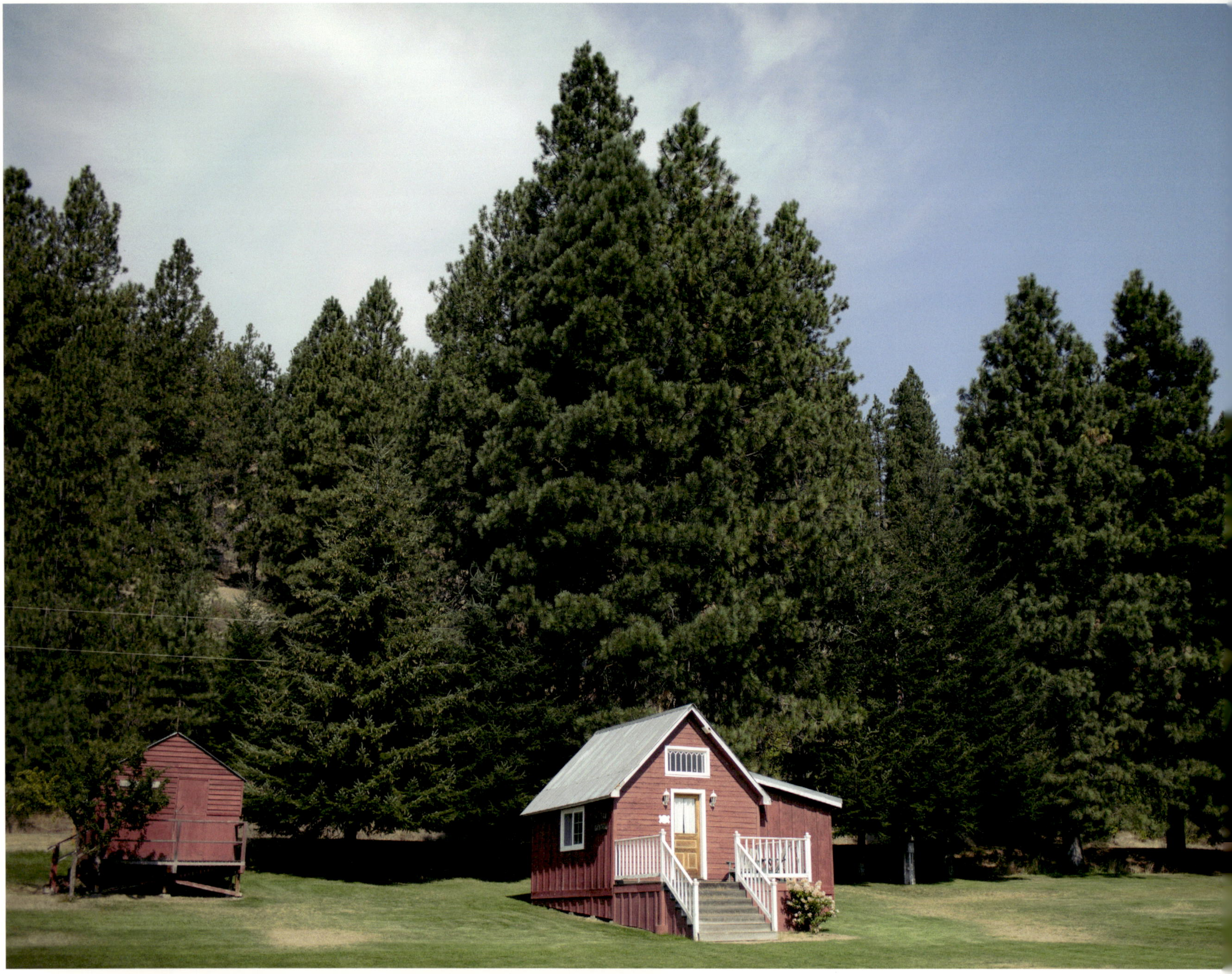

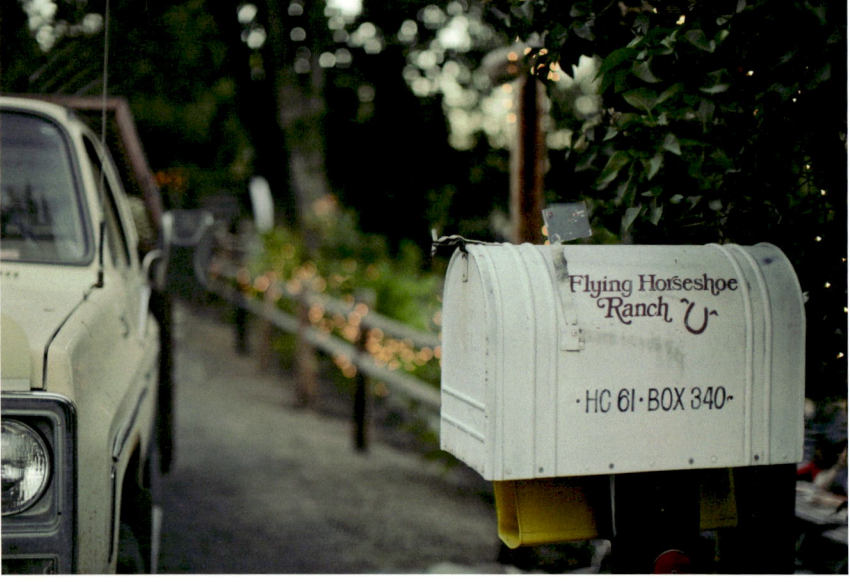

The Setting

Getting out into the country for your wedding can make it seem as if there is no one in the world but you and your guests. A ranch like the one where Kristen and Michael got married will serve up the most wonderful scenery and is just as at home with a romantic, intimate ceremony as it is with a barbecue and festivities under a star-spangled sky.

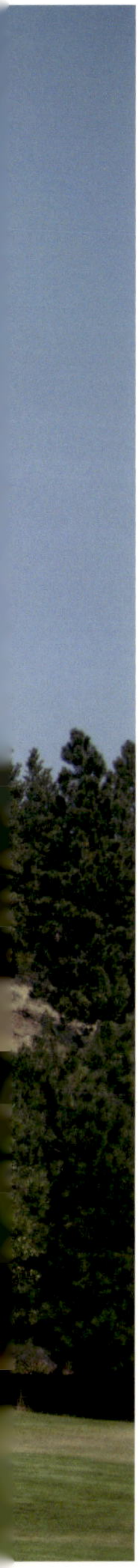

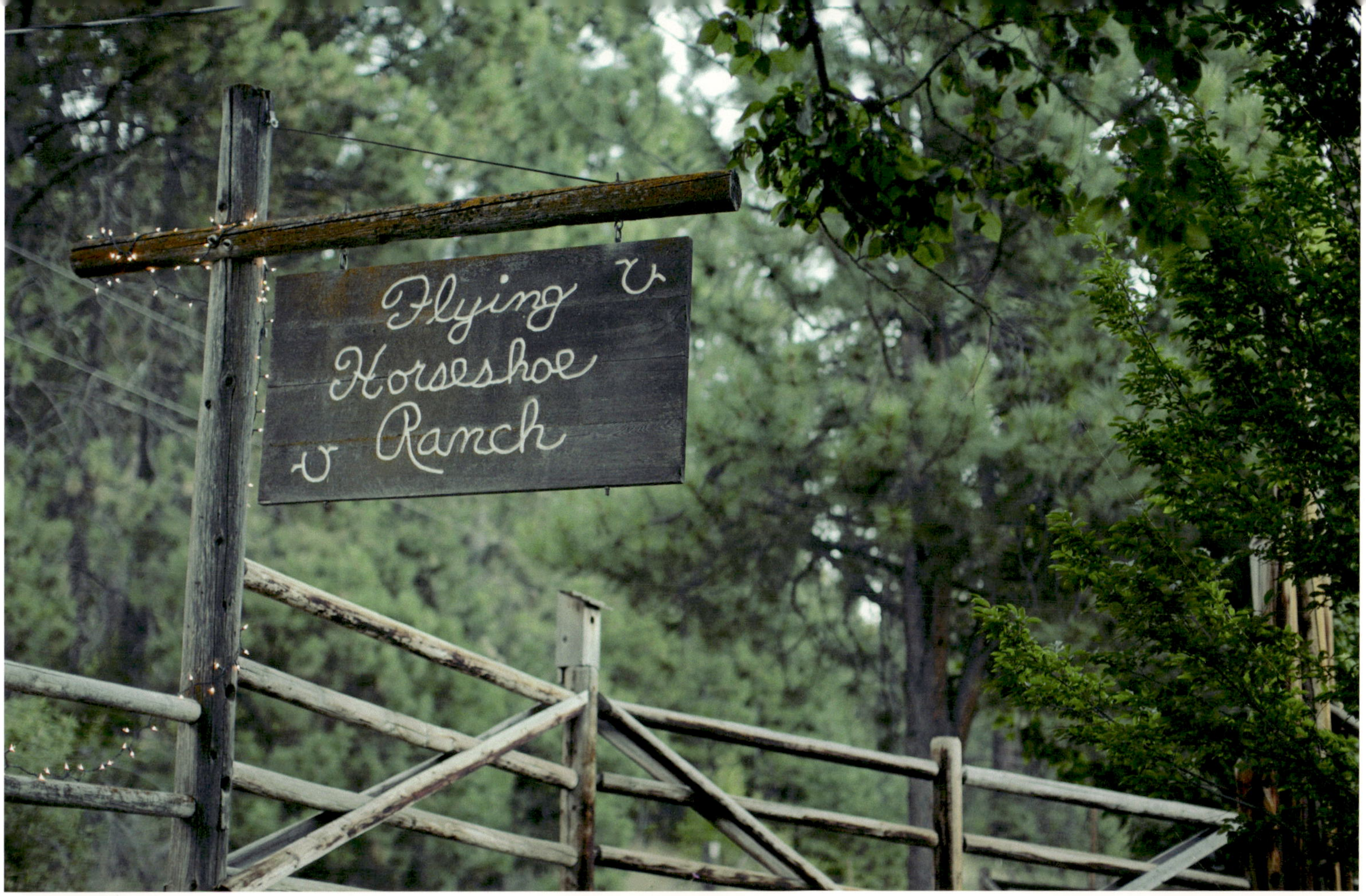
Flying
Horseshoe
Ranch

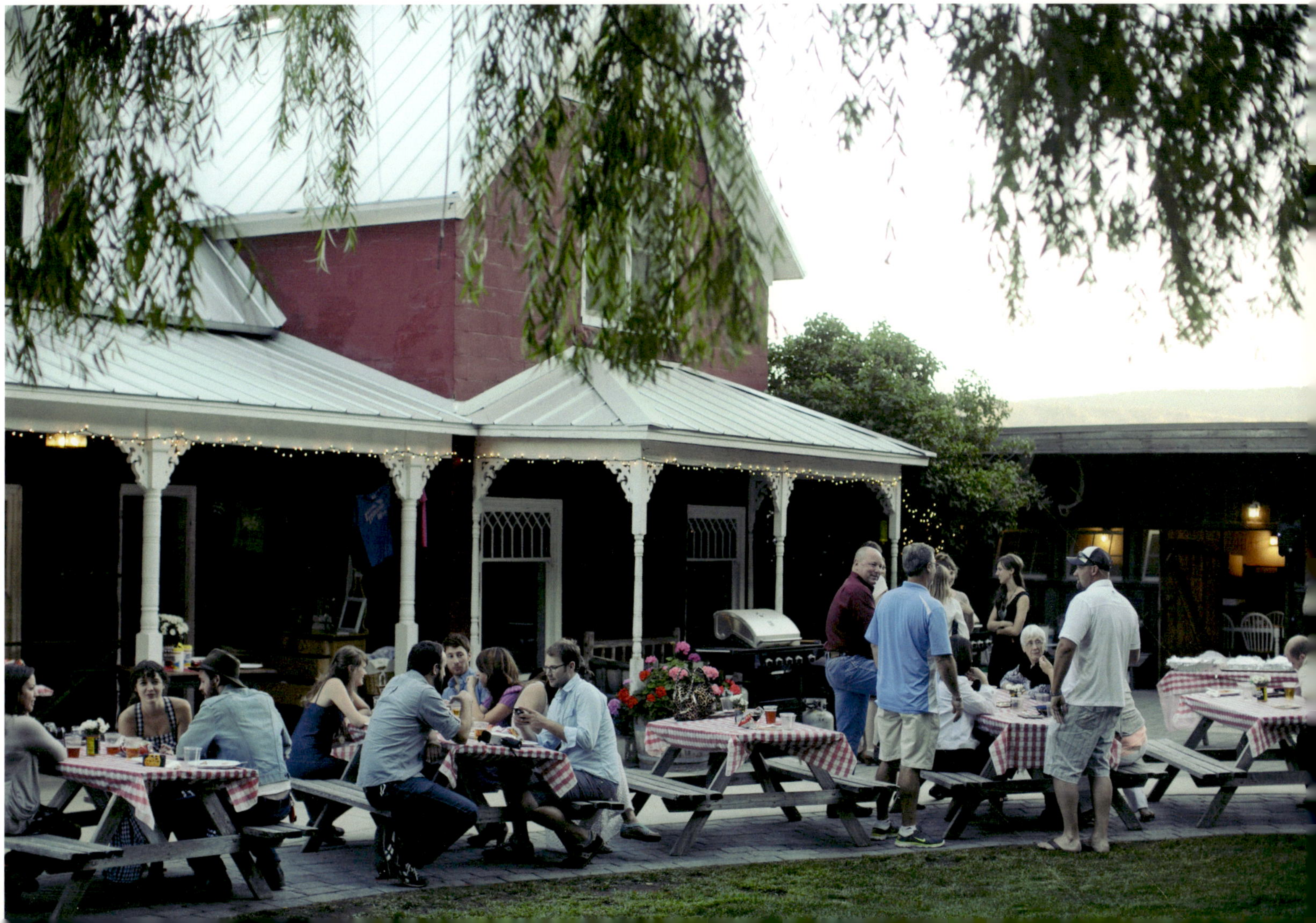

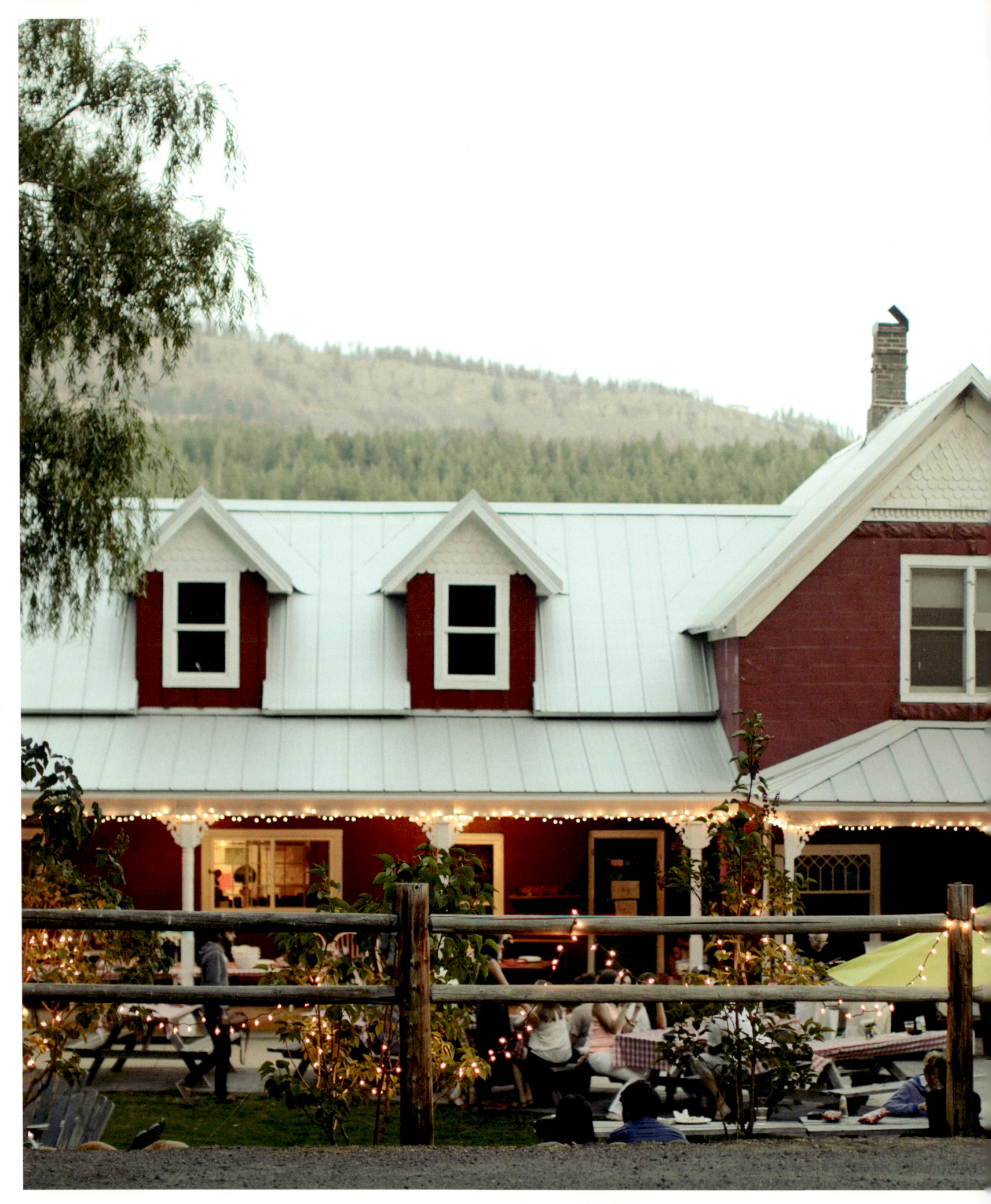

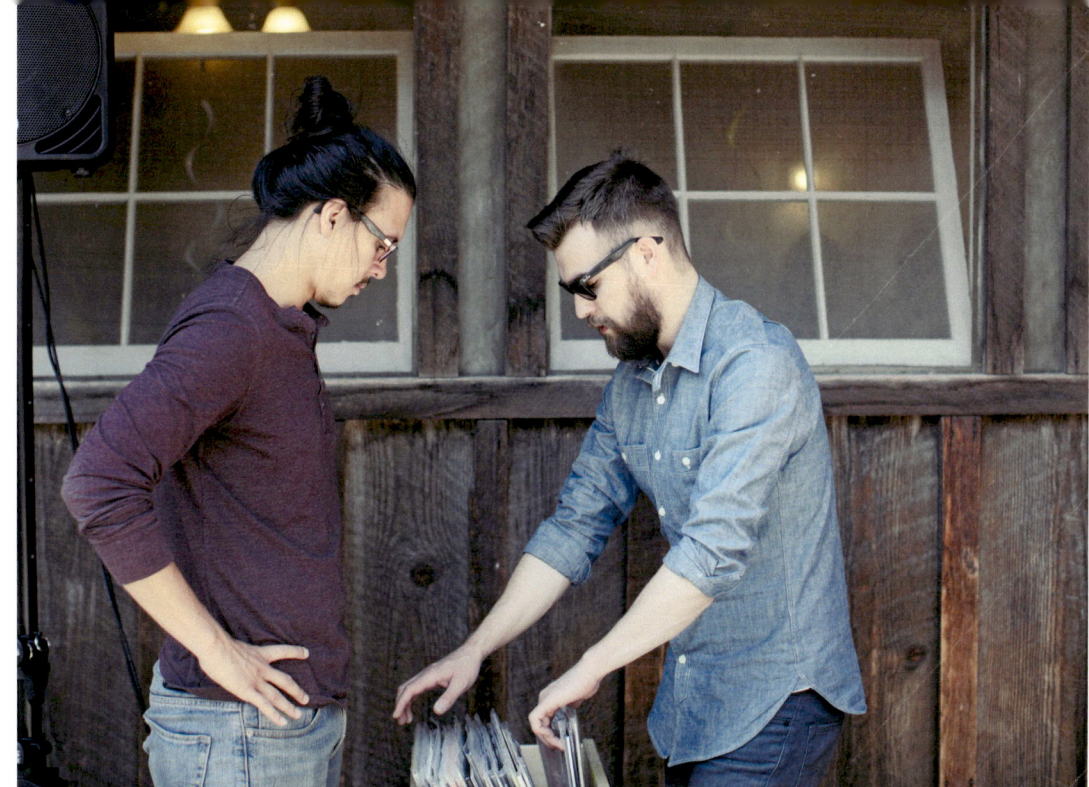

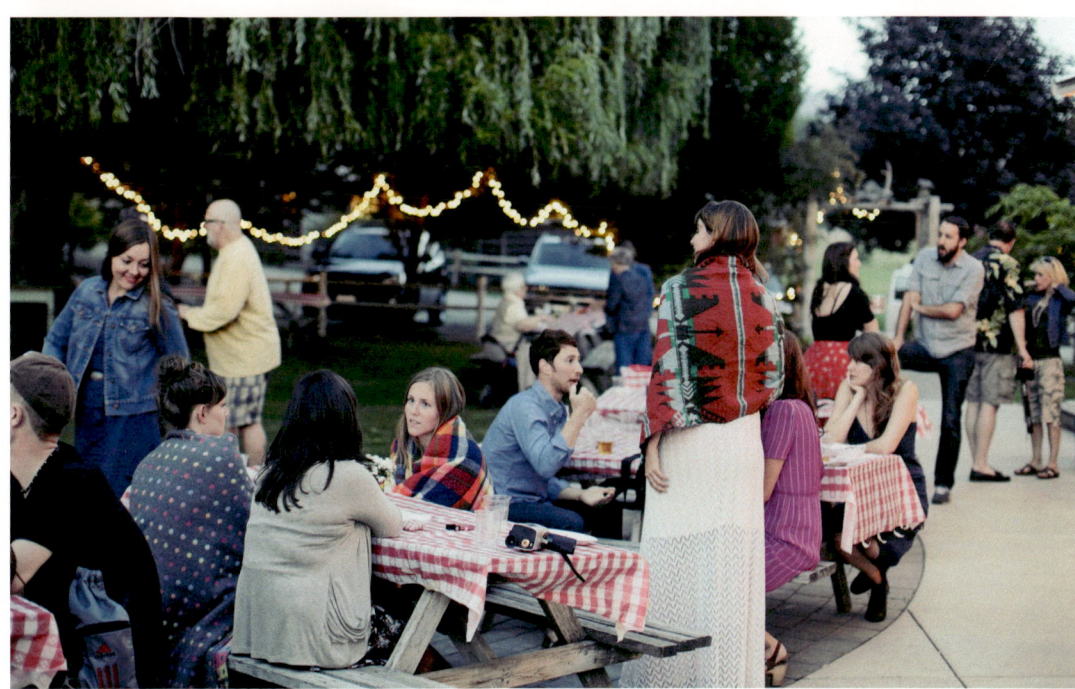

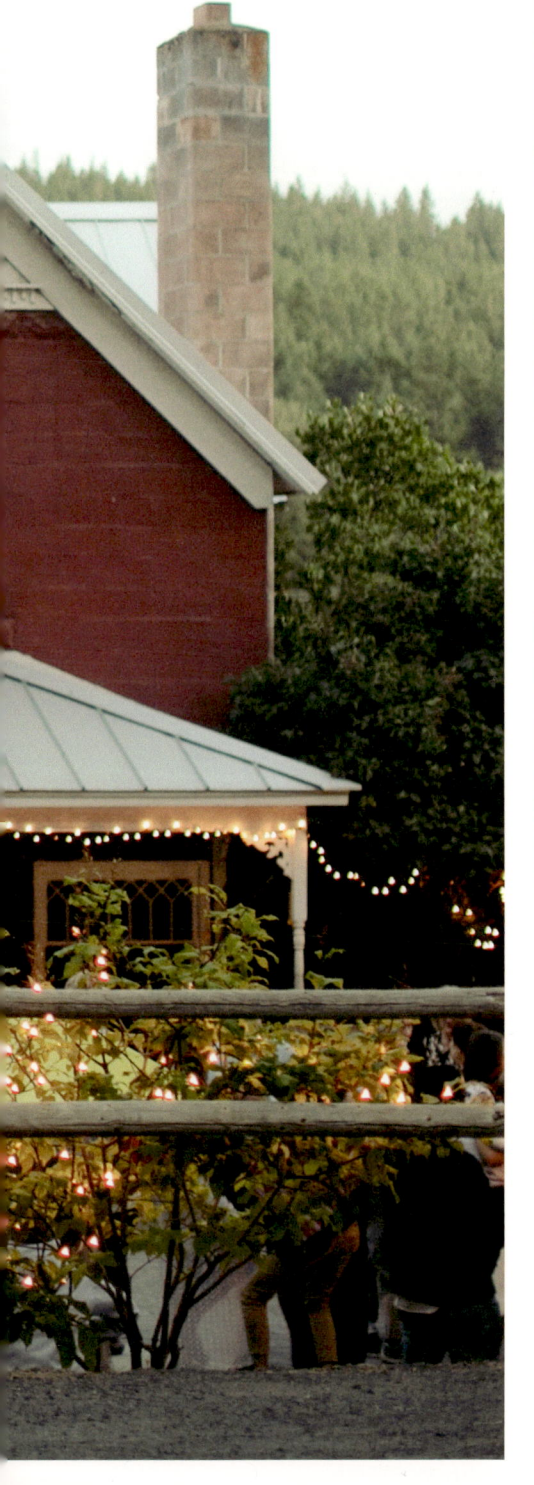

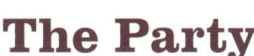

The Party

Checkered tablecloths and picnic benches are a key ingredient for any homestead dinner, and having a stack of brightly-colored blankets on hand will keep everyone warm as the night air breezes in. But judging by the look of that vinyl collection, we doubt anyone stayed wrapped up in them for long.

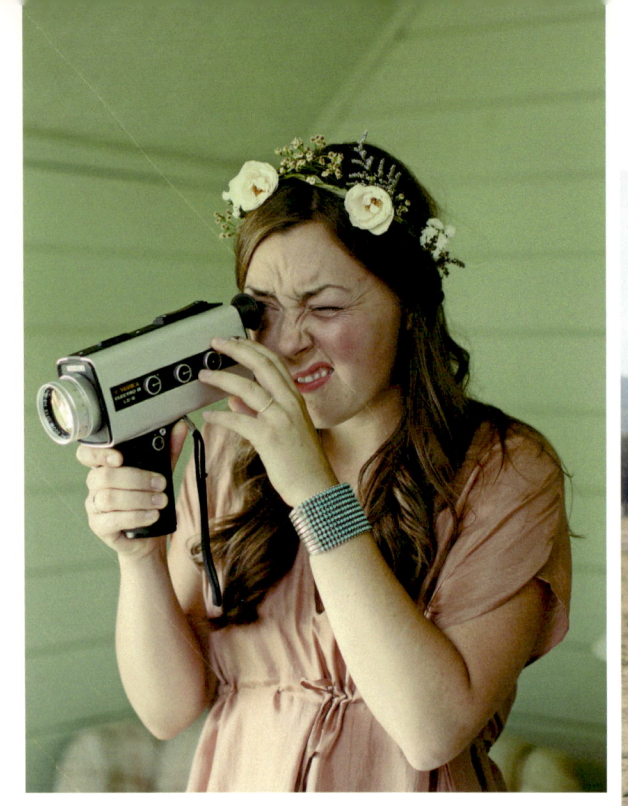
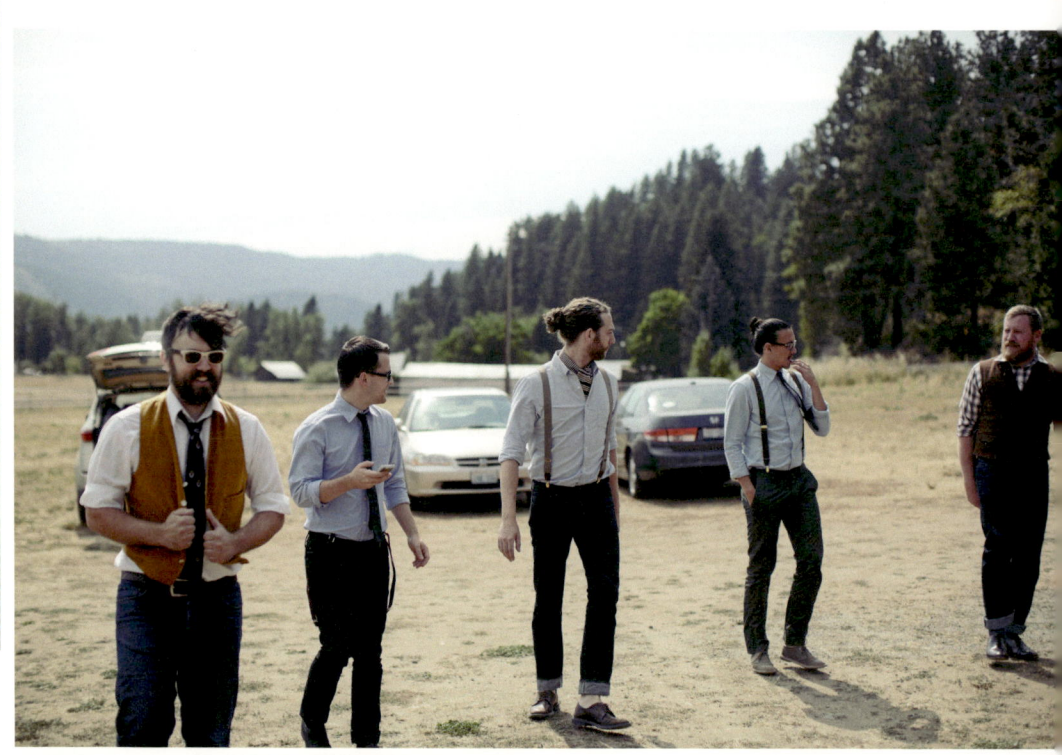

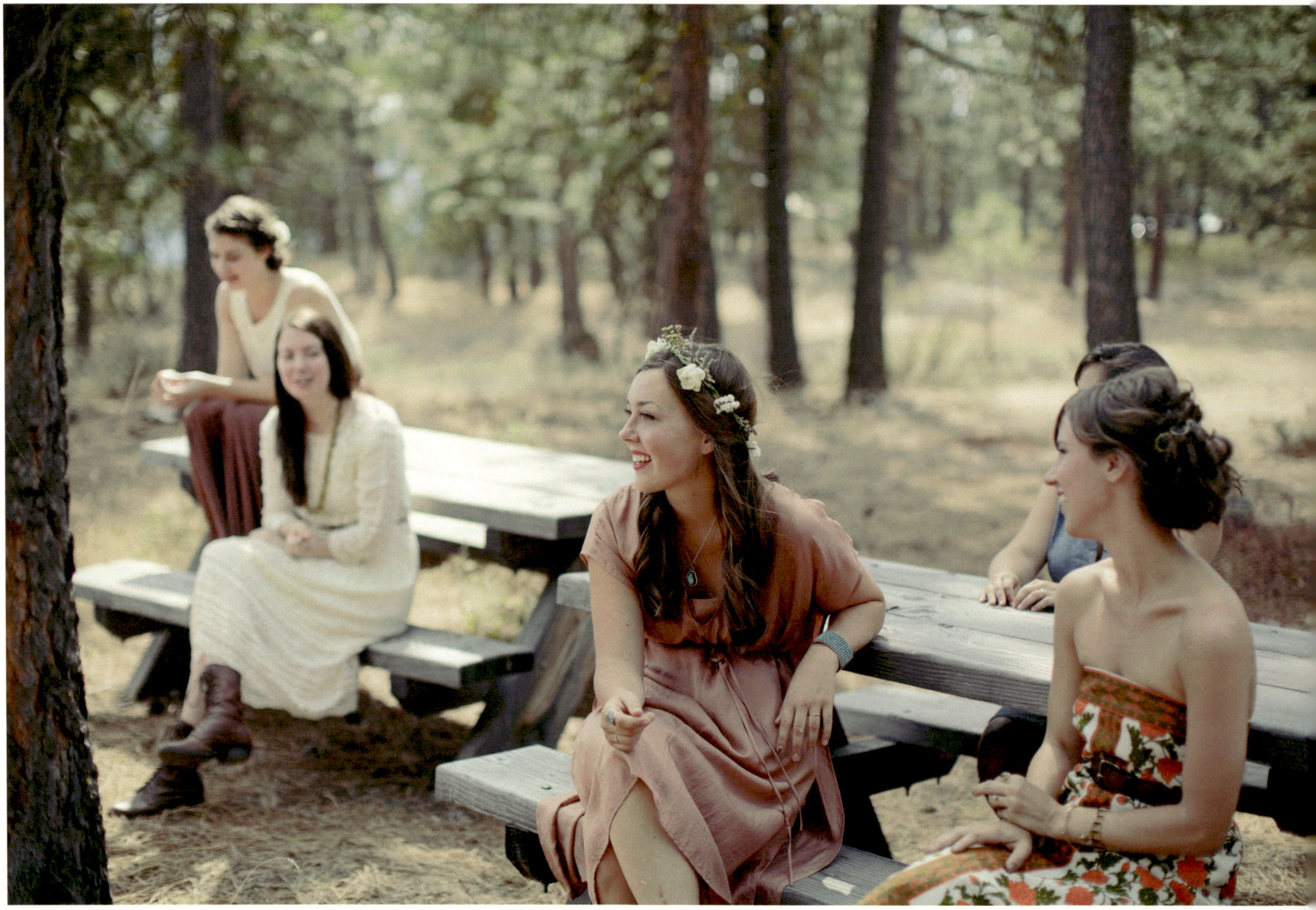

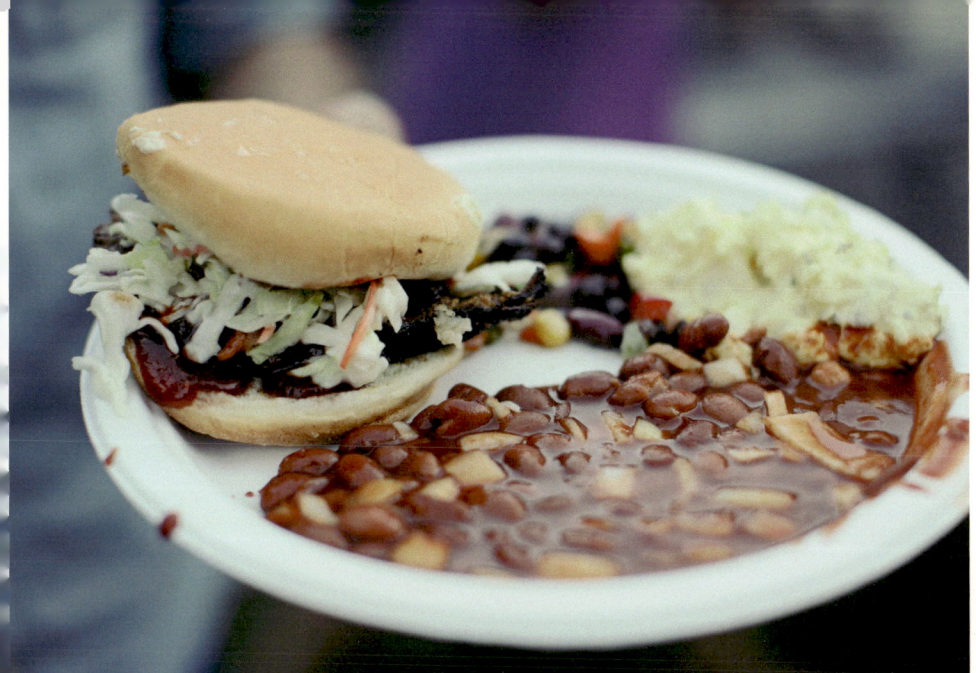

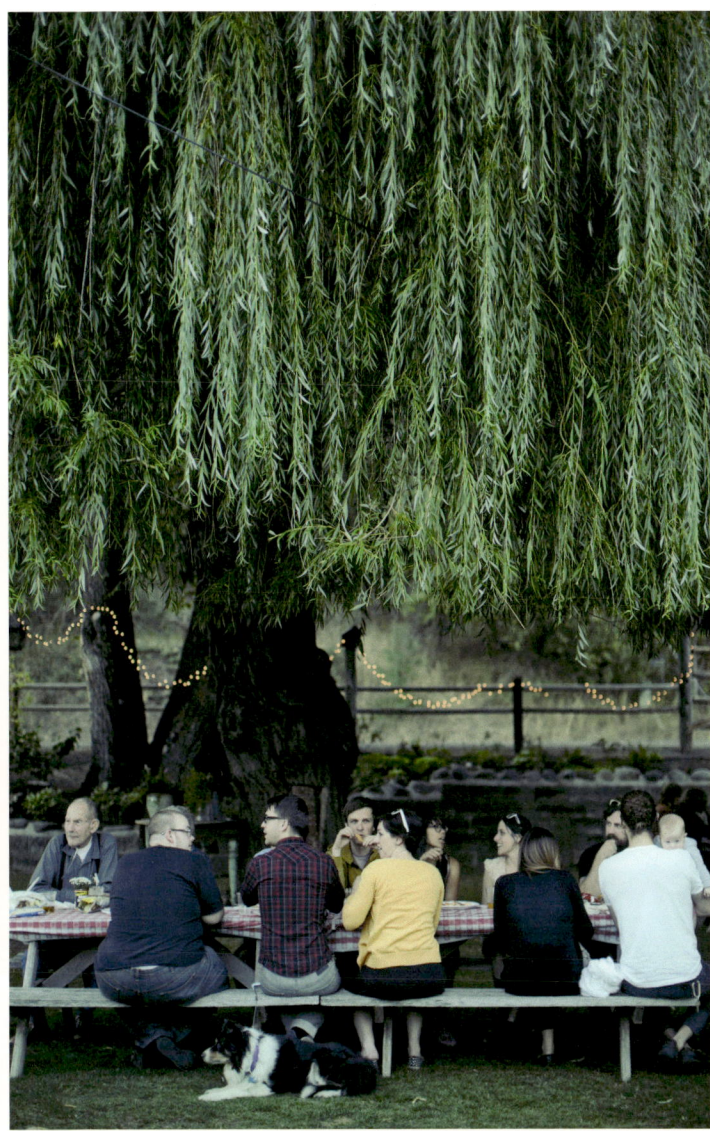

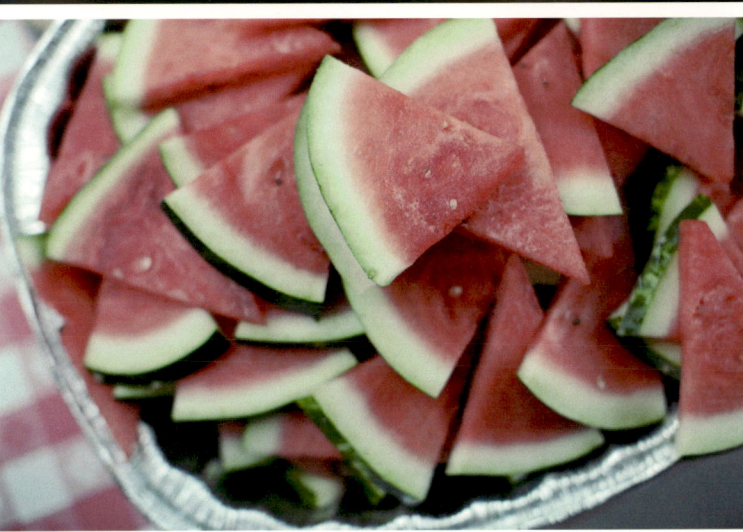

1. Burgers and beans are just right for a ranch.

2. Rows of picnic benches are the ultimate in relaxed, communal dining.

3. One scoop or two? Four? Oh, go on then.

4. There is something undeniably cheerful about a watermelon.

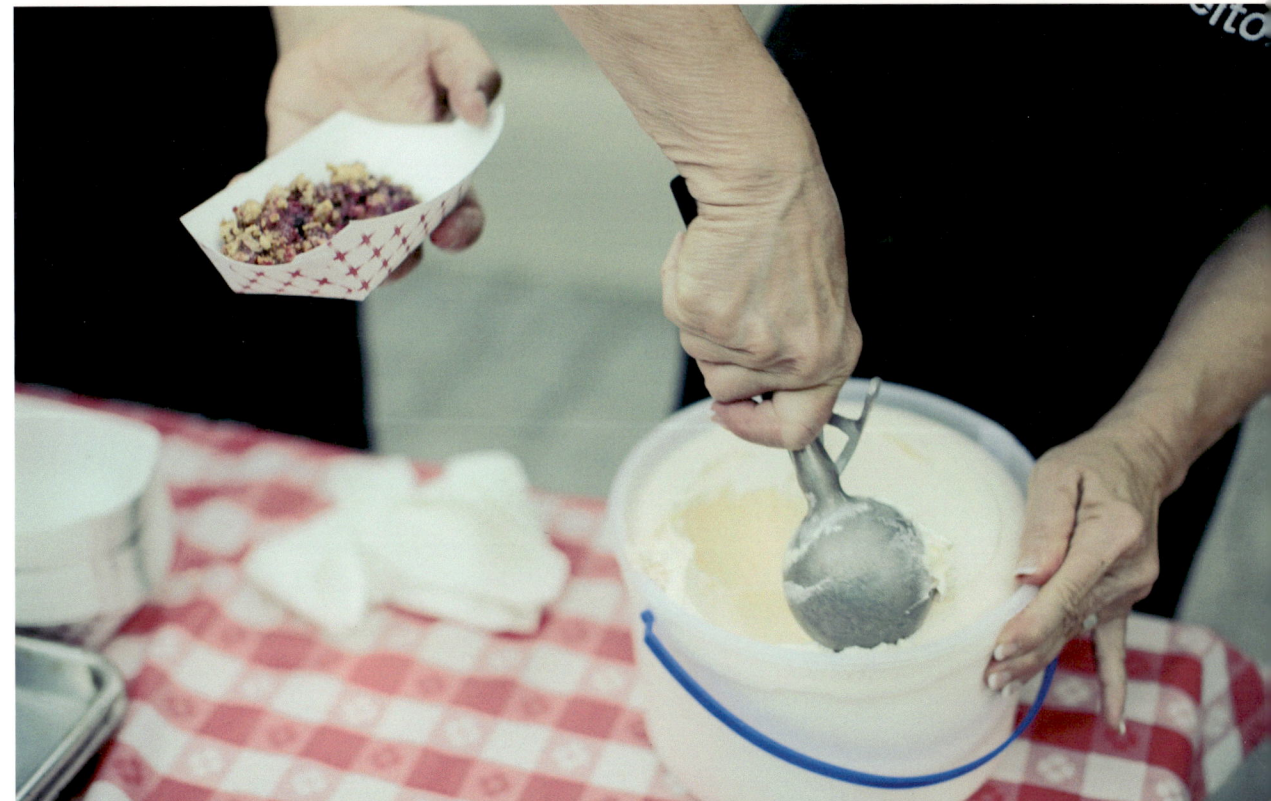

The Invite

Kristen and Michael's invites were as rustic as the ranch. Looping cursive writing gives them a personal feel, and a creative approach to addressing the envelopes makes everything even more special. Working with a graphic designer who will find inspiration in your uniqueness can produce gorgeous results.

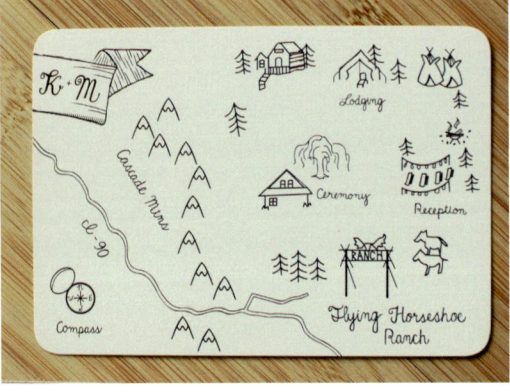

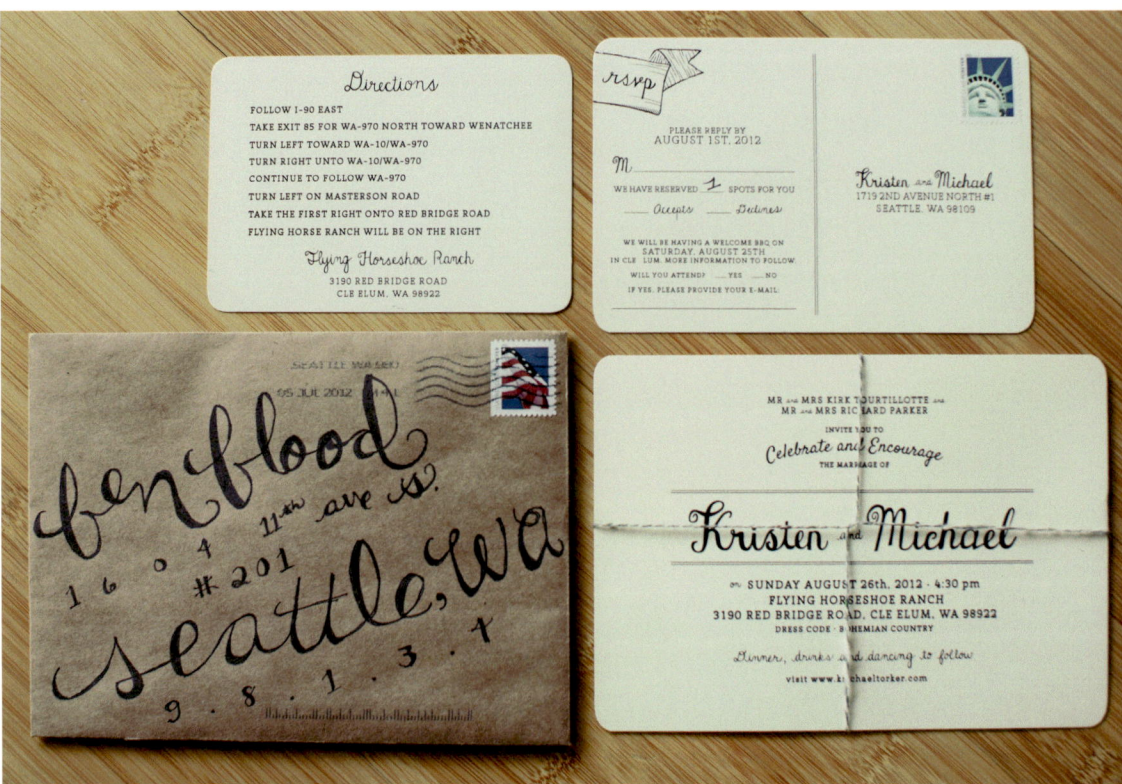

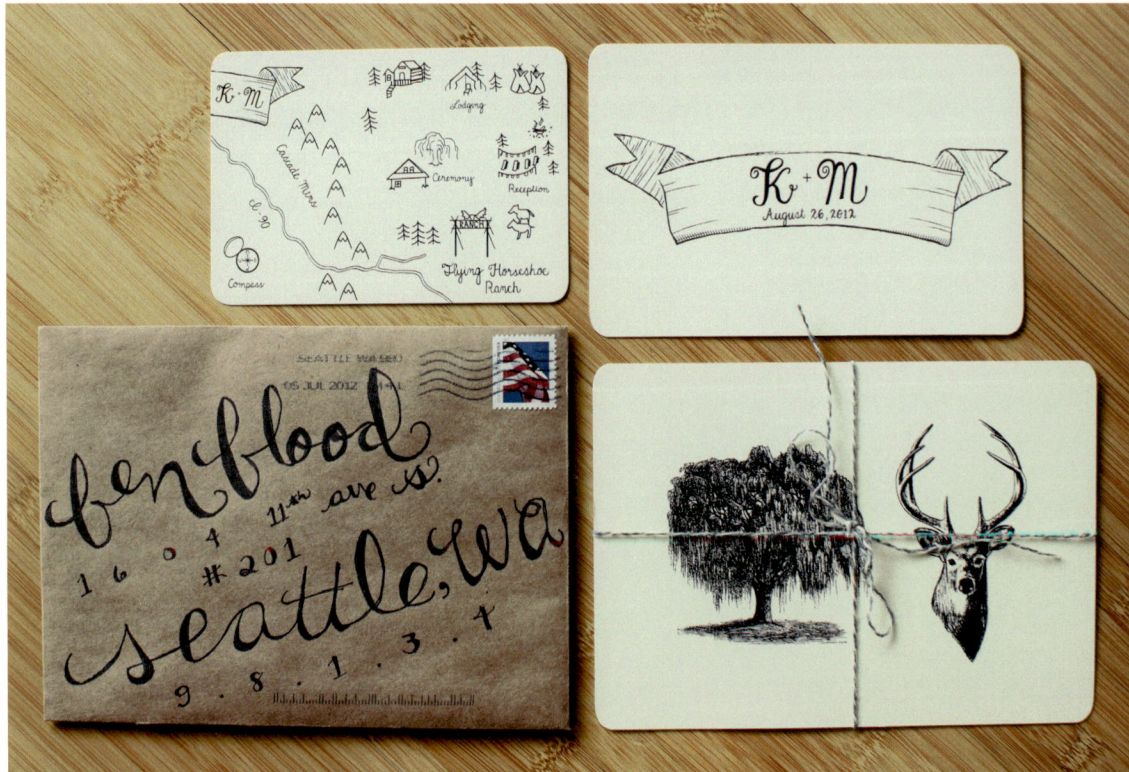

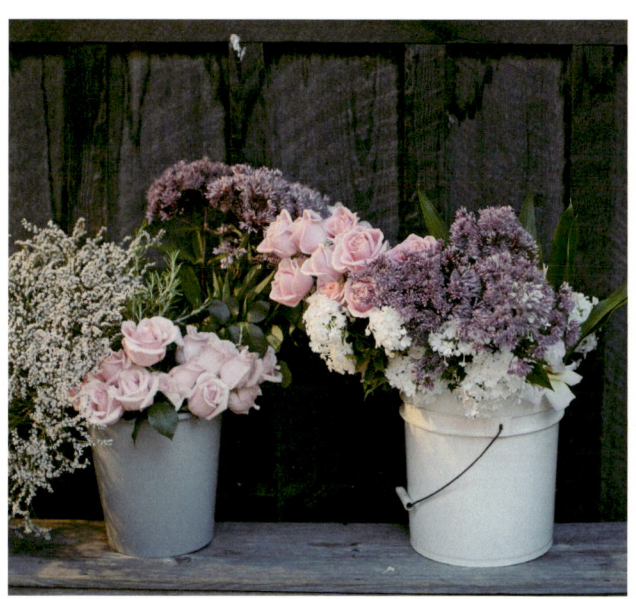

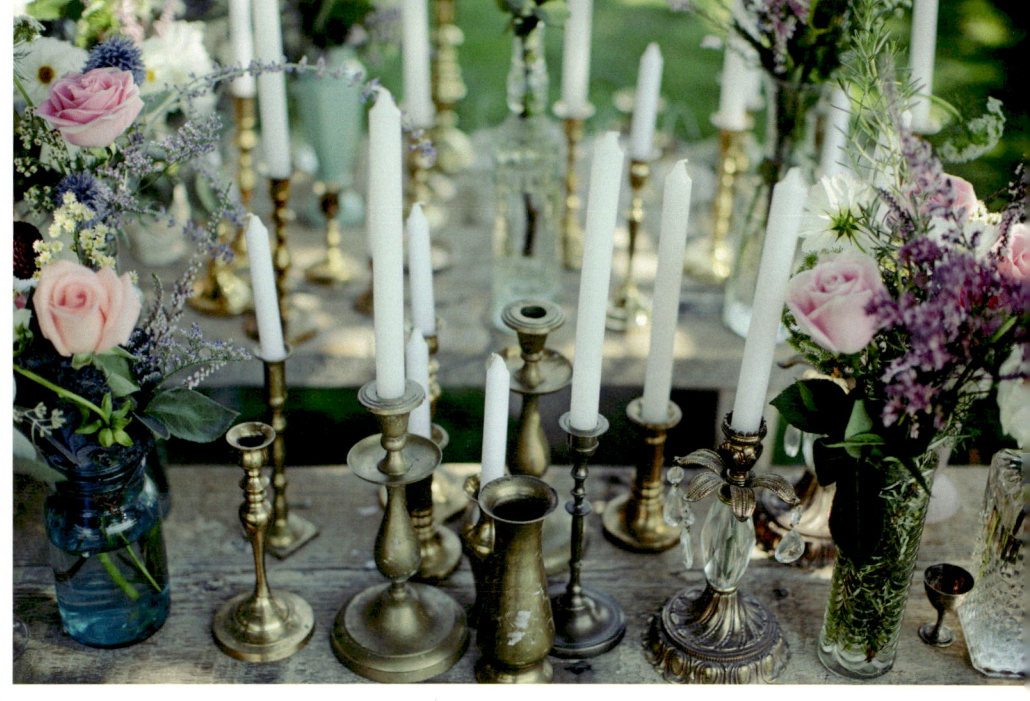

Flowers & Decoration

Jam jars, tin pots, and glass bowls can more than hold their own against crystal vases. Pewter candlesticks bring old-world romance to the table.

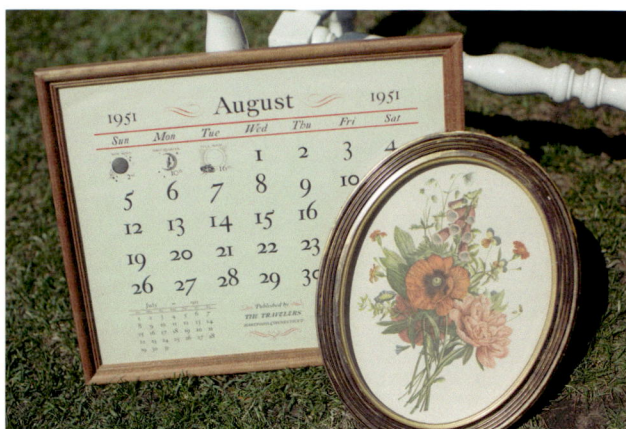

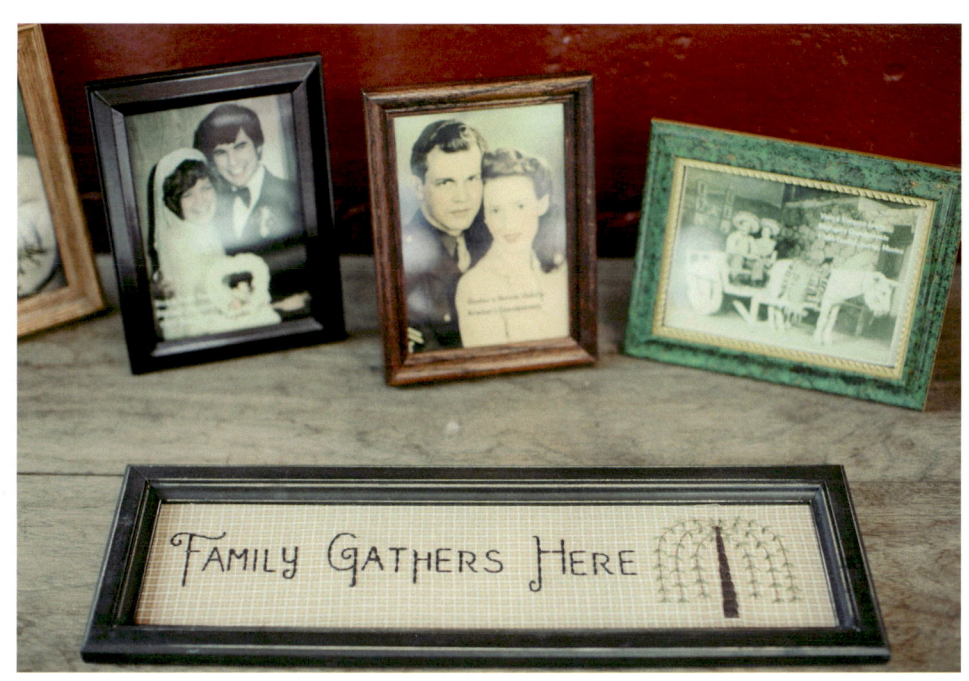

Faded photographs and family heirlooms are right at home at a rural wedding.

The All-Important Location

It's good to be practical, but if there was ever a time to follow your heart and not your head, getting married is definitely it! Choose somewhere that resonates with you; that you feel a connection with. It might be a place that's already dear to you or that holds a special significance. For Rin and Joe it was the familiarity of their own backyard that made it the only place they wanted to say "I do."

On the other hand, it could be somewhere completely random that for some reason you feel drawn towards or a location that, with a bit of attention, can be made special.

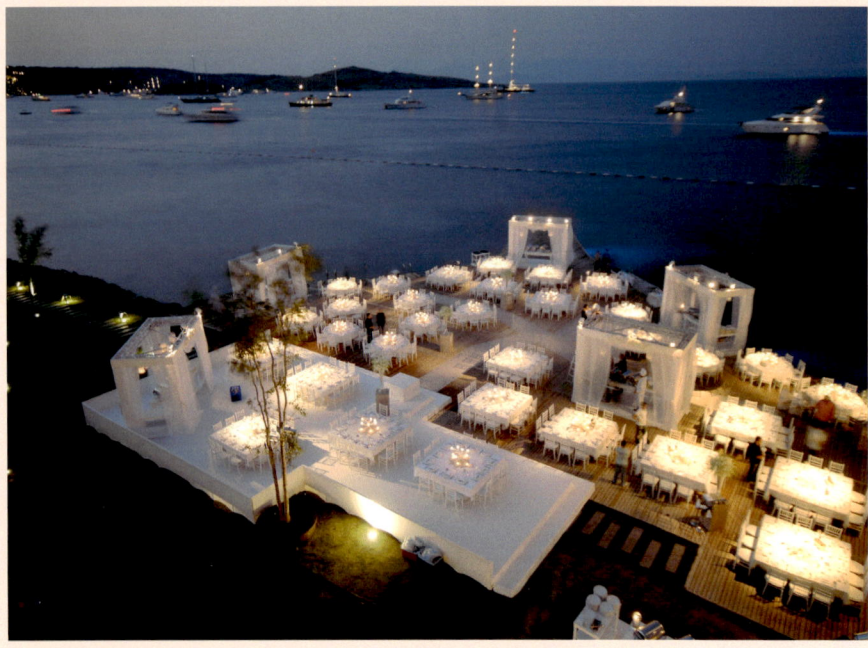

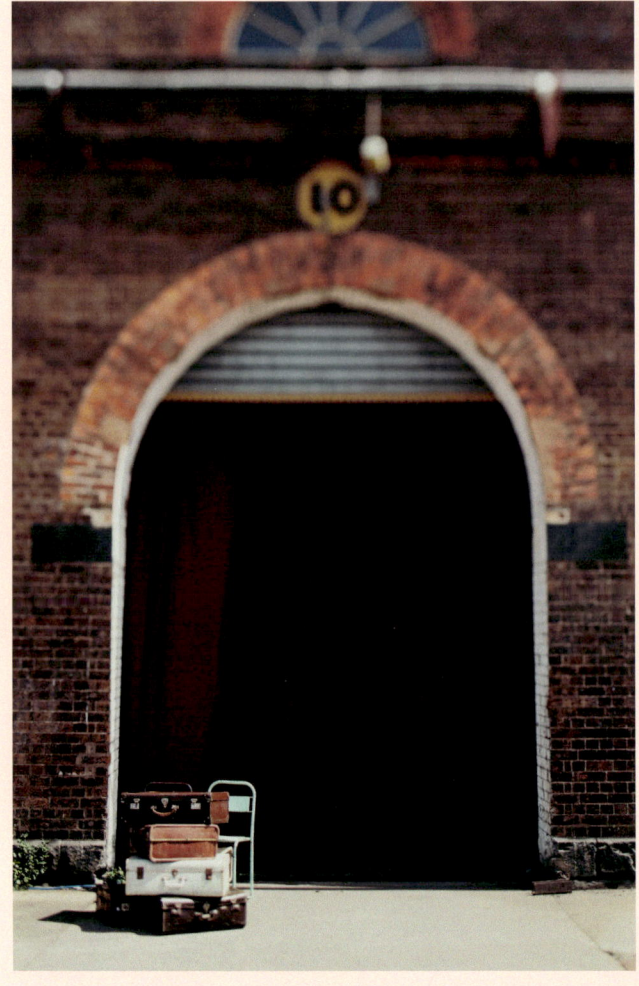

When deciding on your wedding venue, try and visualize how you would like your day to be and find a space that fits. For example, if you see your wedding as organic and natural, then maybe look at outdoor locations. If you want something very traditional, then start by researching places of worship or sites of historical beauty.

It's also helpful to keep in mind what it is about your potential location that means the most to you.

Think about what's at the top of your venue checklist: is it whether it fits with your theme? Or whether it's big enough to fit all of your guests? Does it need to be a multi-functional space that can house different areas? Or are you more excited about architectural aesthetics?

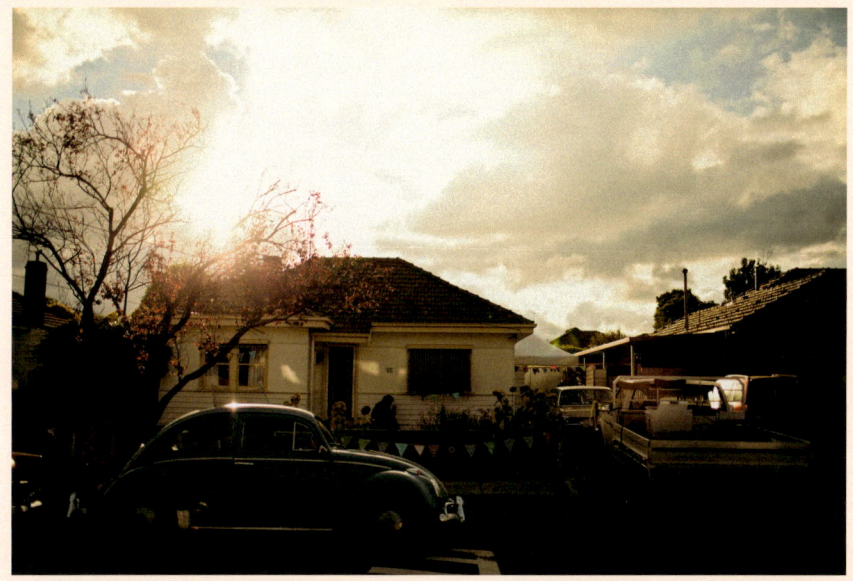

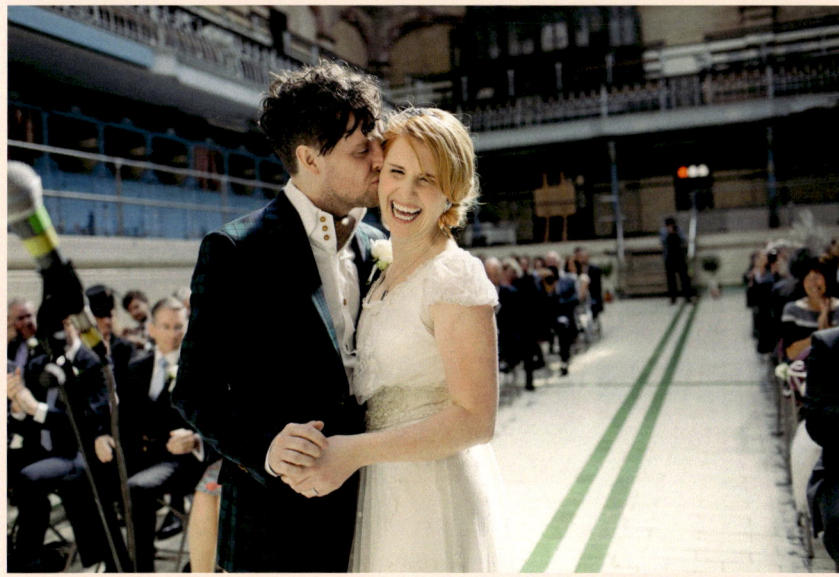

Fiona and Jonny fell in love with the quirky charm of an Edwardian swimming baths. They wanted a memorable location, so the deep end of an empty pool seemed the perfect place for them to take the plunge into married life.

Don't limit your venue options before you have even started looking. I believe it's best to not only look at the typical wedding venues, otherwise you risk discounting some incredible options.

The part of event design that I love the most is the alchemy of creating something that wasn't there before. You can transform even the most unassuming location into the perfect setting for your wedding with some

Your location should be practical yet personal:

1. The backdrop of an industrial venue can be an amazing contrast to the soft romance of a wedding. Old shipyards, airport hangars, and docks are beautiful.

2. The space of a Victorian warehouse has the right balance between a blank canvas and character.

3. If the call of the wild is drawing you outdoors, look for sites of natural beauty and spectacular views. Woodland, deserts, mountain tops, and glaciers all have potential.

4. Think about your passions. Are you both film buffs? Consider art deco cinemas or locations from your favorite movies.

5. If you are looking for somewhere nearby, what could be closer and more personal than your own backyard or that of your family?

Things to consider when celebrating outside:

1. Always have a rain contingency plan. No matter what the weatherman says!

2. Ensure your decorations can stand up to the wind. Paper and tea lights will fall in a big gust of wind.

3. Avoid your guests becoming parched under warm sunlight and provide shaded areas. Shelter from the sun is just as important as shelter from the rain. Equally, have blankets on hand and light fires to provide warmth on a much cooler evening.

4. Bugs and flies are the most irritating gatecrashers. Light repelling scented candles or have a discreet bug-zapper to keep flies at bay.

5. Roaring waves or rushing winds can drown out intimate ceremony moments. Trees, foliage, or even blinding sunlight can all block the view, too.

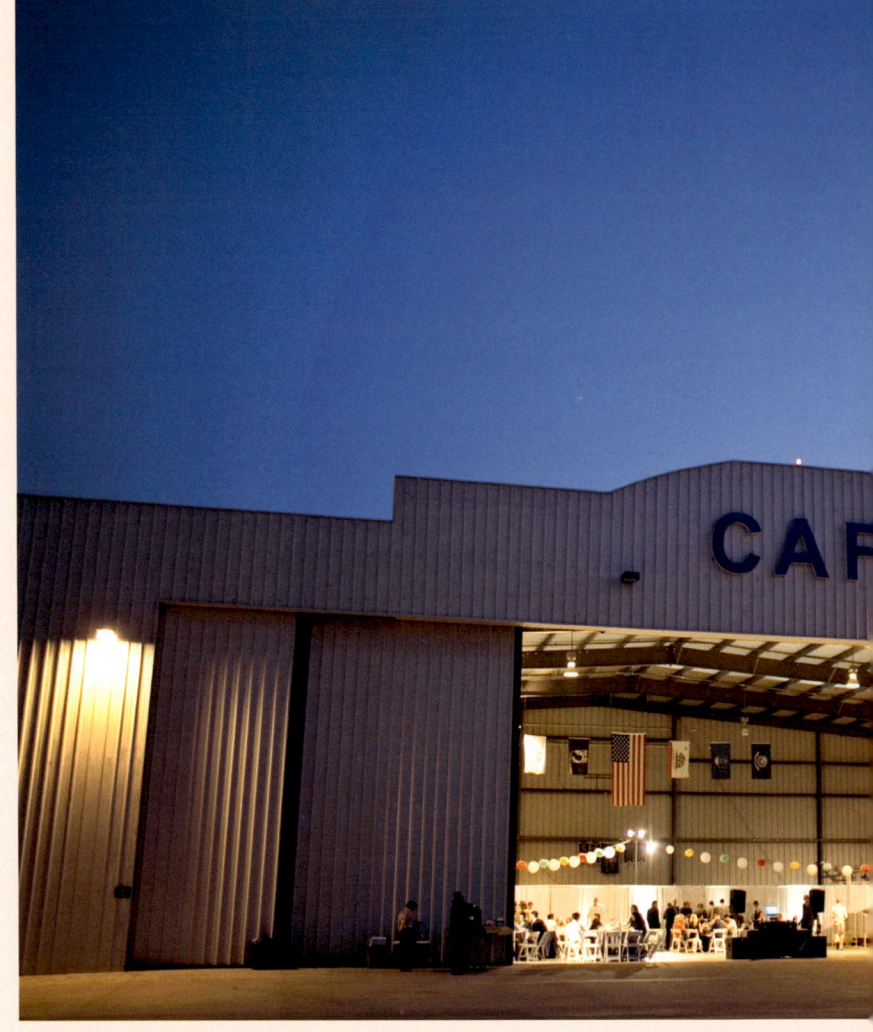

clever planning and imagination. Who would have thought that an airplane hangar could be turned into a beautiful and elegant wedding venue?

Kelly and Curtis saw the potential and did just that. An unusual location can even inspire the rest of your wedding design with fantastic results. As you will see, the fun aerial twist that Kelly and Curtis put on their wedding helped to make it a unique and unforgettable celebration.

Once you have nailed down your venue, embrace your space. Even if your location isn't quite what you had in mind, work with what you've got and make the most of whatever your space has to offer.

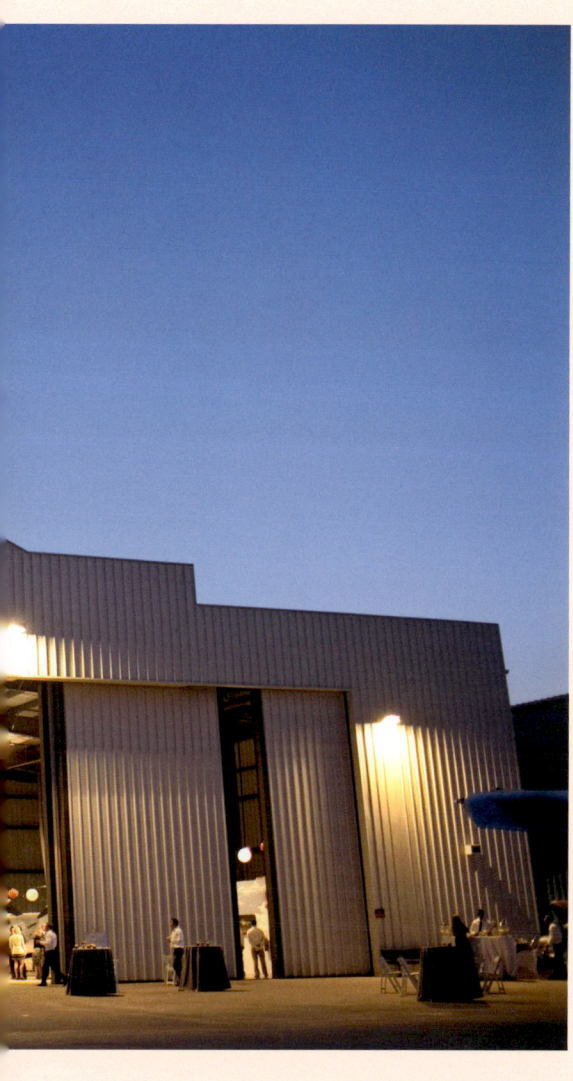

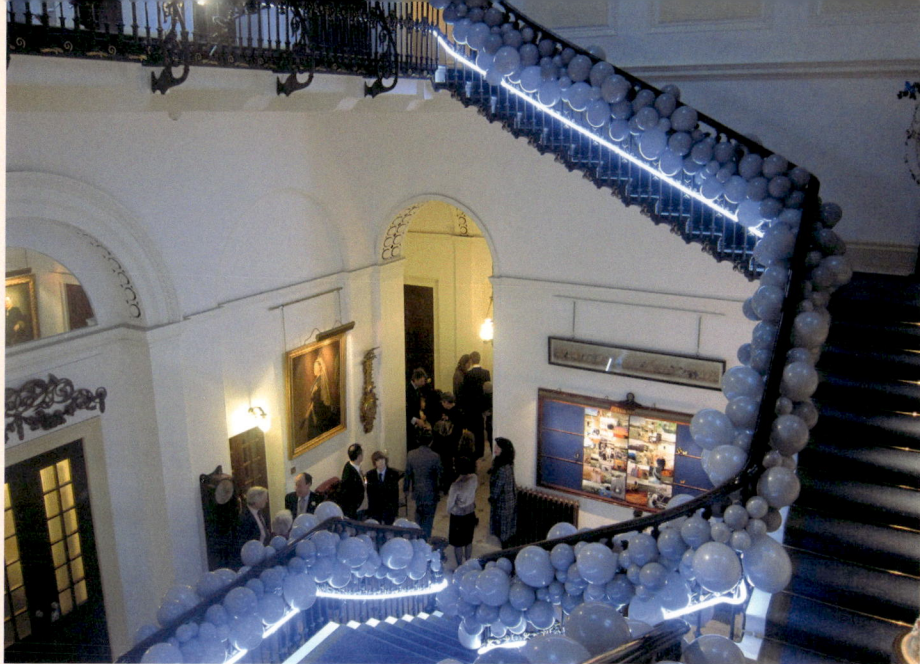

Try to play on your location's best features. If it has fabulous high ceilings, highlight them by taking the decorations skyward. It doesn't have to take much, it could even be as simple as arranging the seats at your ceremony so that you get married against the backdrop of a beautiful view.

Pick an area and really emphasize it: whether it's a grand staircase you adorn with balloons or a beautiful tree you fill with lanterns. Bring to the forefront the assets unique to your location that you want your guests to notice and appreciate.

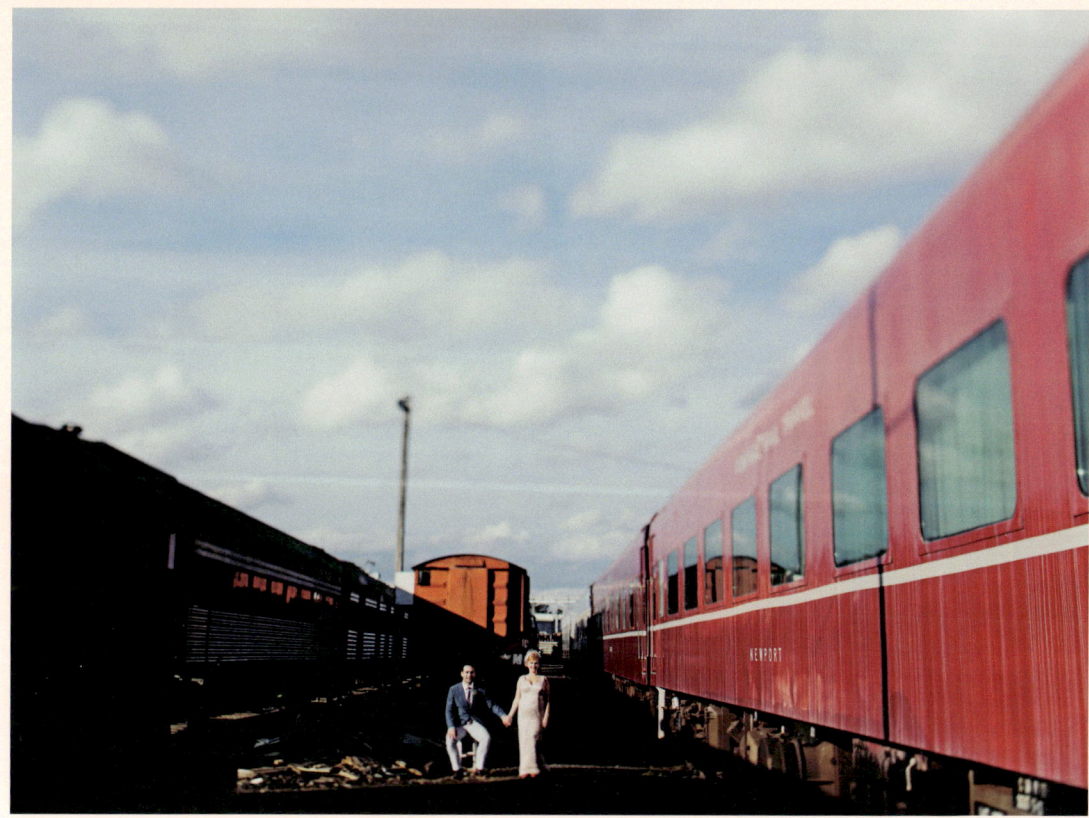

From an underground cavern to an abandoned theme park in North Carolina, throughout this book you will find some of the most inspiring locations from across the world. The couples featured in these pages have managed to transform even the most unlikely spots into stylish backdrops for their celebrations.

It goes to show that the right location can do wonders, from elevating a theme to driving an entire event. Find your perfect place and the rest will follow.

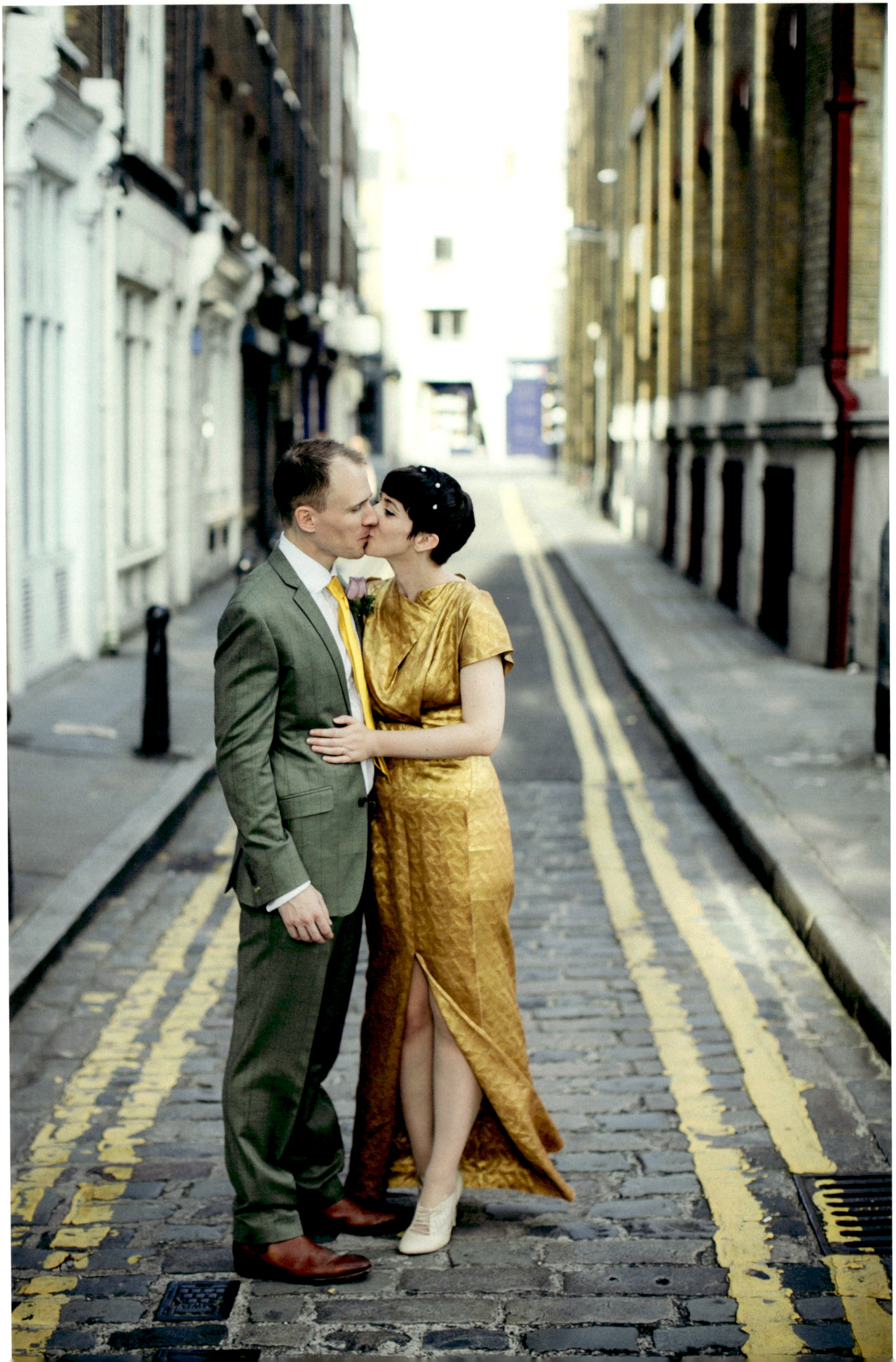

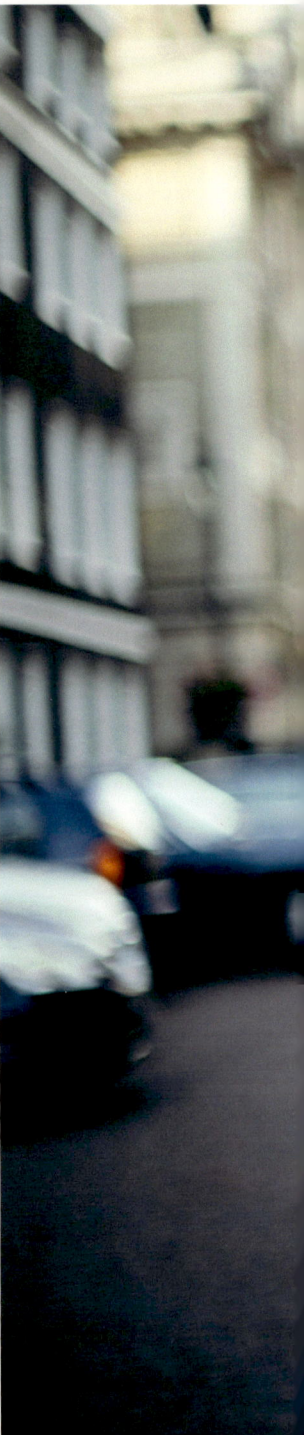

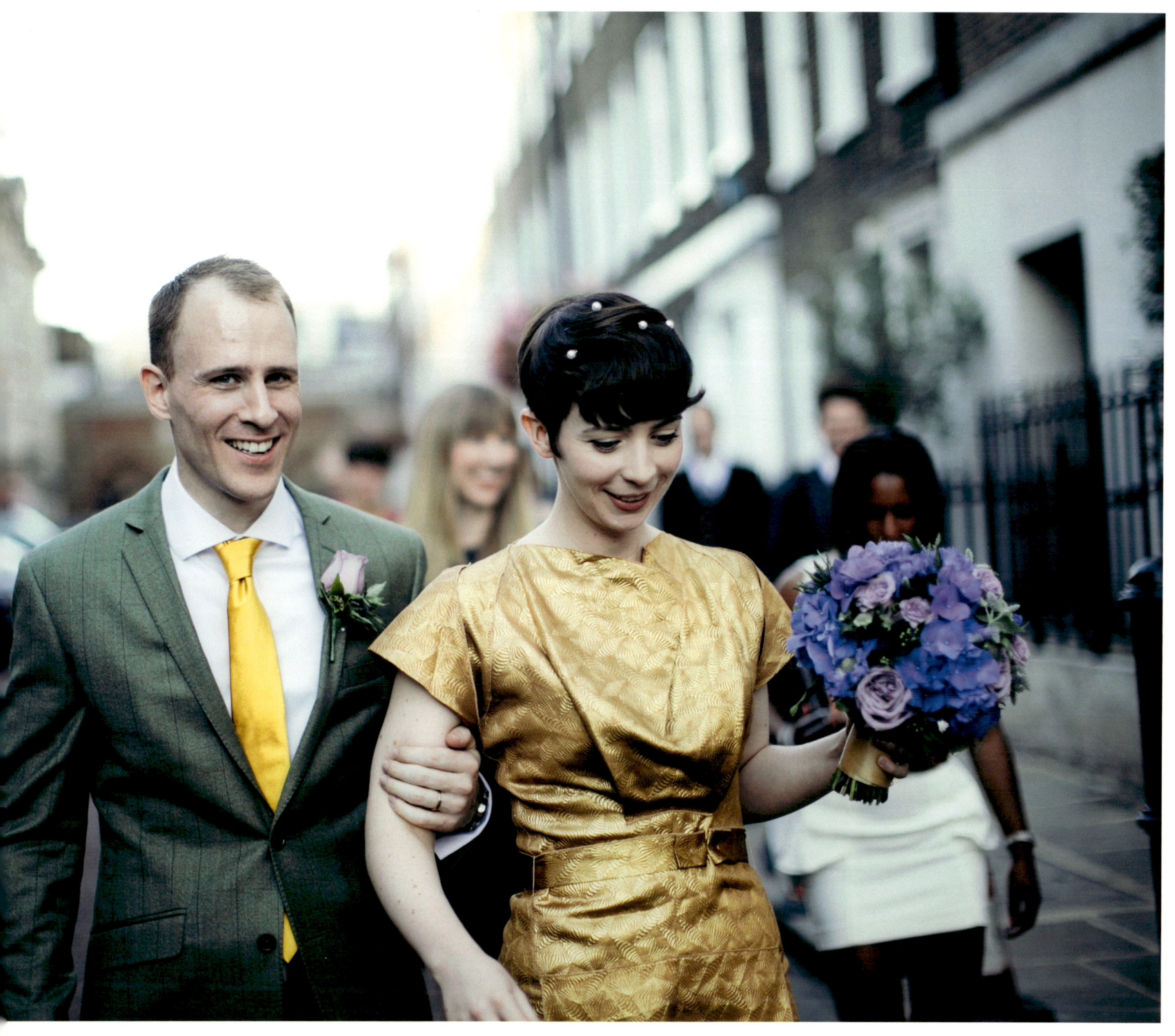

Anna & Paul

Anna and Paul's wedding began in the U.K. The ceremony was held in the most iconic of London boroughs: Camden. The Big Smoke can go from townhouses and cobbled streets to gritty slabs of urban realism in an instant, but this is the city where Anna and Paul met and they love every part of it. Her gold dress and his bespoke tweed suit bucked the usual trends—only natural for a wedding in one of the fashion capitals of the world. As night fell, the festivities crossed the Atlantic (in spirit, at least) to a retro ten-pin bowling alley.

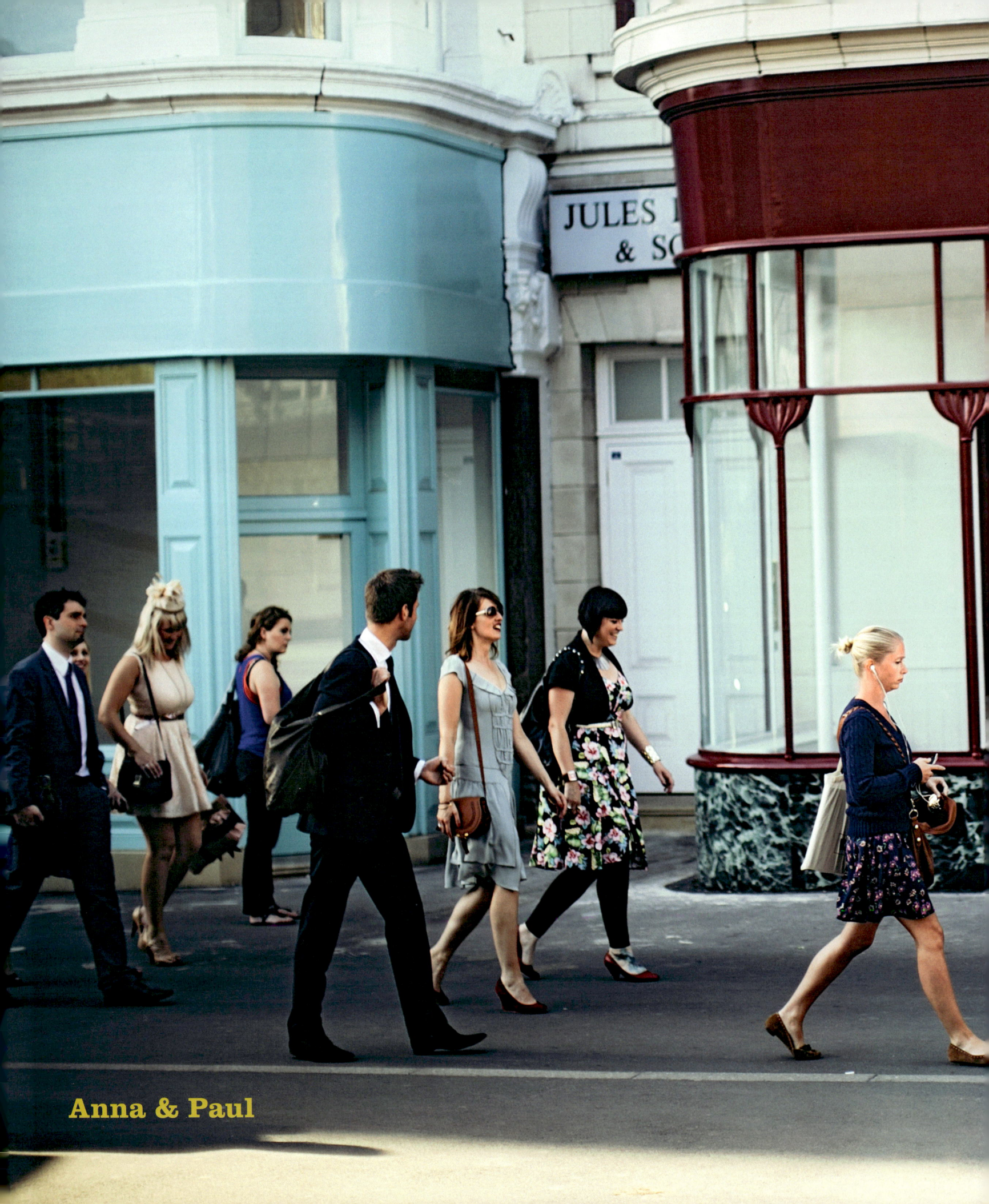

Anna & Paul

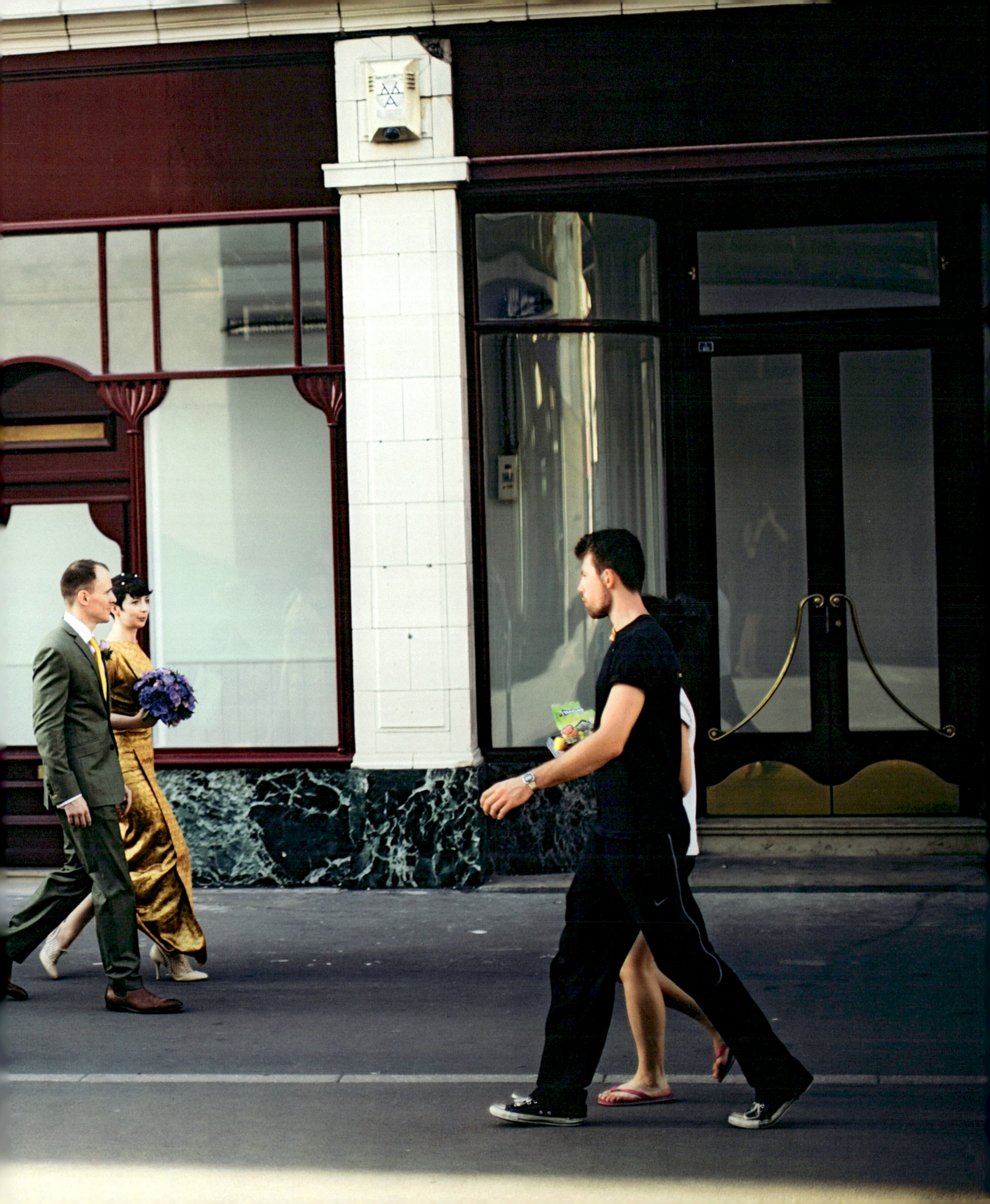

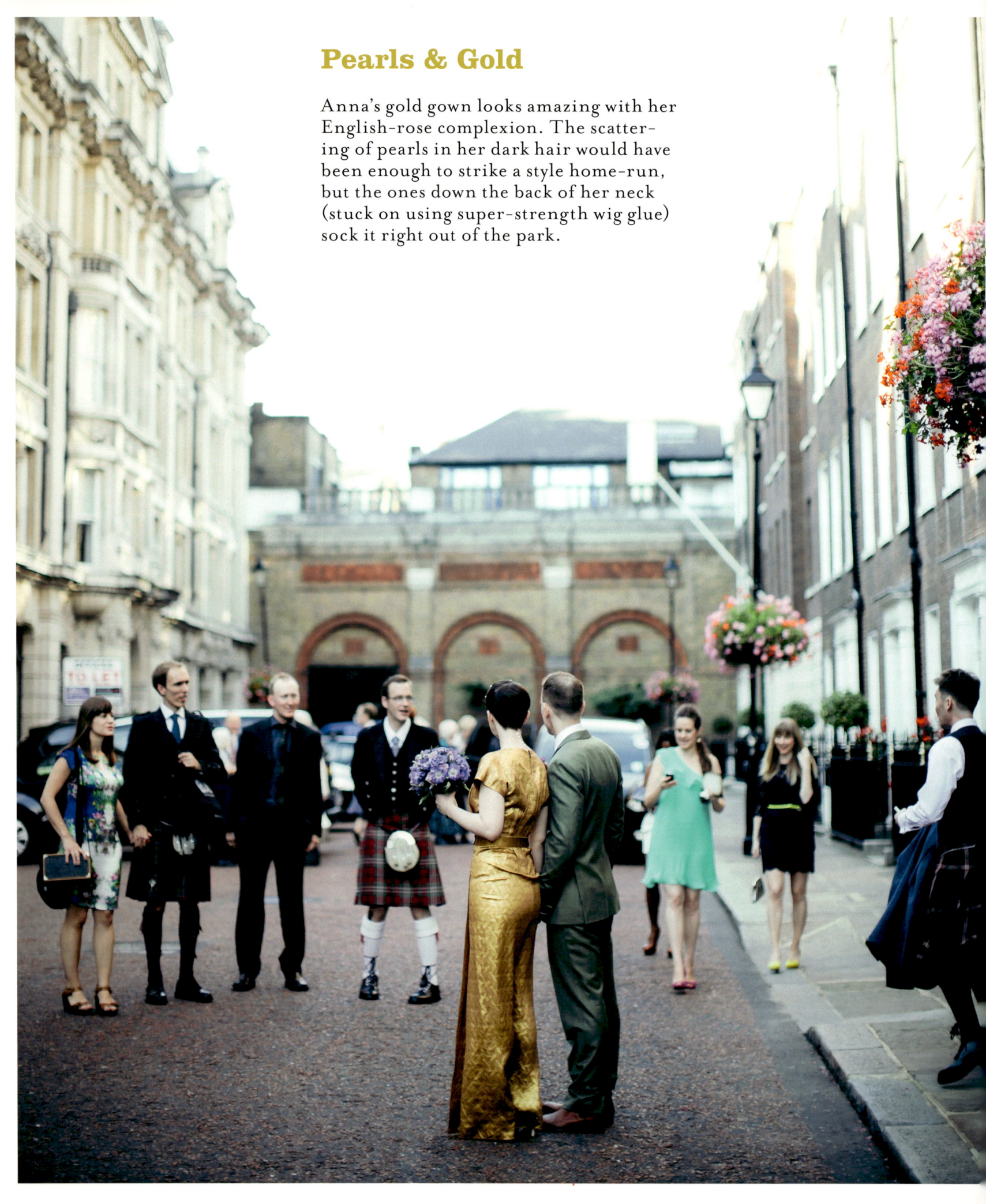

Pearls & Gold

Anna's gold gown looks amazing with her English-rose complexion. The scattering of pearls in her dark hair would have been enough to strike a style home-run, but the ones down the back of her neck (stuck on using super-strength wig glue) sock it right out of the park.

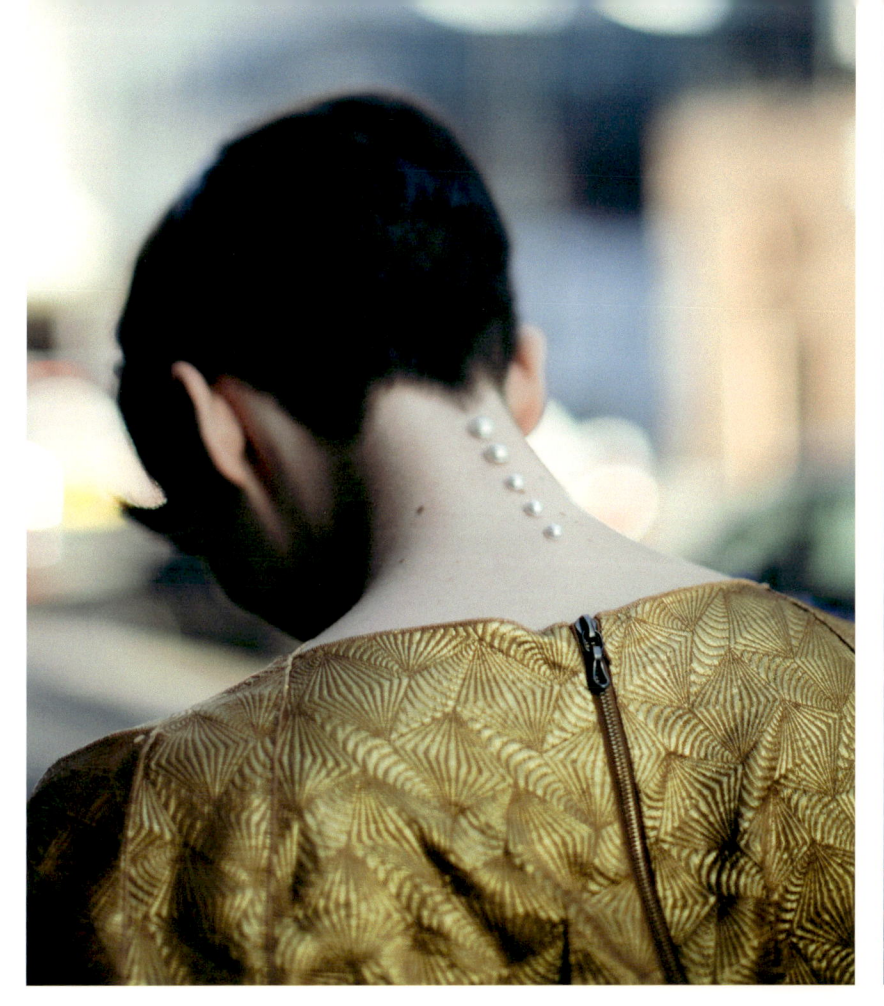
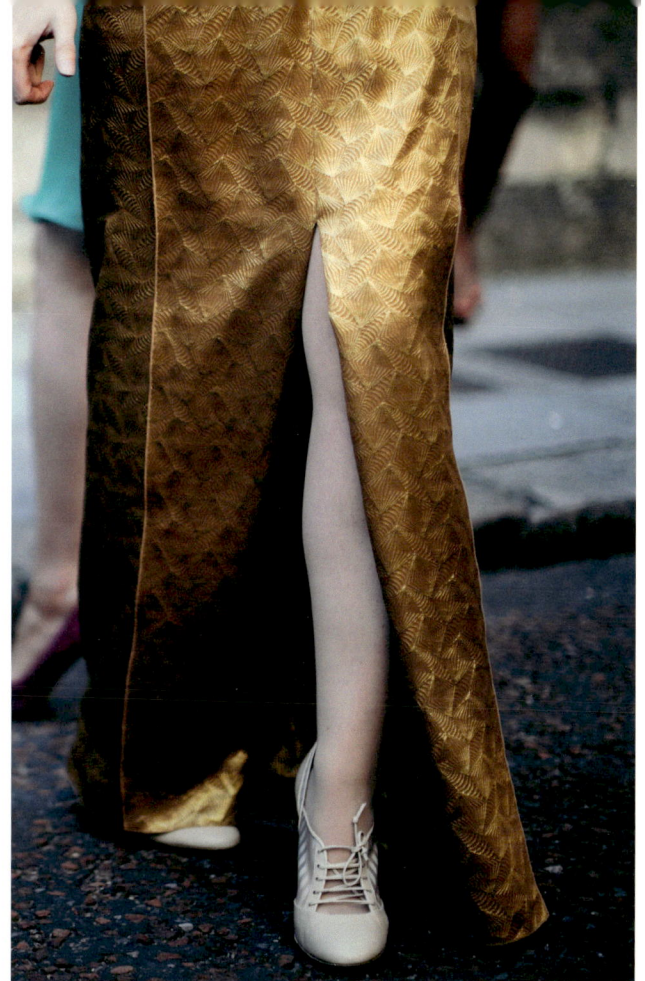

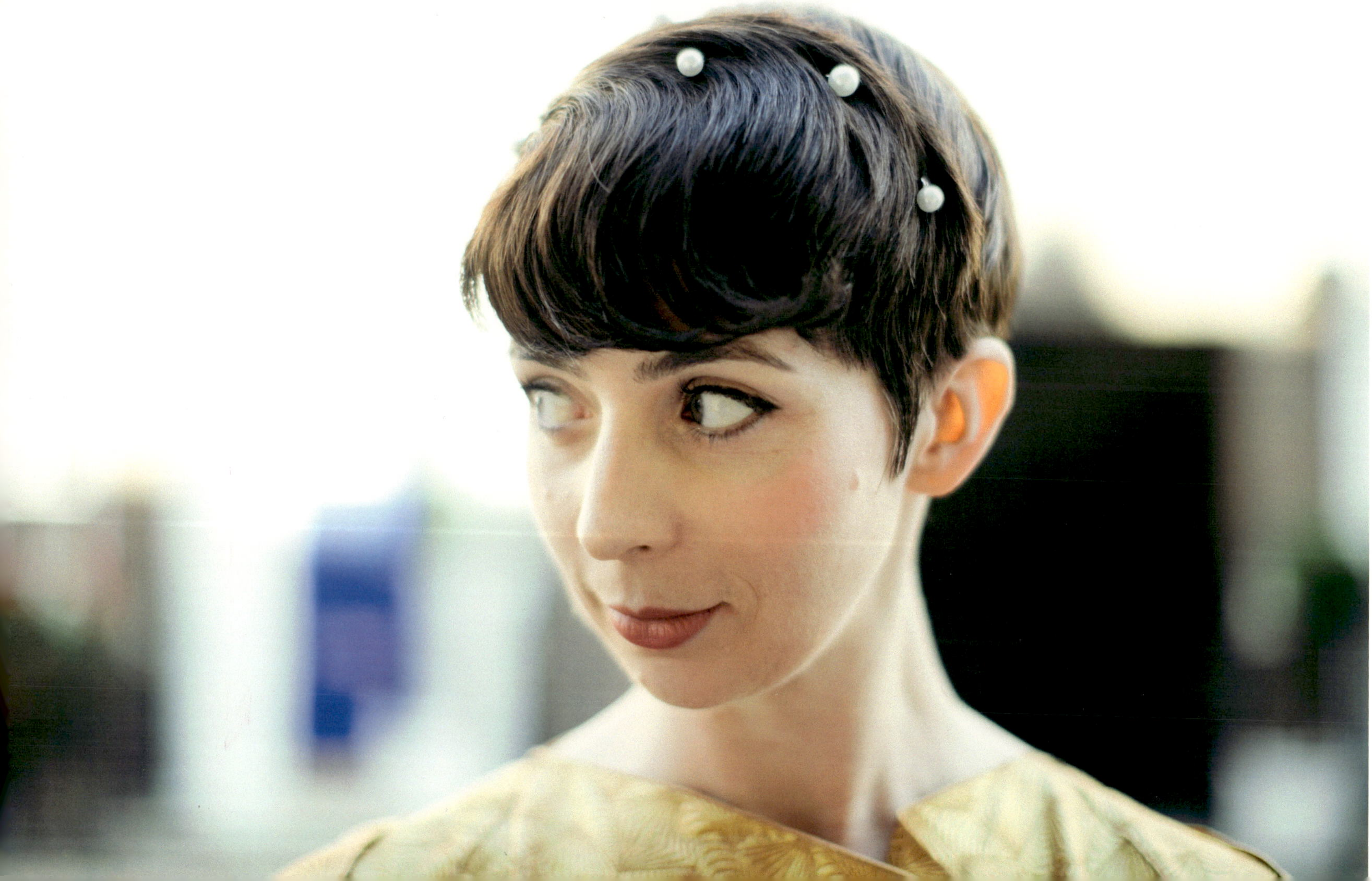

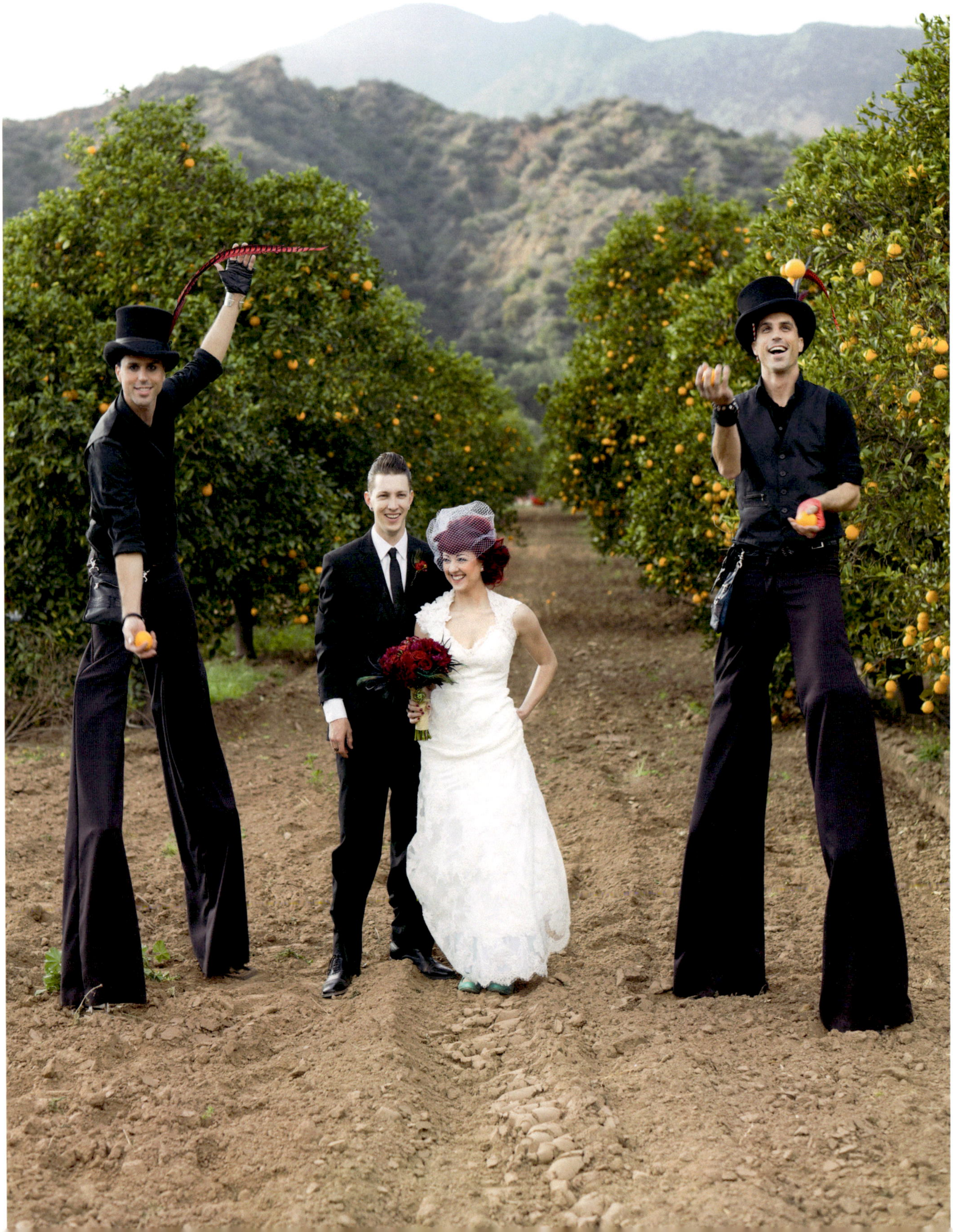

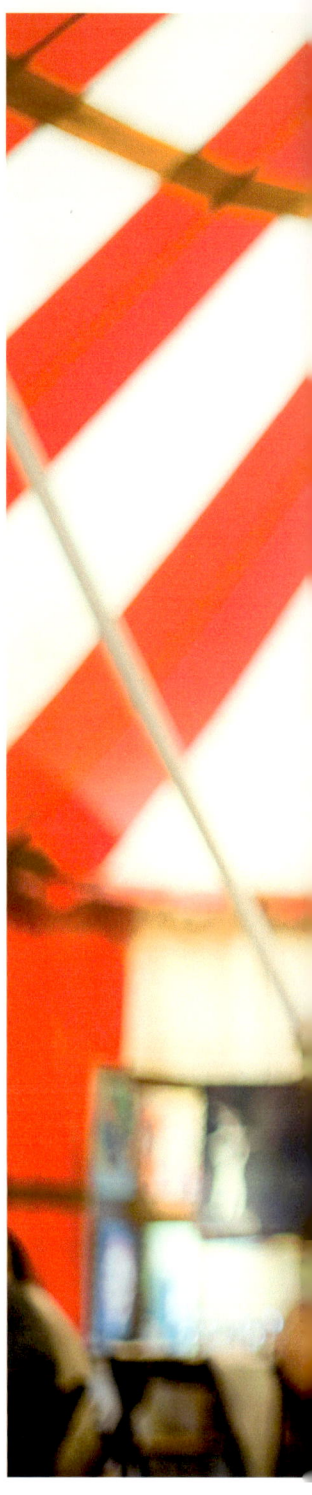

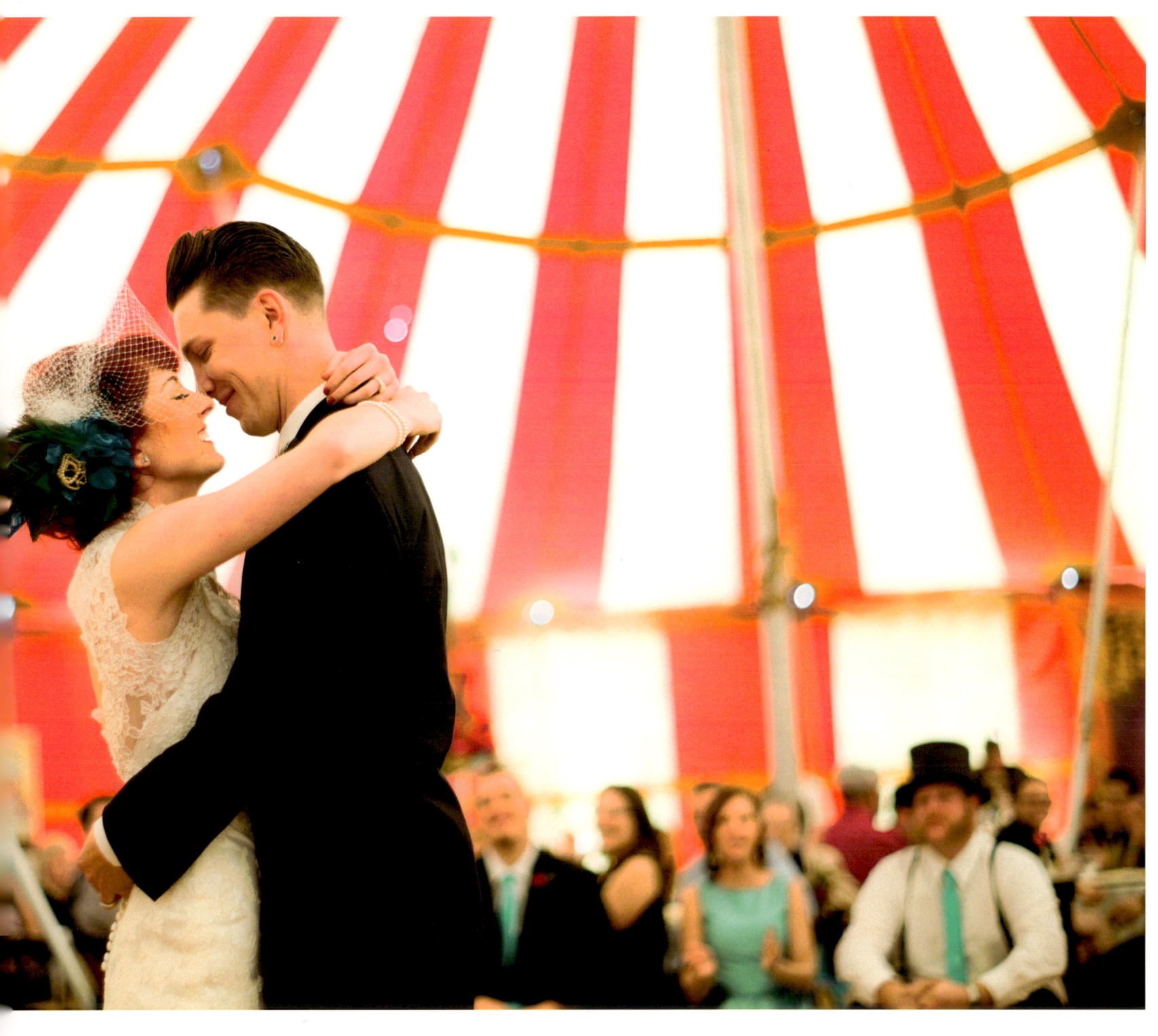

Stacy & Josh

Jugglers, fire breathers, and stilt walkers are not your average wedding-day entertainment. That suited Stacy and Josh just fine, because the last thing they wanted was average. Being massive fans of 1940s circus culture, they decided to hold their big day in a big top. Stacy's lace dress and netting veil were forties through and through, and her green Mary Janes matched the peacock feathers in her hair. Leaning against a rusty vintage car, Josh looked every inch the star performer in his sleek black suit and quiffed hair.

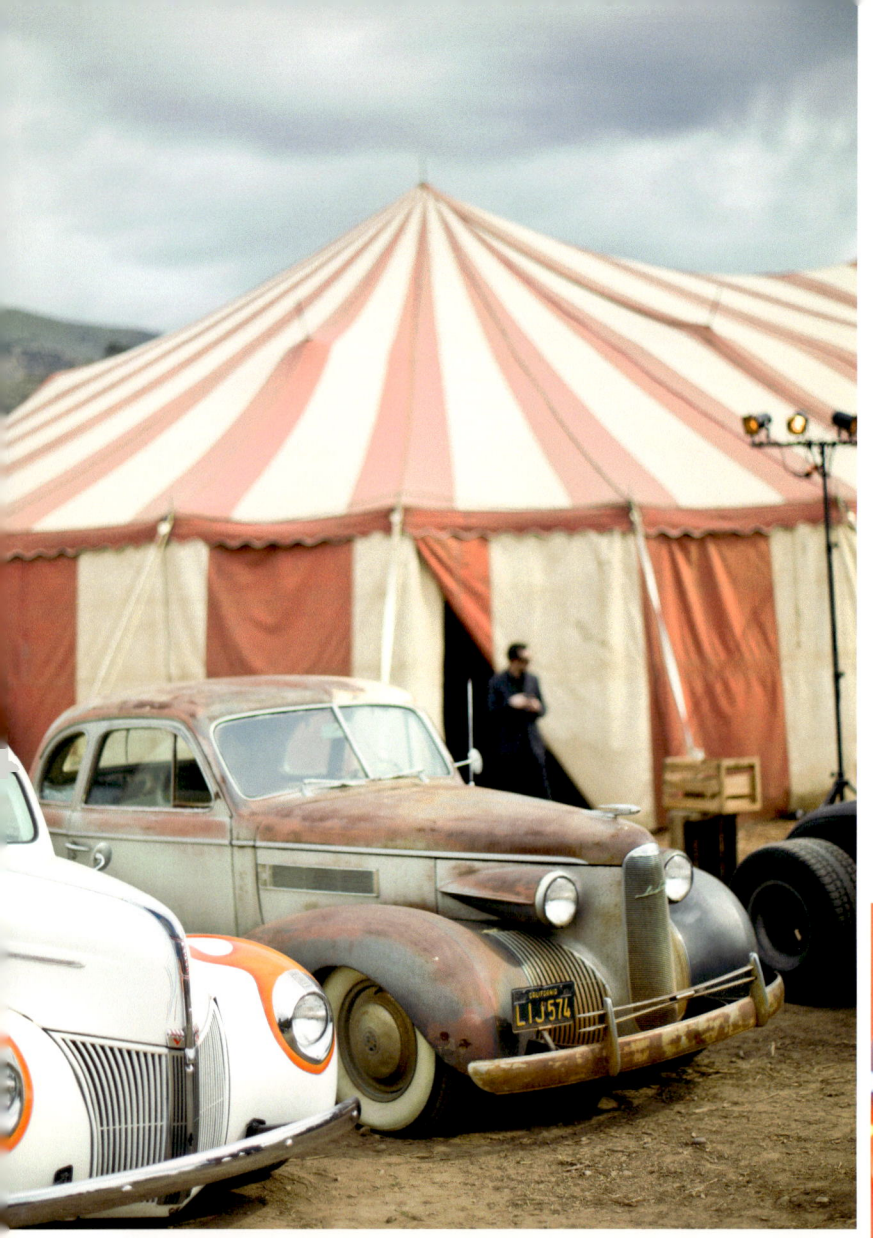

Roll Up, Roll Up!

Like a marquee, but different…
Stacy and Josh's venue gave them
loads of space, and the sun shining
through the red and white stripes
made the roof look incredible.

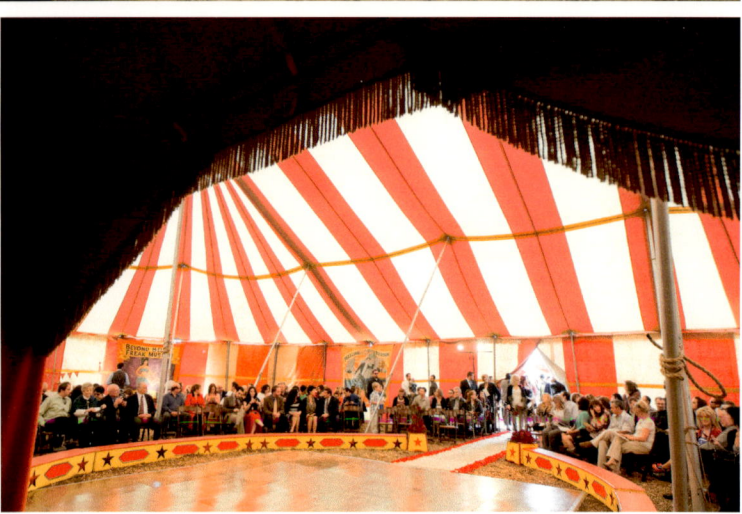

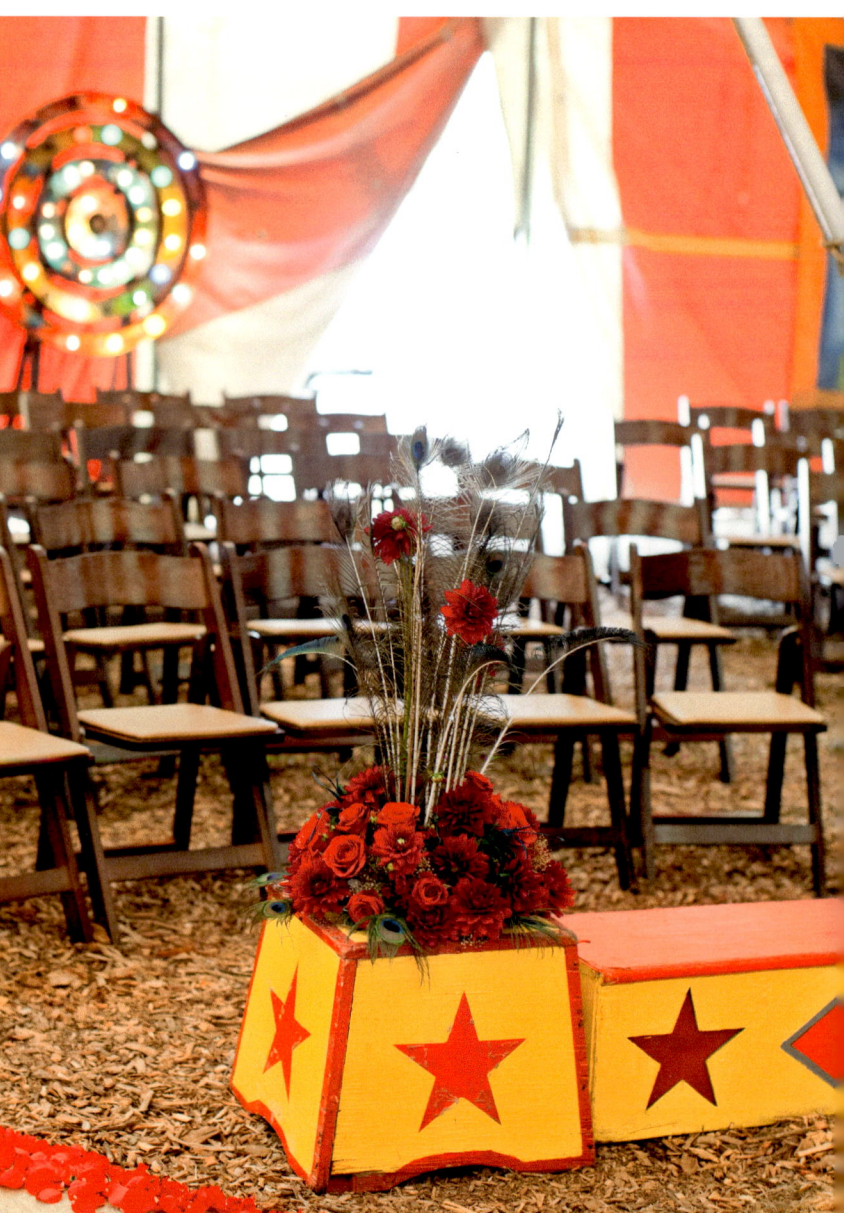

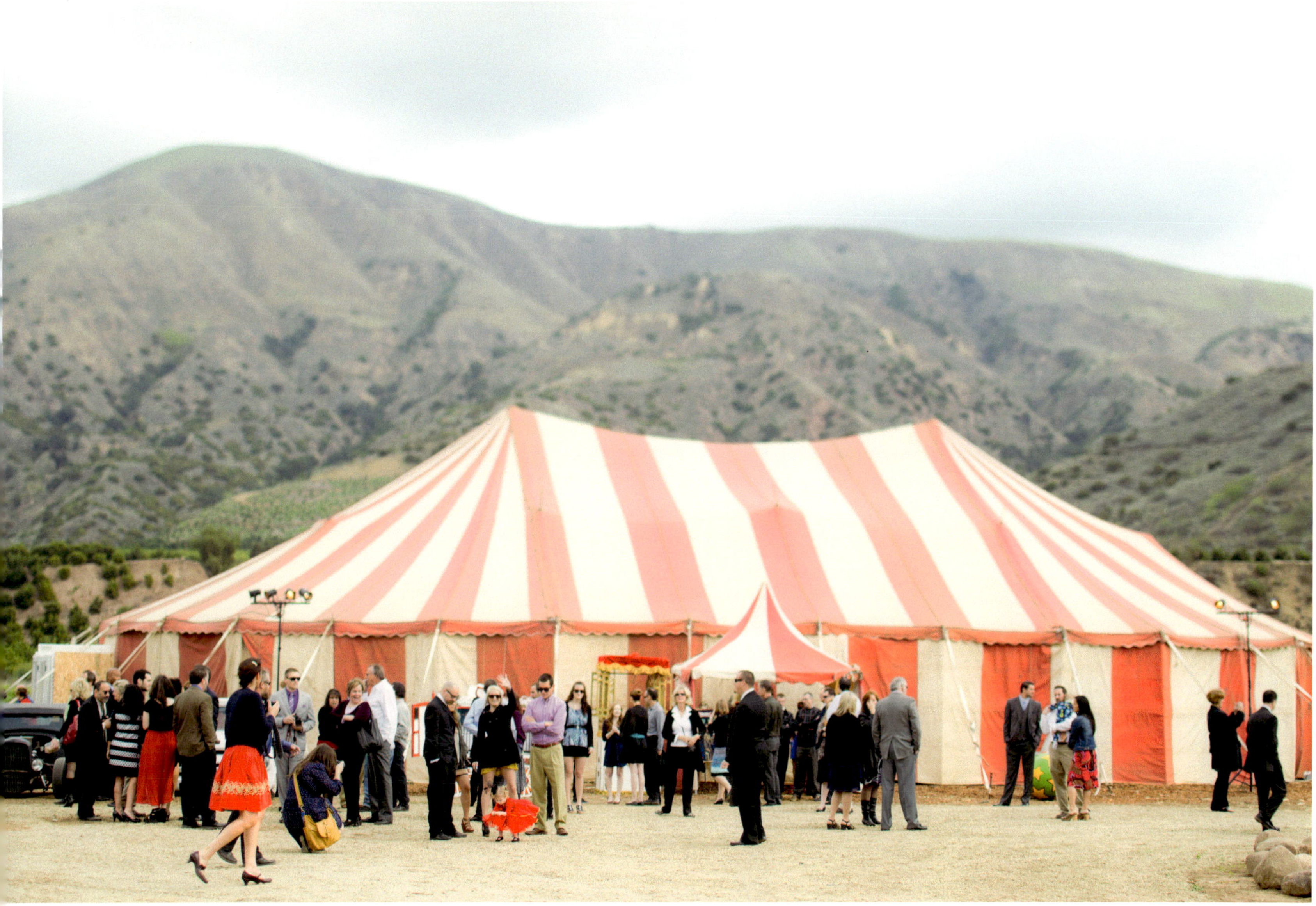

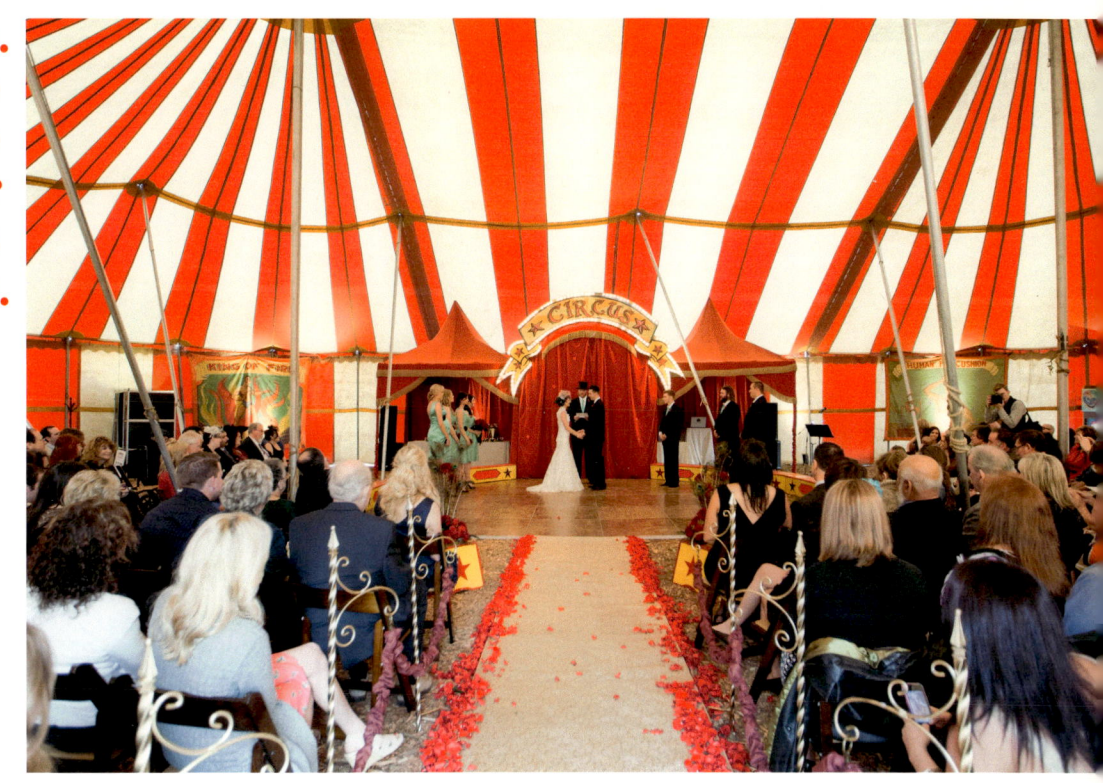

A circus tent. Who would have thought? The possibilities for wedding venues are endless.

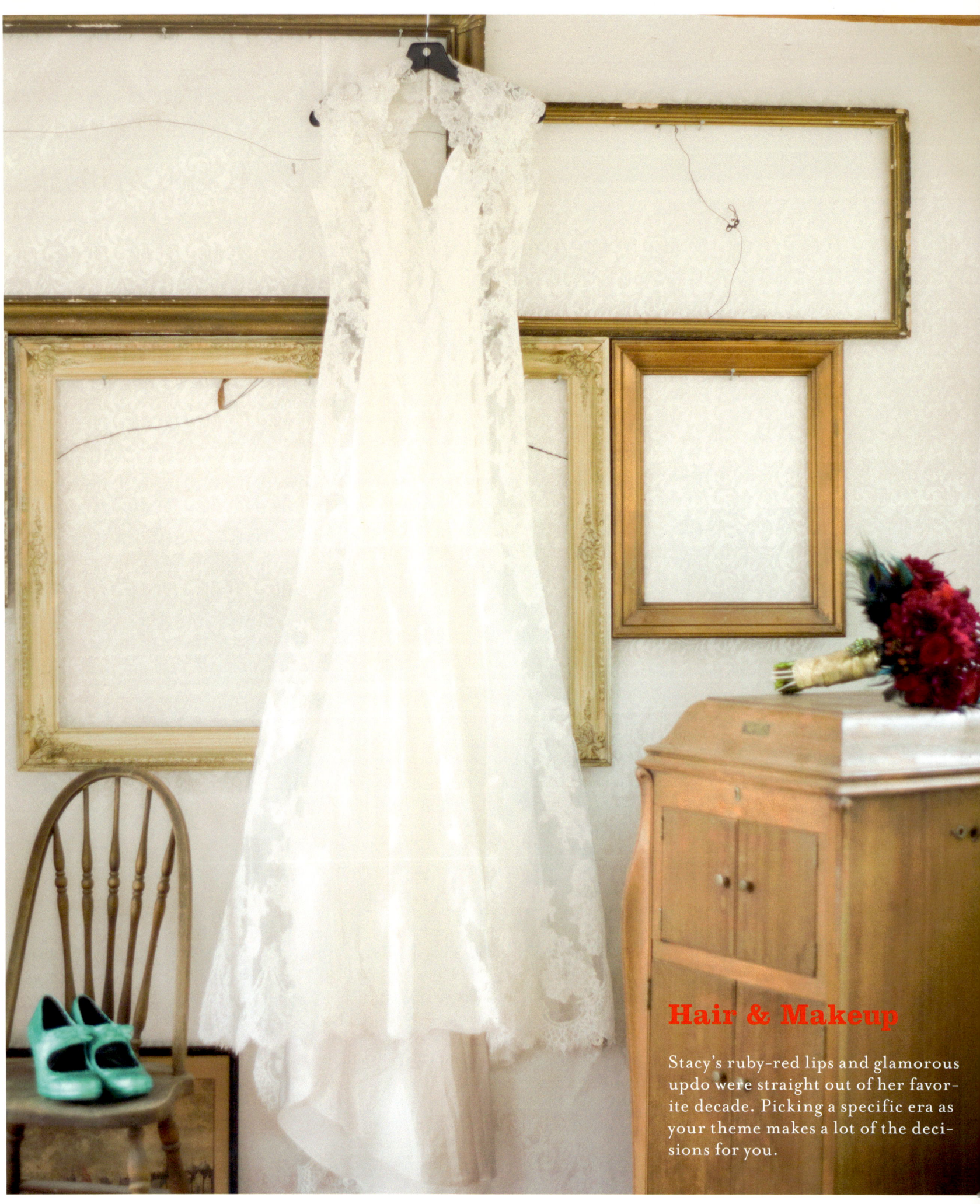

Hair & Makeup

Stacy's ruby-red lips and glamorous updo were straight out of her favorite decade. Picking a specific era as your theme makes a lot of the decisions for you.

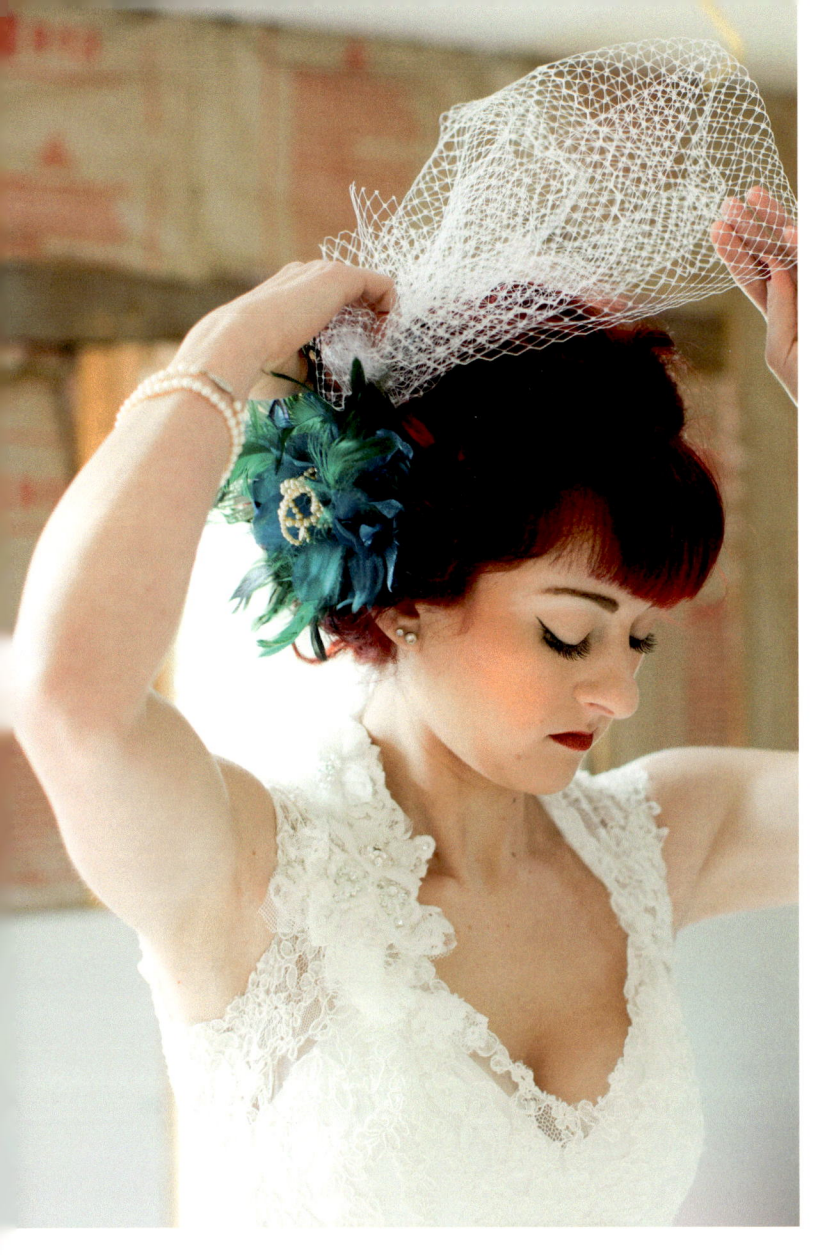
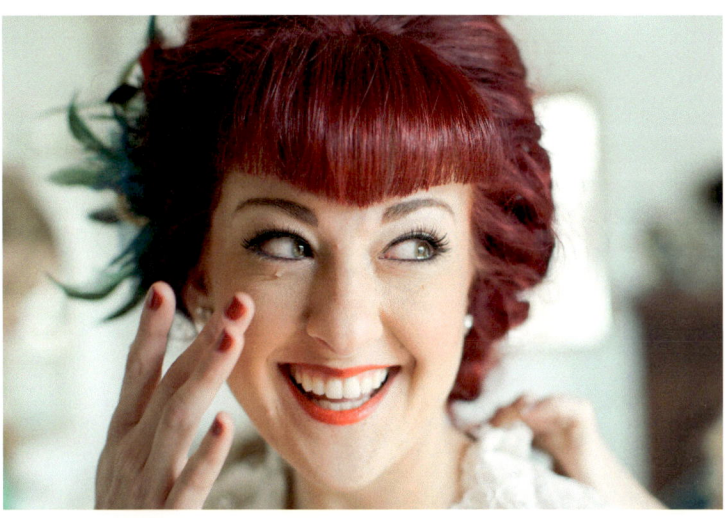
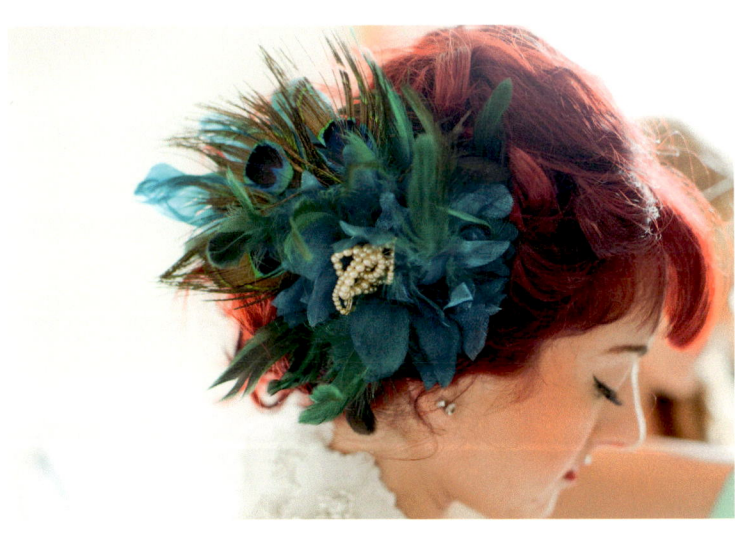
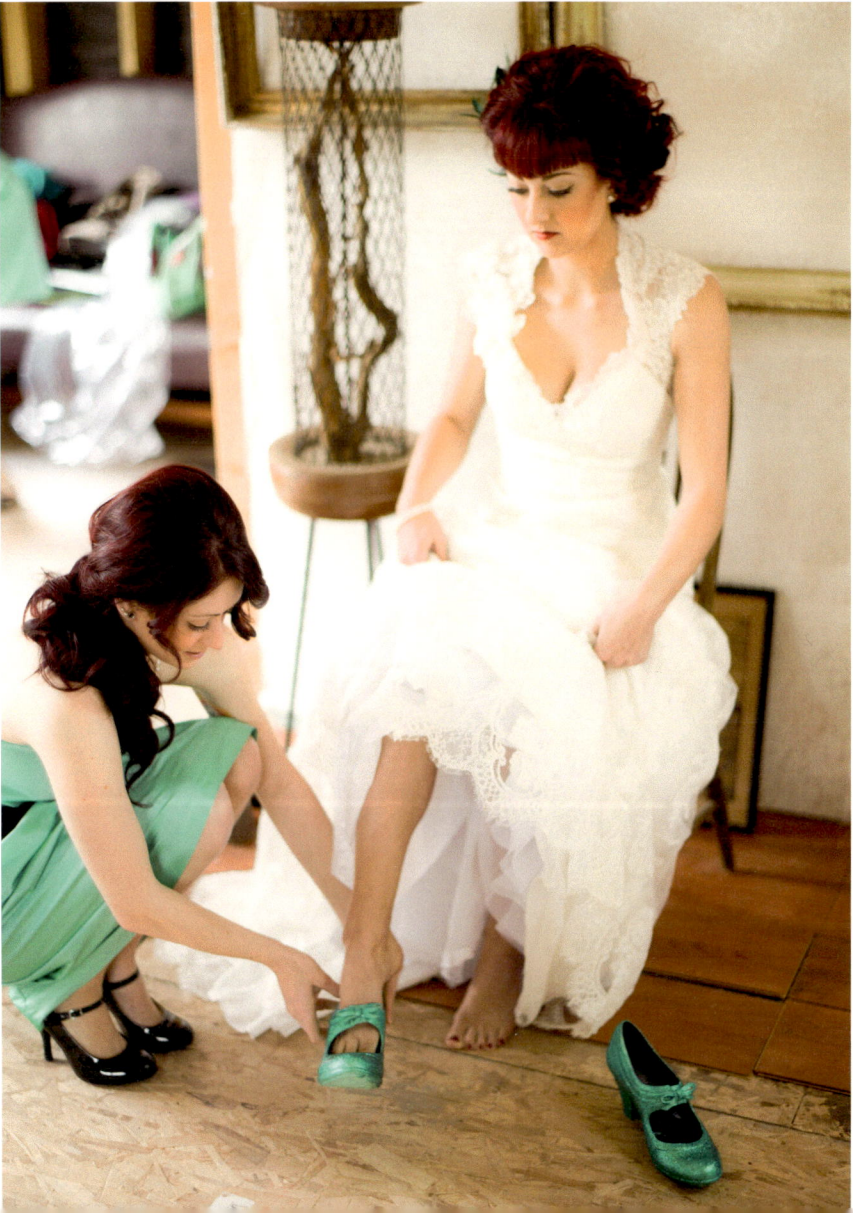

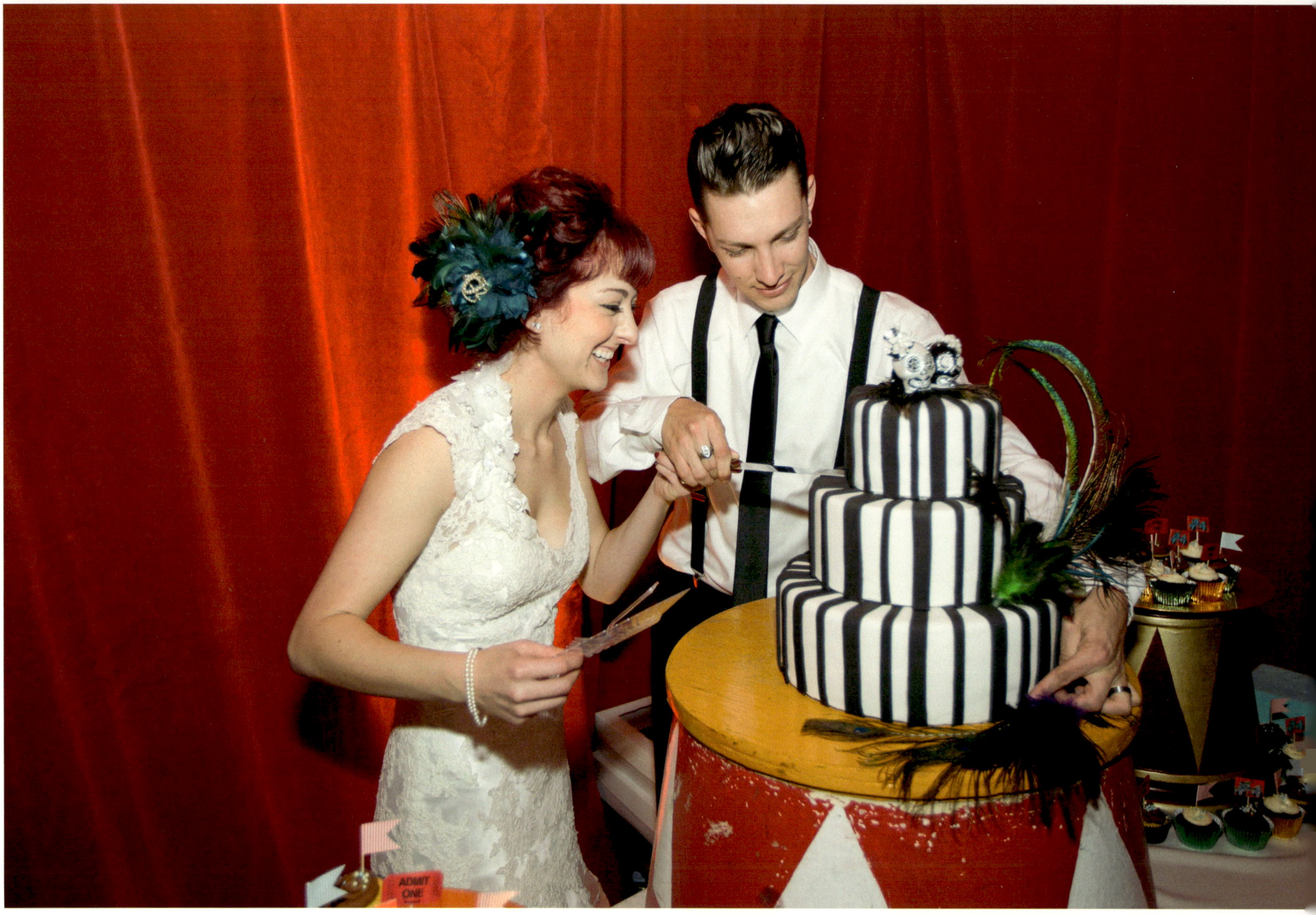

Fun Food

It's amazing how the smallest touches can tie a whole wedding up into one fabulous package. The stripes on the cake matched Josh's outfit, and the peacock feathers on the edge matched Stacy's hairpiece. The cupcakes did their bit for the circus too, with razzle-dazzle cases and admission-ticket toppers.

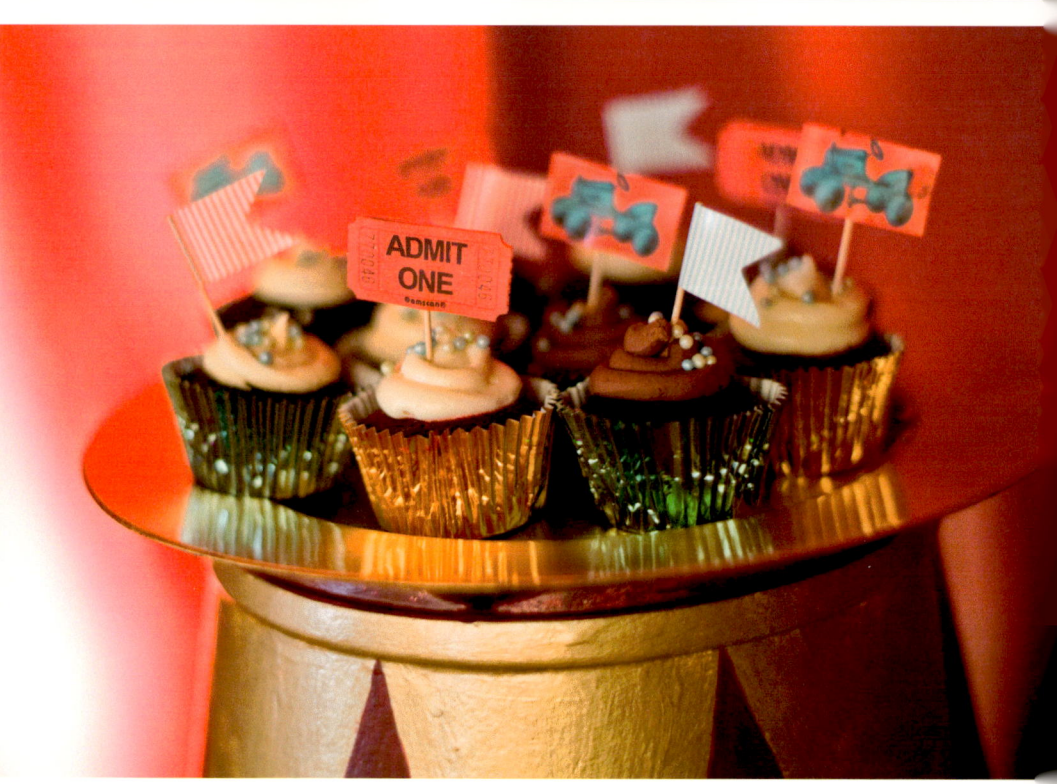

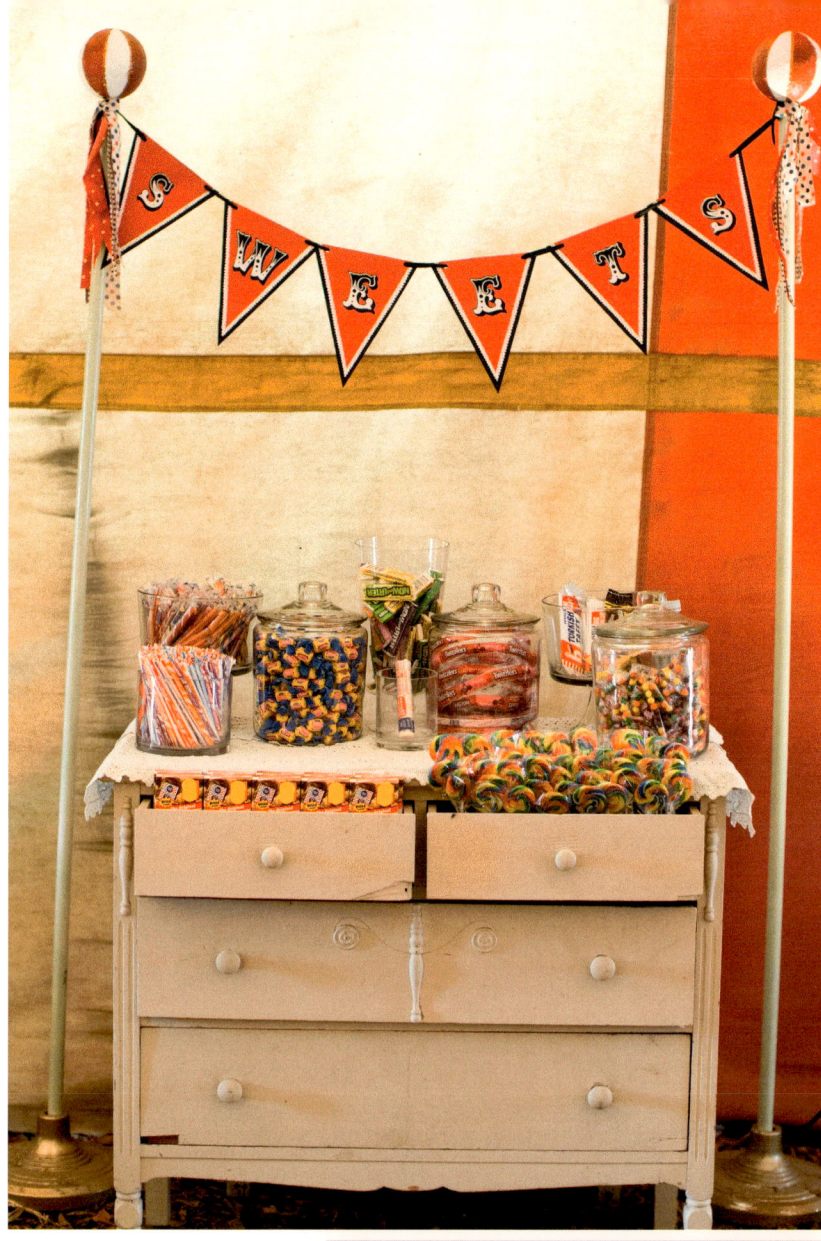

1. No visit to the circus is complete without a sugar high.

2. Park a popcorn machine at your wedding and put a smile on everyone's face.

3. Remember to leave room for dinner!

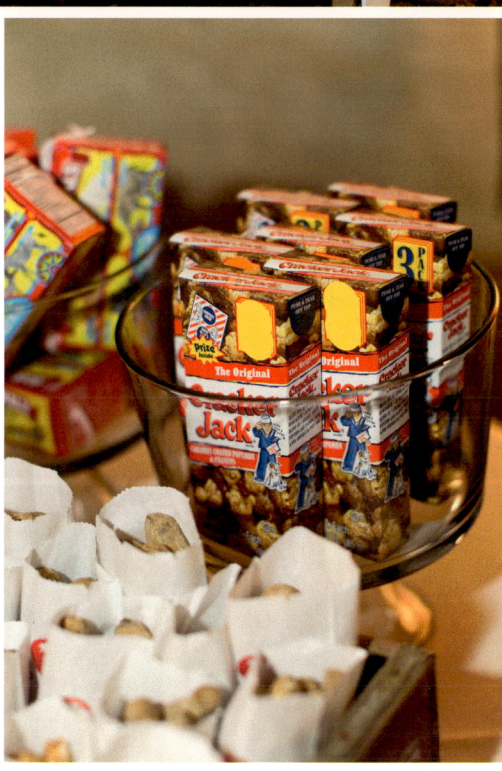

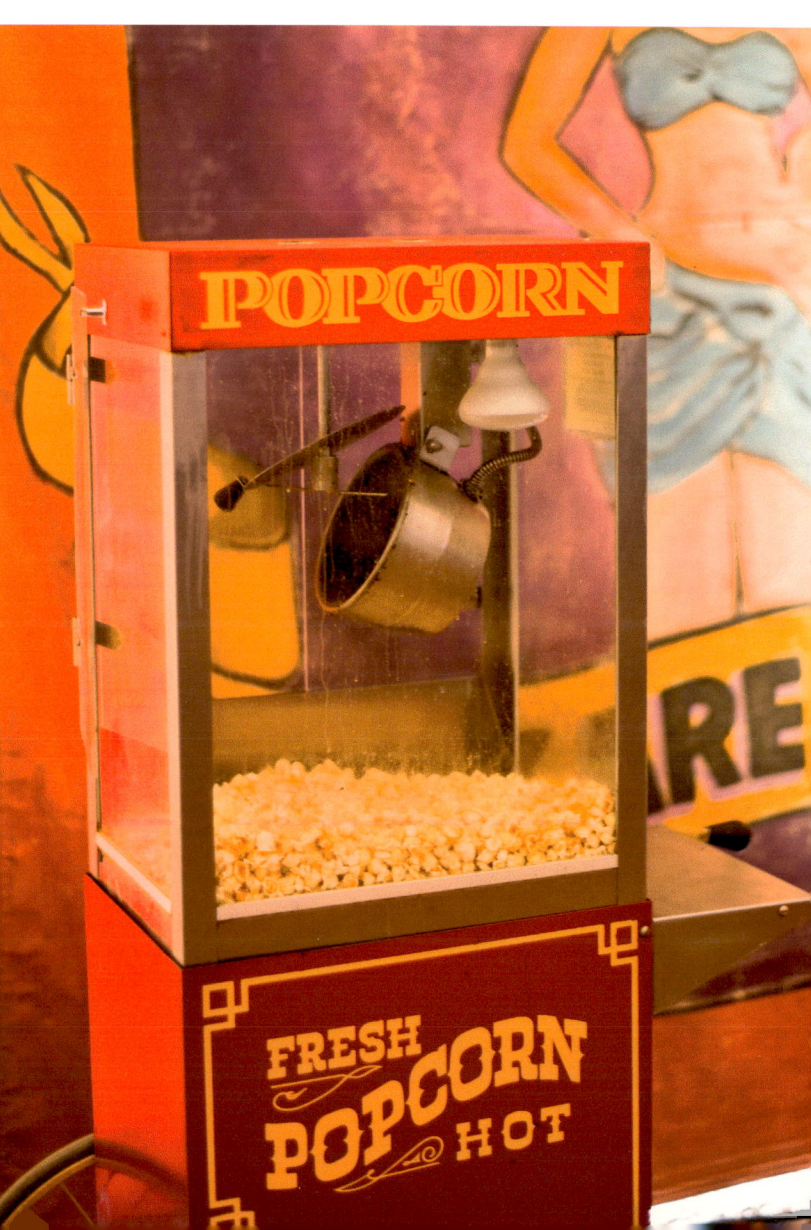

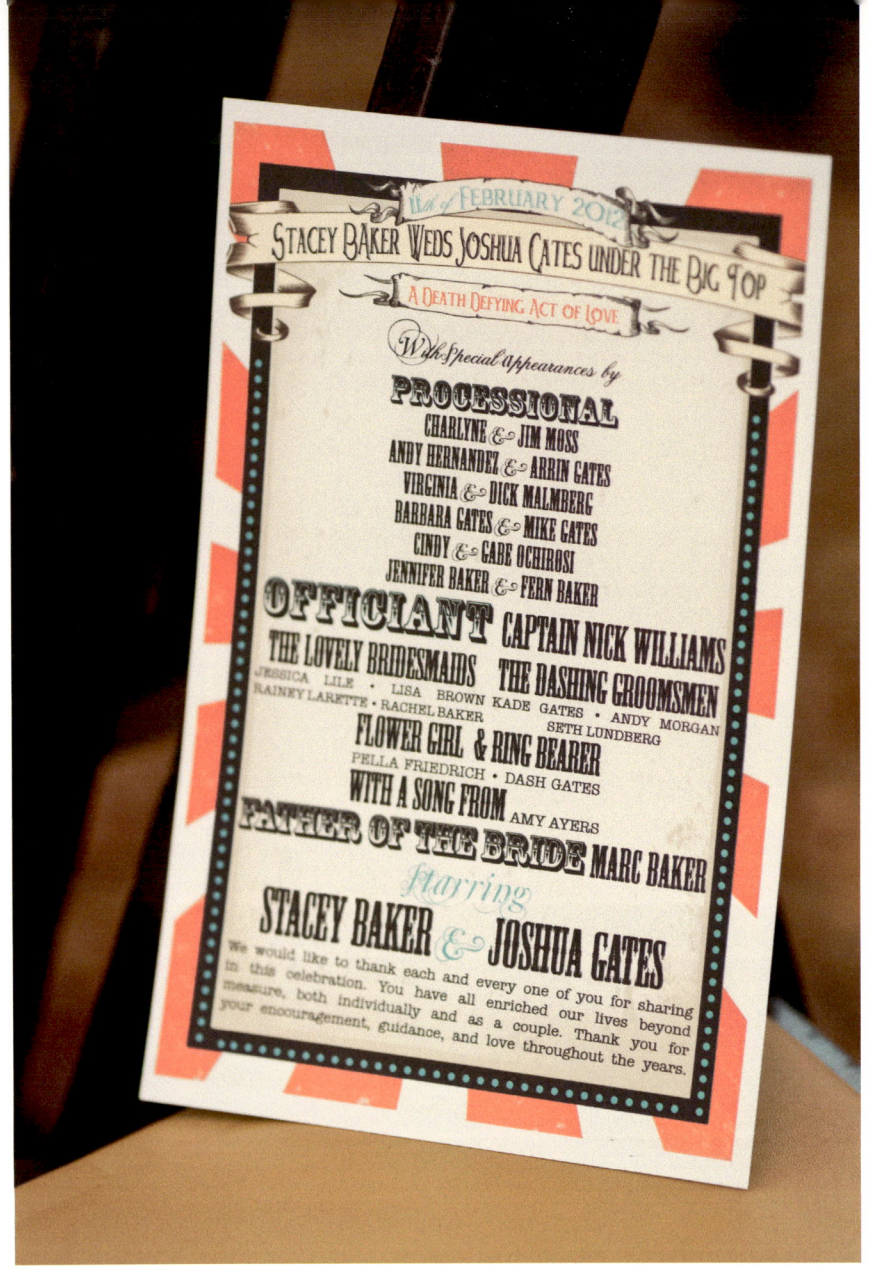

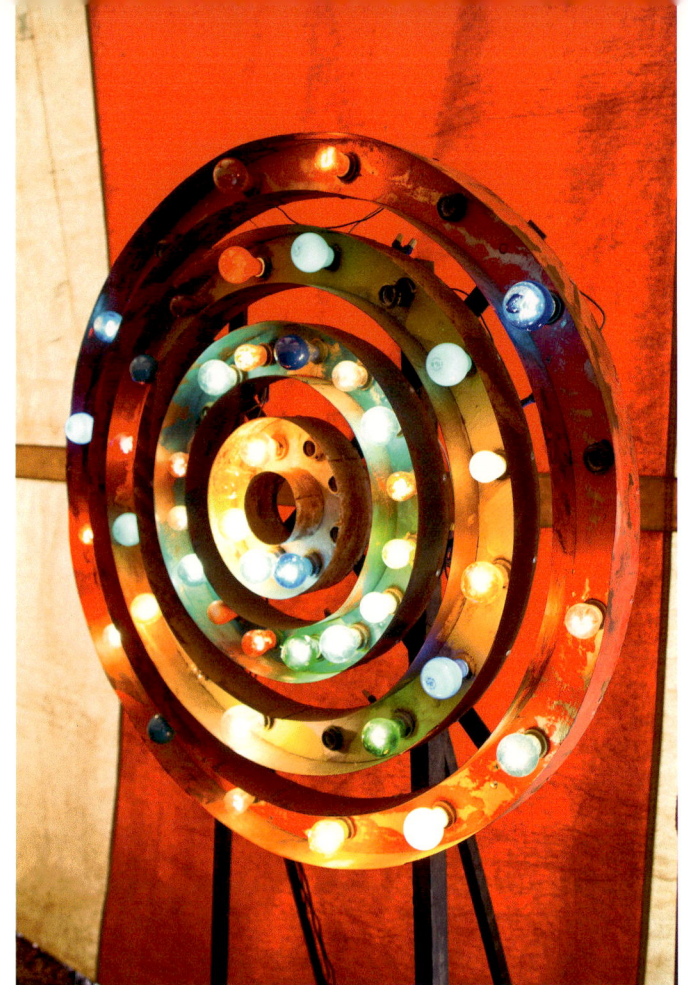

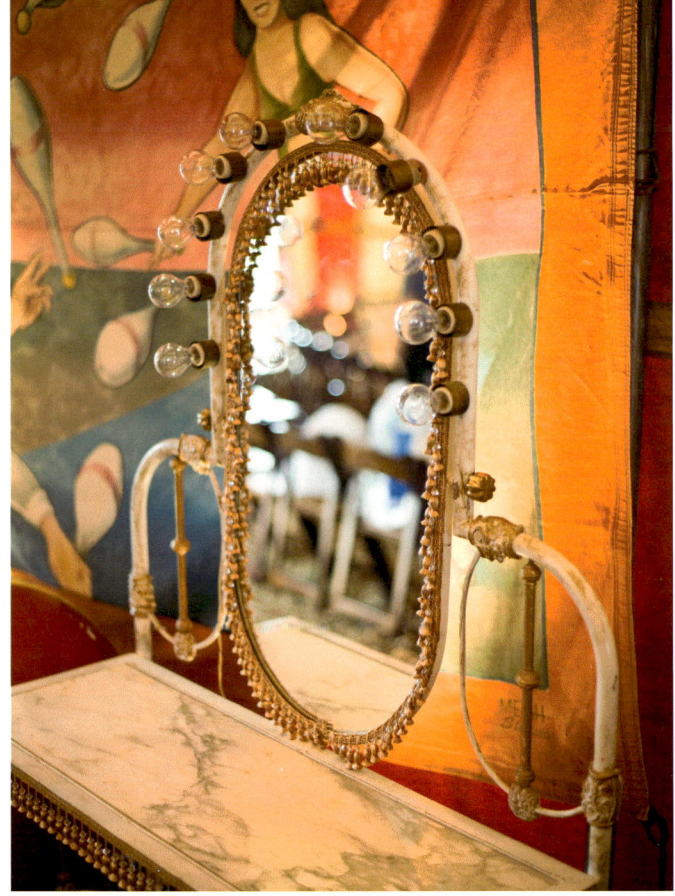

Show Business

You can't be shy with circus decoration. Stacy and Josh went wild with bold colors, gold trimmings, bright lights, and sensational flowers. They even found space in their centerpieces for a nod to that old carnival favorite, the goldfish.

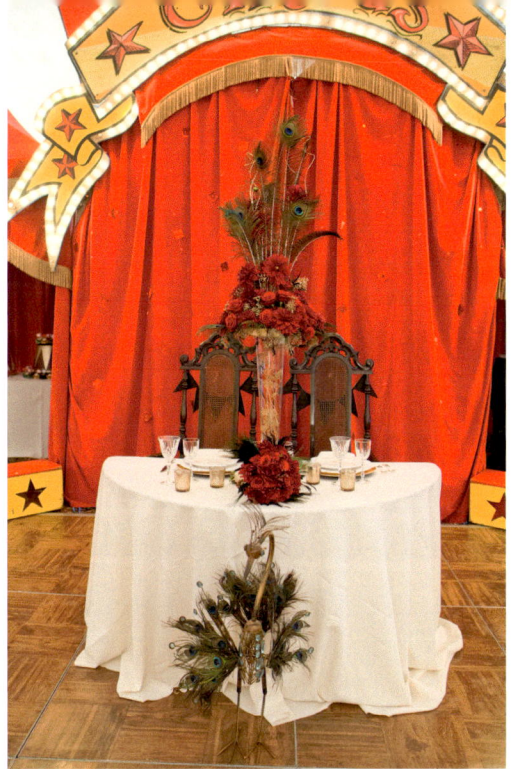

1. A fish would be much happier in these fluted-edged bowls than in a baggie.

2. Thrones for the circus's main attraction.

3. Bride and Groom bunting—the versatility of those little flags knows no bounds.

4. Crockery doesn't have to match to look good.

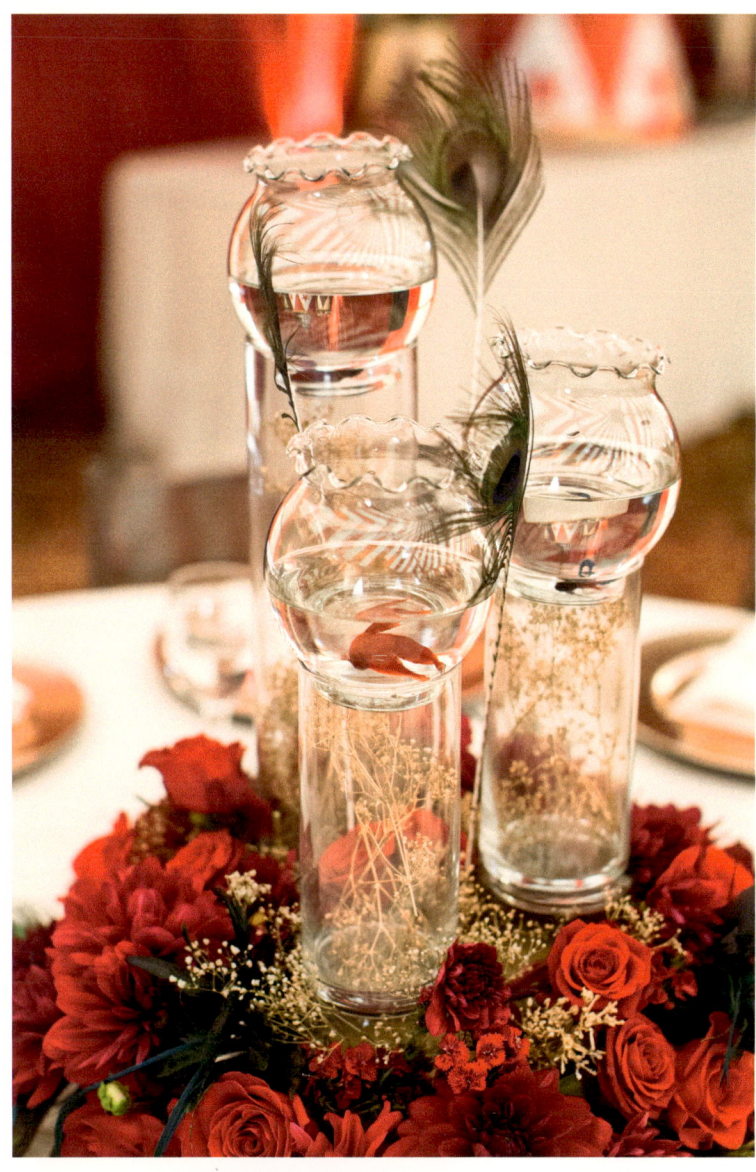

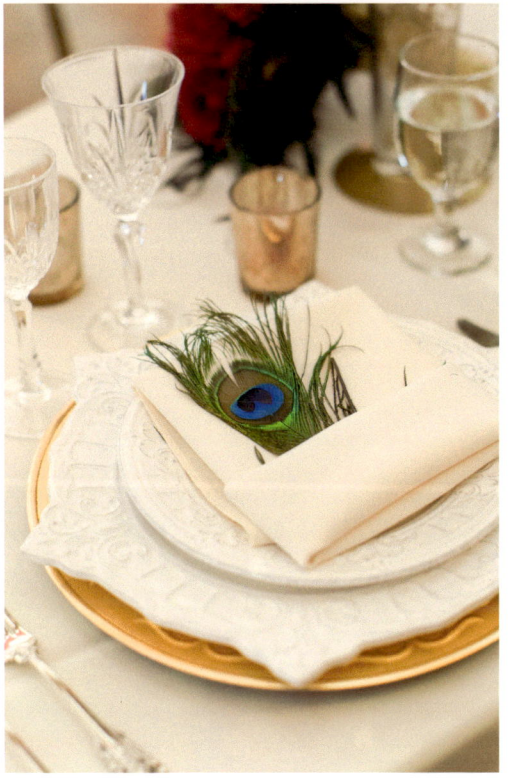

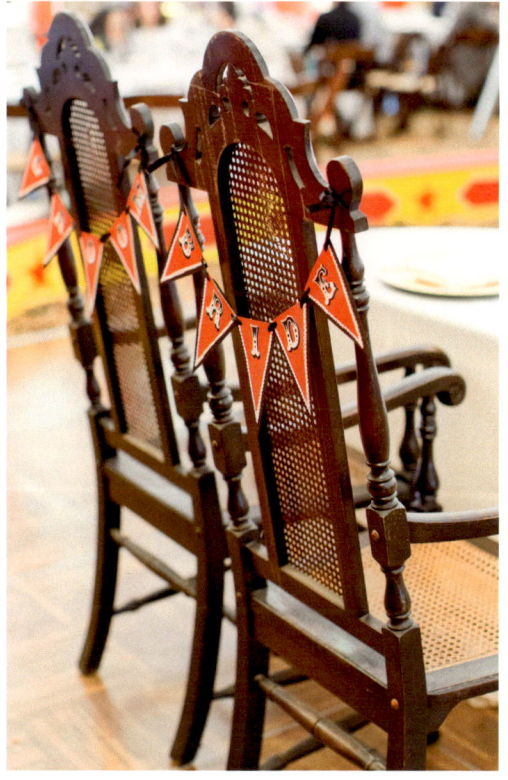

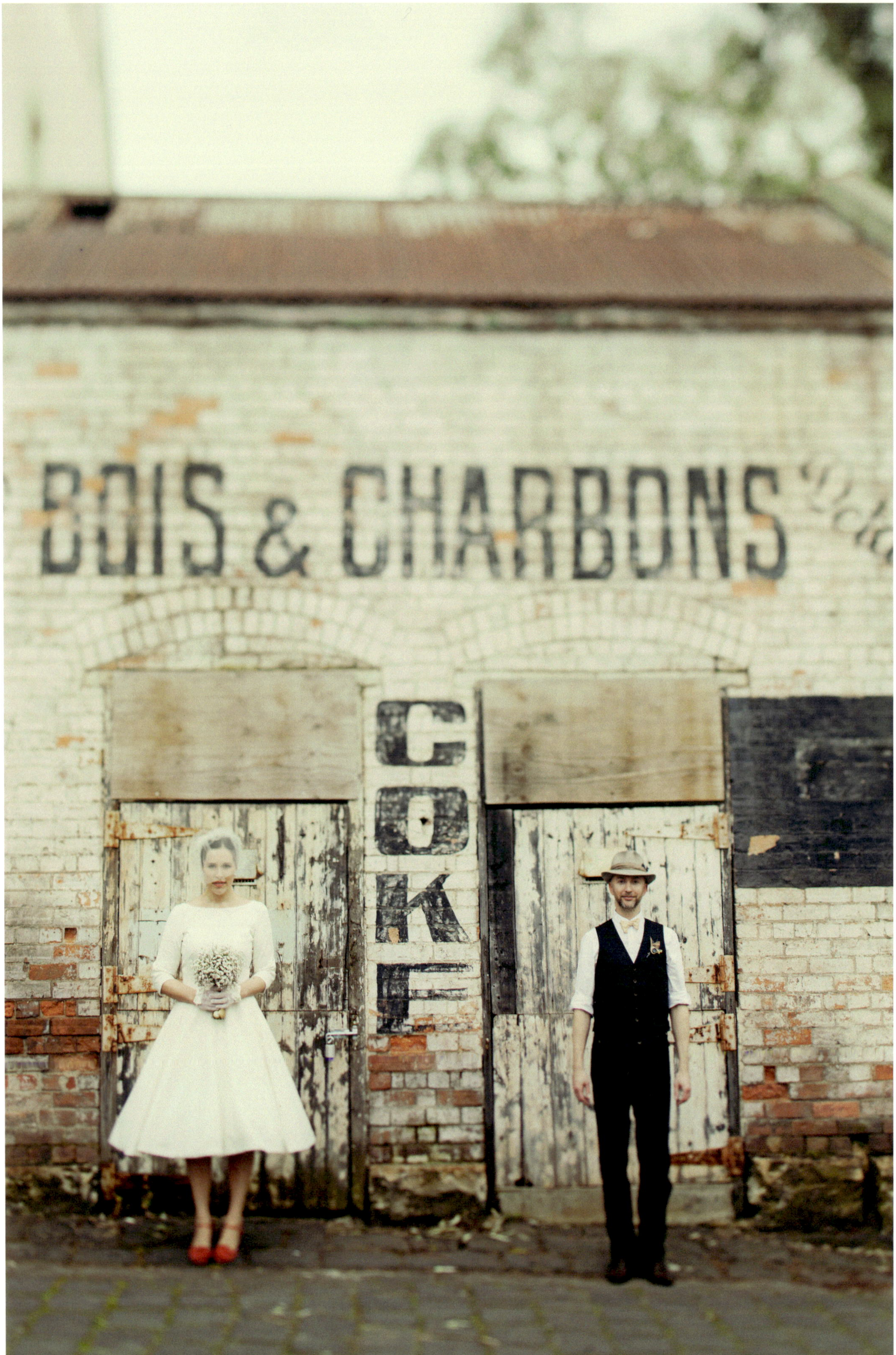

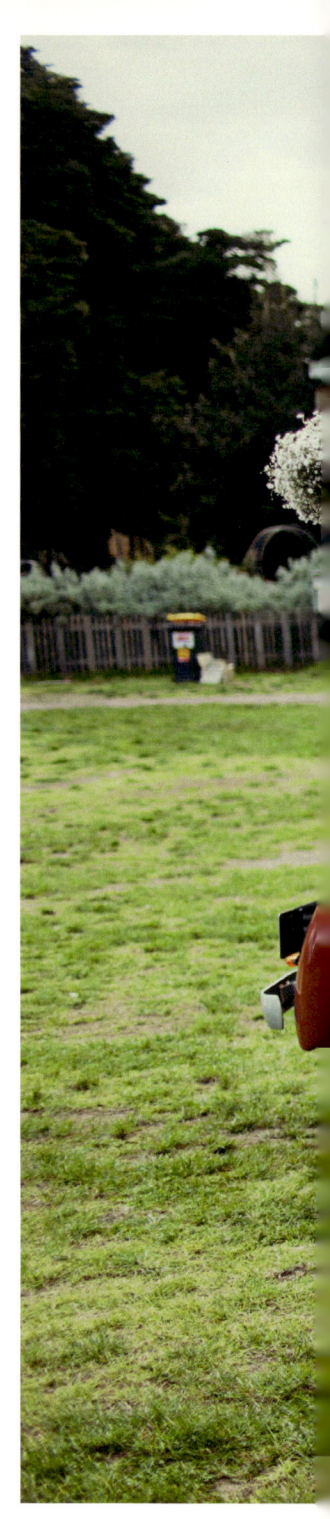

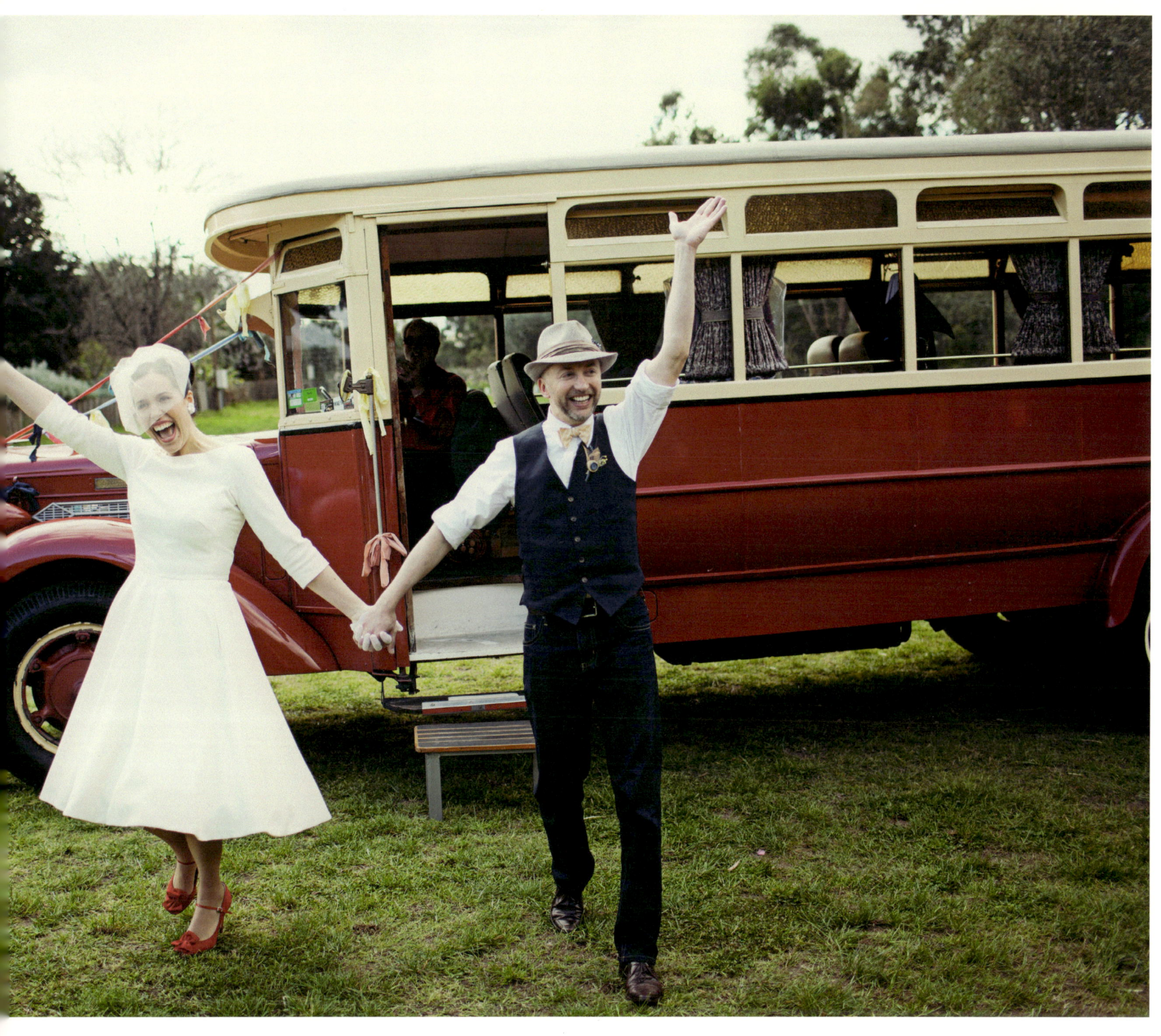

Sarah & Justin

After meeting on the set of a TV show and getting engaged in a theater, Justin and Sarah wanted their wedding to be the biggest, most heartfelt production ever. The "snazzy picnic" dress code set the theme, and the day became a homemade mash-up of Enid Blyton, *The Great Gatsby*, and the spirit of the 1950s. Showing bravery in the face of the old showbiz warning about kids and animals, Justin and Sarah got married on a children's farm. Lawn games and tea in take-home teacups followed. An all-woman tap-dancing troupe opened the reception, which also featured a surprise flashmob dance.

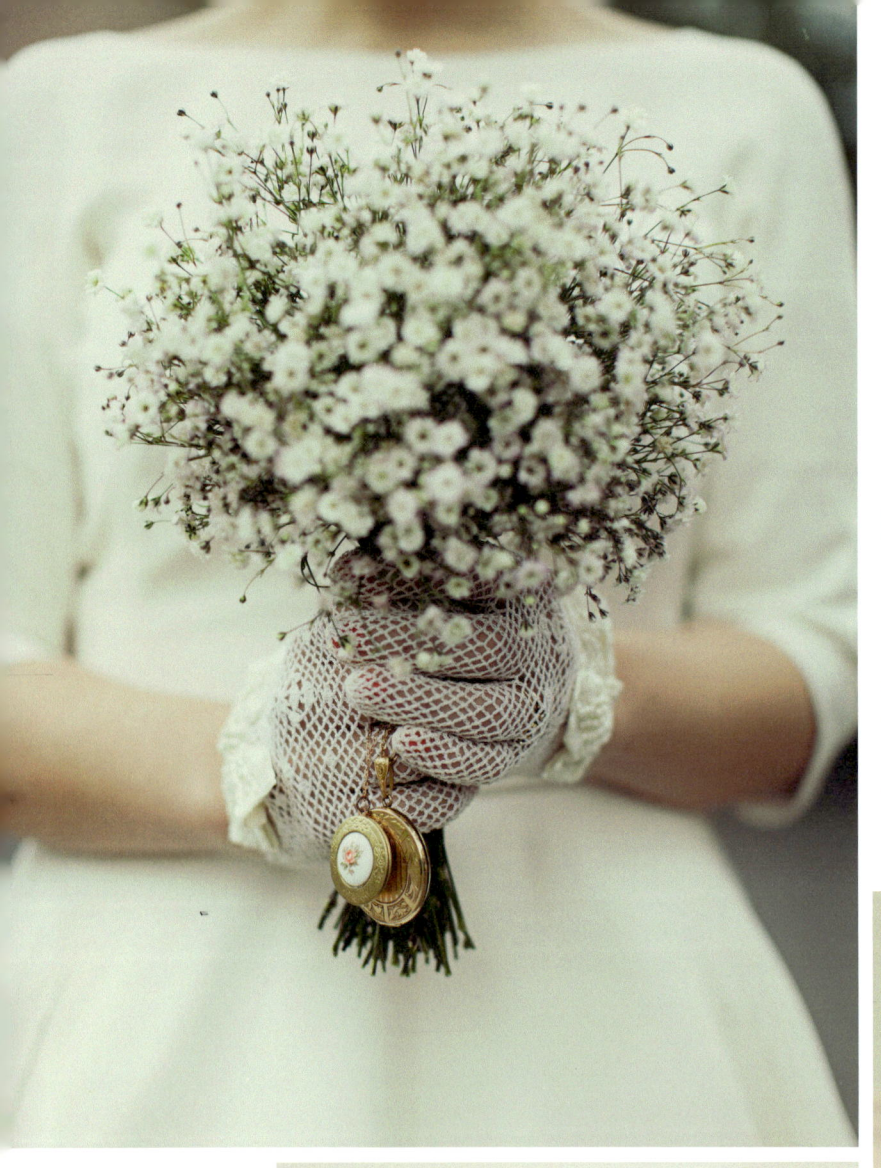

Dressing to Impress

Sarah's dress had no lace, no peals, and no extravagant neckline, but plain doesn't even play into it. The cut alone was enough to raise it above the ordinary, which just goes to show that beauty can lie in the simplest things.

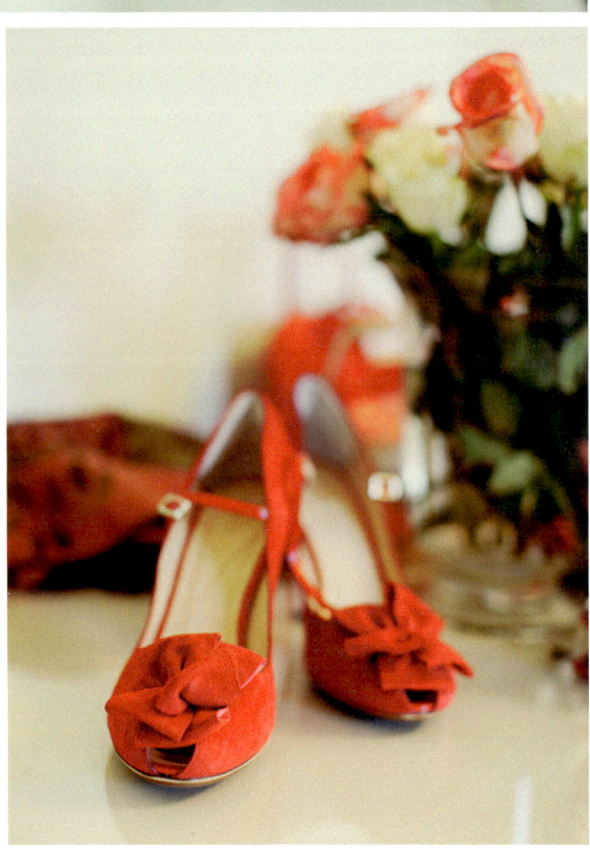

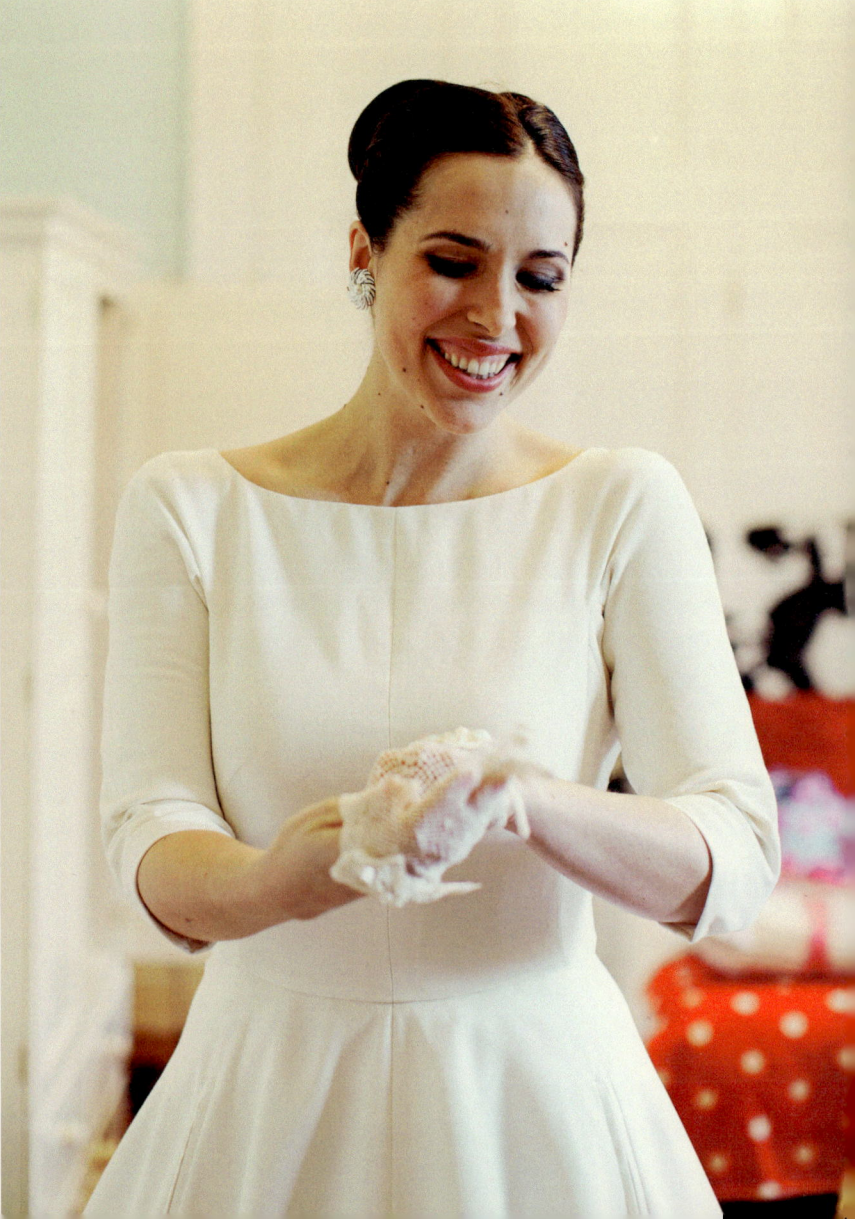

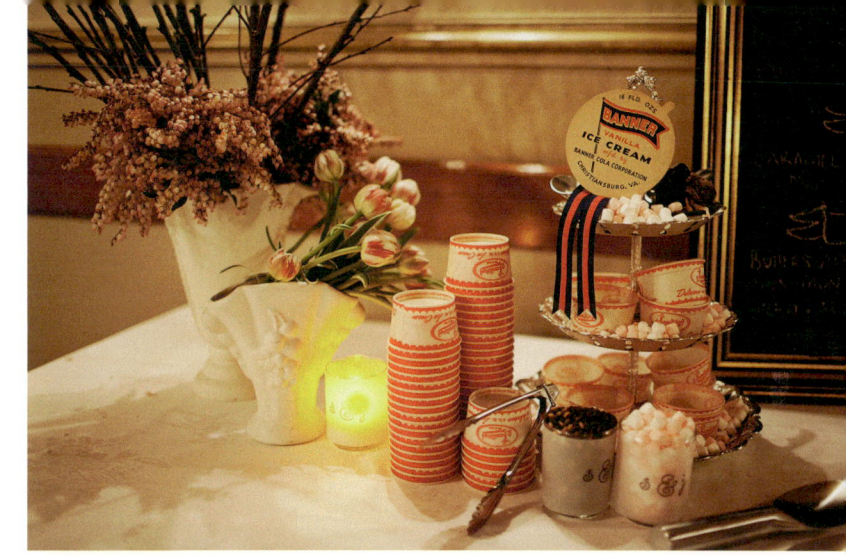

Sweet Idea

When it came time to cut the cake,
152 knives all started slicing at once.
It's not that the bride and groom
have really big hands, it's that each
table had its very own cake so that
everyone could join in!

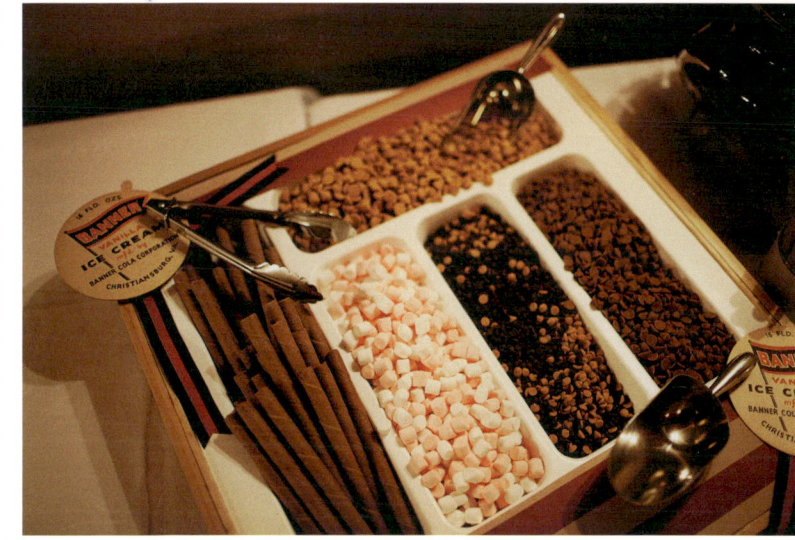

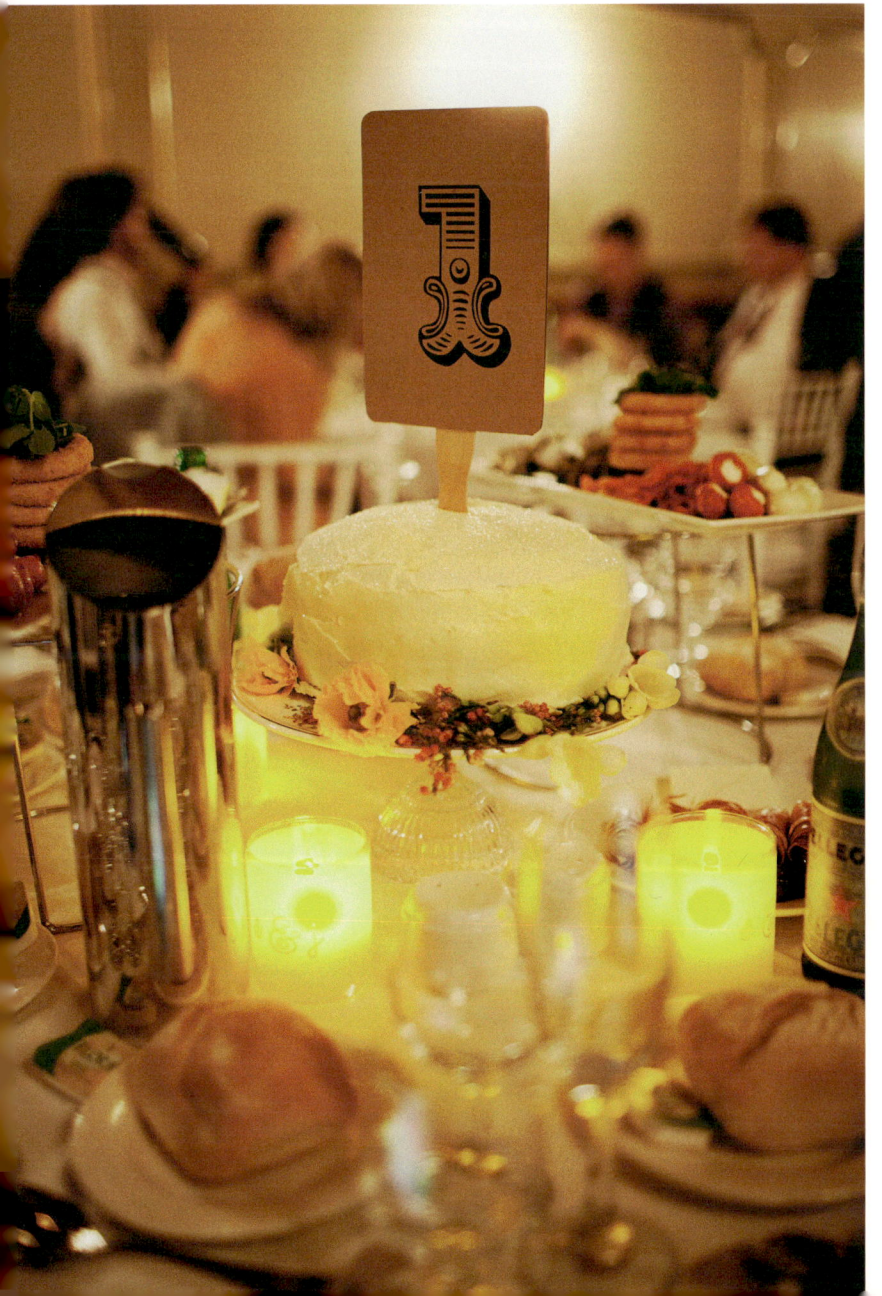

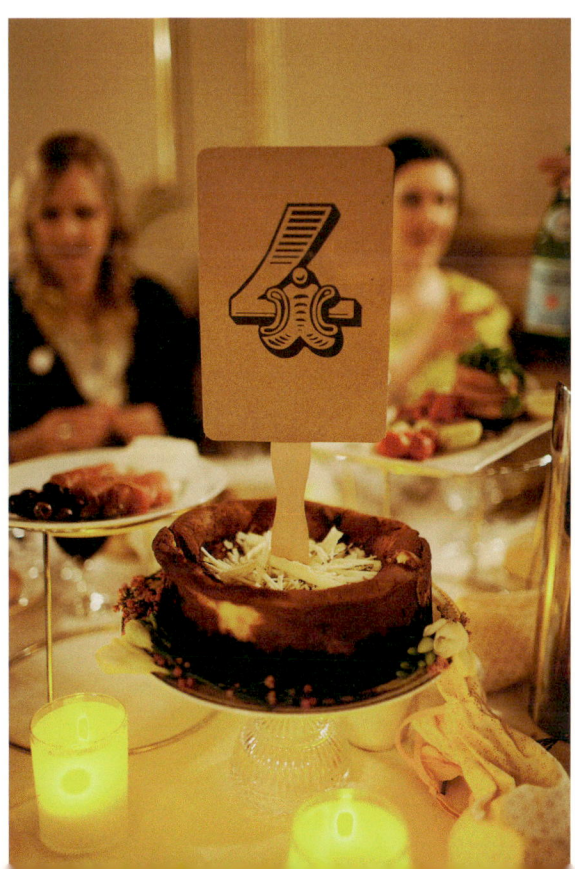

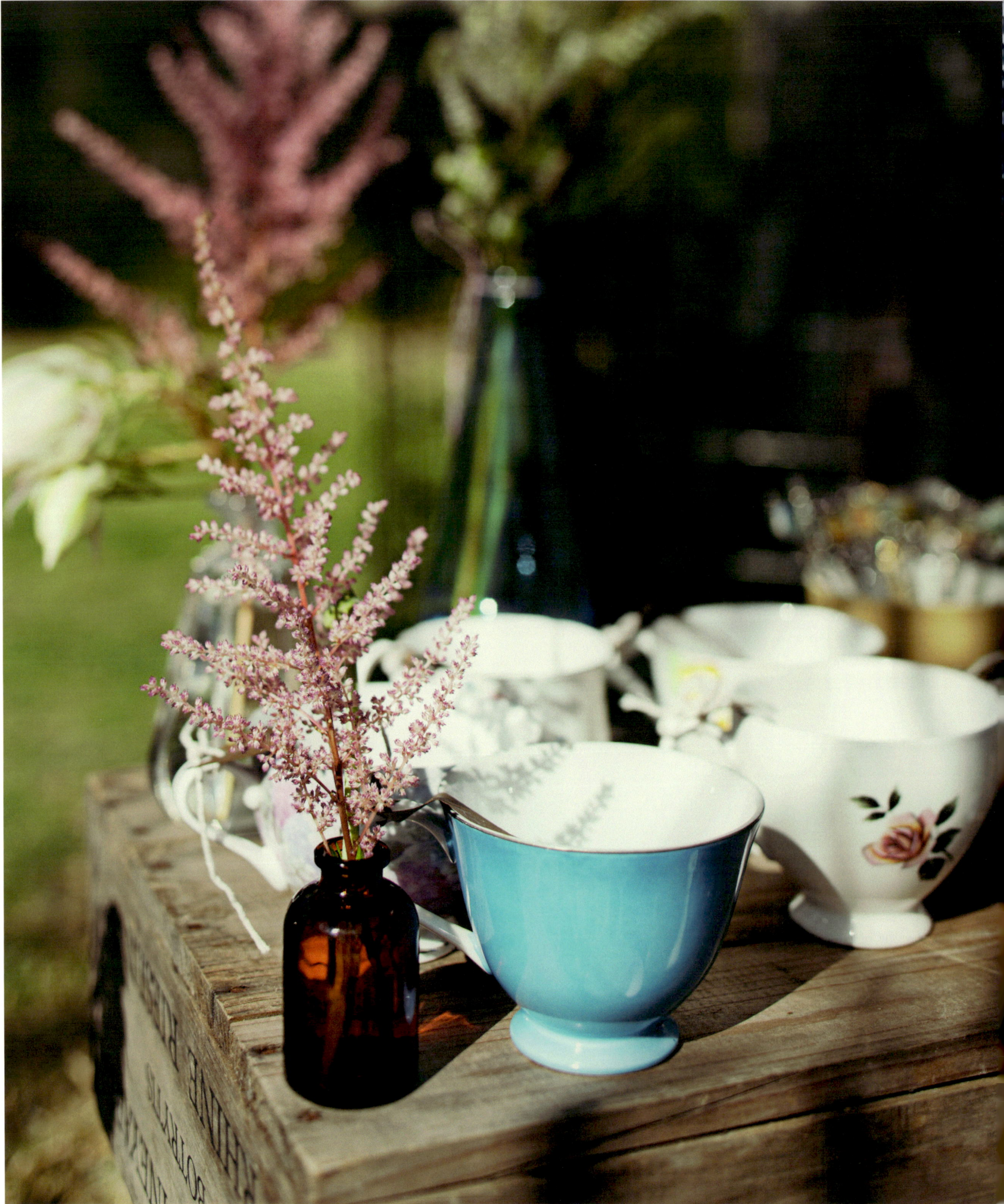

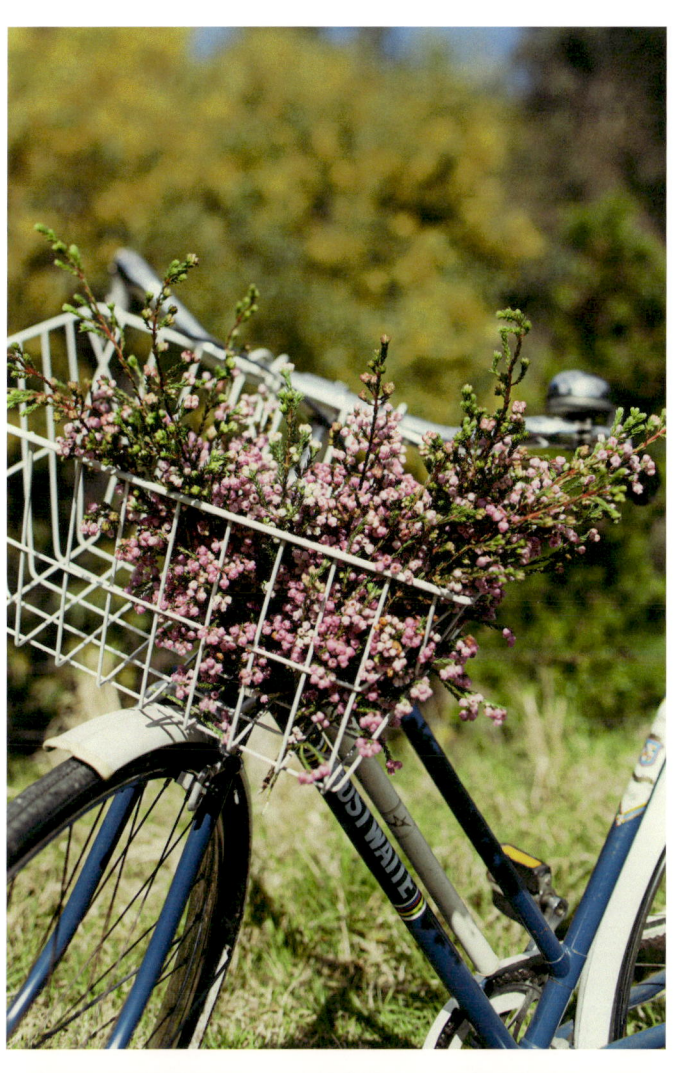

Flowers

We've seen some innovative approaches to vases so far, but this is the first time bicycle baskets and tin cans have turned up. We think they do a sterling job, and we love the idea of using heather and small-blossom flowers too.

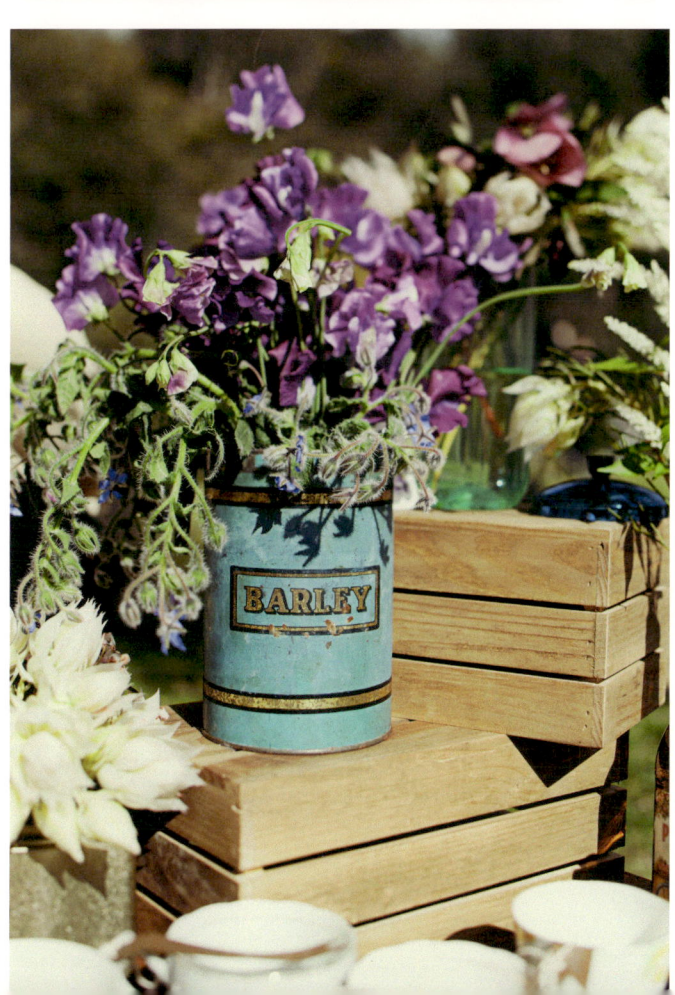

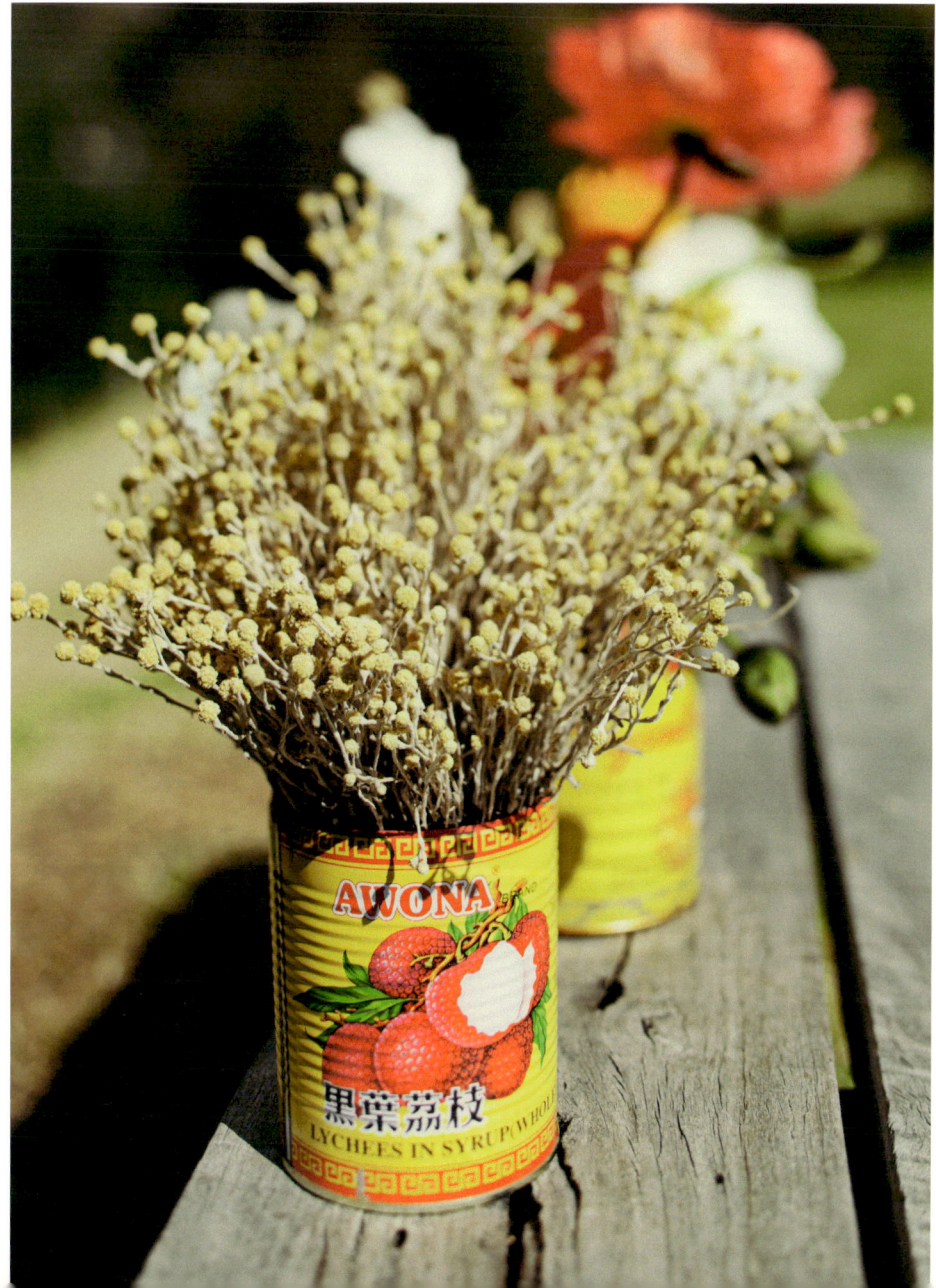

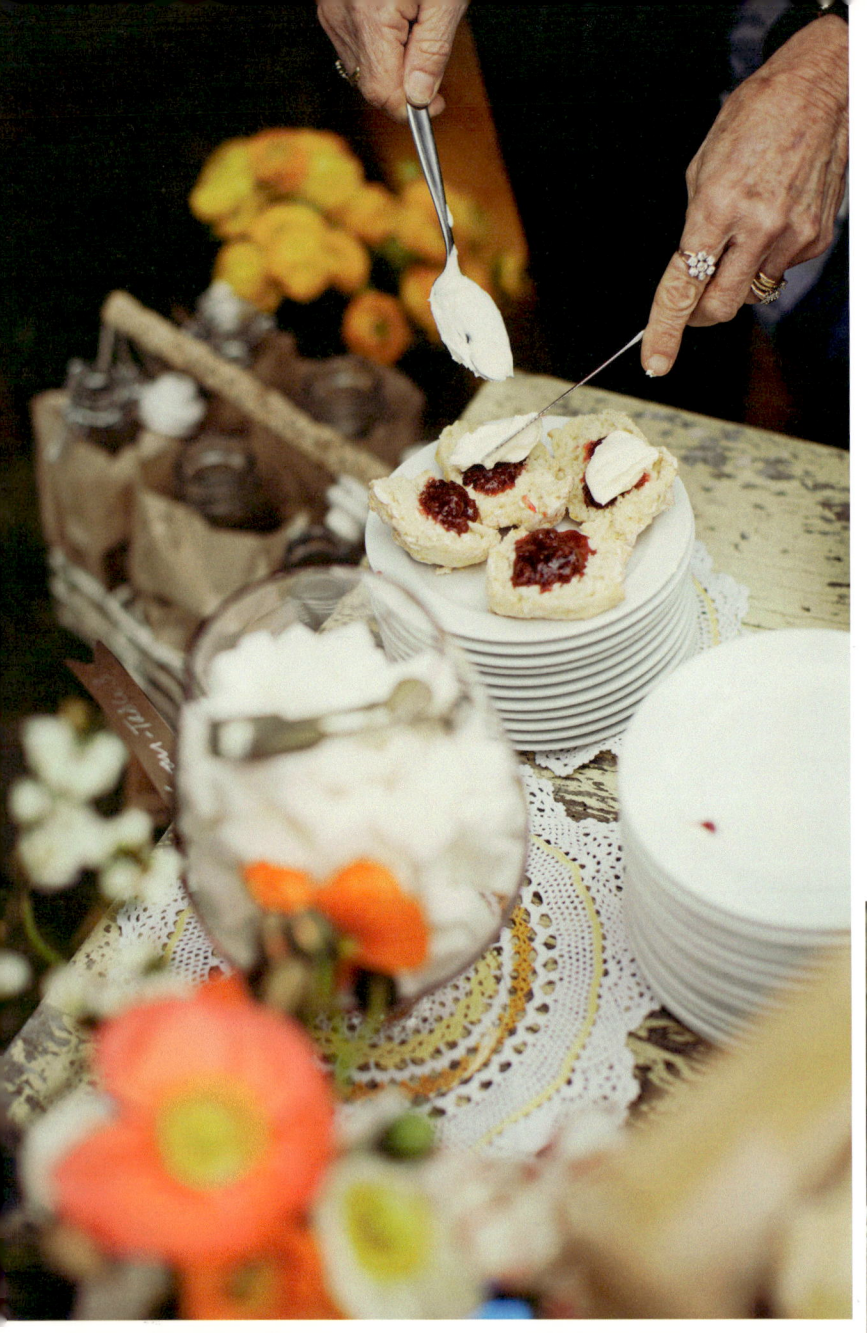

Food & Deco

Hurrah for the humble picnic! Simple and stylish, this kind of outdoor dining can be endlessly adapted to suit your tastes.

1. Fresh scones, raspberry jam, clotted cream. Outstanding.

2. Turns out old suitcases can scrub up pretty well.

3. They dedicated a whole table to scone-serving! And a whole bowl to the cream!

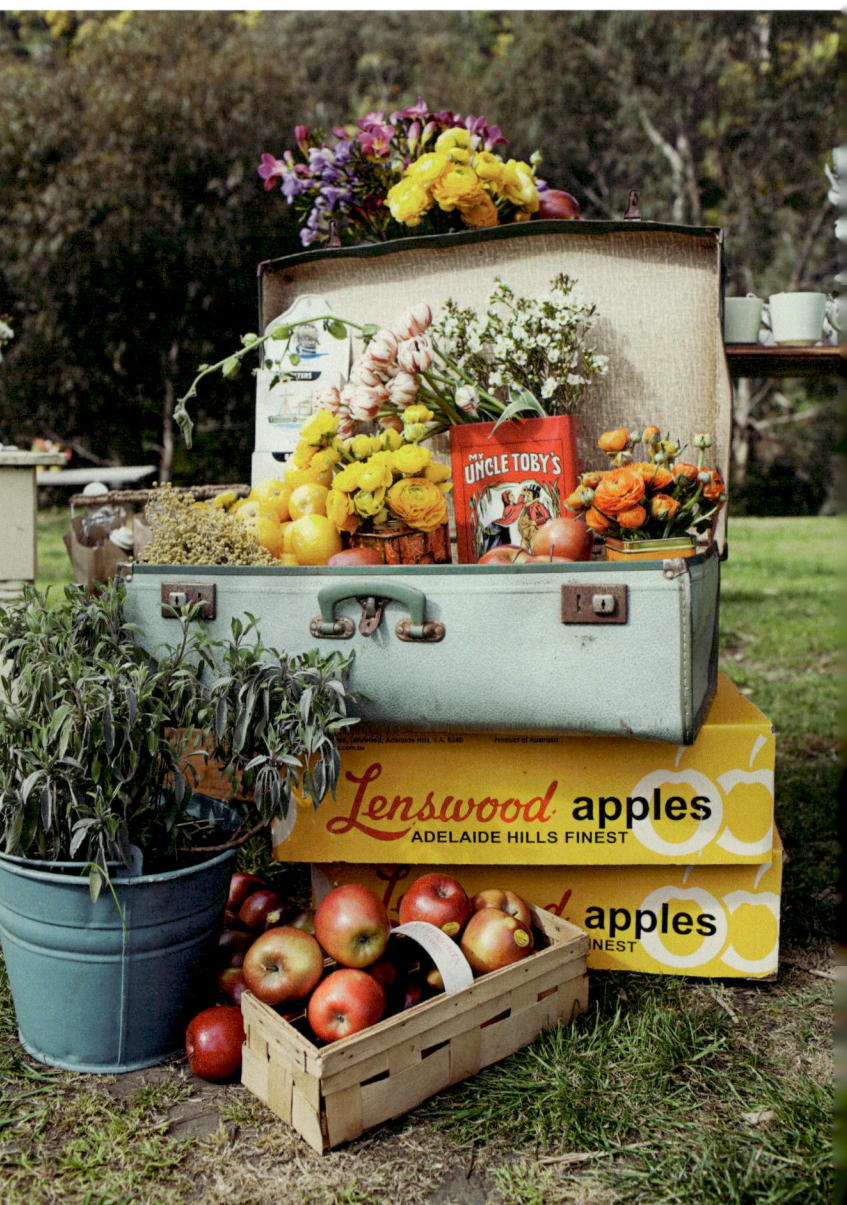

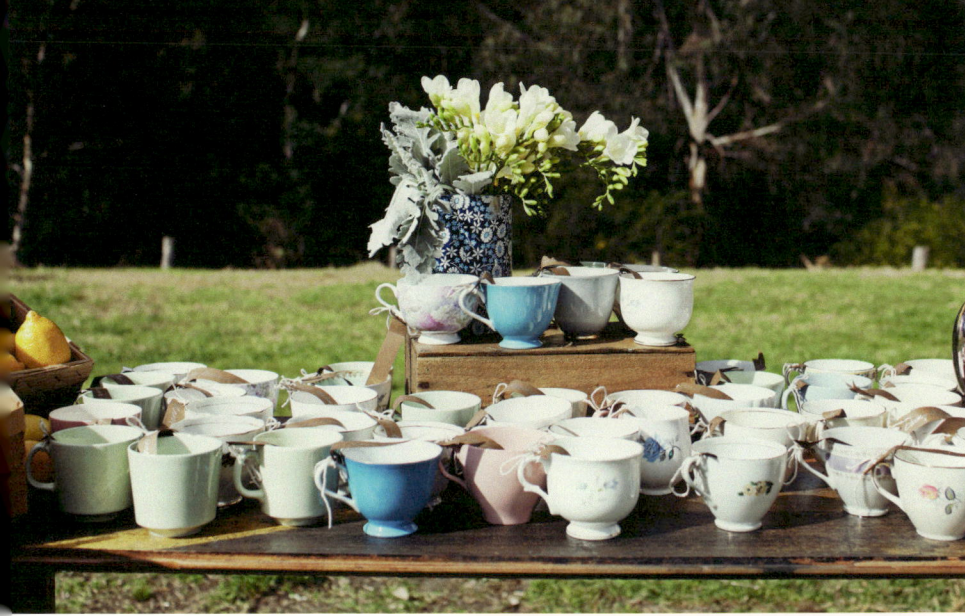

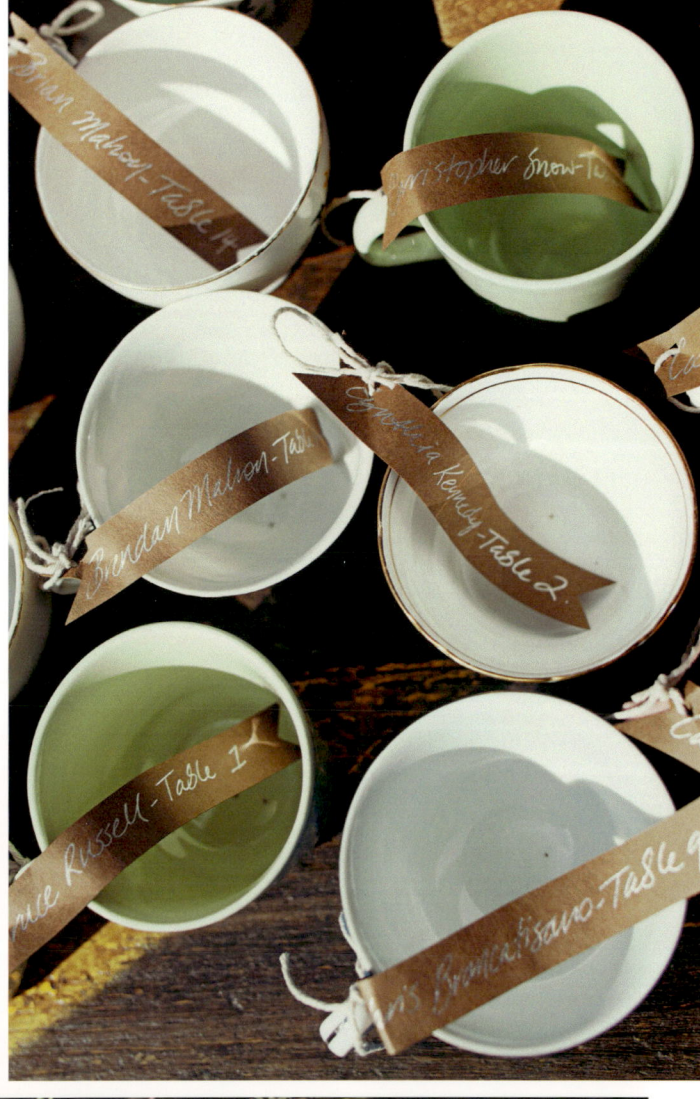

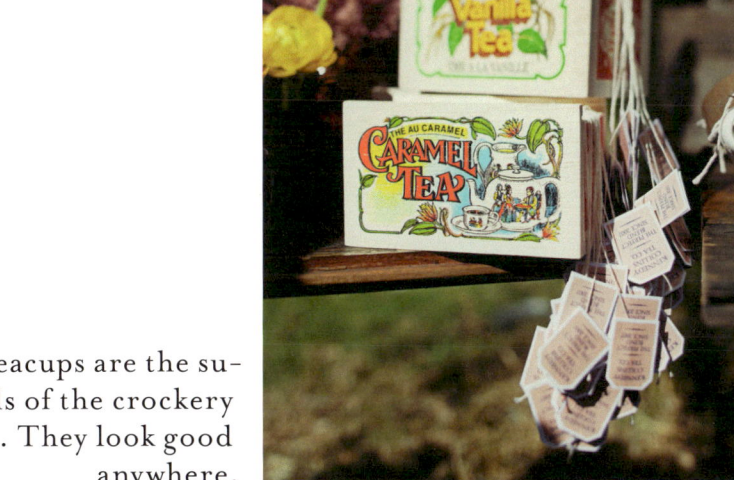

1. Teacups are the supermodels of the crockery world. They look good anywhere.

2. They are also a neat way to tell everyone where they are sitting.

3. Displaying decorations at different levels livens up simple wooden tables.

4. Colorful wooden boxes of tea add an exotic touch to this oh-so-English of scenes.

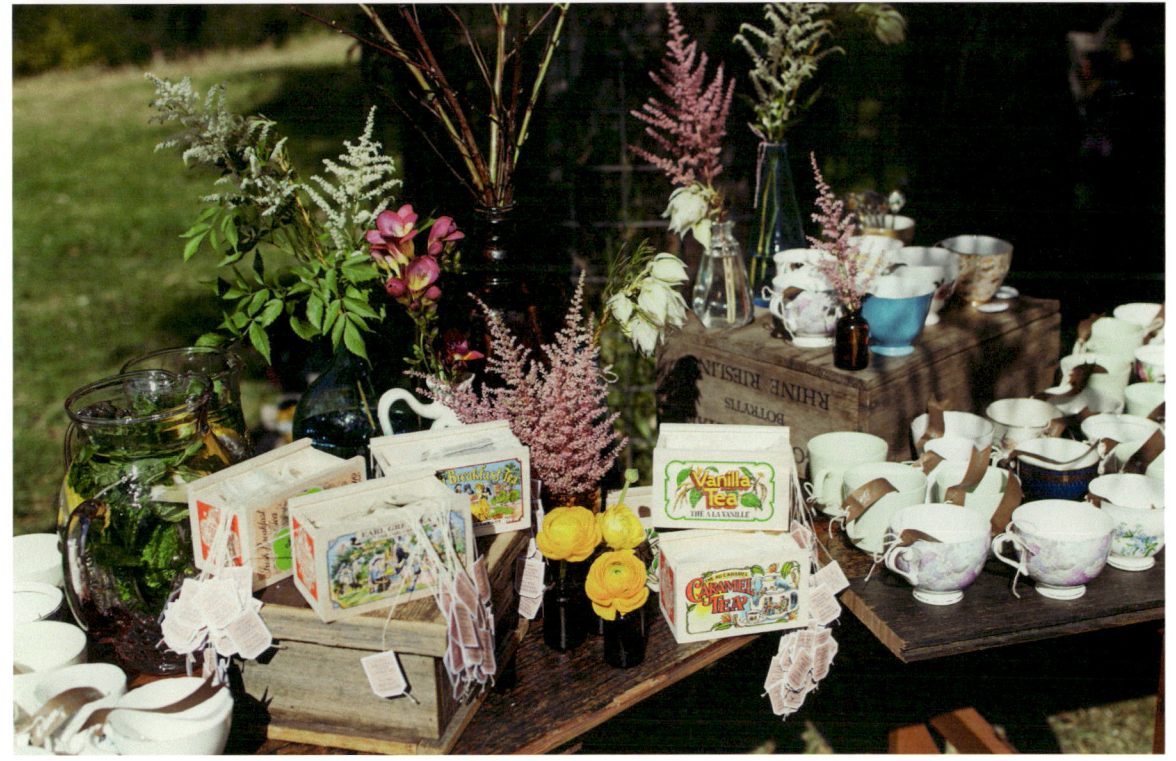

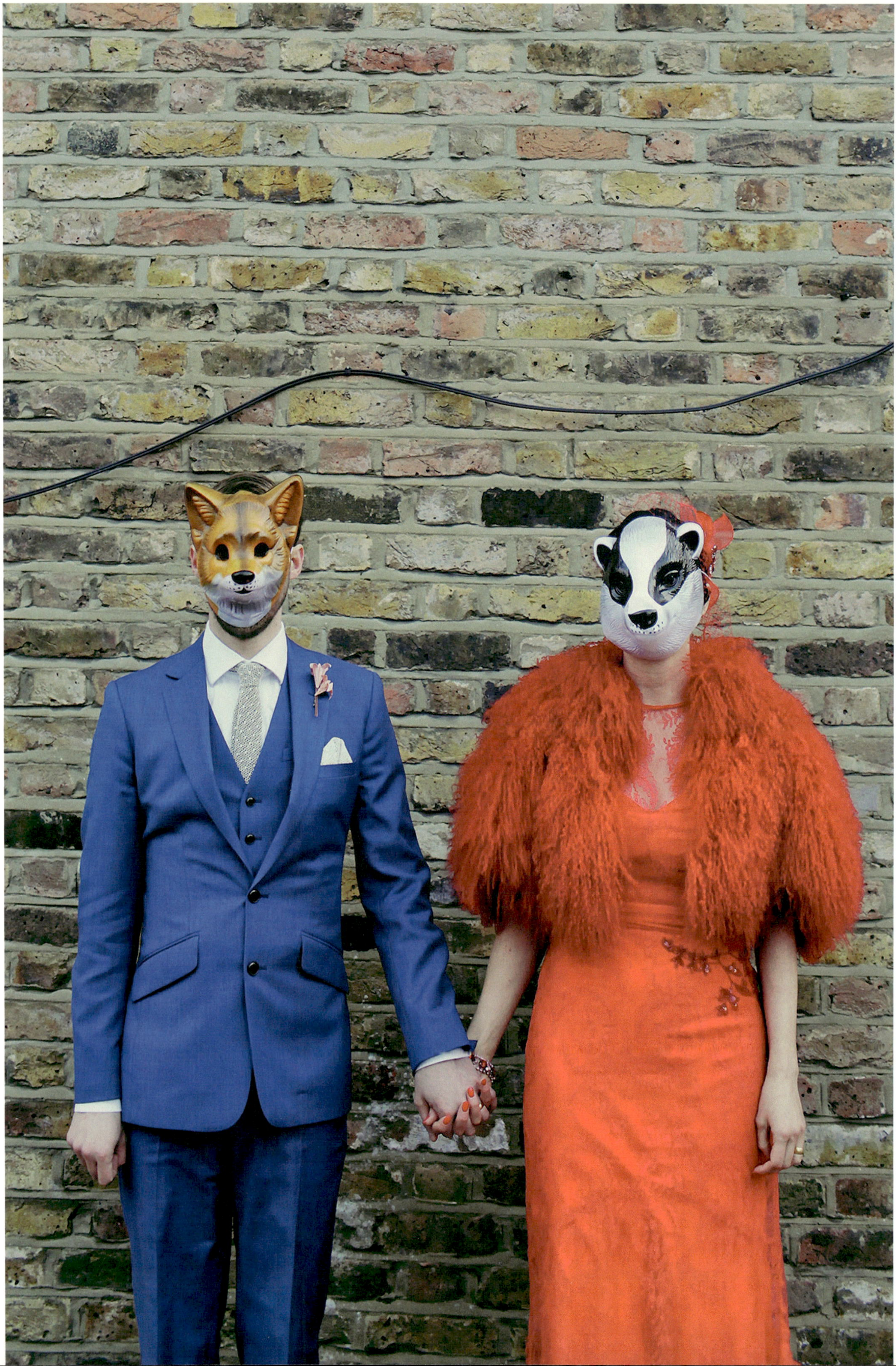

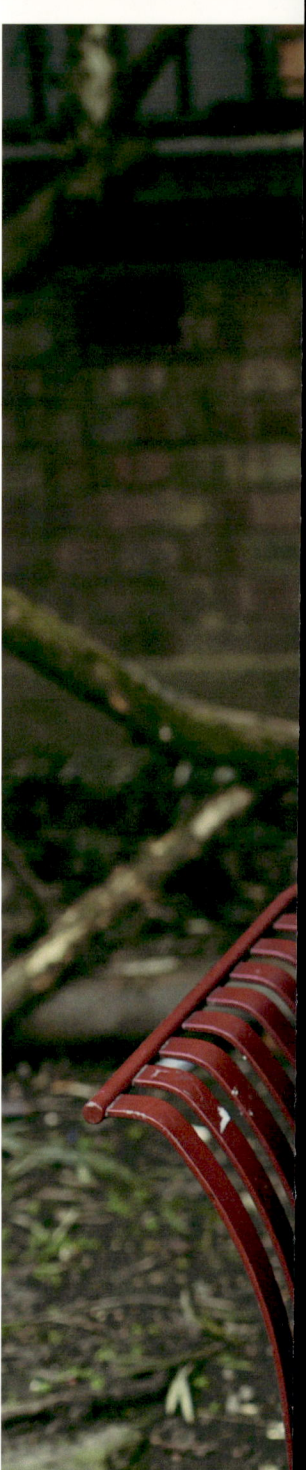

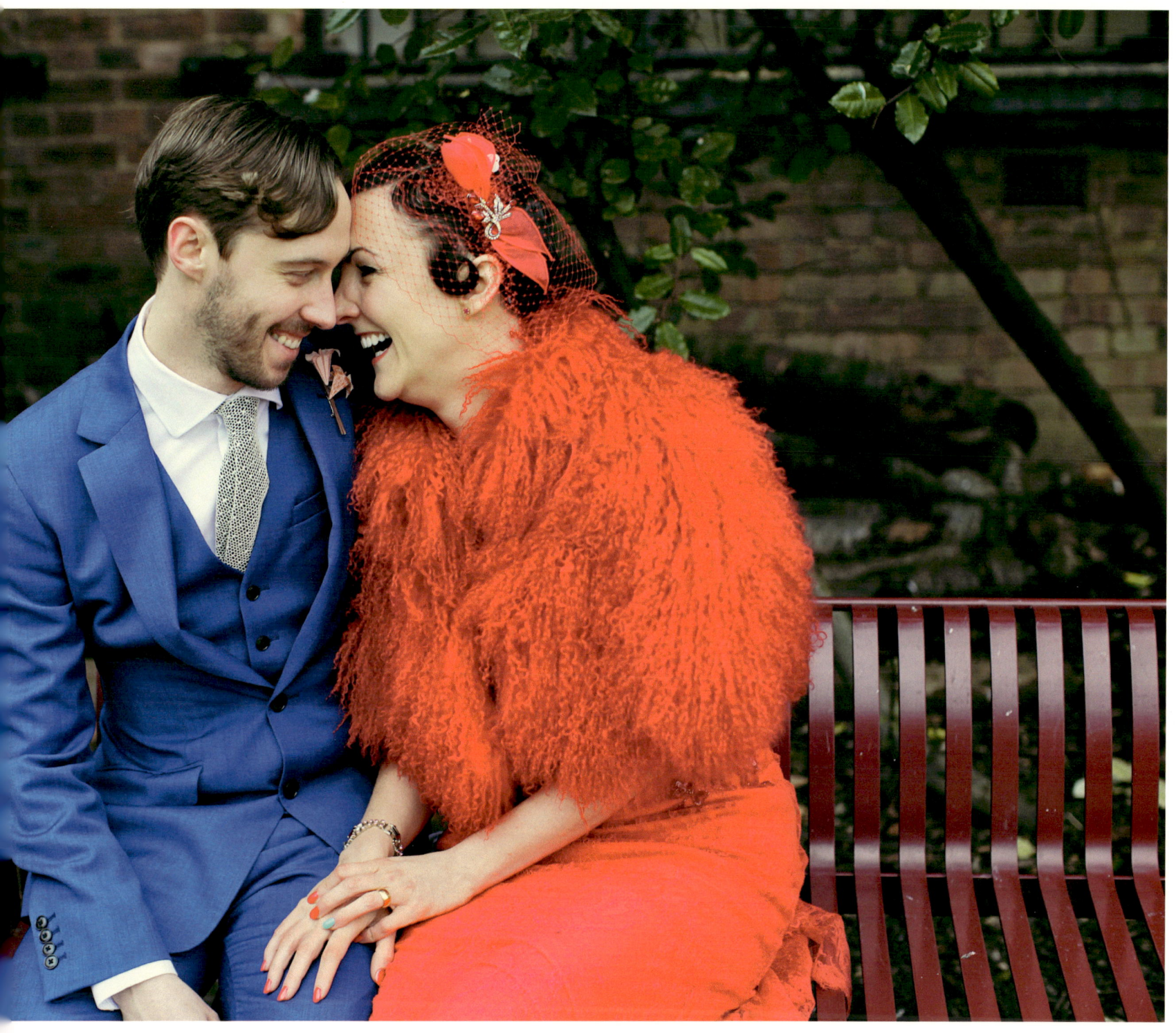

Zoe & Phil

This London wedding took its cues from the glamour of the jazz-infused thirties. Zoe made her own (red) dress, and created the origami bouquets, buttonholes, and table decorations. She says she put the last touches to them over a glass of champagne the night before the wedding, but there are no signs of the bubbles having fuzzied the edges of her precision folding skills! The Old Finsbury Town Hall was a gorgeous art-nouveau setting for the ceremony, and the reception was held in a pub-turned-photography studio where the décor was as eclectic and surprising as any jazz solo.

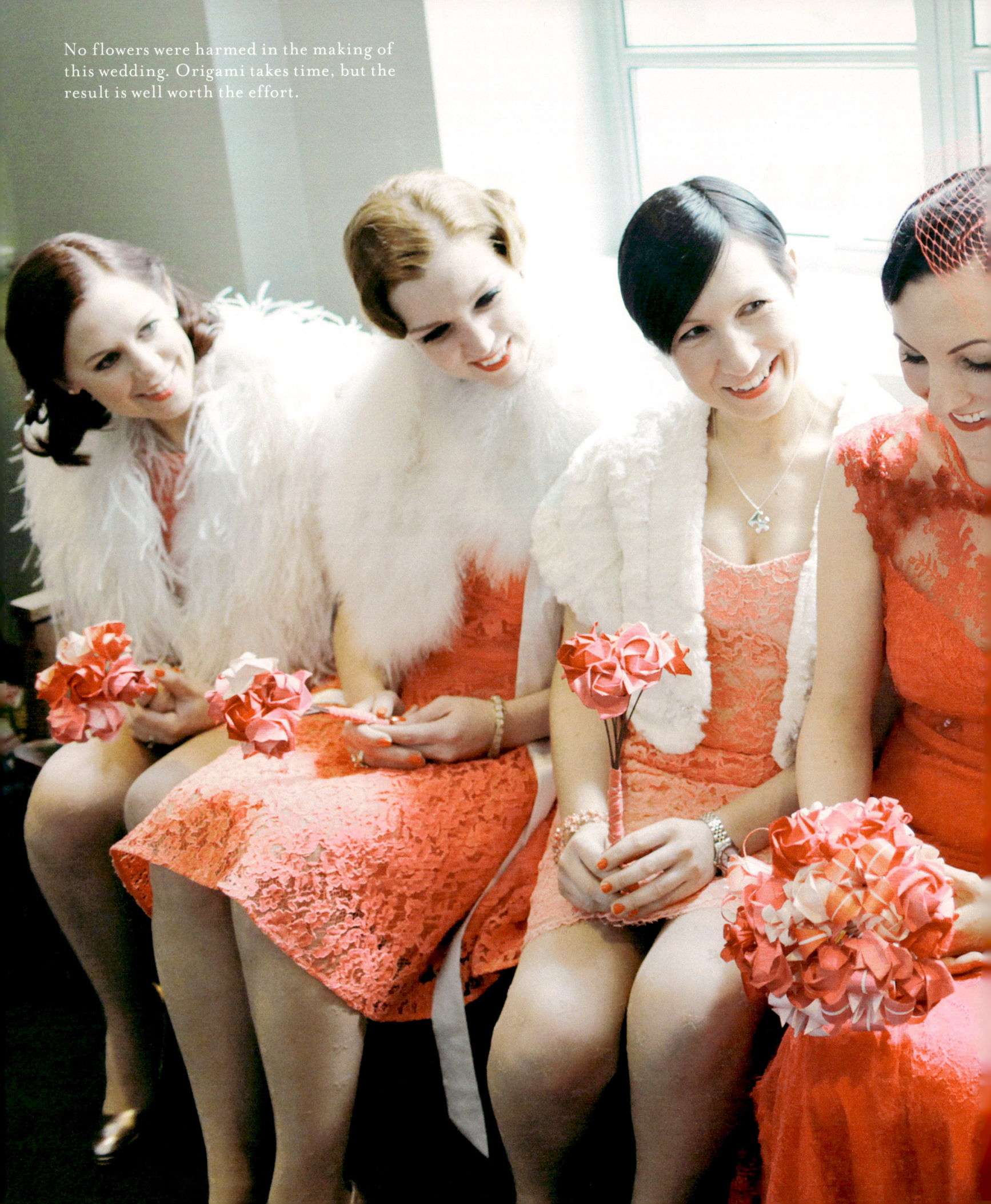

No flowers were harmed in the making of this wedding. Origami takes time, but the result is well worth the effort.

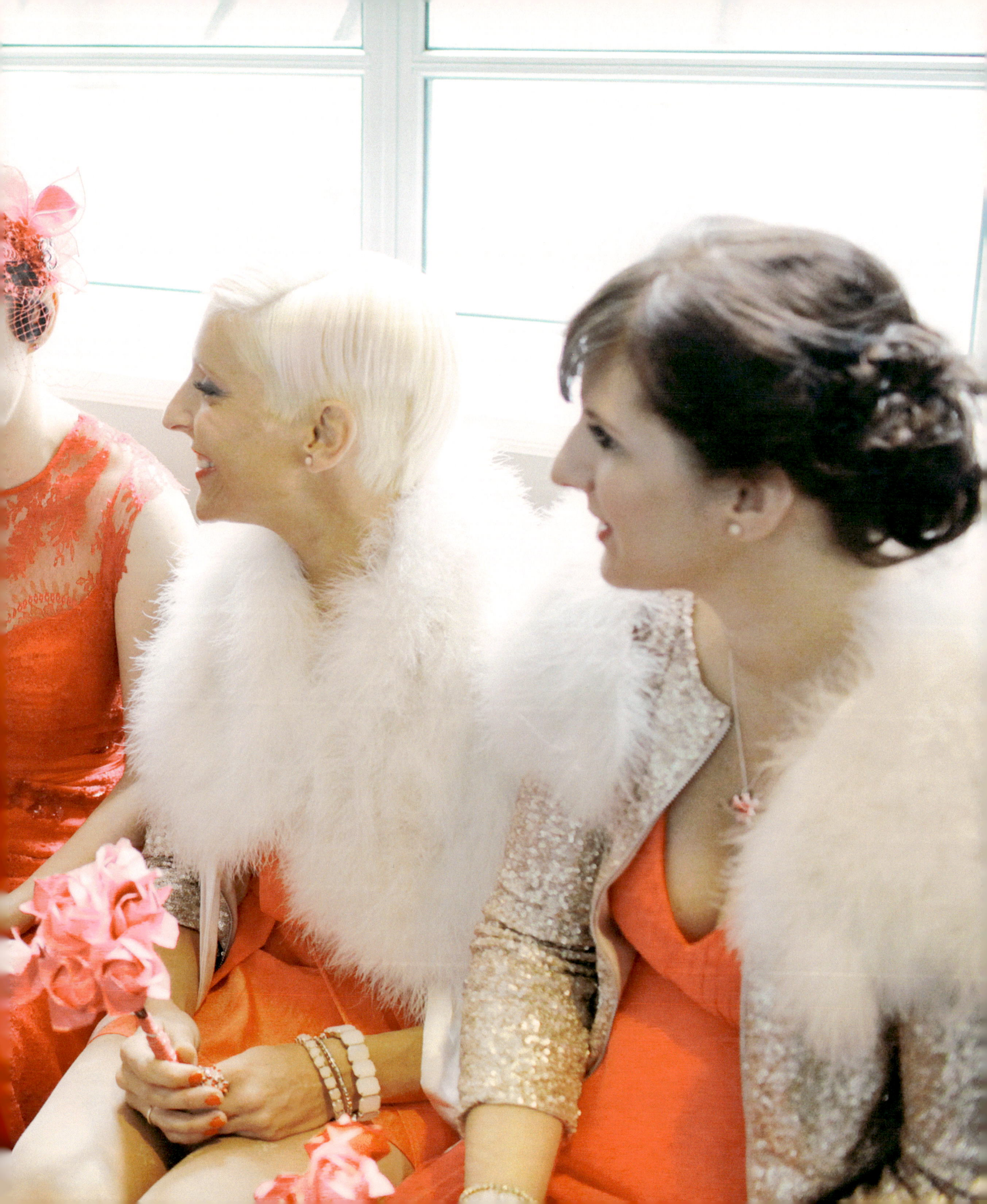

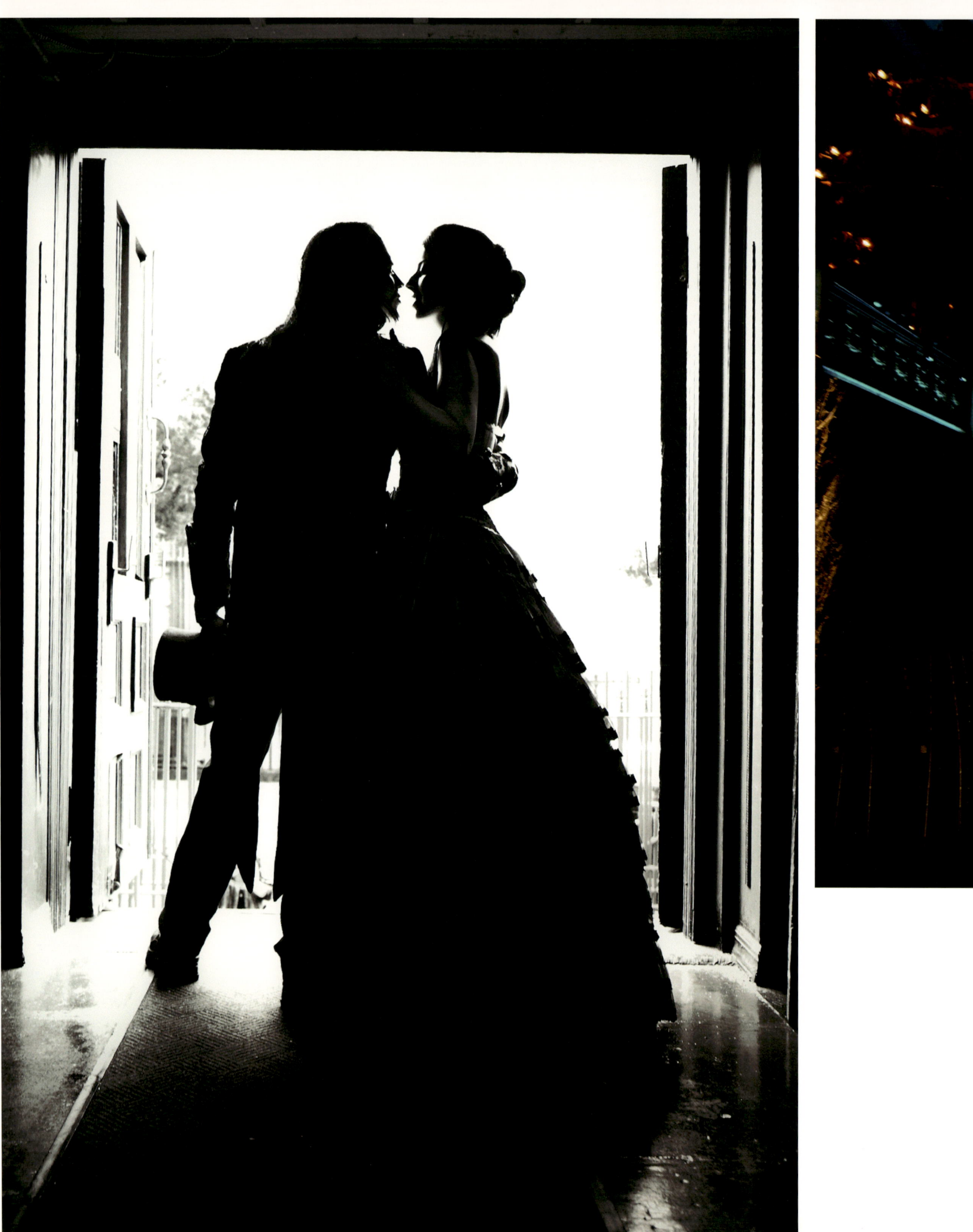

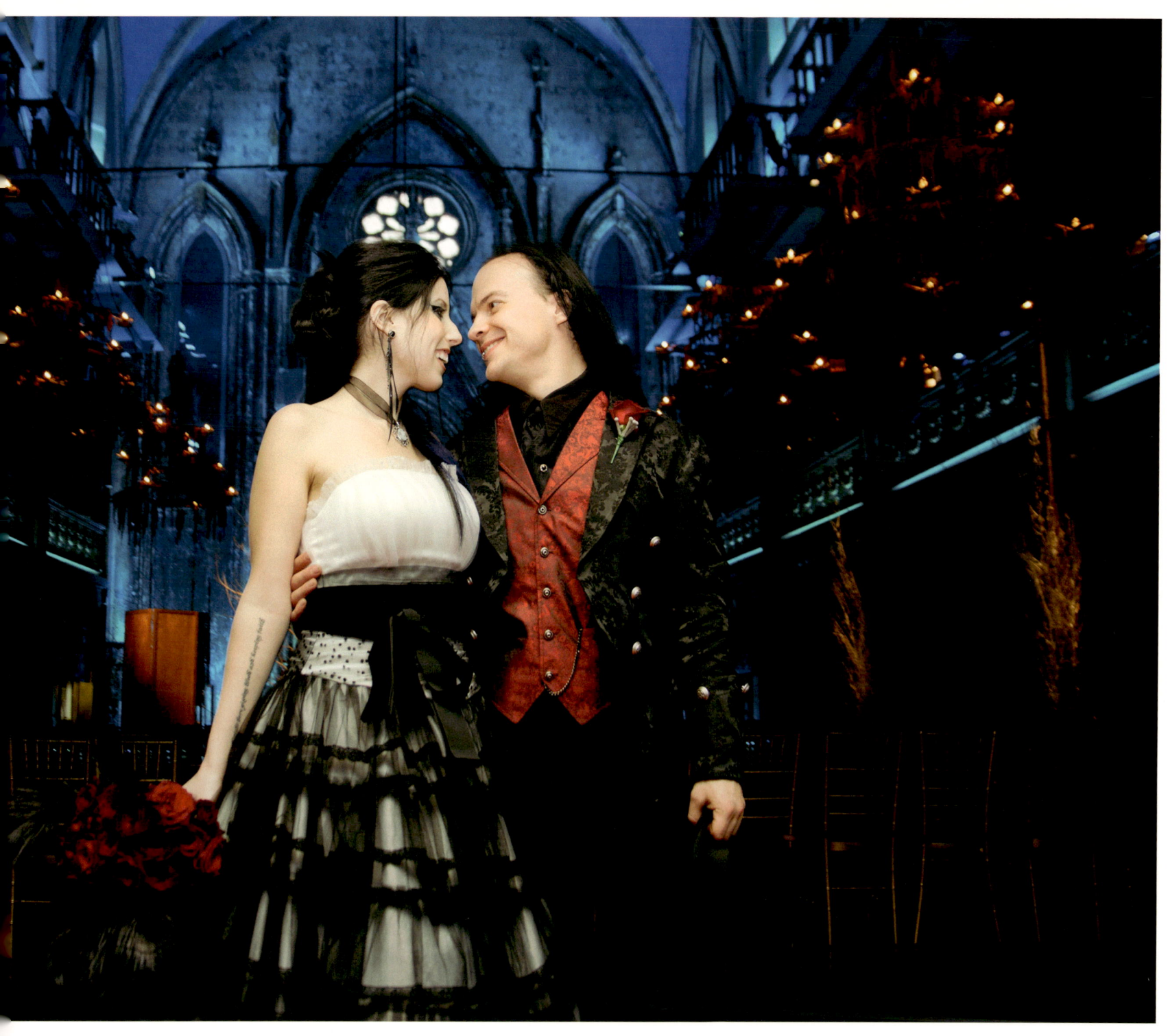

Suzy & Dmitry

Looking at Dmitry and Suzy's wedding, you half expect to see Edward Scissorhands and Jack Skellington celebrating among the guests. The gothic arches of a former synagogue set the scene for a ceremony that would have been at home in any of the superbly dark, kooky stories that Tim Burton has spun over the years. Leafless trees flanked the altar, creating a winter-wonderland theme at odds with the summer outside. A contortionist performing among petals added to the dramatic feel, and napkins printed with two silhouettes hanging from a tree captured the macabre in "till death do us part."

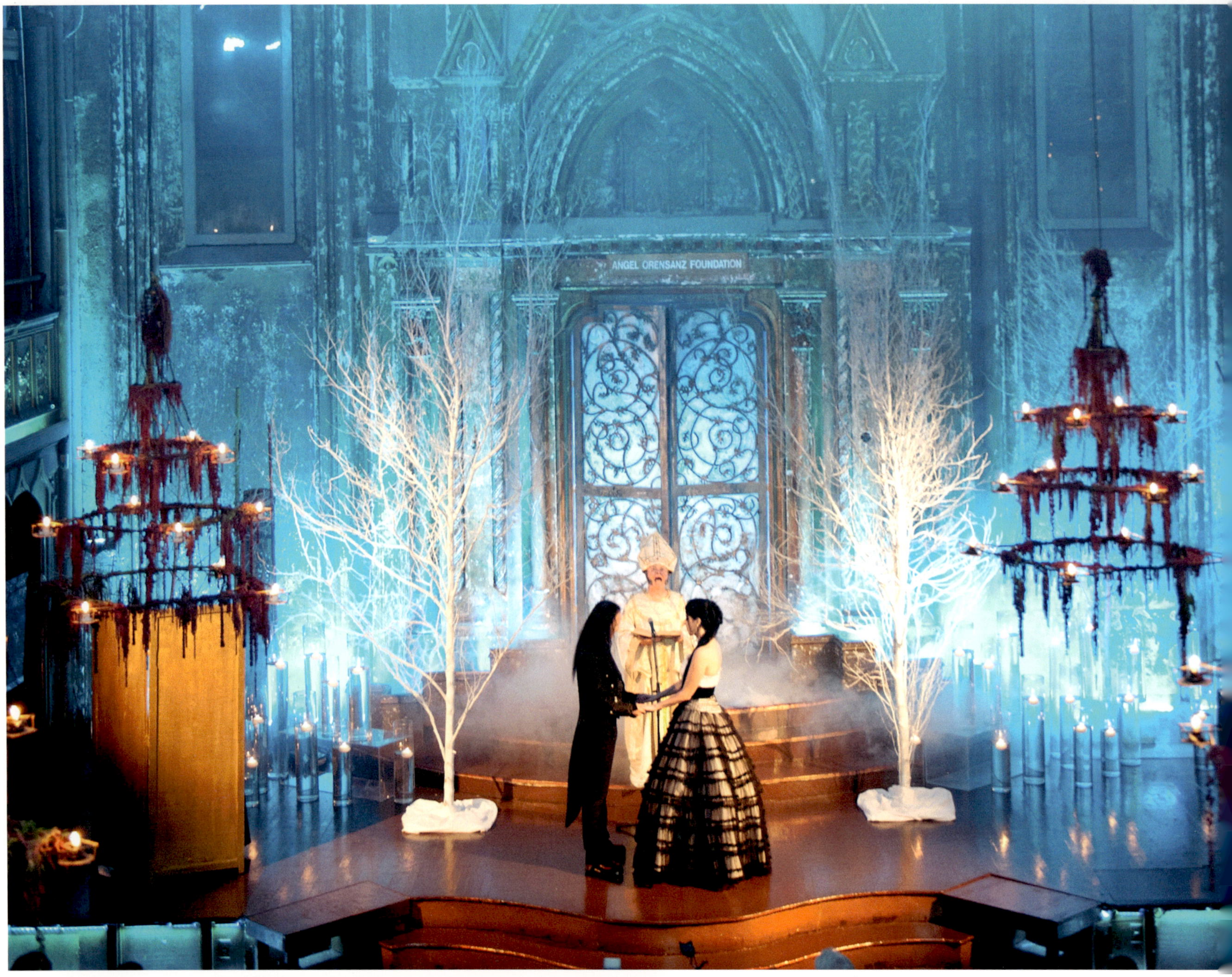

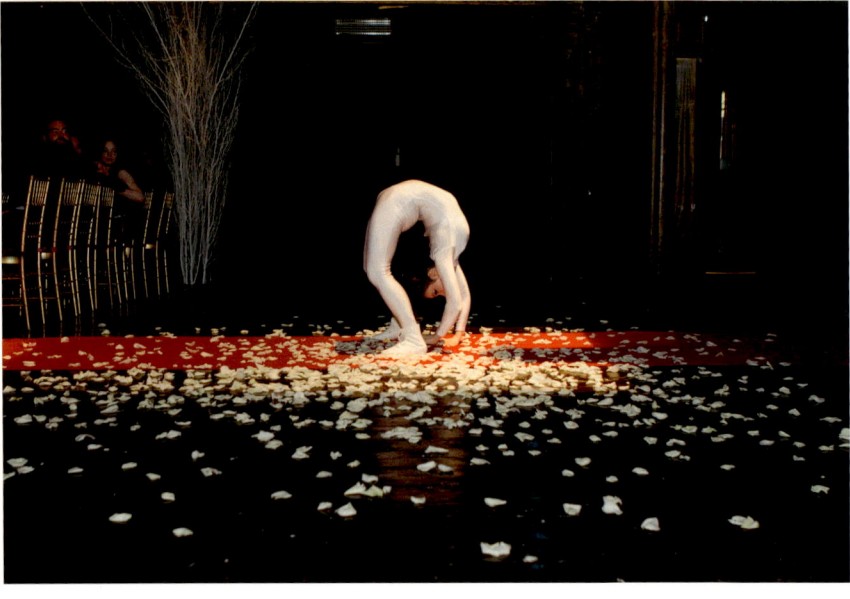

The ceremony
was performed
by a man dressed
up as the bishop
from the movie
*The Princess
Bride.*

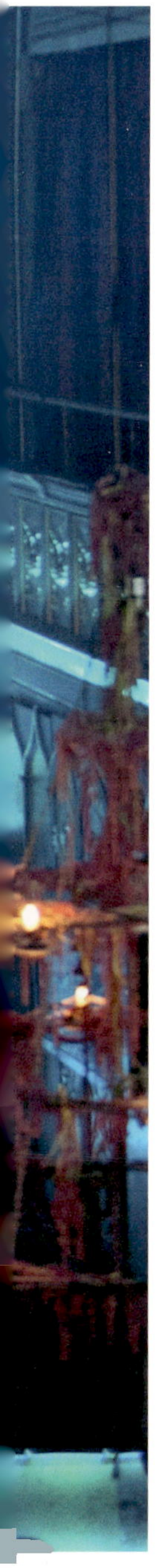

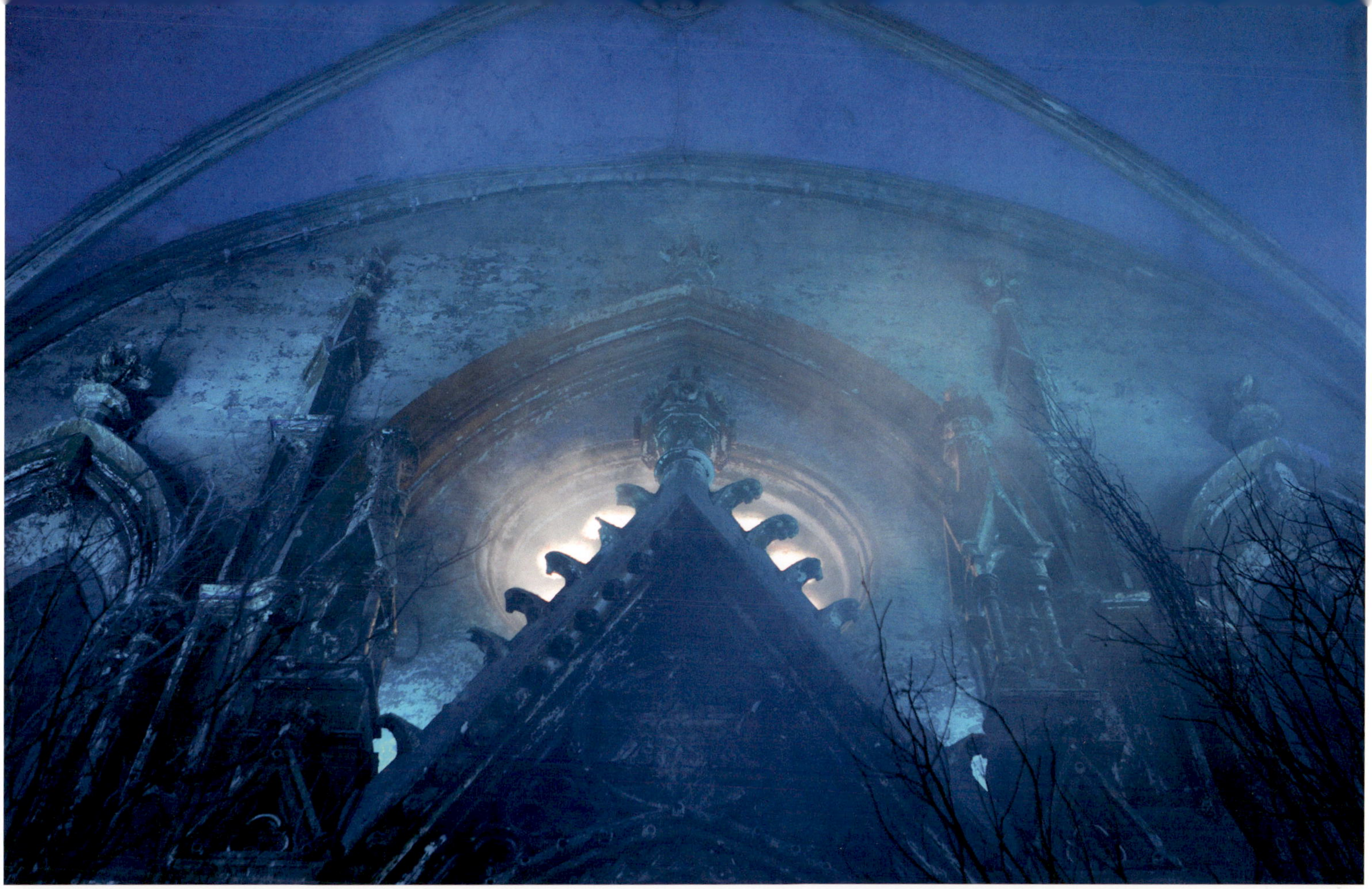

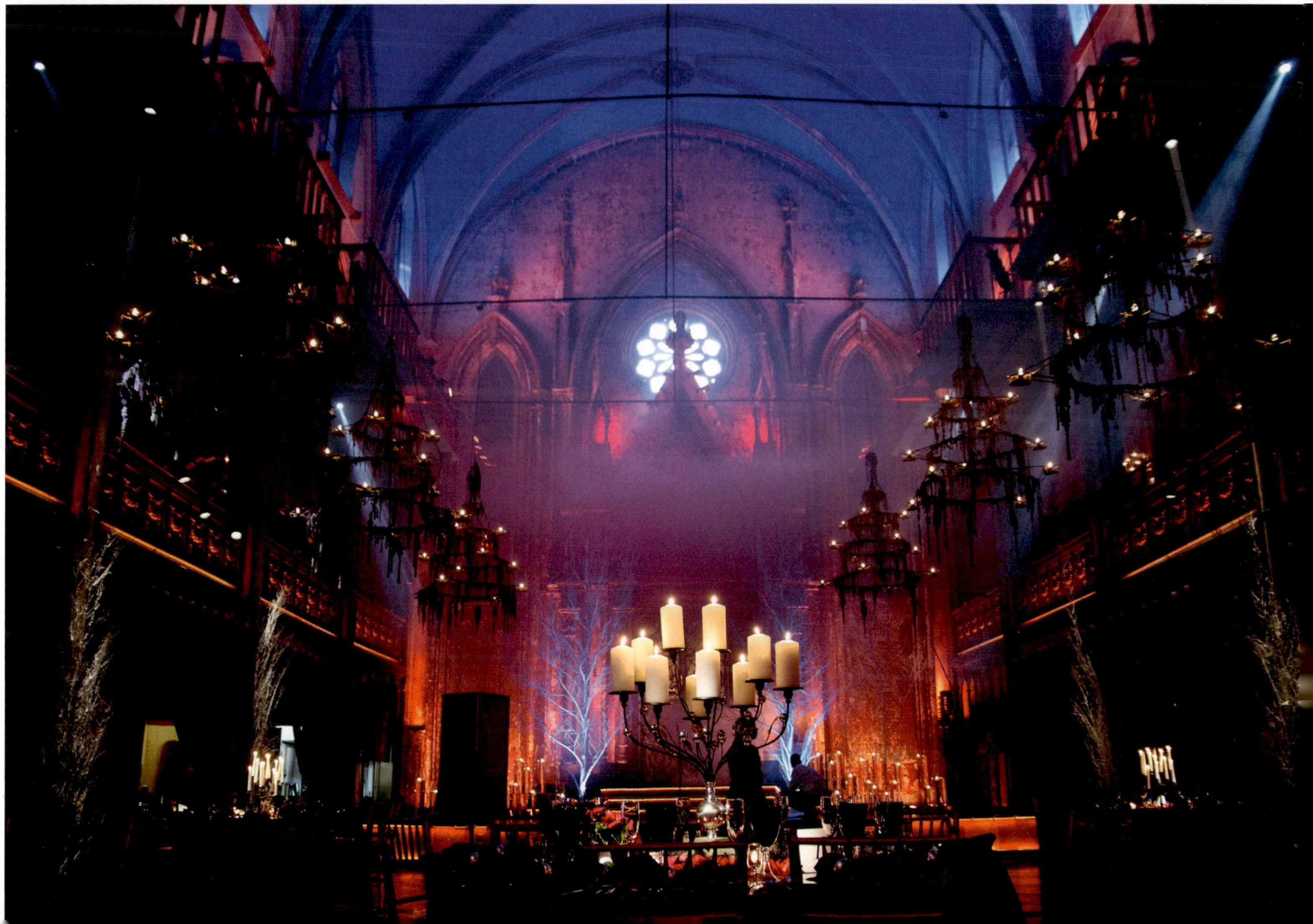

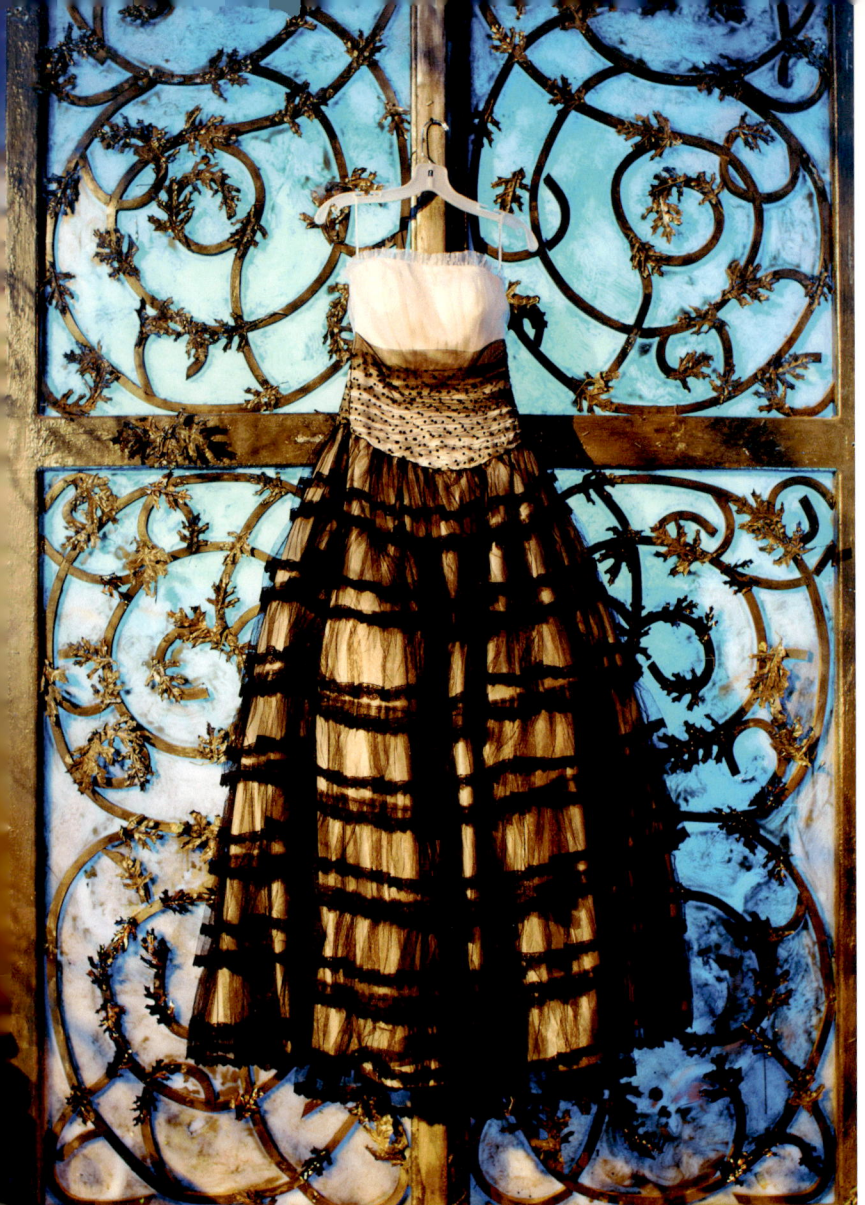

Gowns & Wedding Skulls

Suzy paired her gothic Victorian dress with an elegant cameo pendant and wide black ribbon. She and Dmitry exchanged place cards for homemade miniature plaster skulls stamped with each person's name and table number. They had the hanged-couple design made into a stamp and used it on the napkins and other paper products that were featured on the day.

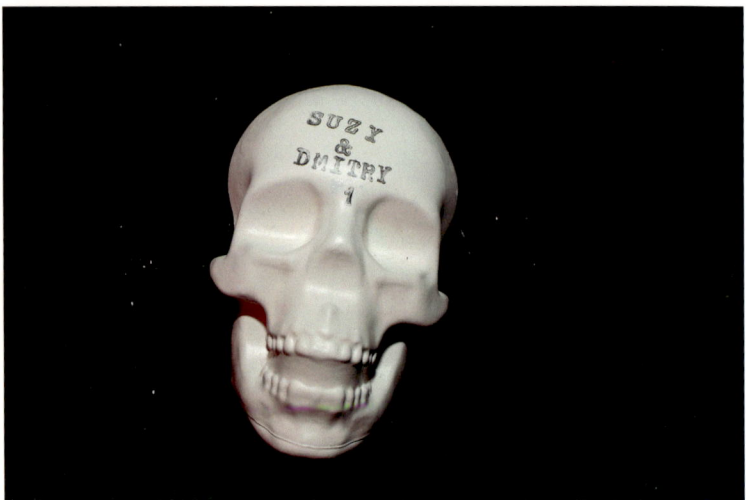

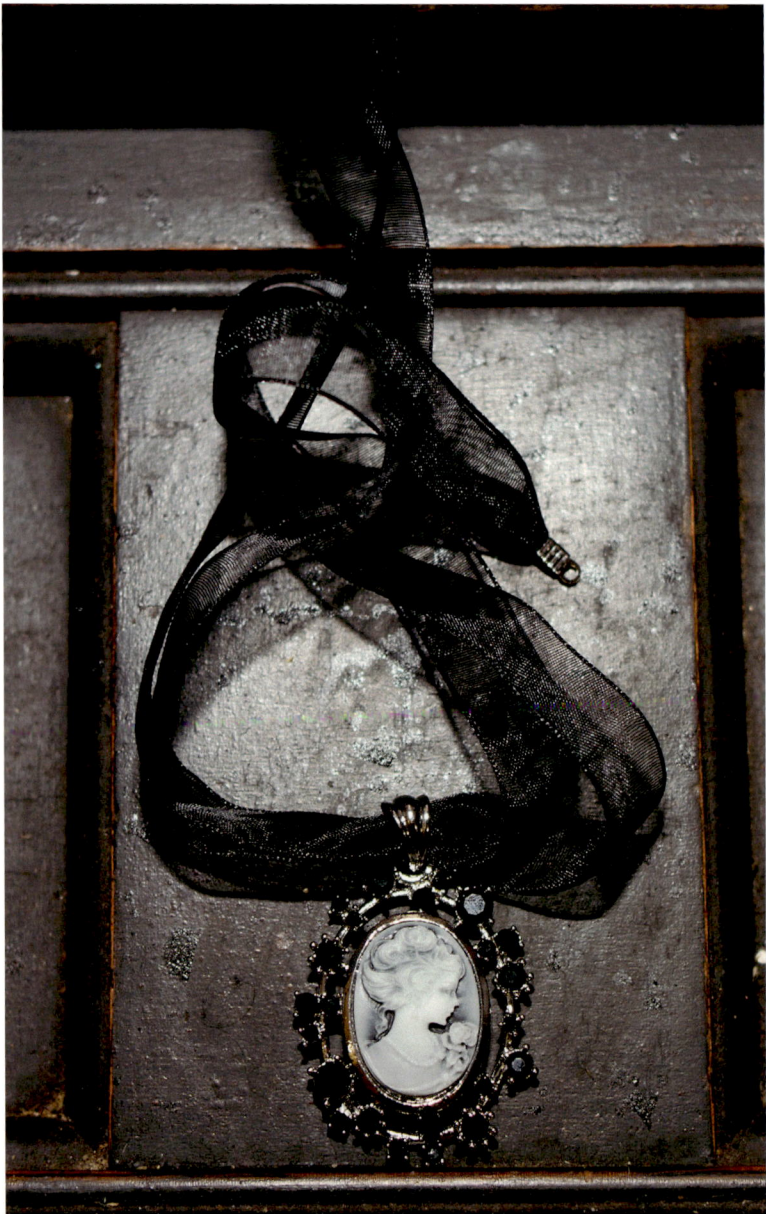

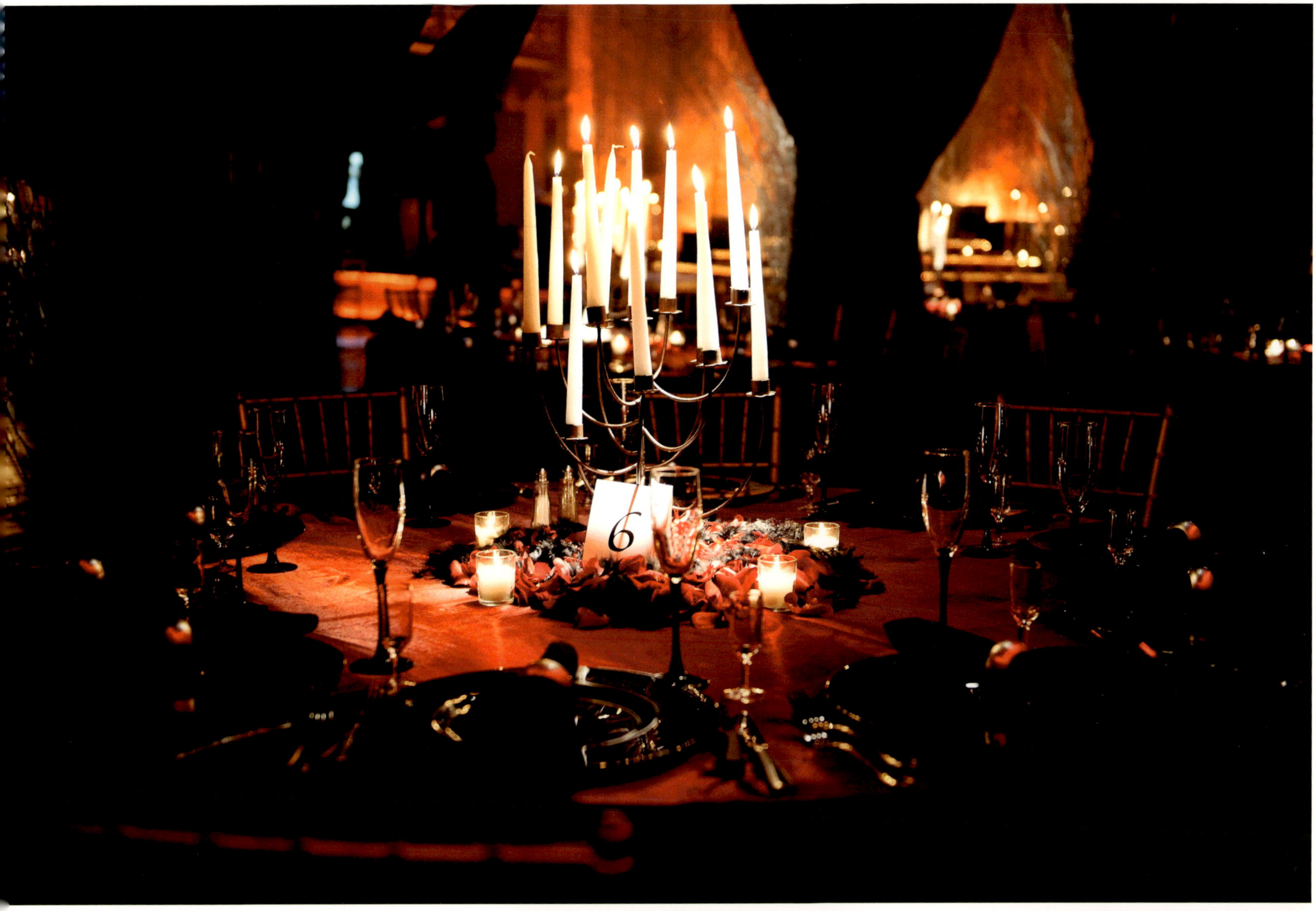

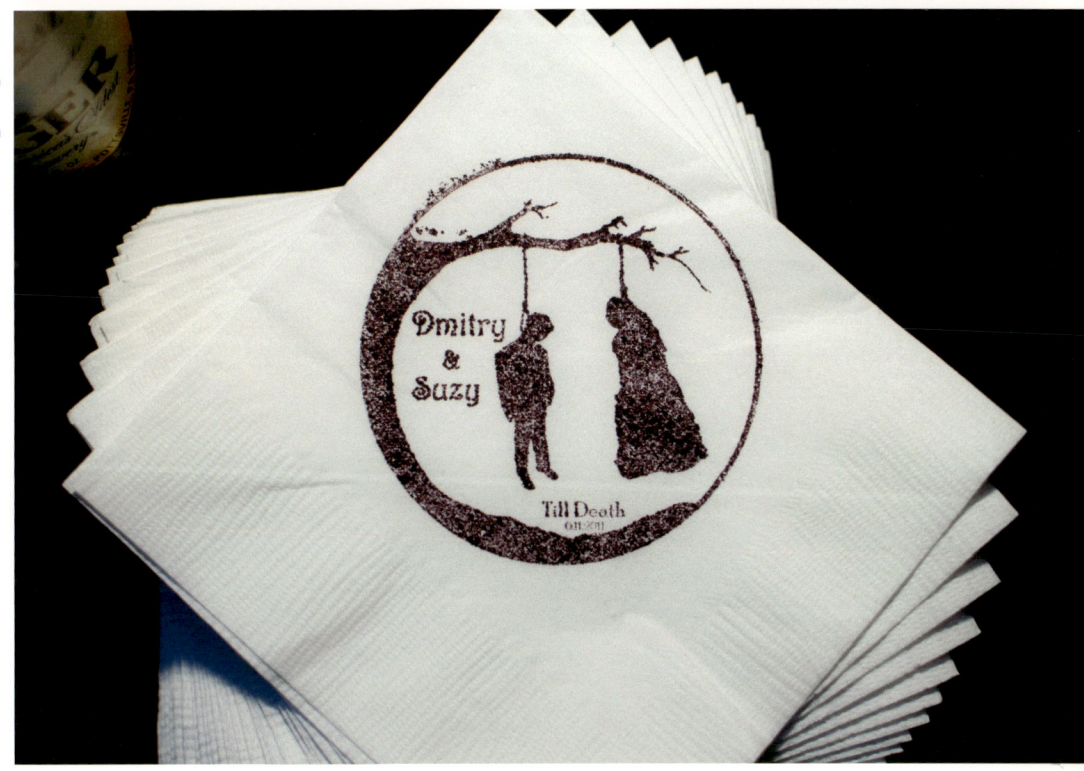

The rose petals and black feathers surrounding the candelabras matched the bouquet that Suzy carried down the aisle.

Dmitry
&
Suzy

Till Death

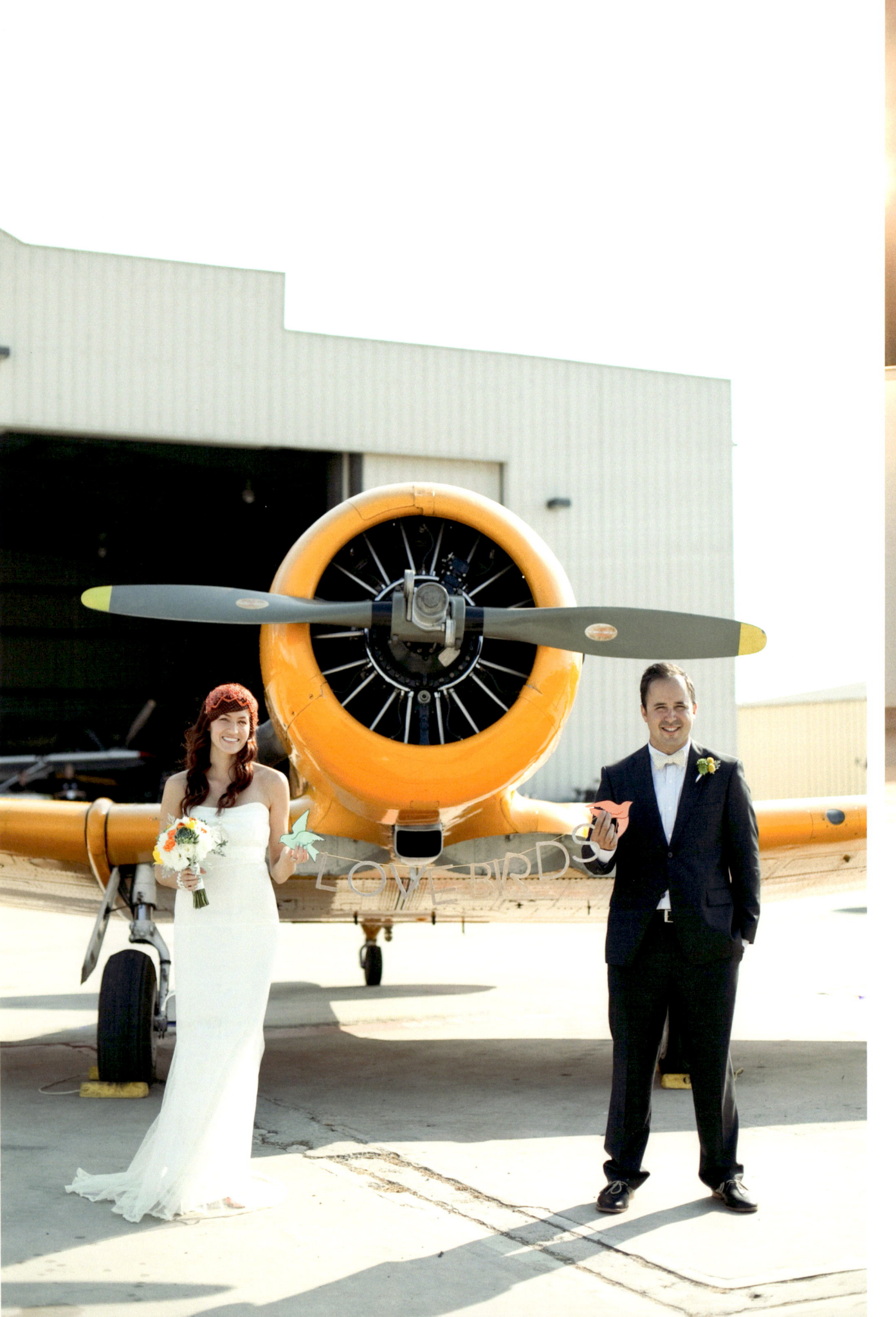

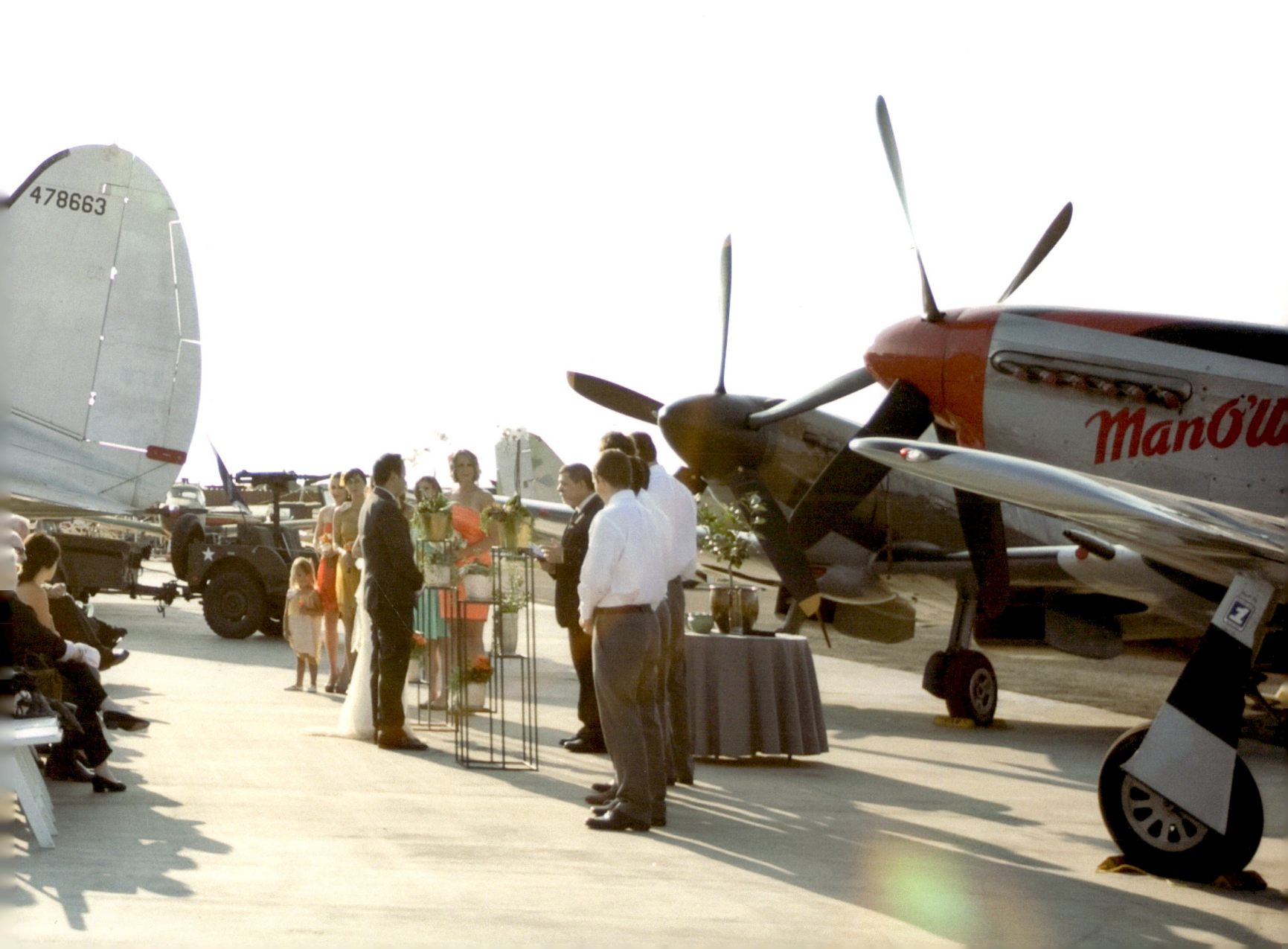

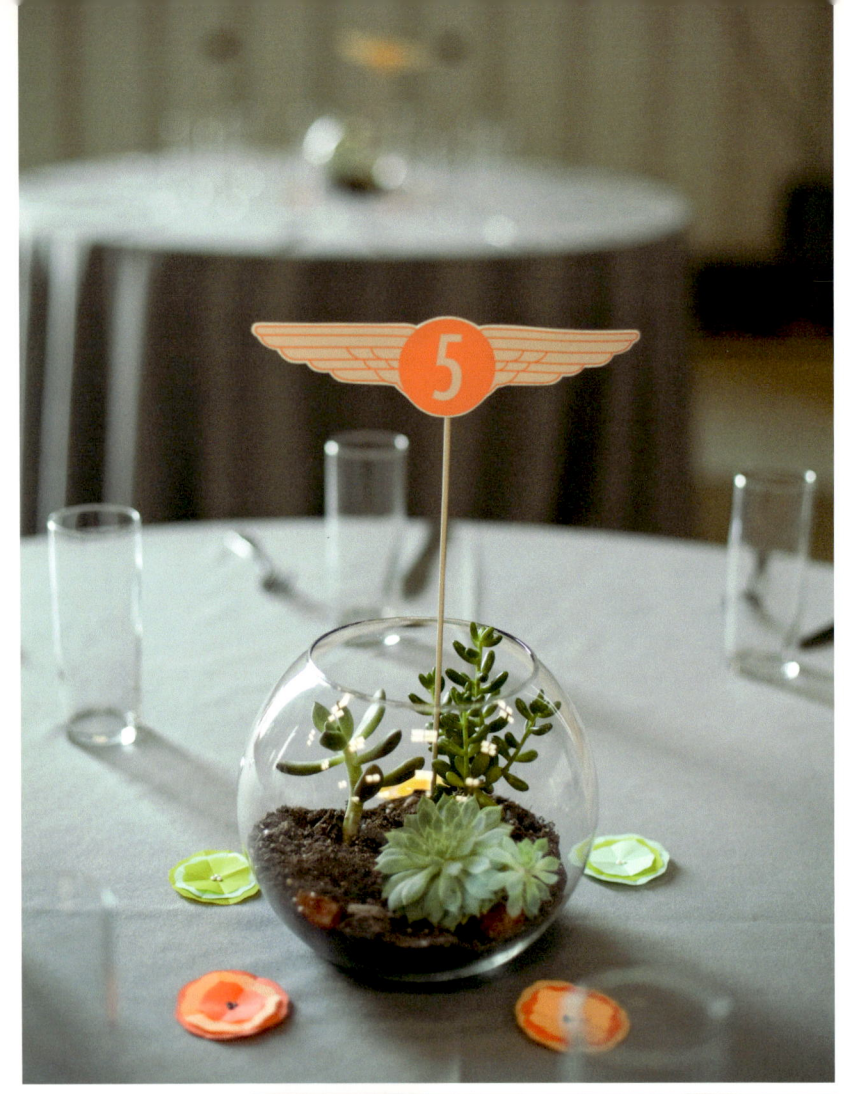

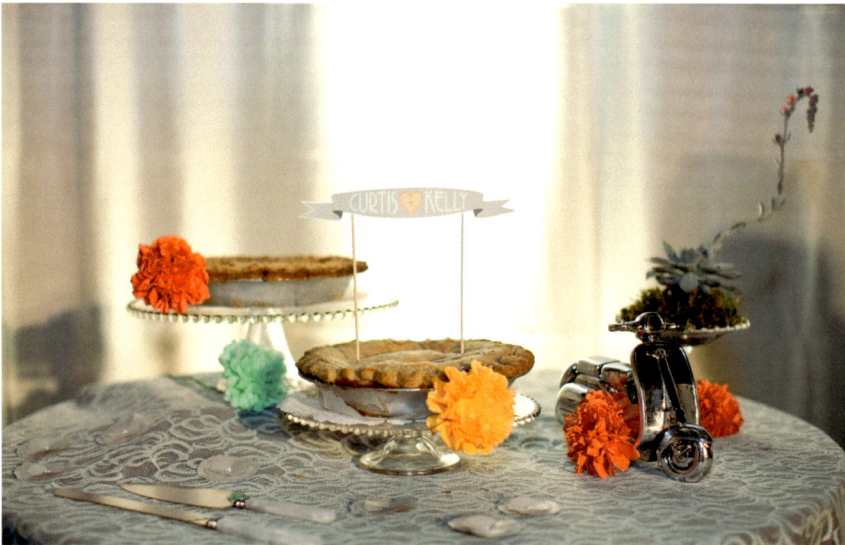

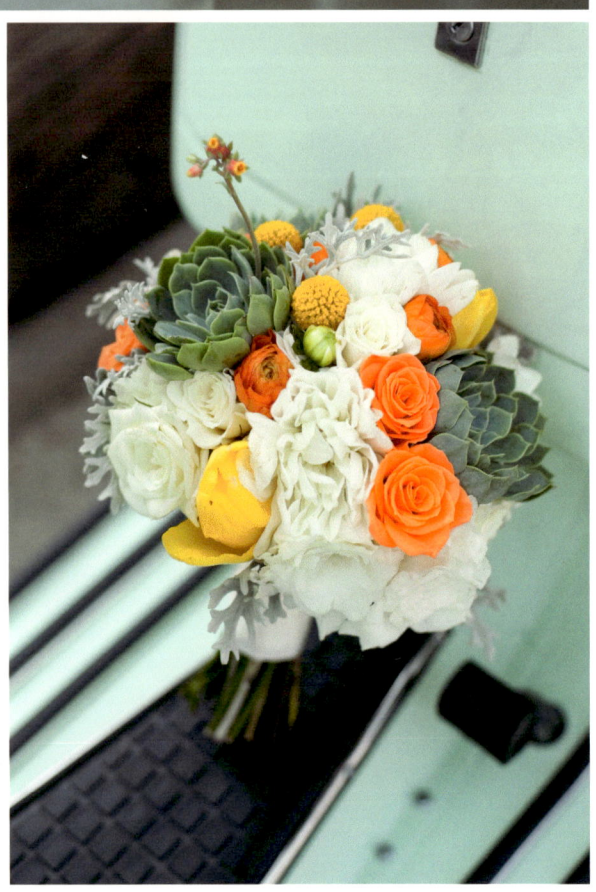

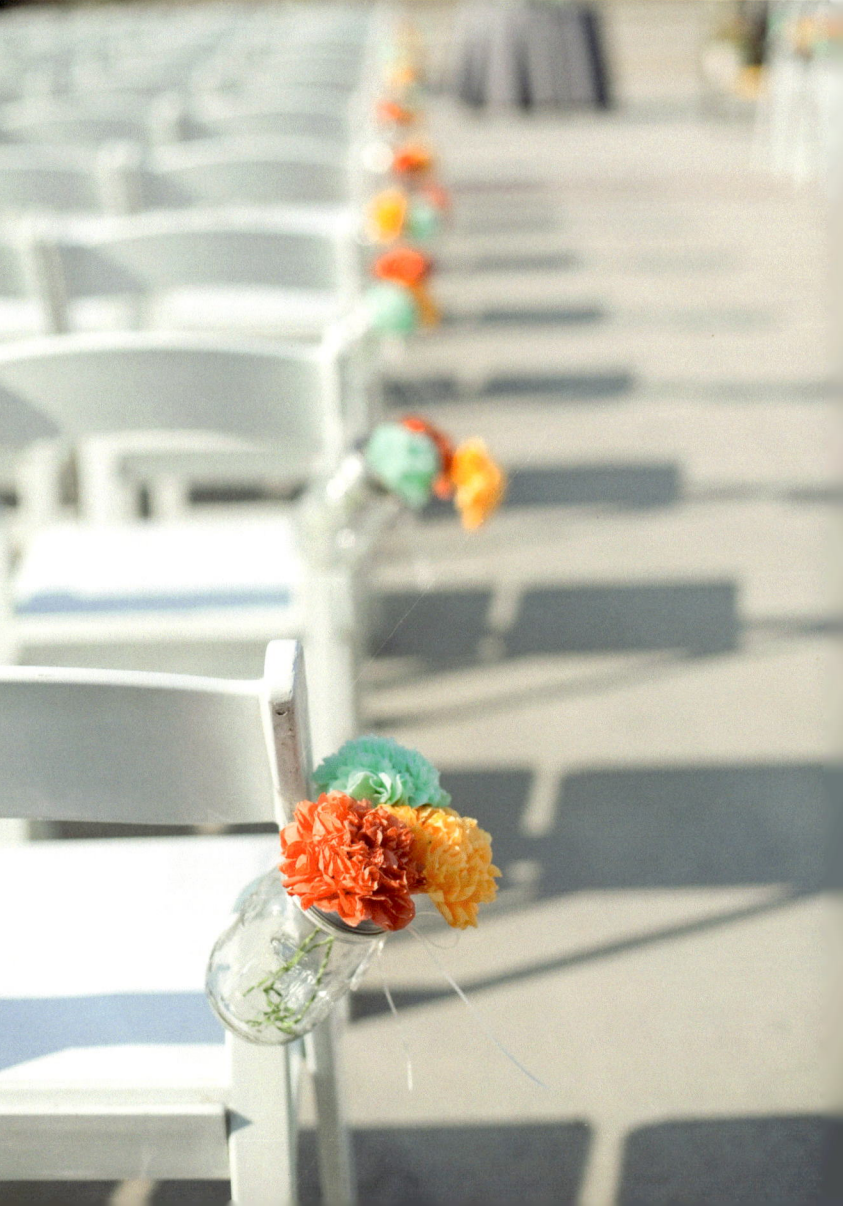

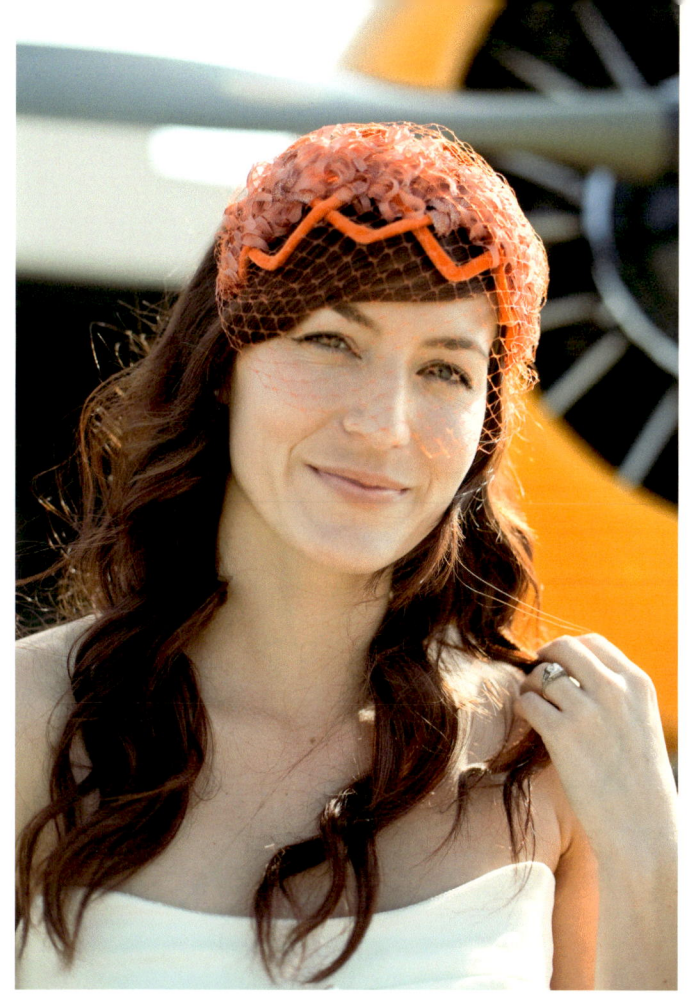

Flowers & Parasols

Pretty in pink, mint, and yellow. Kelly didn't go for cookie-cutter bridesmaids' dresses. Instead, each of the girls got a dress that matched her own coloring—and the color of the flowers that lined the aisle, decorated the pie table, and peppered Kelly's bouquet. Topped off with white parasols and a net headpiece for Kelly, these wedding outfits deserve an honorary flypast.

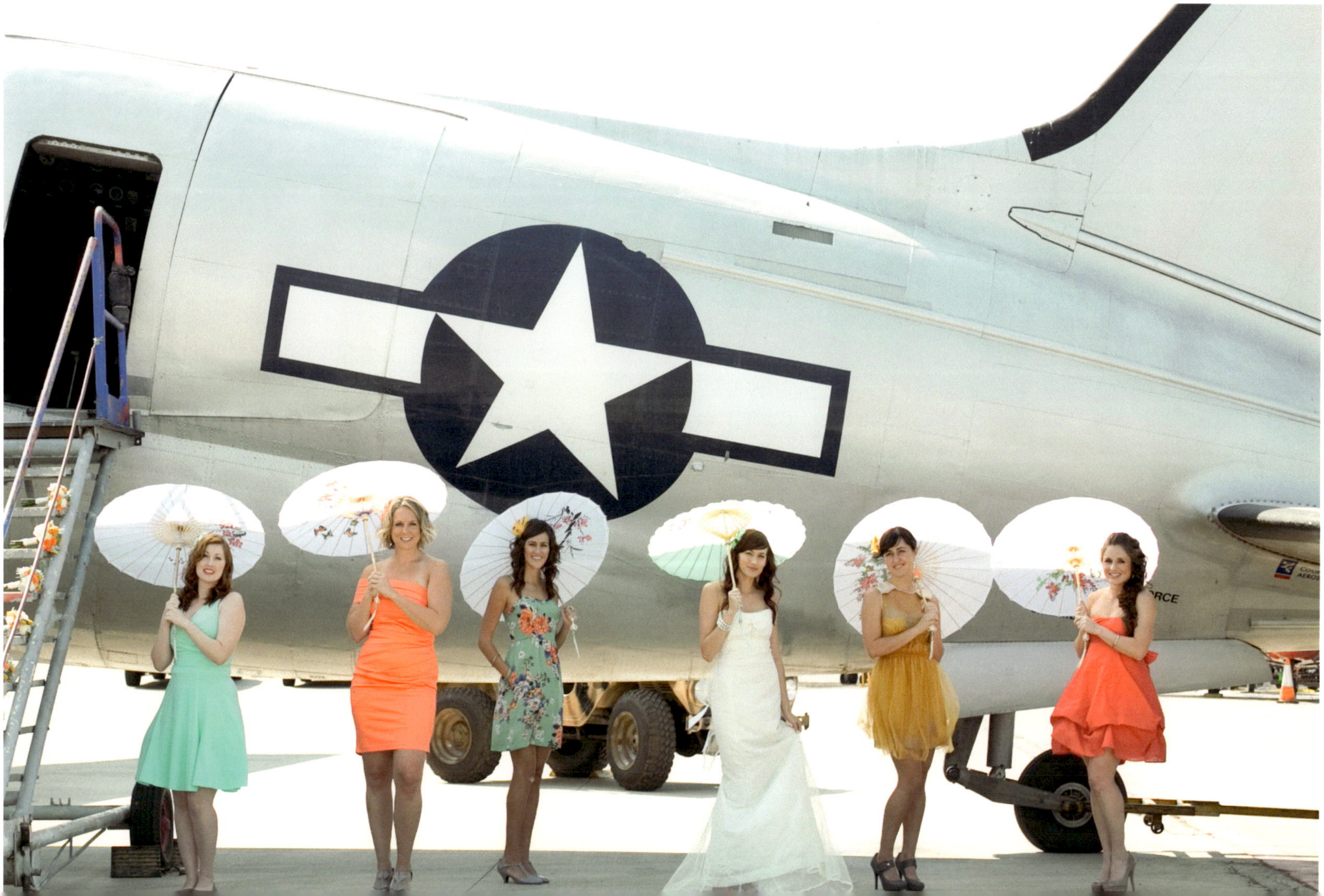

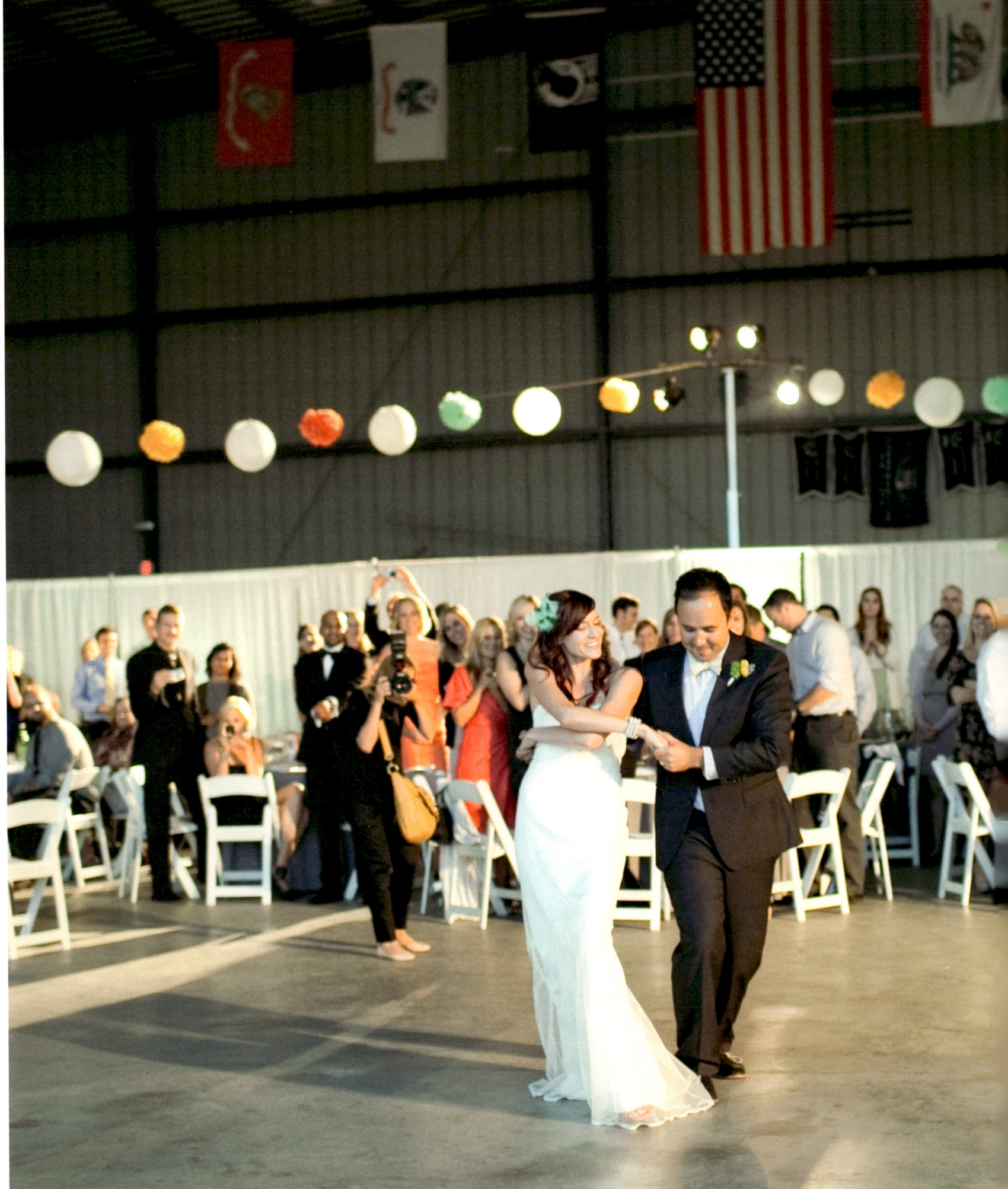

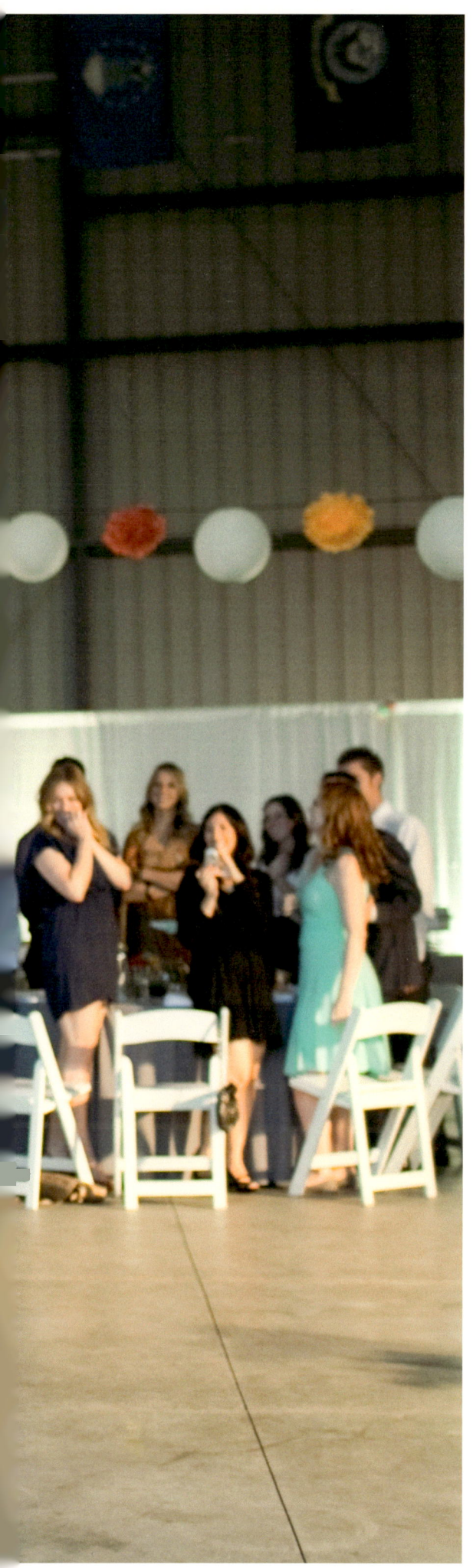

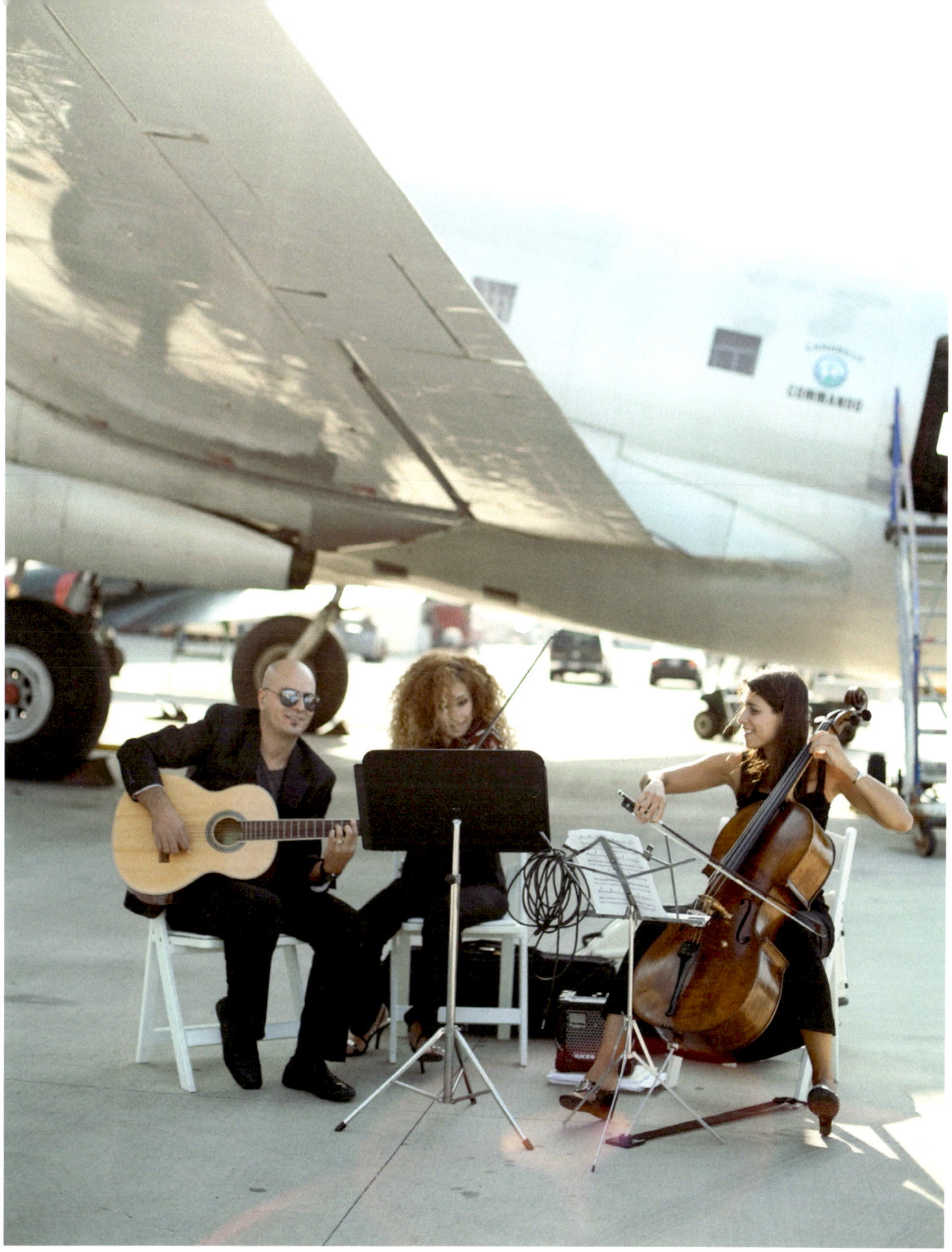

As Kelly and Curtis move across the floor, they look like a Hollywood love story come true... all that's missing is a final shot of the couple flying off into the sunset.

The Guestlist

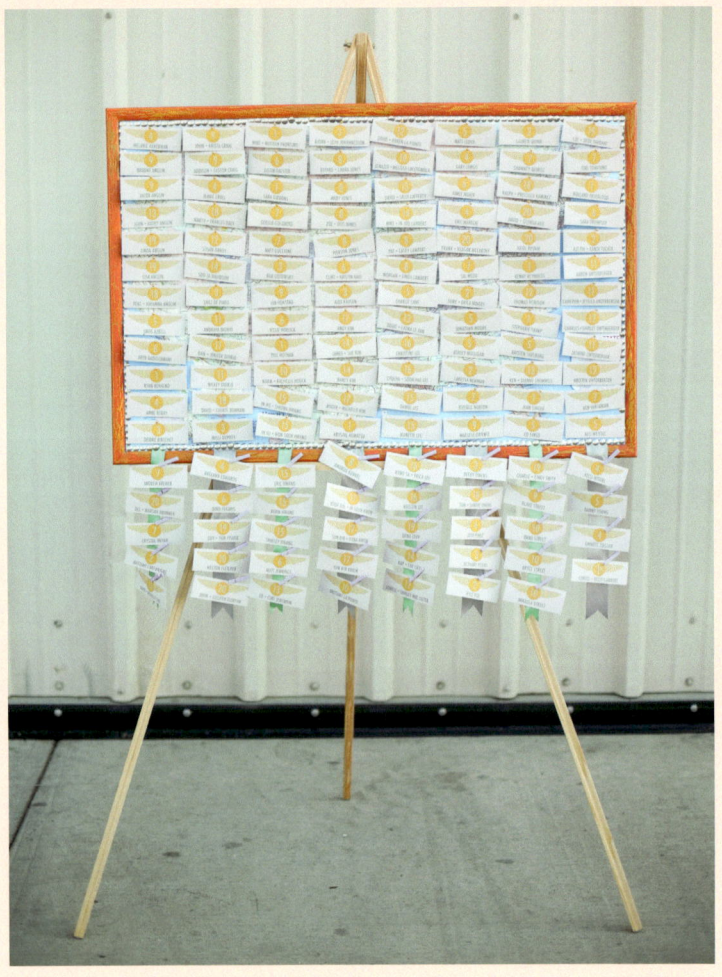

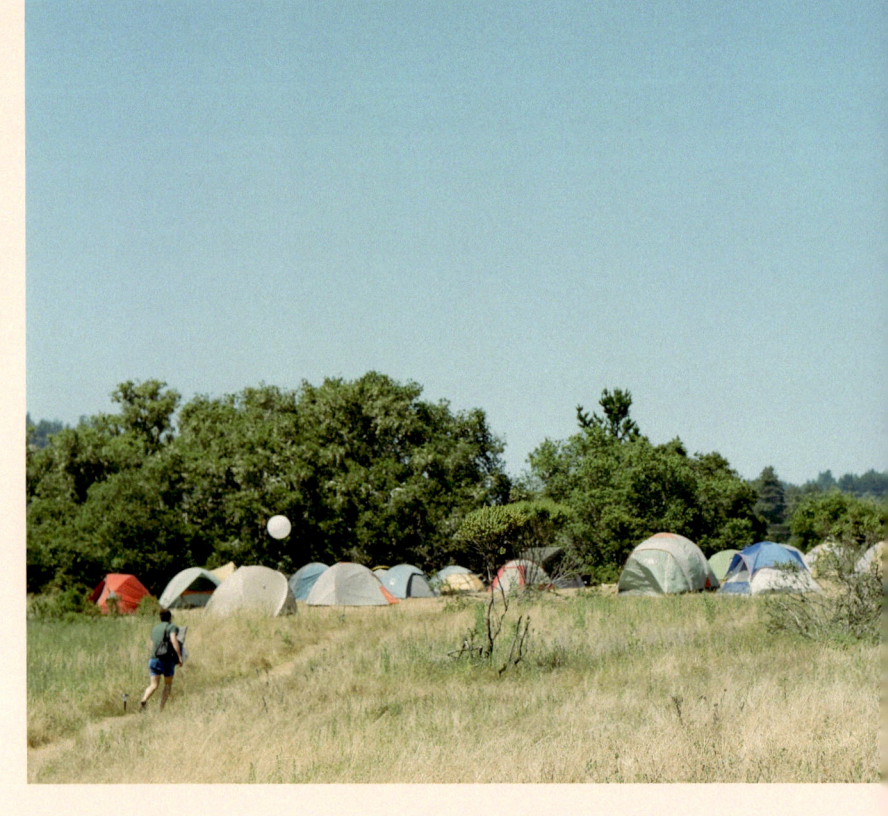

Everyone entertains and interacts with people differently. Some of us enjoy low-key encounters whilst others love large-scale affairs. When deciding on the size of your wedding's guest list, think about what you prefer. If you feel more comfortable connecting with people on an intimate level, opt for a smaller wedding. If you prefer to sweep through a room of hundreds, then a large wedding it is.

There is nothing wrong with preferring a smaller gathering. There is, however, an issue when that's what you are inclined towards but

feel compelled by tradition to have a large raucous wedding. Ignore what you feel you should do and stick to what feels comfortable.

One of my favorite weddings was an elopement. The couple were worried that their nerves would get the better of them in front of a vast congregation of guests so they decided to have their ceremony completely between themselves. With just each other and their officiator, they were married without any fuss or crowd-induced butterflies. It was so beautiful because it really stripped things back down to the very core of what getting married is all about—two people coming together in love.

Consider the impact of size on the dynamic of the day.

What atmosphere do you want to create? Smaller weddings with a selection of your nearest and dearest are close, cozy and affectionate. In comparison, larger weddings, with hundreds of guests, have the celebratory atmosphere of a carnival.

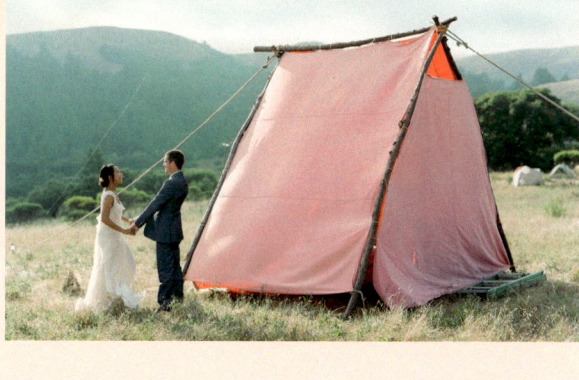

Visra and Chris wanted to create a festival-style ambiance at their celebration, so to make it truly authentic meant inviting a whole campsite of guests.

When planning an event the formula remains the same regardless of the size. It's just a case of scaling up or down. However, keep in mind that more guests means having to stretch your resources further. If you are on a tight budget, a bigger wedding might mean having to cut back on other areas or sacrifice some completely.

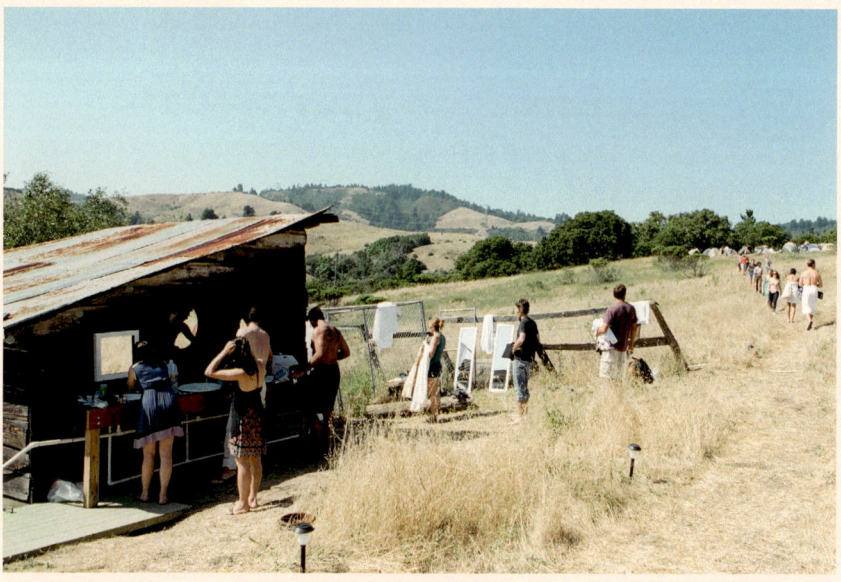

Think about what matters to you the most. For one of our most intimate weddings, that meant filling their celebration with personality and playful details, like the bride drawing the most incredible illustrations of each attendee instead of place cards. This was feasible with an invite list of only a few guests and their dog: had they had a bigger wedding, the mammoth task of hand-painting a portrait for every guest would have been impossible.

A clever seating plan can help guests get to know each other. Here are a few things to get the conversation going:

1. Disposable cameras on tables with a shoot list. Props also work well, like paper hats, vintage sunglasses, or stick-on moustaches. They turn picture taking into storytelling.

2. Crossword puzzles filled with fun questions about the couple and a prize for the winning table.

3. Crackers filled with conversation starters or table tasks.

4. Give each guest a nickname and print it on the place cards—each person has to explain theirs to the other guests.

Things to keep children entertained:

1. Paper tablecloths with cartoon designs for them to color in.

2. Engaging entertainment—a magician or balloon artist.

3. Special kids' menus work brilliantly. An ice cream bar or special dessert table will make them go wild. Not too wild, hopefully.

4. Comfortable seating and hang-out areas. Formal dining and hard chairs make little ones fidget. Bean bags and soft seating are much more child-friendly.

5. Interactive decorations such as piñatas and balloons.

6. Give them tasks and responsibilities on the day to make them feel more grown up.

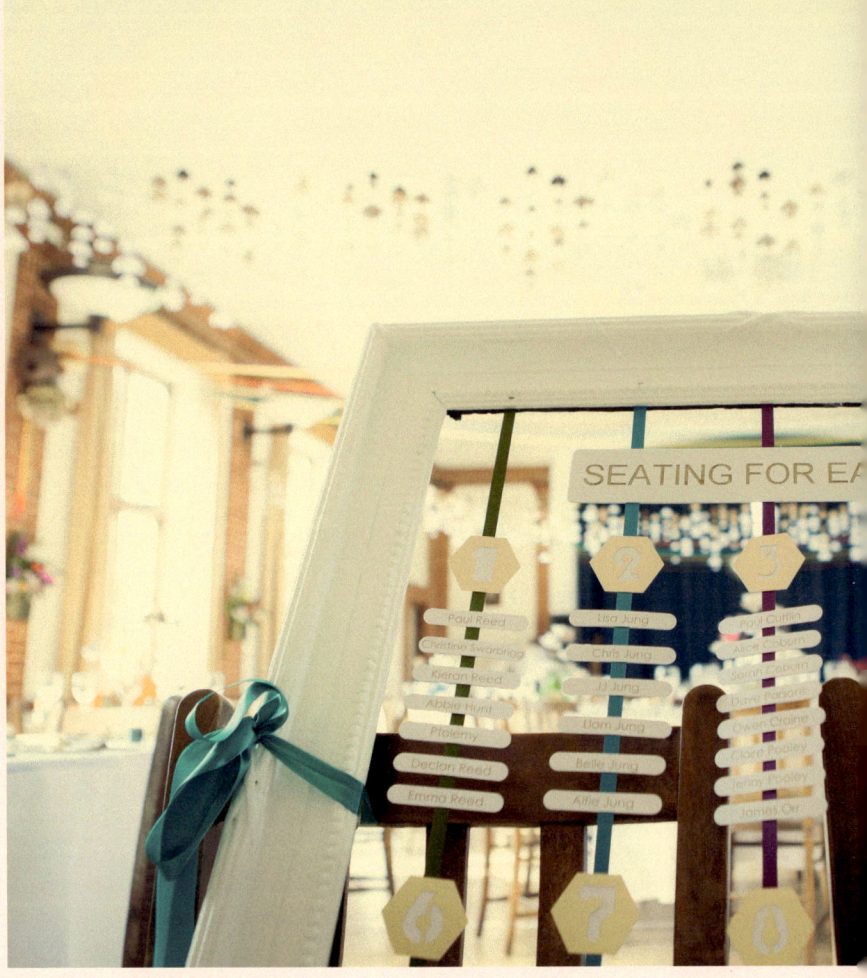

When it comes to your wedding it's not just the size of your guest list that matters but also the names that are on it.
Who you choose to invite will have a dramatic effect on the overall atmosphere.

For example, an event filled with business acquaintances and distant, unfamiliar relatives will have a much more formal tone than a gathering of your closest family and friends.

When writing your guest list it can be extremely difficult to narrow it down, especially if you have a limited number of spaces.

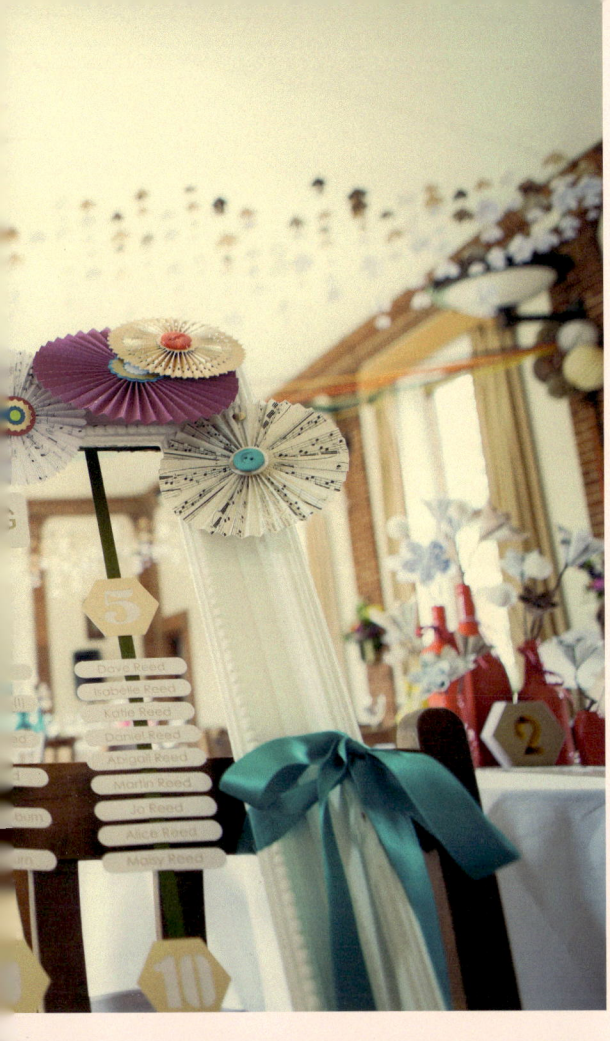

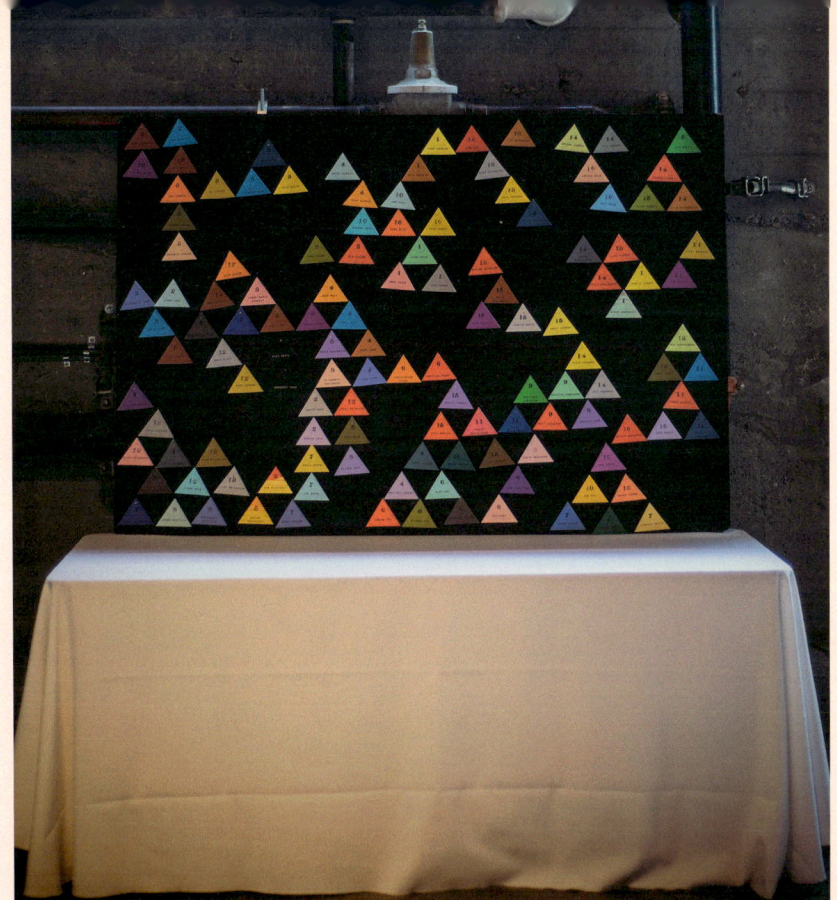

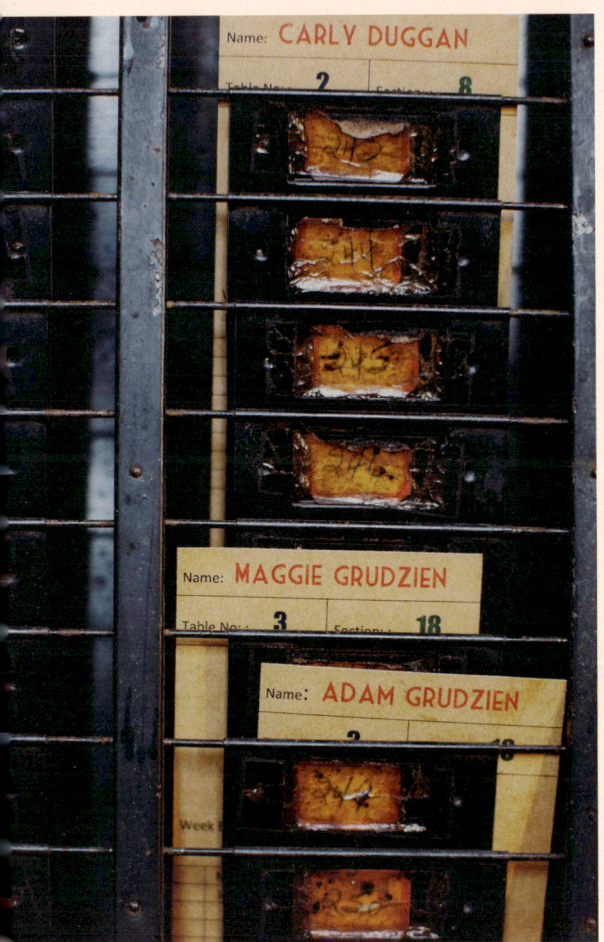

As obvious as it sounds, invite people you like and invite those you want to share this life-changing moment with.

Don't feel pressured into having an enormous wedding with everyone you're "supposed" to invite. My advice would be to consider three key factors. First, who is important to you? These are the people who you couldn't imagine getting married without; when you picture your wedding, their faces are always there.

Who holds meaning in your life? Whether you have shared tough times or happy memories, these are the people who have been present at moments of great importance in your life and who you want to be at the next: your wedding. And, finally, who makes you happy?

This book illustrates that a brilliant wedding can come in all different shapes and sizes; from pocket-sized parties to huge gatherings. Forget the fuss, do what feels right for you and you simply can't go wrong.

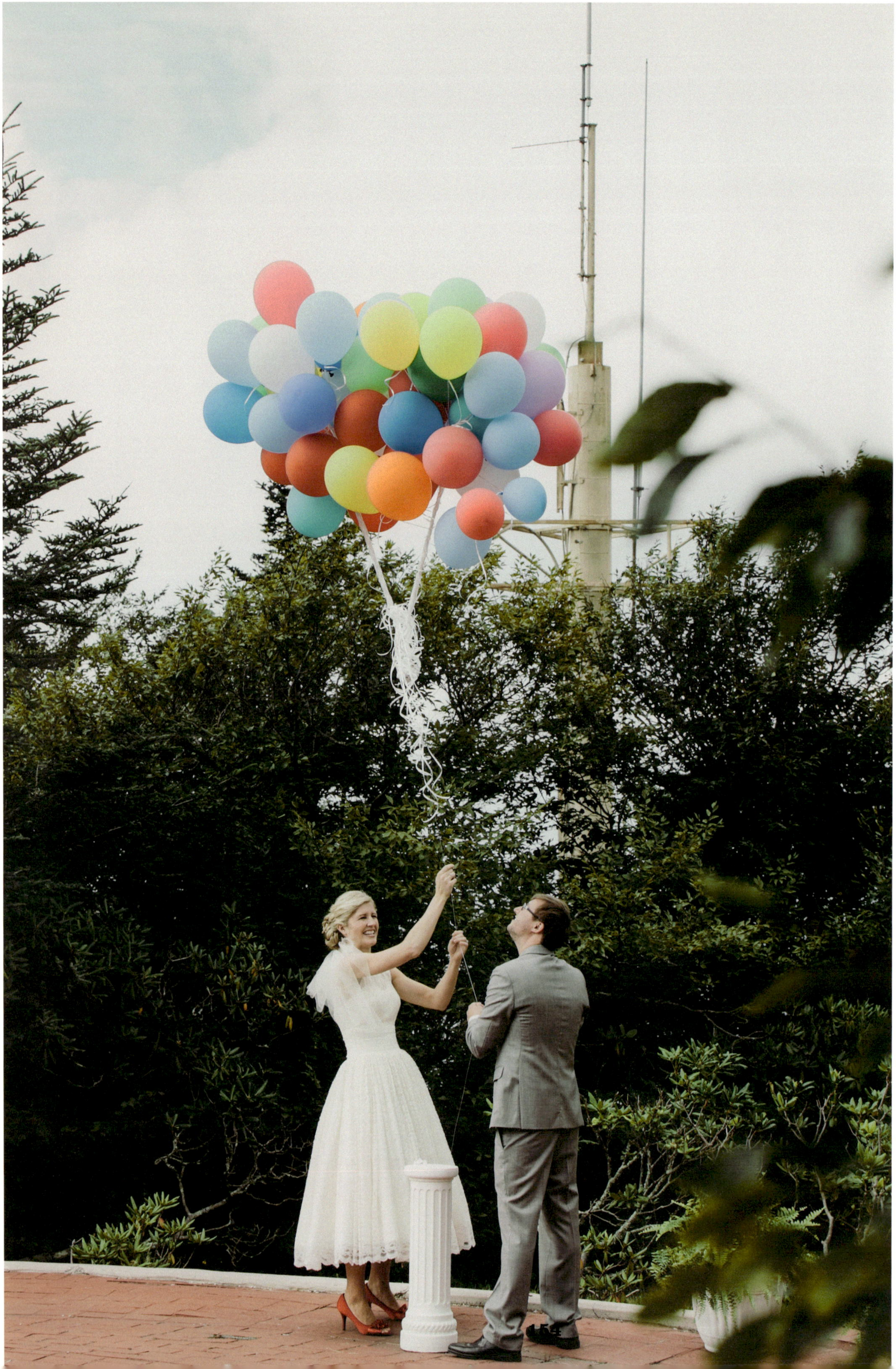

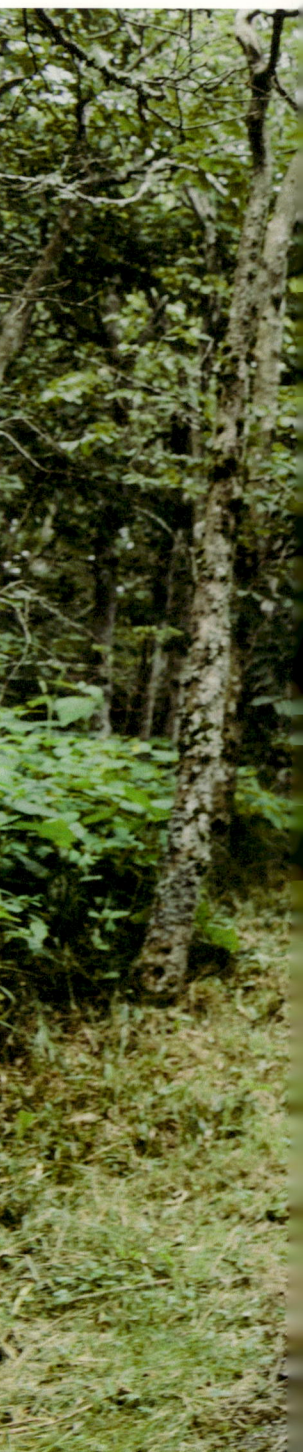

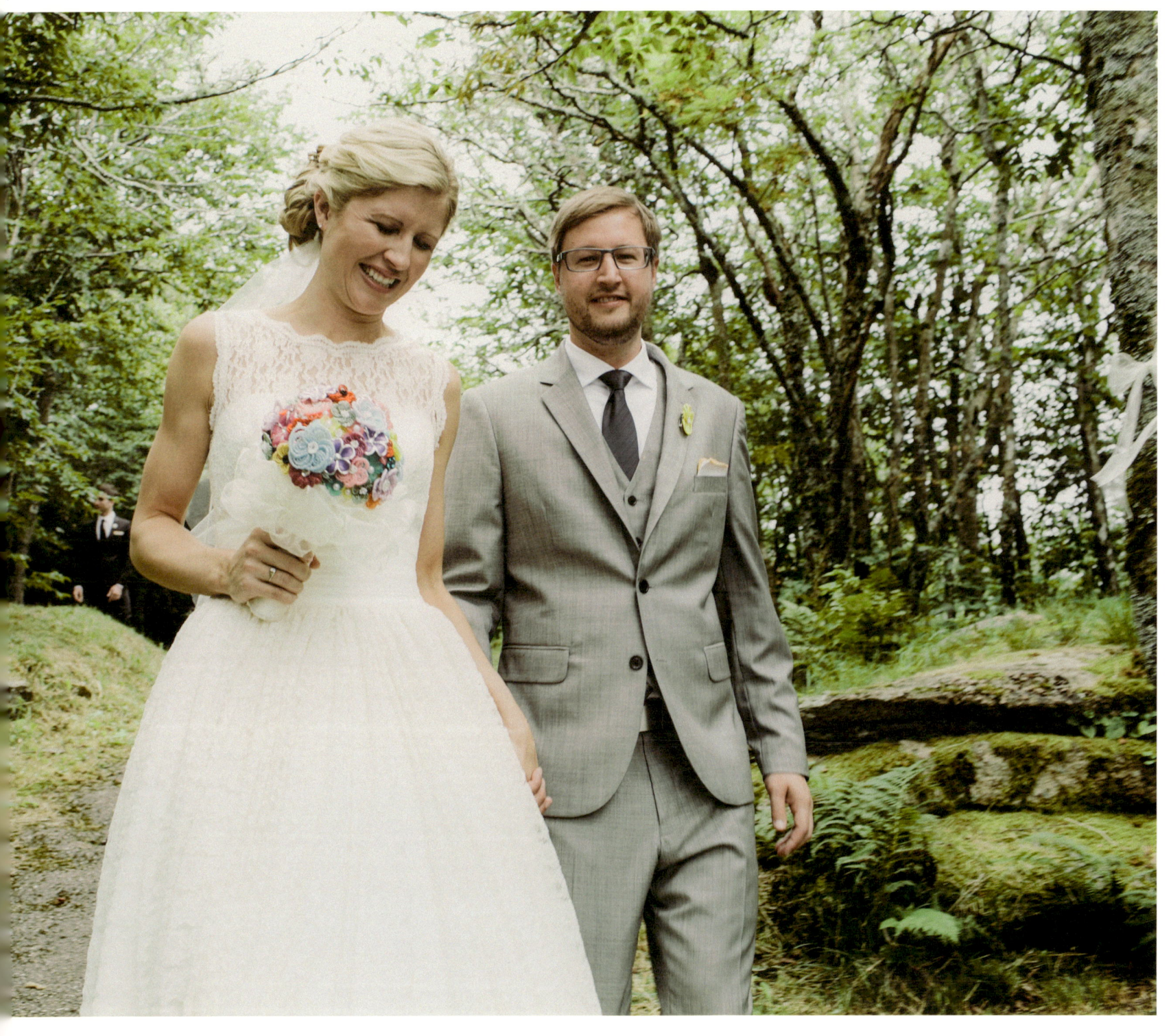

Anna & Brandon

Haunted forest? Witch's castle? Is this a good idea? Thankfully Anna and Brandon are too grown up to be scared of the Wicked Witch of the West, so tying the knot in the Land of Oz suited them just fine. Given the location, Anna must have taken all of two seconds to decide on her shoes. The scarlet heels played their part brilliantly, holding their own against her white dress, the yellow brick road, and the bunches of balloons that brightened the day.

155

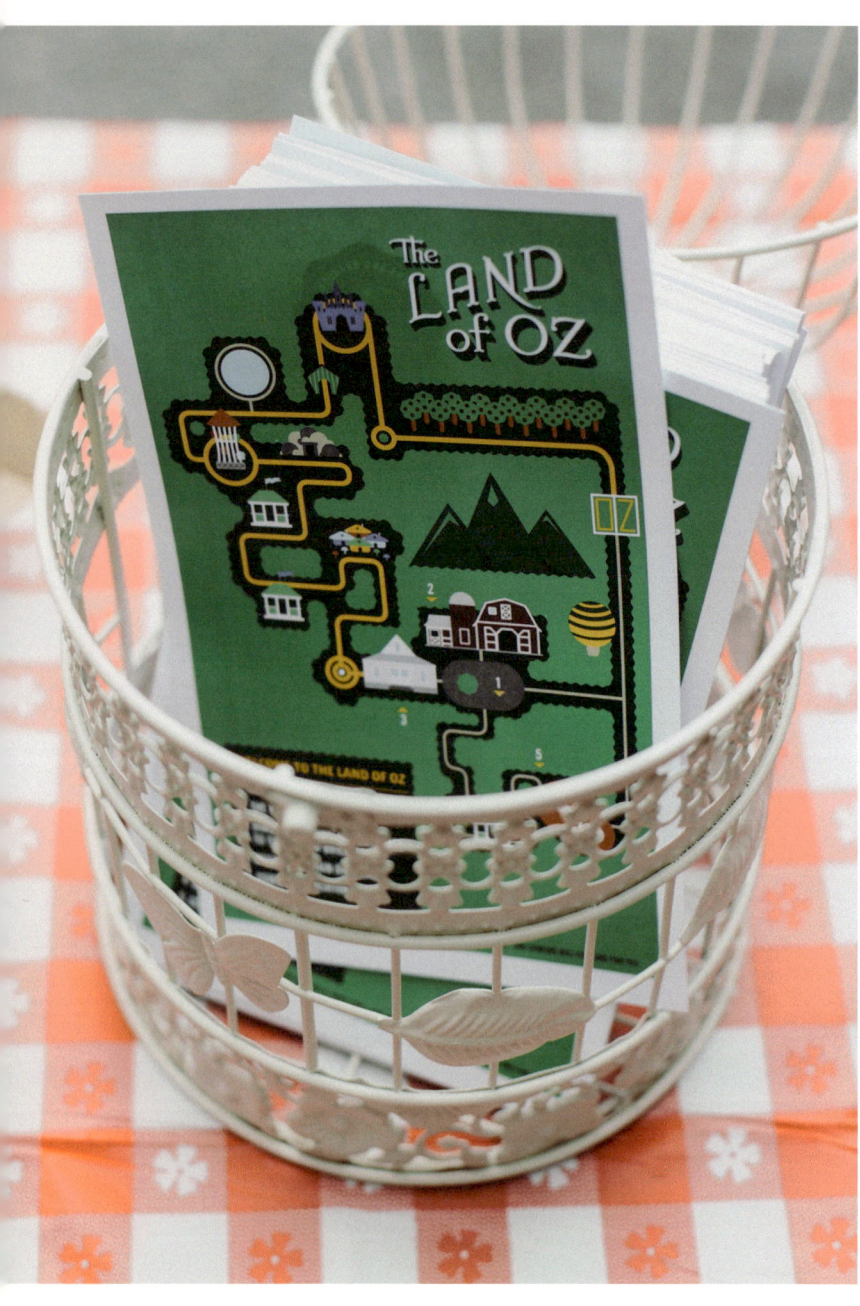

A Wonderful Theme

The Land of Oz theme park is now only open for private events, but it still has everything Anna and Brandon needed for a magical start to their journey together.

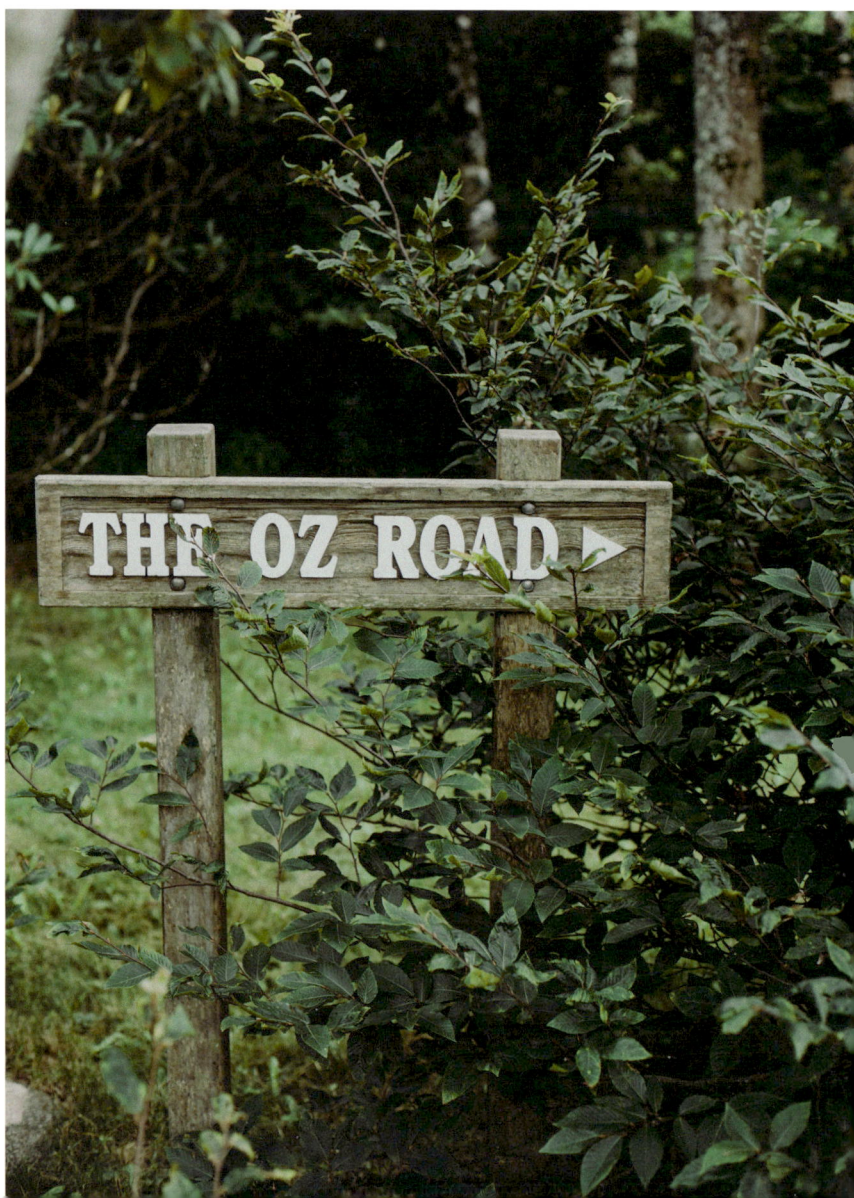

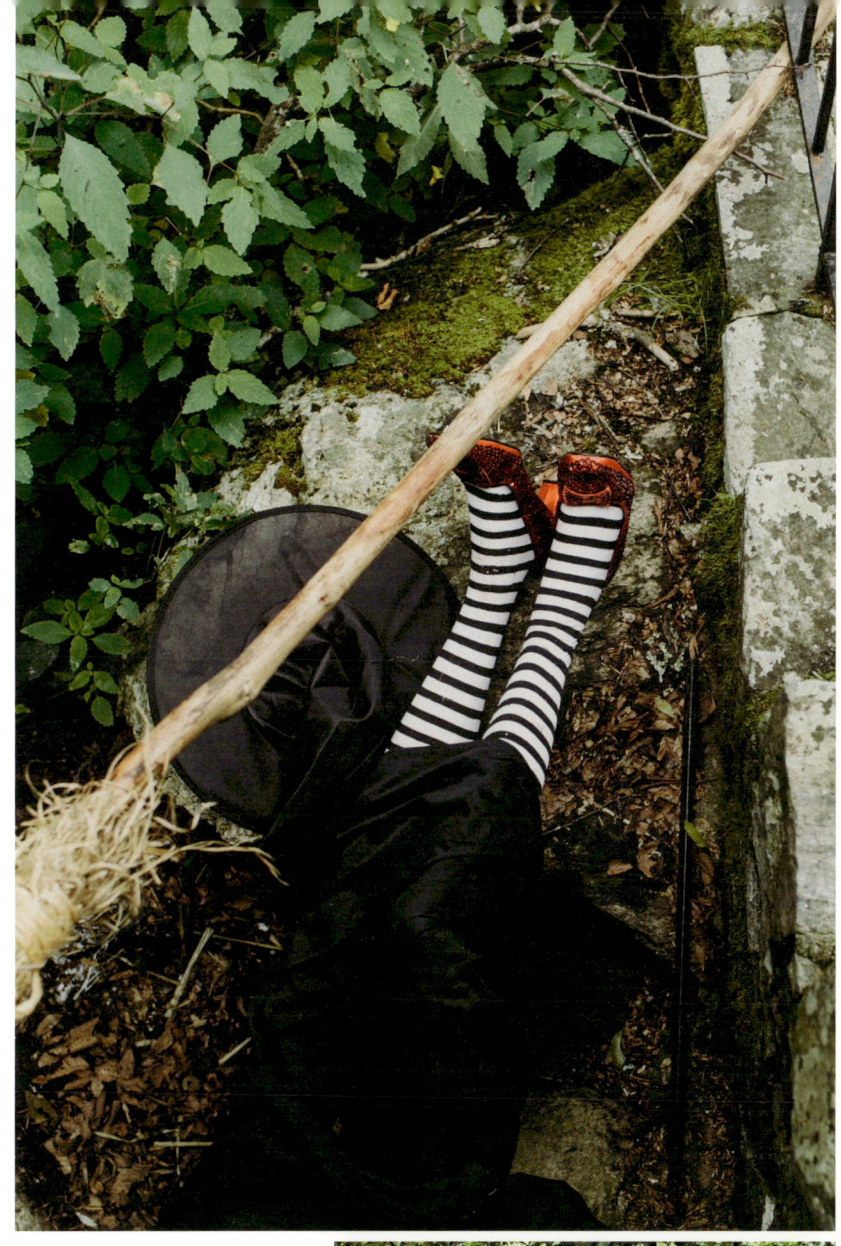

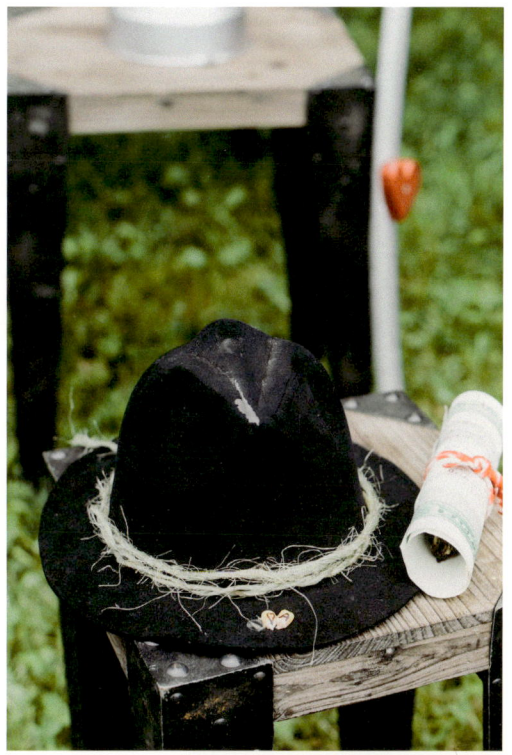

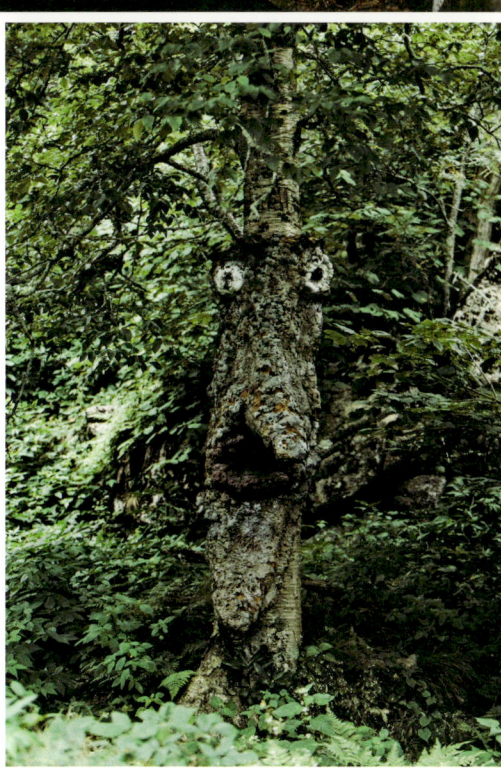

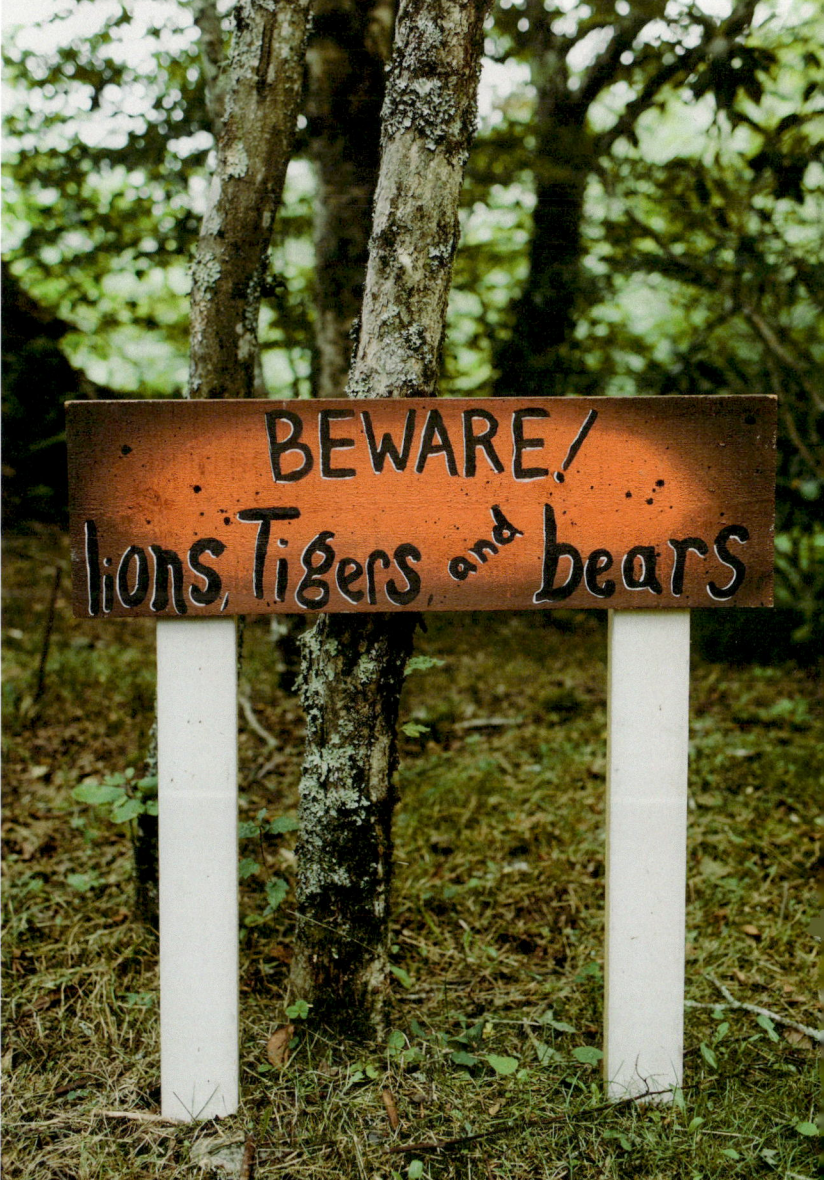

BEWARE!
lions, Tigers and bears

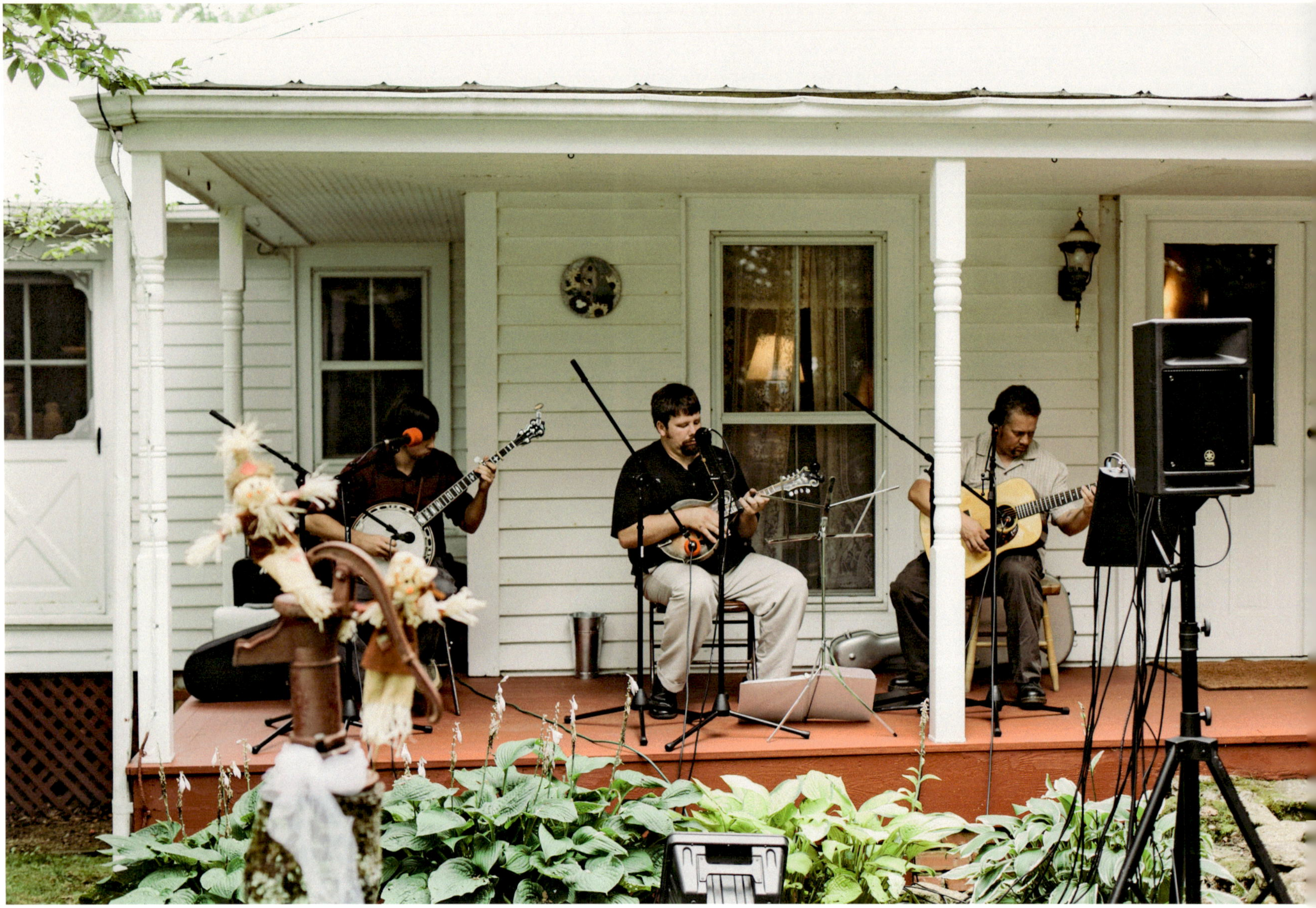

Party & Location

The ceremony began with The Merry Old Land of Oz and ended with Somewhere Over the Rainbow. Then a bluegrass band got on the banjoes and served up some music that was just the ticket for a country girl like Dorothy.

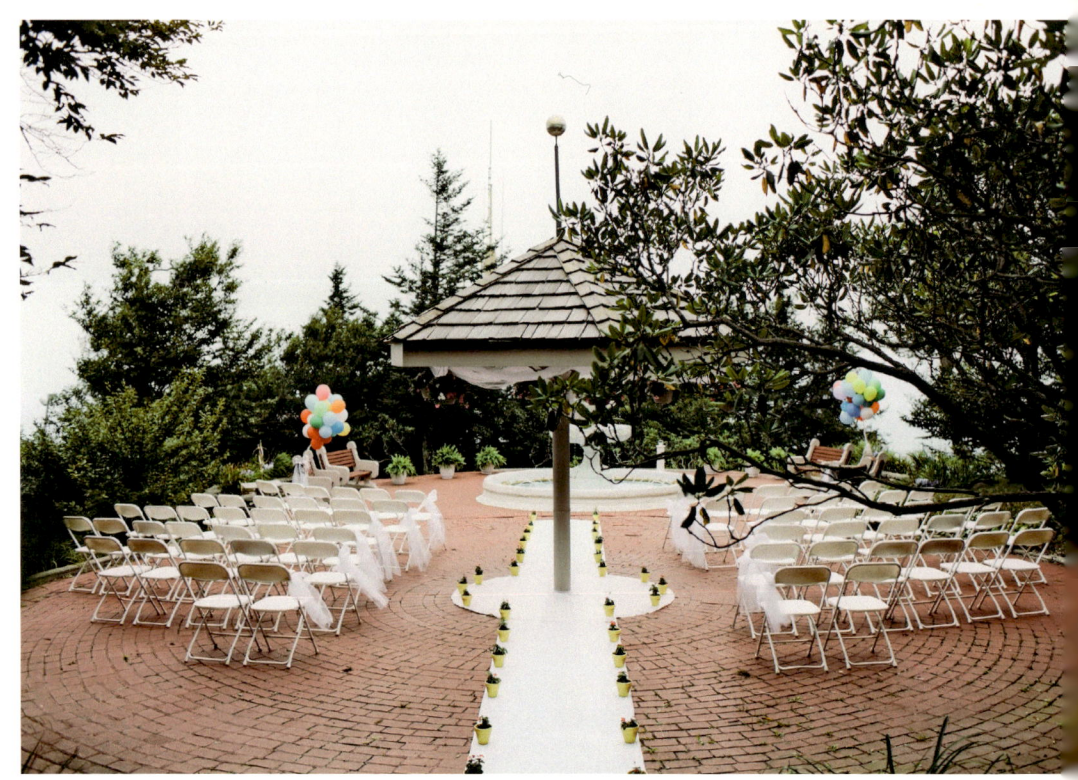

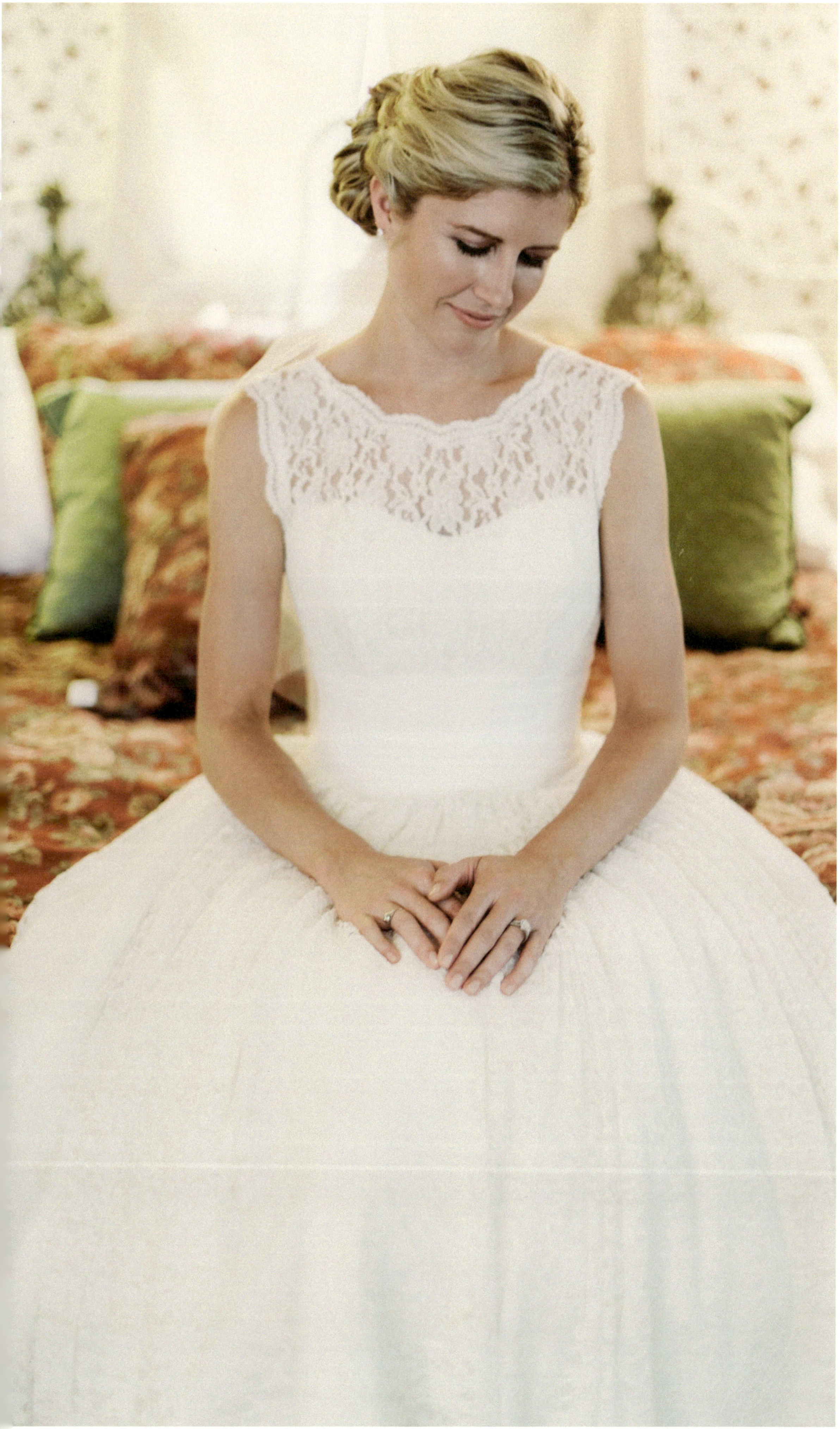

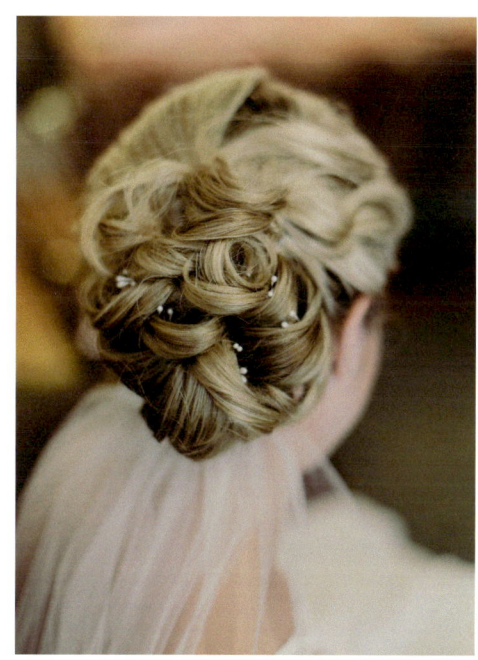
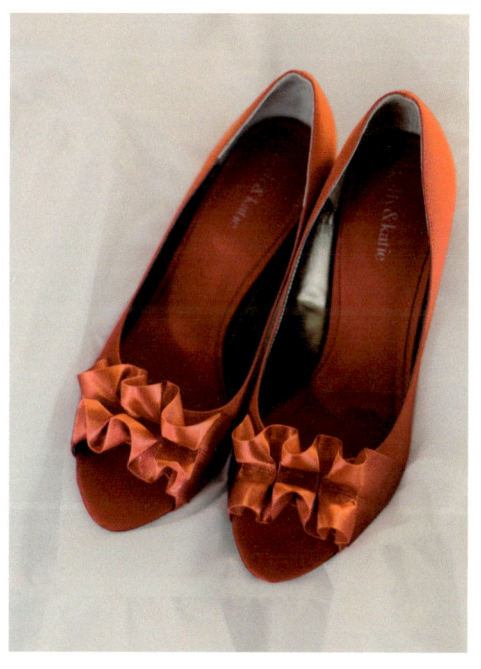

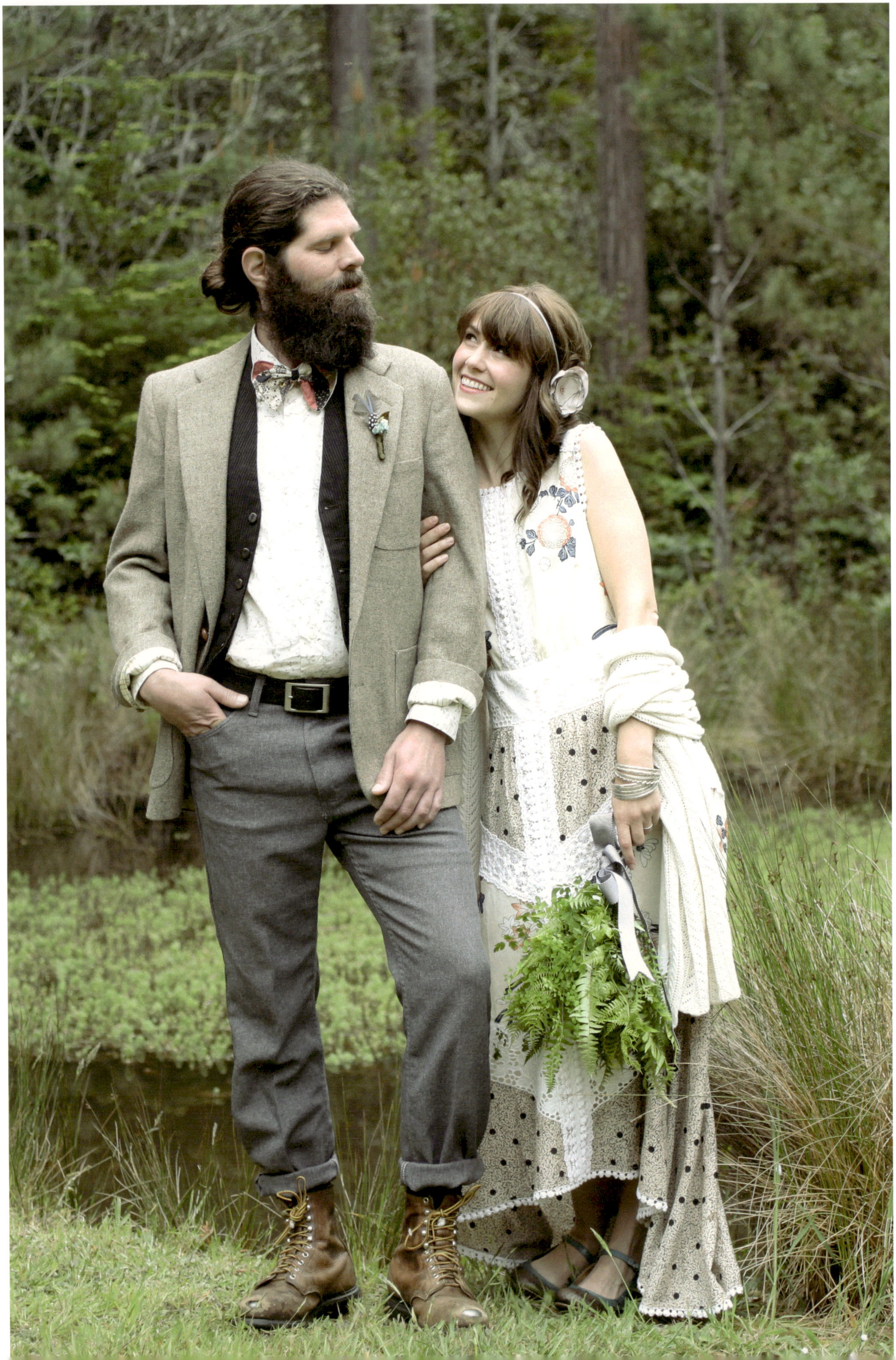

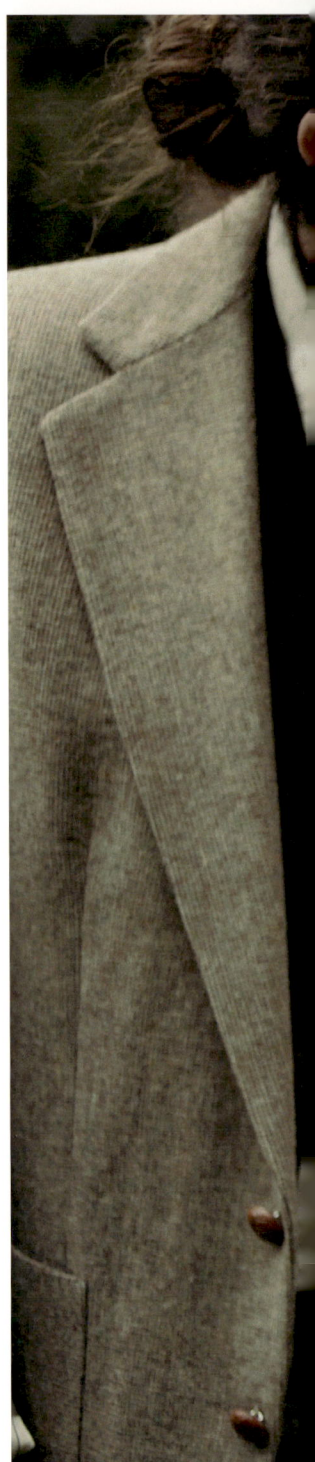

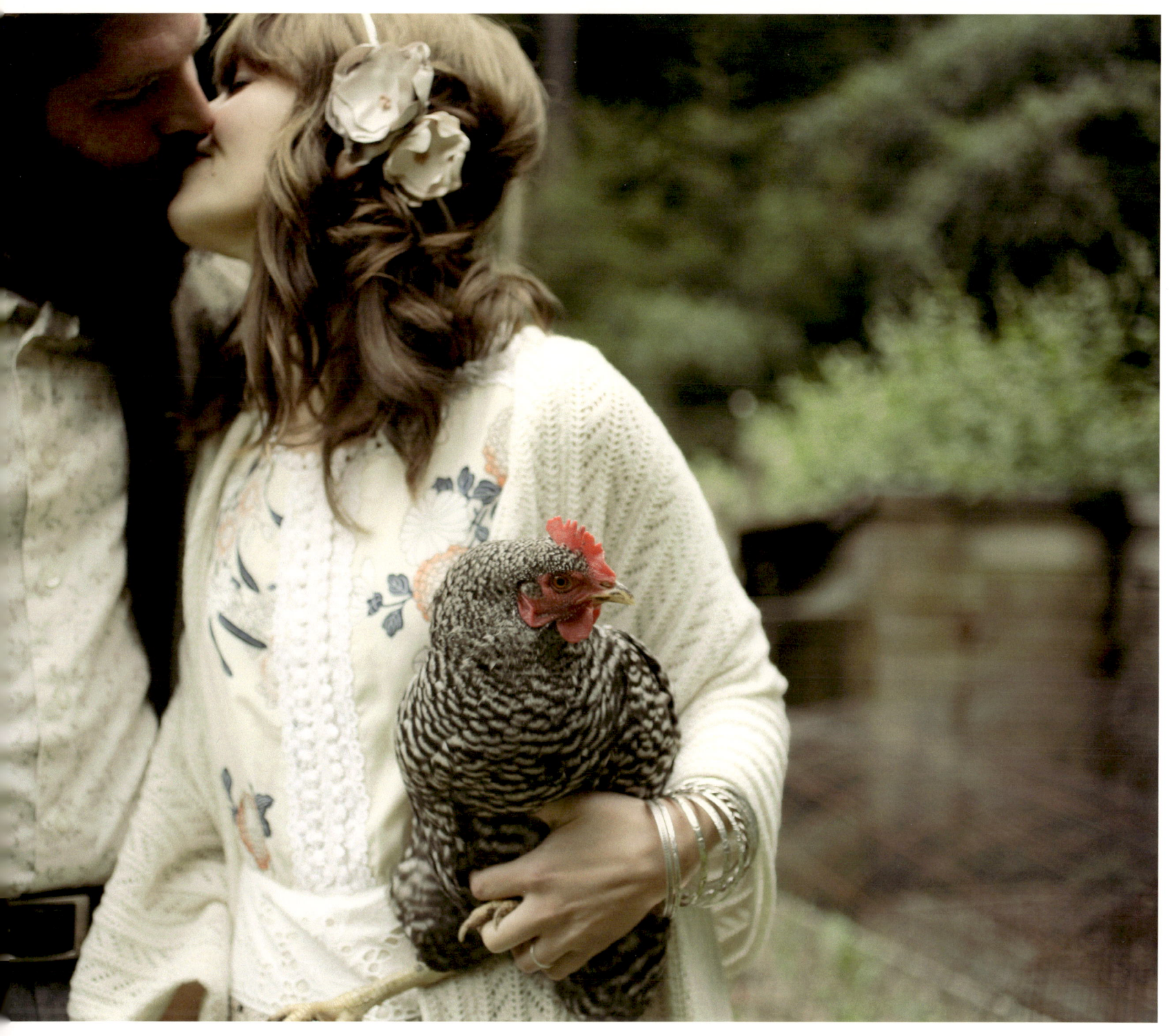

Gwyneth & Monko

This is not a wedding. No, really. We know it looks like one — blushing bride, handsome groom, live band — but it is actually make believe. Clever Girl Consulting and Edyta Photography created these photos to inspire couples looking for an affordable, intimate wedding in the California country-side. The bride's fern bouquet was picked fresh from the redwood forest on the grounds of Mendocino Farmhouse. Folk-singer duo Gwyneth and Monko did a great job playing the newlyweds, but seeing as they really are in love, it can't have been all that hard.

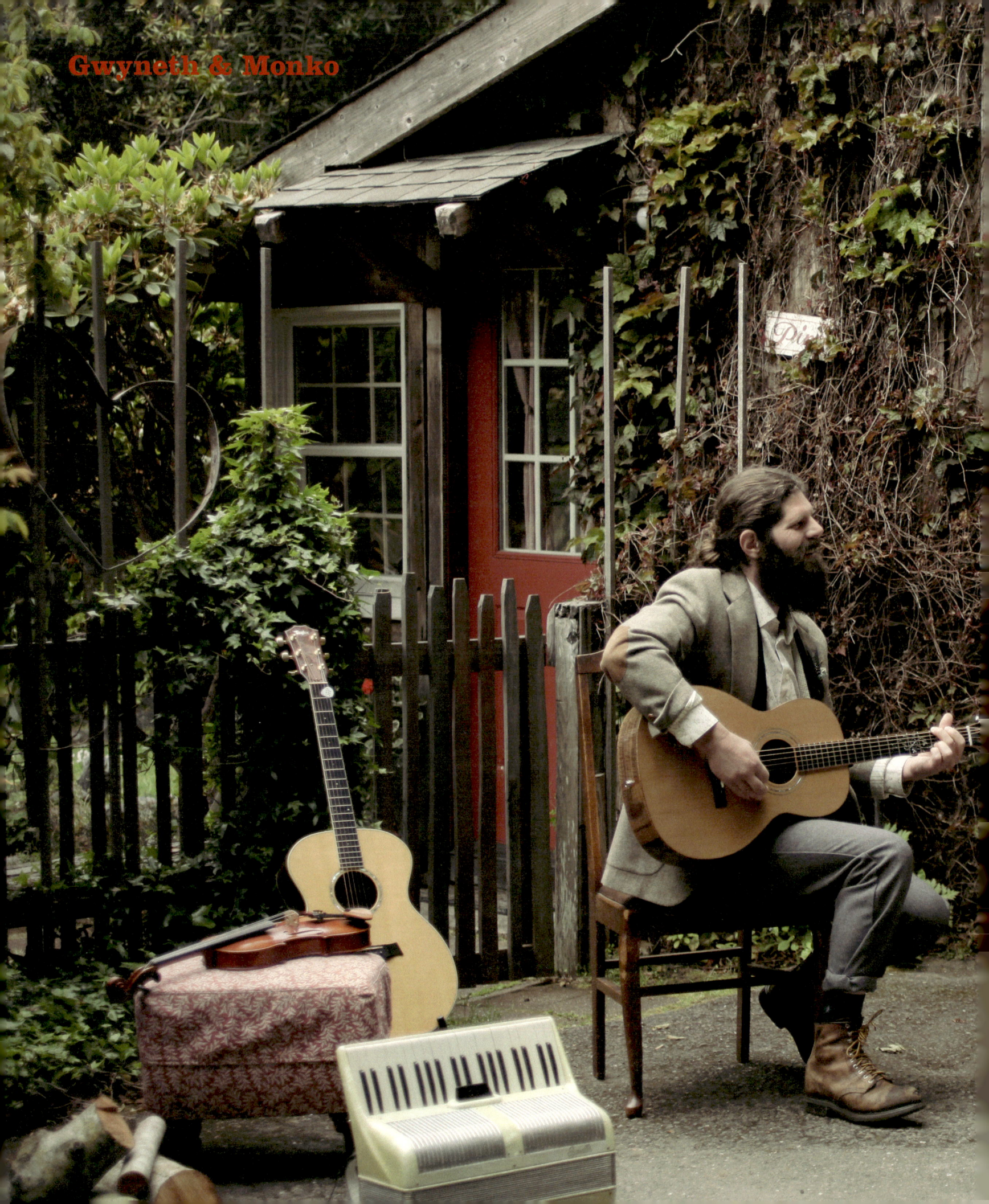

Gwyneth & Monko

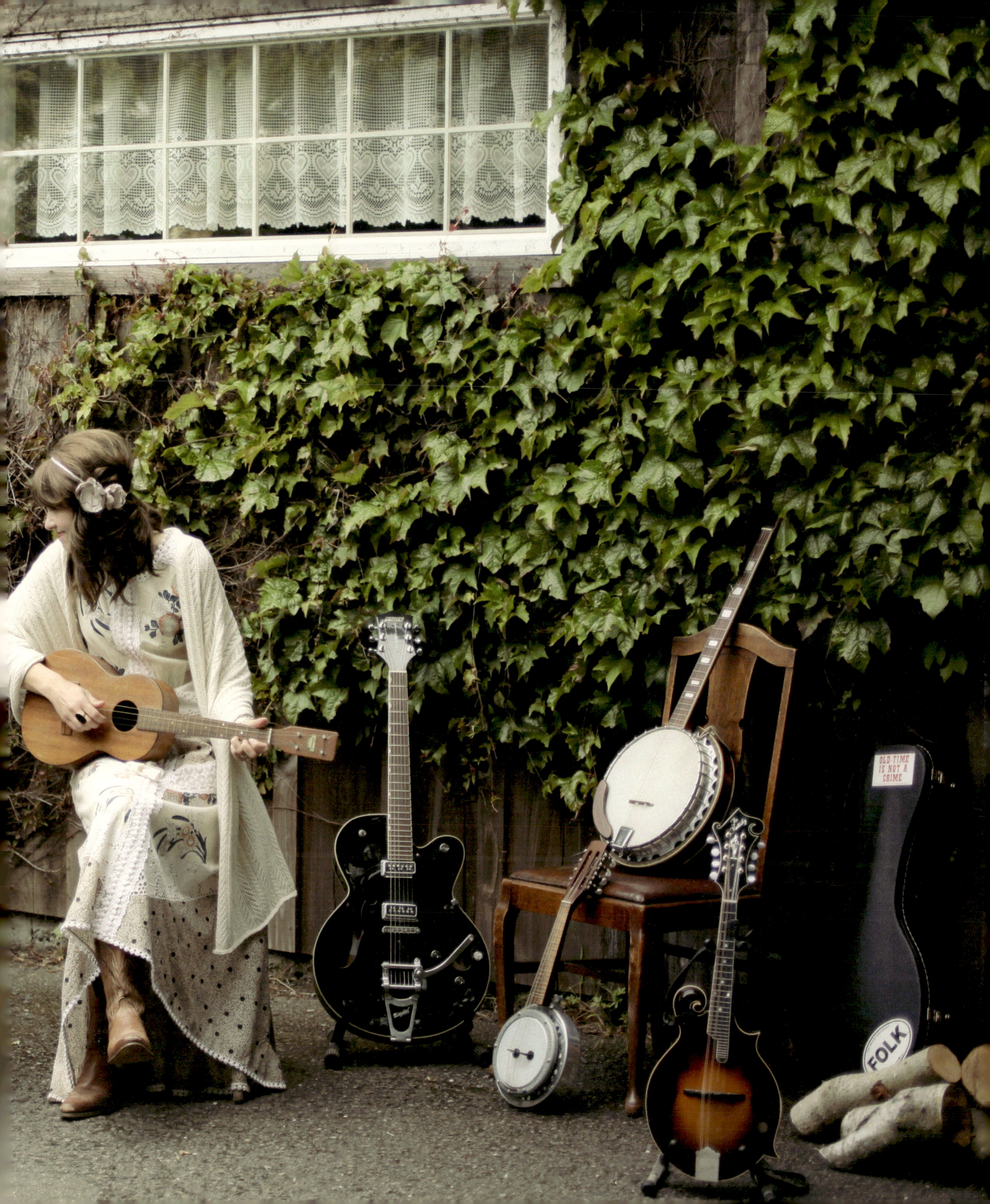

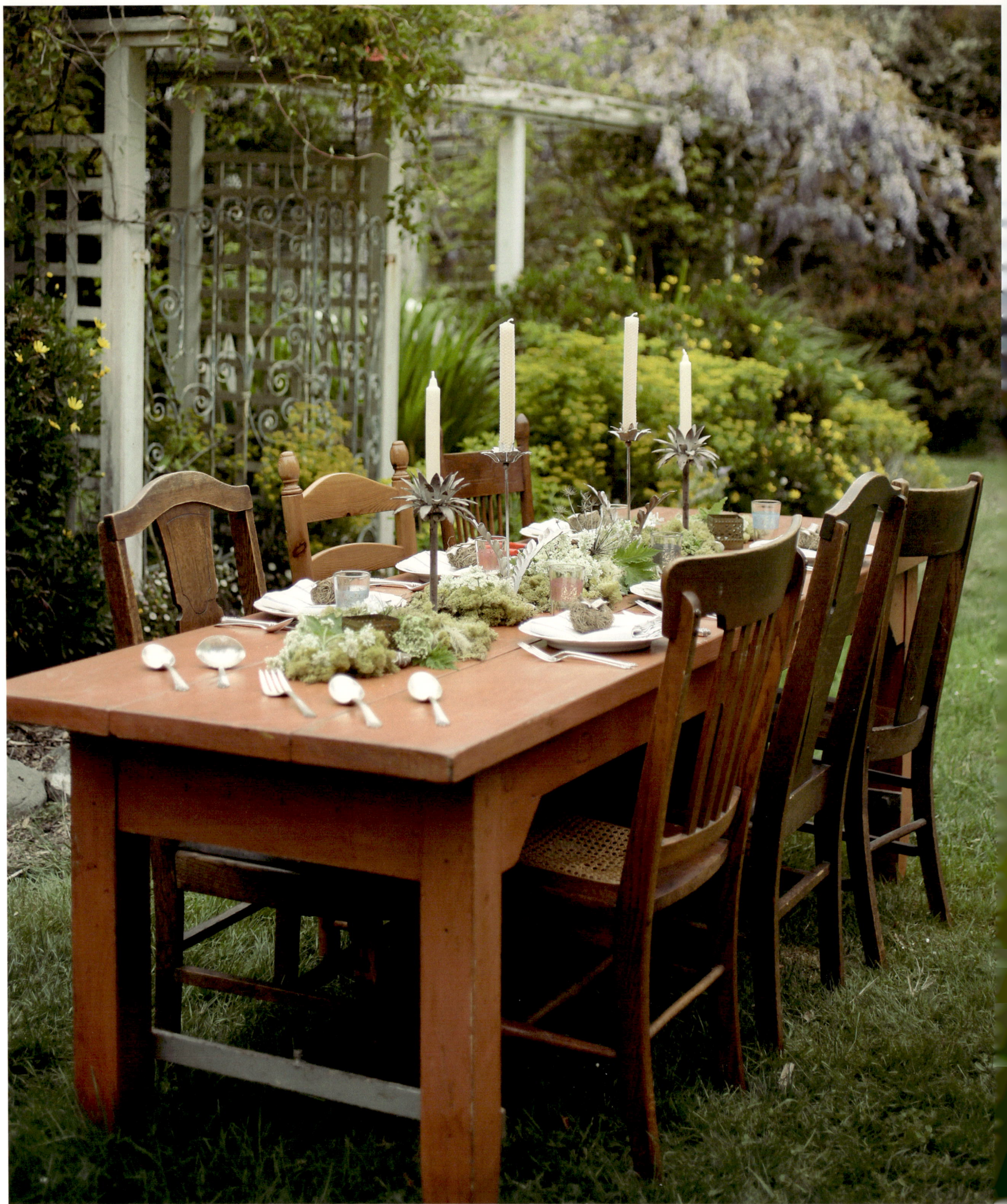

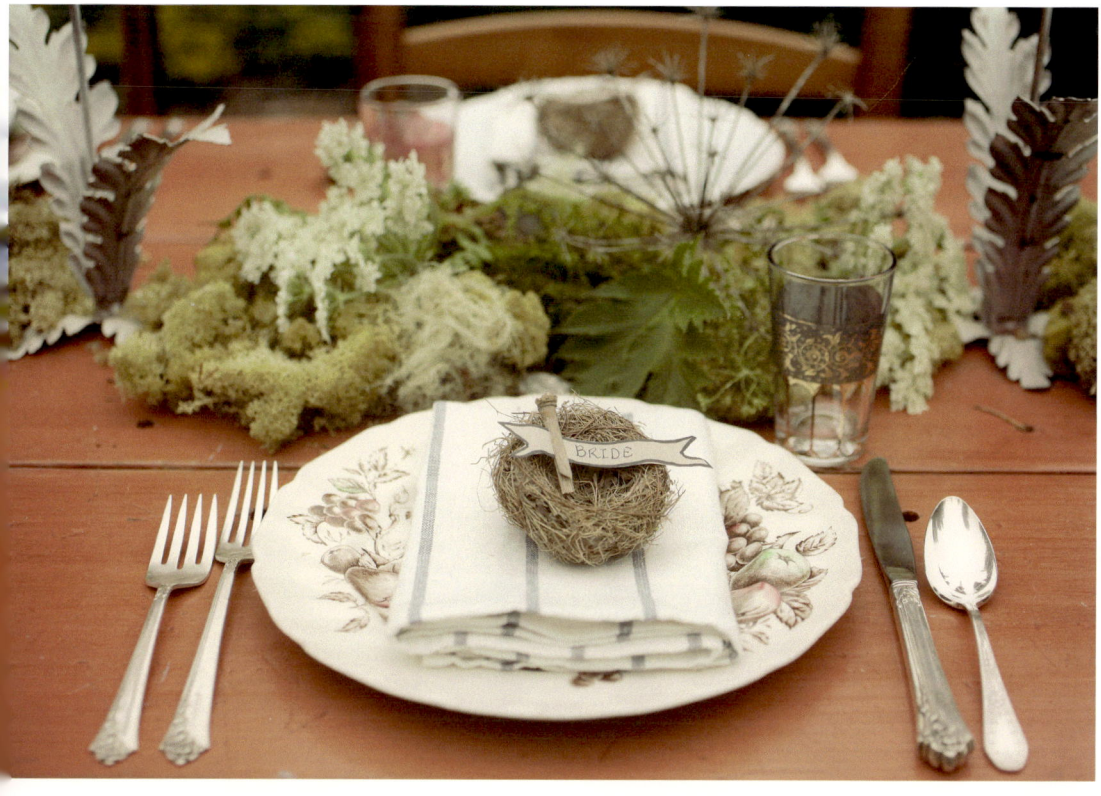

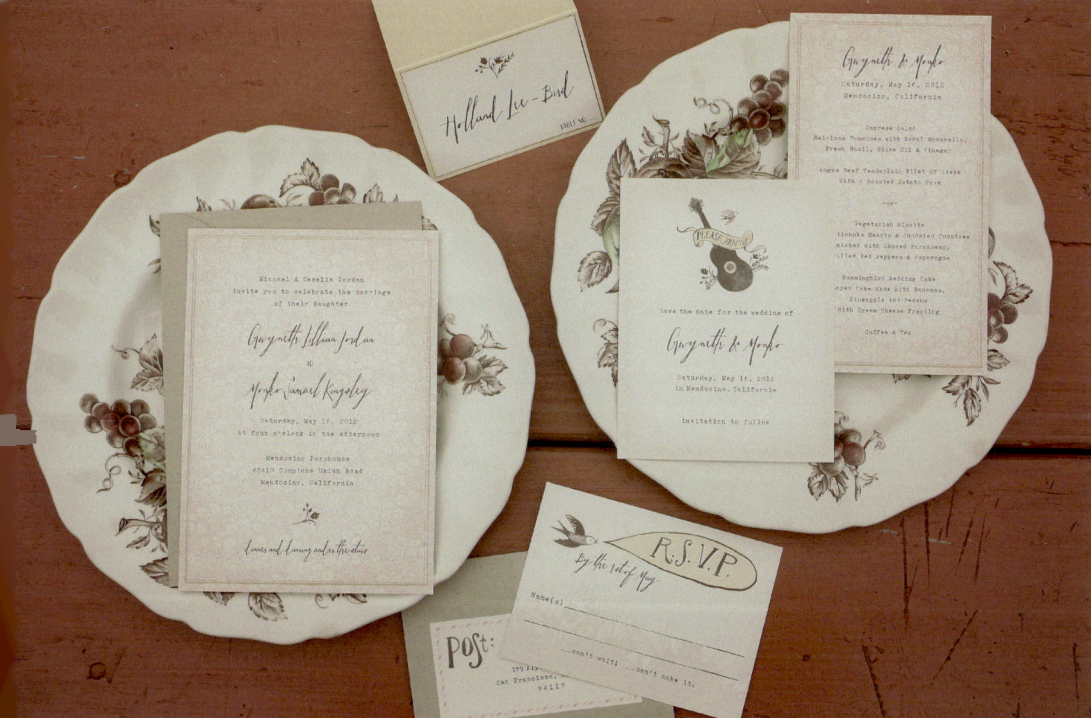

Local is Lovely

Sourcing food and drink from the area around your venue makes sustainable sense. It will also broaden everyone's palate, as they will get to try out little-known beers and other delights that don't line the shelves of your average supermarket chain.

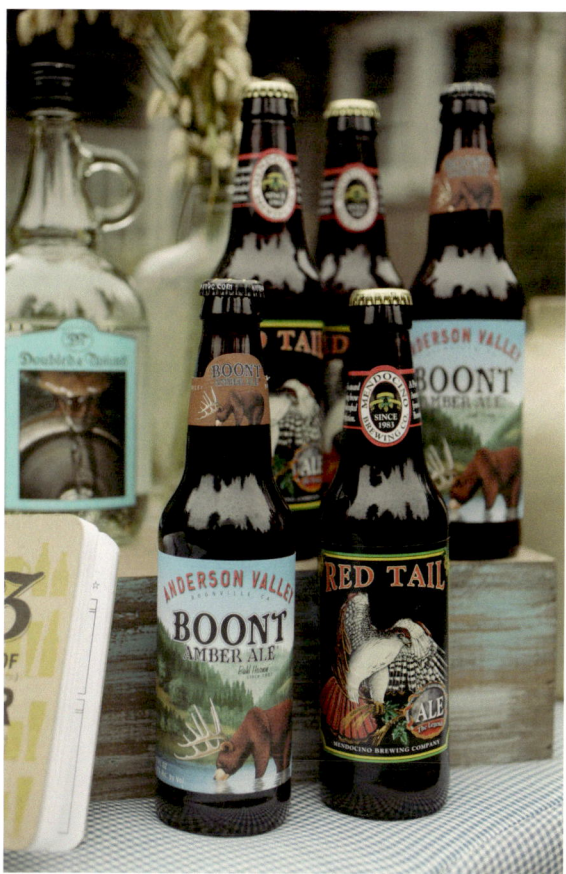

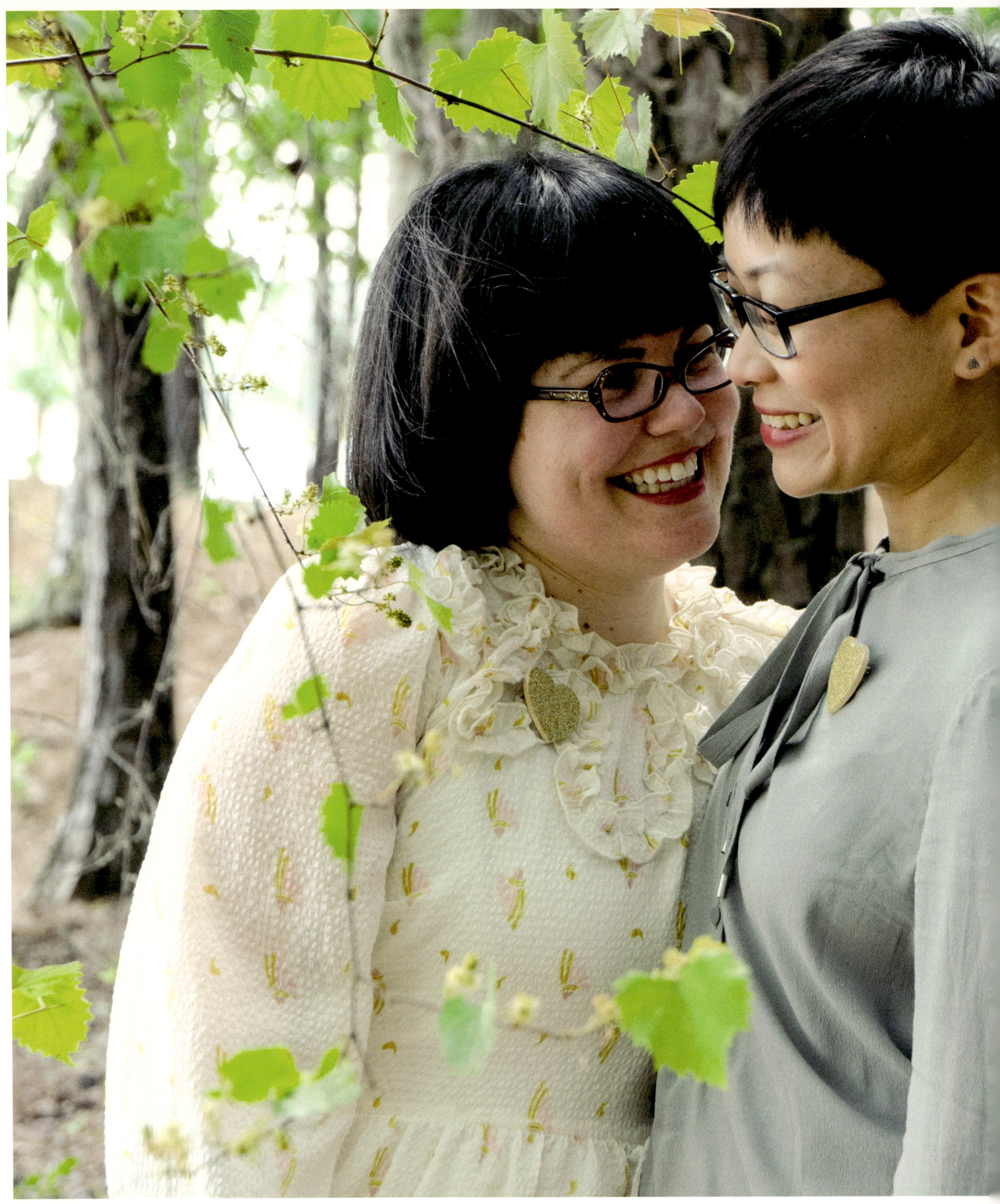

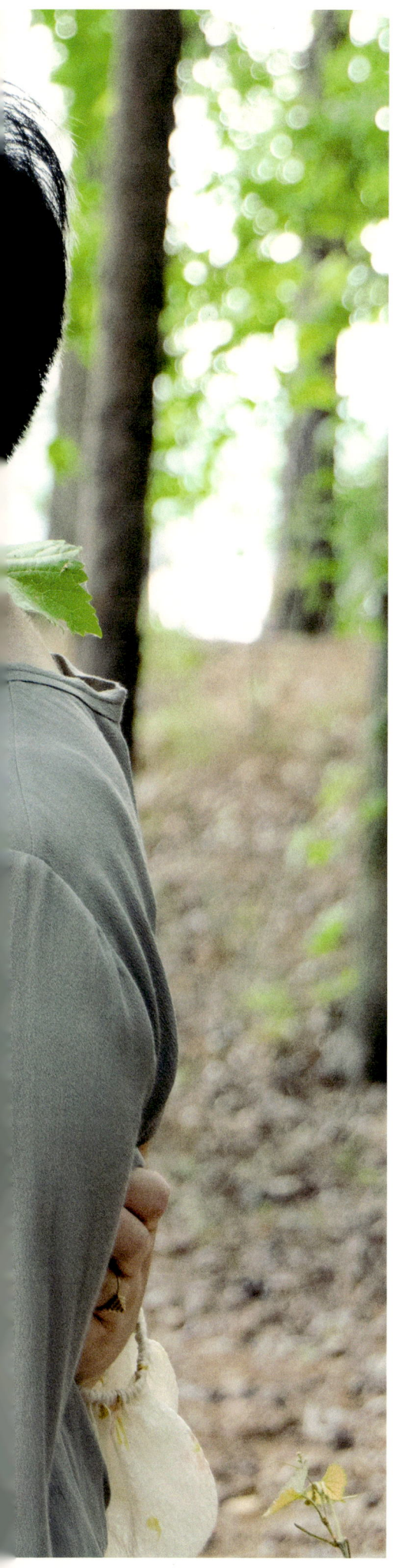

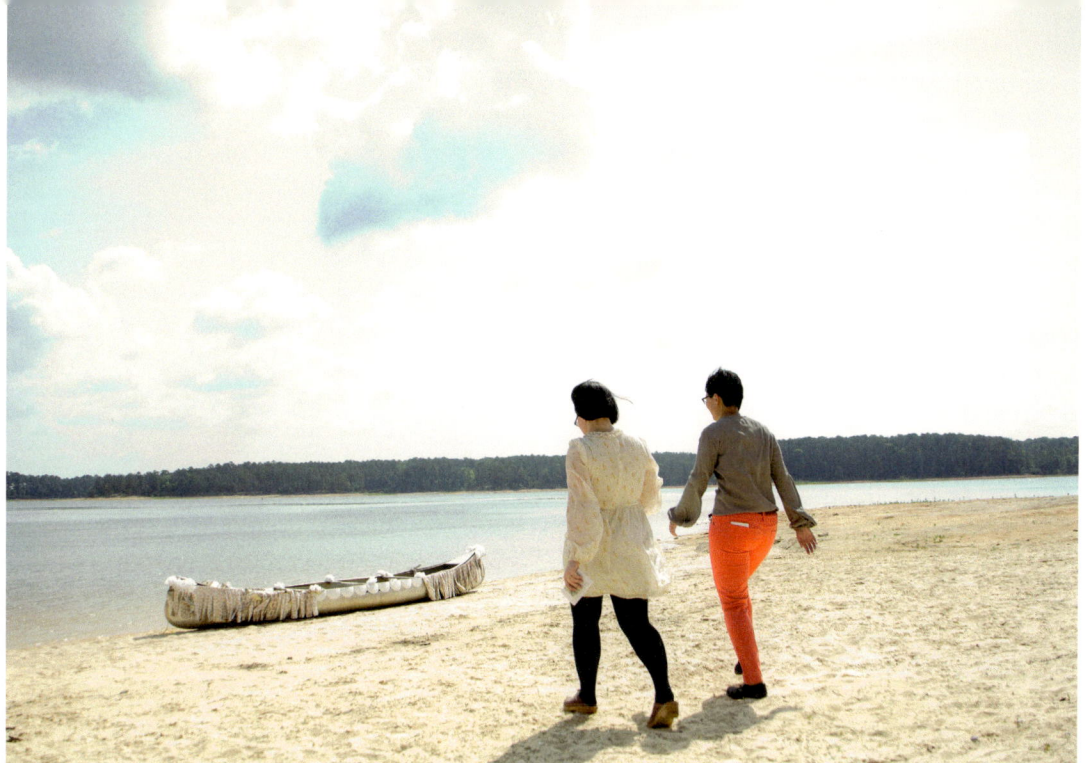

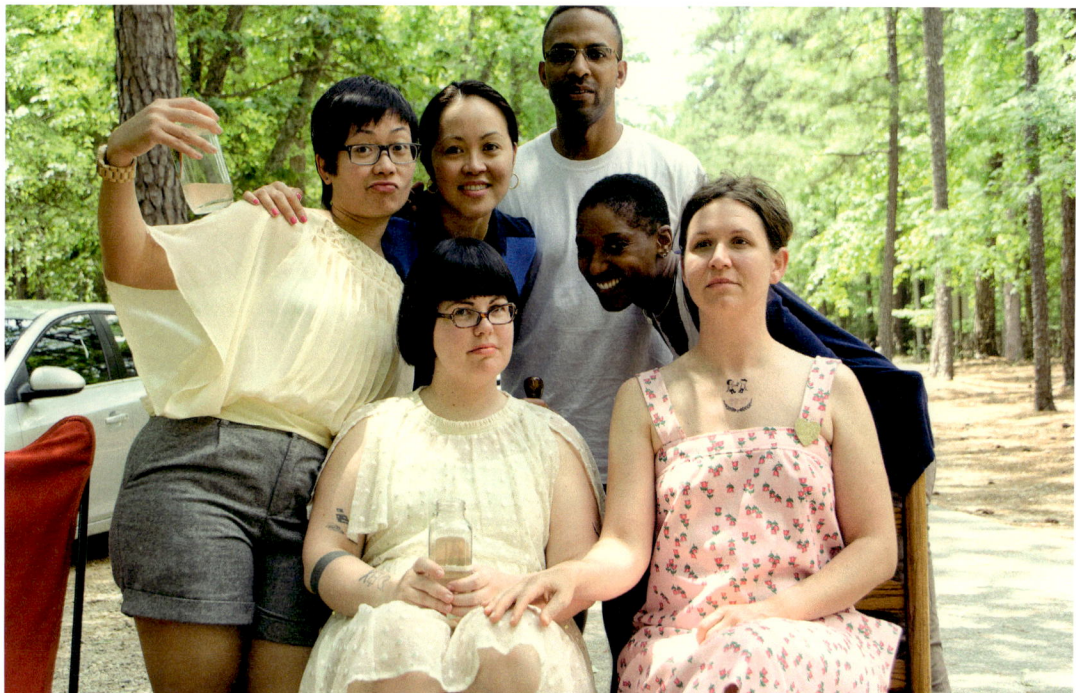

Sarah & Dawn

As sunlight poured down through the trees, a small procession made its way along the forest trail. Some carried huge white balloons bobbing in the lakeside air. In a clearing, they made a circle and the ceremony began. At first Sarah and Dawn were so overcome that they cried. This, they said, was what made their wedding special.

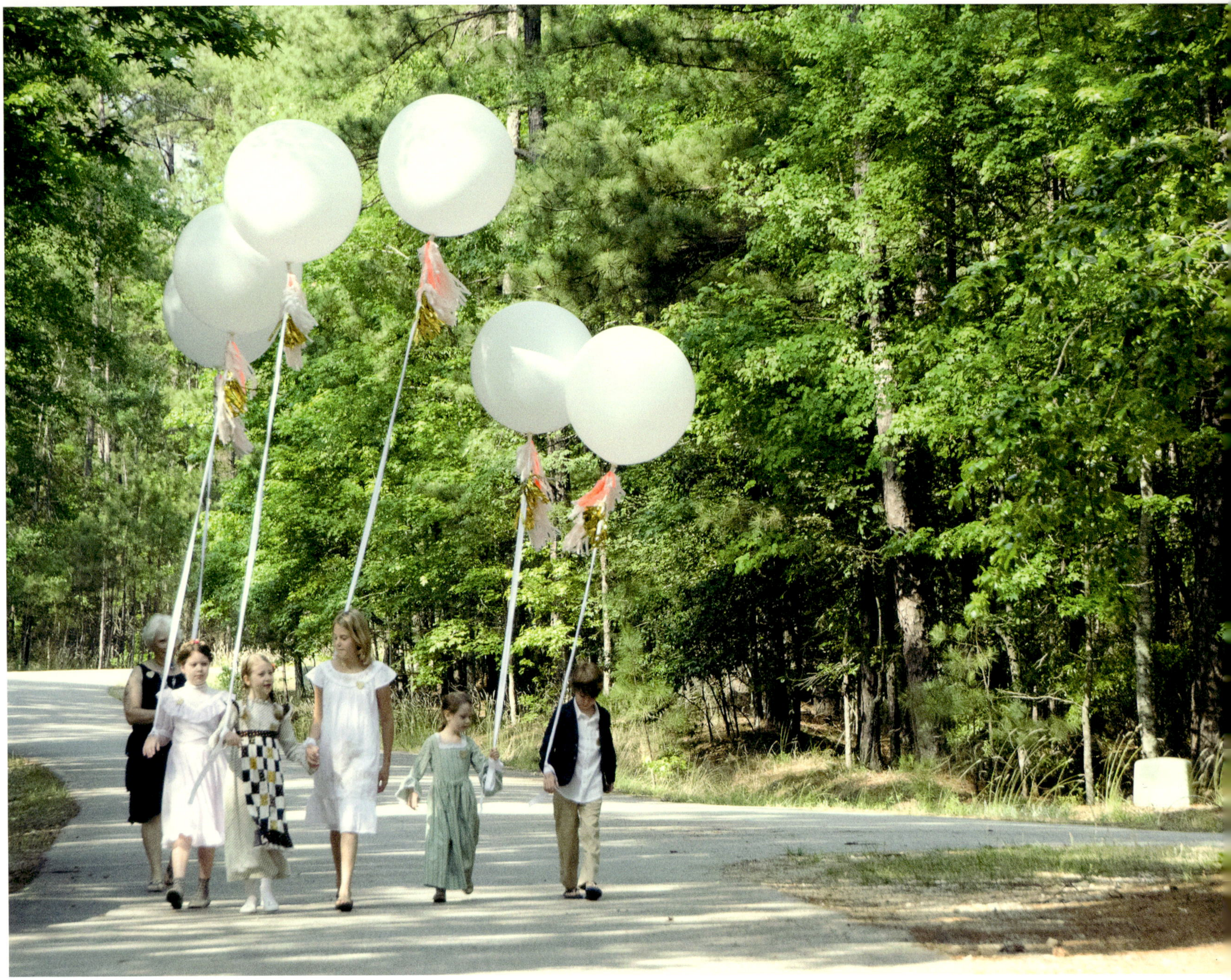

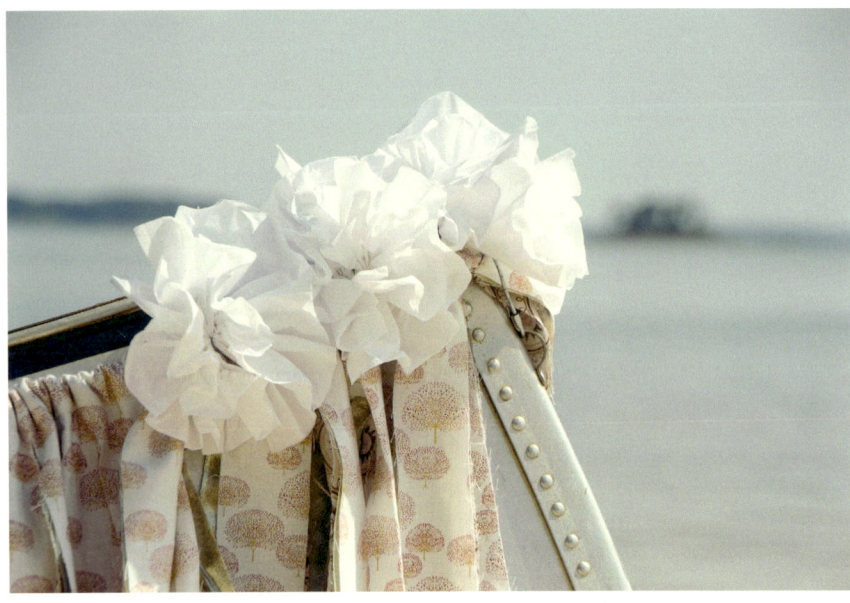

A dreamlike canoe and a sunlit clearing make this wedding seem like something out of another world.

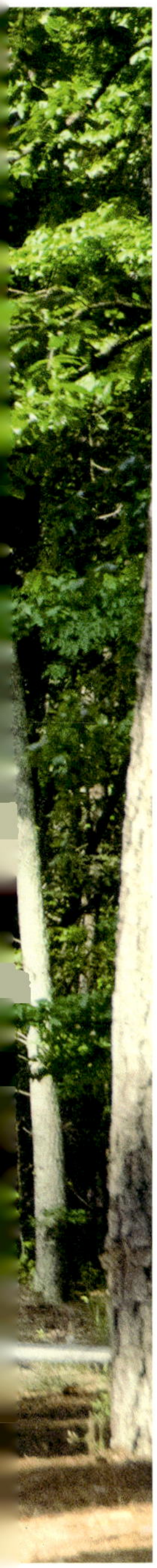
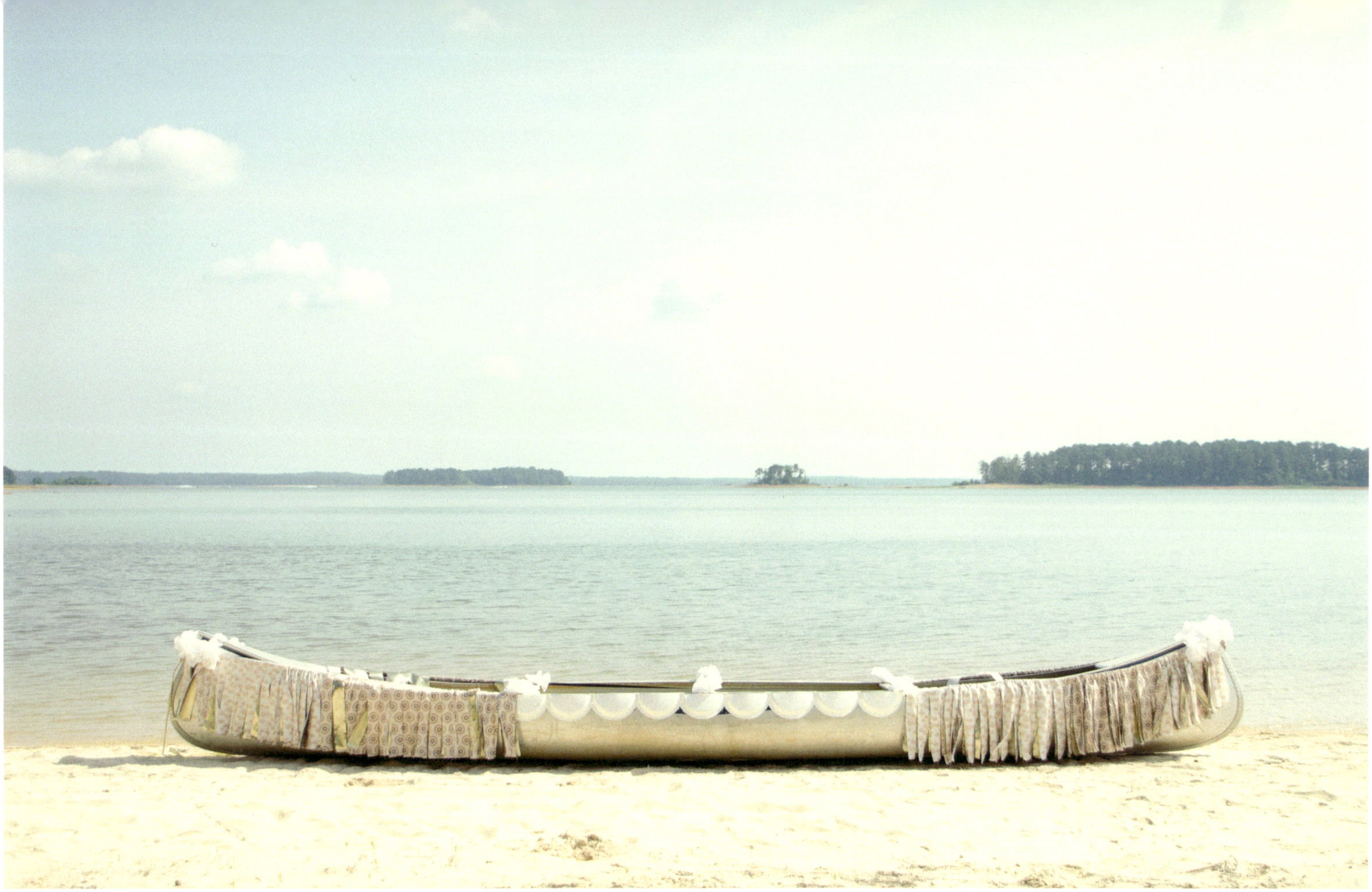
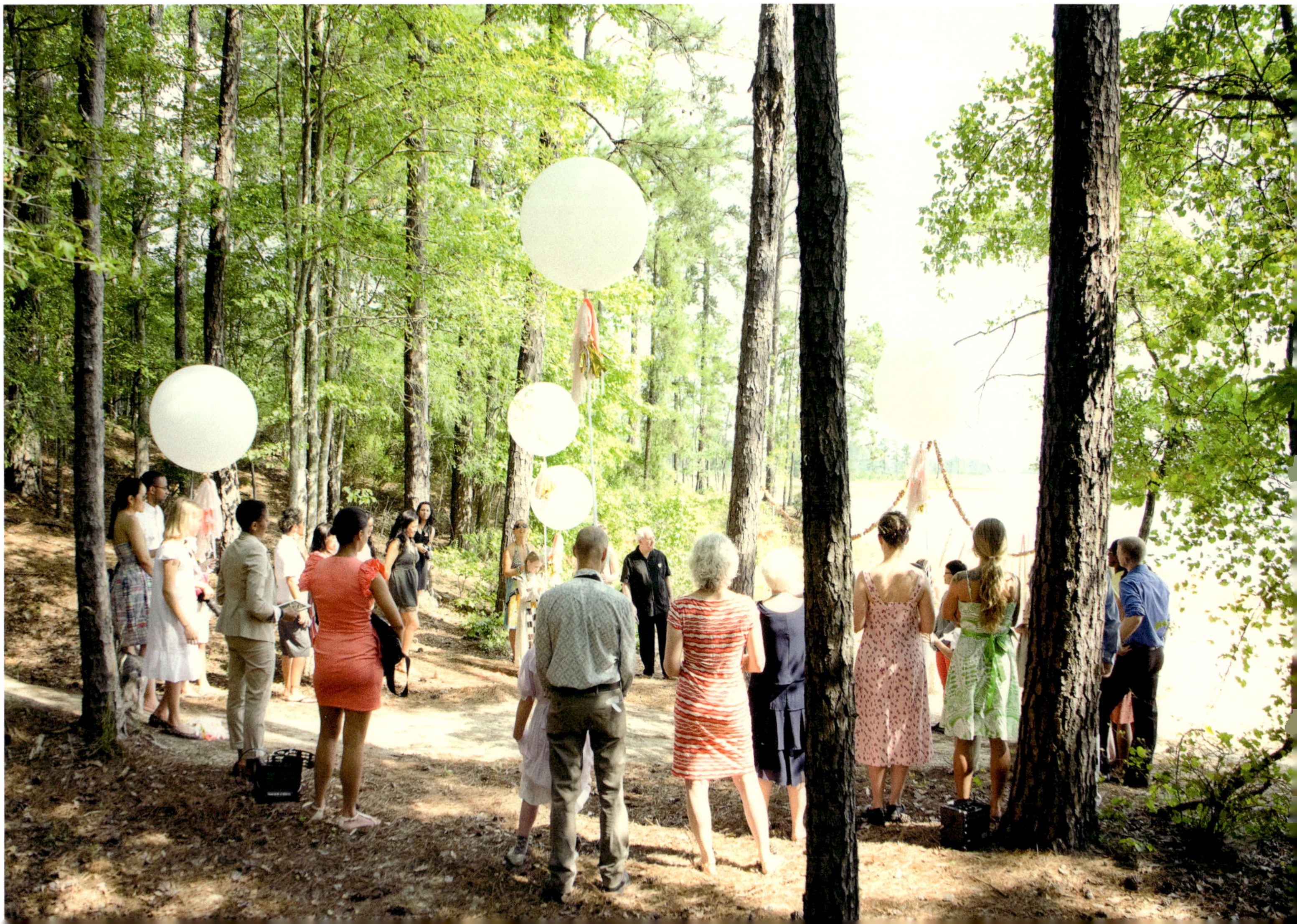

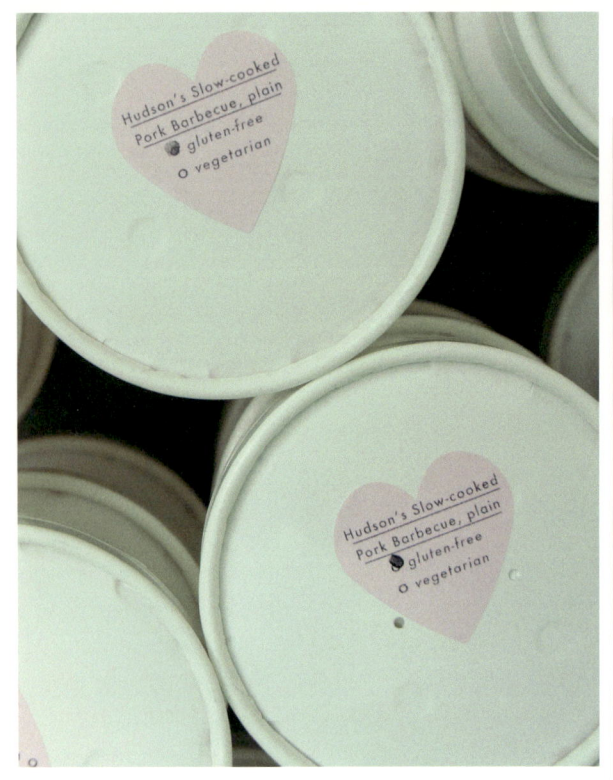

Hudson's Slow-cooked
Pork Barbecue, plain
● gluten-free
○ vegetarian

Hudson's Slow-cooked
Pork Barbecue, plain
● gluten-free
○ vegetarian

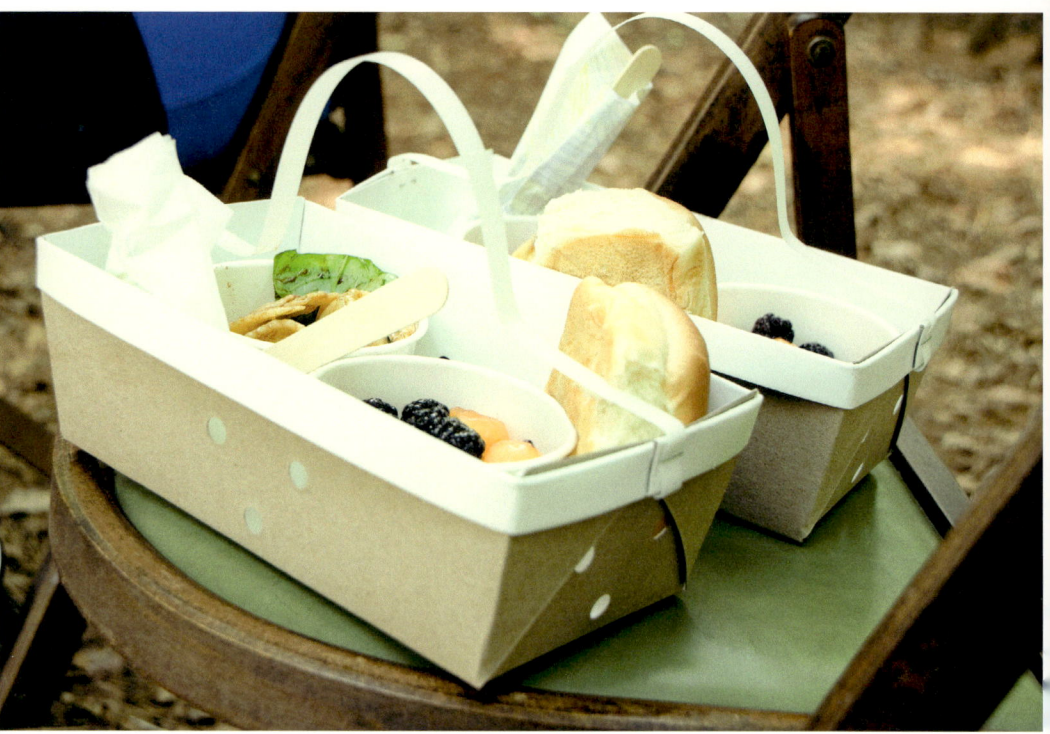

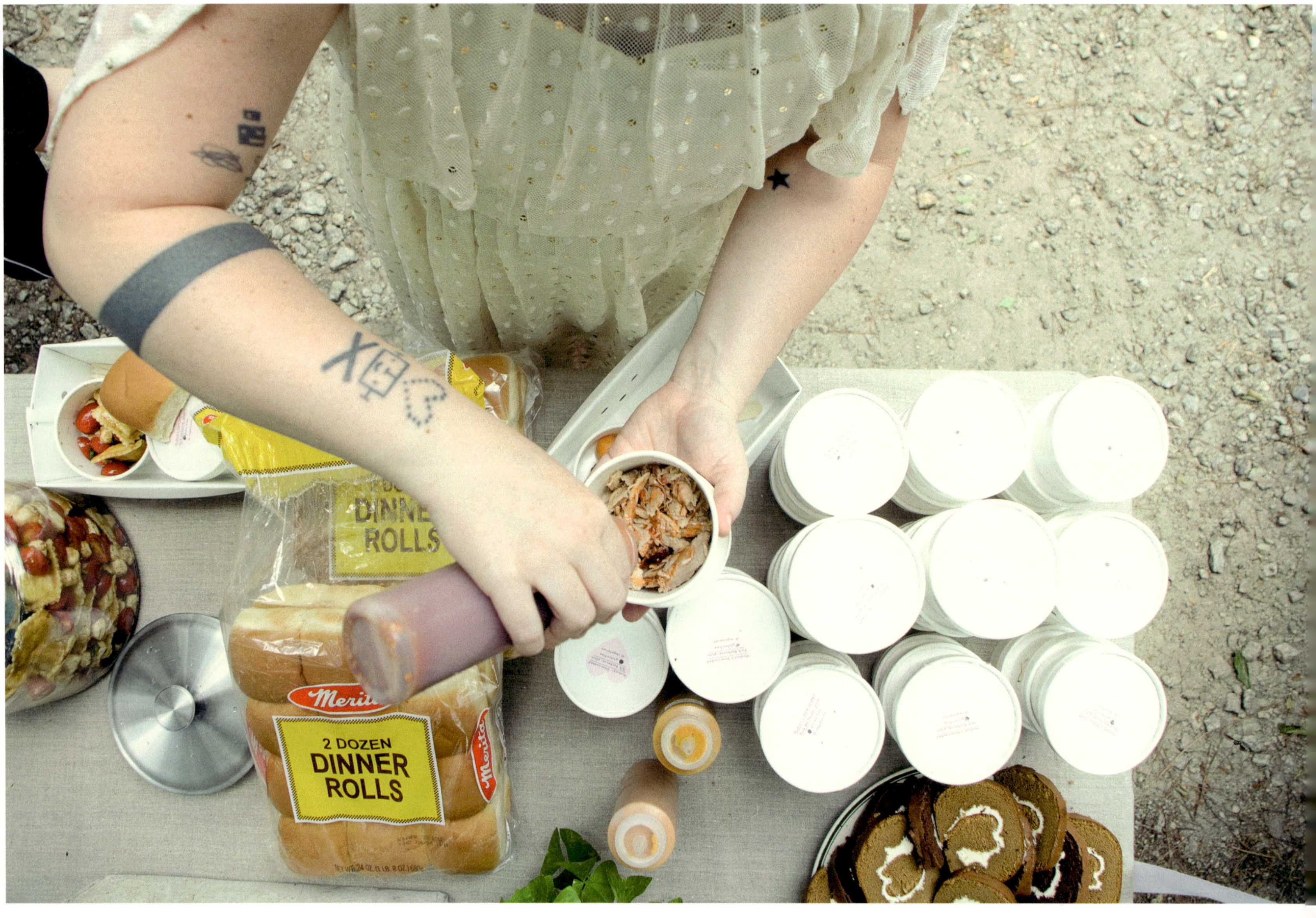

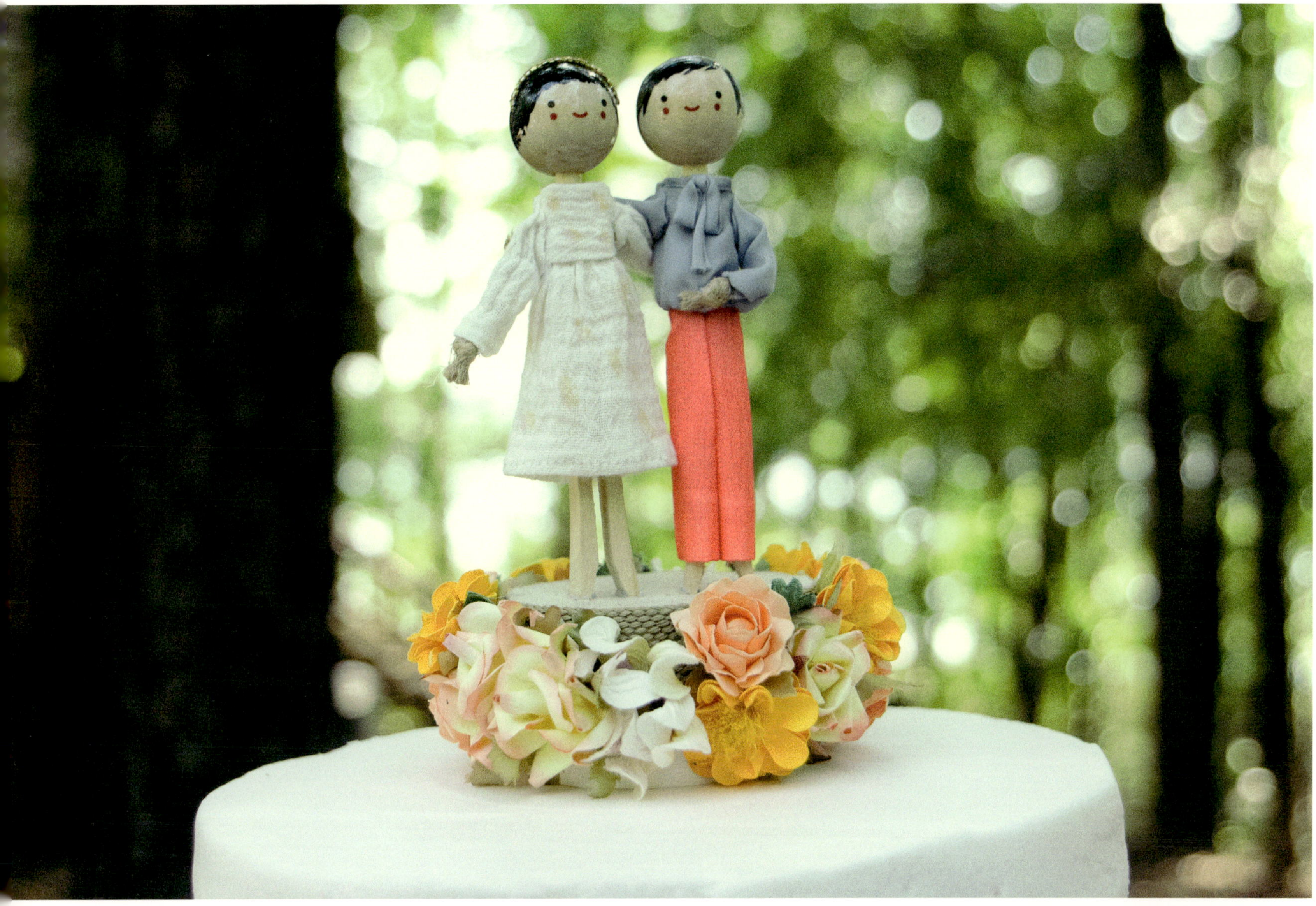

Food & Decoration

Mini picnic baskets, barbecue pork, and help-yourself pots and sauce let guests get creative and put together their own meals for carrying down to the beach. Sarah-and-Dawn matchstick figures made for cute cake toppers, while jars decorated with old-fashioned labels were an inspired alternative to the usual glasses.

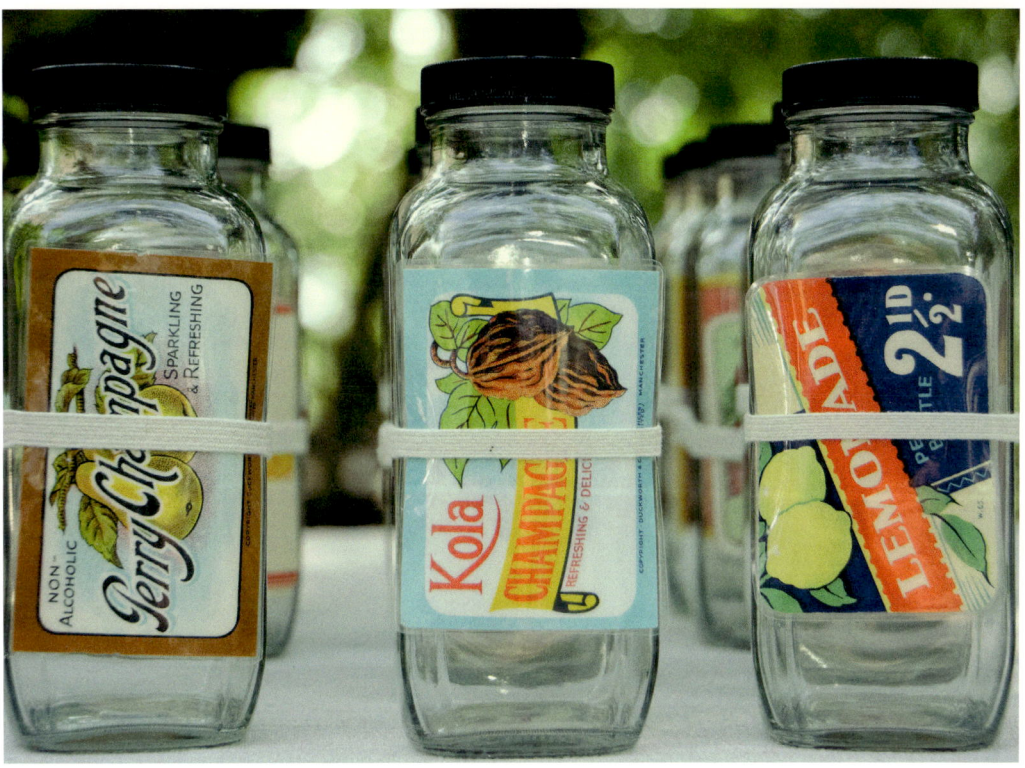

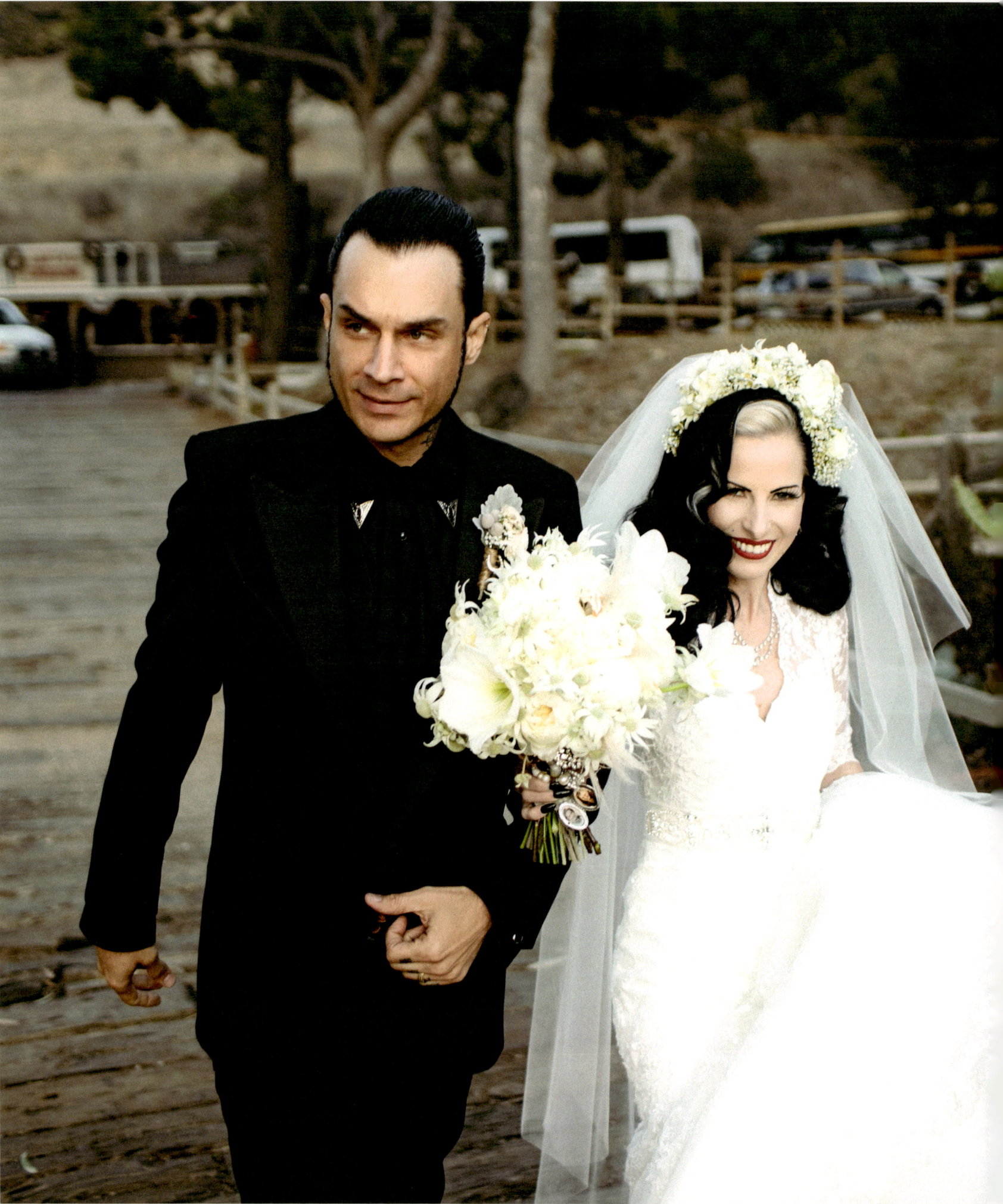

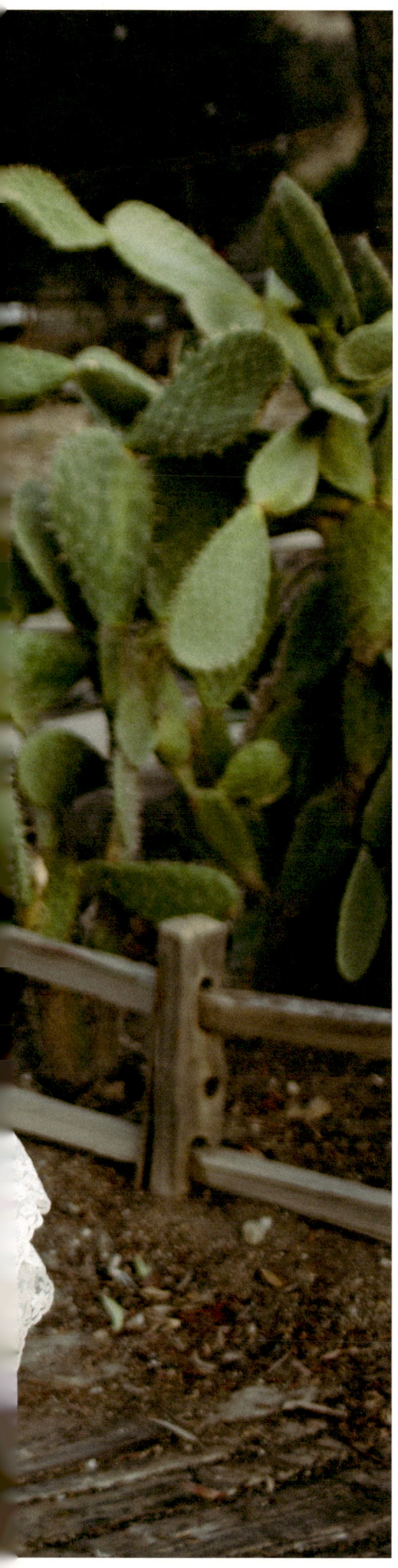

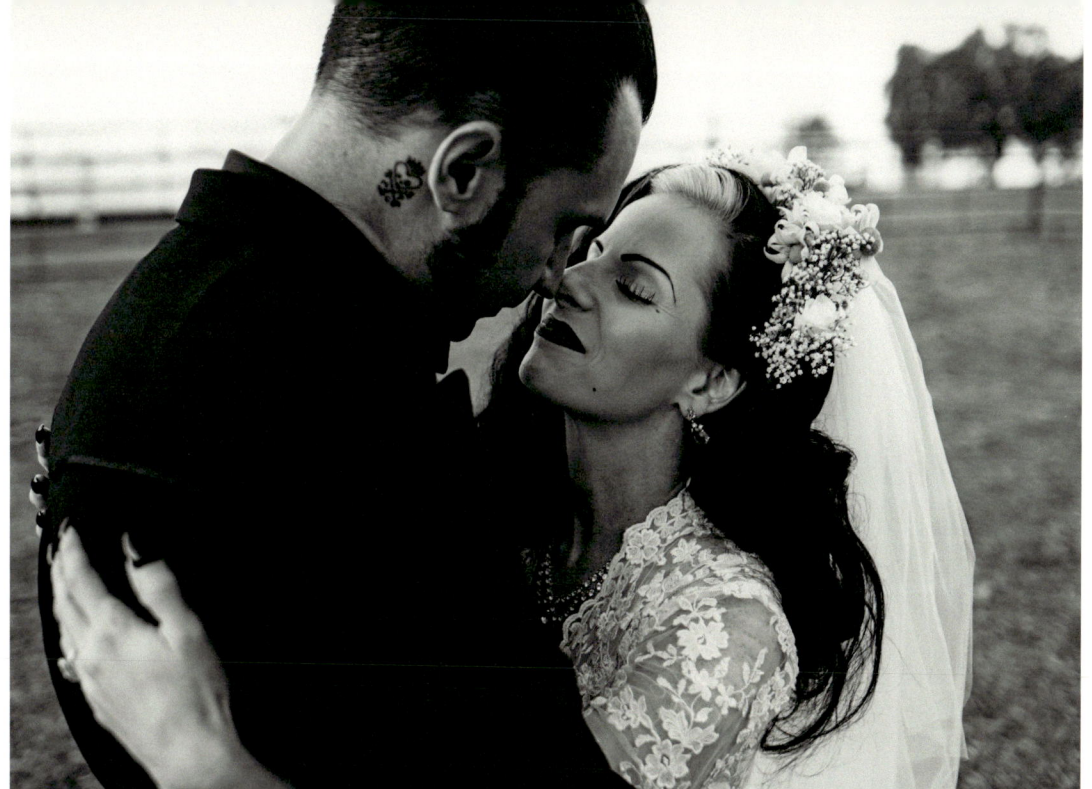

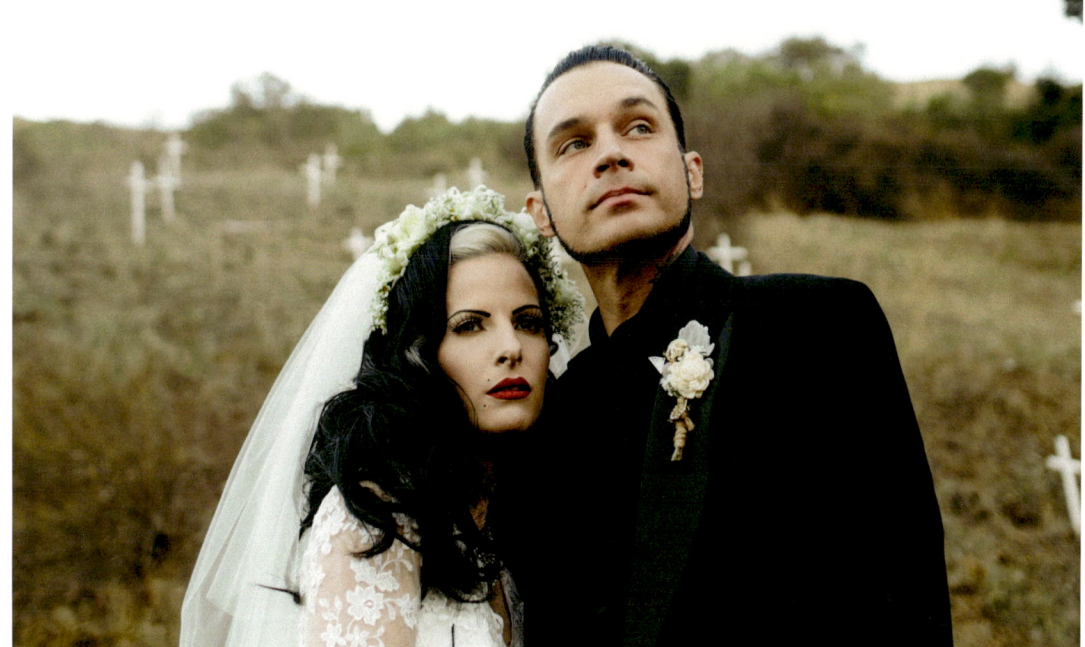

Lynnette & Gris

Where better to find inspiration than driving across America, chasing a horizon lying flush against the vast blue sky? After a trip filled with talk of their heritage and the early pioneers, Lynne and Gris created a day that celebrated their roots and their own unique styles. The ranch setting, groomsmen's outfits, and animal skulls were all about Gris's rural upbringing and the American West.

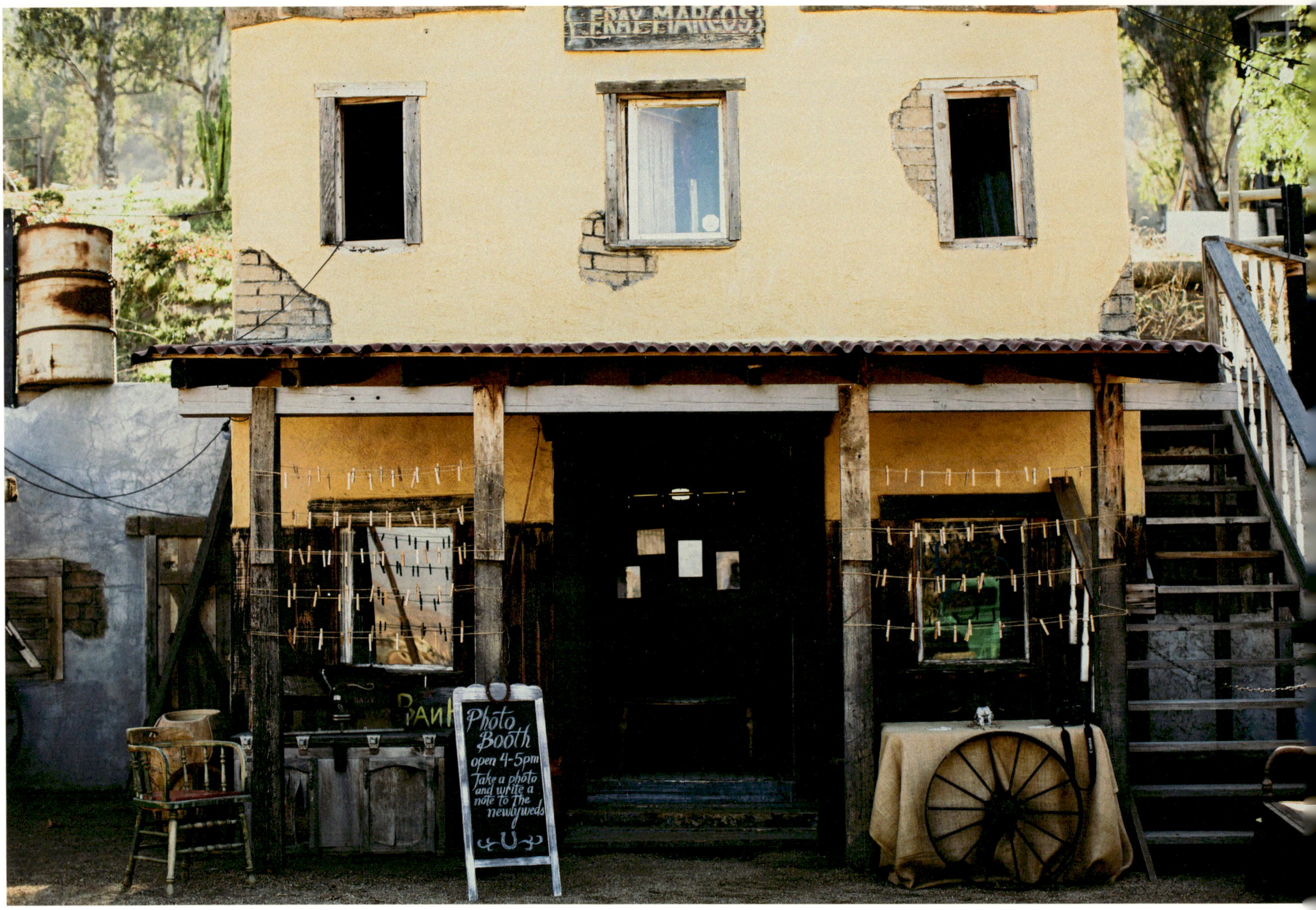

The Ranch

If it wasn't for the baskets of food and bright sunshine, there would be something a little bit ghost-town about this ranch. But that's not a bad thing—in fact, it fit right in with the slightly spooky feel of Lynette and Gris's wedding.

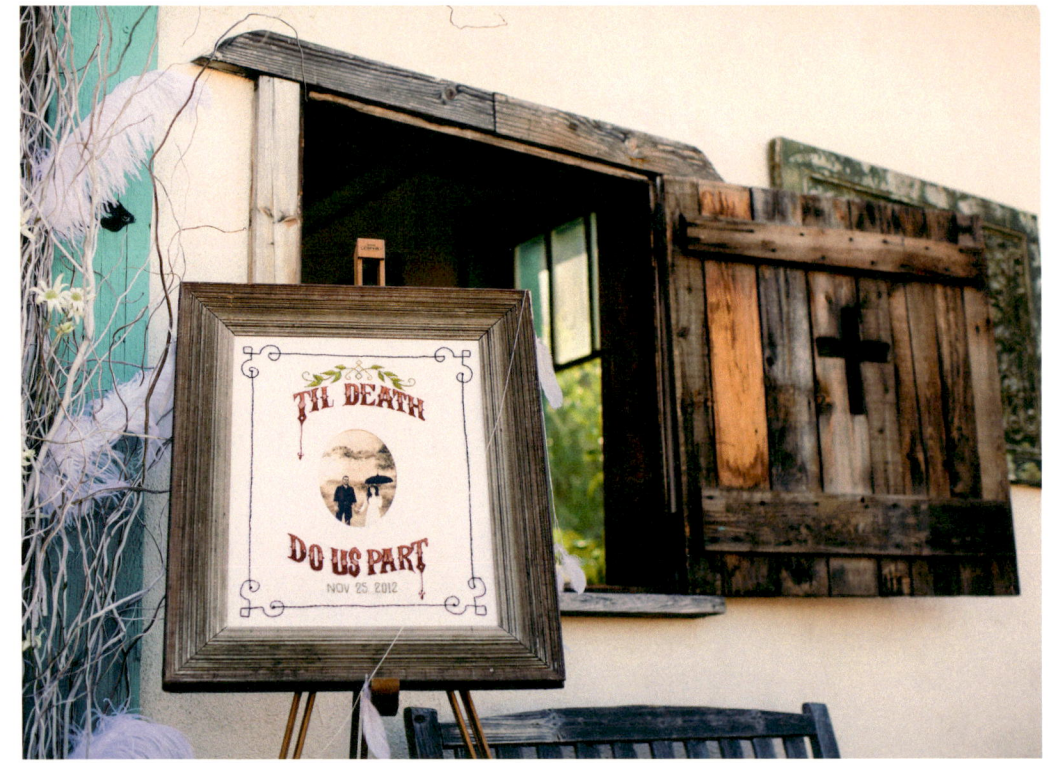

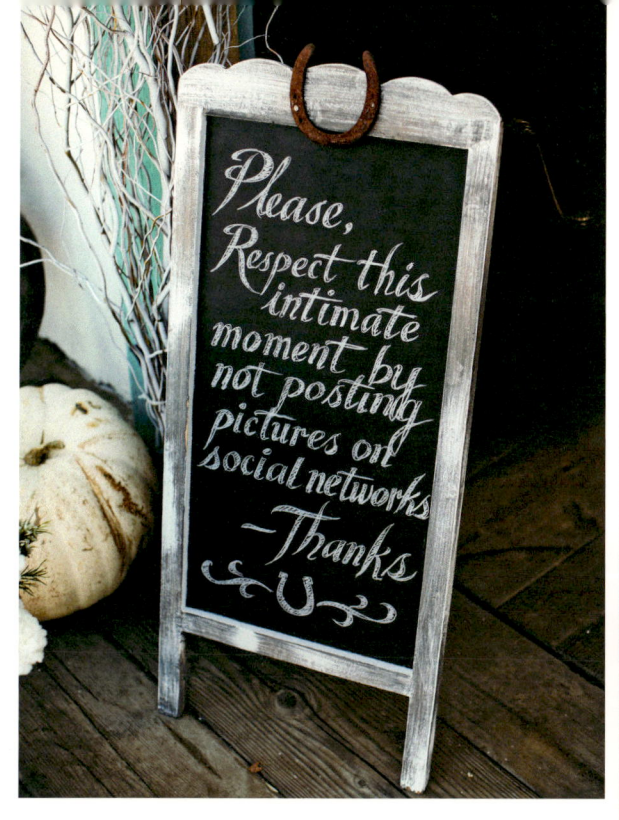

Please,
Respect this
intimate
moment by
not posting
pictures on
social networks
—Thanks

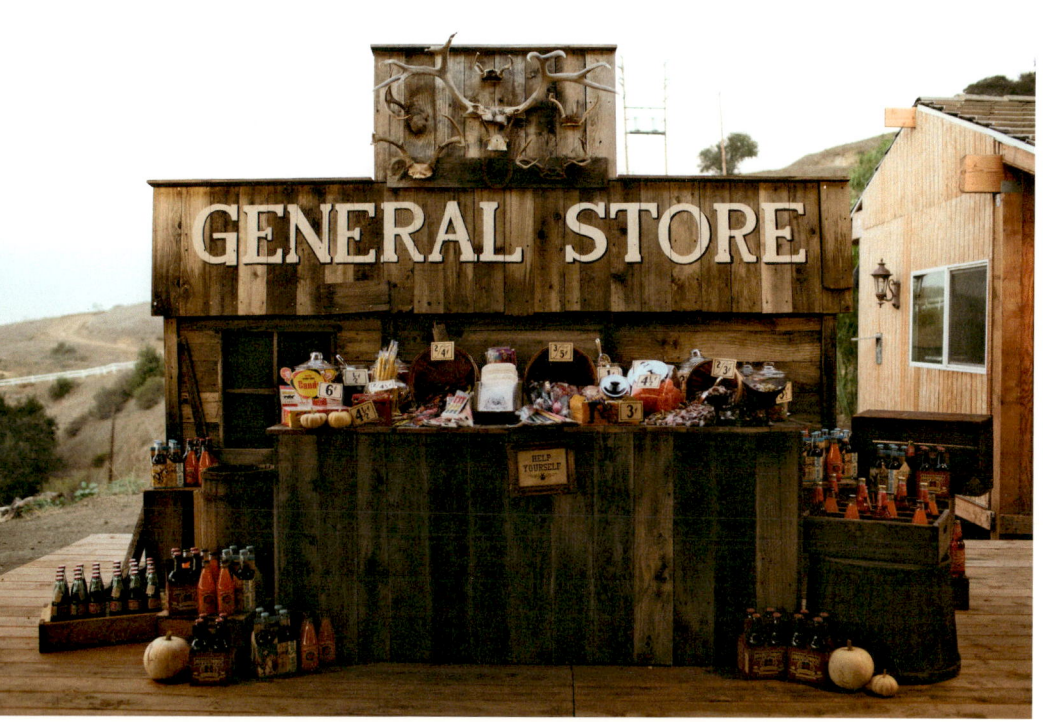

GENERAL STORE

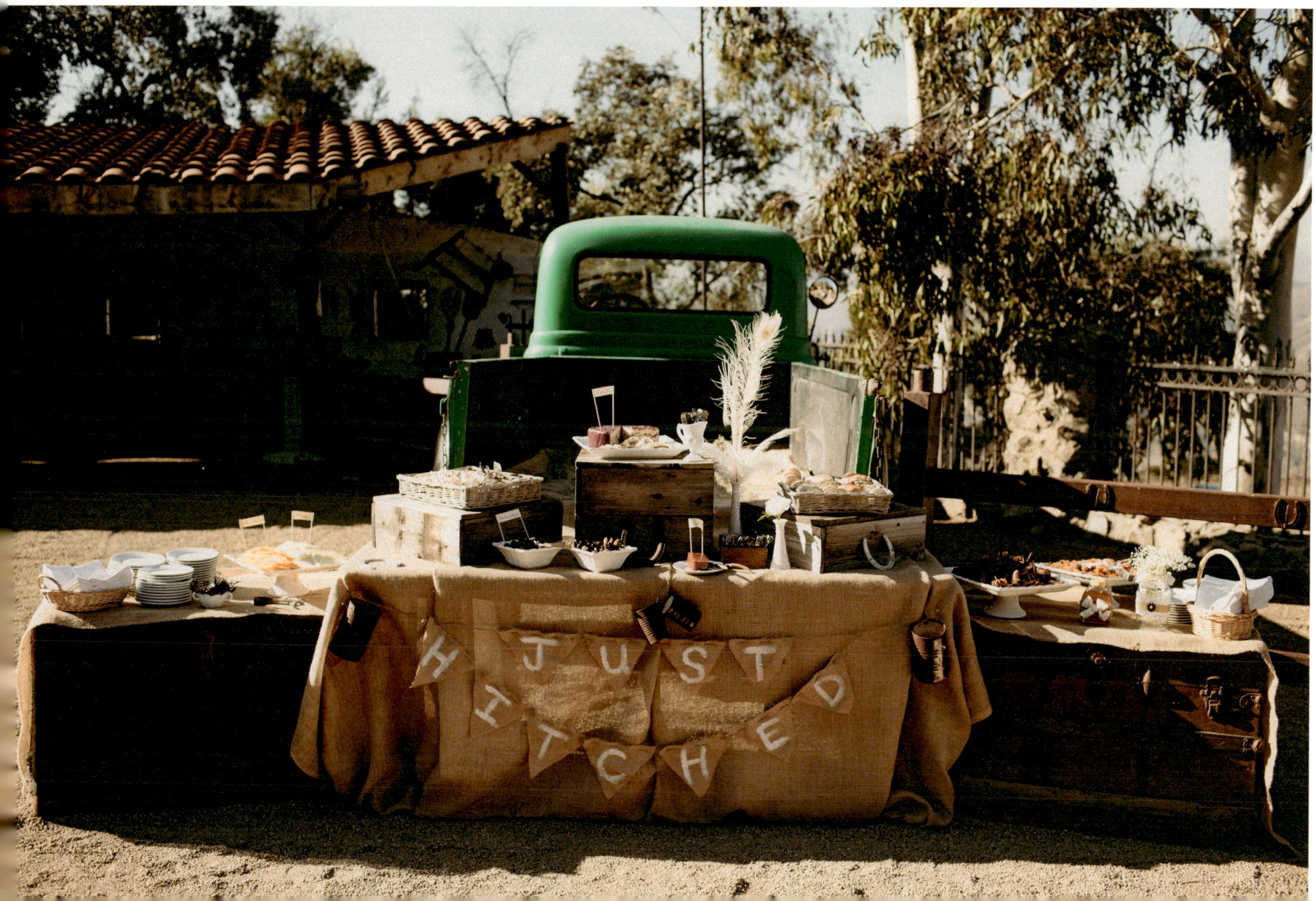

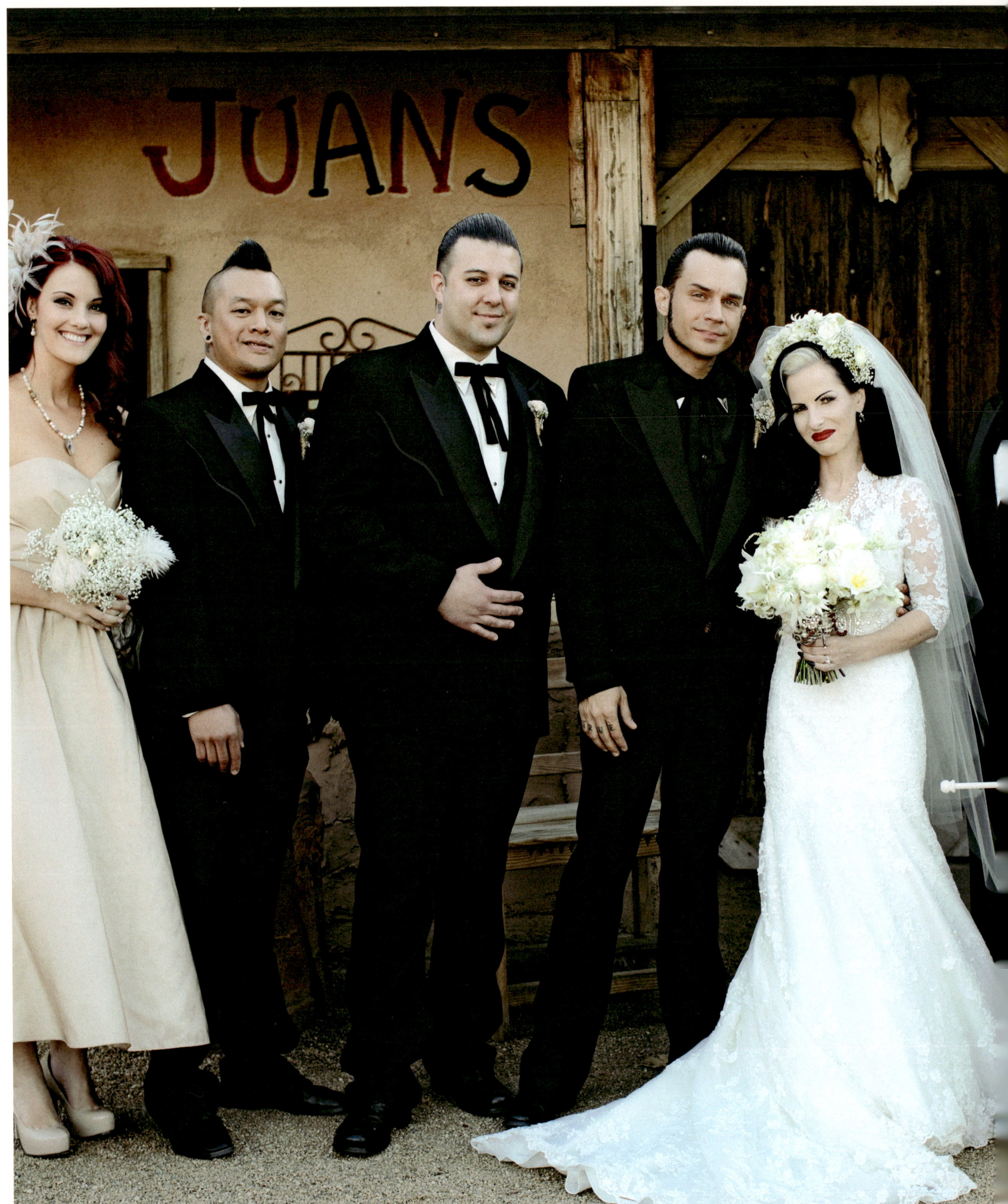

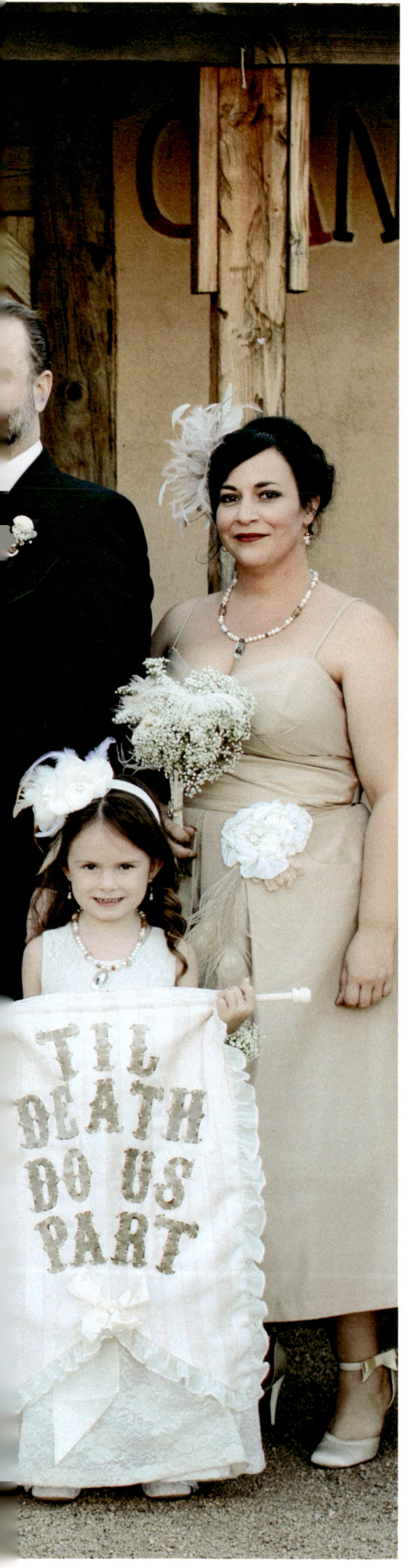

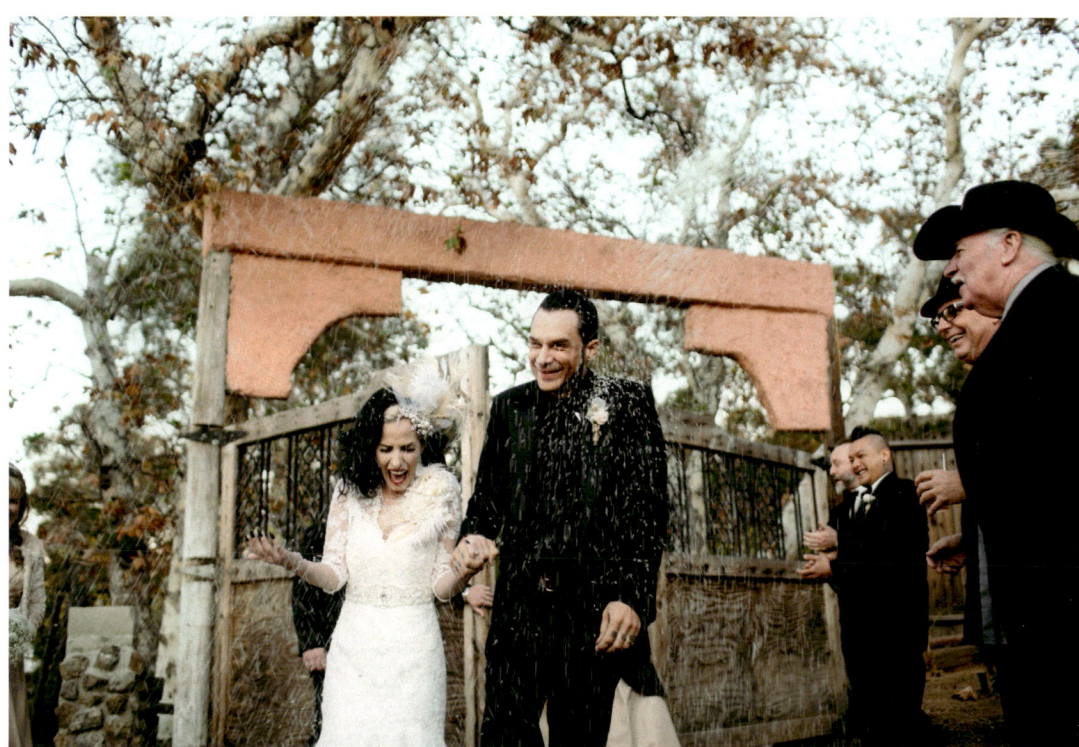

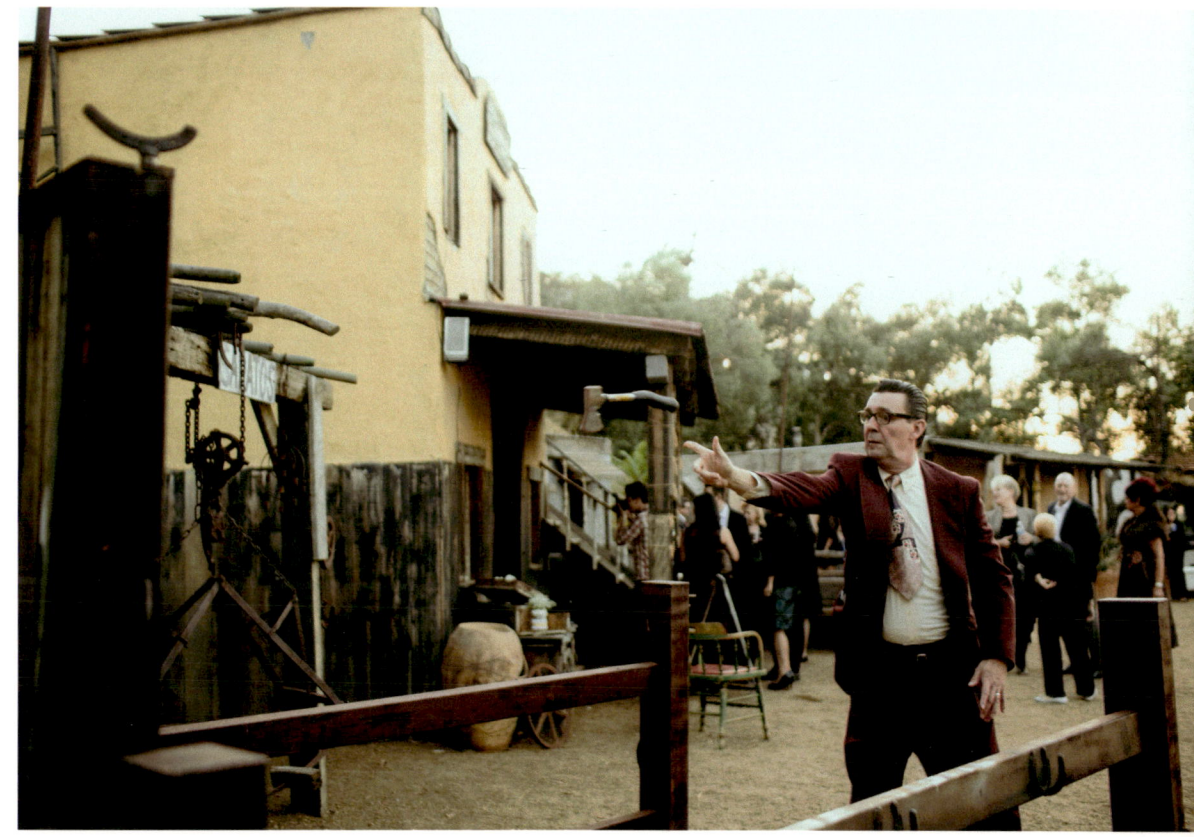

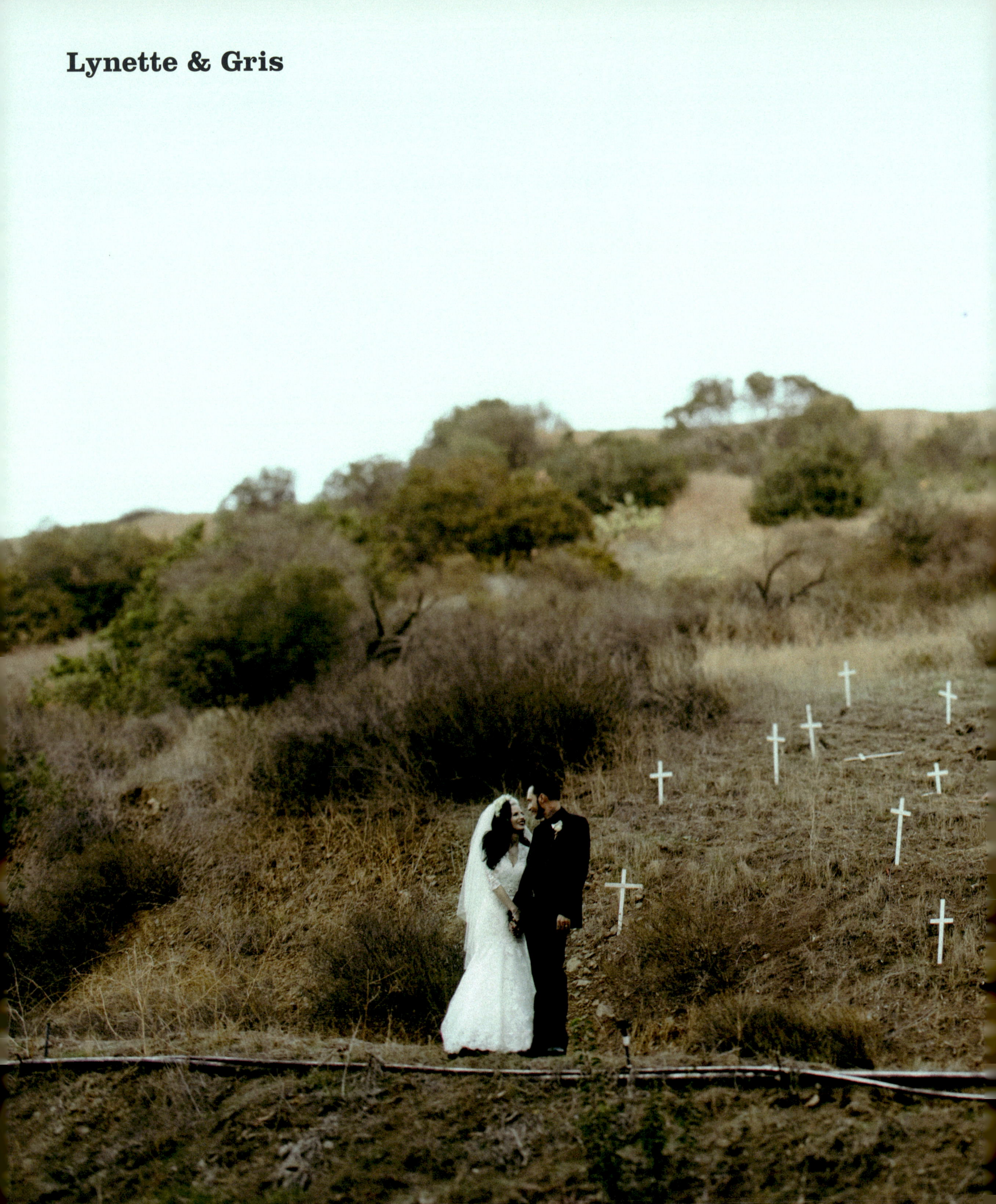

Lynette & Gris

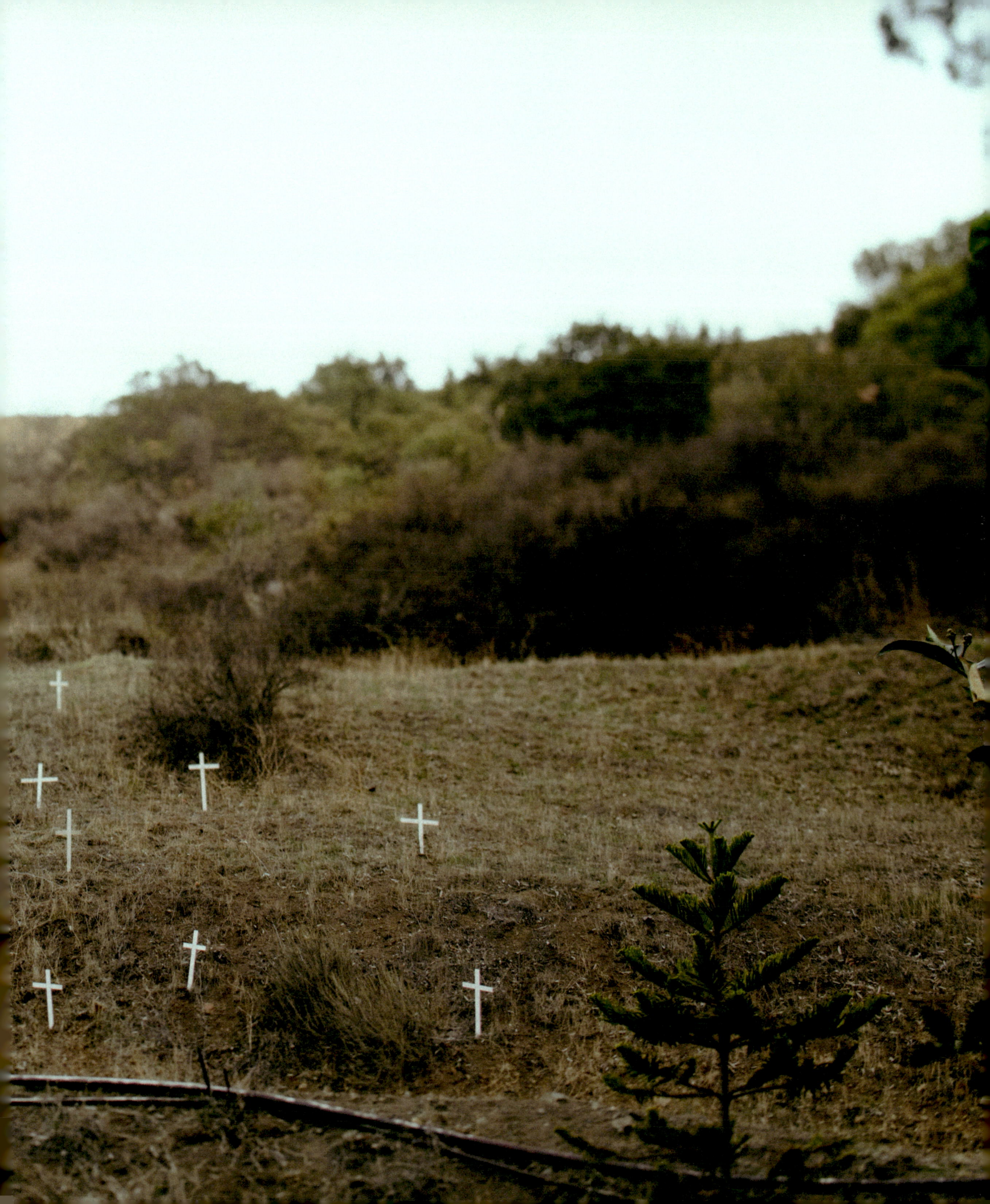

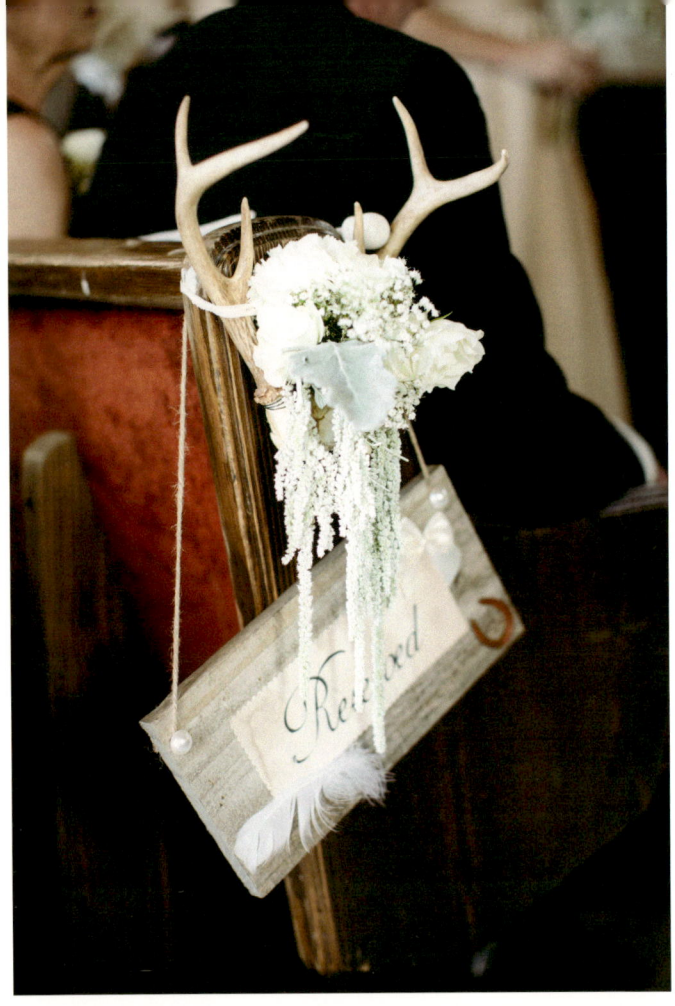

The Decoration

Animal skulls are visually stunning, and they go amazingly well with bouquets. Feathers hanging on invisible threads in the chapel created a kind of heavenly rain that mirrored the tumbling tails of the white peacocks in the background.

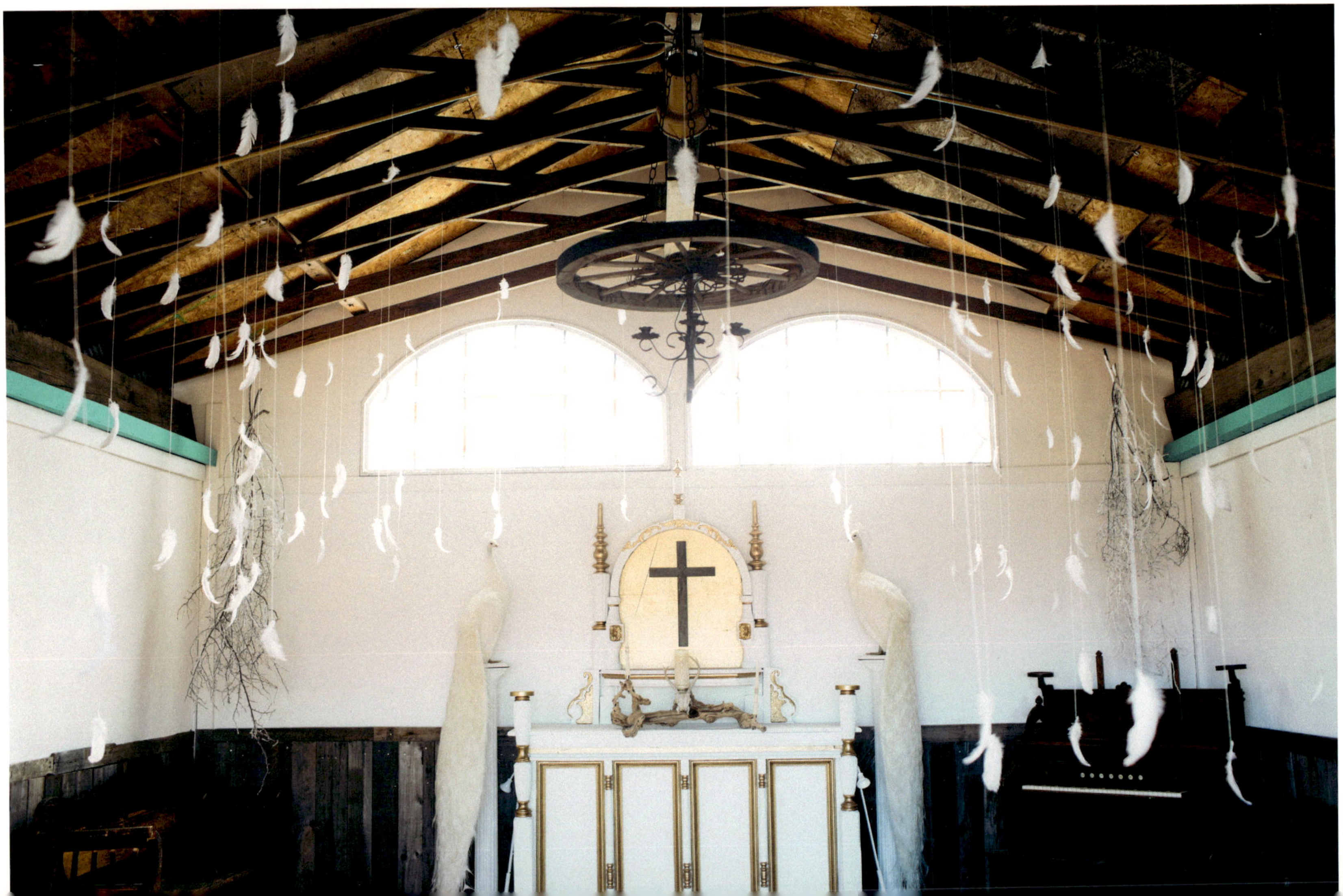

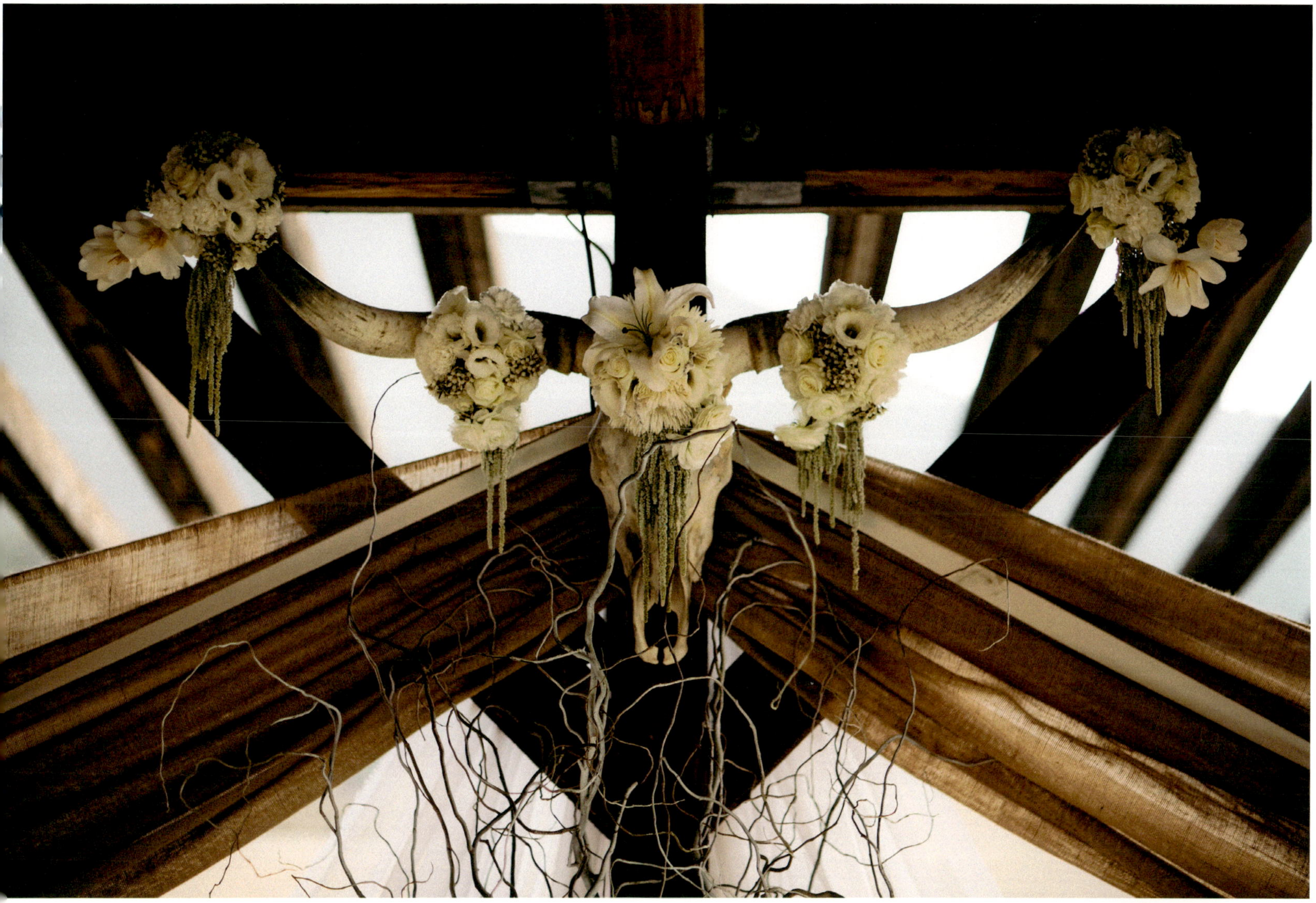

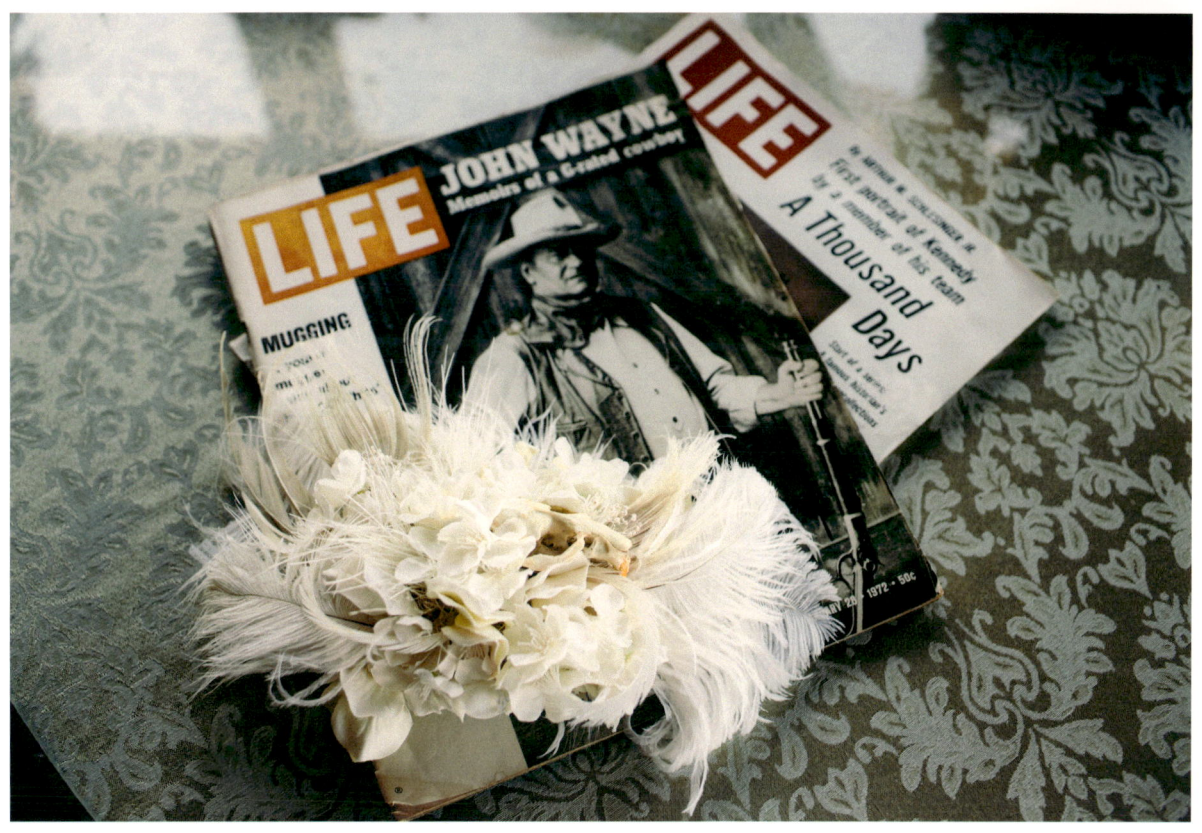

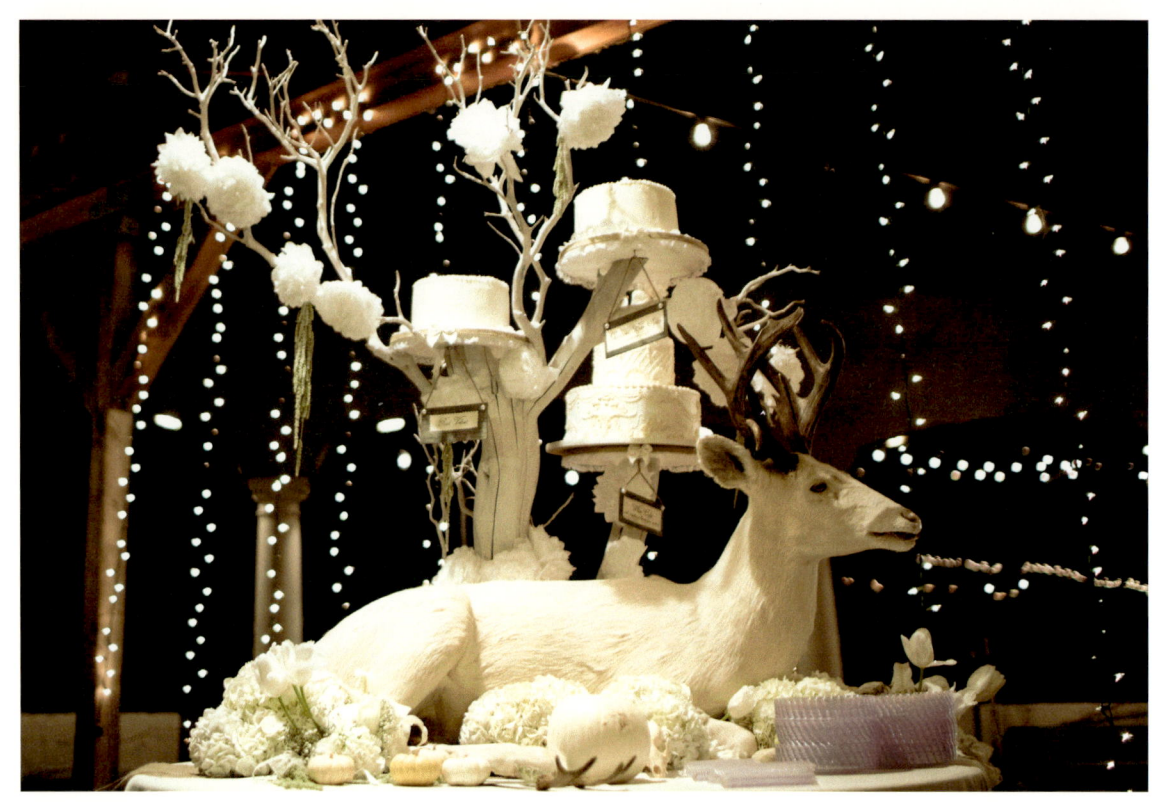

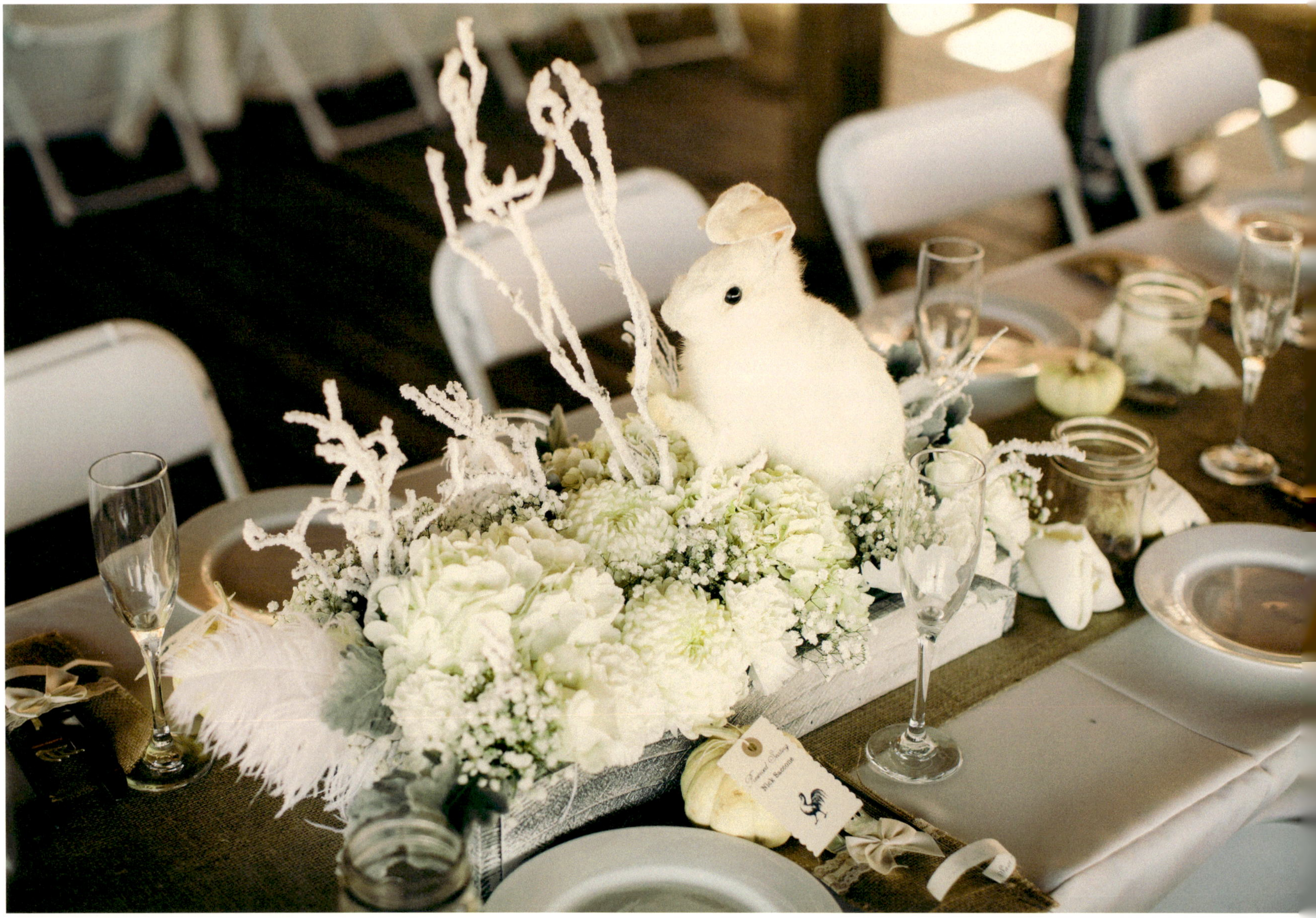

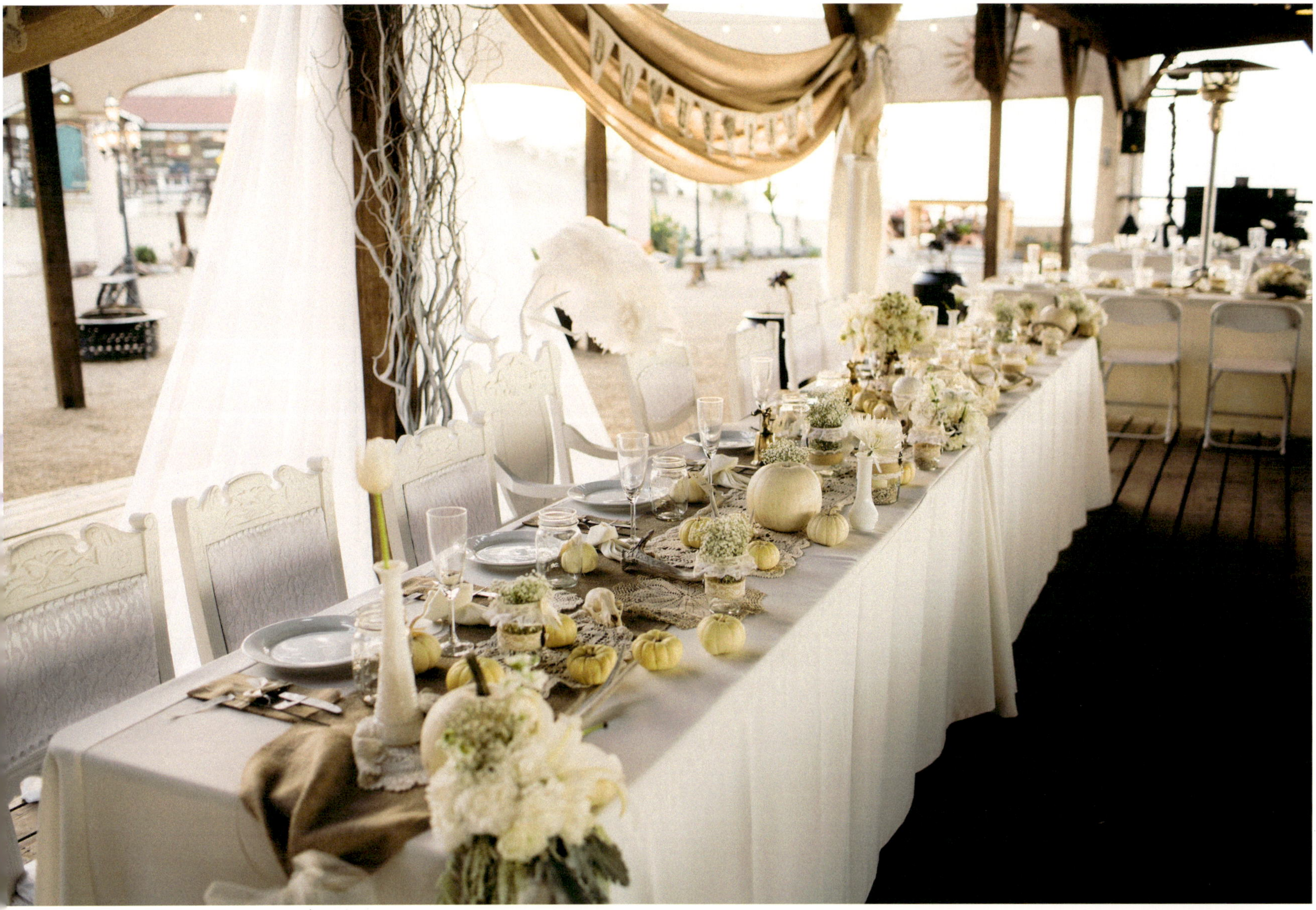

Gris and Lynette both have art in their blood, and nowhere was that more evident than in the extraordinary treetop-and-stag ensemble that held the cakes aloft for all to see.

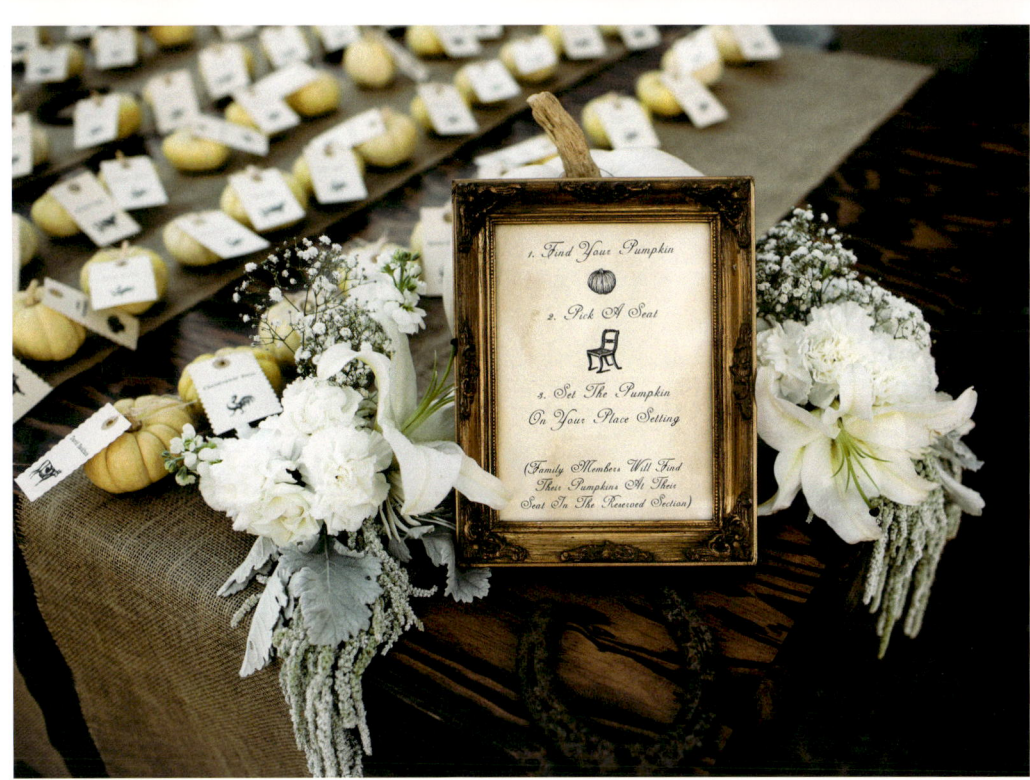

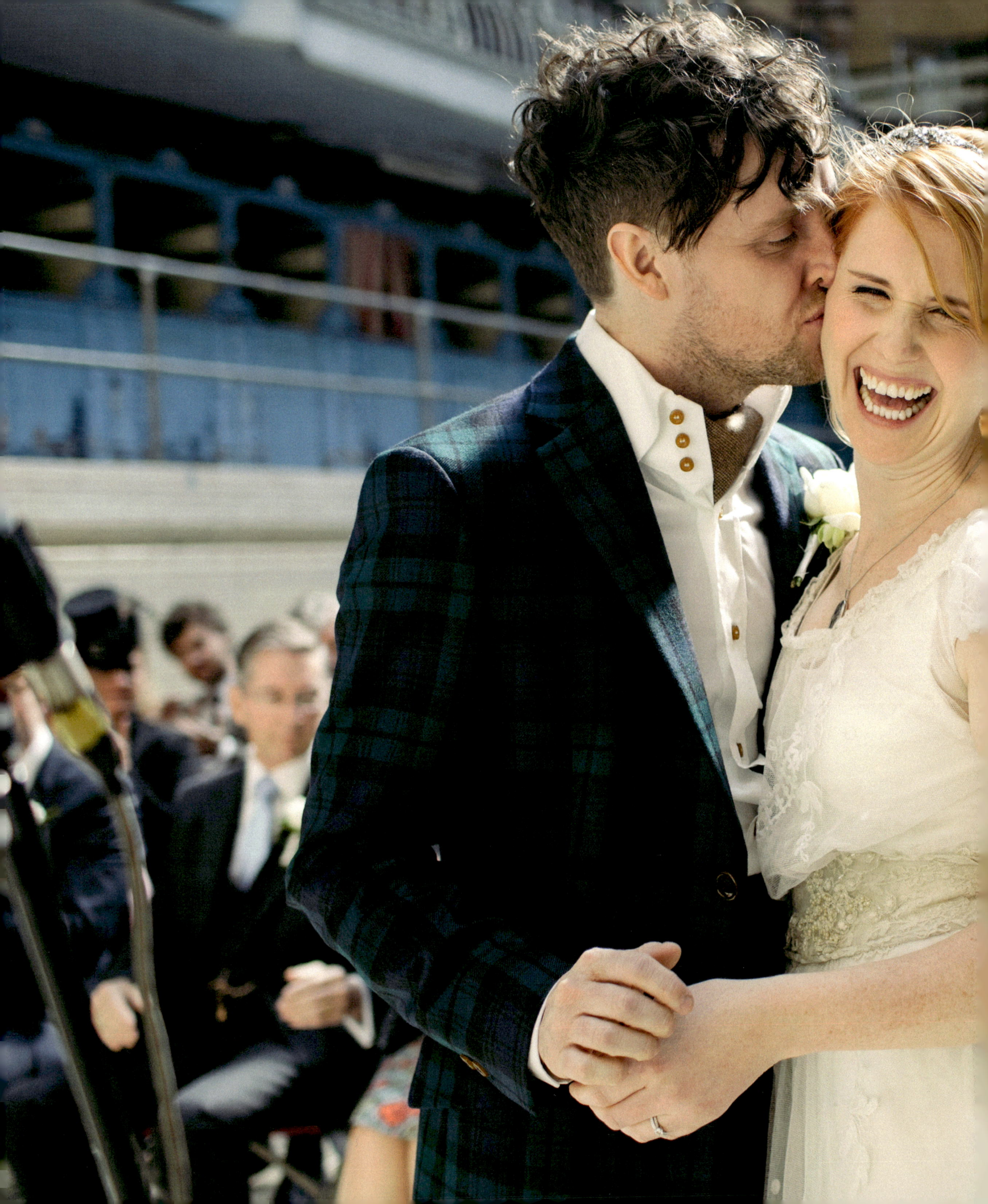

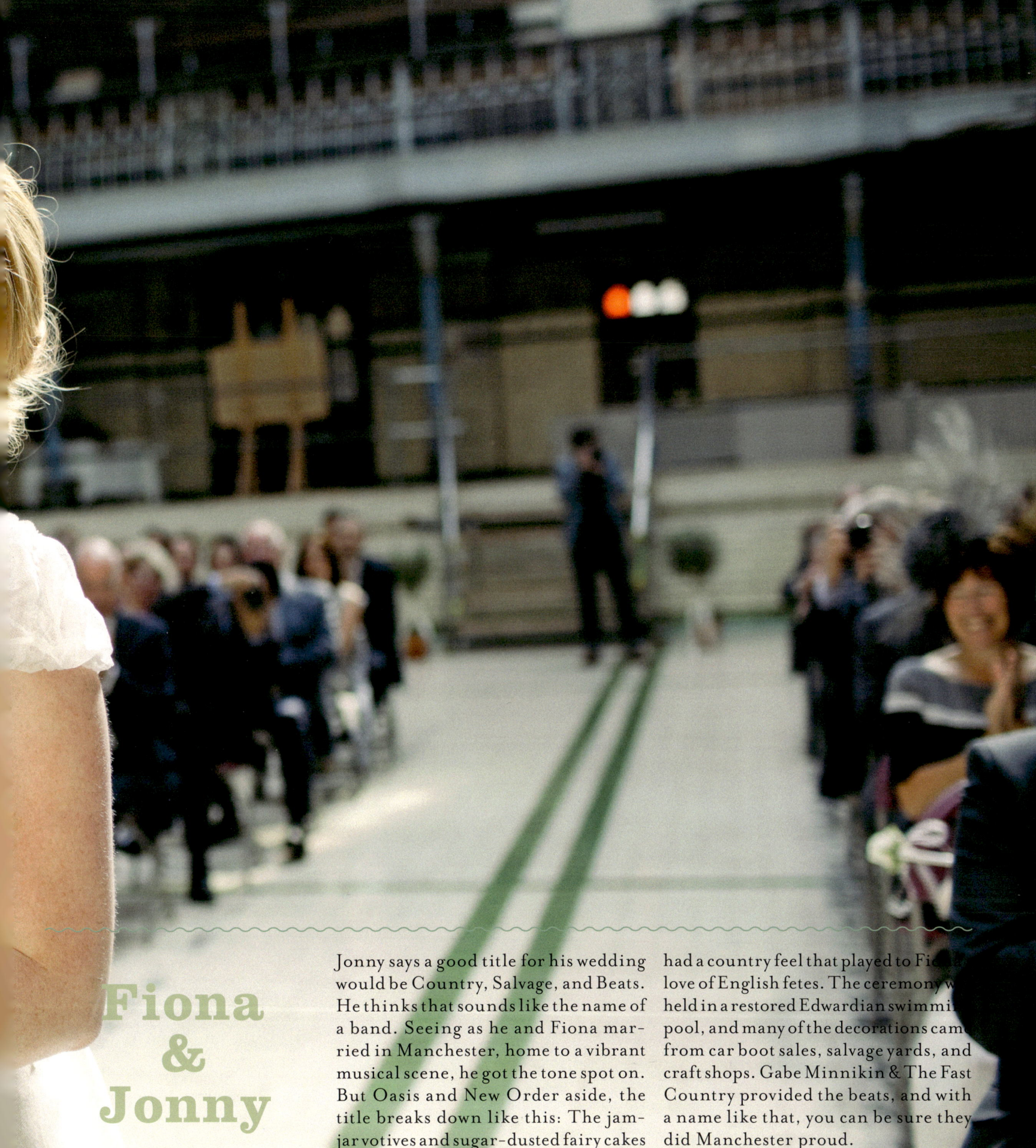

Fiona & Jonny

Jonny says a good title for his wedding would be Country, Salvage, and Beats. He thinks that sounds like the name of a band. Seeing as he and Fiona married in Manchester, home to a vibrant musical scene, he got the tone spot on. But Oasis and New Order aside, the title breaks down like this: The jam-jar votives and sugar-dusted fairy cakes had a country feel that played to Fi[ona's] love of English fetes. The ceremony w[as] held in a restored Edwardian swimmi[ng] pool, and many of the decorations cam[e] from car boot sales, salvage yards, and craft shops. Gabe Minnikin & The Fast Country provided the beats, and with a name like that, you can be sure they did Manchester proud.

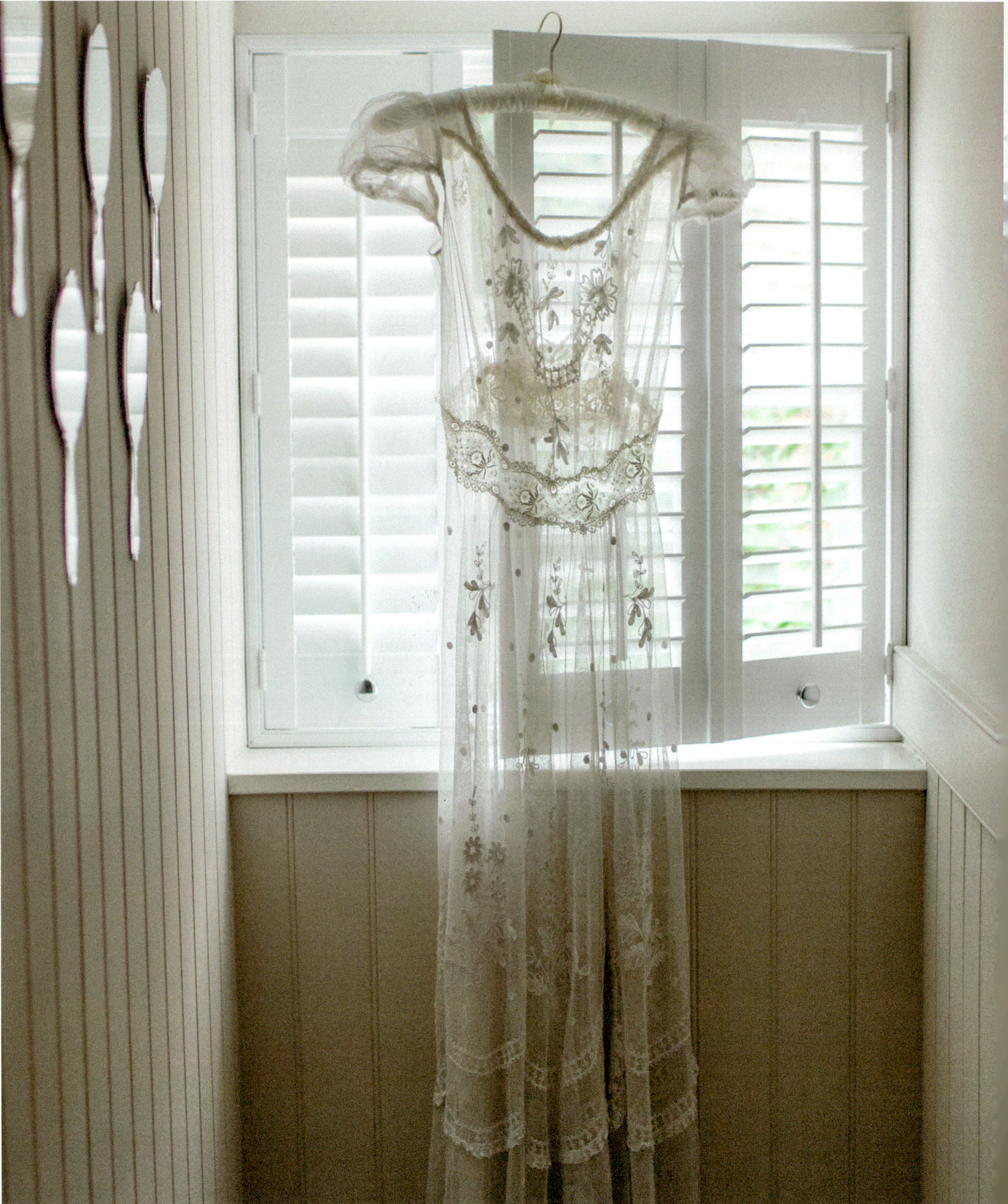

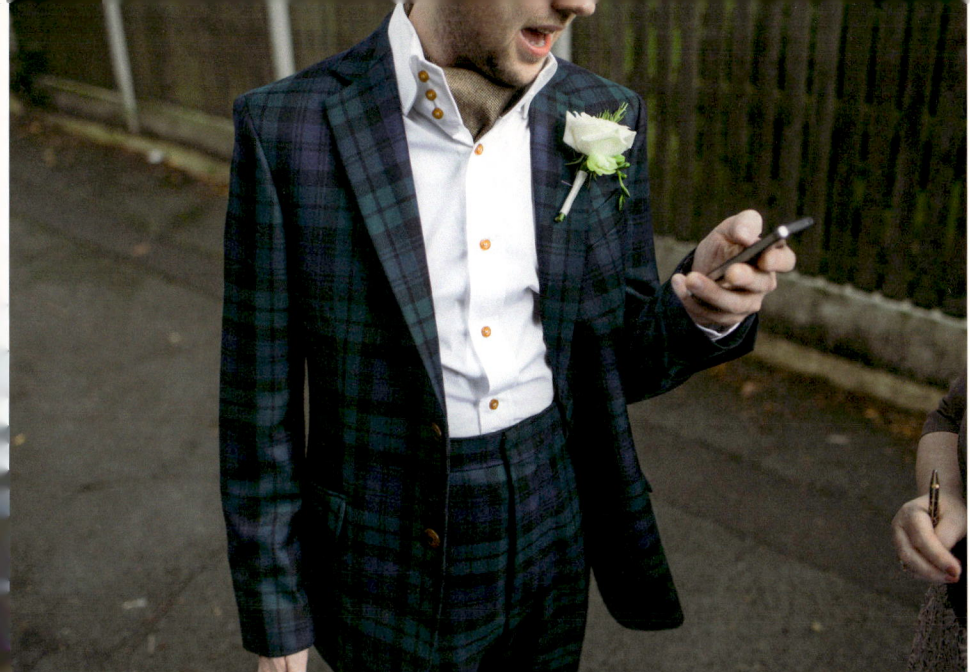

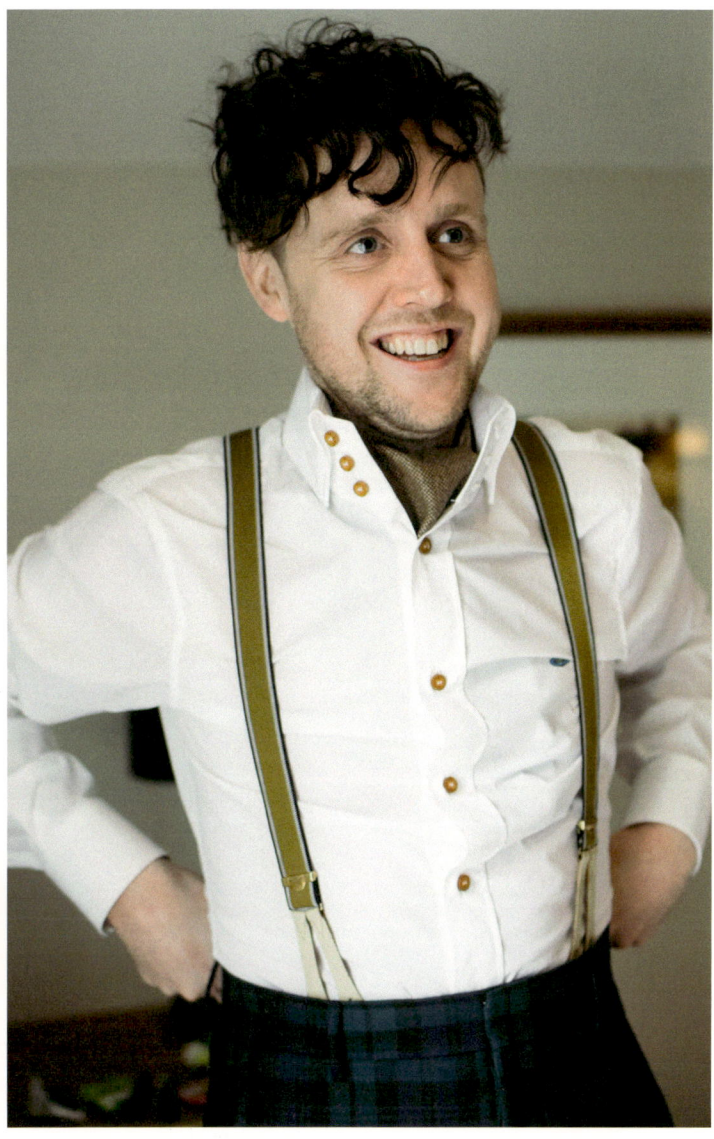

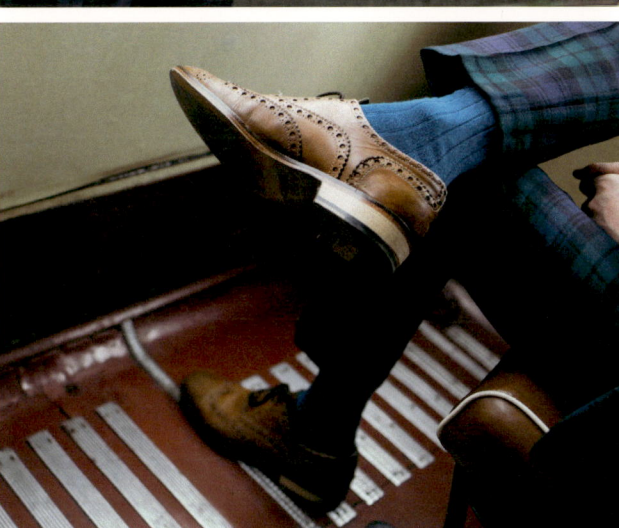

Impressive Dress

The delicate lace of Fiona's dress matched the Edwardian glamour of the pool where they married. Jonny's plaid suit, high-collared button-down shirt, and tan brogues provided a very British backdrop to his brilliantly cheeky smile.

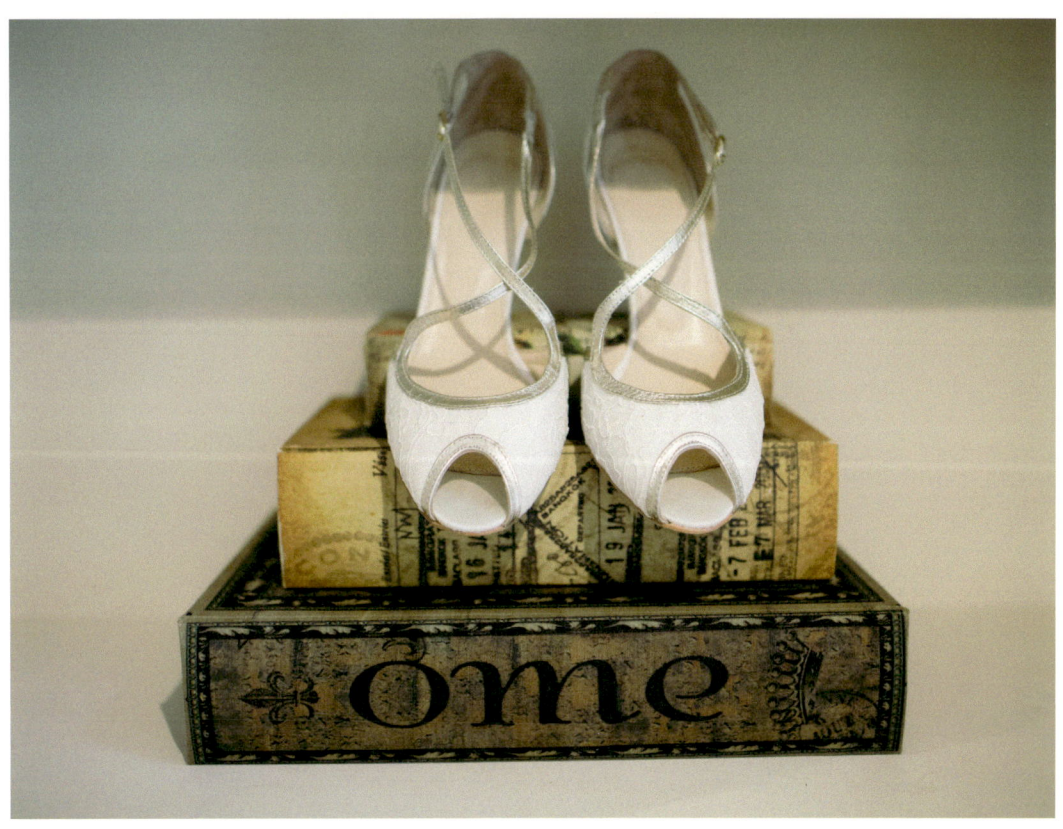

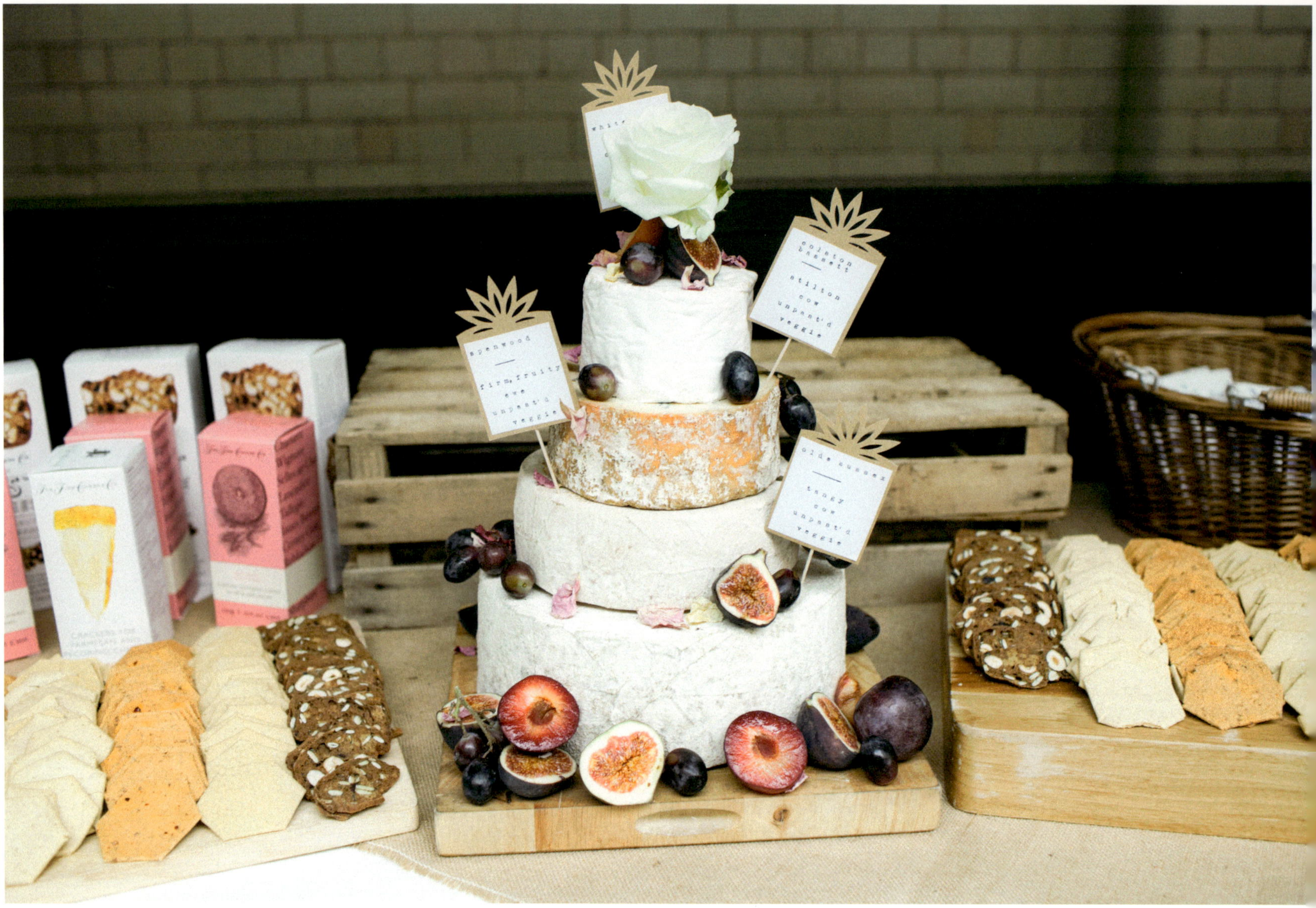

Food & Tables

A cheesecake (no, not the New York kind) is a fun alternative to the usual board. Decorated with fresh figs and grapes, it can look just as pretty as a traditional wedding cake. Emily and Jonny kept their table design simple and let the amazing food steal the show.

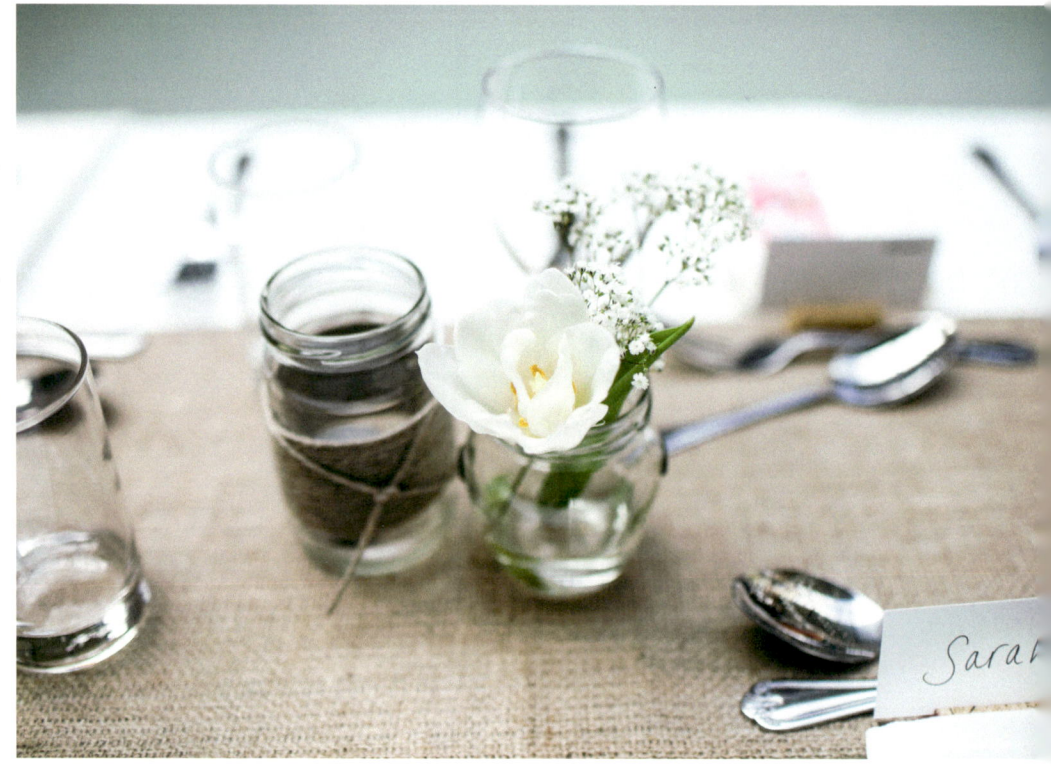

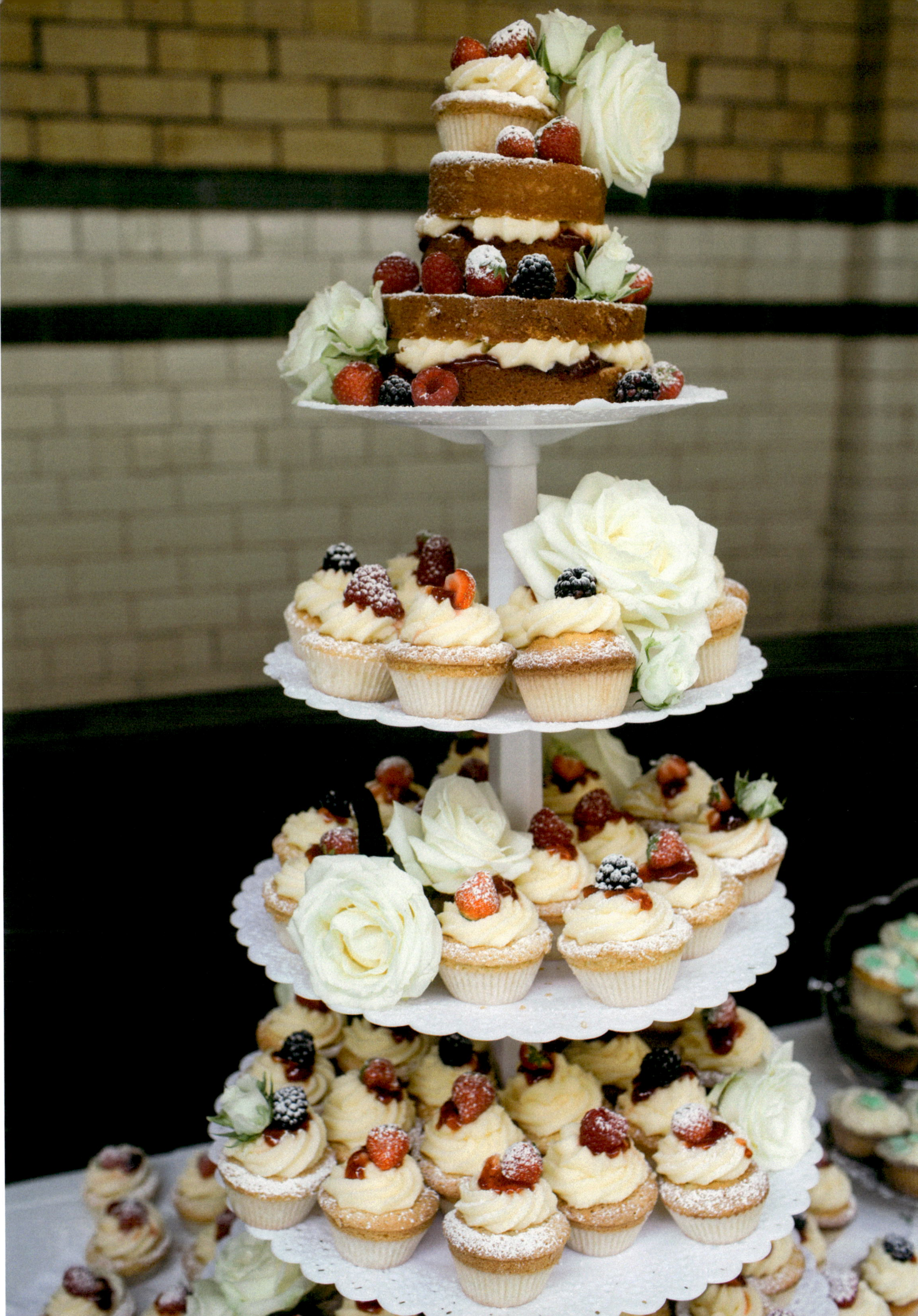

The Journey

Like every other part of your wedding, the schedule should reflect your personality. It could be as simple as including some time to visit a special place to take some meaningful wedding photos. Or it could be on a larger scale, like surprising your guests with bikes and cycling from your ceremony to your reception venue.

At the heart of a wedding is the ceremony. This the moment that the whole day centers around, where you profess your undying love and promise forever to each other. You only get one chance so forget a generic set of rigid vows and say what you want to say.

Bring style to your ceremony without compromising on the substance. Look to traditions of

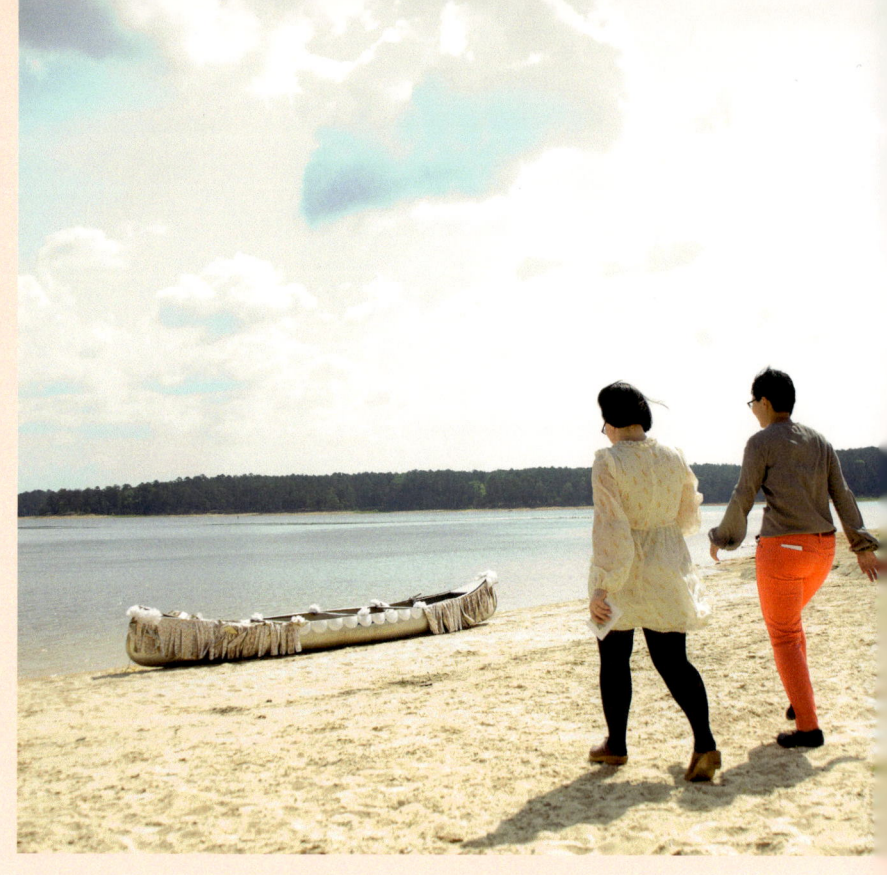

the past or other cultures for inspiration. Take parts you like and make a ceremony that's relevant to you as a couple. Don't be afraid to shake up tradition with your wedding's schedule. You don't have to feel obligated to have a ritual or convention just because "it's what you do." Take inspiration from Toni and Colin who swapped a cocktail hour for getting commemorative tattoos before their ceremony. Turn a negative to a positive; it will make the day feel more natural and will go down a storm with guests.

It's easier said than done but keep a check on what the day is all about — celebrating an amazing connection between two people.

Remember to make some time in the schedule for you as a couple, even if it's just fifteen minutes. It can be so easy to get swept up in the momentum of the day. Take inspiration from Sarah and Dawn. After their ceremony at a lakeside in Georgia, the couple took a canoe out onto the water to spend a quiet moment together as newlyweds before they dived into the reception festivities. Simple moments like this will be the ones you remember. From ceremony to after-party, a wedding can be a long day for you and your guests.

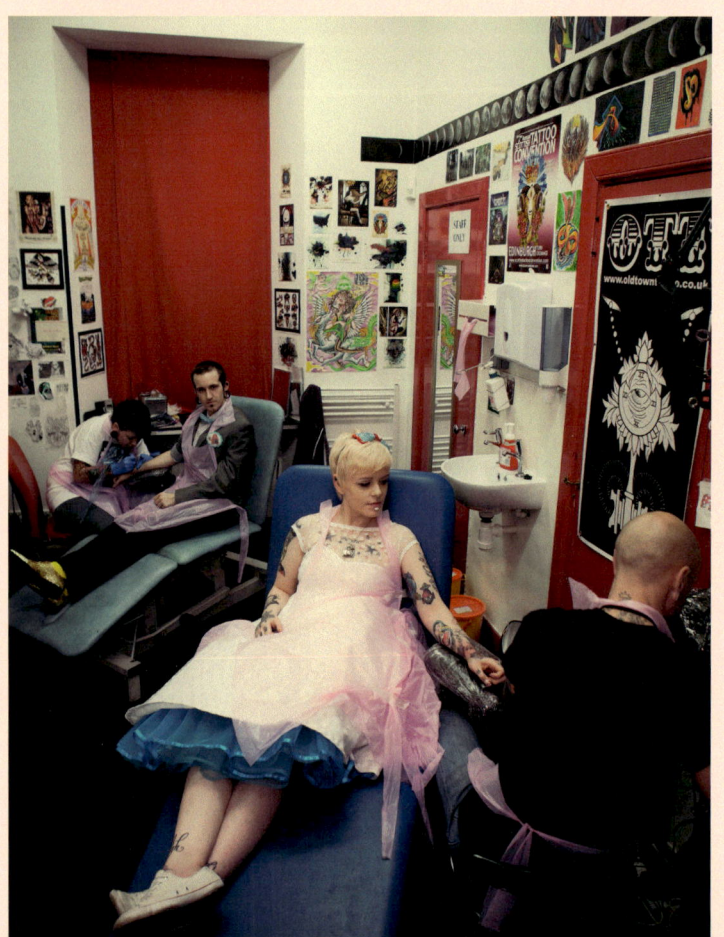

Stop your wedding becoming a snooze-fest by throwing in a few surprises here and there.

Shake things up with a Mariachi band to announce dinner or a flash mob of salsa dancers to kick-start the after-party or even a trip to your favourite ice cream parlor for dessert. Games, photo booths, guest books to write messages in are also great to get everyone interacting. Photo booths have become a big hit recently and there are so many different types. They capture your guests in a way a photographer can't. I find everyone let's go of all inhibitions with photo booths.

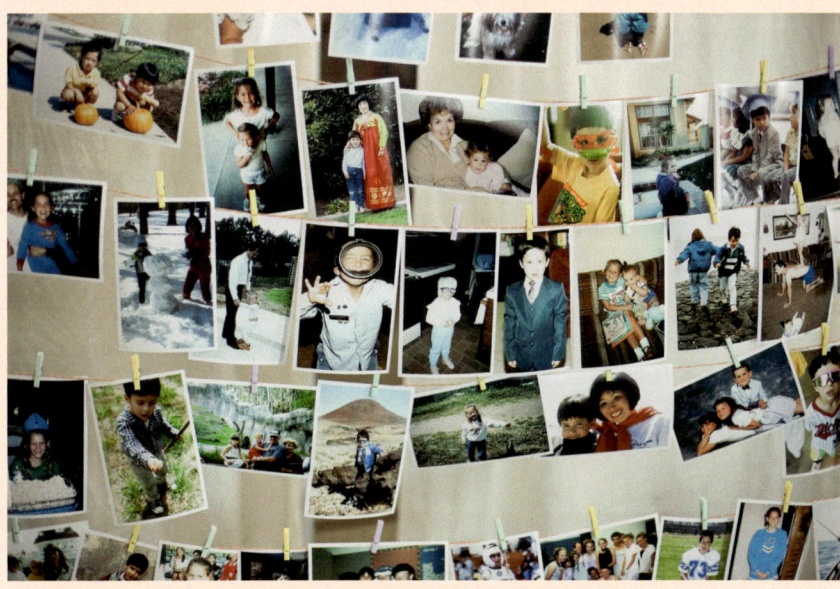

Food is such an important part of any event but especially so at a wedding where guests need sustaining through the duration. When designing your day, remember that food is as much a form of artistic expression as the decorations you hang or the tables you lay. You can convey so much through your edible elements. It could be pay tribute to your heritage, showcase your travels, enhance your theme, or take you back to childhood with a much-loved family recipe. Sprinkle an extra special something on your wedding banquet by making your menu meaningful. Julie and Bo had an entire banquet of Deep South home-

These are the essentials to make your day run smoothly:

1. Master of ceremonies—someone to keep the day's schedule on track, like calling guests to dinner or pulling the groom's party over for photographs.

2. Someone to take care of the children—during the day and just as importantly in the evening when they get tired and their parents start to party.

3. Transportation—getting guests to and from venues can be a nightmare. Organizing transport ensures no one gets lost, turns up late or risks loosing a driving license on the way back.

4. Clean up team for afterwards—no one wants to be taking down decorations or sweeping up confetti on their post-wedding day. Hire a team to handle the de-rig operation.

Music you might have not think of but which will get the party started:

1. Punk-rock cover band

2. Top of Pops Karaoke—think Dancing Queen by ABBA

3. Friends who are musicians —anyone from a singer to a cellist or a piano plater

4. Ceilidh band to get everyone really moving

5. Personal performance from the bride and groom

cooking, including a signature cocktail, which they called the "Mississippi Medicine," to reflect their roots. It doesn't have to be a Michelin starred dining experience; a thoughtful selection can be far more stylish.

Hire a food truck like an artisan ice-cream van or tuctuc serving lobster rolls.

Not only is the food fantastic but it will add a fun, uplifting energy to your day that you wouldn't get with a formal sit down dinner. Drinks act in the same way. If your wedding is outside on a warm summer's day think about refreshing drinks like pink lemonade in cute soda bottles or jars with themed straws.

Having a proper cocktail maker, even for an hour or so at the drinks reception is a really great way to shake things up and you can work with them to create a cocktail menu you both love. Alternatively fill glass urns with your favorite punch mix for people to pour their own. The point is, it doesn't need to be all about wine and champagne fountains!

Another way to get guests onto their feet and interacting is through music. It is such a useful tool than can elevate spirits or emphasize a touching moment. Match your music to the mood you want to create at different stages of the wedding Your guests will really respond to the sensory engagement. You need to decide whether you want a live band or a DJ or even a simple playlist. Do you want a piper to greet guests on arrival or strings through the drinks reception. Whatever you decide, something I love to give guests on their way out the door is a mix CD of songs and music from throughout the day.

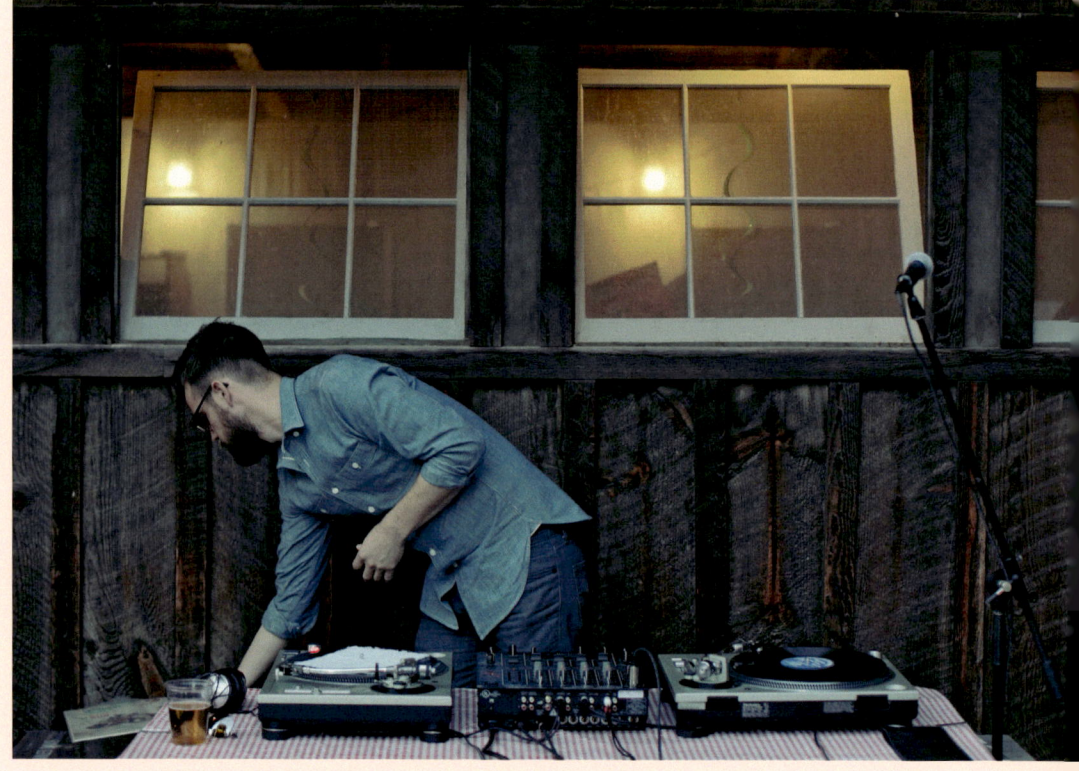

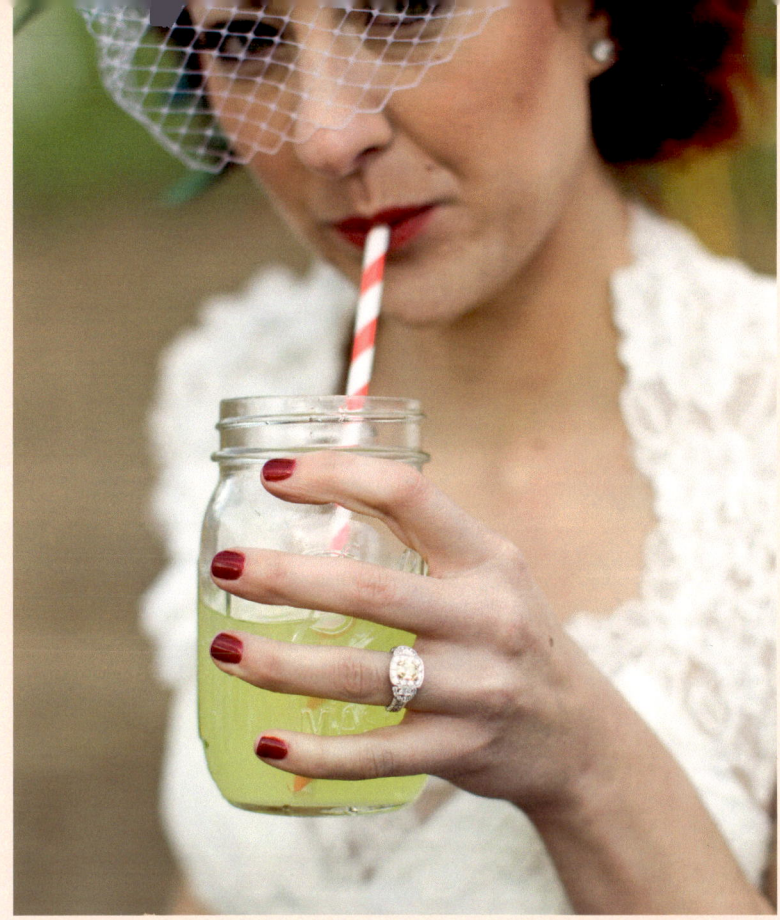

modes of transport, it's incredible all the different parts of the design to consider when creating your wedding. It can be so easy to forget the nitty-gritty production required on the day. Yes, the hand-made decorations are beautiful but who is going to put them all up?

It's the one-day in your life where it'd be great to have an assistant to do the logistics and generally take care of the business of getting married. Hiring someone is always a good idea but not essential. You could appoint a friend, just as long as they are someone you trust to run the schedule and keep everything on track. Don't try to manage everything yourself; delegate different tasks to a trusted team of those happy to help.

Most importantly remember to enjoy yourself! Keep it calm and relax. No matter how much you prep and plan, mishaps are bound to happen. Don't let them spoil your day—after all you are marrying THE love of your life! If everything went wrong but you still got to marry your soul-mate then it would still have been a pretty perfect day.

The day passes in the blink of an eye so make every moment special. Even the logistics of getting from place to place can be made fun with clever transport choices.

If within walking distance, lead guests in a parade to the reception venue accompanied by a marching band or ringleader. For a night-time wedding, light the way using candles or hurricane lamps. If there is a bit more of a way to go, surprise guests with bikes and cycle to the next destination. Choose matching frames and tie streamers to the handlebars for a cohesive aesthetic.

If a more traditional transport option, such as a bus, takes your fancy opt for a beautiful vintage model. Make it your own by filling with streamers or decorating with vinyl stickers. For longer journeys, be sure to provide guests with a little hamper of something edible. Miniature bottles of champagne and popcorn will make them feel special.

Keep energy and spirit levels high with an amazing playlist or by hiring a band to set up stage in the back seats for an unexpected performance. It'll be the best bus ride they've ever had! From music to

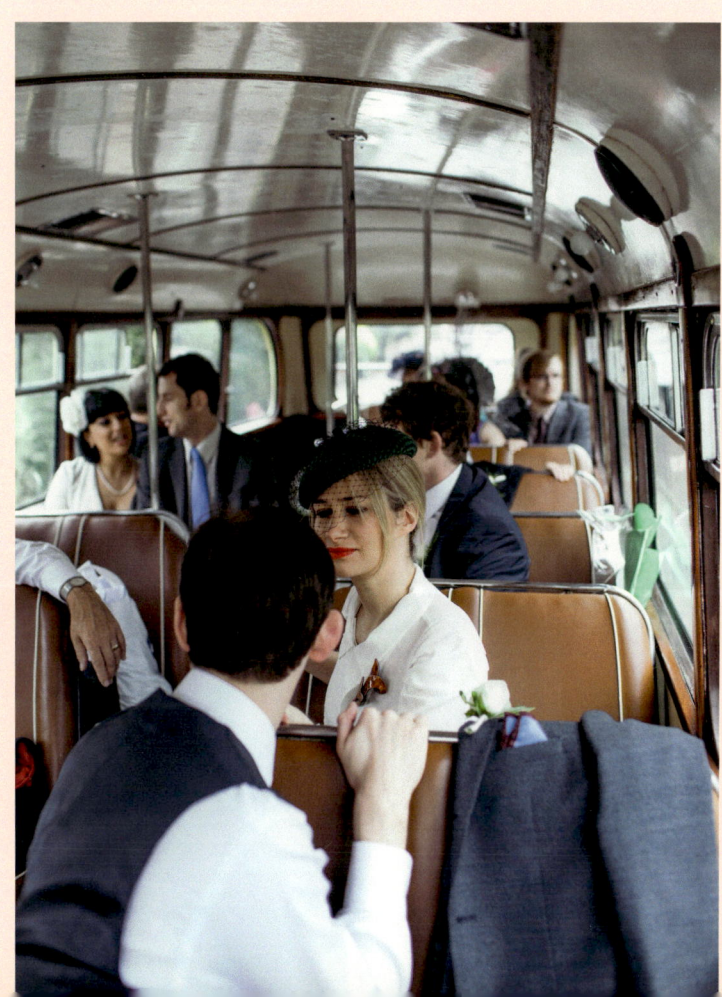

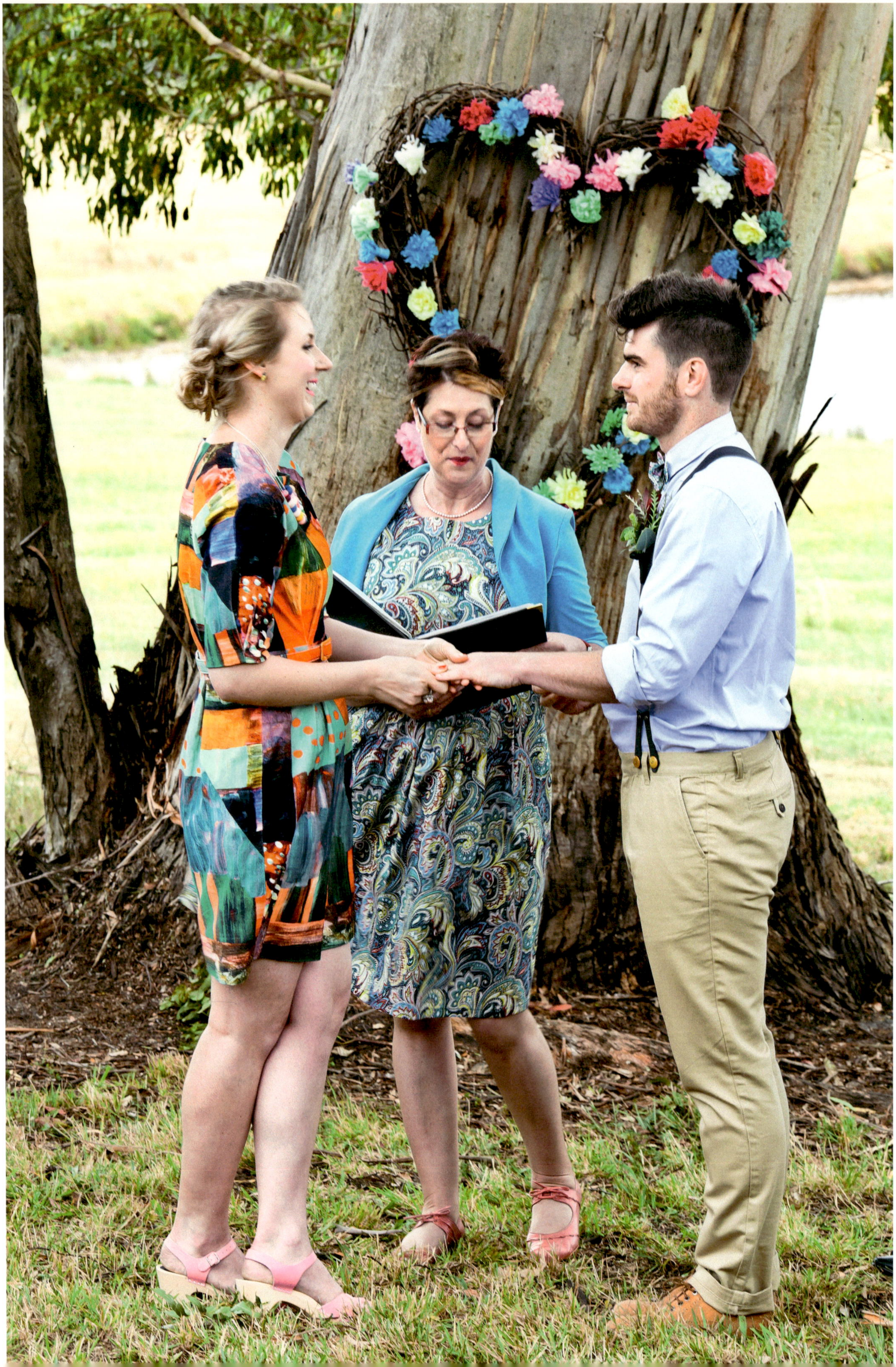

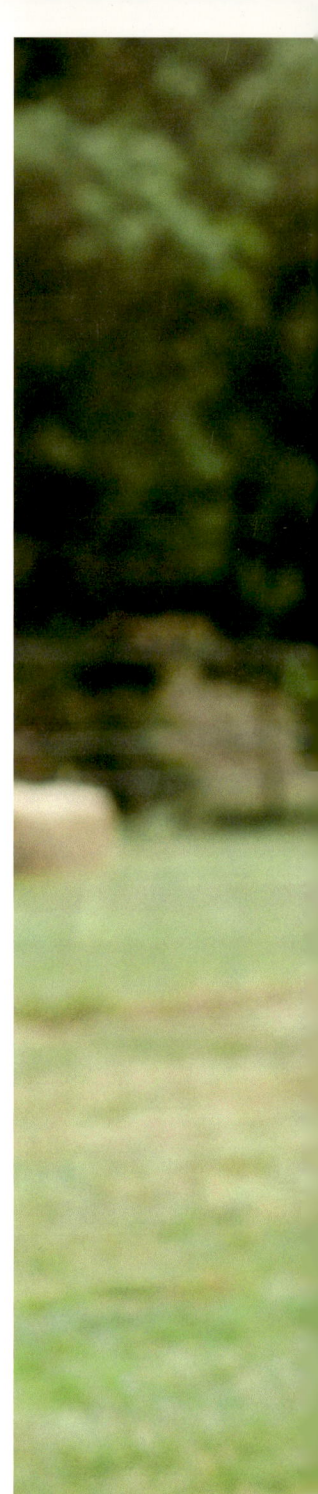

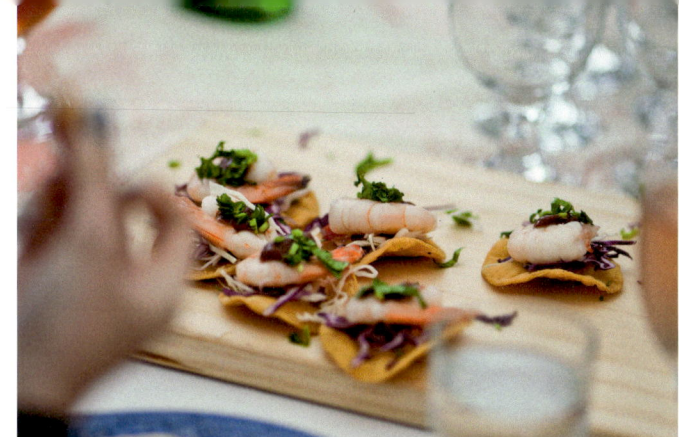

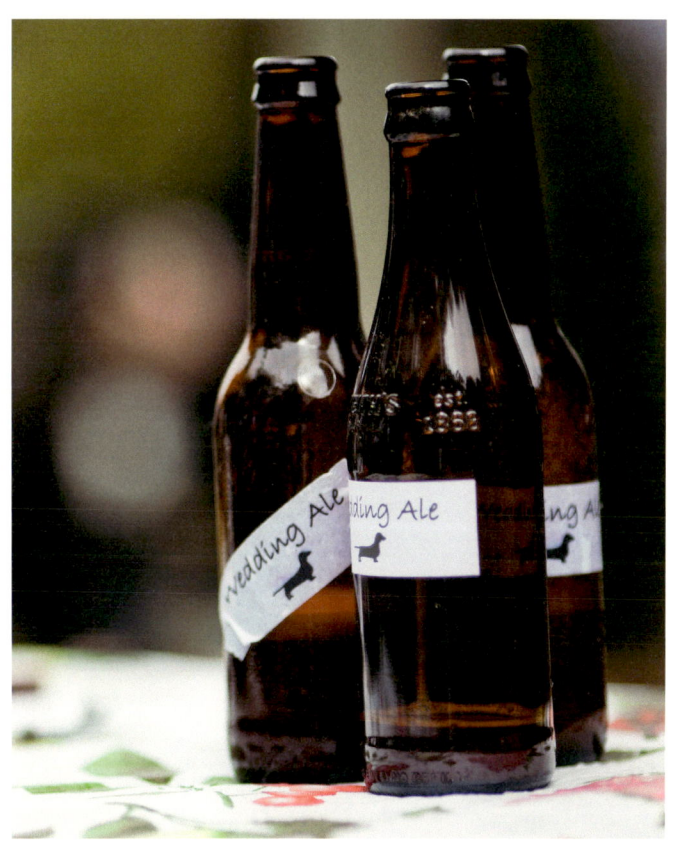

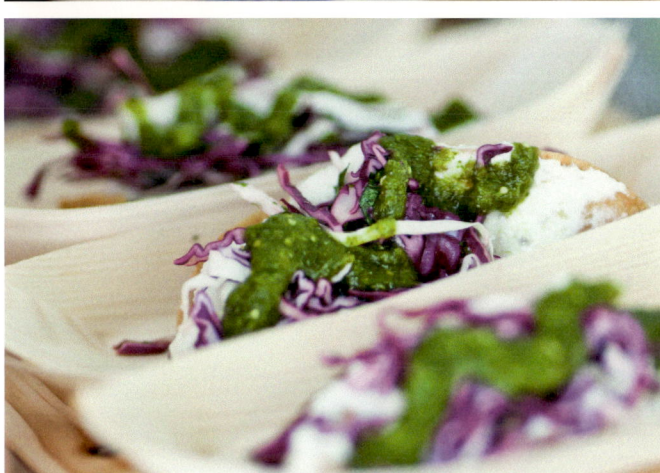

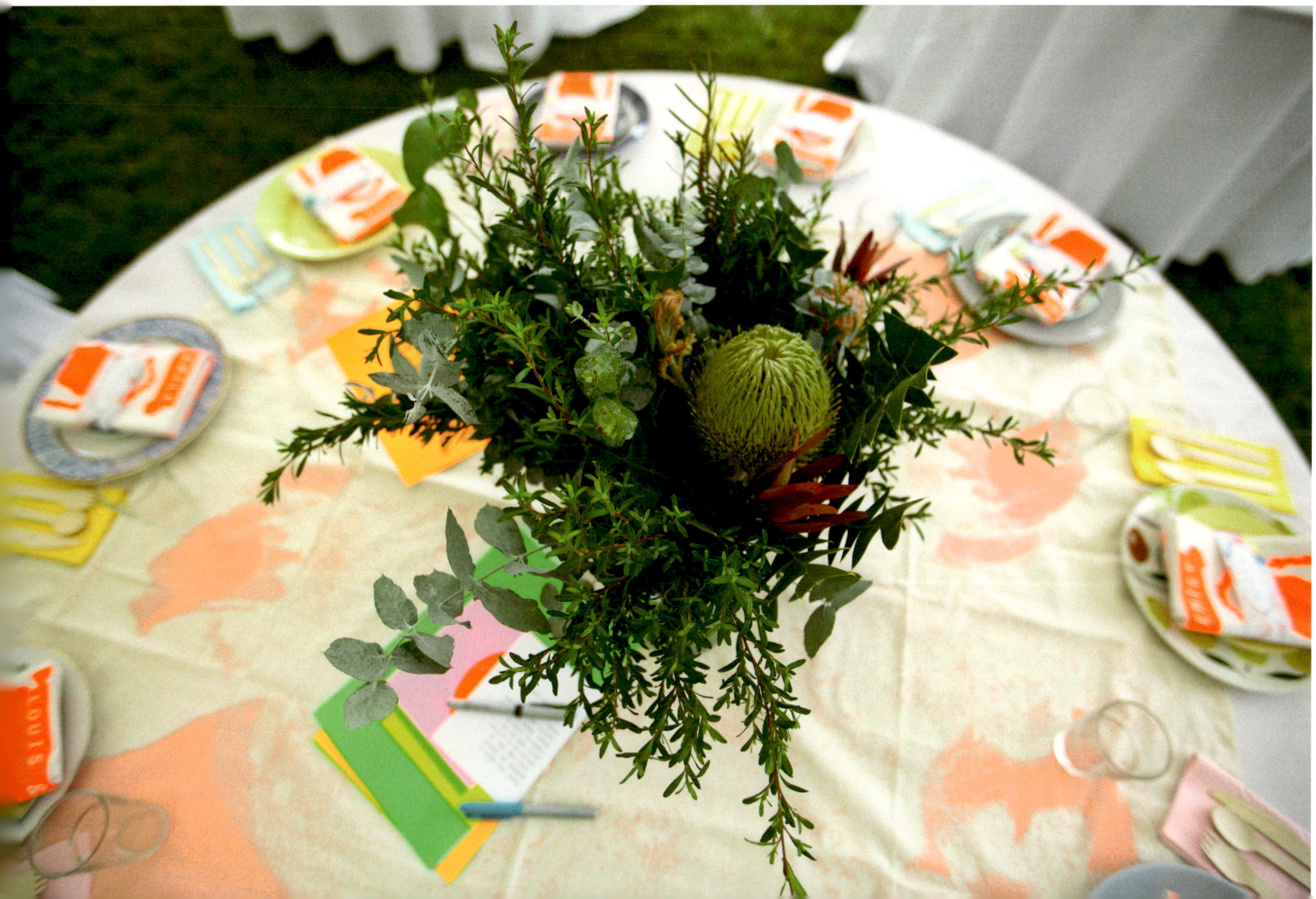

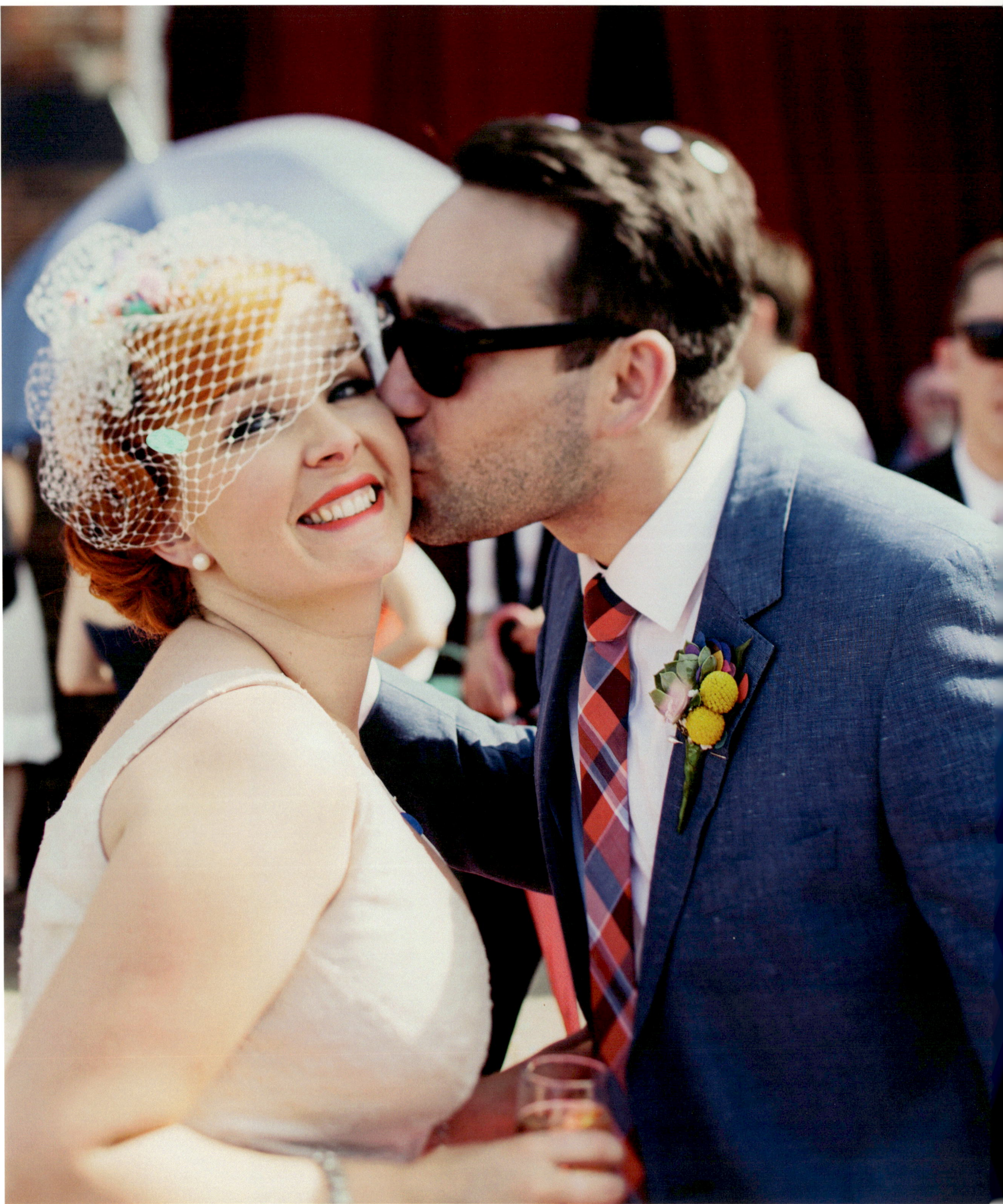

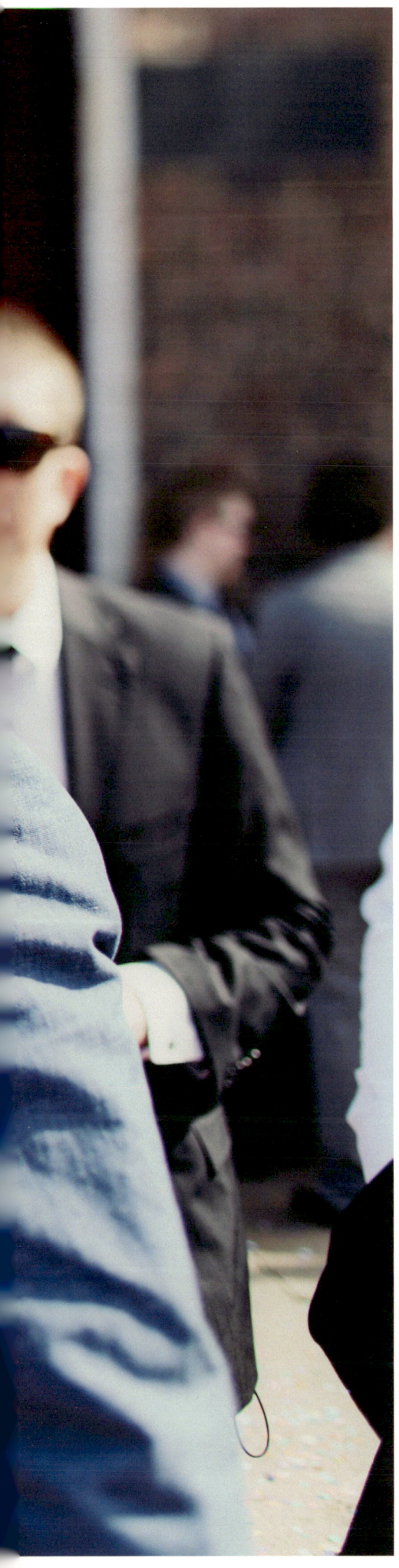

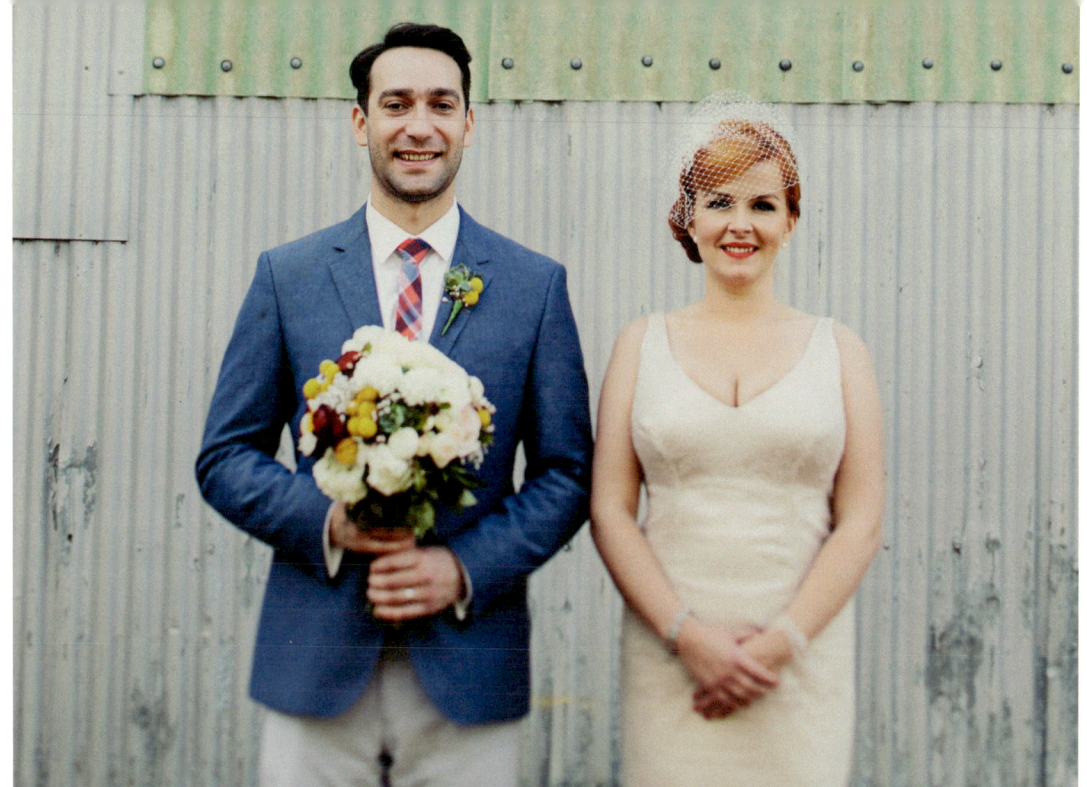

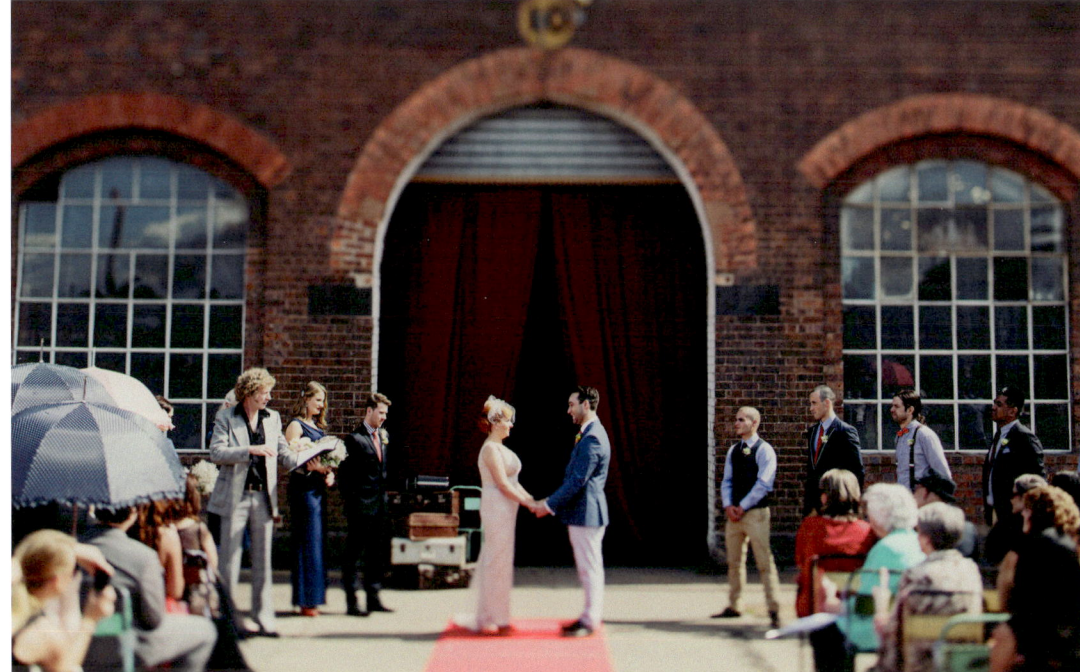

Kirstyn & Adam

The red carpet leading to a brick archway framed with thick velvet curtains set a dramatic scene for Adam and Kirstyn's wedding ceremony. The theater theme reflected her love of performance and his fascination with the spaces themselves. In between the vows and cocktail hour, the second theme rolled into town in the form of a 1940s carnival.

The Fashion

Royal blues, navy blues, sky blues…
everyone's wearing them but no one
has got them. Just look at all those
happy smiles! No one could be glum
on a wedding day when they get to wear
cherry-red shoes (the girls) or fabu-
lously flamboyant socks (the boys are
wearing those, trust us).

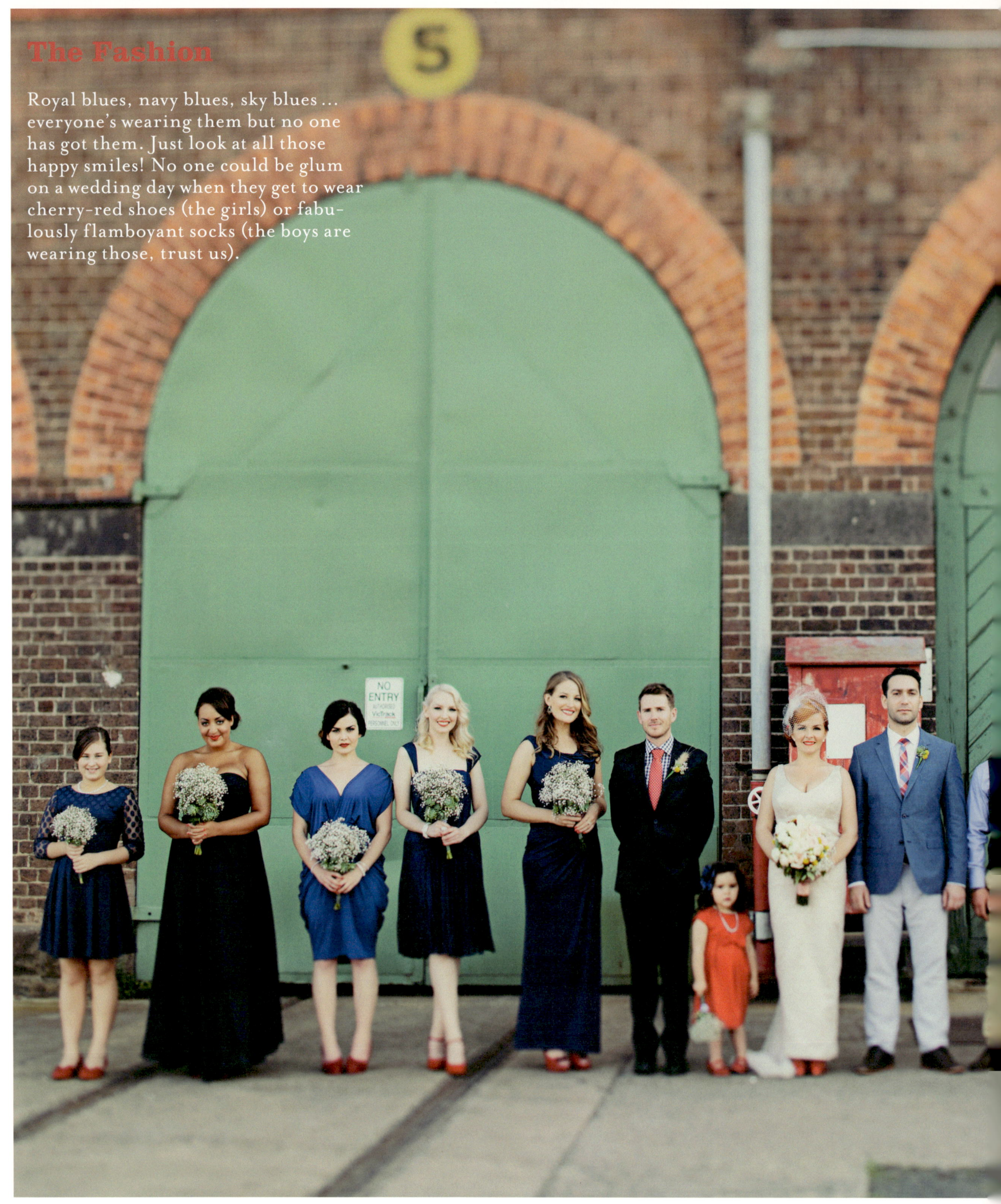

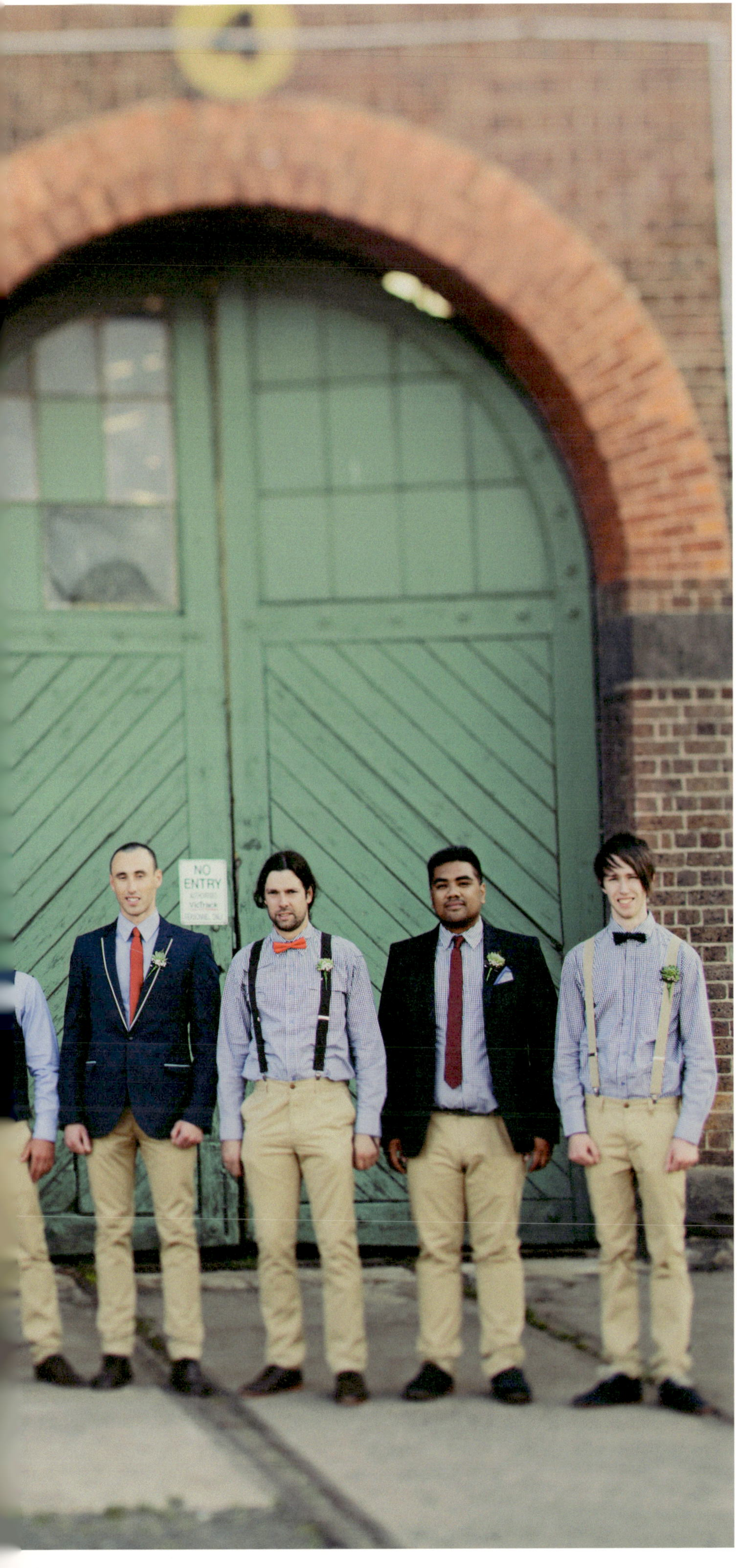

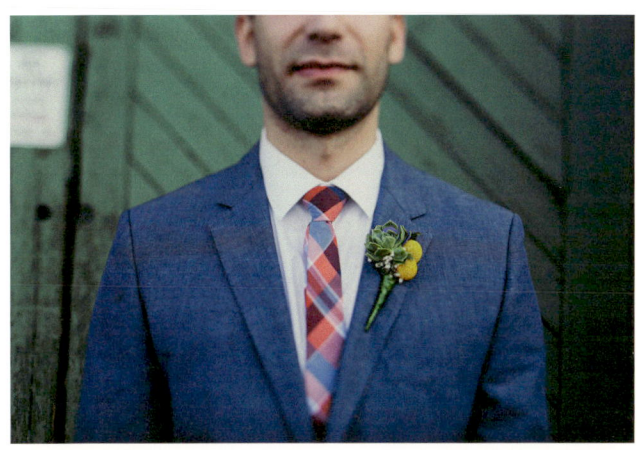
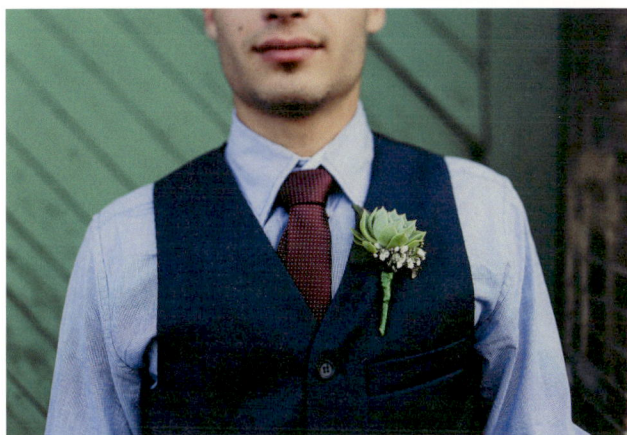
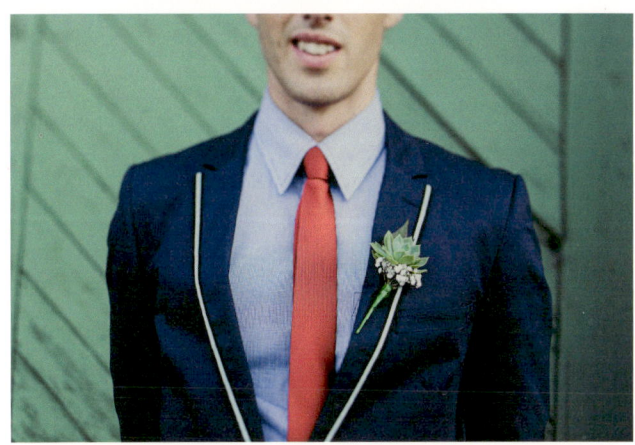
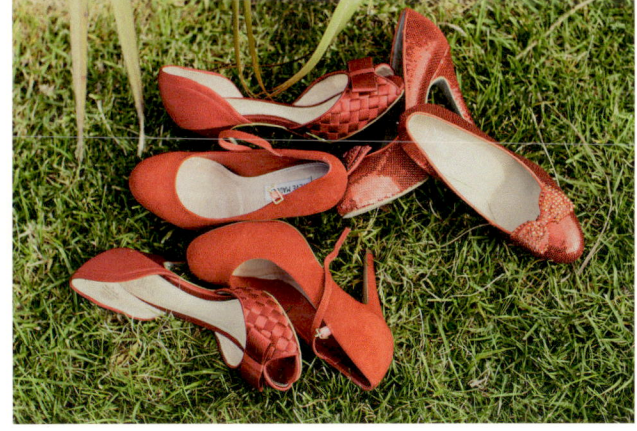

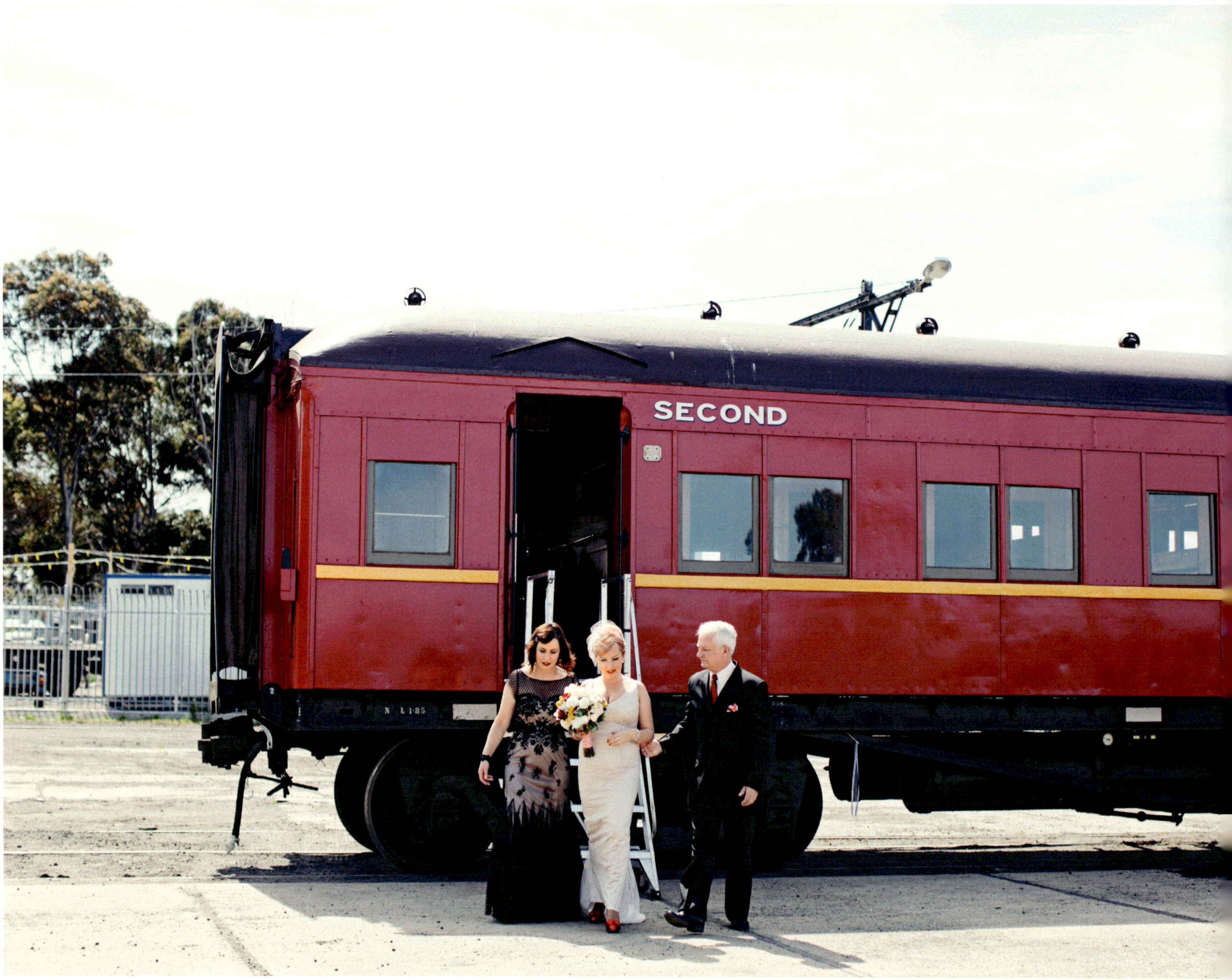

Location

The Old Newport Railway Workshops in Melbourne gave Kirstyn and Adam the theatricality they were looking for in a ceremony venue. As evening fell, they moved on to the nearby Substation, where theater and carnival came together in a glittering reception. Sky-high windows were hung with red drapes, and the ceiling featured a lighting installation that very nearly stole the show.

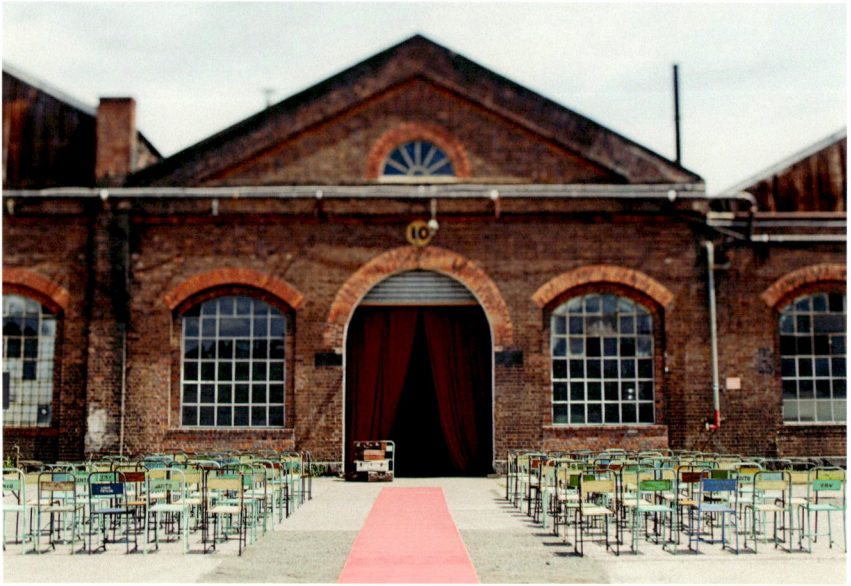

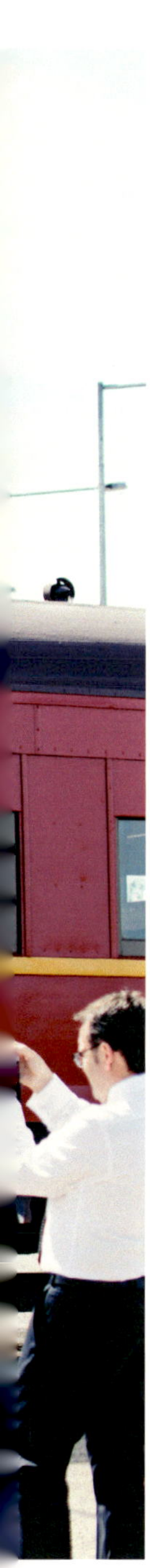

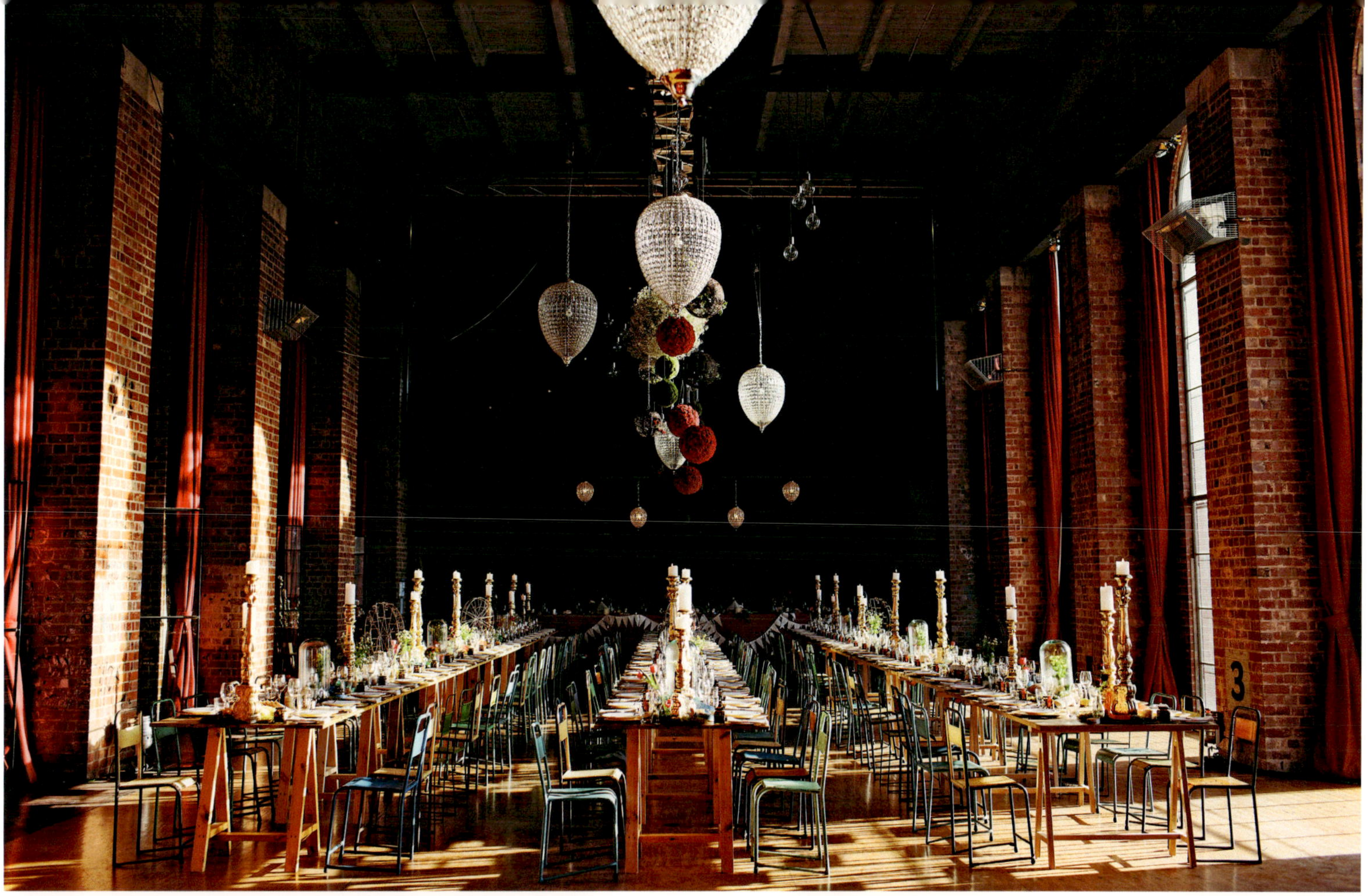
3

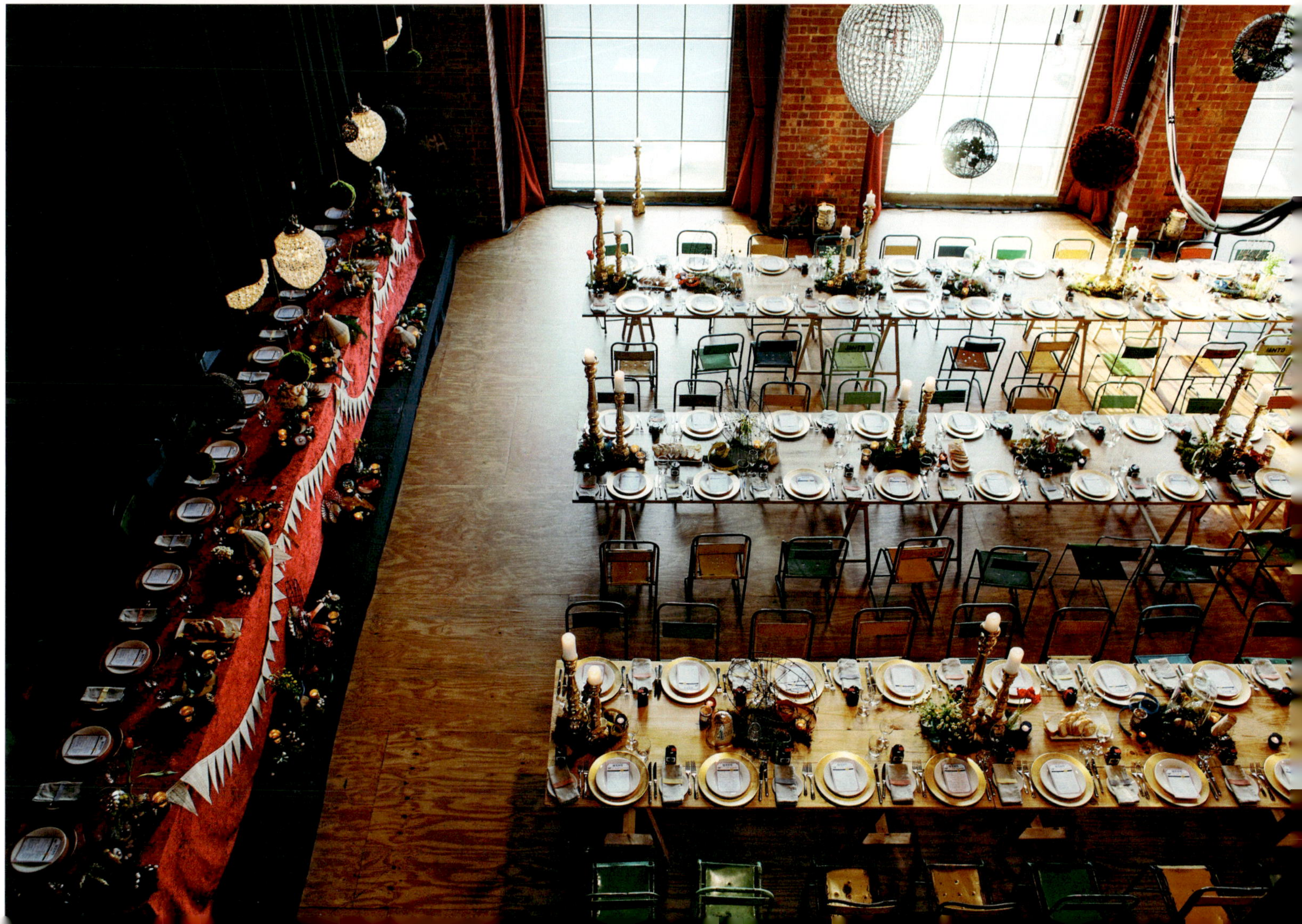

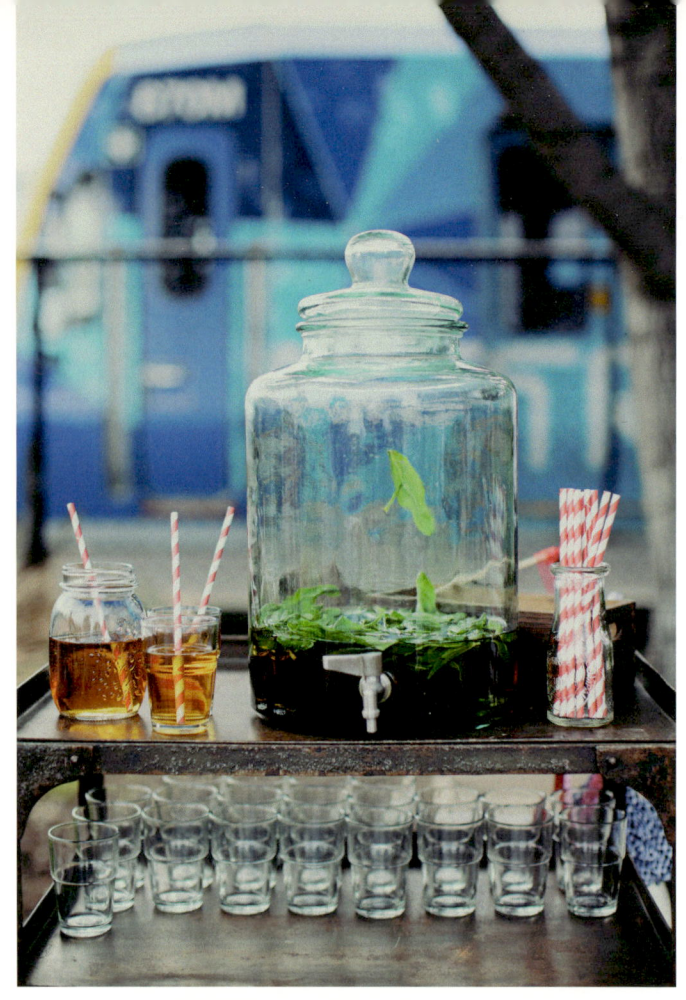

Drinks & Ice Cream

Vintage glass dispensers and old-fashioned straws are a stylish way to serve afternoon drinks. Ice cream cones are also a welcome addition to a summer wedding. There is a chance yours might drip on your dress or your tie, but it's a risk worth taking.

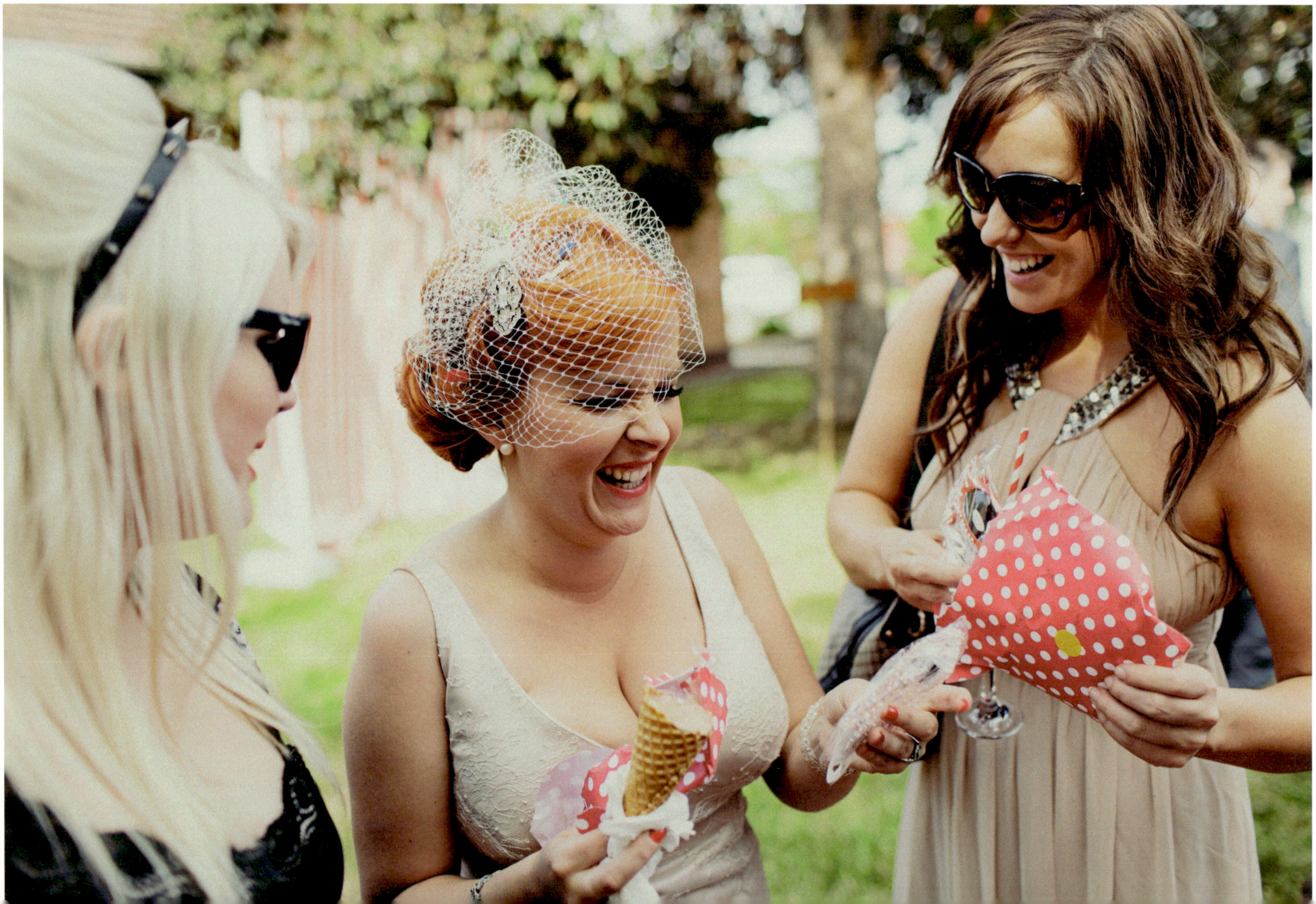

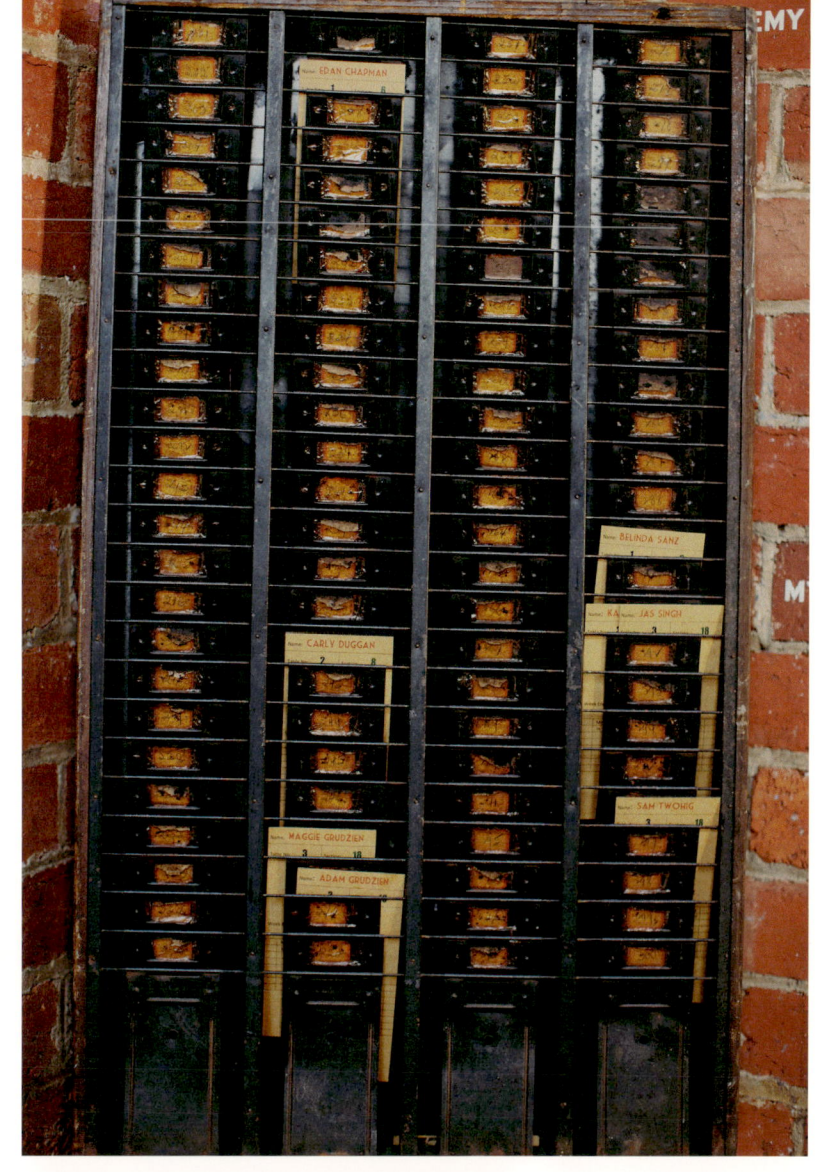

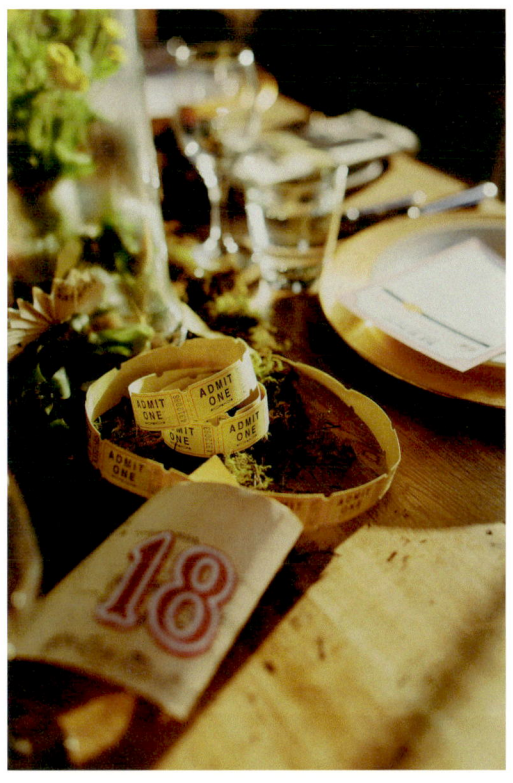

Tables

Clock-in cards were the inspiration for the escort cards, which were made by Kirstyn's mom and displayed in the original holders. Kirstyn was the brains behind the design for the vintage menus (clearly creativity runs in her family). Each table had fairground centerpieces interspersed with jars of flowers, golden candlesticks and peals of laughter as the speeches got underway.

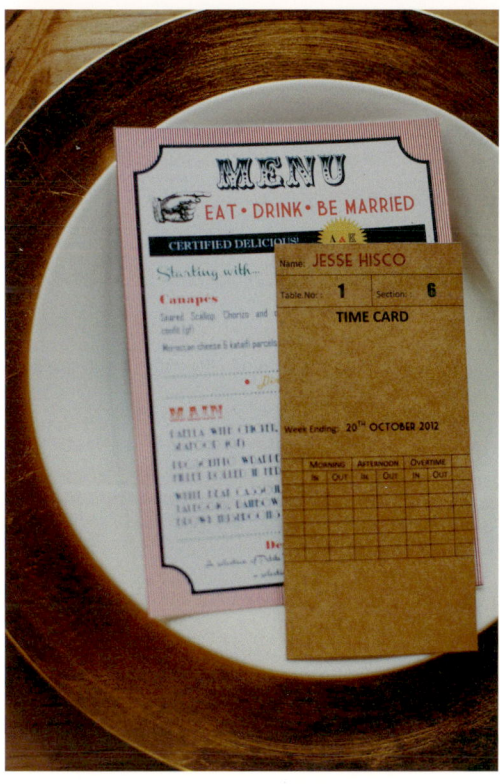

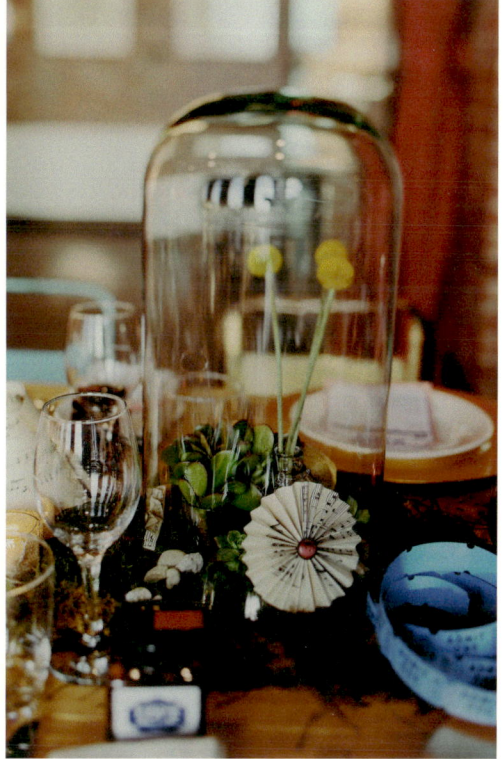

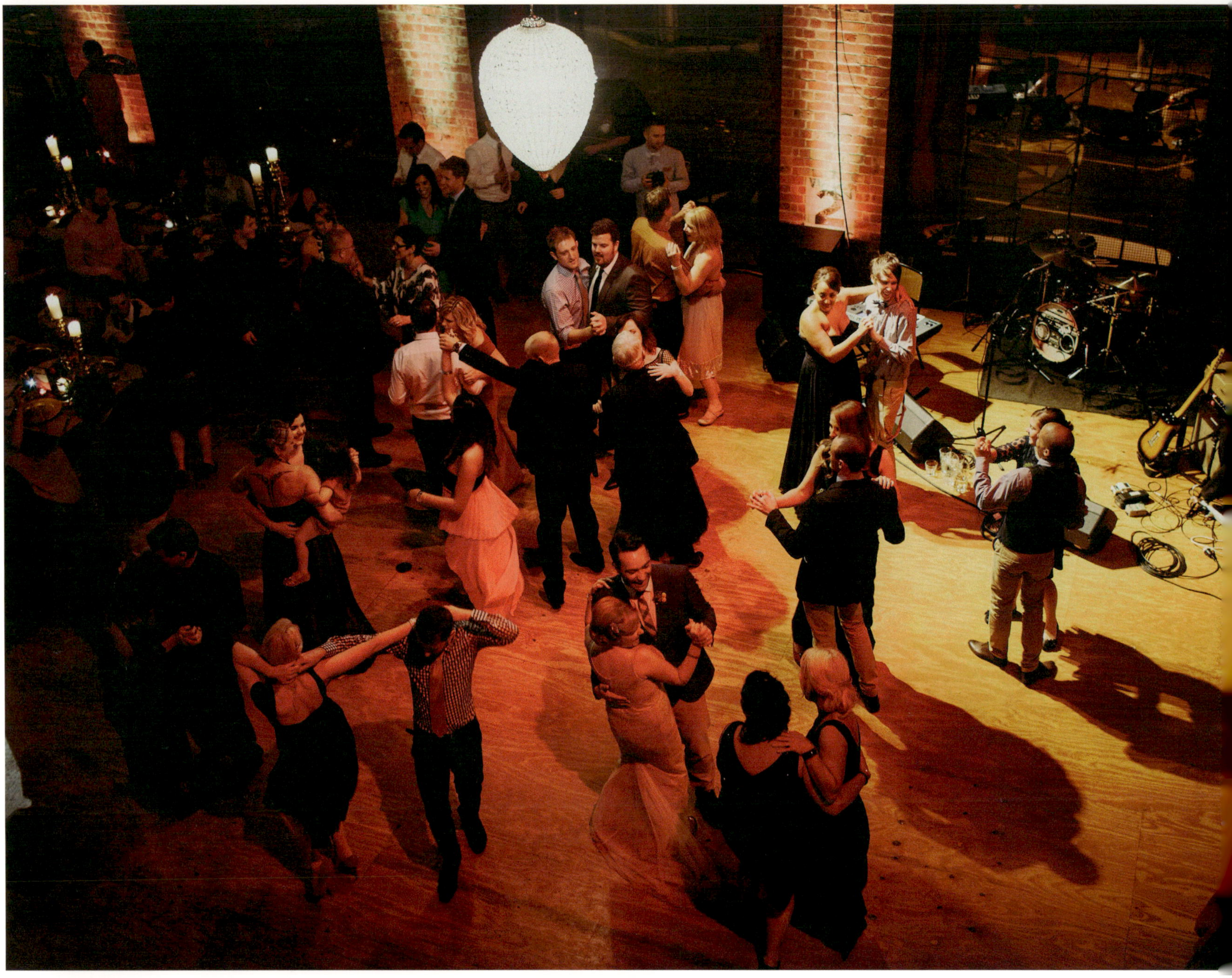

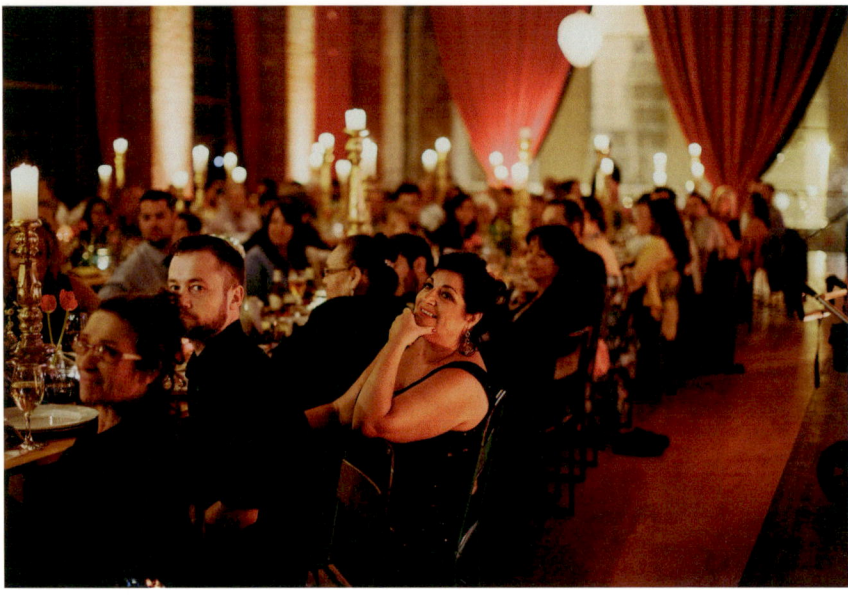

A soul and funk band, made up of close friends of the couple, played late into the night.

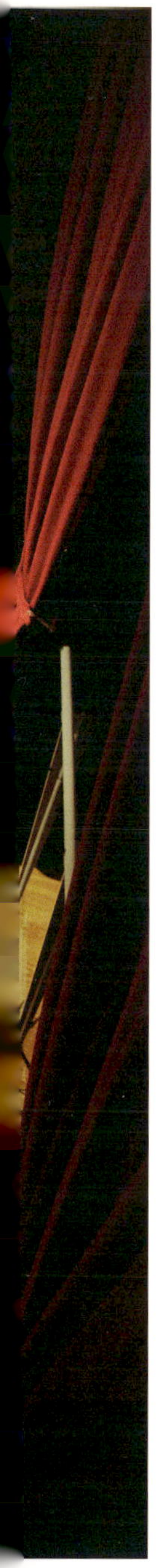

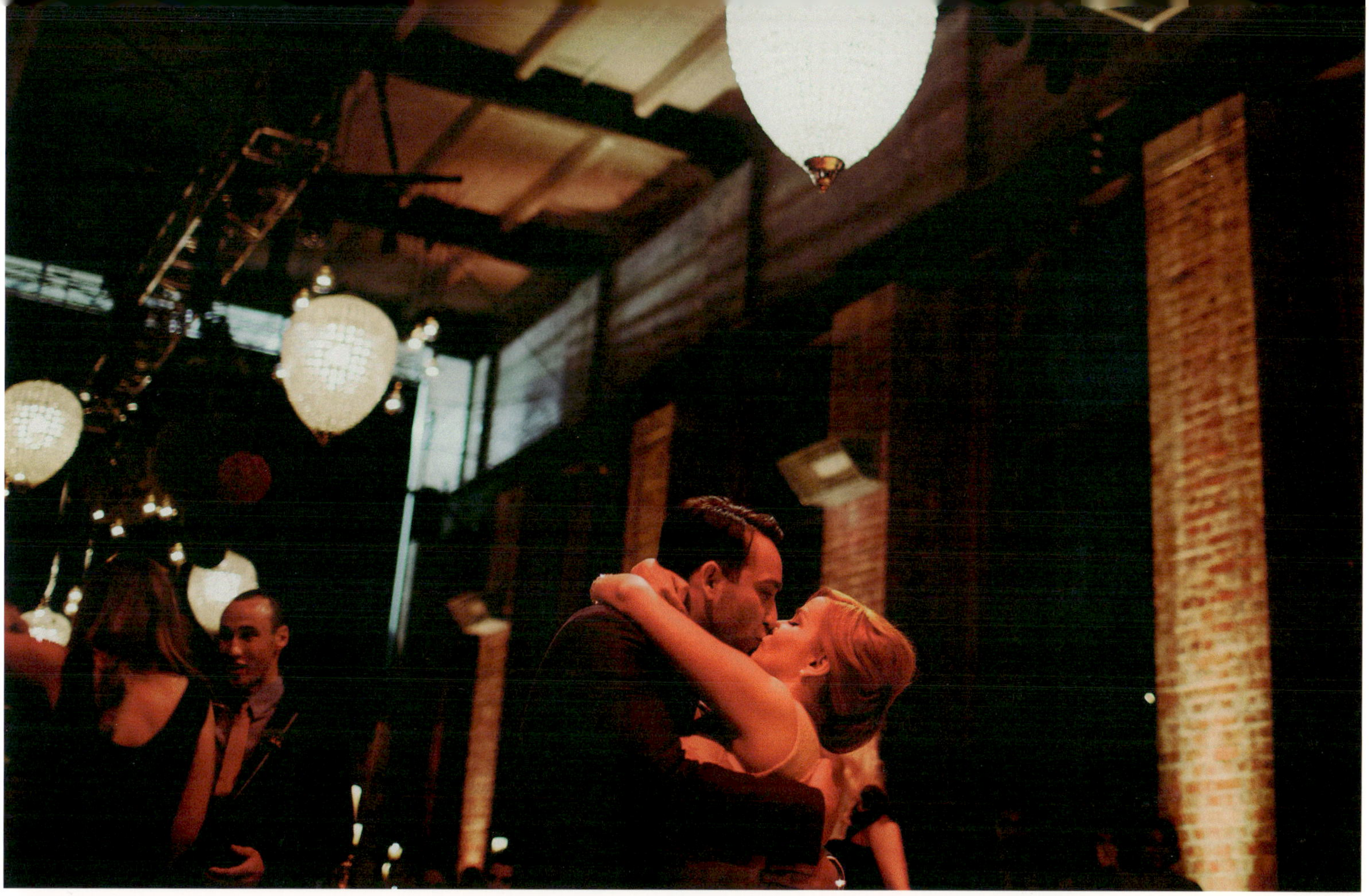

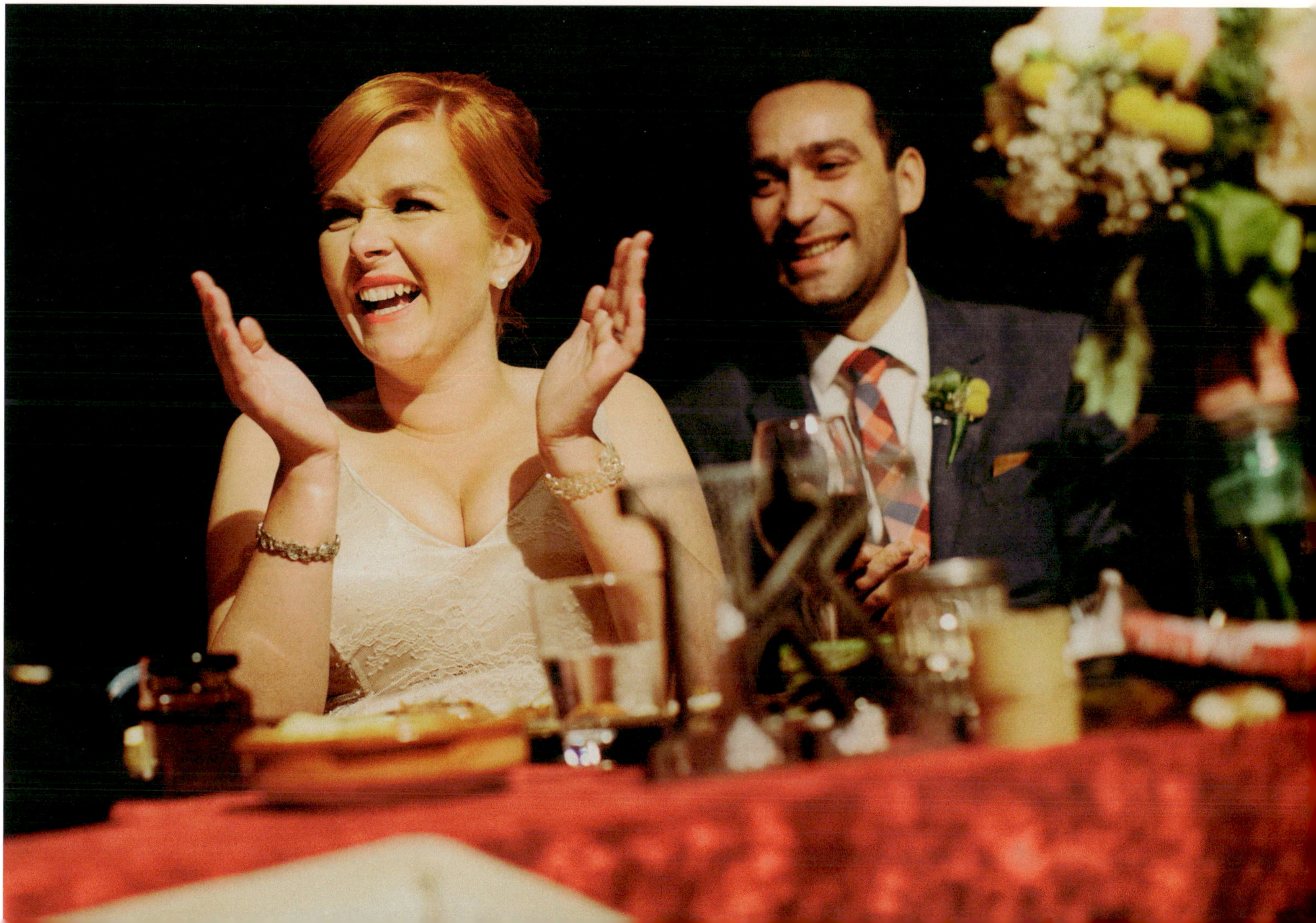

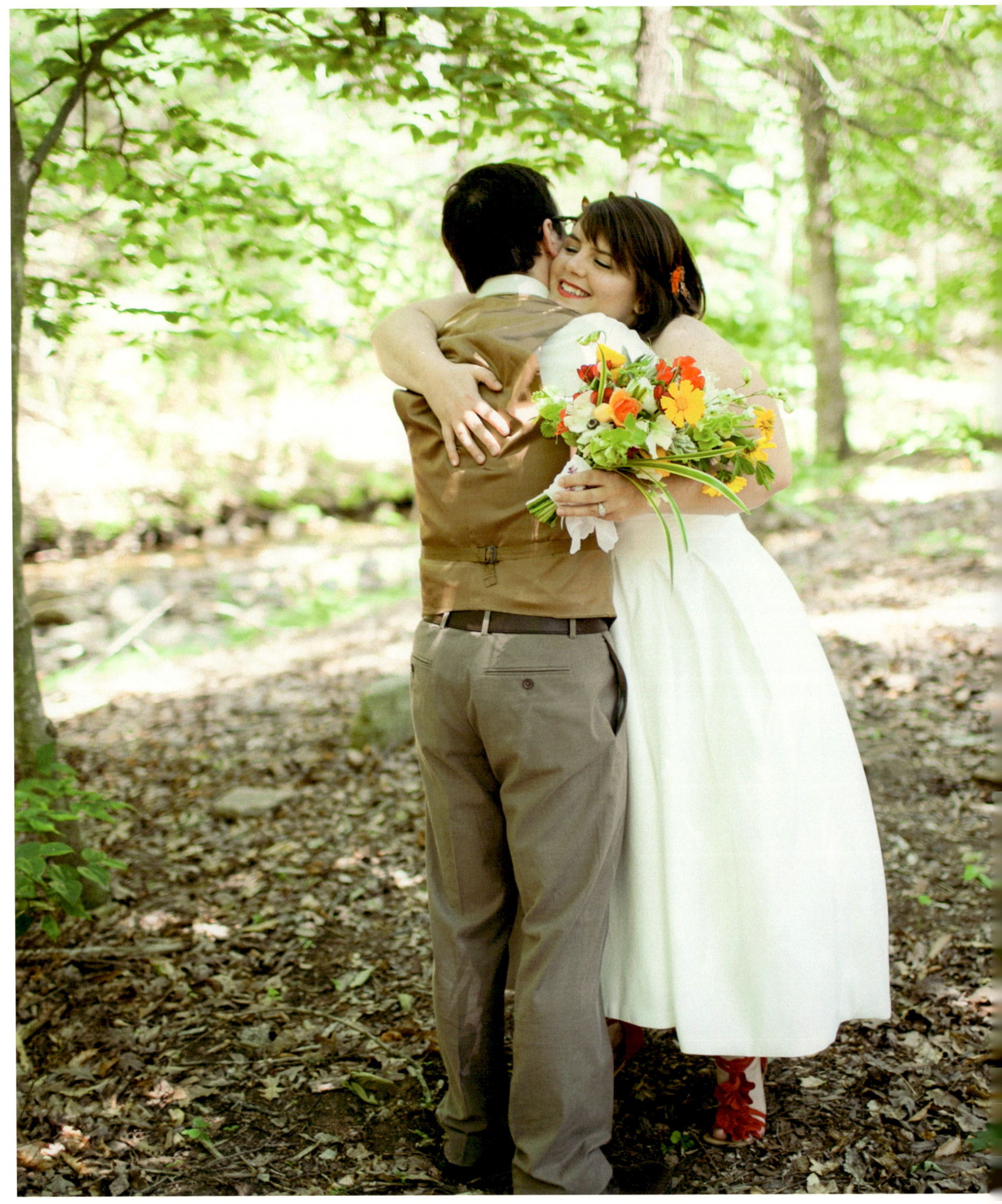

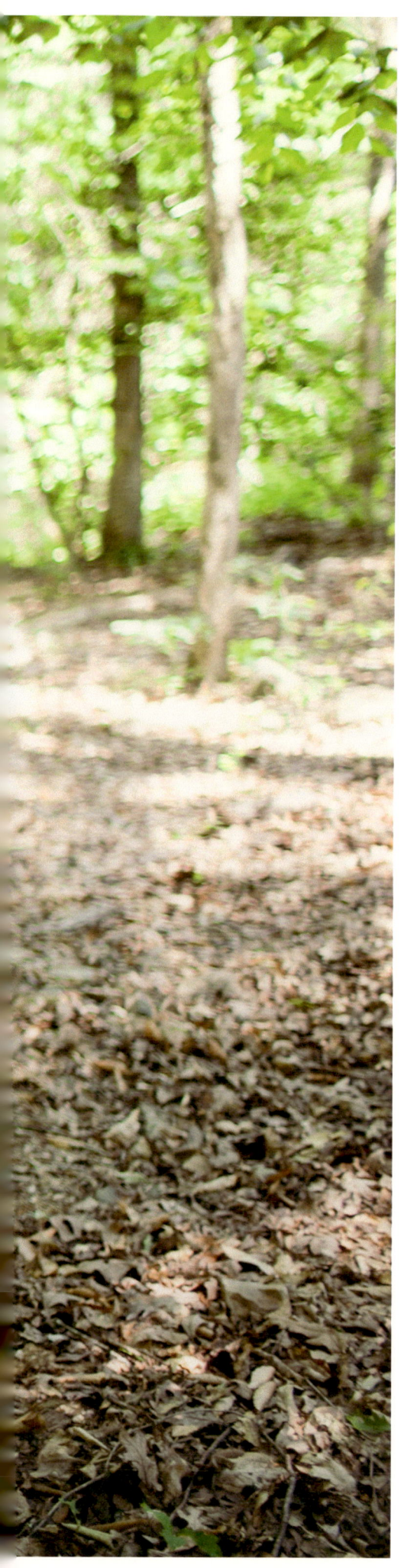

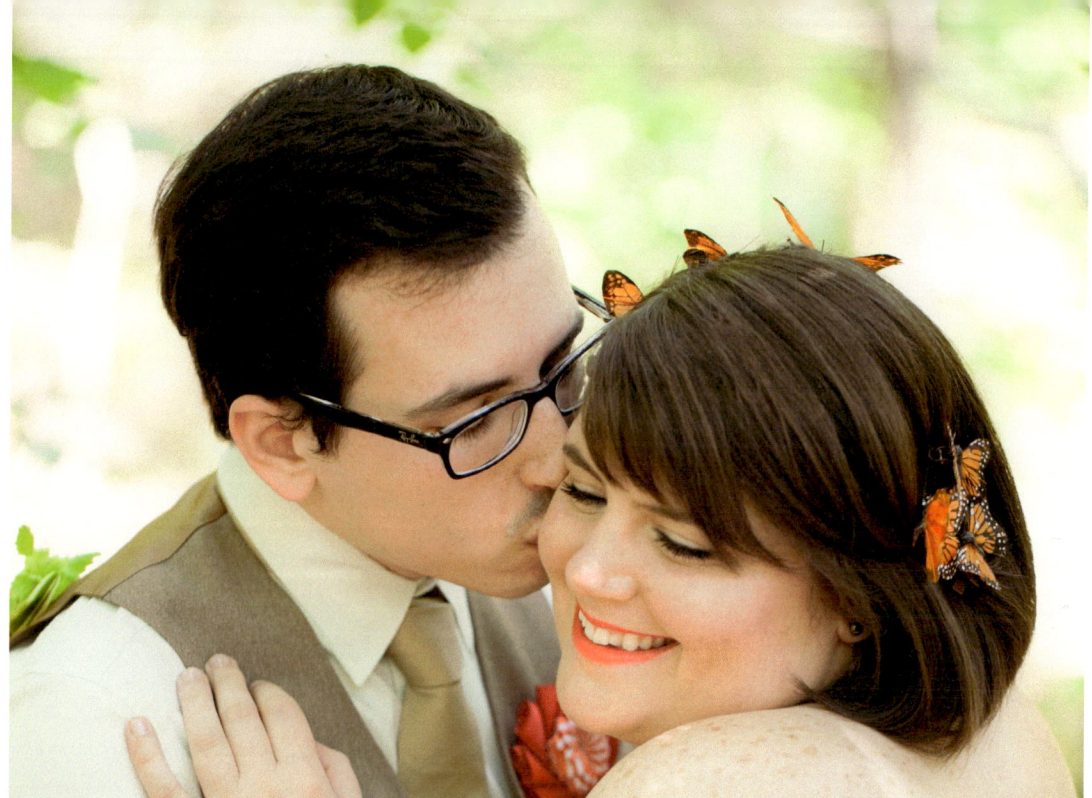

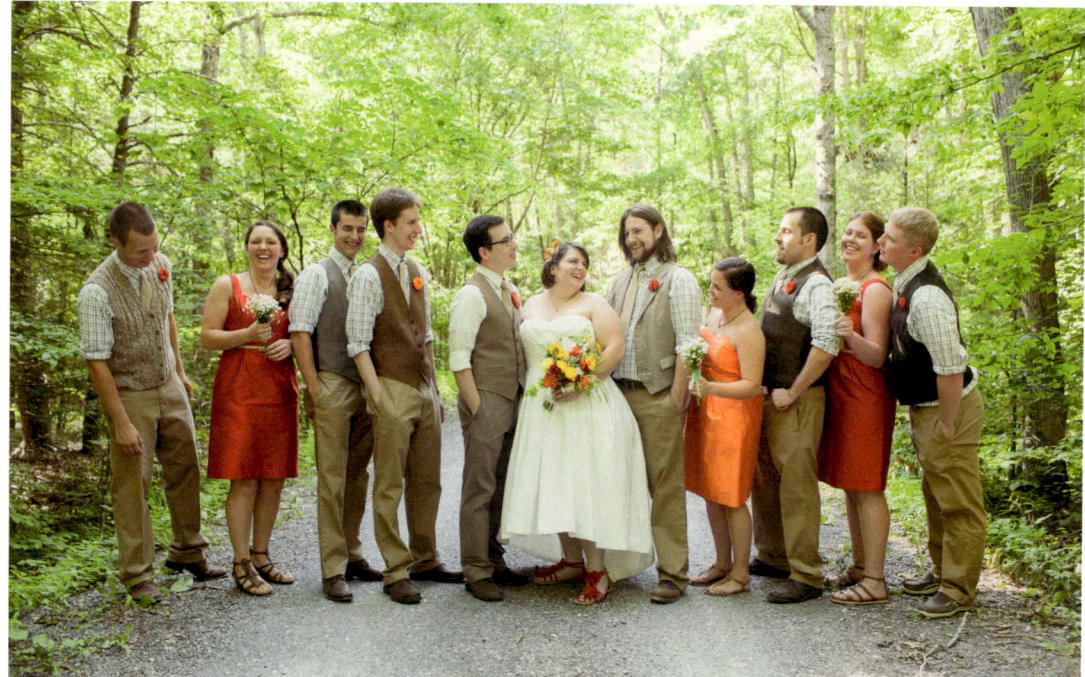

Trishia & Justin

If Mother Nature ever finds herself at a loose end, she could always do a sideline in wedding planning. Along with Trishia, Justin, and many of the guests, she helped create a woodland wedding that was a riot of greens, golds, browns, and yellows. The ivy crowning the outdoor stone chapel was all her work, but the huge flower heart and curtain were down to Trishia and her team.

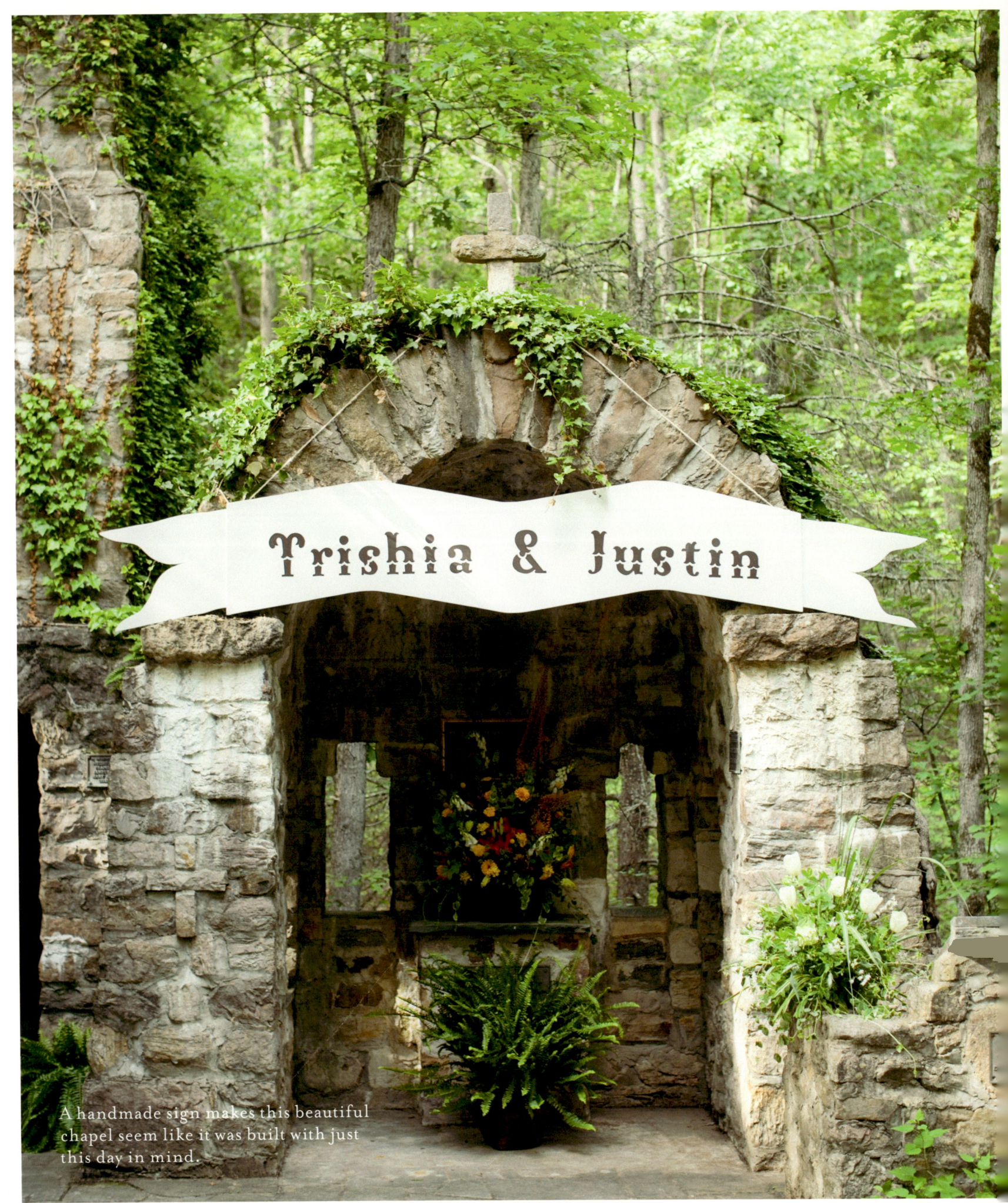

Trishia & Justin

A handmade sign makes this beautiful
chapel seem like it was built with just
this day in mind.

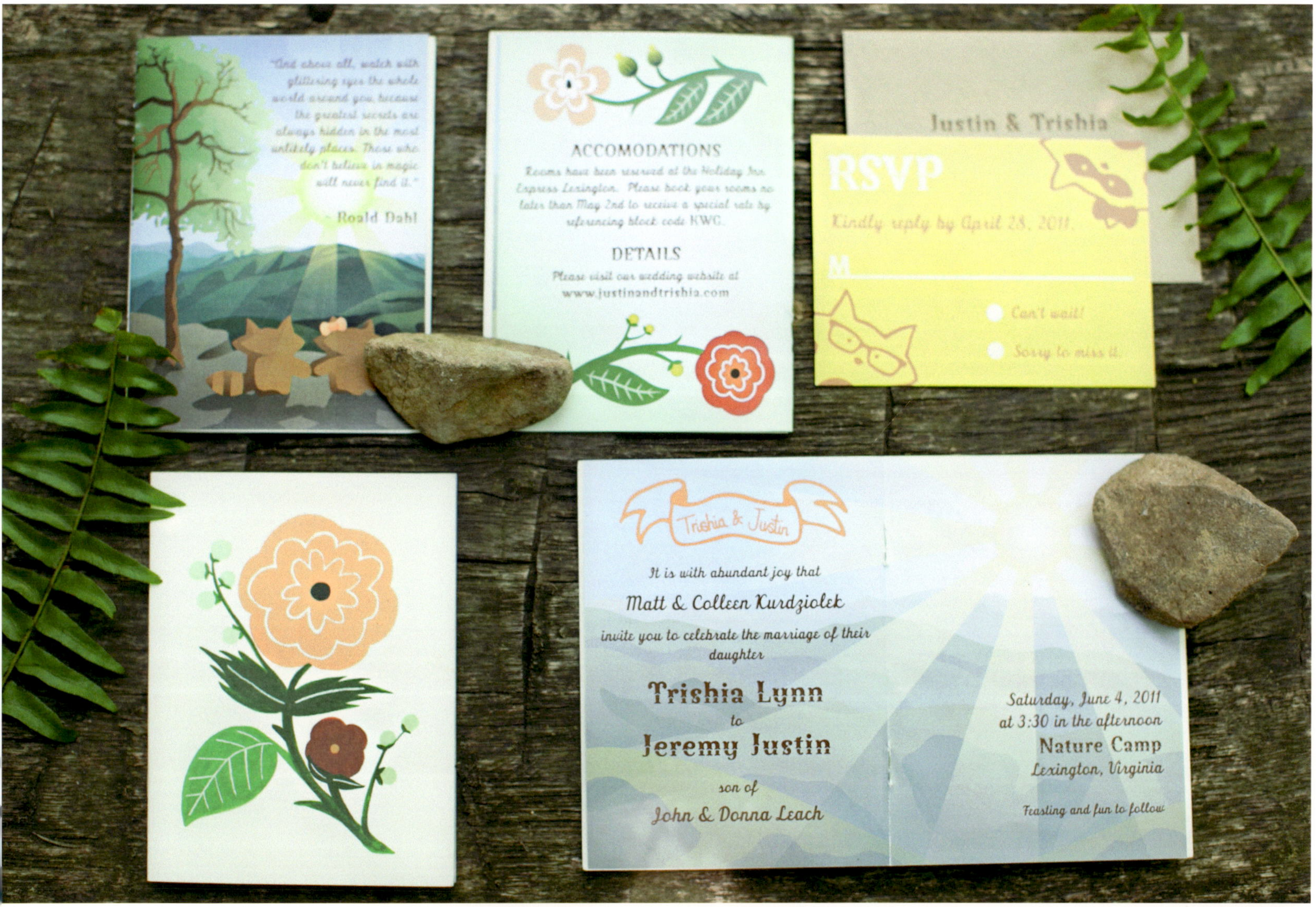

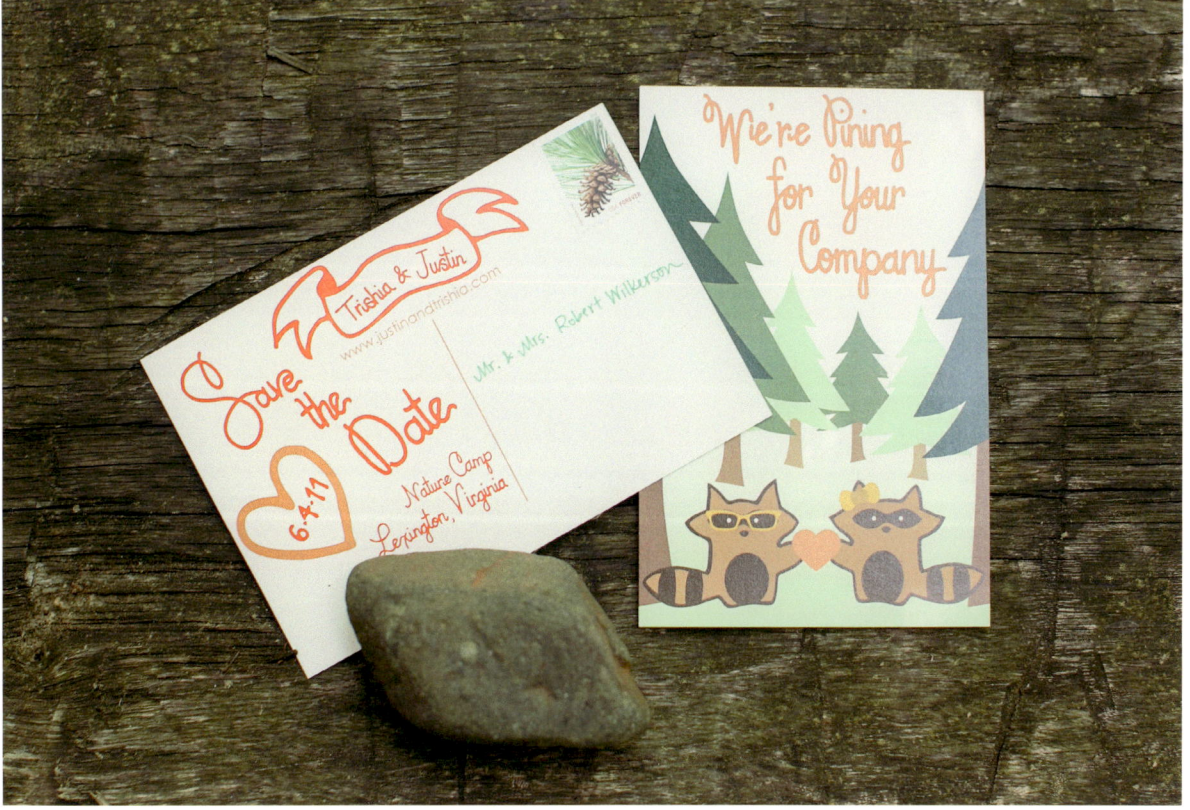

"And above all, watch with glittering eyes the whole world around you, because the greatest secrets are always hidden in the most unlikely places. Those who don't believe in magic will never find it."

Roald Dahl

ACCOMODATIONS

Rooms have been reserved at the Holiday Inn Express Lexington. Please book your rooms no later than May 2nd to receive a special rate by referencing block code KWC.

DETAILS

Please visit our wedding website at www.justinandtrishia.com

Justin & Trishia

RSVP

Kindly reply by April 28, 2011.

M _____

○ Can't wait!

○ Sorry to miss it.

Trishia & Justin

It is with abundant joy that

Matt & Colleen Kurdziolek

invite you to celebrate the marriage of their daughter

Trishia Lynn
to
Jeremy Justin

son of
John & Donna Leach

Saturday, June 4, 2011
at 3:30 in the afternoon
Nature Camp
Lexington, Virginia

Feasting and fun to follow

Lighthearted invites feature the smitten raccoons.

Trishia & Justin
www.justinandtrishia.com

Save the Date
6.4.11

Nature Camp
Lexington, Virginia

Mr. & Mrs. Robert Wilkerson

We're Pining for Your Company

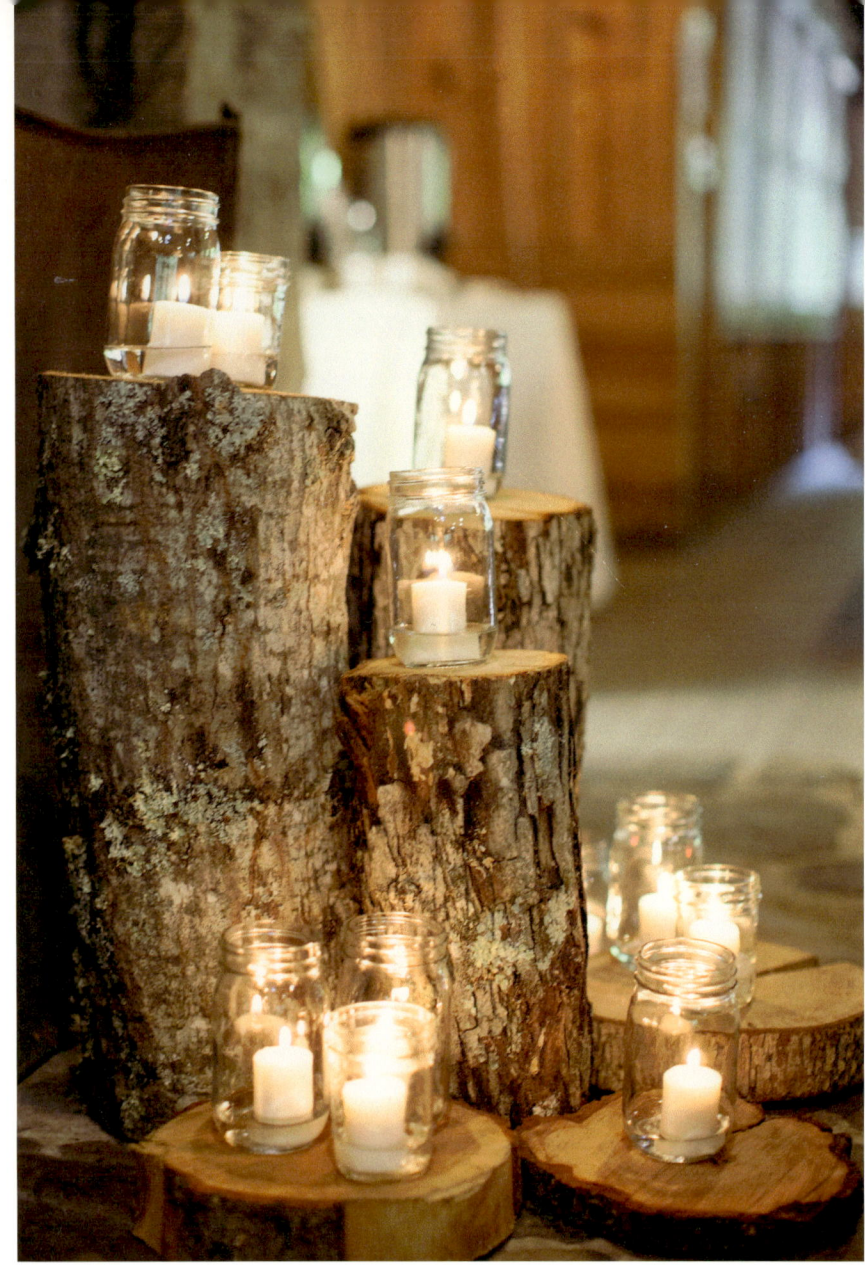

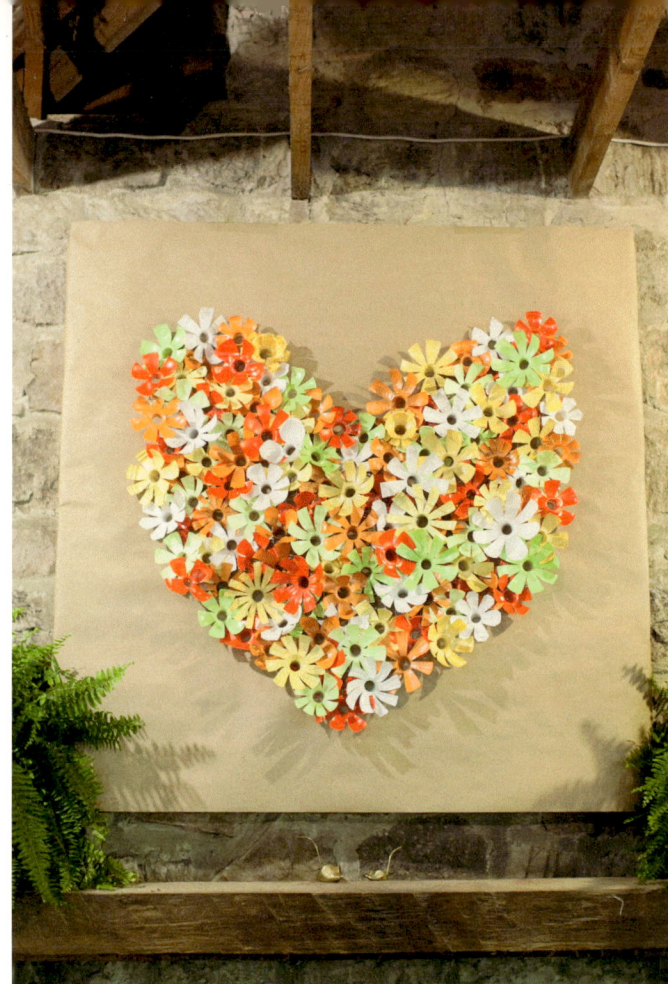

Decoration

1. A log-and-candle display like this is so easy to make. For Trishia and Justin, it brought the magic of a nighttime forest indoors to their reception.

2. These bold blossoms made of spray-painted soda bottles were the perfect partners to the bride's bouquet and brides-maids' dresses.

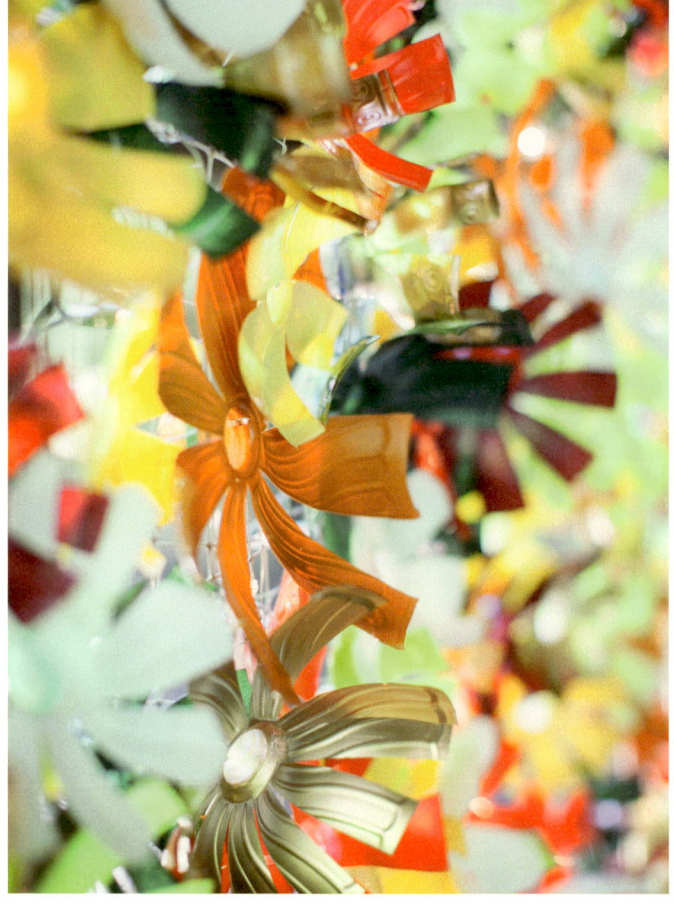

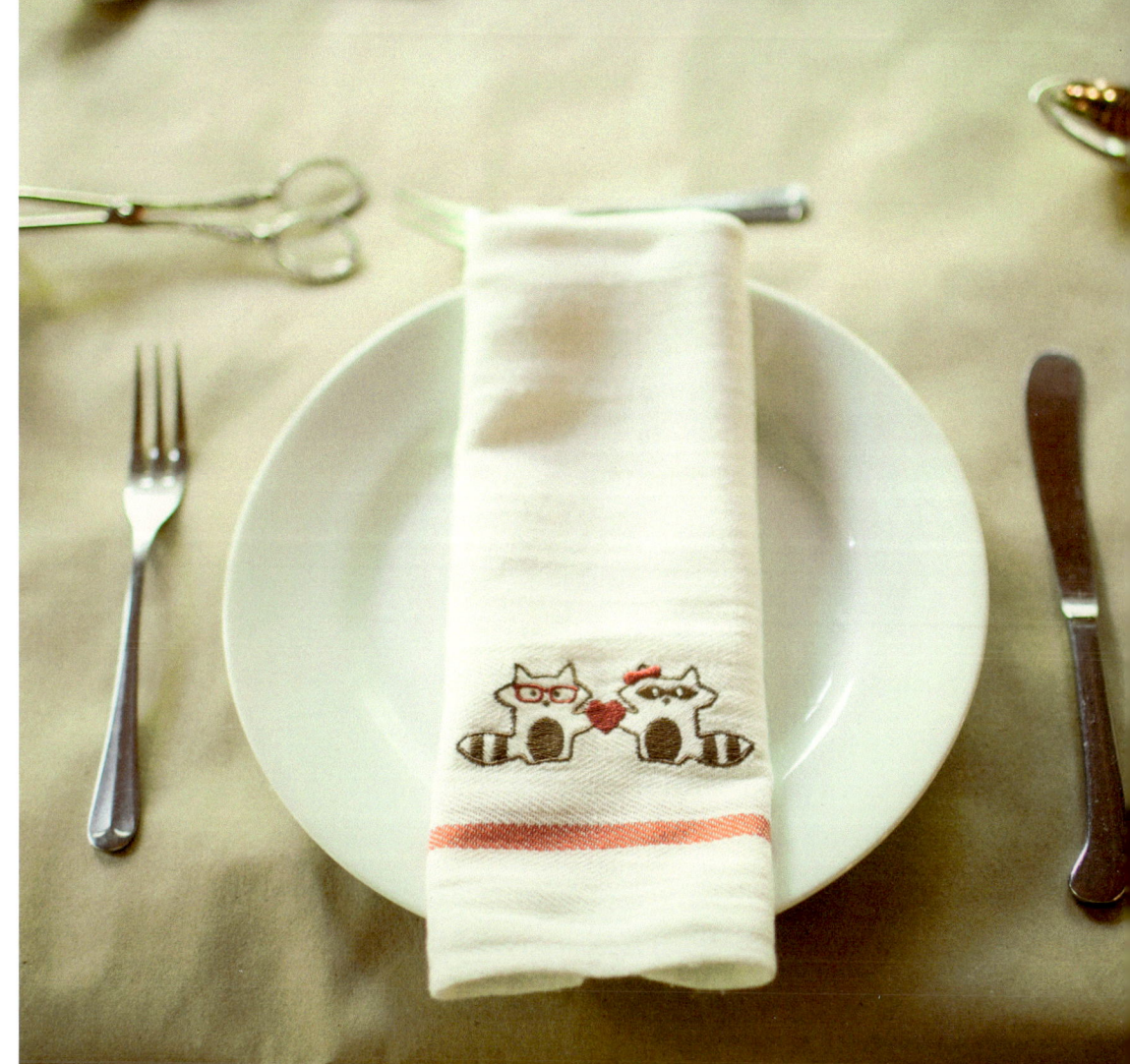

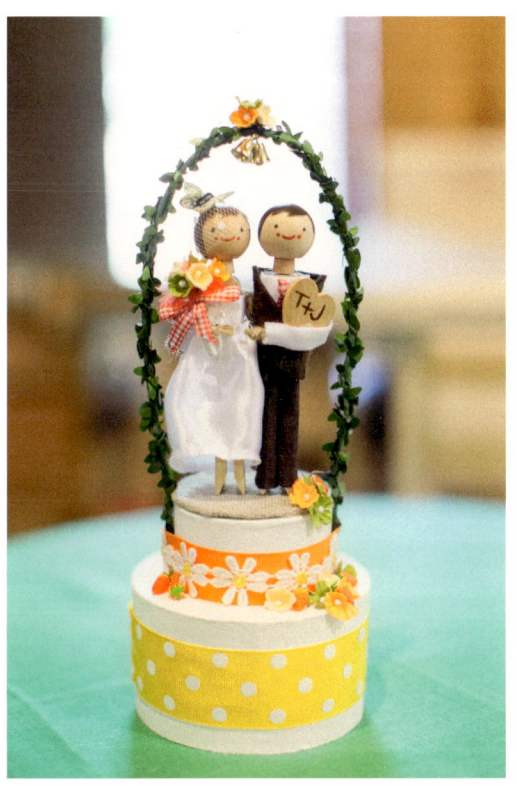

Time for Dinner

The raccoons kept popping up throughout the wedding—this time on the menus and embroidered napkins at dinner. As a locally sourced, seasonal feast, the food had the blessing of the forest dwellers that shared their habitat with Trishia and Justin for this happy day.

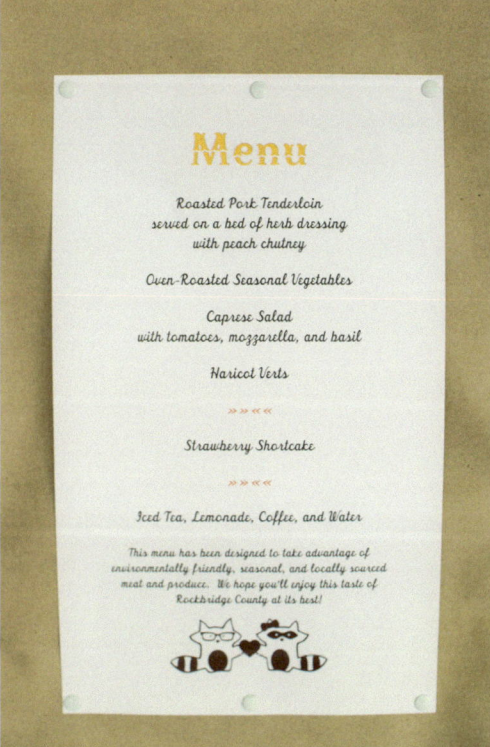

Menu

Roasted Pork Tenderloin
served on a bed of herb dressing
with peach chutney

Oven-Roasted Seasonal Vegetables

Caprese Salad
with tomatoes, mozzarella, and basil

Haricot Verts

≫ ≫ ≪ ≪

Strawberry Shortcake

≫ ≫ ≪ ≪

Iced Tea, Lemonade, Coffee, and Water

This menu has been designed to take advantage of
environmentally friendly, seasonal, and locally sourced
meat and produce. We hope you'll enjoy this taste of
Rockbridge County at its best!

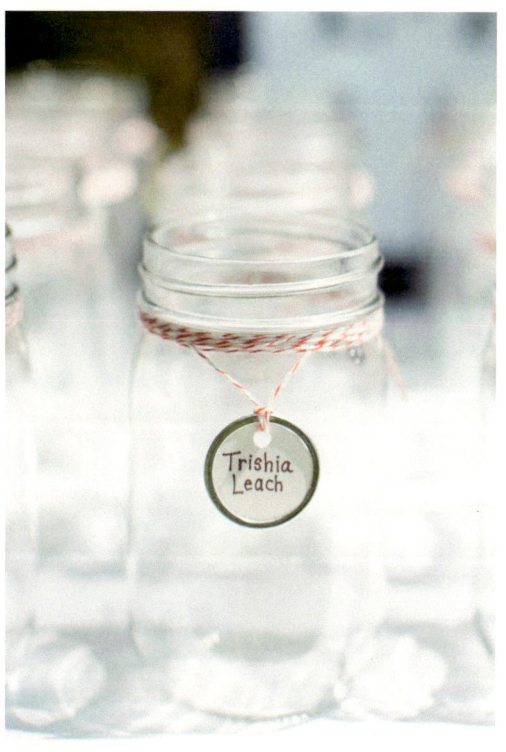

The Decadence is in the Decoration

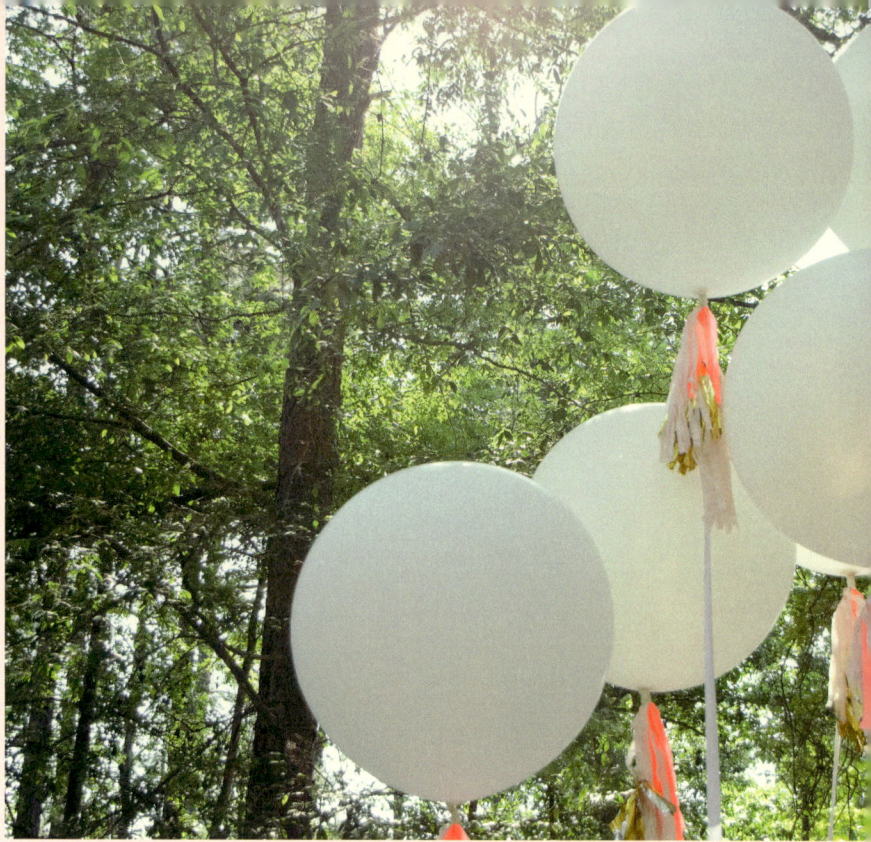

Deciding on the décor is one of the most exciting parts of wedding design. It is living art that, beyond making your wedding a pretty party, infuses personality and enhances the overall visual experience.

When creating your wedding, take inspiration from what you are passionate about or what you hold close to your heart and incorporate it into your design. It doesn't have to be in an obvious way; the gentler touches work the best. You can find many lovely examples of meaningful design details in this book.

Your wedding day should celebrate your past, present and future together, so try and express this in your décor.

Think about where have you come from? What defines you at the moment? And how will you move forward together?

Don't be afraid to be playful. Of course getting married is a serious, life-changing experience, but there will always be room for a few laughs.

A cheeky wink or a hint towards a long-running joke or a shared memory will not only add personality to your wedding, but also make great conversation starters.

It's always good to include your guests in the fun, too. The more you get them involved, the more they will connect with the event and enjoy sharing this special occasion with you. Do something personal for them like making custom friendship bracelets and using them as napkin rings, or printing off name labels and sticking them onto mason jars for personalized drinks. Little details that engage your

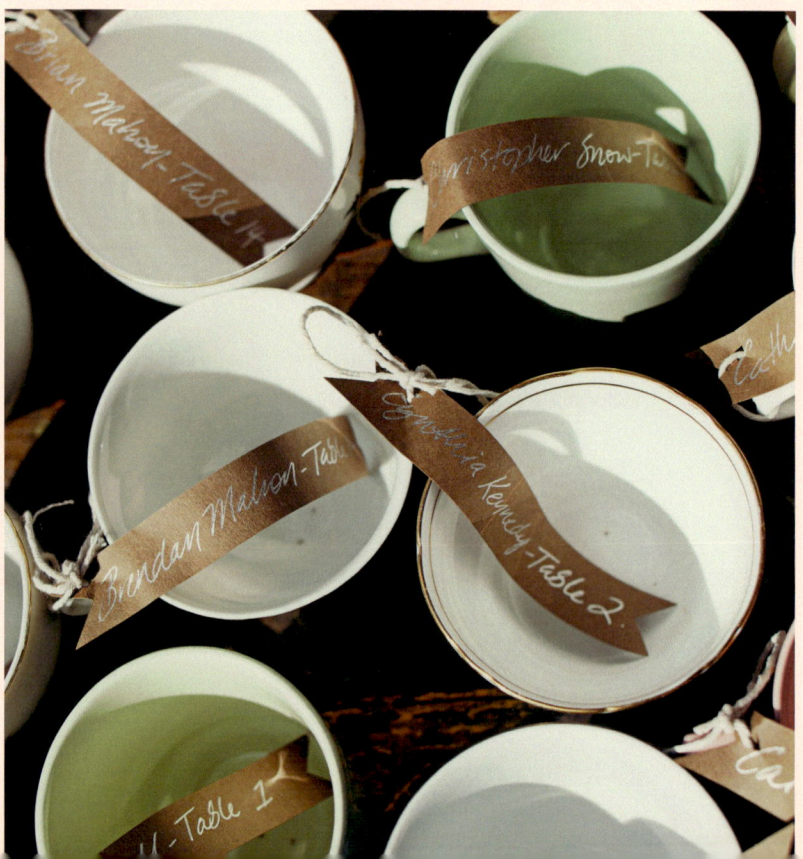

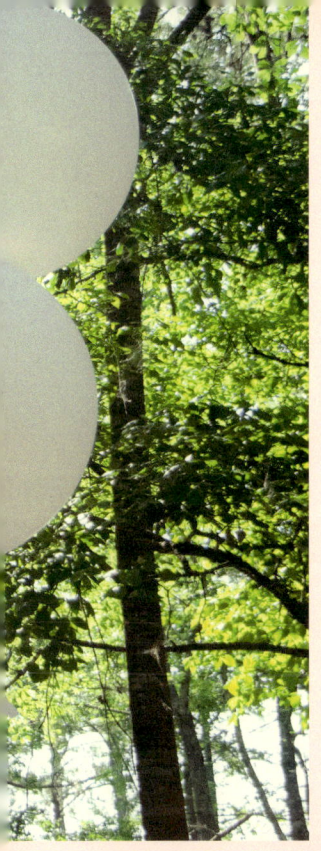

guests don't have to be expensive, but will always go down well.

The lovely thing about decorating an event is that you can create something spectacular for next to nothing if you have to. There are a number of ways to keep costs down without scrimping on style.

Firstly, flowers. Don't get me wrong; I am the first one to admit I'm a floral fanatic. But as beautiful as blooms may be they are quite the budget buster.

Whether you are keeping an eye on your spending or not, sometimes it's all about keeping it simple. Bulbs in apothecary jars bought

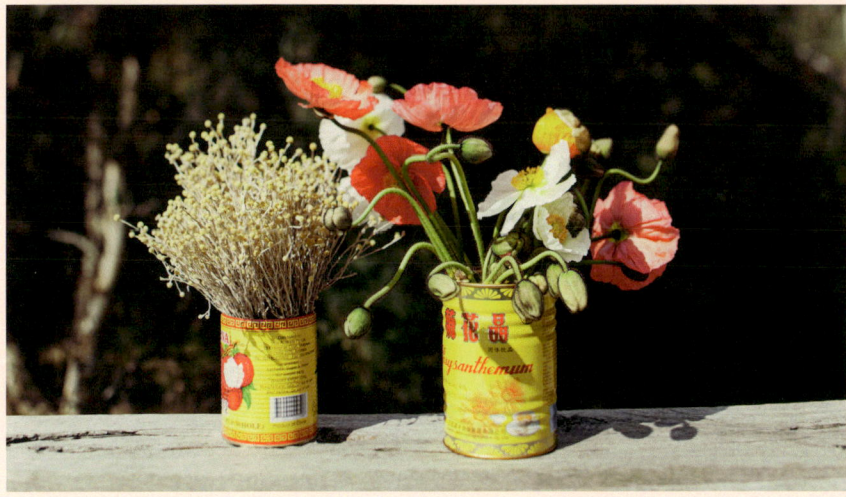

from a junk shop, or vintage eggcups with a single bud are more chic than statement arrangements. Who says you even have to use any flowers at all? In the past I've used towers of macaroons and medicine jars filled with sweets as table decorations. I love the Victorian idea of using jellies as centerpieces. Not just because they look incredible, but because they can be eaten as a dessert—or thrown!

Another trick would be to use what is available to you—including friends and family. If your grandmother makes amazing fudge, wrap some up and use as wedding favors; if you have a friend who is a graphic designer, ask for some help on your invitations. Generally you will find people are honored to even be asked

Ideas that make a beautiful yet surprising wedding:

1. Inspired food choices—rather than the traditional fare do something different such as truffle popcorn, a martini trolley, or a retro sweets bar.

2. Personal placements—try Scrabble letters to spell out names, friendship bracelets, or a personalized trinket that has meaning for your guest.

3. Interpret the traditional—instead of real flowers try paper ones. Lots of them!

4. Volume—decorations used en masse is something I stand by every time.

5. Great music choices—personal performances, themed bands, great singers or dance acts.

Things to provide guests with on their way home:

1. Flip-flops

2. Aspirin

3. Bottle of water

4. Piece of wedding cake

5. Photograph from the booth

6. Flowers—they take a bit of effort, but wedding flowers can be dismantled into individual bouquets for your guests.

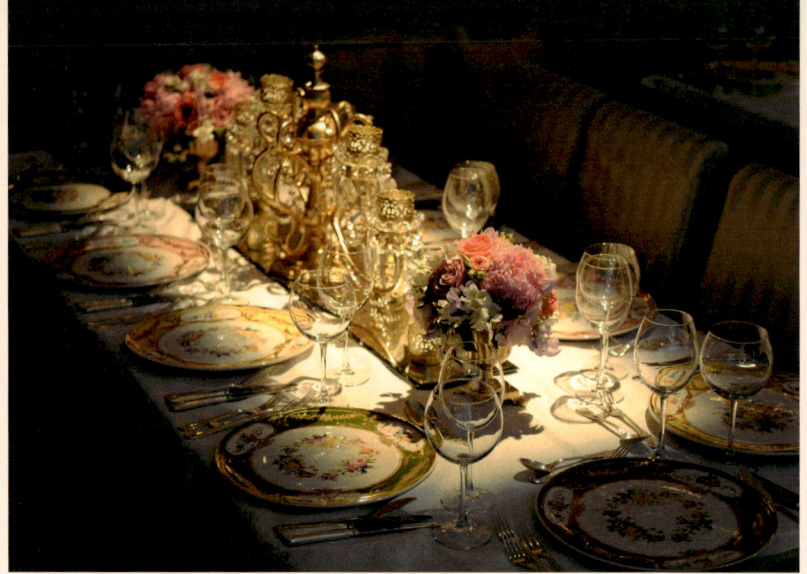

and love to get involved with such an important occasion in your life. Even if it's just making the most of the extra hands, it not only helps you get things done: it also makes those close to you feel part of the wedding and builds up extra excitement leading up to the day. In a clever design, it's not what you use; it's how you use it. Elevate the mundane to something exciting and wonderful. Use compact mirrors as place settings with guests' names scrawled on in scarlet lipstick or make a seating plan out of lottery tickets. I love to take everyday items and turn them into pieces of art.

Use objects out of context for a stylish contrast, whether it's building a bar out of books or hanging piñatas from the ceiling.

A visual juxtaposition can create a unique dynamic and add an element of surprise to your wedding that will keep energy levels high and guests entertained.

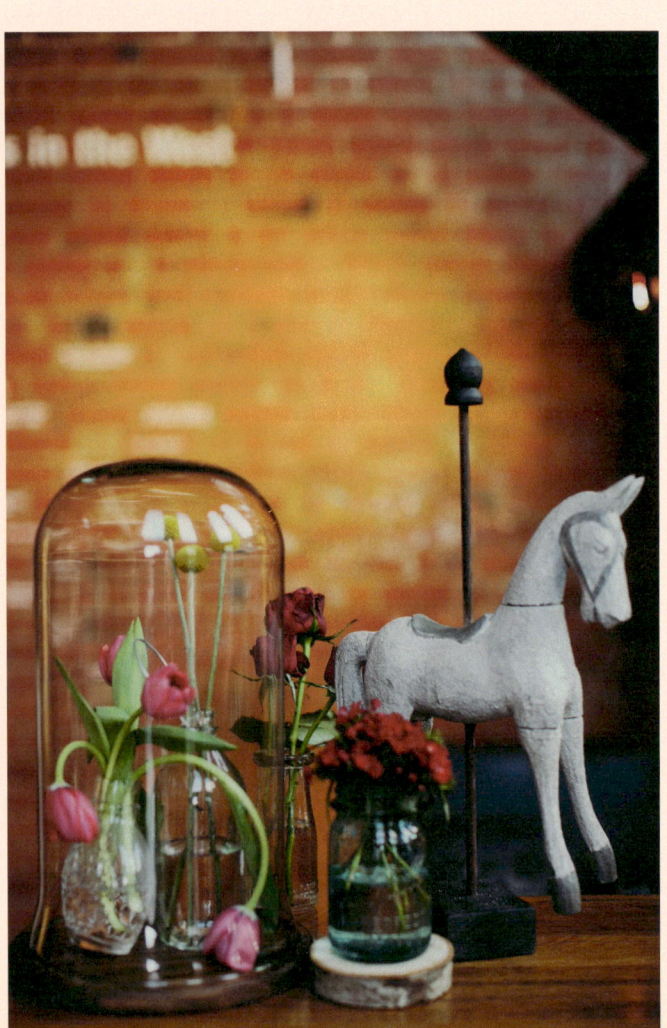

When sourcing design props, my first ports of call would be Ebay, junk shops and antiques fairs. It's amazing what unique treasures you can find there! I'd definitely say to start searching early. Make sure to give yourself enough time because it can take a while to find exactly what you are looking for. Don't get disheartened; the extra effort will definitely be worth it in the end. When you look back on the journey to track down your decorations it will only add an additional value and meaning to them. As you'll see, part of what made Emily and Louis's day so charming was the garage sale bounty that decorated their outback wedding. As passionate thrift store scourers, each item, from the champagne saucers to the tableware, had been carefully collected over a period of months. At this couple's wedding, a plate wasn't simply a plate: it was a labor of love. No matter how ordinary an object might be, you can add significance and create impact by using multiples. A lone tea-light is just a tea-light but a thousand tea-lights is a stunning, dramatic visual effect.

Personally, I'm a maximalist — for me abundance is key.

I like to create volume with things in large groups, whether it's balloons, flowers, vases, or whatever else you fancy. In the past I have used walls of balloons and ceilings of paper flowers.

When it comes to choosing your dress (and shoes) it's really important that you are comfortable and you choose something that suits your body shape. Don't get too caught up in trying to theme your dress to the decorations. You might long for 20s-style Gatsby glamour, but a flapper dress just isn't your thing. Most importantly, if you're wearing the dress all day and night, you have to be comfortable.

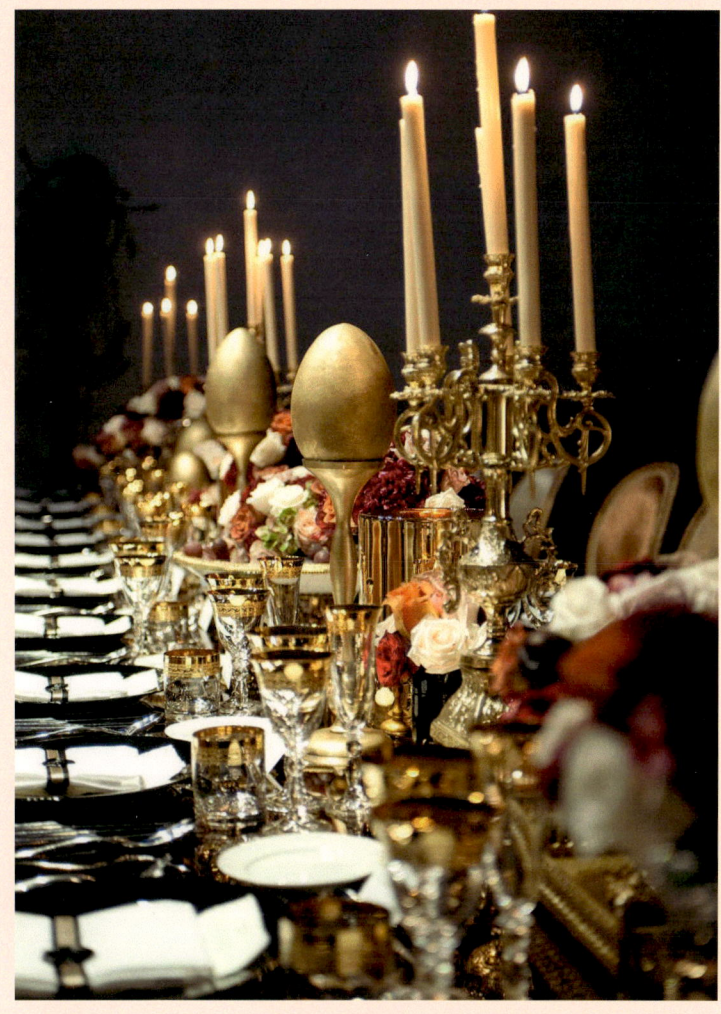

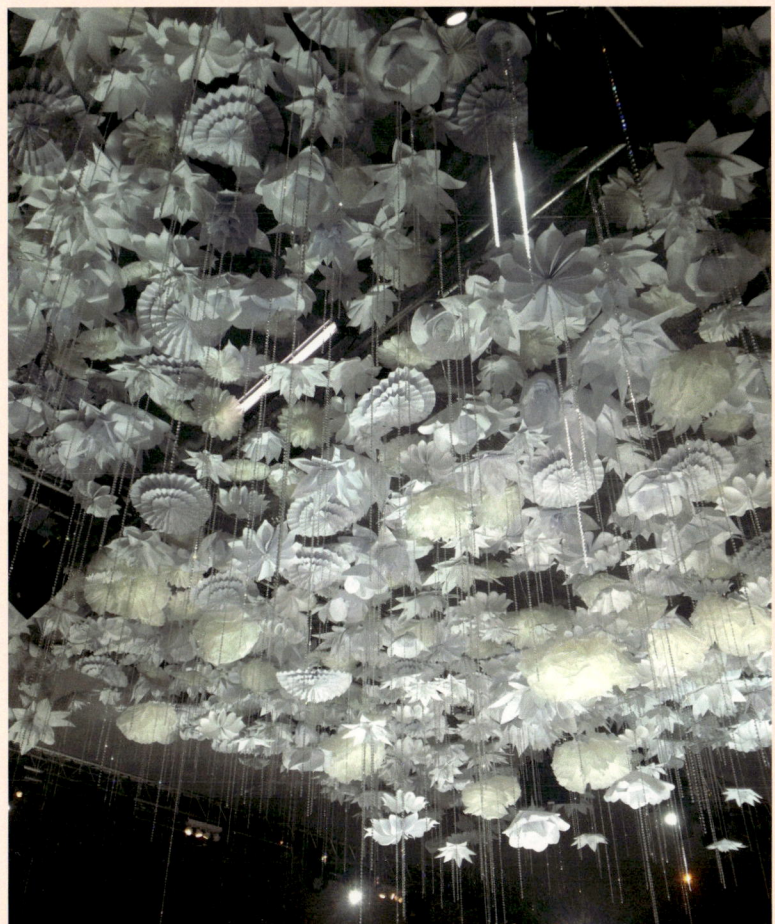

It's the worst thing in the world not to have comfortable shoes. This is the difference between dancing until dawn or smiling through gritted teeth when saying farewell to your guests. Think about terrain and where you're getting married. Grass and stilettos don't work. A friend of mine said to me the other day that there is no such thing as bad weather; it's just being badly attired. When thinking of what you're wearing, also consider your guests and alert them to any "terrain issues" they might encounter, like a sandy beach or a grassy hill.

All that said if you do love the 50s and look great in a 50s wedding dress you might carry that era all the way through. You could have a pastel color theme and a Buddy Holly and the Crickets-type band. This can evolve into themed food such as a retro sweets bar and could inspire an American classic car that gets you to the church on time.

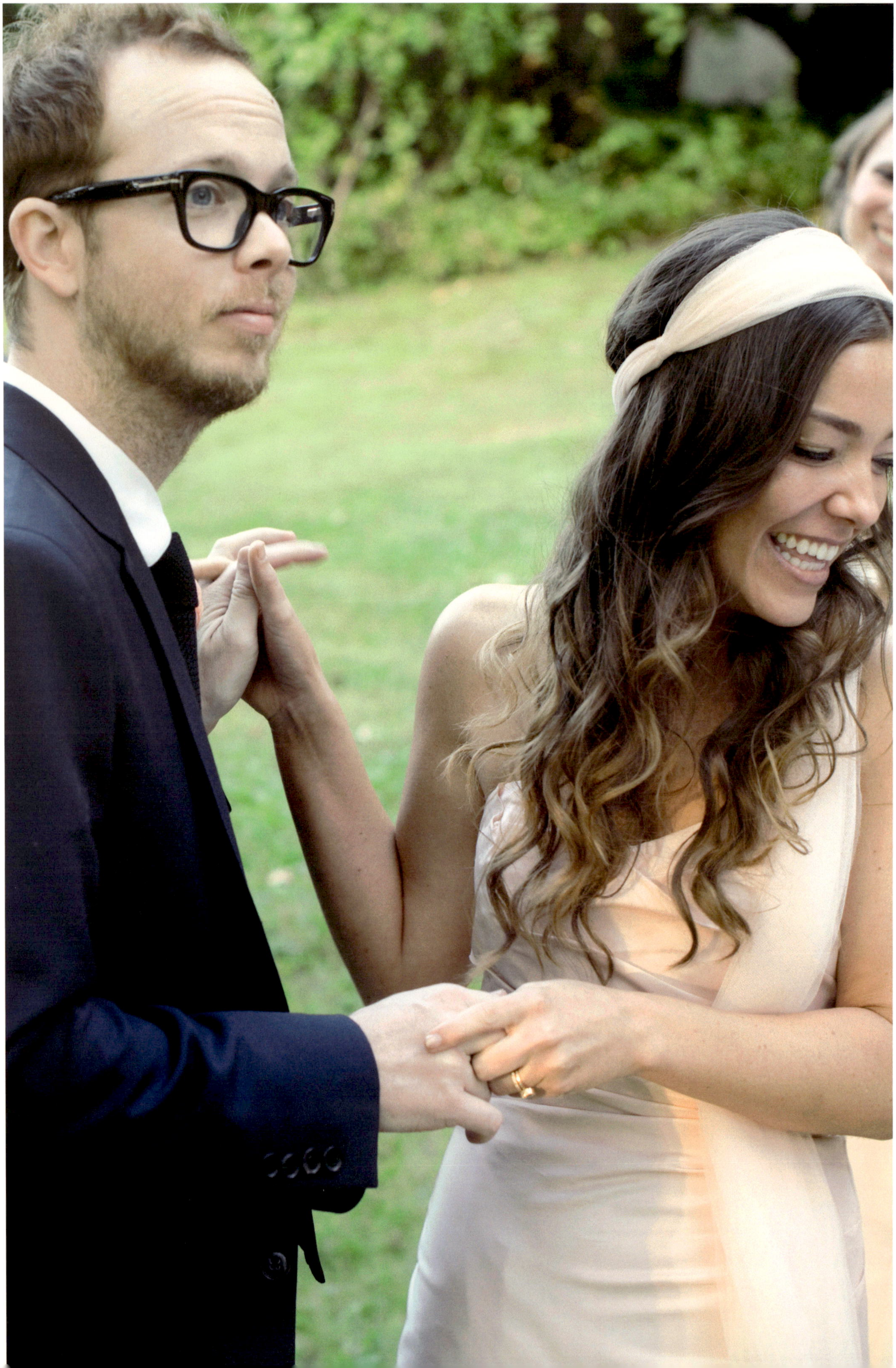

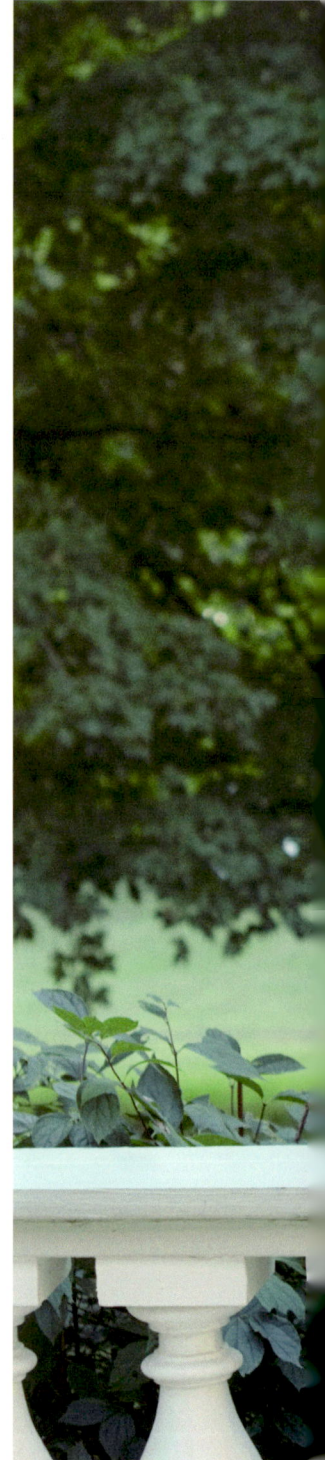

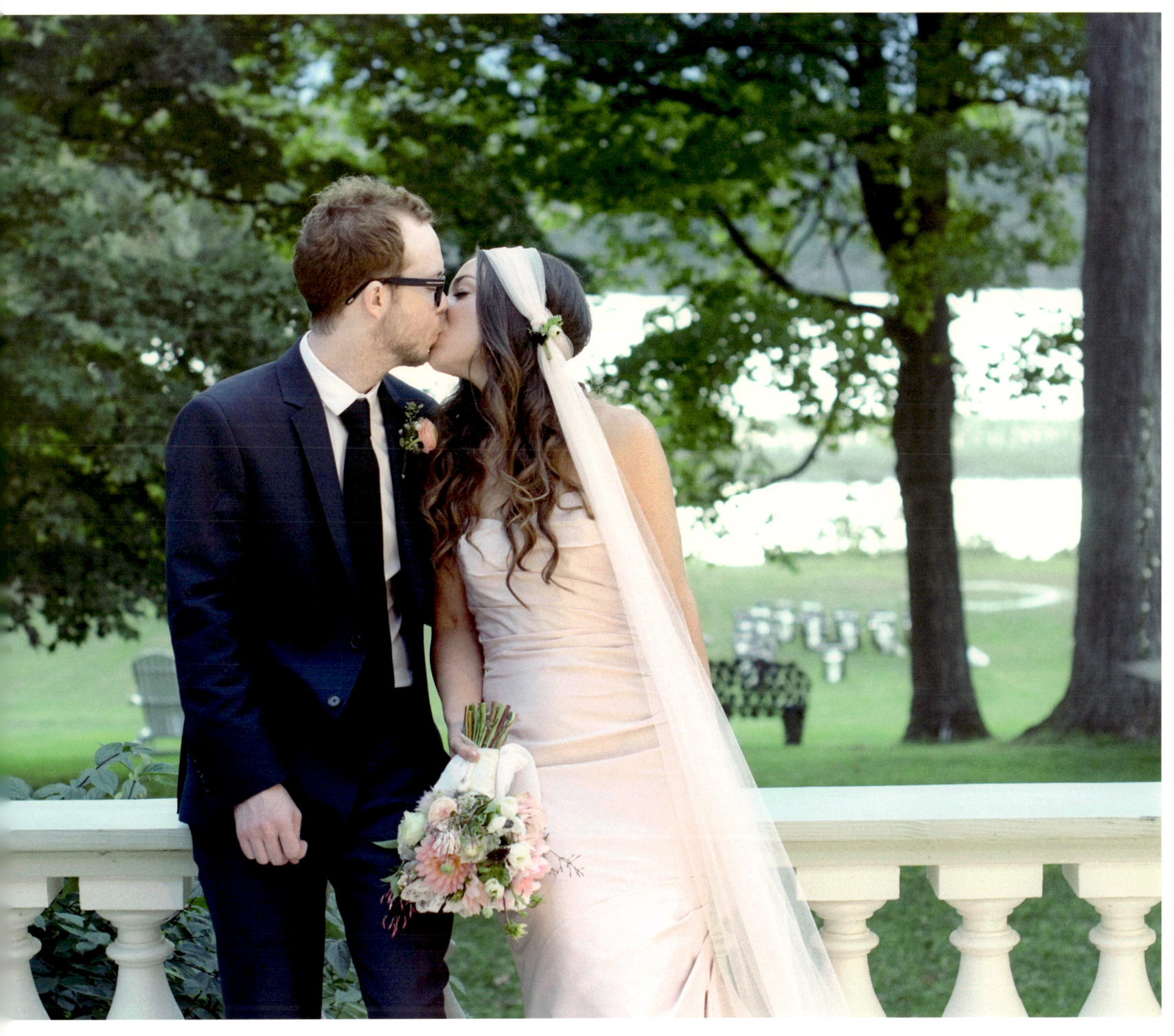

Julie & Bo

Julie and Bo wanted a fun, relaxed, and just plain lovely day. They had a woodland photobooth, served a champagne surprise, and played croquet on the lawn. The ceremony overlooked the Hudson River, and guests sat on seats tied with wide ribbons and tiny flowers. Yet for all its bohemian style — the loose curls, the floor-length dresses — the day brings to mind a play written long before the word "bohemian" even existed. When night fell and fairy lights pierced the darkness, it was as if fireflies had come out to create one more beautiful memory for this midsummer night's dream of a wedding.

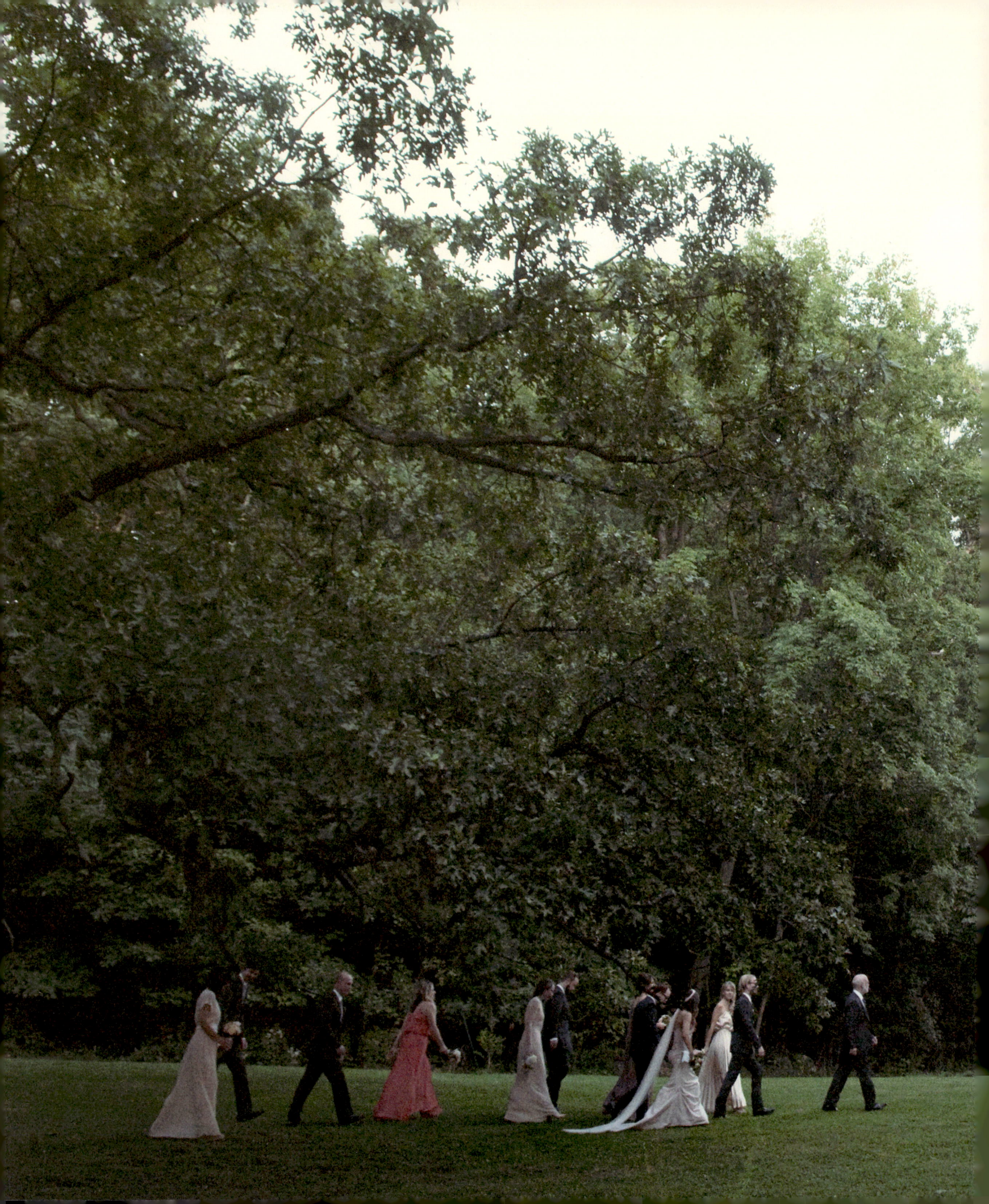

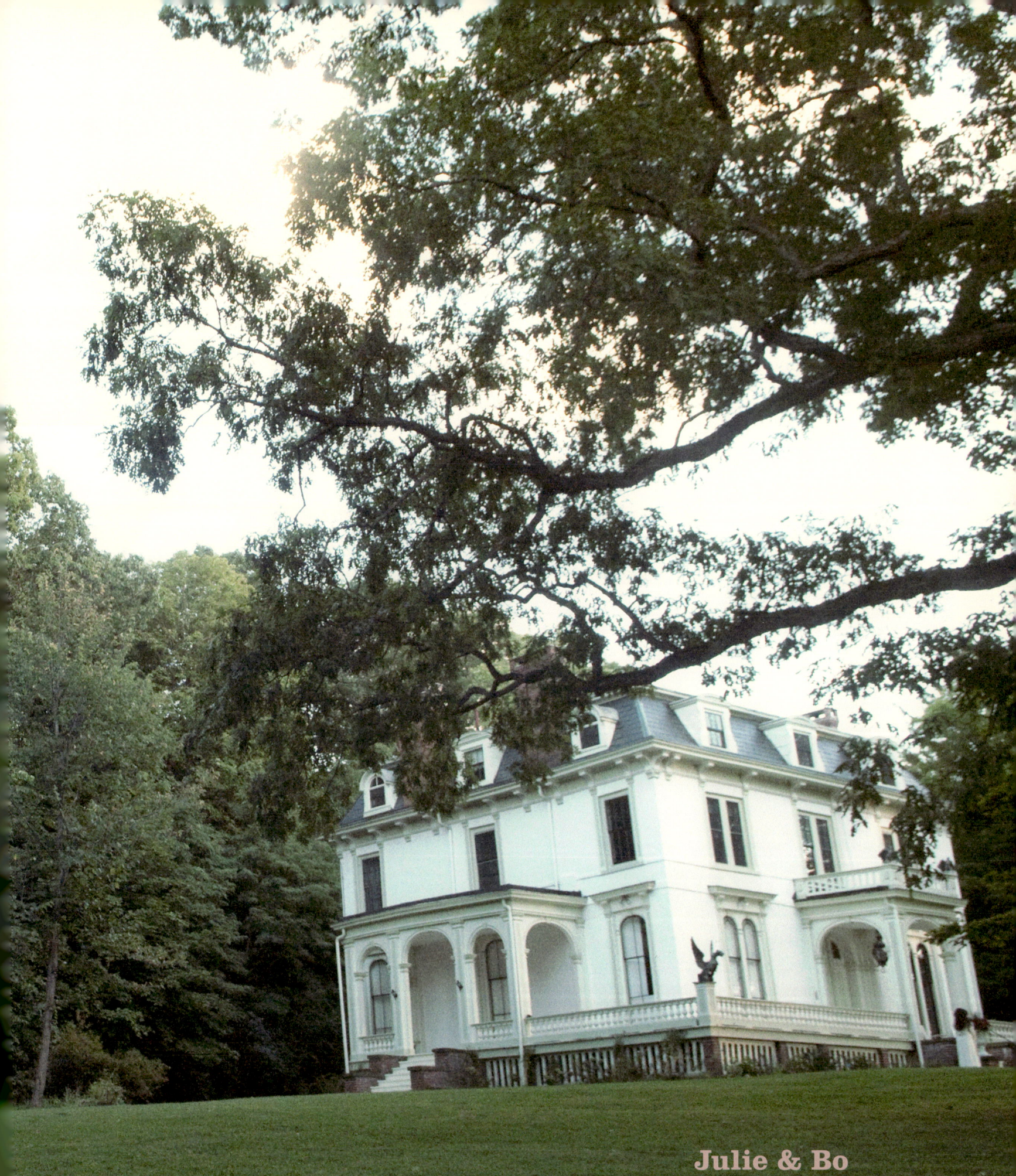

Julie & Bo

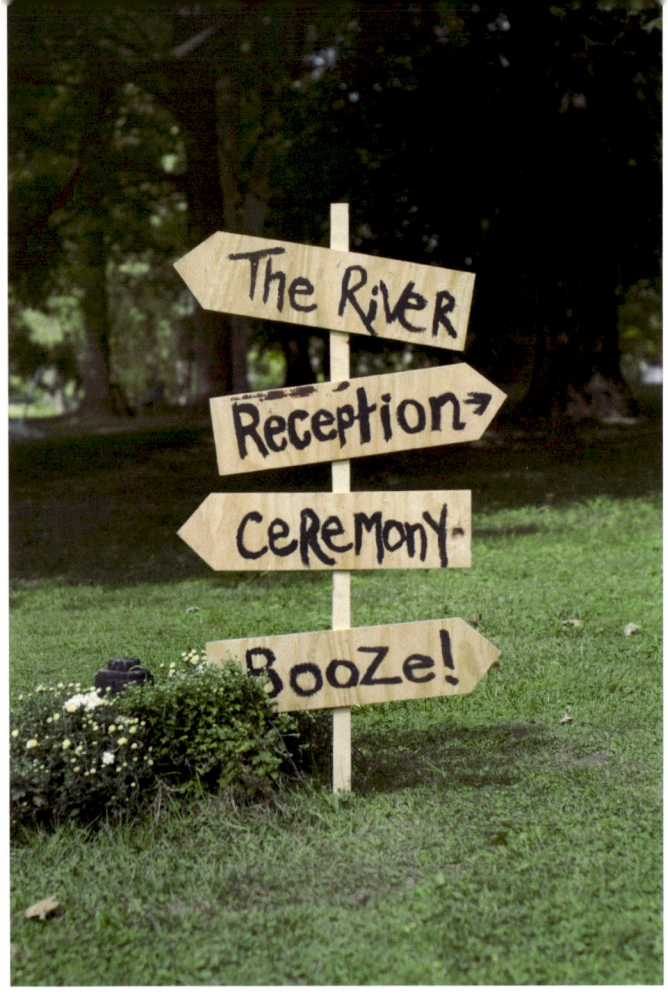

Location

Bo and Julie married at A Private Estate, a nineteenth-century estate deep in the Hudson Valley. They made their vows as the sun glinted on the water and lit up the majestic oaks and lush grass. The main house provided an elegant backdrop for photos, and the reception was held in one of the converted barns.

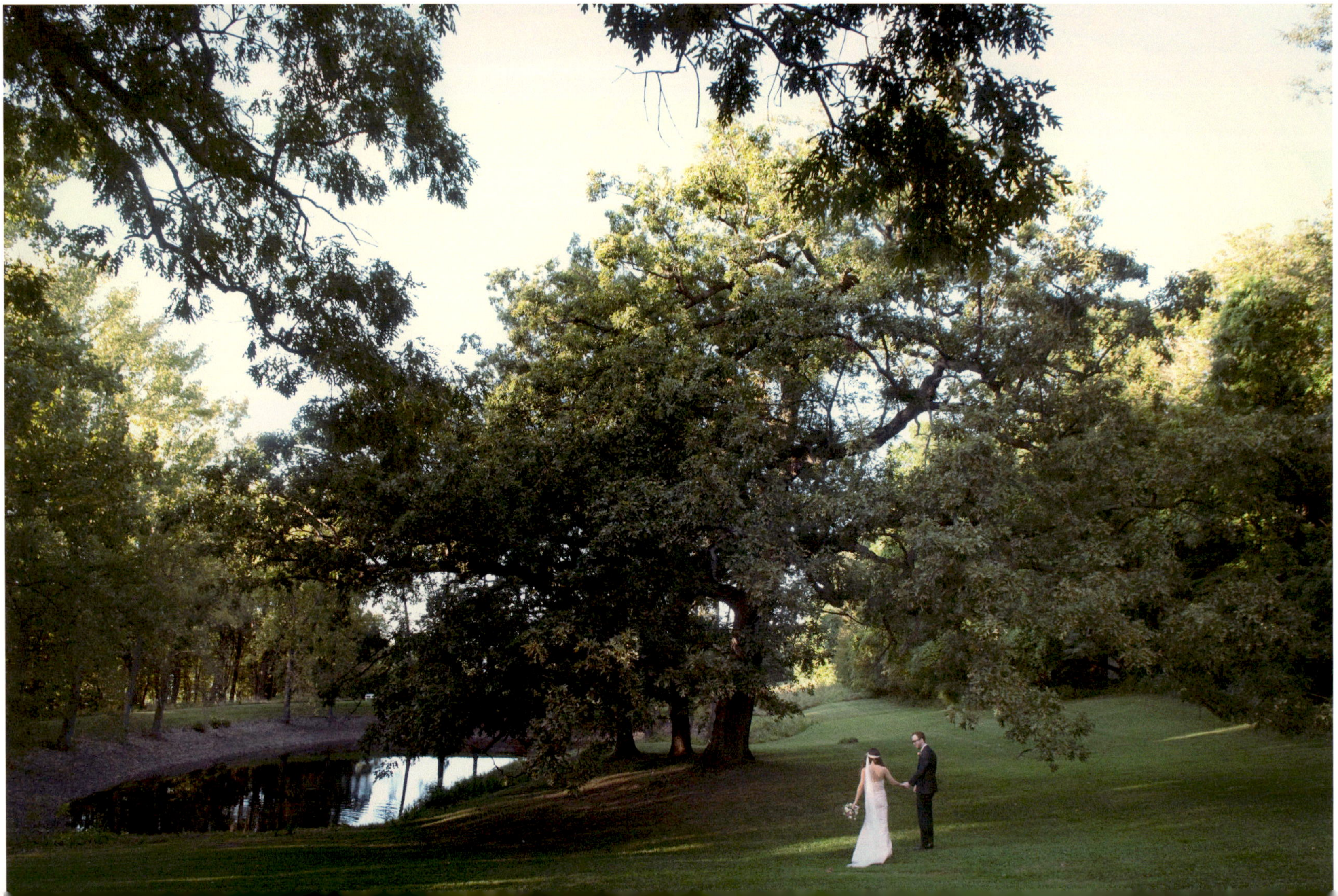

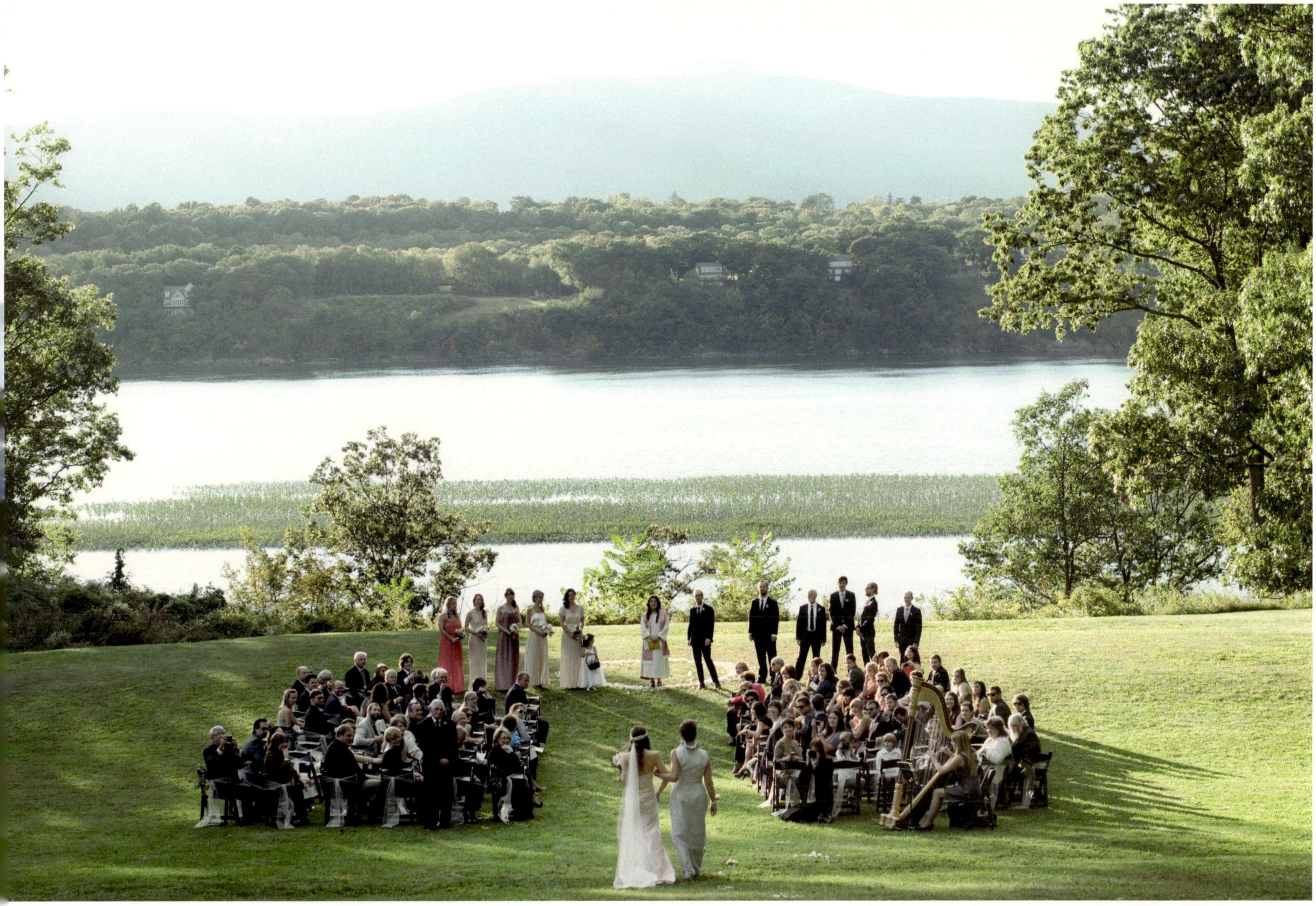

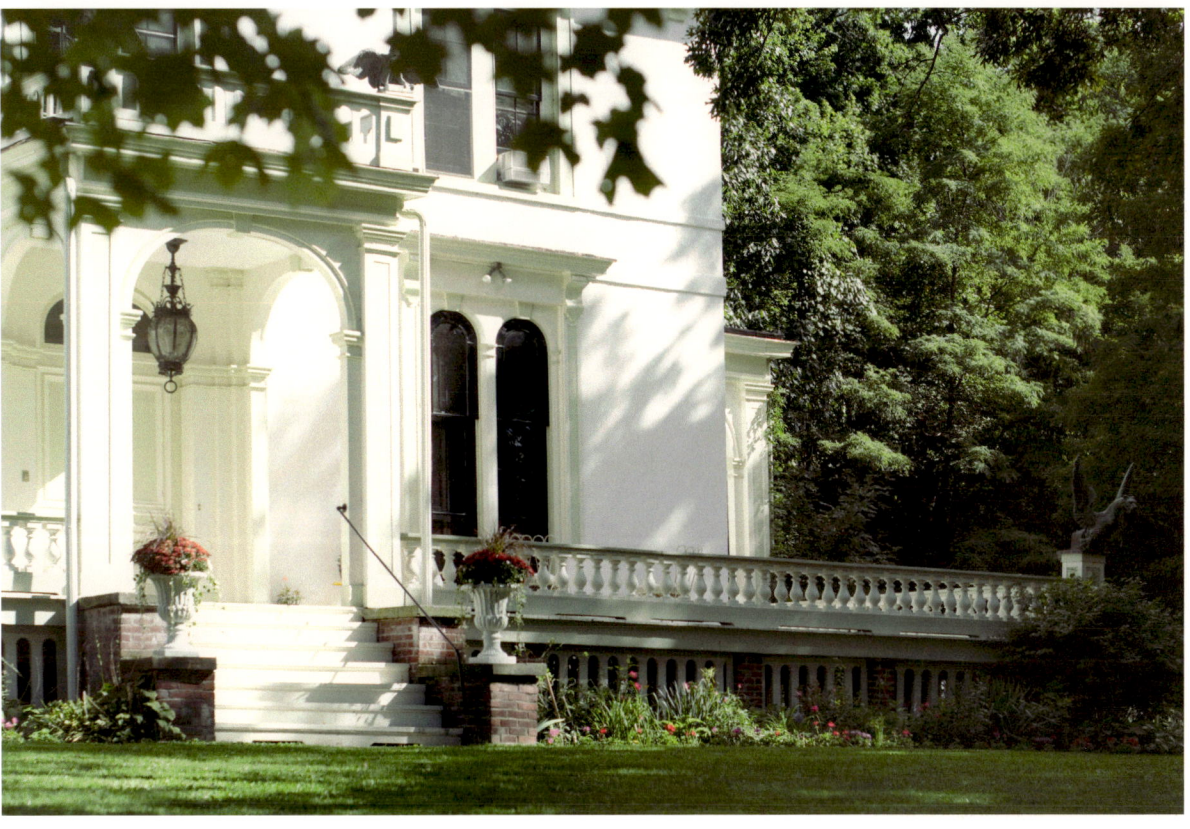

Tickled Pink

The invitations were handpainted with watercolors and the text was letterpressed on top. A special wax seal held the envelopes shut and put the finishing touches to the graceful design. Bo and Julie also had a wedding website, which was decorated with logos designed just for them.

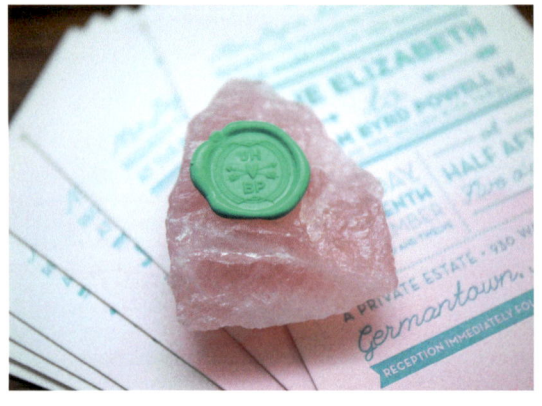

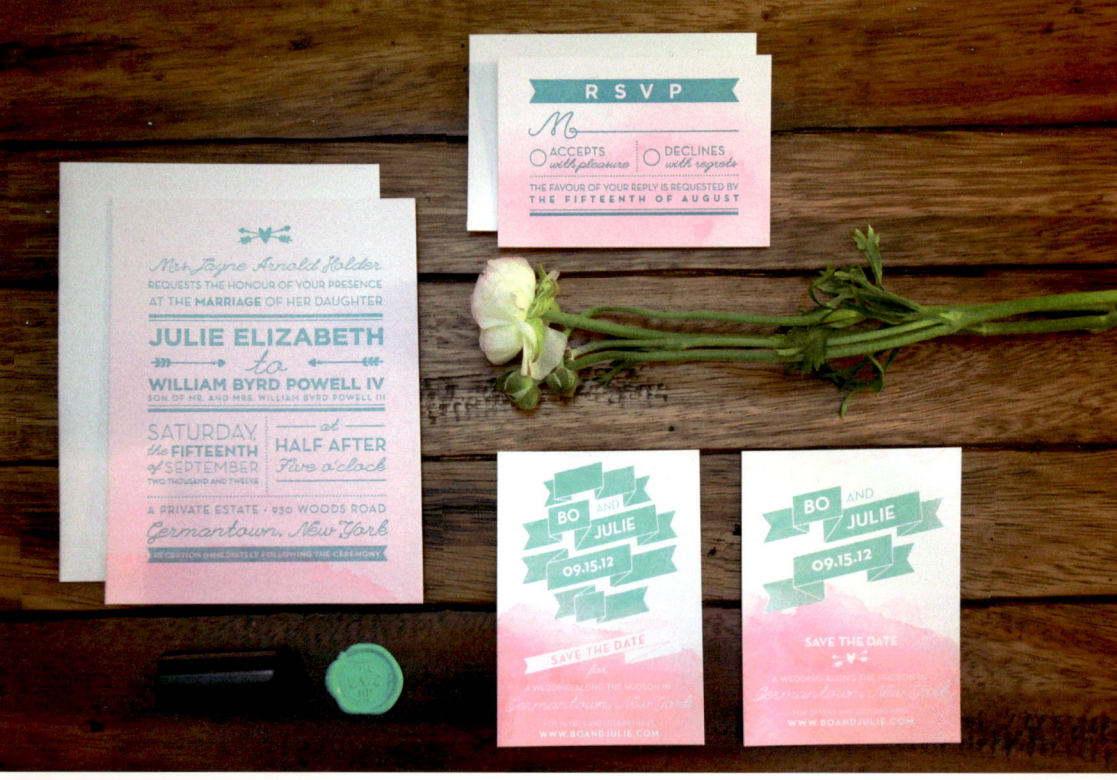

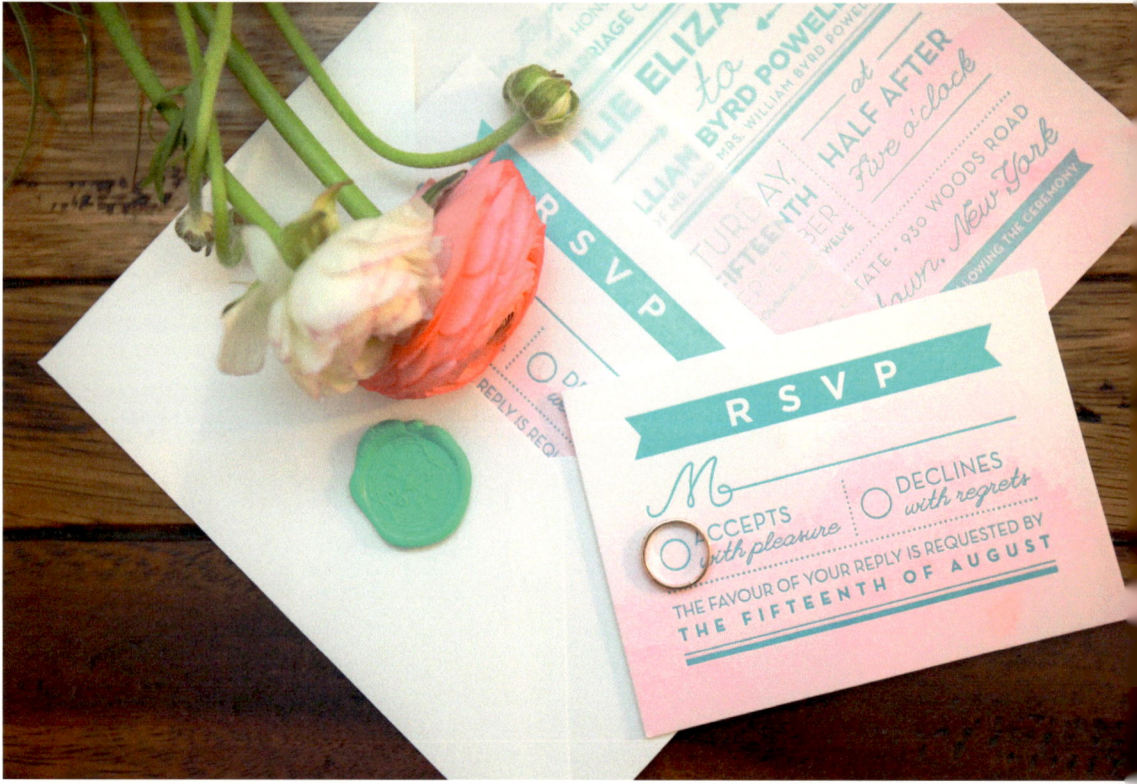

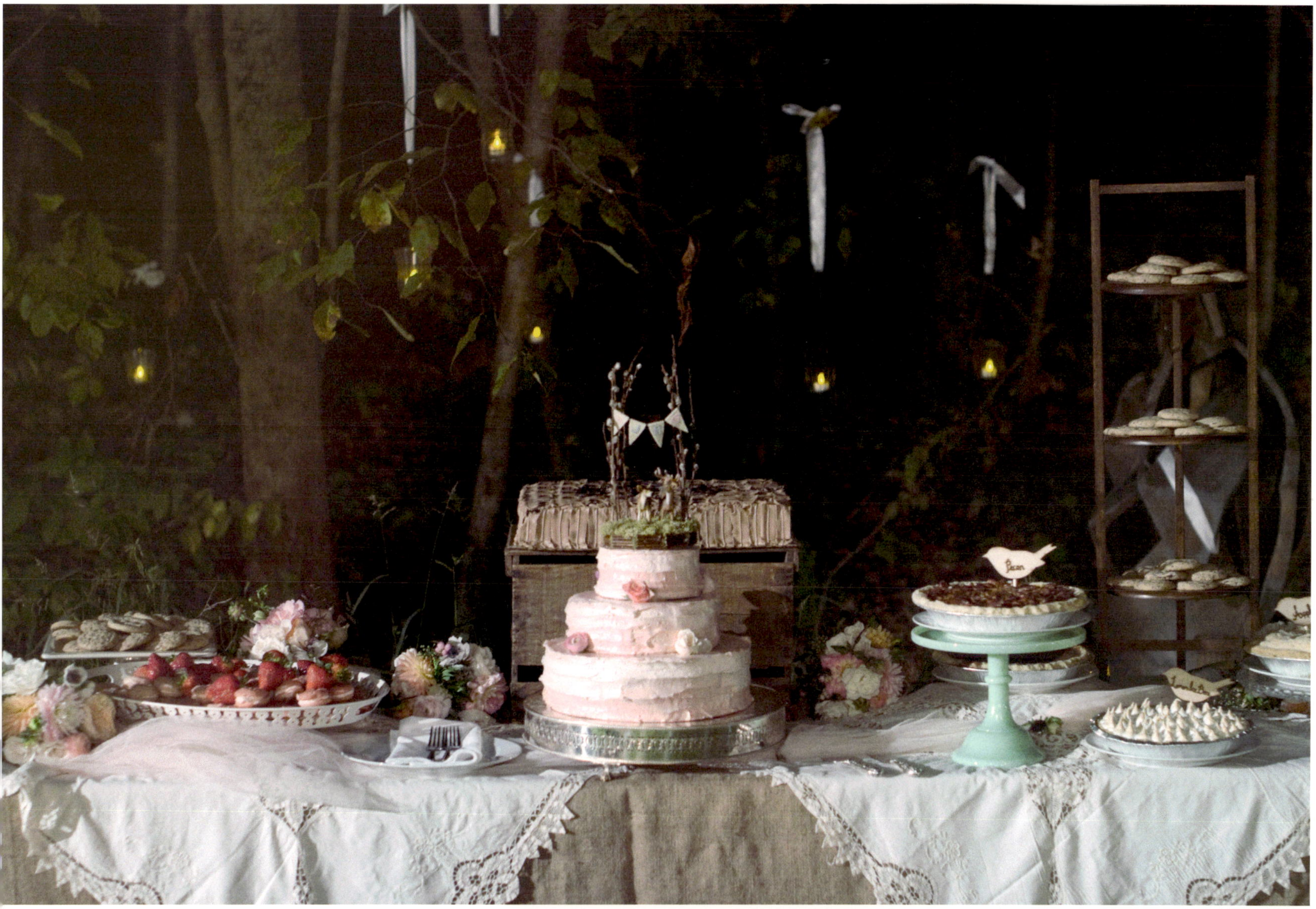

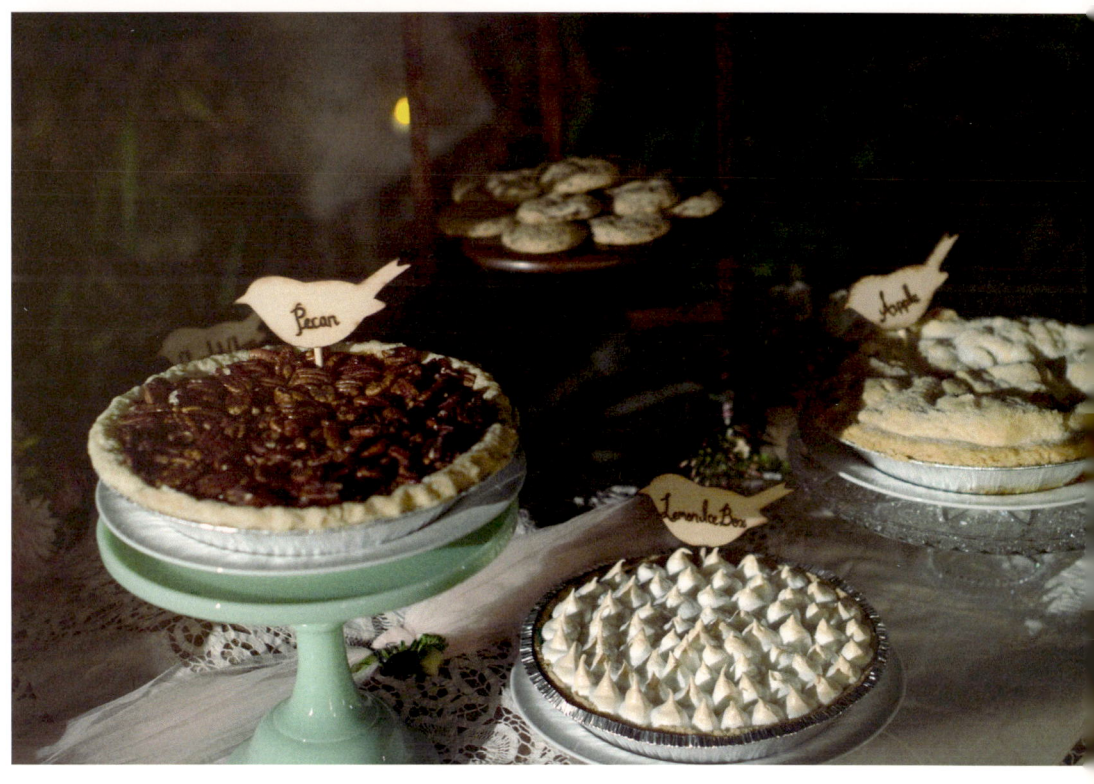

Even the cakes,
pies, and cookies
fit in with the
color scheme.

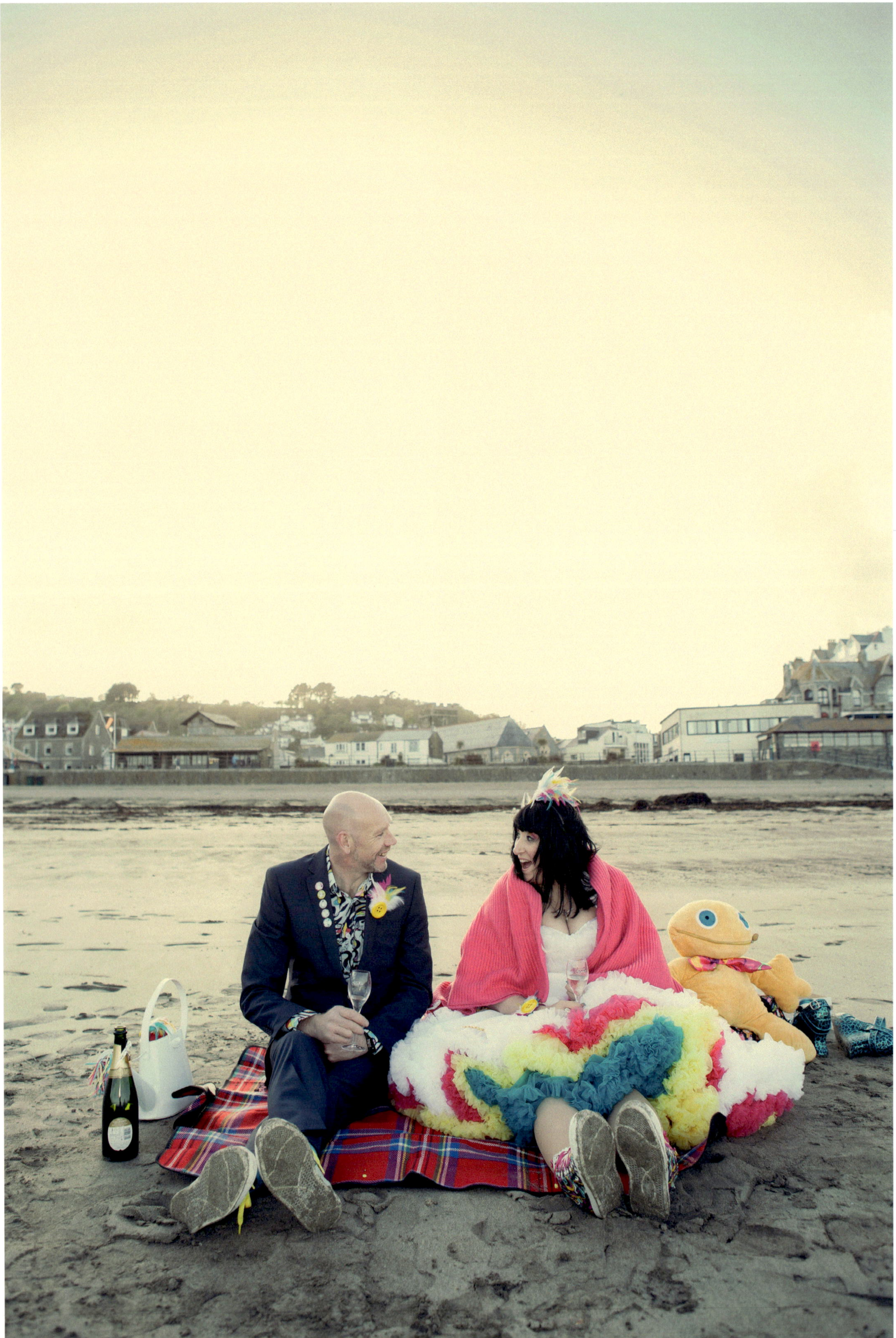

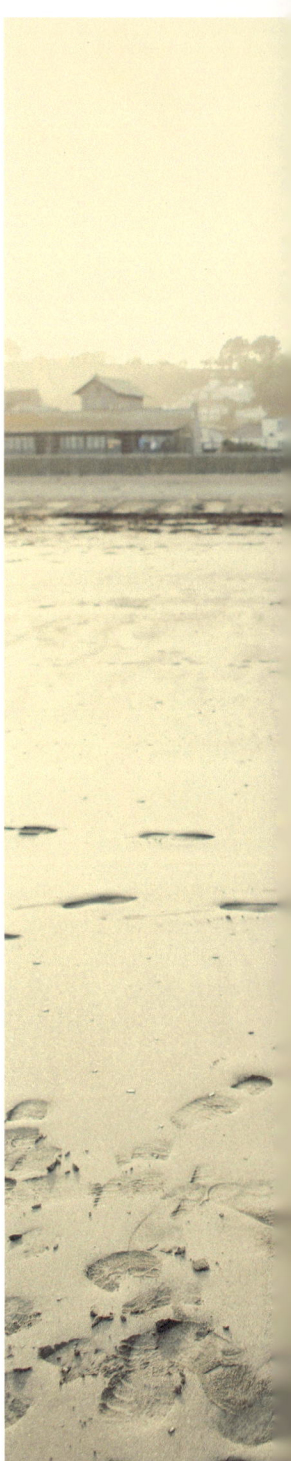

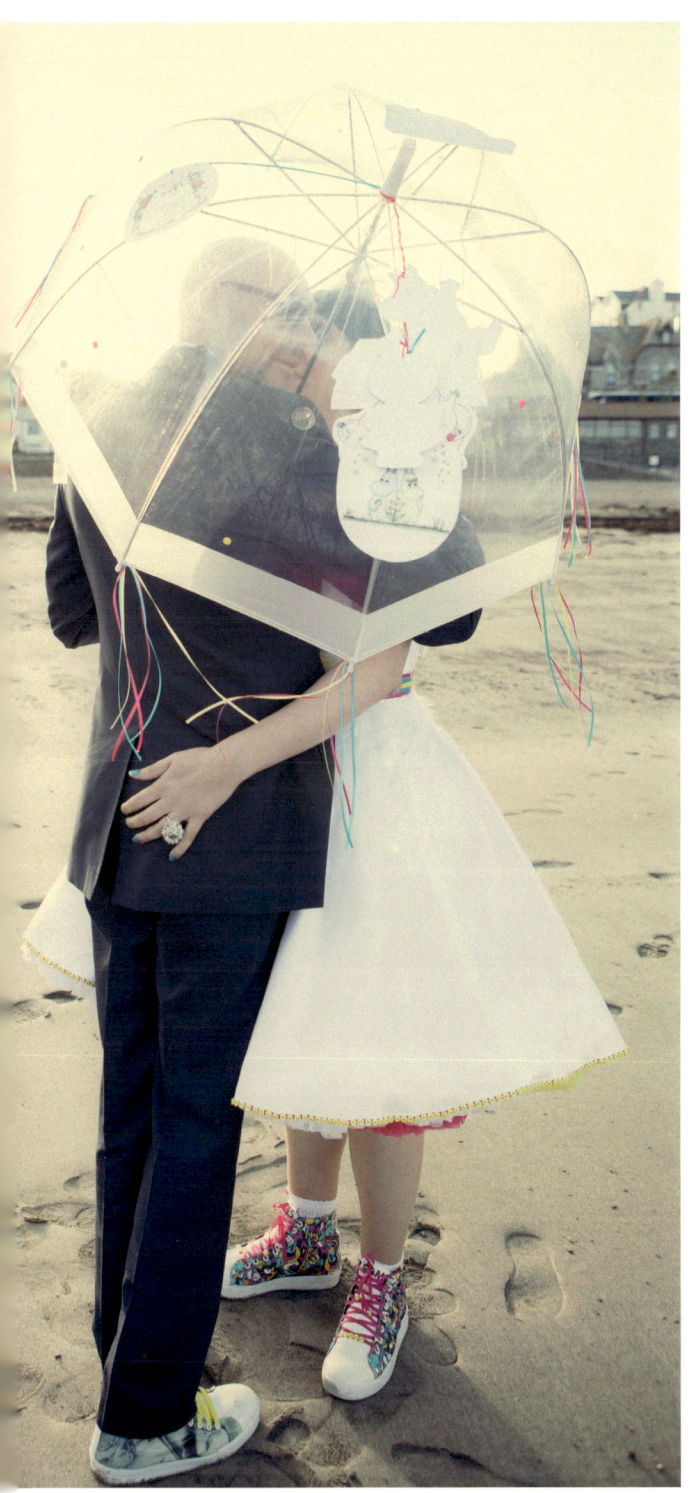

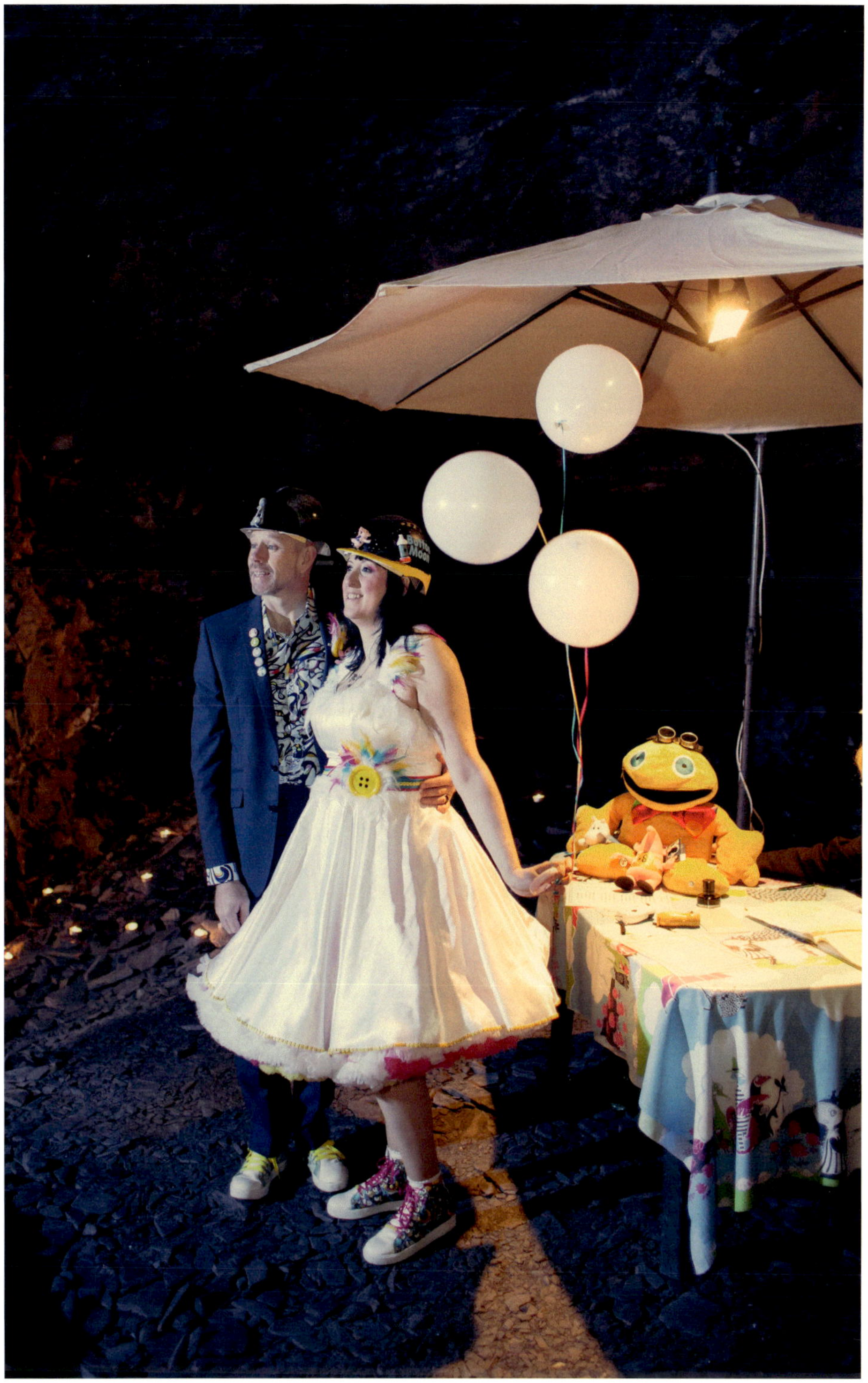

Caroline & Johnny

A wedding that started in a cave, went to a jail, and ended on a beach — if that's not original, we don't know what is. But Caroline and Johnny didn't just want unusual locations, they wanted to make the whole day about them. Caroline bought a 50s-style dress and added bright feathers, colorful petticoats, and yellow buttons. Johnny designed his own shoes and then turned his creativity loose on the hard hats for the cave. And throughout it all, they were accompanied by the TV characters they had both loved so much as kids.

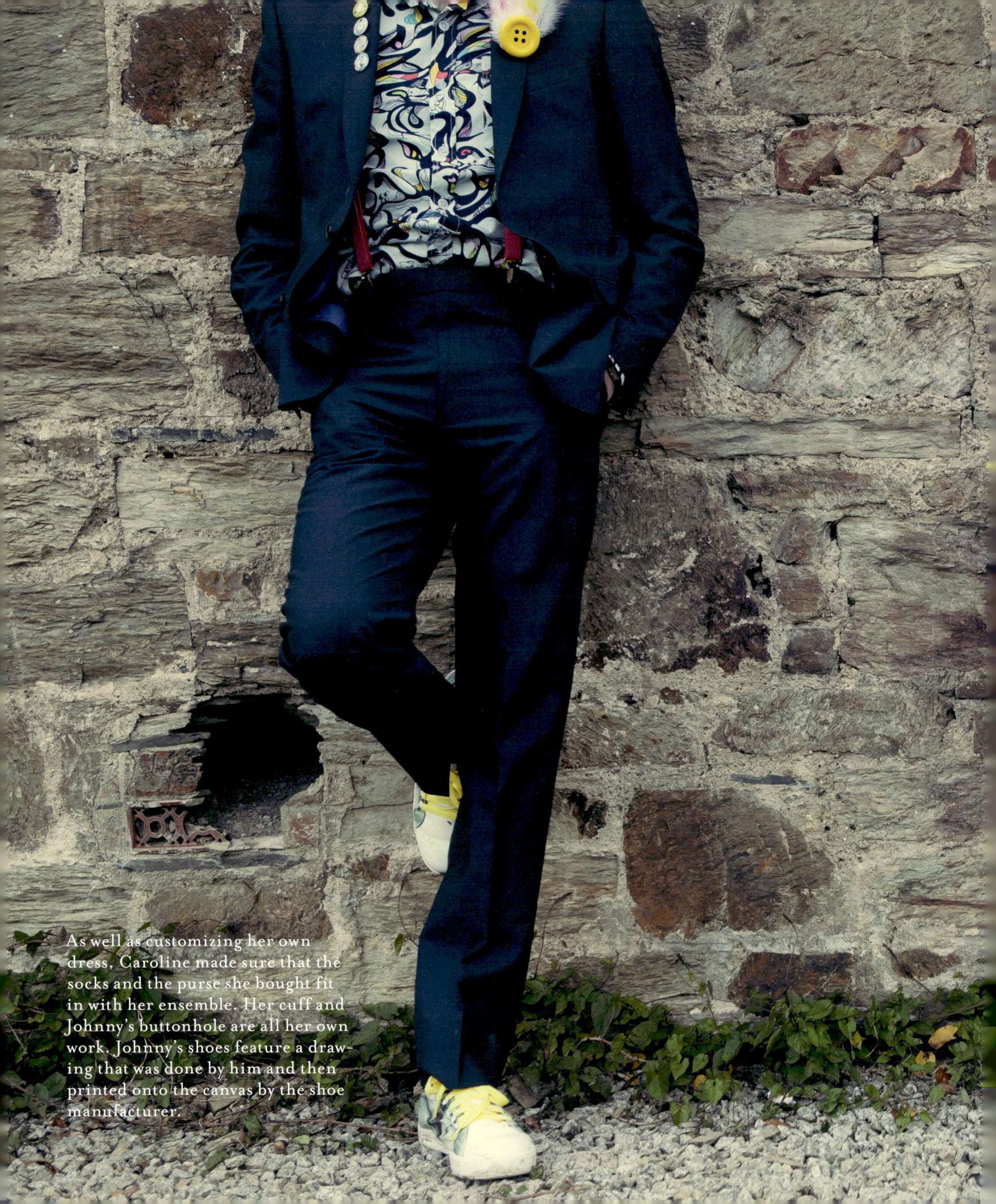

As well as customizing her own dress, Caroline made sure that the socks and the purse she bought fit in with her ensemble. Her cuff and Johnny's buttonhole are all her own work. Johnny's shoes feature a drawing that was done by him and then printed onto the canvas by the shoe manufacturer.

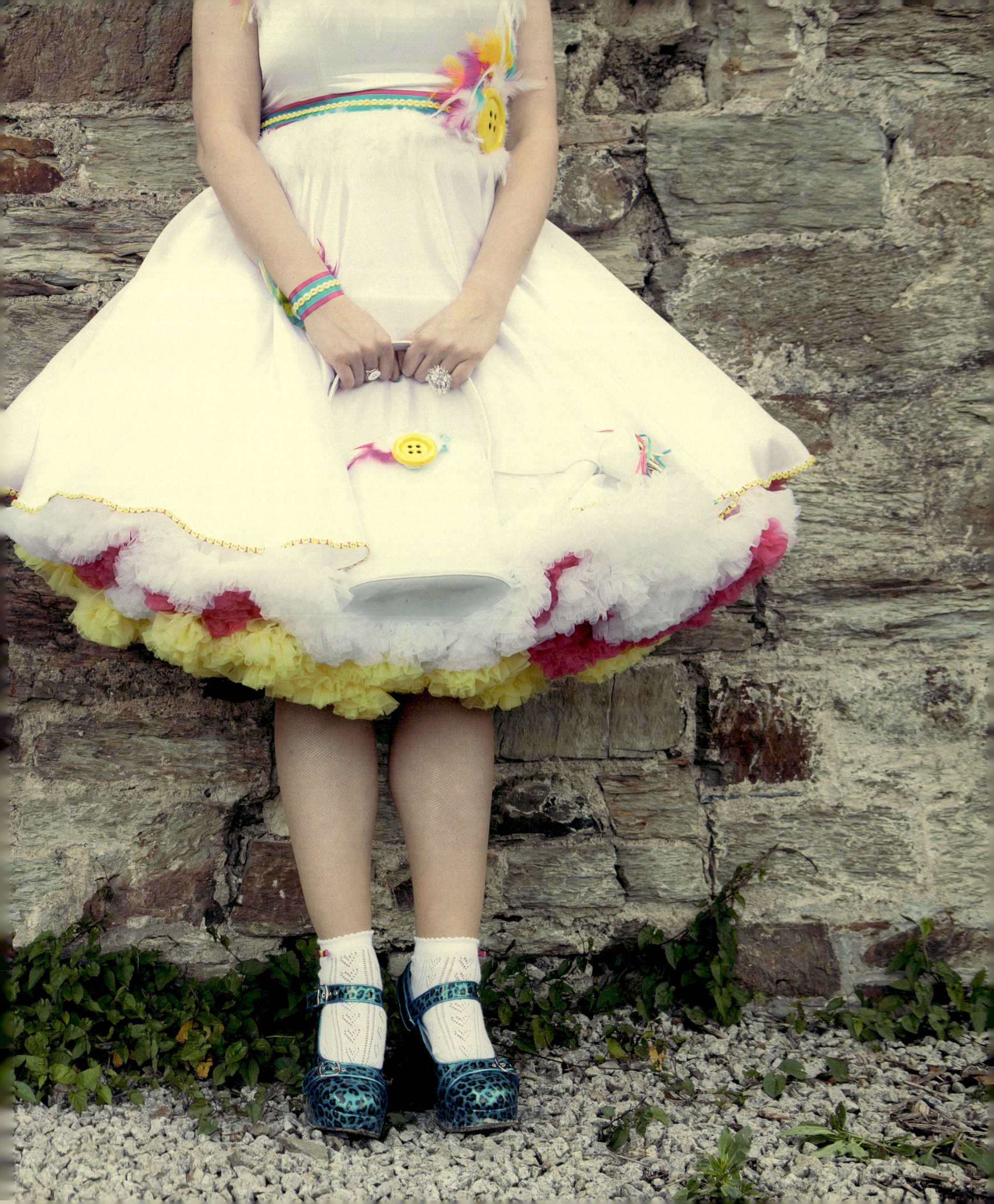

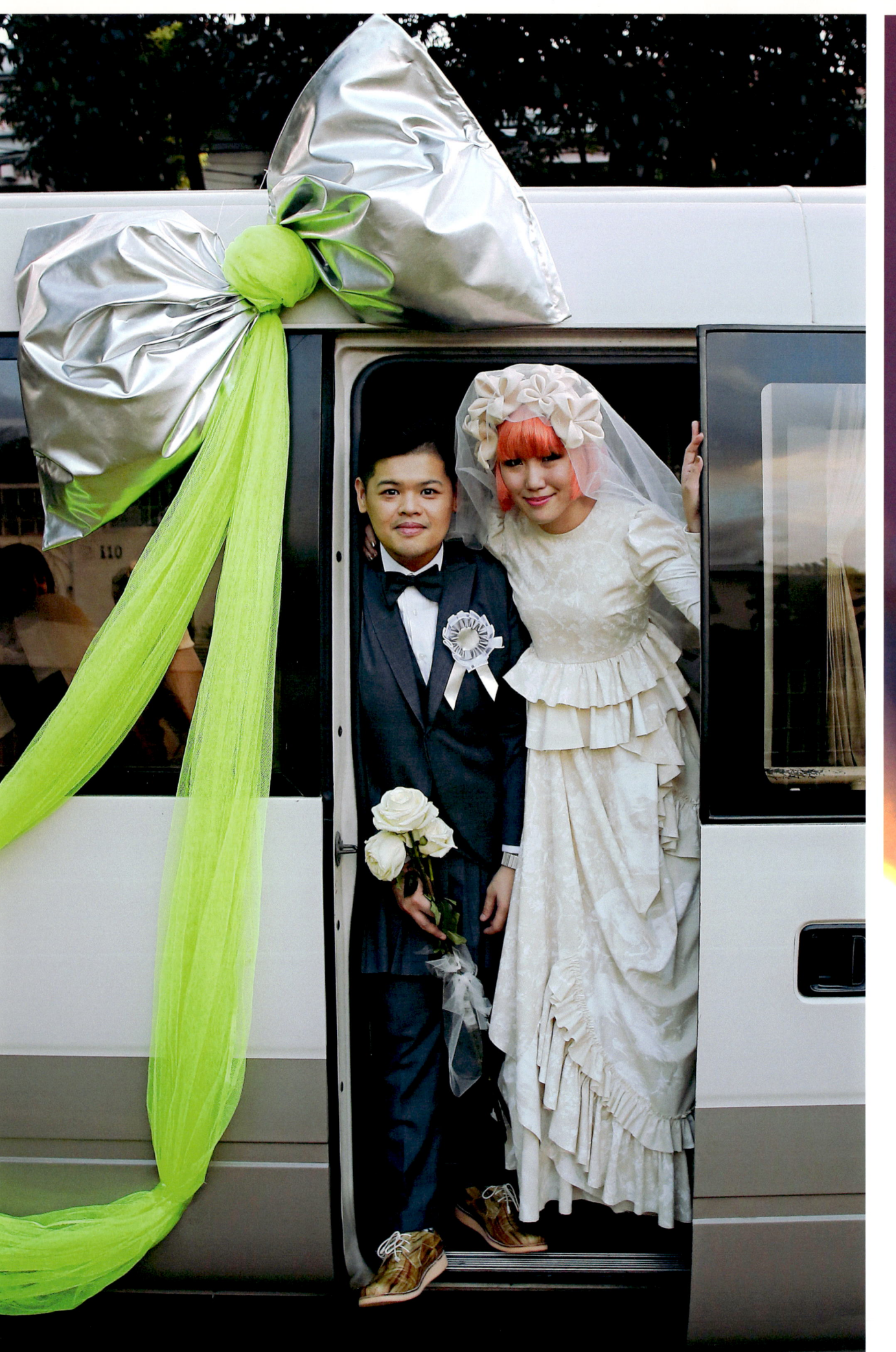

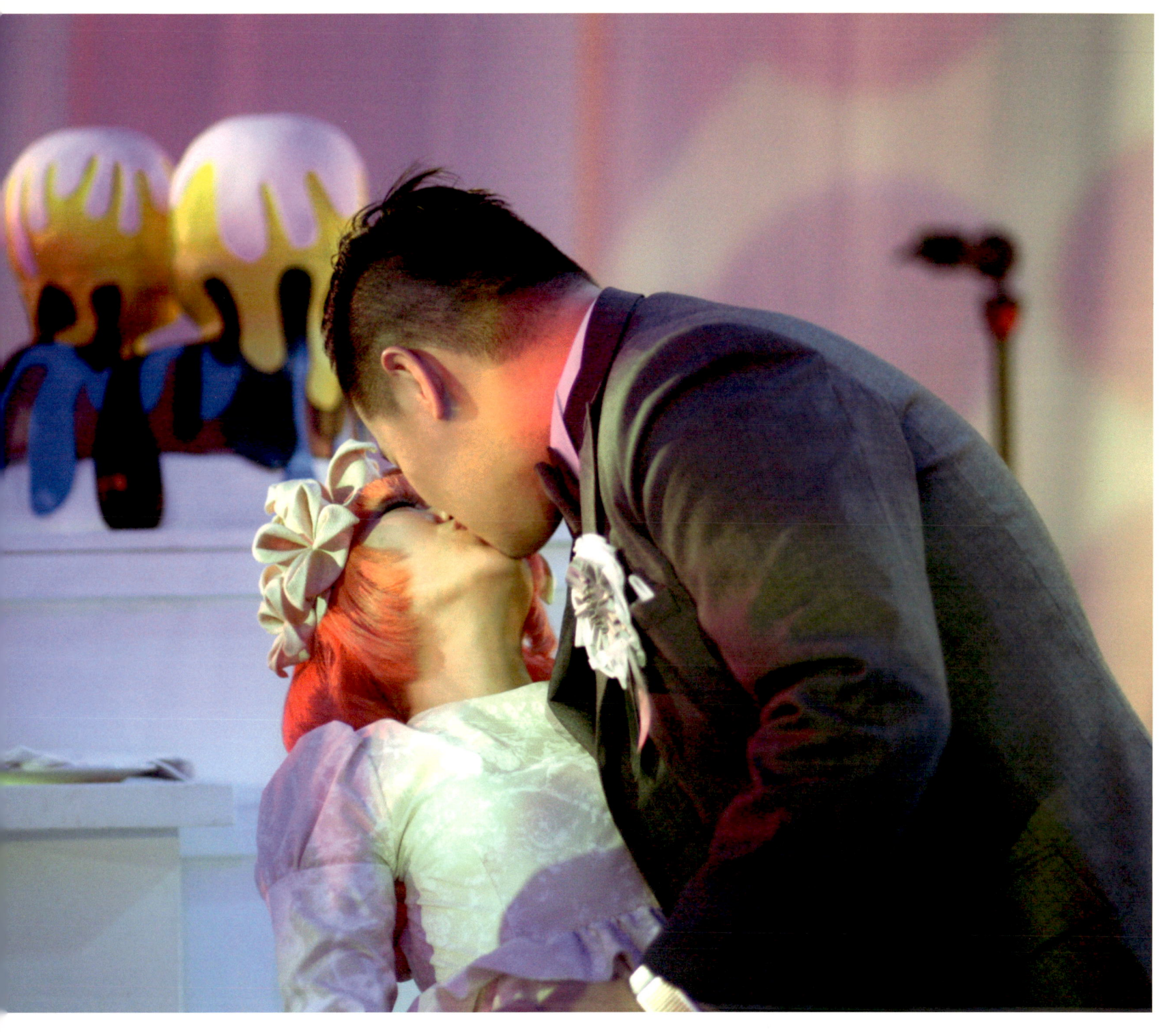

Garovs & Ryan

For their wedding day, Ryan and Garovs wanted to share what they were feeling with their family and friends. Everything began with a walk in the clouds, as swathes of cotton wool created a sense of weightlessness during the ceremony. At the reception, guests made their way through a series of spaces, each designed to create a different sensation — of being at a circus, say, or an art exhibition. The pale centerpieces on the tables created a striking contrast with the cartoon cake that was a patisserie pastiche of the rock-star smooch that Ryan gave his bride in the spotlight.

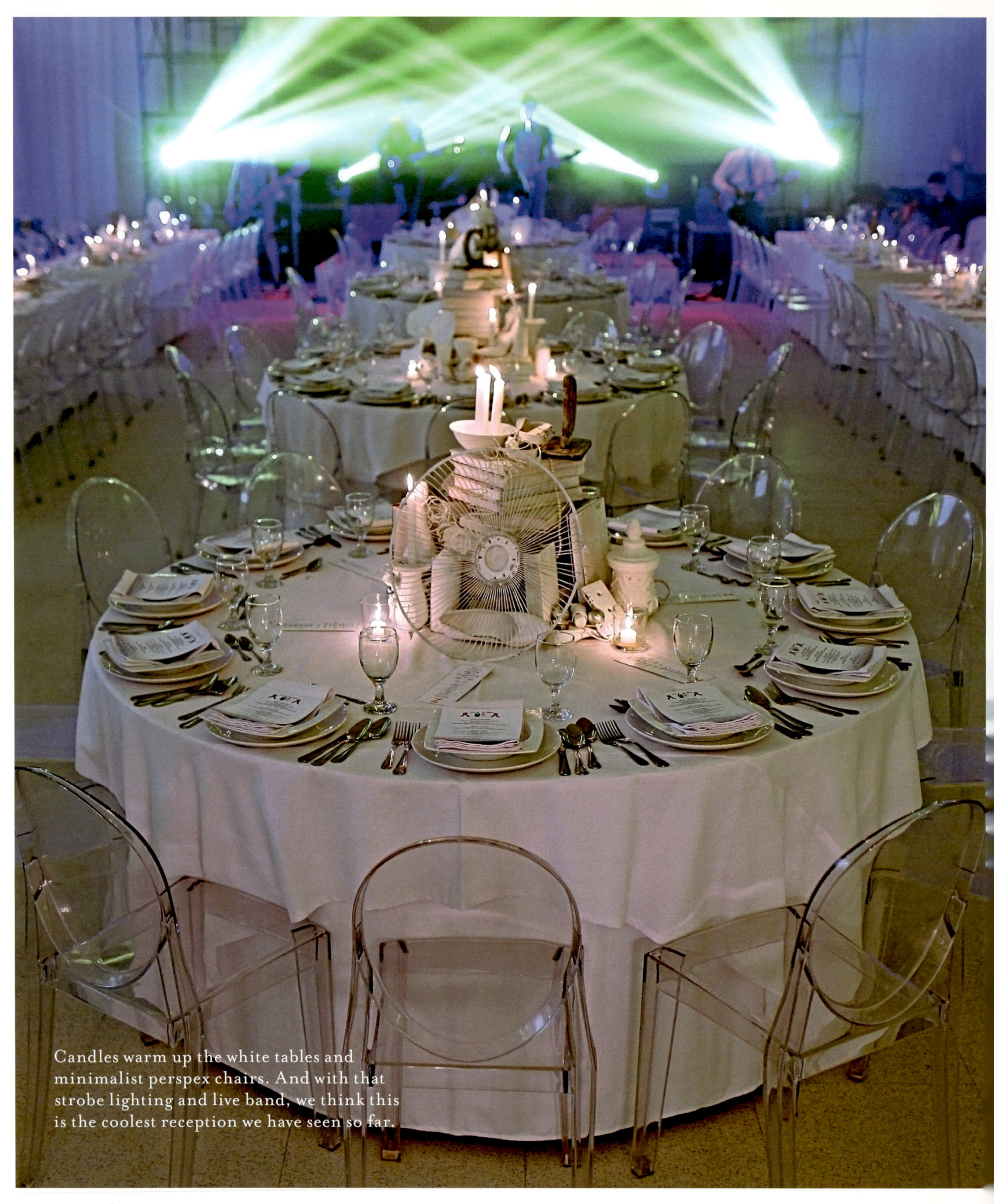

Candles warm up the white tables and minimalist perspex chairs. And with that strobe lighting and live band, we think this is the coolest reception we have seen so far.

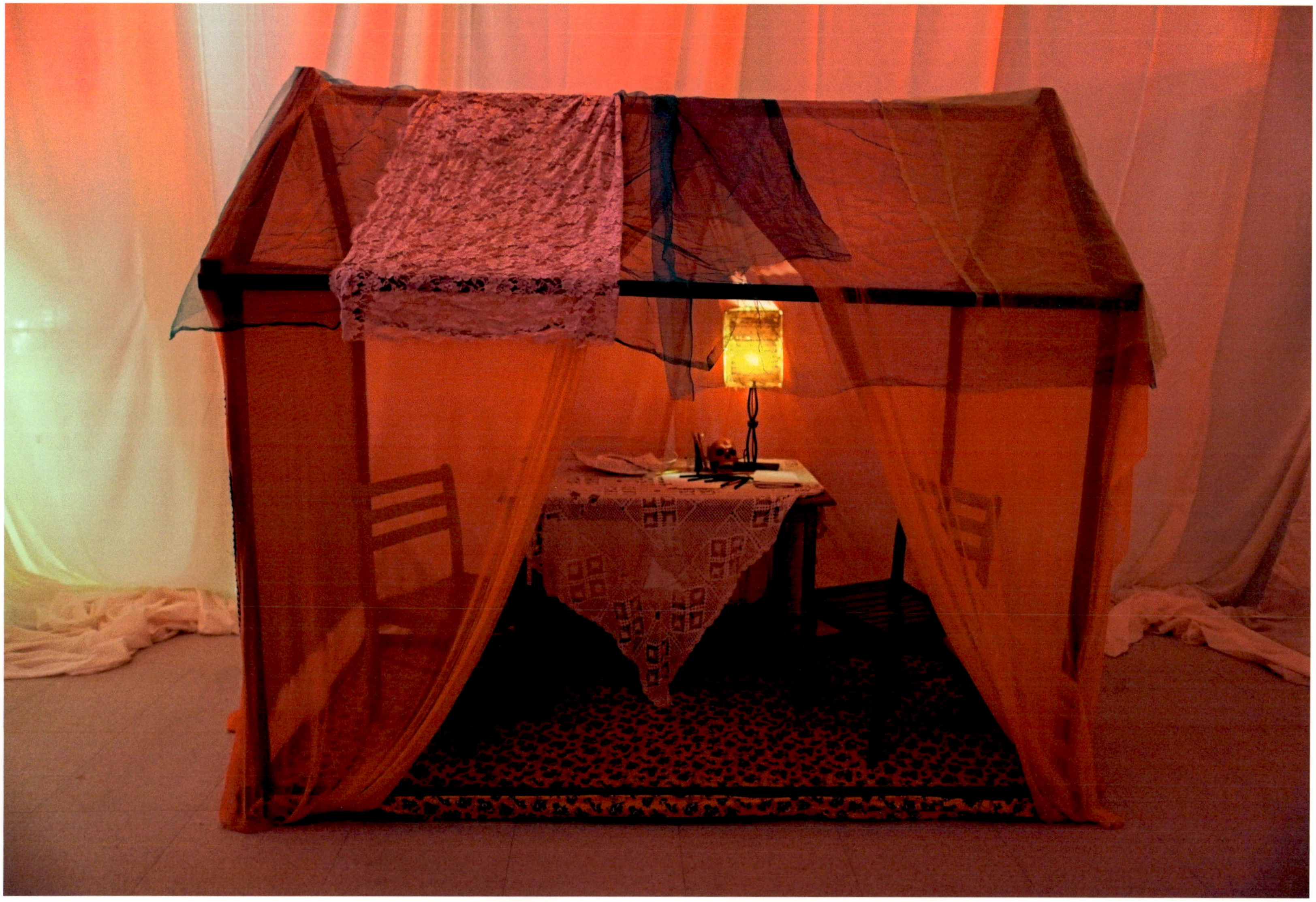

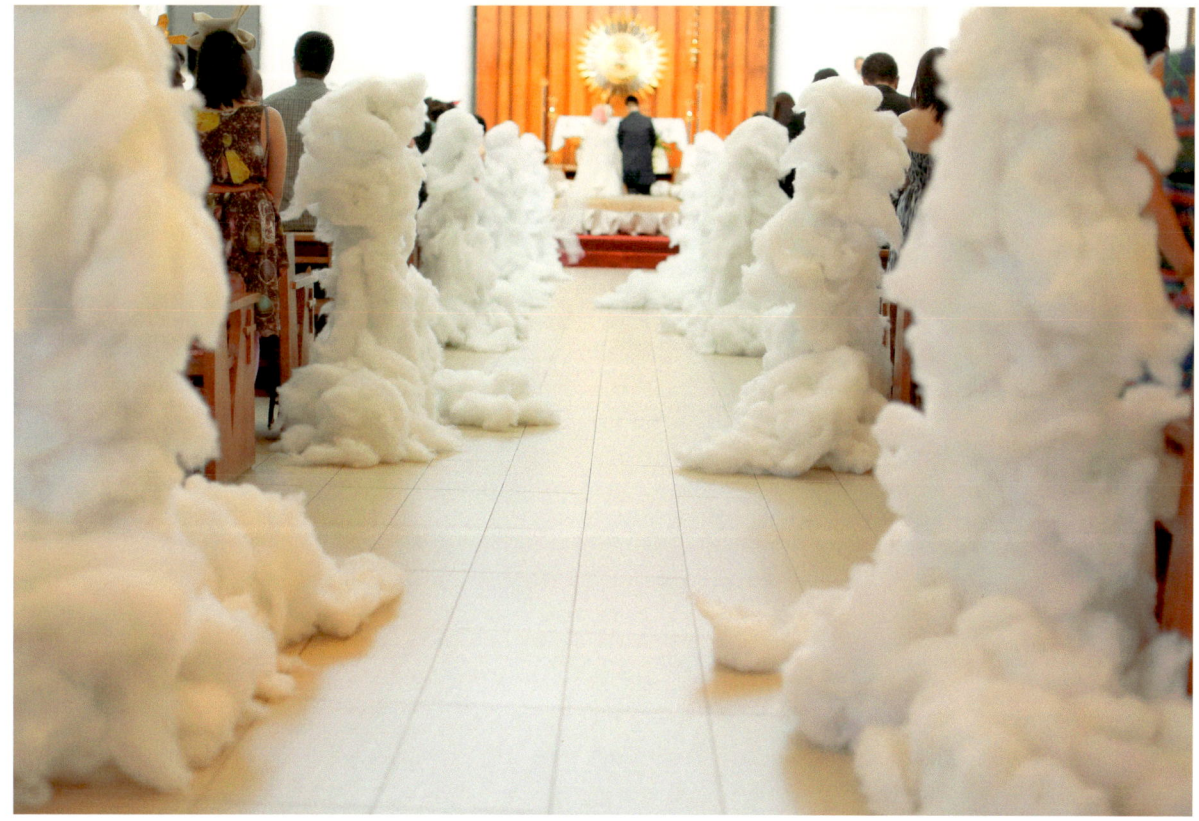

You don't have
to limit your
wedding to a
single style.

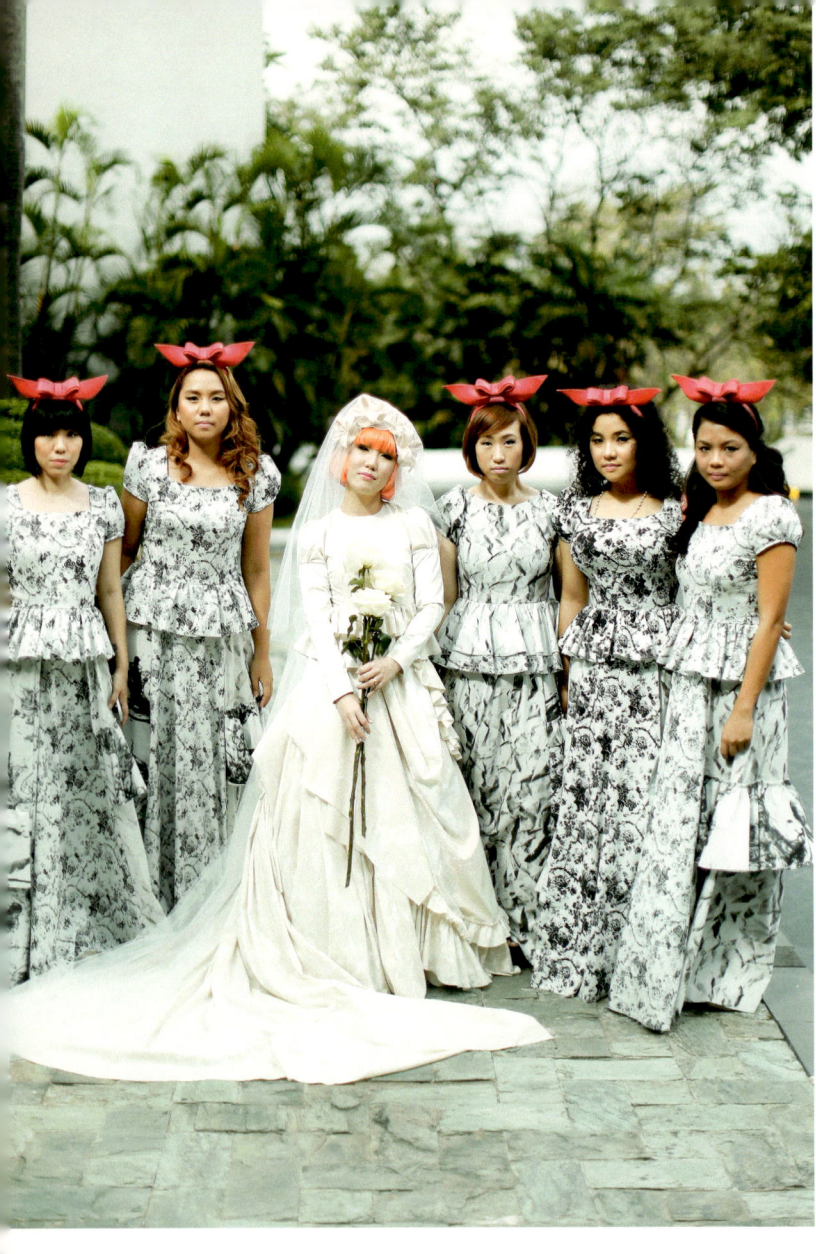
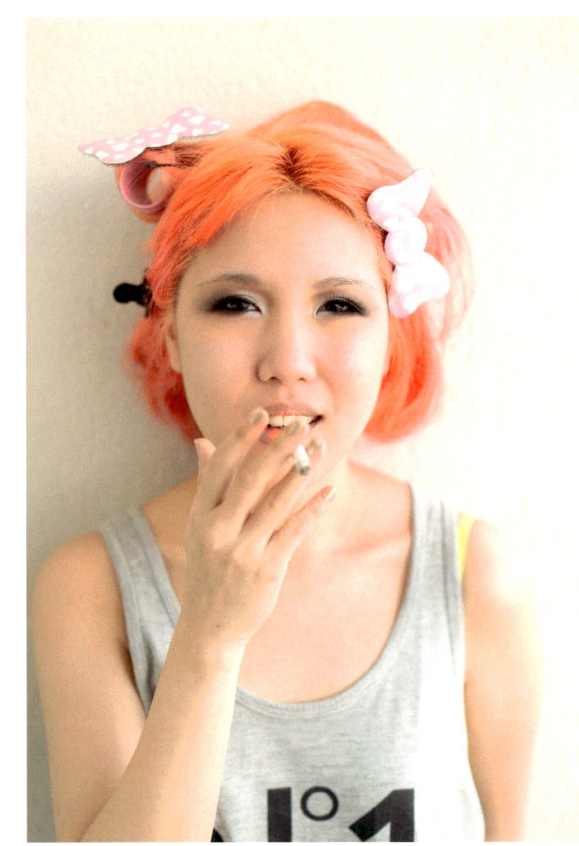
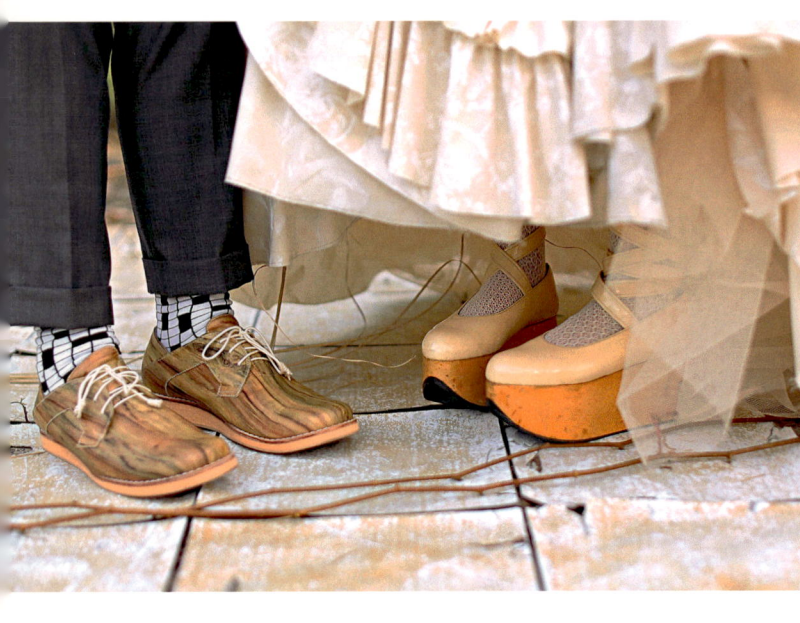
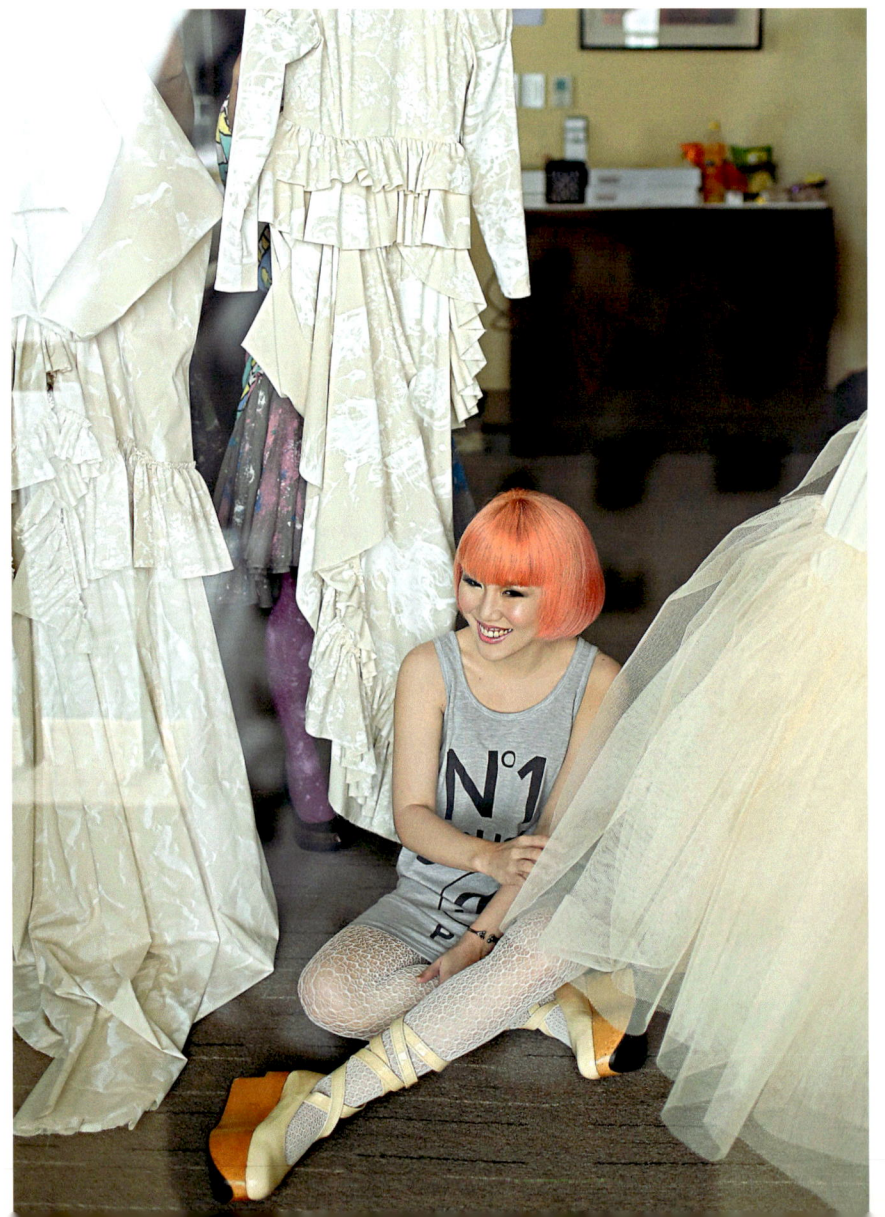

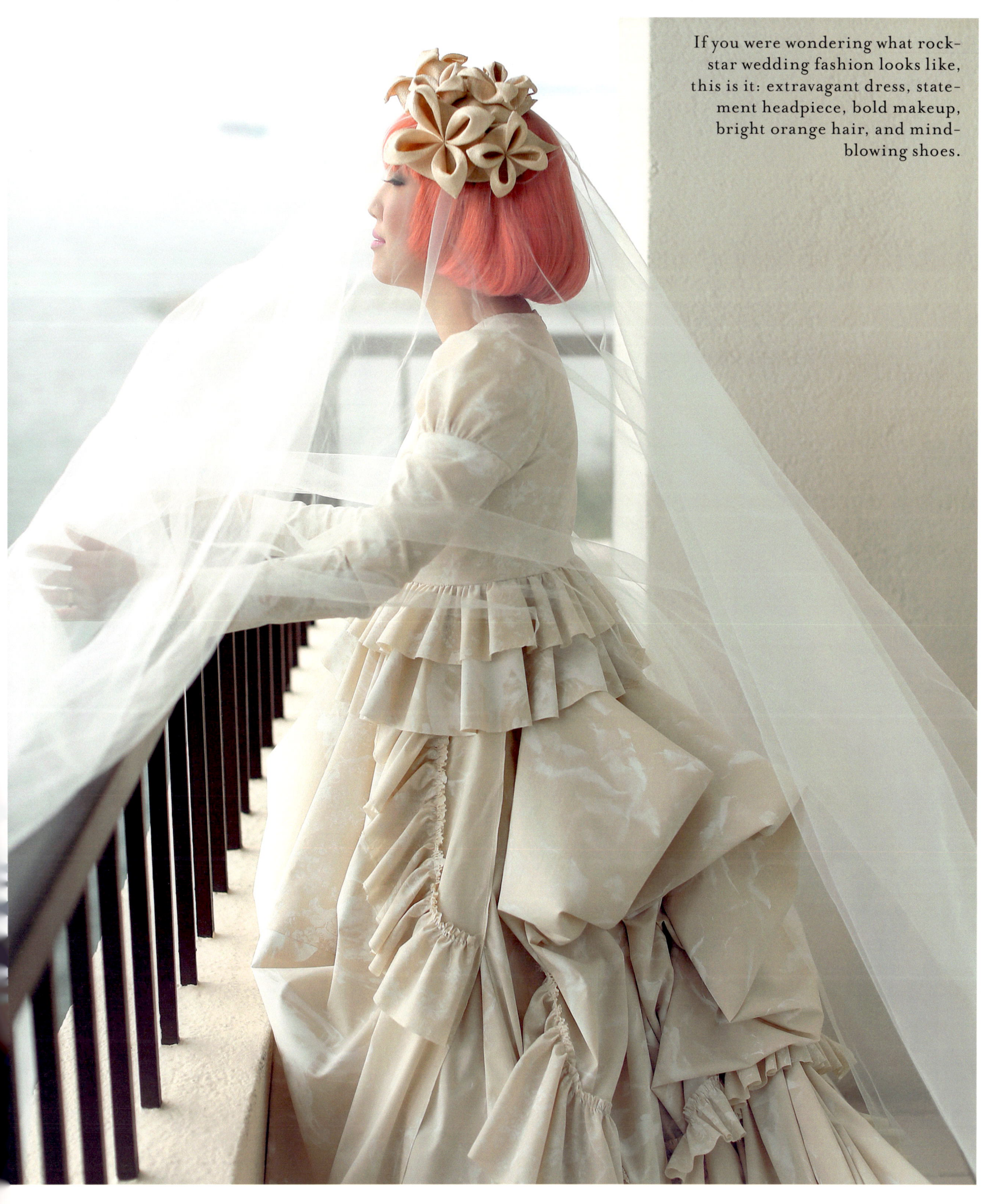

If you were wondering what rock-star wedding fashion looks like, this is it: extravagant dress, statement headpiece, bold makeup, bright orange hair, and mind-blowing shoes.

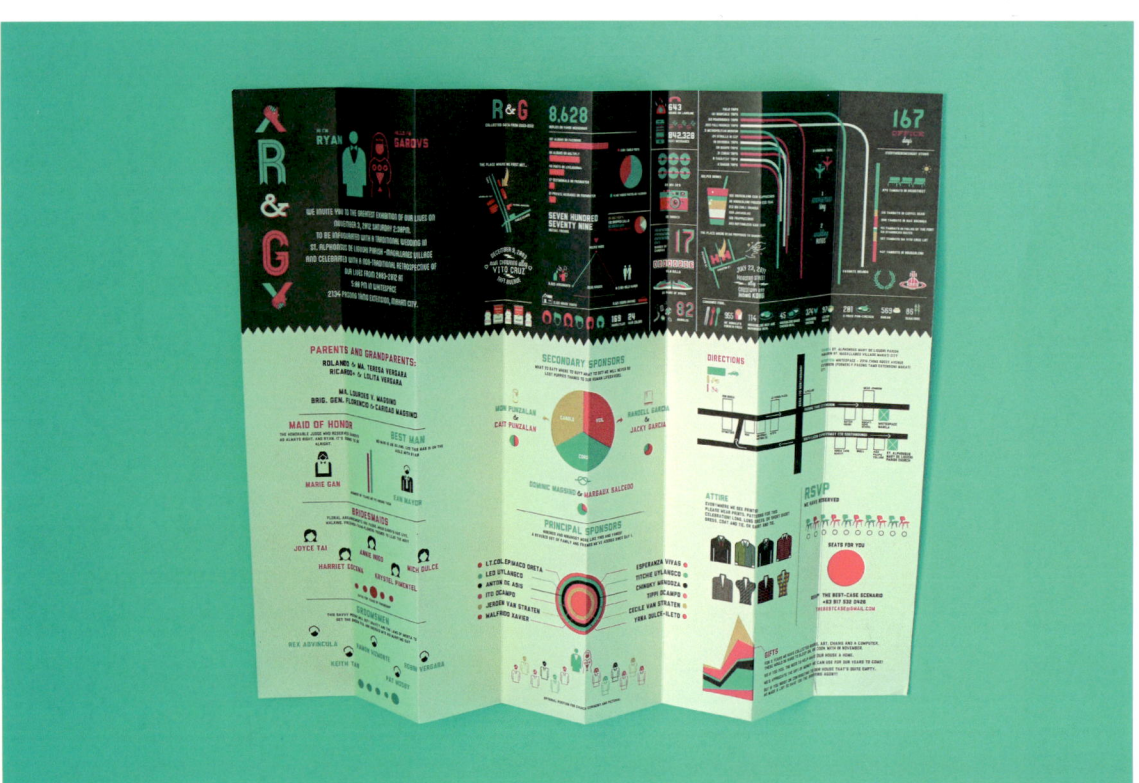

The Invite

On one side, an intricate layout that looks like the graphics you might see displayed on the screen of the latest slice of state-of-the-art technology. On the other, a concertina collage of the happy couple. Ryan and Garovs are all about the eclectic.

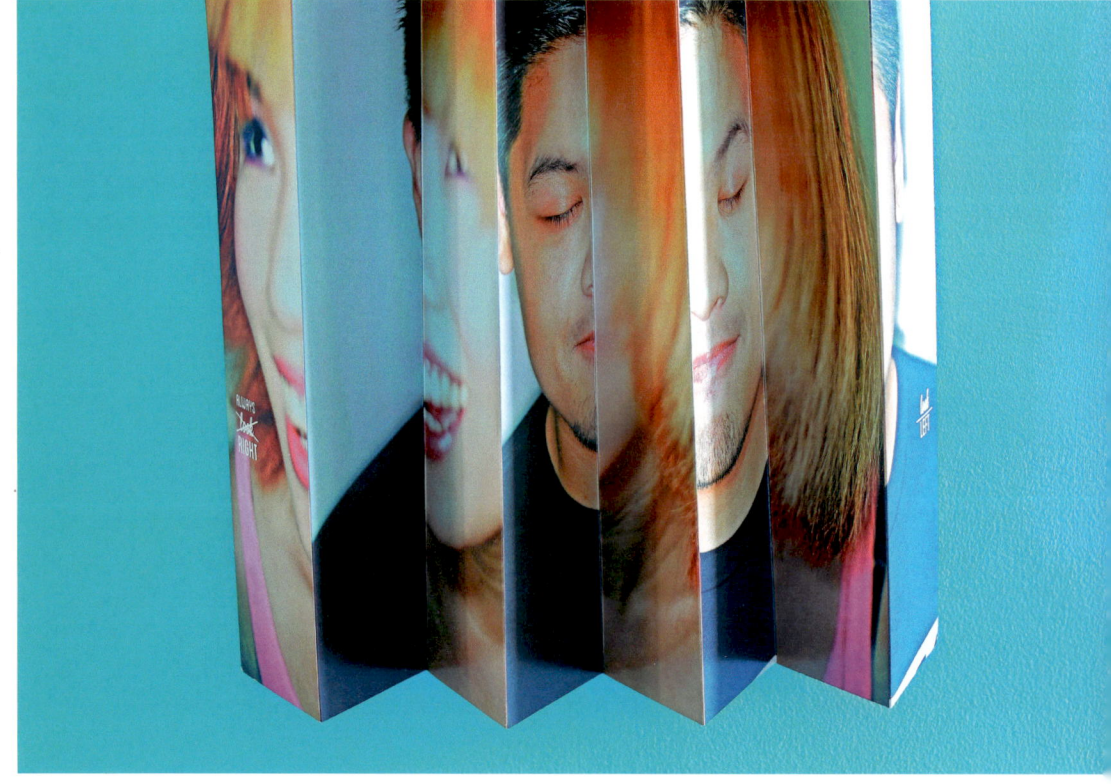

Decoration

1. Centerpieces made of stacks of books, top hats, and old bottles.

2. No need for bride-and-groom cake toppers—this cake has got it covered!

3. Mini packages of personalized candy make a neat take-home treat.

4. An amazing cake installation... but is it art?

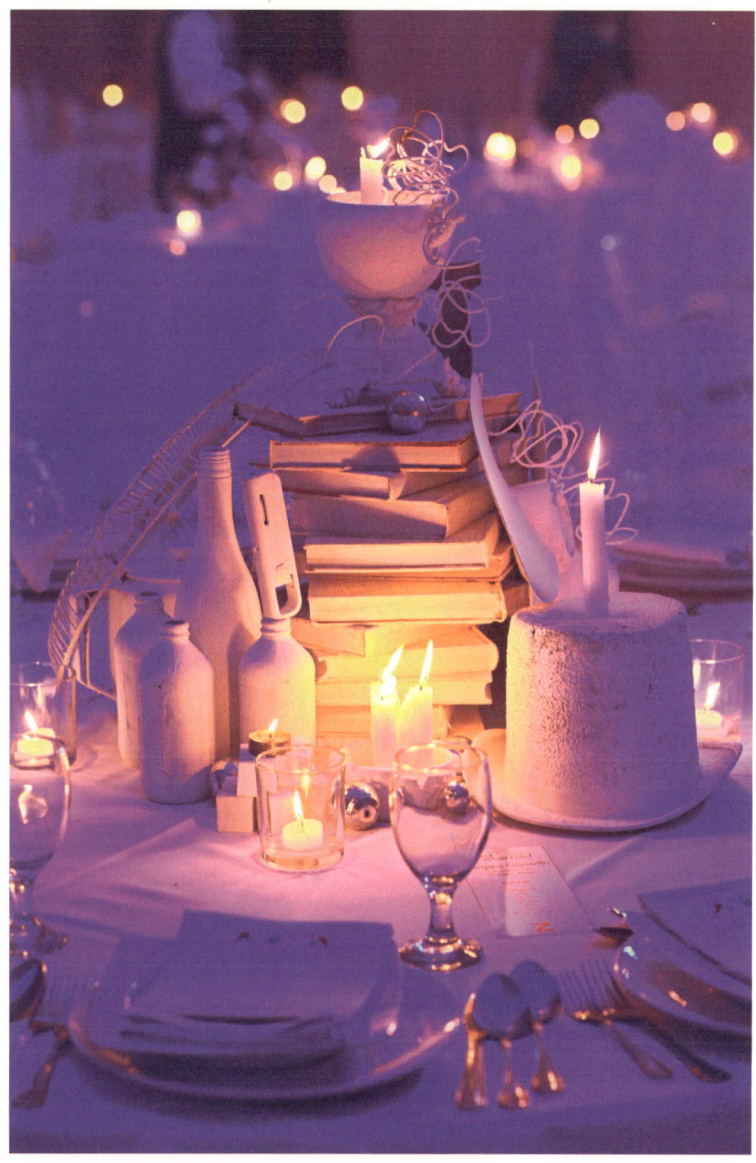

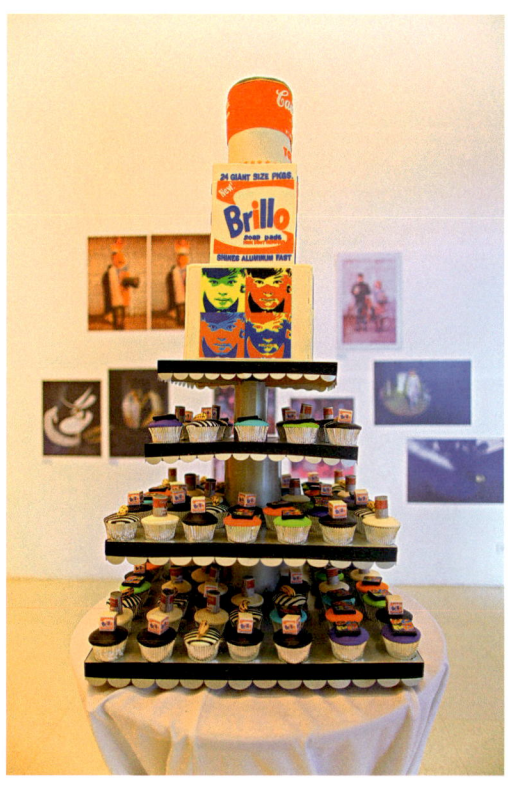

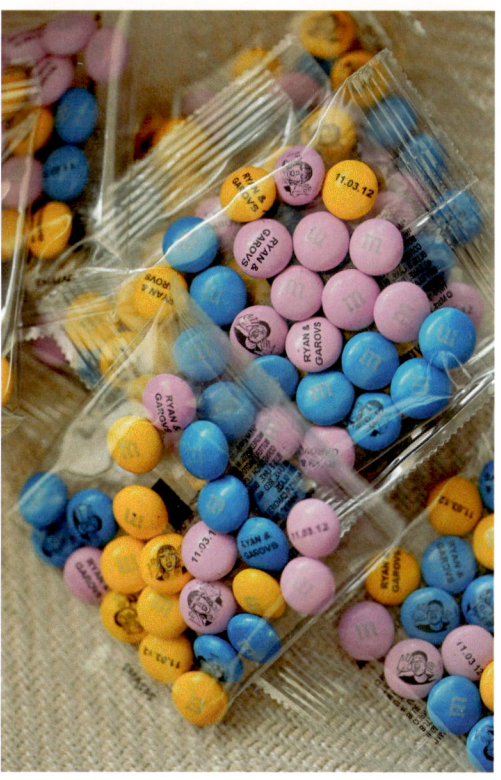

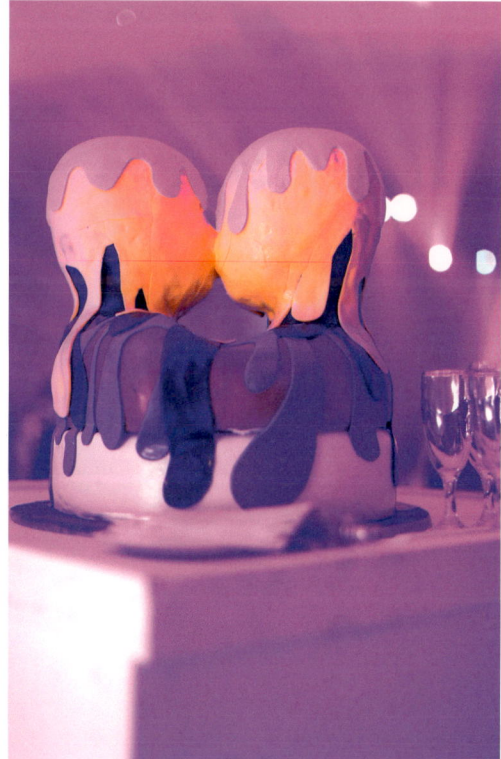

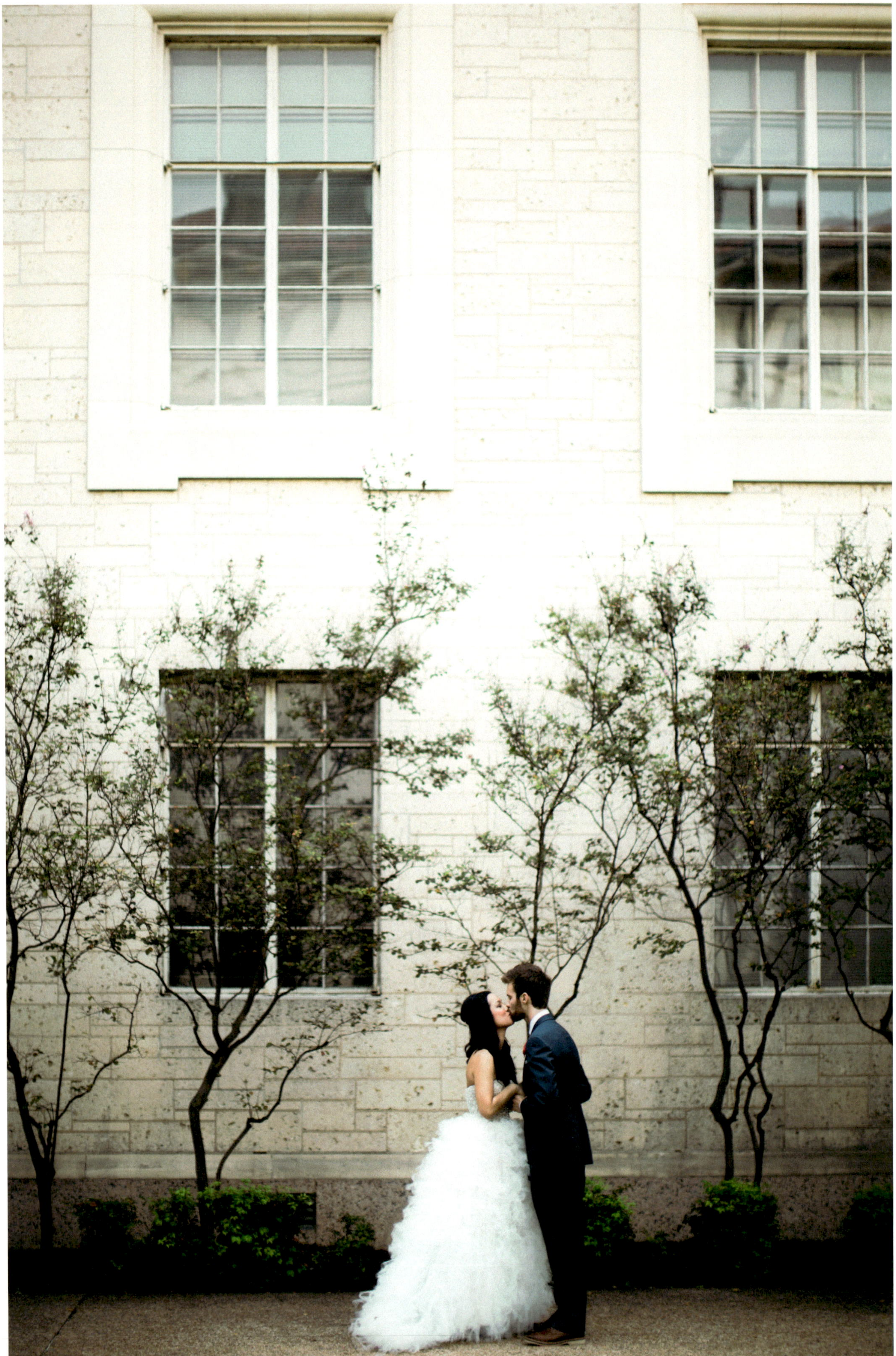

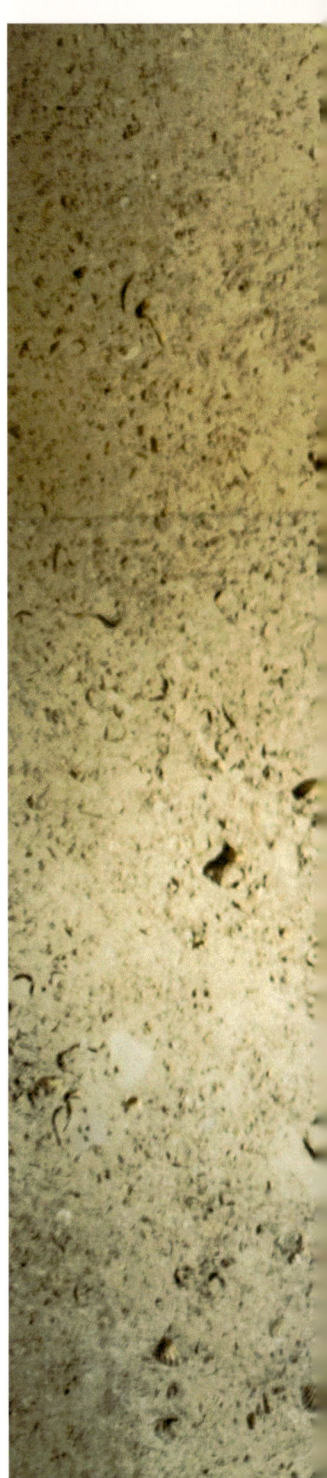

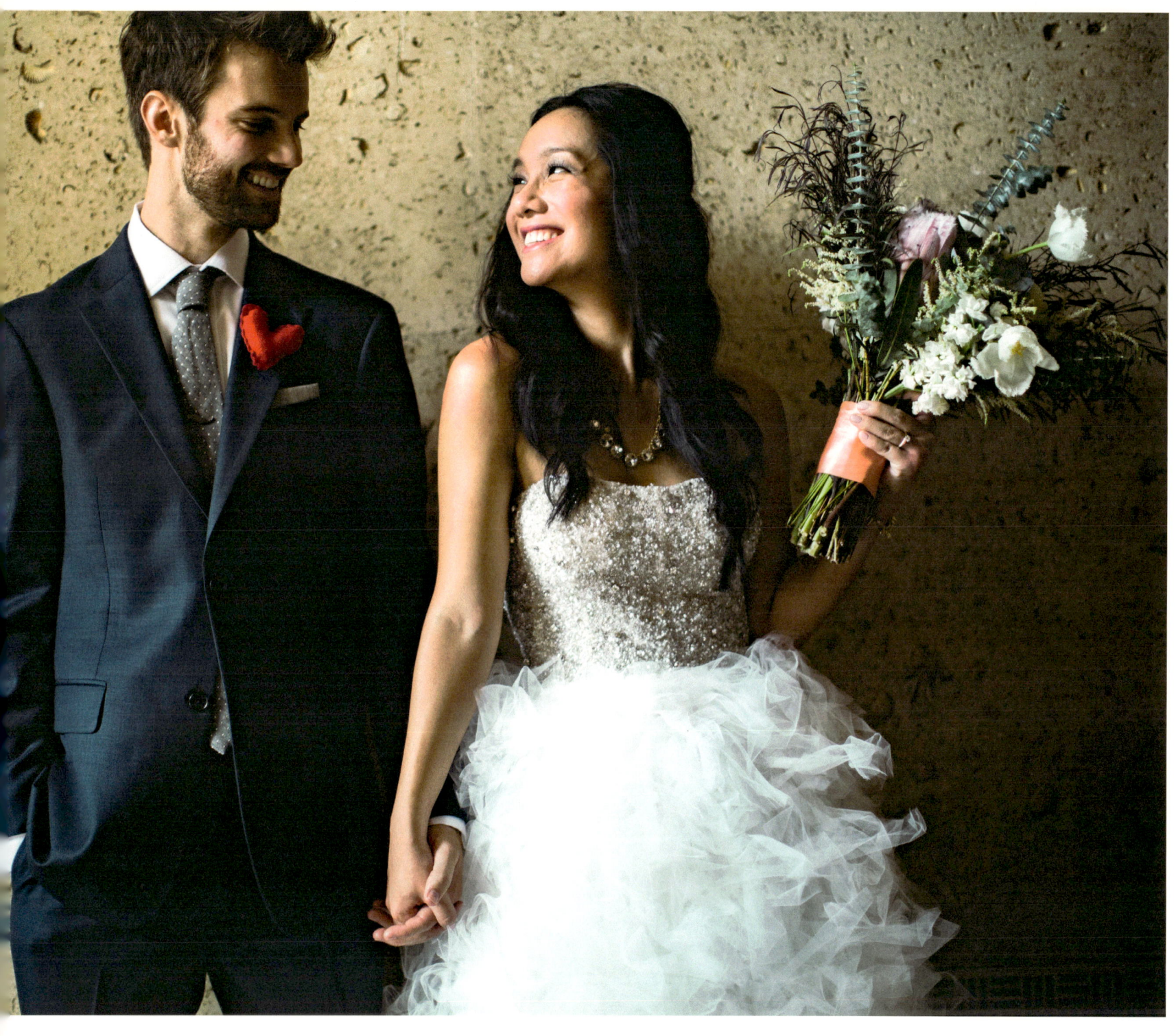

Kim & Robbie

Kim and Robbie love each other. They also love partying and the film *Napoleon Dynamite*. Can you see where this is going? Yup. A wedding that was the raddest party ever, done in the inimitable style of the biggest nerd ever to hit Hollywood. Toy dinosaurs roamed around, quotes of Napoleon's best lines decorated the tables, and the whole reception space was done out in colors from the school in the film. The only exceptions to the geek-chic were the bride's dress, the groom's suit, and the stylish attire of their sidekicks.

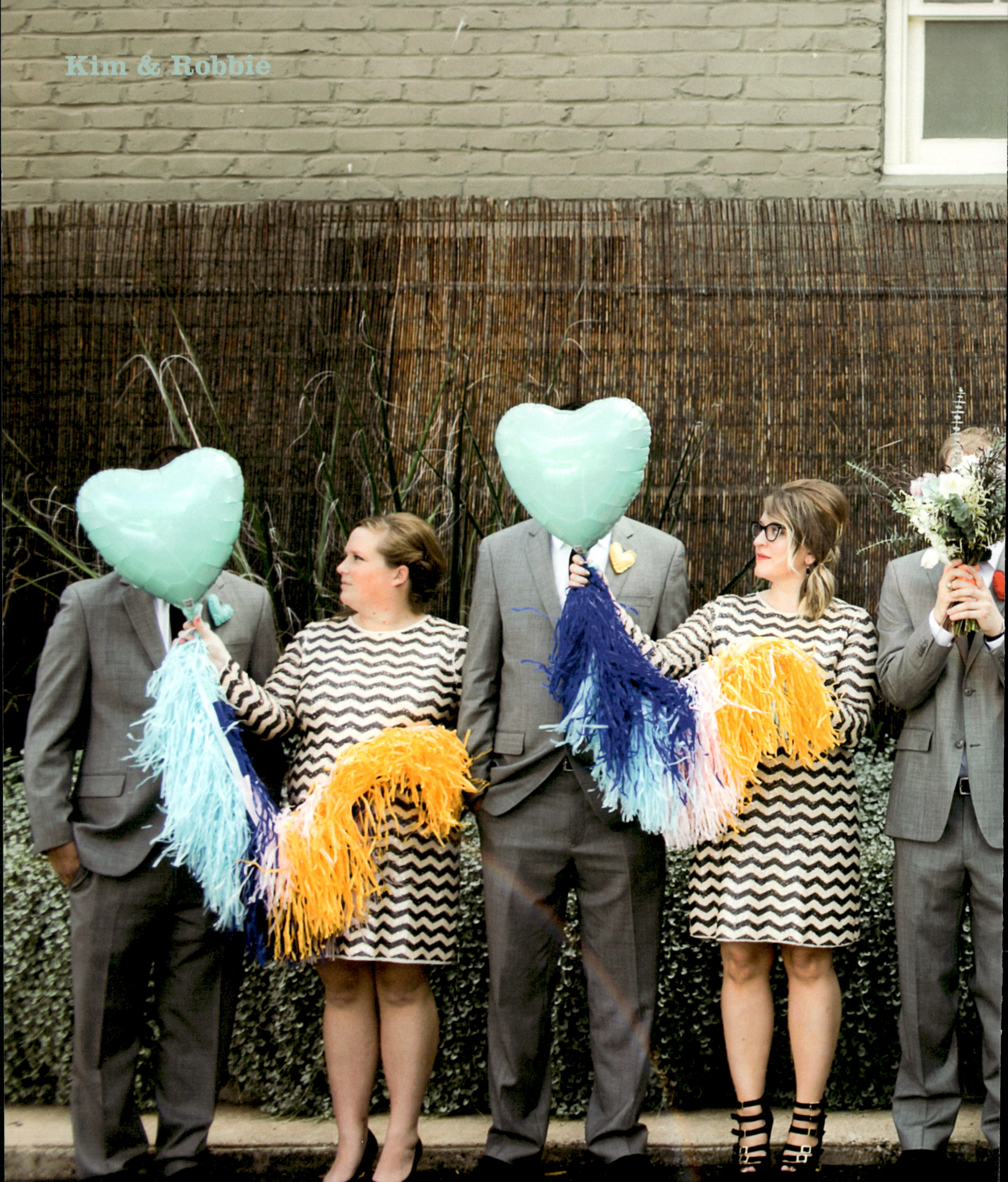

Kim & Robbie

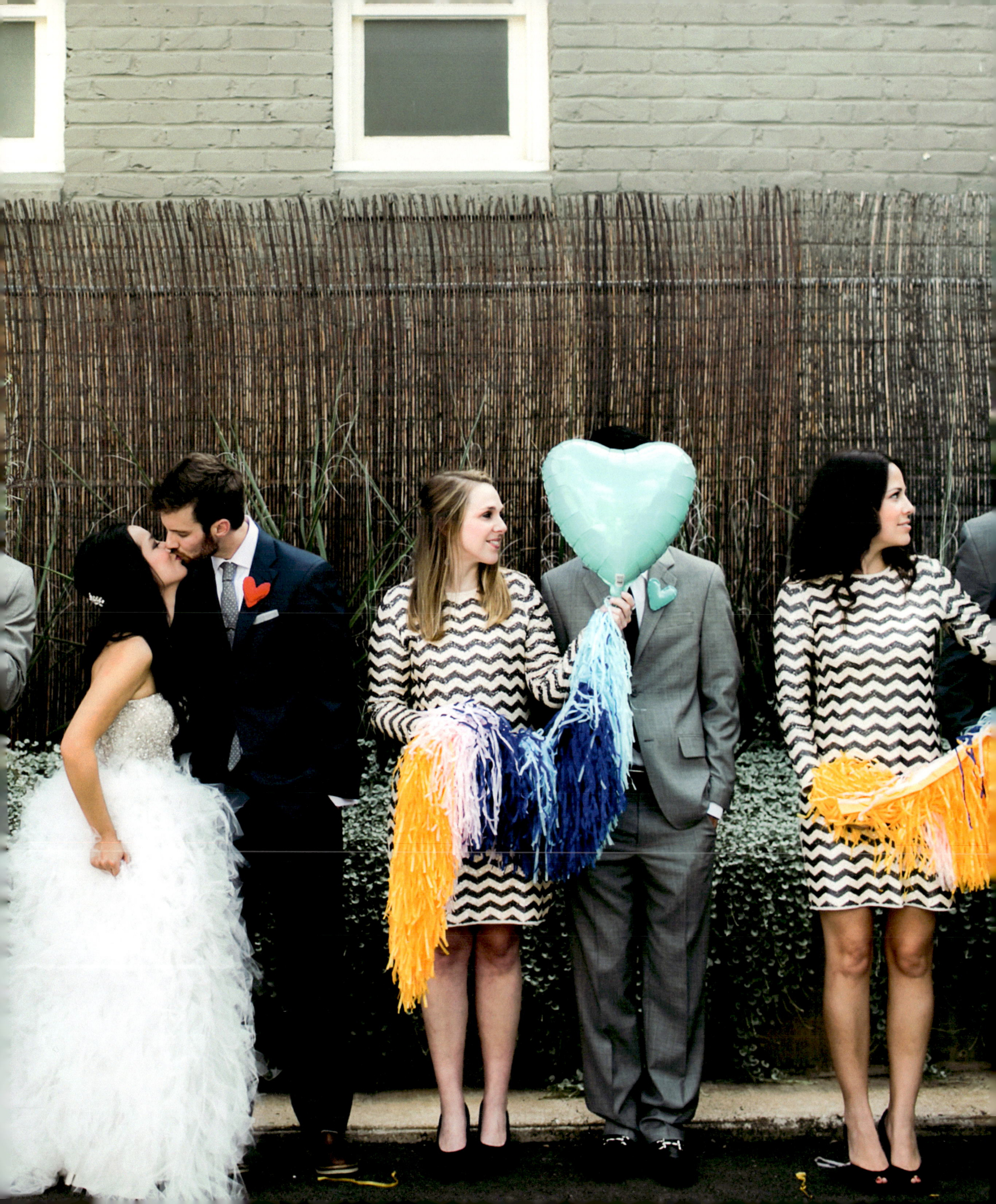

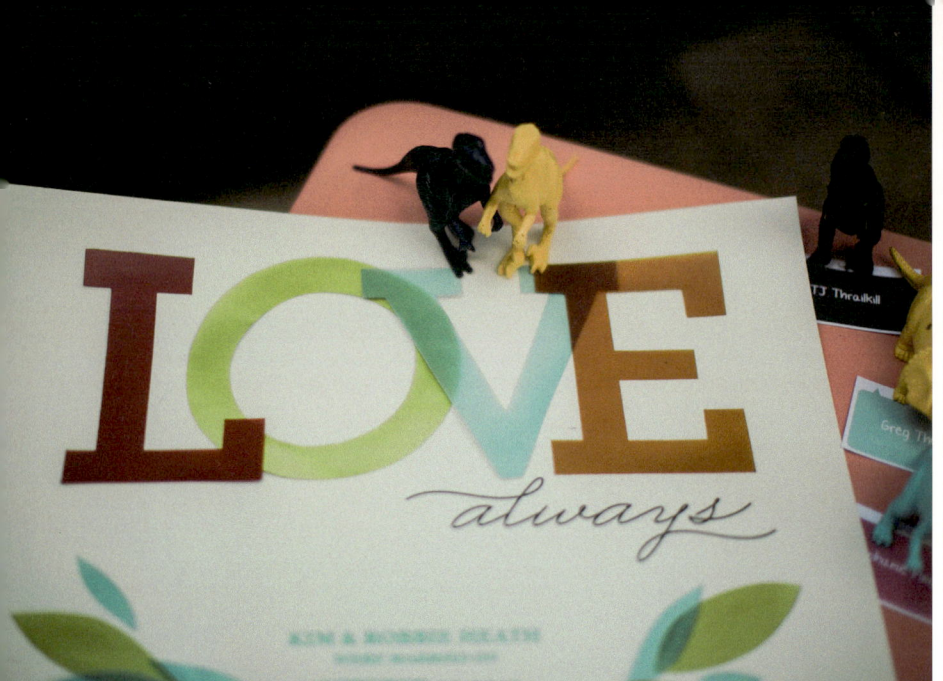

LOVE always

KIM & BOBBIE HEATH

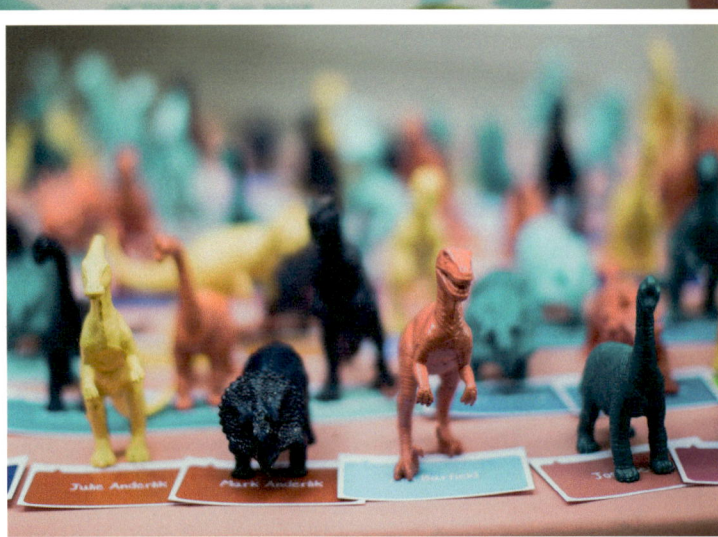

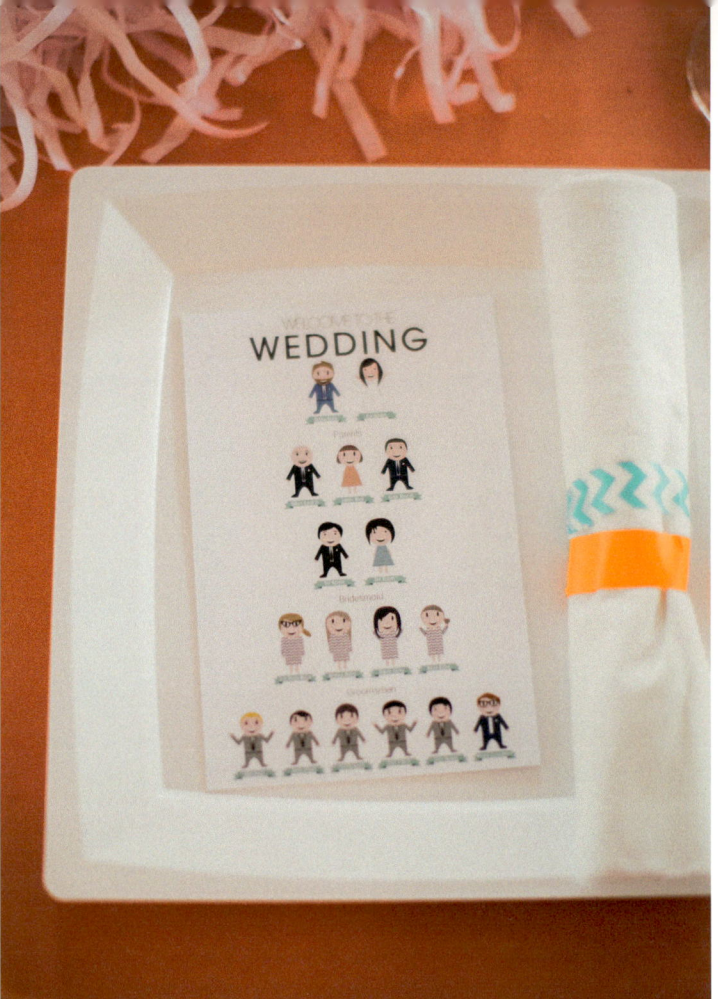

WELCOME TO THE
WEDDING

Kind of like a school cafeteria, but way more awesome.

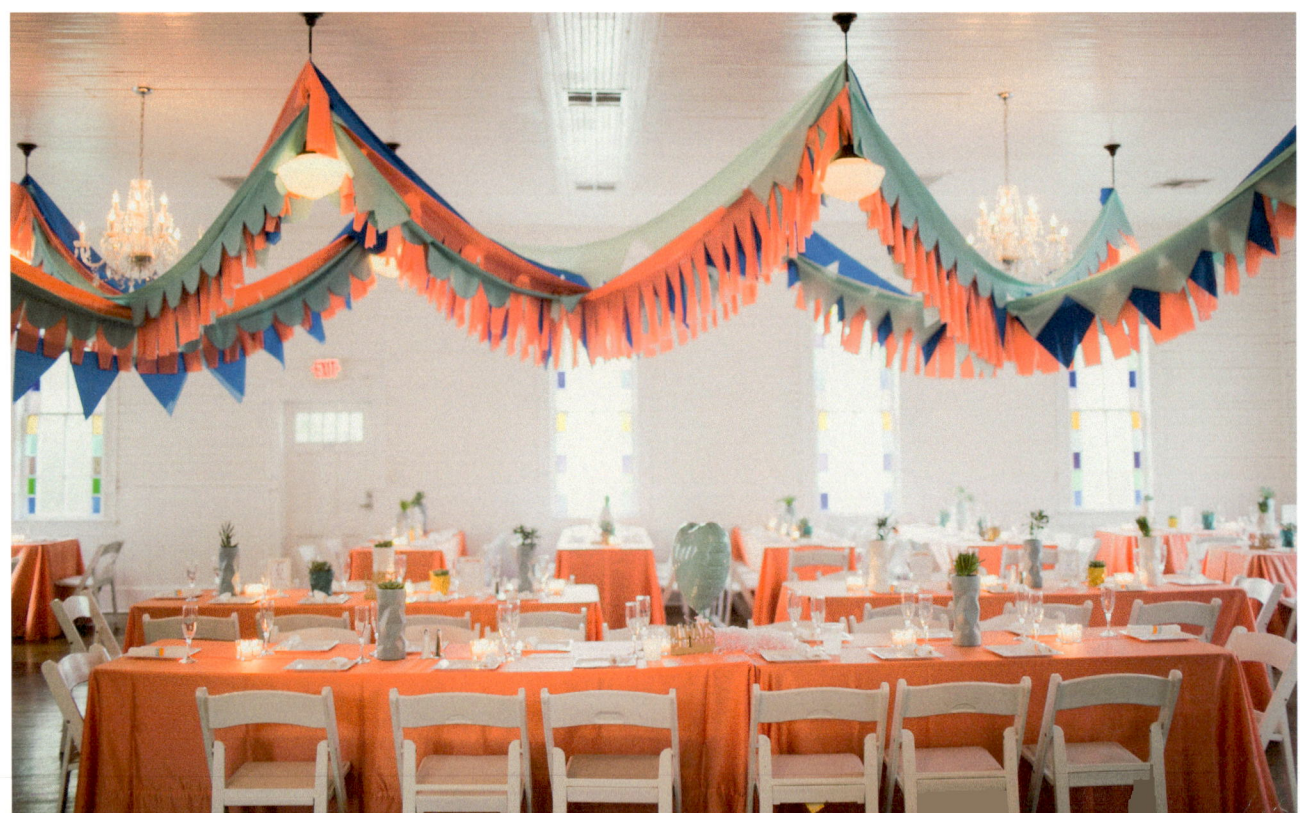

"Heck Yes We Did"

The motto for Kim and Robbie's wedding came straight from the mouth of Napoleon Dynamite—as did the laser-cut quotes leaning against the centerpiece succulents. The geometric decorations hanging over the dessert table were truly nerd-tastic, but no wedding would be complete without the sleek cut-off ovals of champagne flutes.

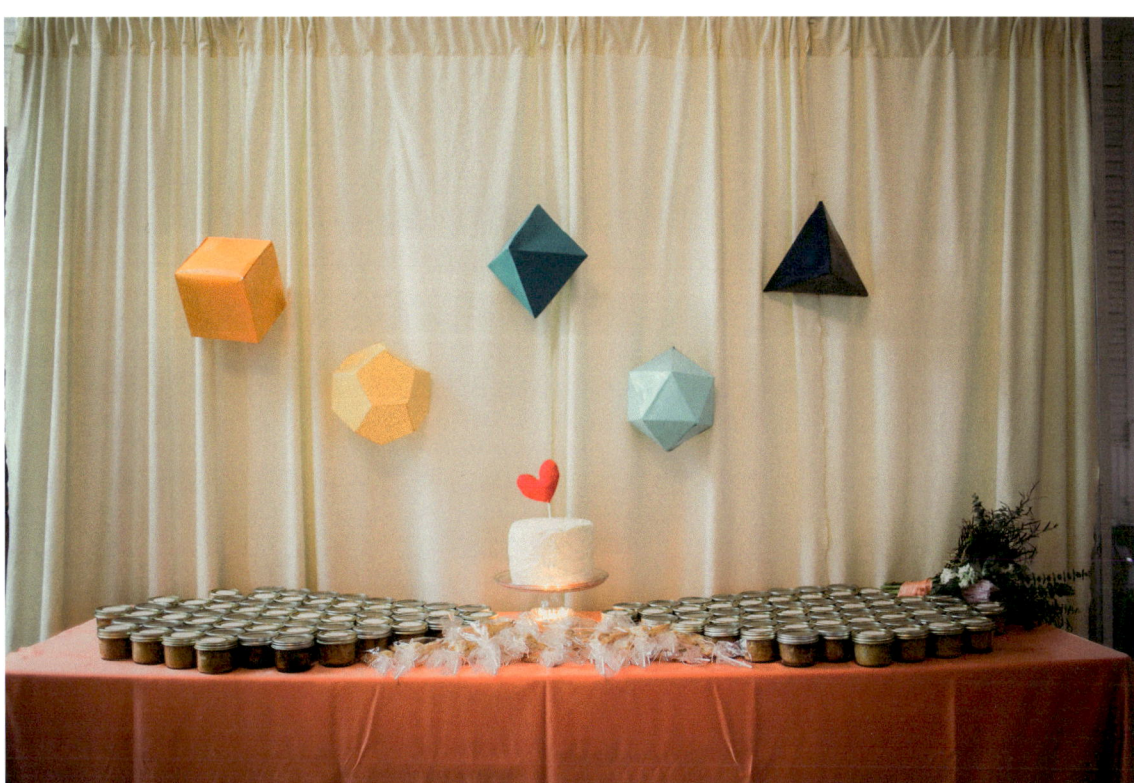

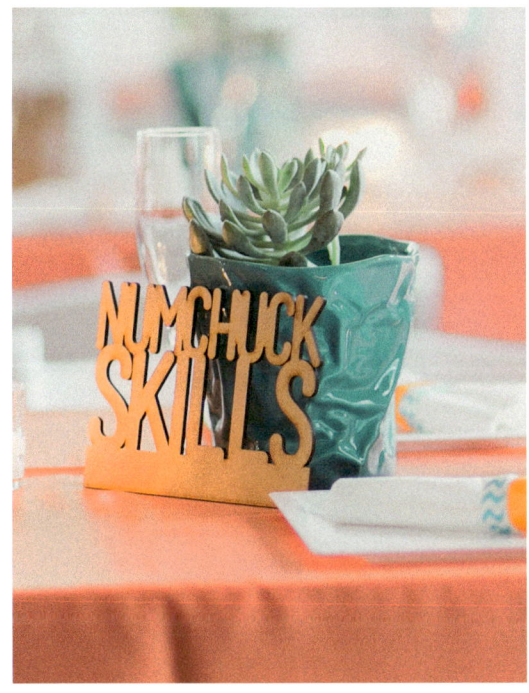

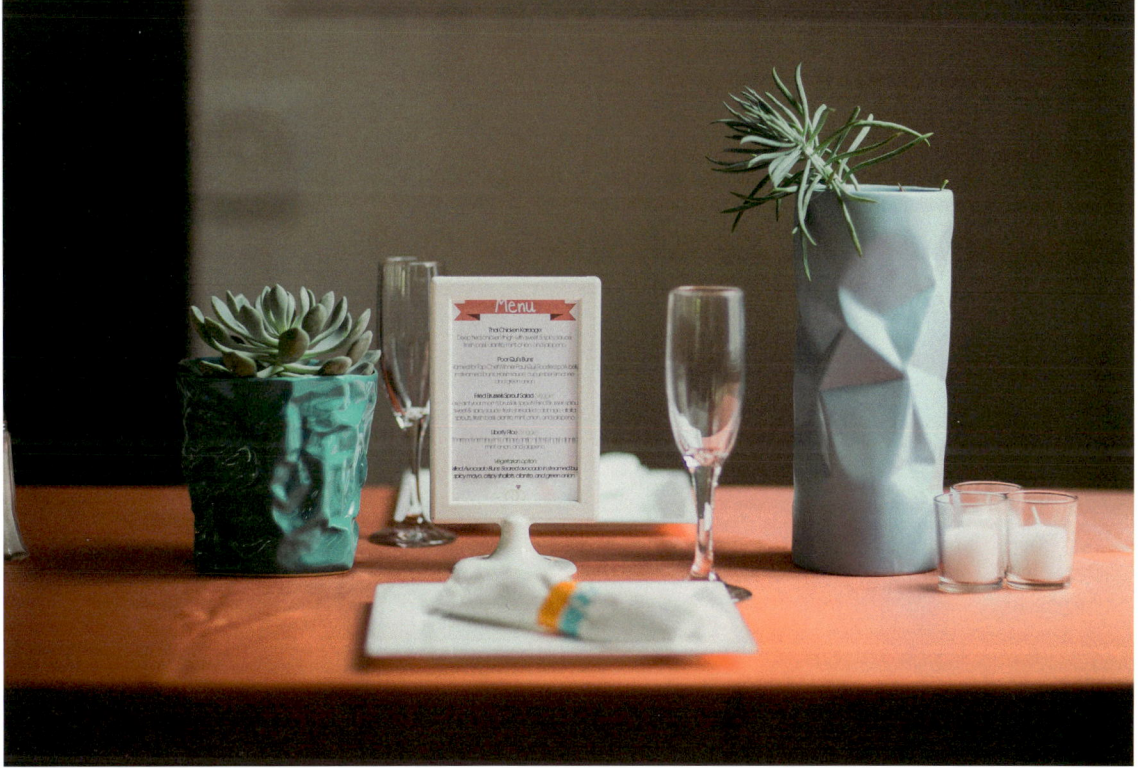

Index

Anna & Brandon (p. 154–159)

Photo Credits: Brett and Jessica Donar
www.brettjessica.com
Bride's Dress: Olga's Bridal and Formal
Couture in Raleigh, NC
Groom's Attire: Indochino
Bridesmaids' Dresses: White House
Black Market
Flowers: Anna made them herself
Stationery: Brandon, the groom
Entertainment: Bluegrass Band,
Brian Hicks
DJ: Carl Griewisch

Anna & Paul (p. 102–107)

Photo Credits: Naomi Goggin
www.naomigogginblog.com
Ceremony Venue: Saint Etheldreda's
Church, Ely Place, London
Reception Venue: The Modern
Pantry, Clerkenwell/All Star Lanes,
Brick Lane
Bride's Dress: by Roland Mouret for
NET-A-PORTER
('Wallis' design, inspired by the
infamous Wallis Simpson)
Bride's Shoes: Beatrix Ong, snapped up
at the Jaeger sale
Groom's Attire: Bespoke tweed suit by
Ben Sherman, Savile Row. His shoes
were a cowboy-cum-chelsea boot.
Cake: Red velvet cake from
Hummingbird Bakery, London
Flowers: Bouquet and buttonholes by
McQueen, London
Hair: Accessories and styling by session
stylist Angela Hertel. The bride didn't
wear jewellery or a veil, but wanted
pearls in her cropped hairstyle, and
Angela had the idea to fix pearls
down the back of her neck using super-
strength wig glue. They were a real
talking point.
Stationery: Cool tattoo-inspired,
hand-drawn design by Jayne Travis. The
design featured two holding hands, a
swallow and a classic scroll.
Transport: Addison Lee black taxis

Caroline & Johnny
(p. 232–235)

Photo Credits: Assassynation
www.assassynation.co.uk
Ceremony Venue: Carnglaze Caverns,
Liskeard, Cornwall
www.carnglaze.com
Reception Venue: Squid Ink Restaurant,
Looe, Cornwall
www.squid-ink.biz
Bride's Dress: Dress Vivien of Holloway
www.vivienofholloway.com
Petticoats: Vivien of Hollway and
Swingtime, www.swingtime.co.uk
Socks: Primark and customized
by the bride
Watering: Pylones and customized by the
bride,
www.pylones.com
Bride's Shoes: Alternative Footwear
www.alternative-footwear.co.uk
Bride's Pumps: MES footwork
MES footwork allows you to upload your
own pictures or images to be printed
on the sides of a pair of pumps. Johnny
is inspired by HR Giger's work and had
done a fabulous pencil drawing a little
while back so we took a photo of it and
uploaded it to MES's website who then
printed it onto the pumps. A completely
unique pair of pumps!
Bride's Headpiece: DIY by the bride
Bride's Jewellery: Necklace 'Guardian
Angel' by HR Giger. HR Giger Museum,
Gruyères, Switzerland
www.hrgiger.com
Cuff Links: DIY by the bride
Groom's Suit: Suit Marks and Spencer
Moomin Badges: Moomin shop,
Covent Garden
Buttonhole: DIY by the bride
Groom's Shirt: Chenaski
www.chenaski.com
Cake: Local bakery, cake topper
Miss Cake
www.misscake.co.uk
Hair: DIY by the bride,
Makeup: DIY by the bride
MAC cosmetics
www.mac.com
Stationery: Invite DIY by the bride
Reception Décor/Props: Teacup
wineglasses, DIY by the groom
Transport: Barry from Looe Taxis
www.looetaxis.com

Claire & Gary (p. 082–085)

Photo Credits: Modern Hearts |
Wedding Photographs
www.modernhearts.co.za
Dress: Elizabeth Dye, Portland, USA
www.elizabethdye.com
Groom's Suit: Ben Sherman
www.bensherman.com
Cake & and Décor: Homemade by family
members
Invites: Designed by the groom
Rings: Tommy D
www.tommyd.co.za

Emily & Louis (p. 194–199)

www.emilygreen.net
Photo Credits: Luke Lornie
Photography
www.lukelornie.com.au
Hair and Makeup: Dana Leviston of
Lady Day
www.ladyday.com.au
Flowers: Entwine Florist
(wedding bouquets and buttonholes)
Food: The Taco Truck
www.tacotruck.com.au

Fiona & Jonny (p. 184–189)

Photo Credits: Emma Case Photography
www.emmacasephotography.com
Venue: Victoria Baths
Bride's Dress: Jane Bourvis
Bride's Shoes: Rachel Simpson
Bride's Headpiece: Jenny Packham
Hair: Mai
Makeup: Kerri-Ann
Groom's Attire: Vivienne Westwood and
Oxfam Originals, Manchester
Bridesmaids' Dresses: Jane Bourvis
Cake: Sarah Tildsley
Flowers: Jo Wood, Manchester Flower
Company
Band: Gabe Minikin & The Fast
Country
DJ: Patrick Ryder
Stationery #1: Wedding Tea Towels
Stationery #2: Antiquaria
Catering: Pieminister
Cheese: The Fine Cheese Company
Snacks: Seabrooks
Lighting: Hipswing

Garovs & Ryan (p. 236–243)

Photo Credits: MangoRed
www.mangored.com
Wedding Coordinator:
The Best-Case Scenario

Gwyneth & Monko
(p. 160–165)

Photo Credits: Edyta Szyszlo
Photography
www.edytaszyszlo.com
Venue and Food: The Mendocino
Farmhouse
www.mendocinofarmhouse.com
Styling and Design: Karin Kamb,
Clever Girl Consulting
www.clevergirlconsulting.com
Models: Gwyneth & Monko, local folk
singers

www.gwynethandmonko.com
Florals: Karin Kamb, Clever Girl
Consulting
www.clevergirlconsulting.com
Makeup: Amy Wall of
Mendocino Beauty
www.mendocinobeauty.com
Hair: Marianella Brey for
Mendocino Beauty
www.mendocinobeauty.com
Stationery: www.hellolucky.com

Jose & Joel (p. 036–043)

Photo Credits: Elizabeth Messina
Location: Figueroa Mountain
Farmhouse
Event Design & Production: Lisa Vorce
of Lisa Vorce
www.lisavorce.com
Wedding Photography: Elizabeth
Messina
Floral and Event Design: Mindy Rice
Floral and Event Design
Catering: New West Special Occasion
Catering
Stationery: Tiny Pine Press, Papel Paper
& Press
Calligraphy: Anne Jones
Cake: Sweet and Saucy Shop
Lighting: Bella Vista Designs
Wedding Filmmaker: Joe Simon
Wedding Films
Groom's Attire: Hugo Boss (suits and
shirts), Ben Sherman (Jose's tie);
Forage (Joel's bow tie), Santoni (shoes)
Ceremony and Cocktail Music:
Bolero Soul
Reception Music: Michael Antonia of
The Flashdance
Rentals: Classic Party Rentals
Specialty Décor: Barker Décor Service
Wedding Bands: Waxing Poetic

Julie & Bo (p. 220–231)

Photo Credits: The Weaver House
www.TheWeaverHouse.com
Venue: A Private Estate
www.aprivateestate.com
Event Planner: Danielle DeFreest of
Every Little Detail
www.everylittledetails.com
Floral Design: Sprout Home
www.sprouthome.com/stores/brooklyn
Bride's Dress: Gina DeSilva
Hair Pieces: Sprout Home for flower
crowns
www.sprouthome.com/stores/brooklyn
Adrienne's Bridal NYC for veil
Shoes: Jimmy Choo
Bridesmaids' Dresses: Vintage, Asos,
American Apparel, NeedSupply
Hair and Makeup: La Tua Bella
www.latuabella.com
Groom's Suit: Billy Reid
Invitations/Paper Goods: Meghan
Sokarai—she is amazing. She hand-
painted every invitation and RSVP card
with watercolors for an ombre look.
They were letter-pressed on top of the
watercolors. She also made all the logos
on our website and the wax seal stamps
we used for the invites. We loved them so
much!
www.and-hereweare.com
Catering: New World Catering
www.ricorlando.com
Cake: Flatiron Restaurant
www.flatironsteakhouse.com
Ceremony Music: Kristi Shade, harpist
www.kristishade.com
Reception Band: Nu-Cullers (Gene
Dobbs Ult. Band)
www.gigmasters.com/Dance-Band/Nu-
Cullers

Kelly & Curtis (p. 140–149)

Photo Credits: Ashley Rose Photography
www.ashleyrosephotography.com
Design (save the dates, invitations, menu
and programs): CRAFTË Design
www.craftedesign.com
Wedding Coordinator: Heather Hoesch
of LVL Events
www.lvlevents.com
Flowers: Randi Tucker of Tucker Floral
www.tuckerfloral.com
Catering: Tender Greens
www.tendergreensfood.com
Dessert: Julian Pie Company
www.julianpie.com
Espresso Cart: Cafecito Orgánico
www.cafecitoorganico.com
Photo Booth: Photo Booth Moment
www.photoboothmoment.com
DJ: Nicholas of Coastal Entertainment
Group
www.cegevents.com
Ceremony Music:
International String Trio
www.internationalstringtrio.com
Rentals: Event Rents
www.eventrents.com

Kim & Robbie (p. 244–249)

Photo Credits: Studio Castillero
www.studiocastillero.com
Additional Credits: Jesi Haack Design

Kirstyn & Adam (p. 200–209)

Photo Credits: Jonathan Ong
www.storytelling.jonathanong.com
Hair Stylist: Mary Posterino, Salon
Symmetry
www.facebook.com/SalonSymmetry and
Adam DiBiase, HOT HOUSE
www.facebook.com/pages/HOT-
HOUSE/422265184526616
Makeup: Sadie Tate Makeup Artist www.
facebook.com/SadieTateMakeupArtist

Bouquets and Buttonholes: Connie
Fedele
Stationery and Paper Goods: I worked on
the design for the invites with a fabulous
woman on Etsy called B. Designs, they
really set the tone for the day.
www.etsy.com/shop/Bdesignsinvitations
I designed the menus myself and my
very talented mother designed the
clock-in cards that were used as escort
cards for the guests.
Ceremony Venue: The Old Newport
Rail Workshops
www.steamrail.com.au
Reception Venue: The Substation,
Newport
www.thesubstation.org.au
Celebrant/Officiant: Jon Von Goes
www.jvgcelebrant.com
Reception Music: A friend, Austin Busch
played during cocktail hour and to kick
off the reception. Then another dear
friend Anthony Murray and his band
Mamakusa took us all through the night
with amazing soul and funk tunes!
www.facebook.com/pages/Austin-
Busch/13106433458
www.myspace.com/shortythadrumma
Wedding Favors: We picked olives off
our tree six months before our wedding
and cured them for four months before
putting them in jars with a secret recipe
mixture. We had gorgeous little labels
made by Lajari. The best part was they
really were a gift of love because we had
invested effort and love into creating
them.
www.facebook.com/lajaridesign
Caterers: Melbourne Catering Company
who are the in-house caterers for The
Substation. The food was definitely one
of the highlights of the whole day.
www.melbournecateringcompany.com.au
Cake: Our wonderful and talented
friend Jennifer Kidd. We weren't going
to have a cake until she offered. And it

worked out perfectly. It was rainbow on
the inside—just like us!
www.pinterest.com/madelinimoo
Wedding Rings: Adam's ring is from
Dora. My engagement ring is from
Keshett and my wedding ring was
custom-made by Fedele Jewelworks
www.dora.com.au; www.keshett.com.au;
www.fedelejewelworks.com.au

Kristen & Michael
(p. 086–097)

Photo Credits: Ben Blood
www.benblood.com
Venue: Flying Horseshoe Ranch, Cle
Elum, WA
Day-of Coordinator: Emily Murphy of
Manette Gracie
Flowers: from mom and grandma's
gardens, local markets, bulk wax flowers
and sister's floral wreath from Henshaw's
Floral
Bride's dress: Custom by Knar Bridal in
Kirkland, WA
Hair and Makeup: Jenny Bowker
Shoes: Bernardo
Groom's suit: J. Crew
Invitations: Sam and Dale Ahn
Catering: Twelve Baskets
Plates: Thrifted, heirlooms, Rad
Crockery Rentals
Cake: Alyson and Ashley Redding, Top
Pot Doughnuts,
Cookies: Aunt, mom and grandma
Music: Michael (the groom), vinyl

Laura & Mike (p. 048–057)

Photo Credits: Assassynation
www.assassynation.co.uk
Ceremony Venue: Winchester Guildhall
Reception Venue: Rotherwick Village
Hall
Styling: Laura
www.thingsbylaura.co.uk

Bride's Dress: Bride's design
(embroidered by the bride and made by
Rosemary Pitkin)
Bride's Headpiece: Laura
www.thingsbylaura.co.uk
Bride's Jewellery: Earrings made by the
bride, necklace borrowed
Groom's Attire: British Heart
Foundation Charity Shop
Bridesmaids' Dresses: Made by mother
of the bride
Bridesmaids' Accessories: Poetry Jewelry
on Etsy
Cake: Mother of the bride and guests
(inc. fifi and lola, www.fifiandlola.com)
Flowers: Bride (ceremony, buttonholes
and bridesmaids)
Bride's Bouquet: Bride's boss
Venue: Mother of the groom
Hair: DIY, Moko Sellars
Makeup: DIY, bride
Band: Barn Dance, Dance On
DJ: DIY, groom's own ipod mix
Stationery: Laura
www.thingsbylaura.co.uk
Caterers: Organic Hog Roast and father
of the bride
Reception Décor/Props: Bride
Transport: 1949 Bedford from Mervyn's
Coaches

Leigh & Brad (p. 020–029)
Photo Credits: Modern Hearts |
Wedding Photographs
www.modernhearts.co.za

Lynette & Gris (p. 172–183)
Photo Credits: Phil Chester
www.philchester.com
Styled by: The couple,
Assistant: Nick Radford
Flowers: The Little Branch
Cakes: Sweet Art Cakes and Nickel Diner

Natasha & Len (p. 070–075)
Photo Credits: Modern Hearts |
Wedding Photographs
www.modernhearts.co.za
Wine: Solms Delta
www.solms-delta.co.za
Venue: Oppi Duin at the Grootvlei
Guest Farm
www.grootvleiguestfarm.co.za
Music: Peachy Keen
www.facebook.com/PeachyKeenSA

Rin & Joe (p. 062–069)
Photo Credits: Eric Ronald
www.ericronald.net
Photographer: Eric Ronald
Bride's Dress: Online
Bride's Veil/Hair Accessories:
Flowers Vasette
Hair and Makeup: Lady Day
Ceremony Officiant: Susan Ellis,
Soul Mate Ceremonies

Sarah & Justin (p. 118–129)
Photo Credits: Jonathan Ong
www.storytelling.jonathanong.com
Ceremony Location: Collingwood
Children's Farm/Reception Venue: The
Regal Ballroom
Event designer: Georgie Kay and Erin
Lilja from Georgeous Events
Flowers: Melanie Stapleton from
Cecilia Fox
Bride's Dress: Alice Haute Couture
Blusher Veil: Etsy seller Portobello
Shoes: Darla from Kate Spade Gloves:
BHLDN
Bracelet: J. Crew/Vintage Sarah
Coventry Earrings from Etsy
Custom wedding rings from Chris Parry
Hair: Marie Uva and Giovanni Tedesco
at Rokk Ebony South Melbourne
Makeup: Rosemary Walsh
Bridesmaids' Dresses: Stop Staring

Raileen dresses in navy
Groom's suit: J. Crew vest, bow tie by
xoelle on etsy, Eugenia Kim hat from
The Hat Mansion, shirt by French
Connection
Groomsmen wore shirts by French
Connection, vests by Charles Tyrwhitt,
and jeans from Carhartt Celebrant: Jon
Von Goes
DJ: Brendan and Liam at DJ Masters
and friends, Lauren Glezer and Keren
Leizerovitz from Melbourne band
Pleasing Anna sang at their ceremony
and Andy McLelland of Mr McClelland's
Finishing School DJ'd their reception
Caterer: Tom Hay at The Farm Cafe did
their devonshire tea and catering by The
Regal Ballroom Wedding
Dessert: DIY ice cream sundae buffet
styled by Georgeous
Wedding Invitations: Bride's cousin
Caitlin Gahan designed the invitations
(caitlingahan@hotmail.com), and the
bride and groom designed their brown
paper bag envelopes.
Videographer: Sarah Walker from Sarah
Walker Photography
Transportation: 1938 Diamond T Bus
from Vintage Fun Hire Cars

Sarah & Dawn (p. 166–171)
www.thesmallobject.com
Photo Credits: Mark Tioxin
LeahAndMark.com
Custom Cake Topper: The Small
Object, made by Sarah
Cakes: Icing Cake Design
Ring Pouch: Mimi Pong
Invitations: Racing Snail Press

Shona & Luke (p. 058–061)

Photo credits: AmyMurrell/
Especially Amy
www.especiallyamy.co.uk
Designer: Fiona Leahy Design
www.fionaleahy.com

Stacy & Josh (p. 108–117)

Photo Credits: Cameron Ingalls
www.cameroningalls.com
Event Coordinator/Designer:
Saralee Franchi of XOXO Bride

Suzy & Dmitry (p. 134–139)

Photo Credits: Photo Pink
www.photopinknyc.com

Talia & Zac (p. 006–019)

Photo Credits: Eric Ronald
www.ericronald.net
Photography: Eric Ronald
Wedding Planner: Us!
Celebrant: Matt Finch
Ceremony Venue: Boyd Baker House
Reception Venue: Boyd Baker House
Bride's Dress: Vintage
Bride's Shoes: Peeptoe
Bride's Headpiece: Isobel Badin
Bride's Jewellery: vintage
Hair: Candice deVille
Makeup: Candice deVille
Groom's Attire: Ralph Lauren
Groom's Shoes: Cole Haan Lunergrand
Groom's Cap: Norse Projects
Cake: Sticky Fingers Bakery
Flowers: Fowlers Flowers
Stationery: Designed by the bride,
printed by The Hungry Workshop
Caterers: Taco Truck
Band: Shamdoogie
Any Reception Décor/Props:
Signage made by bride's brother Ben,
rest of décor by the bride

Toni & Colin (p. 076–081)

Photo Credits: Assassynation
www.assassynation.co.uk
First Look and Couple Shot Location:
www.thecitycafe.co.uk
Venue: The Quay, Musselburgh
Wedding Tattoos:
www.oldtowntattoo.co.uk
Bride's Dress: Pixie Pocket
Bride's Headpiece: Janine Basil
(customized)
Bride's Shoes: Converse & Irregular
Choice
Groom's Attire: Various inc Red Bird
Makes (bow tie), Ask The Missus at
Office (shoes), The Doll City Rocker and
Paper and String (buttonholes)
Bridesmaids' Dresses: Hell Bunny
Cupcakes: Marks & Spencer
Toadstool Cake: Bibi's Bakery
Flowers & Bouquets: DIY
DJ: Chaplin's Disco

Trishia & Justin (p. 210–215)

Photo Credits: Jodi Miller Photography
www.jodimillerphotography.com
Venue: Nature Camp
www.naturecamp.net
Bride's Dress: Oleg Cassini for
David's Bridal
Hair and Makeup: Jenny Beckner
of the Salon of Lexington
www.thesaloneflex.webs.com
Shoes: Flora Sandal by Dollhouse
via Endless
www.endless.com
Butterfly Clips: Colleen Kurdziolek,
mother of the bride
Bridesmaids' Dresses: Simple Silhouettes
via Bella Bridesmaid
www.bellabridesmaid.com
Bridesmaids' Necklaces: Designed and
made by Emily Schweitzer
Bridesmaids' Hairpieces: Colleen
Kurdziolek, mother of the bride

Groom's/Groomsmen's Custom Vests:
Erik of Brightwall
www.etsy.com/shop/brightwall
Groom's Wedding Band: Zoe and Doyle
www.etsy.com/shop/ZoeandDoyle
Pinwheel Bouts: Blue Lemon Provisions
www.wedzu.com/seller/
BlueLemonProvisions
Photography: Jodi and Kurt of
Jodi Miller Photography
Raccoon Logo: Josh Gulley, groomsman
Décor: Styled by Trishia Soda Bottle
Flowers: Inspired by Anthropologie
window displays, made by Trishia, bride,
mother of bride, and family and friends
(used Krylon spray paints)
Menu/Signage: Trishia and family
and friends
Cake Topper: made by mother of bride
Embroidered Tea Towel Favors: Towels
via Ikea, embroidery by Colonial Sports
Custom Screenprinting and Embroidery
www.colonialsportscustom.com
Table Quilts: Trishia
Buri Animals: Christmas Mouse
www.christmasmouse.com
Ritual Box: John Leach,
brother of groom
Flowers: Bouquets and ceremony
arrangements by Susan Roepke of
Flower Fields
www.flowerfields.webs.com
My Mom is a former florist and she
made/planted all of the arrangements
you saw during the cocktail hour and
reception dinner.
Catering/Shortcake: Jenny Elmes of
Full Circle Catering
www.fullcirclecatering.com
Rentals: Festive Fare
www.classicpartyrentals.com
Invitation Books: Book cover by Rifle
Paper Co.
www.riflepaperco.com
Interior Illustrations and Reply Card: by
Trishia and Josh Gulley (logo designer)